ISBN 978-1-331-82005-5
PIBN 10238999

1 MONTH OF
FREE
READING

at
www.ForgottenBooks.com

By purchasing this book you are eligible for one month membership to ForgottenBooks.com, giving you unlimited access to our entire collection of over 1,000,000 titles via our web site and mobile apps.

To claim your free month visit:

www.forgottenbooks.com/free238999

English
Français
Deutsche
Italiano
Español
Português

www.forgottenbooks.com

Mythology Photography **Fiction**
Fishing Christianity **Art** Cooking
Essays Buddhism Freemasonry
Medicine **Biology** Music **Ancient**
Egypt Evolution Carpentry Physics
Dance Geology **Mathematics** Fitness
Shakespeare **Folklore** Yoga Marketing
Confidence Immortality Biographies
Poetry **Psychology** Witchcraft
Electronics Chemistry History **Law**
Accounting **Philosophy** Anthropology
Alchemy Drama Quantum Mechanics
Atheism Sexual Health **Ancient History**
Entrepreneurship Languages Sport
Paleontology Needlework Islam
Metaphysics Investment Archaeology
Parenting Statistics Criminology
Motivational

A

·VINDICATION

OF THE

DOCTRINE OF SCRIPTURE,

AND OF

THE PRIMITIVE FAITH;

CONCERNING

THE DEITY OF CHRIST:

IN REPLY TO DR PRIESTLEY'S HISTORY
OF EARLY OPINIONS, &c.

———

IN TWO VOLUMES.

———

BY JOHN JAMIESON, D. D. F. A. S. S;

MINISTER OF THE GOSPEL, FORFAR.

VOL. I.

Behold, this *Child* is fet for the fall and rifing again of many in Ifrael;
and for a fign which fhall be fpoken againft:—that the thoughts of many hearts may be revealed. LUKE.

Omnes hæretici perverfa credentes, panem de cœlo defcendentem co-
medere non poffunt: fed obftupefcunt dentes eorum, non ciborum aufte-
ritate, fed vitio dentium. HIERONYM.

EDINBURGH:

PRINTED BY NEILL AND COMPANY, FOR C. DILLY,
POULTRY, LONDON; AND SOLD BY J. OGLE,
PARLIAMENT SQUARE, EDINBURGH.

M.DCC.XCIV.

1 MONTH OF
FREE
READING

at

www.ForgottenBooks.com

By purchasing this book you are eligible for one month membership to ForgottenBooks.com, giving you unlimited access to our entire collection of over 1,000,000 titles via our web site and mobile apps.

To claim your free month visit:

www.forgottenbooks.com/free238999

English
Français
Deutsche
Italiano
Español
Português

www.forgottenbooks.com

Mythology Photography **Fiction**
Fishing Christianity **Art** Cooking
Essays Buddhism Freemasonry
Medicine **Biology** Music **Ancient
Egypt** Evolution Carpentry Physics
Dance Geology **Mathematics** Fitness
Shakespeare **Folklore** Yoga Marketing
Confidence Immortality Biographies
Poetry **Psychology** Witchcraft
Electronics Chemistry History **Law**
Accounting **Philosophy** Anthropology
Alchemy Drama Quantum Mechanics
Atheism Sexual Health **Ancient History**
Entrepreneurship Languages Sport
Paleontology Needlework Islam
Metaphysics Investment Archaeology
Parenting Statistics Criminology
Motivational

THE

PREFACE.

THE idea of this work was firft fuggefted by a letter which appeared, under Dr Prieftley's fignature, in one of the London prints, about four years ago. The defign of this letter was to ftate that, although fome years had elapfed fince the publication of his *Hiftory of Early Opinions concerning Jefus Chrift*, no anfwer had been given to it ; and that, if the fame filence fhould be obferved during a certain time which he is pleafed to limit, he would confider it as an acknowledgment, on the part of the whole Chriftian world, that it was unanfwerable.

For a confiderable time, I hefitated, expectingthat fome more able combatant would enter the lifts againft this literary giant, who has *defied the armies of the living God*. But a full conviction that I have truth on my fide, emboldened me to engage in this work ; and, notwithftanding various difcouragements, to proceed in it. The fatal influence of the Socinian fcheme, in throwing open the fluices to Infidelity, and in hurrying forward thofe whom this torrent has already fwept away ; the fafcinating power which it inva-

riably

riably difcovers, in bereaving its votaries of all that diftin-
guifhes Chriftianity but the name ; their unwearied affi-
duity in extending the delufion ; with its rapid progrefs
in this age ; undoubtedly lay the ftrongeft obligations on
every one who really believes the gofpel, to exert himfelf to the utmoft, according to his place or ability, for the
prefervation and defence of the truth *as it is in Jefus.*

It feems to be the plan of modern Socinians, to carry the
controverfy as much as poffible out of the boundaries of Revelation. The voluminous and inaccurate works of the
Fathers afford them a more ample field for mifreprefenta-
tion, for cavilling, or at leaft for conjecture. Therefore, as
far as the nature of the work would admit, I have endeavoured to reftore the controverfy to its proper limits. With
this view, I have not only confidered the principal arguments from fcripture contained in the Hiftory, but occafionally introduced others which Dr P. has publifhed diftinctly ; efpecially as he refers to thefe for further illuftration.

Confidering the many able replies that have been formerly made to writers of the fame clafs, to fome this work
may appear fuperfluous. But error, although ftill fubftantially the fame, affumes a diverfity of forms in different pe-
riods. This has been remarkably the cafe with refpect to
the Socinian herefy. Thofe who now appear as its friends
deny the force of the reafoning of many former writers, becaufe they have renounced the grounds on which that reafoning proceeded. In the laft century, they acknowledged
that the Logos was a perfon, and affirmed that this perfon
was the mere man Jefus Chrift. They now maintain that
the fame Logos is merely an attribute of God. Then they
worfhipped the Son. Now they refufe that he is entitled

to

to religious worſhip of any kind. In lieu of their former interpretations of ſcripture, they have deviſed a great many new ones; which, although equally weak, and in many inſtances more ridiculous, are ſtill calculated to enſnare the ignorant, and the unwary.

Some may imagine that it was quite unneceſſary to enter into the controverſy, as far as it reſpects the Fathers; becauſe the deciſion of the general queſtion cannot depend upon their doctrine. I am as fully ſatisfied as they can be, that the word of God is the only teſt of divine truth, and that any human authority, as far as it oppoſes this, is of no weight. Although the majority of Chriſtian writers, in the age immediately ſucceeding that of the Apoſtles, had held a doctrine directly contrary to the obvious meaning of ſcripture, they would not have merited our regard. For if the ſcriptures were written for the uſe of mankind in all ages, and were therefore to be interpreted according to the plain ſenſe of language; we, humanly ſpeaking, muſt be as capable of underſtanding them in all things neceſſarily connected with ſalvation, as thoſe who lived in that early age, or even as thoſe to whom they were immediately directed.

However, when our opponents appeal to the Fathers, it is of importance to ſhew that they appeal in vain. For it cannot be denied that, did the current of antiquity in this reſpect ſeem to oppoſe the Trinitarian doctrine, with many it would be a powerful argument againſt it. But it being once eſtabliſhed that this is the doctrine of ſcripture, according to its obvious meaning; when it is alſo proved that the church from the beginning has adhered to it, although this circumſtance can add nothing to the authority of the doctrine itſelf, it is very confirming to the mind in a ſubordi-

nate

nate refpect ; fhews that the caufe of our opponents is inde-
fenfible on every quarter ; tends to filence their vain boaft-
ings ; may have weight with thofe who will not attend to
any other kind of argument ; and illuftrates the unity of the
church, in her fucceffive generations, with refpect to a doctrine which conftitutes the very bafis of revelation, deeply
affects almoft every article of her faith, and immediately
characterizes the whole of her worfhip.

But in the prefent inftance, the Fathers have been appealed to, not properly with refpect to opinions, but with
refpect to facts ; not as themfelves interpreting the fenfe of
fcripture, but as declaring the fenfe in which it was interpreted by others. From their teftimony Dr Prieftley has
attempted to prove that all the Hebrew Chriftians were E-
bionites, or what he calls Unitarians, and that the majority
even of Gentile Chriftians, in the firft ages, were of the
fame opinion. Were it poffible to prove only the firft of
thefe pofitions, I do not fay that we ought to renounce the
doctrine of the Trinity, but that we ought to renounce Chriftianity entirely. For it would follow that, in the New
Teftament, the faith and practice of the primitive church
are exhibited as directly the reverfe of what they really
were. But a proof of this kind is in fact impoffible. For
did the Fathers affert fuch things, there would be an evident neceffity for rejecting their teftimony as falfe or adul-
terated. For they fubject it to the authority of fcripture :
and the fcriptural narrative of facts, as far as it extends, is
fully as intelligible as theirs. But although their teftimony
could not invalidate that of revelation, they may be fuftained as competent witneffes of the ftate of facts in their
own times ; when there is no certain evidence that they
were themfelves mifled, or that they were difpofed to
miflead others.

It

It has been my wish, as far as possible, to avoid going over the same ground with those learned gentlemen who have animadverted on the *History of the Corruptions of Christianity*. But this could not be entirely avoided, without an absolute disregard to connexion. The substance of the arguments contained in that work, is republished in the *History of Early Opinions*. But it is so interspersed with a variety of new evidence, that the one could not well be separated from the other. Besides, as the *History of Opinions* did not make its appearance till the controversy with respect to the former work was terminated, or nearly so, Dr P. has exhibited many of his old arguments in a new form; meaning, doubtless, that this last statement should be considered as the result of all the investigation on both sides of the question. I am far from flattering myself, that any thing I can say will have more weight with *him*, than what has been advanced by preceding writers. But perhaps, it may appear to others, that some additional light has been thrown even on those points which have been already debated. As no reply has professedly been made to what the Doctor calls his *large* work, an ample field has hitherto remained unoccupied.

That able and elegant writer Mr Whitaker, in his *Origin of Arianism disclosed*, has chiefly directed his attention to the faith of the ancient Jews. This work was transcribed for the press, before I knew that he had wrote on the subject. I was apprehensive that what he had published might have superseded the necessity of any thing further with respect to the Jewish creed. But he has taken a general view of the subject; whereas I have considered it particularly, in relation to the objections made by Dr P. Thus, even where there is some coincidence in the reasoning, it assumes a very different form. There are also several points in which we materially differ.

This work has swelled so much beyond what was originally designed, that it has been necessary to overlook various articles of importance which have received a place in, the *History of Early Opinions.* I particularly regret that I could not enter on the consideration of what is advanced on the doctrine of the *Miraculous Conception.* But if this attempt meet with a favourable reception from the public, that may be the subject of a future discussion.

It would be presumption to imagine, that there are no mistakes in a work of such extent and variety. But I am conscious that I have in no instance wilfully misrepresented the meaning of our modern historian, or misinterpreted the language of any ancient writer quoted on the subject. Nor have I followed the ordinary plan of Socinians, in disregarding what may be reckoned the strongest arguments on the opposite side; but have endeavoured, on the contrary, to give every one its full force.

In the course of this work, those whom our author acknowledges as brethren are often designed by that name which they have assumed. They, indeed, call themselves *Unitarians,* as pretending that they alone hold the divine unity. I need not say that, in this sense, every Trinitarian must deny their title to the name; as being fully convinced that those only who believe in three Persons hold the scriptural doctrine of one God. But as this work contains so many quotations, in which the name occurs in the sense imposed by Socinians; I could not, without confusion or frequent circumlocution, avoid the use of it in this sense. Therefore, it is used merely as a general distinctive appel-

lation

lation claimed by the party, without the moſt diſtant idea of acknowledging the juſtneſs of the claim.

Always, when it has been attainable, I have conſulted the original writers referred to, unwilling to take the quotations of others upon truſt.

It is not one of the leaſt diſadvantages to which this work is ſubjected, that it makes its appearance at a time when the public attention ſeems to be confined to the management of the kingdoms of this world. But there are ſtill many, it is to be hoped, who have their eye principally directed to that kingdom *which cannot be moved*. Others may look on, as nowiſe intereſted in the iſſue of this controverſy; or may conſider it as of no moment, compared with that which engroſſes their attention. But *they* will contemplate all the *ſhakings of nations*, in their certain ſubſerviency to the more eminent coming of the *Deſire of all nations*. As the defence of *his* eſſential rights has been my great deſign in this work, I am not aſhamed to avow that I humbly commend it to his all-powerful protection.

C O N-

N. B. b signifies *from the bottom of the page.*

Page 23, line 15, *for* not out, *read* formed out
—— 96, line 1, *for* in, *read* it
—— 105, line 2, (*b*) *for* Now *read* How
—— 139, line 7, *read* natural
—— 149, line 4, (*b*) *read* communicative
—— 176, line 8, *for* formerly, r. which will be afterwards explained
—— 209, note, *for* 185 *read* 199, 200
—— 215, note, *for* Ηροσχυνεω *read* Προσχυνιω
—— 230, line 3, (b) *for* At *read* As
—— 235, line 1, *for* as fuch *read* as able to
—— 251, line 9, *for* out *read* our
—— 278, line 10, for חרא *read* הדא
—— 288, line 2, *for* writers, *read* writer
—— 360, line 22, *where the letters are dropt out, read* evidence
—— 532, line 10, *for* mention *read* mentioned

CONTENTS

OF THE

FIRST VOLUME.

BOOK I.

THE DOCTRINE OF THE ANCIENT JEWS CONCERNING THE MESSIAH.

CHAP.

BOOK II.

THE DOCTRINE OF THE NEW TESTAMENT CONCERNING JESUS CHRIST.

═══════

BOOK III.

OF THE EVIDENCE OF THE DEITY OF CHRIST FROM THE
USE OF THAT EXPRESSION, THE SON OF GOD.

CHAP.

BOOK IV.

OF DR PRIESTLEY's ARGUMENTS AGAINST THE DEITY OF
CHRIST.

CHAP.

A

VINDICATION

OF THE

DOCTRINE OF SCRIPTURE, &c.

BOOK I.

THE DOCTRINE OF THE ANCIENT JEWS CONCERNING THE MESSIAH.

CHAP. I.

Of Dr Prieſtley's Hypotheſis on this Subject; and of Philo's Doctrine concerning the Logos.

IT is of conſiderable importance, with reſpect to the deciſion of this controverſy, to know what was the faith of the Church before the coming of the Saviour. Dr Prieſtley, in the firſt form which he gave his work, introduced the prophets as his witneſſes. "The Jews," he ſays, "were "taught by their prophets to expect a Meſſiah, who was to "be deſcended from the tribe of Judah;—but none of their "prophets gave them an idea of any other than a man like "themſelves, in that illuſtrious character, and no other "did they ever expect, or do they expect to this day *."

Vol. I.   A   The

* Hiſt. of Corruptions, vol. i. p. 1.

The learned Gentleman was himſelf ſo fully ſatisfied of the truth of theſe aſſertions, that, important as they are in their connexion, he does not ſeem to have thought it neceſſary to add a ſhadow of proof. He makes bare aſſertion the very baſis of his fabric, as if he meant fairly to ſhew the world what they were to expect from the whole.

However, in the enlarged form in which the ſame work makes its ſecond appearance, the author deſcends a little from this dogmatical elevation, and deigns to favour the reader with ſome kind of evidence. But it is partial and inconcluſive. He endeavours to prove that the Jews, without exception, at the time of our Saviour's appearance, expected no other than a human Meſſiah; and that they had no higher expectations in any ſucceeding period. But he offers no proof of his aſſertion with reſpect to the doctrine of the prophets. Indeed, if the determination of this diſpute were left to the prophets alone, and if their teſtimony met with the ſame juſtice, in interpretation, that is ordinarily allowed to human writings, the diſpute would ſoon be at an end. It would appear, that, if there be any meaning in language, if the prophetical writings were not deſigned as an impoſition on the common ſenſe of mankind, *all* the prophets, who particularly wrote of the Meſſiah, give the moſt diſtinct idea of a divine Perſon. But as Dr P. leaves his aſſertion with reſpect to them without ſupport, it is unneceſſary to conſider it particularly. He wiſhes to take a leſs tedious and difficult plan, than that of exploring the depths of prophecy. If he can firſt eſtabliſh it as fact, that the Jews expected merely a human Meſſiah, it will, in his account, be a ſufficient preſumption with reſpect to the truth delivered to them in Scripture.

That the generality of the Jews, at the time of our Saviour's appearance, had very confuſed ideas of the character of Meſſiah, few, perhaps, will be diſpoſed to doubt. But it may afterwards appear that they entertained

ed apprehenfions of his character, not eafily reconcileable with the idea of his being a mere man.

According to Dr P., " Our Saviour could not poffibly " have puzzled the Jewifh Doctors as he did, by afking " them how David could call the Meffiah his Lord, when " he was his Son, or defcendant, on any other principle. " For if they had themfelves been fully perfuaded that " the Meffiah, though defcended from David, was the Ma- " ker and God of David, a fatisfactory anfwer to his que- " ftion was very obvious." But how could that be a *fatif- factory anfwer* in the mouth of a Jew, which is foolifhnefs when uttered by a Chriftian? For once, it would feem, the diftinction of natures in the perfon of the Meffiah may be admitted, as a fatisfactory folution of the difficulty arifing from the apparent oppofition of the characters afcribed to him. But, kind reader, you muft not prefume to plead this as a precedent. It is only meant to ferve a prefent purpofe.

However, as the Jewifh Doctors did not give this *fatisfac- tory anfwer*; it is fair to conclude that they were greatly at a lofs for one that was fo. But they could not *poffibly* have been *puzzled*, had they not been confcious that the words of David implied an acknowledgment of dignity, and therefore of defcent, more than human. Or, fhall we rather fuppofe that thefe Jewifh Doctors were not fo well acquainted with Hebrew idioms and ideas as thofe of our time? *A fatisfactory anfwer* would have been *very obvious* to the mereft novice in Socinianifm. Without any hefita- tion he would have told Jefus, that it was no wife repug- nant to their traditionary and eftablifhed, nay, to their fcriptural ideas of Jehovah, to believe that a mere man fhould fit on his right hand, as fharing in his power and glory. But, furely, a good caufe never had more wretch- ed advocates. For *no man was able to anfwer him a word.* Mere daftards muft they all have been. For *neither durft*

any

any man from that day forth aſk him any more queſtions, Matth.xxii. 46.

But if Jeſus had no ſonſhip ſuperior to that by his deſcent from David, it will be difficult to vindicate his conduct on this occaſion. For if Chriſt was only to be the ſon of David, the Phariſees declared the whole truth in anſwer to our Saviour's queſtion, *What think ye of Chriſt, whoſe ſon is he?* The queſtion was reſtricted to his *Sonſhip.* They could not, with propriety, take greater latitude in their anſwer. *They ſay unto him, The Son of David.* It is allowed that this to a Jew, was a character of the ſame meaning with that of Meſſiah. Now, as they anſwered diſcreetly, if they told the whole truth concerning the Sonſhip, what good end could it ſerve for our Saviour to *puzzle* them? Did it become the great Prophet, when men had juſt and diſtinct ideas of truth, to excite doubts in their minds, and to expoſe them to the danger of Scepticiſm? Undoubtedly, if there was any propriety in the objection made by Jeſus, he wiſhed them to believe, that the character given him by the ſpirit of prophecy neceſſarily implied a ſuperior filiation. He might juſtly leave them in their perplexity, becauſe they ought to have known his character from their own ſcriptures; and becauſe he knew that they wilfully and obſtinately reſiſted the light which theſe afforded.

According to our author, " Facundus very properly " ſays, that Martha and Mary would never have ſaid to " Chriſt, *If thou hadſt been here,* had they thought him " to be God omnipreſent *." But if Jeſus be not God omnipreſent, he could never have *properly* ſaid to Martha, *I am the reſurrection, and the life,* John xi. 21. 25. It ſeems abundantly evident, that even the diſciples had very
.confuſed.

I

* Ibid. p. 35.

confused notions with respect to the character of Jesus, before the effusion of the Holy Ghost, who was to teach them all things. But it is unfair to judge of the fixed principles of the disciples, from the occasional workings of unbelief; especially when their minds were in great perturbation, or under peculiar temptation. It is clear, that our Lord had reproved Martha as indulging this sin ; " *Said I not unto* " *thee that if thou wouldest believe,*" *&c.* ver. 40. Whence proceeded his tears and groanings in spirit, but from the grief of his holy human soul on account of the power of this iniquity, as displayed in the conduct, not of the other Jews only, but of Martha and Mary? But even while their unbelief appears in their virtually ascribing the death of Lazarus to the absence of Jesus, they in the very same words discover a conviction of his being possessed of power more than human. They declare their persuasion of his sovereign authority over death. But the sentiments of the Jews concerning the Messiah, especially as illustrated by the gospel-history, shall be more particularly considered afterwards.

Our author also argues from the interpretations given by their later writers of those passages of the Old Testament, which have been supposed by Christians to contain the doctrine of a Trinity, or of a plurality in the divine essence. When mentioning that passage, Gen. i. 26. *Let us make man,* he acknowleges that it has received a variety of interpretations *. It has been understood as signifying that God spoke to all second causes, or to " intelligences " only, or to the elements, or to souls ;" or that he used the style of a king ; or that he excited or commanded himself. This variety of ridiculous interpretations shews how much the Jews are at a loss. The most general opinion, that he spoke to angels, though designed to exclude a plurality of

A 3   pesons,

---

* Vol. iii. p. 26. 27.

perſons, if it has any meaning, neceſſarily ſuppoſes a plurality of gods.   For God cannot reaſonably be ſuppoſed to
ſpeak in this ſtyle to his inferiors.   Nothing can be more
evident, than that the Jewiſh writers themſelves are conſcious that their interpretations of this paſſage, and of
others of the ſame kind, are far from being ſatisfactory.
They even acknowledge, that they draw a veil over their
true meaning.   Maimonides explains the plural language
aſcribed to God in ſcripture, as referring to his *houſe of
judgment*. that is, to angels *.   But even after he has given this view of it, he ſays ; " All things which are men-
" tioned in the hiſtory of the creation, are not to be under-
" ſtood according to the letter, as the vulgar imagine.
" For otherwiſe our wiſe men would not have command-
" ed the concealment of theſe things, nor would they have
" exerciſed ſuch care in hiding and involving them in pa-
" rables.   Nor would they have even ſo ſtudiouſly pro-
" hibited the mention of ſuch things in the preſence of
" the ignorant rabble.   For the literal ſenſes of theſe
" things either beget wicked thoughts, imaginations and
" opinions concerning the nature of God, or certainly
" ſubvert the foundations of the law, and introduce
" ſome hereſy.—Whoever has any ſkill in theſe ſubjects,
" ought to be on his guard that he do not divulge them ;
" as we have many times given warning in our commen-
" tary on the *Miſchna*.   Hence, alſo our Rabbies plainly
" ſay, that *it is for the glory of God to conceal theſe things
" that are written from the beginning of the book to this
" place*.   But they have ſaid this after what is written con-
" cerning the works of the ſixth day.   Hence, the truth
" of what we have obſerved is evident.   But becauſe he
" who has acquired any perfection is bound to communi-
" cate it to others,--it will unavoidably follow, that thoſe
                                                        " whe

---

* More Nevochim, Par. 2. cap. 6.

" who have apprehended any of these secrets, whether by
" their own diligence, or by the help of a master, will at
" times utter a few of them. But this must not be done
" openly and plainly, but under cover, and only by signs
" and symbols, such as are to be found scattered, and blend-
" ed with other things, in the sayings of our more cele-
" brated and excellent Rabbies. Therefore I also, as you
" may observe, in these mysteries only mention one word
" or expression, as the hinge of the whole. But I leave
" the rest to others, to whom it is to be left *."

What reason can the learned Jews have for speaking of
secrets and *mysteries*; for commanding the *concealment* of
these from *the common people*, the use of *parables*, of *single
words*, or *phrases, blended* with extraneous matter; and for

A 4   giving

* Non omnia secundum literam intelligenda et accipienda esse, quæ
dicuntur in opere *Berefchith* seu creationis, sicut vulgus hominum existi-
mat. Nam alias non præcepissent sapientes illa occultari, neque tanta
cura in eis abscondendis et parabolis involvendis usi fuissent, neque etiam
tam studiosè prohibuissent, ne de iis sermo fieret coram imperita plebe.
Sensus enim illorum litterales vel gignunt pravas cogitationes. imagina-
tiones et opiniones de natura Dei Opt. Max., vel certè fundamenta legis
evertunt, hæresimque aliquam introducunt.—Quicumque verò aliquam
in illis scientiam habet, cavere debet, ne illa divulget, sicuti sæpiùs mo-
nuimus in Commentario nostro in Mischnam. Hinc claris verbis dicunt
quoque Rabbini nostri; *A principio libri usque hûc gloria Domini est
celare verbum :* dixerunt autem hoc post ea, quæ scripta sunt de operibus
fexti diei, ex quo patet veritas illius quod nos diximus. Quia verò is,
qui perfectionem aliquam nactus est, tenetur et obligatur illam aliis quoque infundere et communicare,—ideo fieri non potest, quin illi, qui ali-
quid ex secretis istis, sive proprio Marte et industria, sive ope præceptoris
alicujus, apprehenderunt, nonnunquam pauca quædam dicant. Verùm
non apertè et clarè hoc faciendum est, sed tectè, et non nisi per signa et
indicia, qualia sparsim, et aliis rebus permixta in verbis celebriorum ac
præstantiorum Rabbinorum nostrorum inveniuntur. Ideoque et ego, ut
observabis, in istis mysteriis sæpe unius alicujus verbi vel dicti solùm
mentionem facio, quod cardo quasi est totius rei; cætera vero illis relinquo, quibus relinquenda sunt. Ibid. Par. 2. cap. 29. p. 273, 274.

giving *frequent warnings* to this purpoſe; if they really believe the interpretations which they give openly? When
this intelligent writer ſays, that the literal ſenſe of the
ſcriptural language concerning creation introduces *hereſy*,
he undoubtedly refers to the ſupport that it gives to the
Chriſtian doctrine, which they diſtinguiſh by this name;
and eſpecially to that of the Trinity. For when the Rabbies, according to his acknowledgment, particularly apply
the ſaying quoted from them to what is written concerning
the works of the *ſixth* day, they plainly intimate, that the
great *myſtery*, with reſpect to creation, lies in the language
aſcribed to God in the creation of man. When Maimonides
ſpeaks of a *few ſecrets* being unavoidably *uttered* at times, is
it not implied that many more are intentionally concealed?
What truſt can any man of ſenſe repoſe in ſuch interpreters, as to their faithfully declaring the hereditary doctrine of
their nation? In a word, is it not evident that the difference
between Jews and Socinians is conſiderably wider than the
latter pretend? For the very uſe of the term *myſtery*, in
relation to theſe words, *Let us make man*, muſt be exceedingly ungrateful to a Socinian ear.

R. Huna is introduced in a Jewiſh work, as ſaying, that
if this kind of language had not been written, it would
not have been lawful to ſay, *The Elohim hath created*,
&c *.

On this ſubject Dr P. alſo calls in the aſſiſtance of the
Chriſtian fathers †. They may, indeed, be ſuſtained as
giving a juſt enough account of what they knew. Their
teſtimony is alſo of weight as to the ſtate of the Jewiſh
creed in their own times. But they were not ſufficiently
acquainted

---

* Dixit R. Huna in nomine Bar Cappara, niſi hujuſmodi ſermo ſcriptus
eſſet, non fuiſſet licitum dicere, *Dii creavit cœlum*, &c. Martini Pugio
Fidei, p. 388.

† Ear. Op. vol. iii. p. 8.

acquainted with the writings of the ancient Jews, to be admitted as witnesses. It would appear, however, that in some instances when they only spoke of the Jews in our Saviour's time, or in their own, our author has understood them as expressing the faith of that people in every age. But I shall not lose time on this point, as the assertions of the fathers cannot bring conviction in opposition to other evidence. Some of them might infer from what they knew of the Jews in their own times, that their ancestors held the same sentiments. This seems, indeed, to be our author's plan of reasoning. But it is inconclusive. For with equal propriety may we infer from their later interpretations of prophecy, either that Christians have erroneously believed in a suffering Messiah, or that the Old Testament exhibits two persons under this character, the one as a sufferer, and the other as a conqueror. Justin Martyr not only shews that the ancient believers of the Jewish church considered the Word as a distinct and divine Person [*]; but speaks in such a manner to Trypho, of some of the Rabbies in his own age, that we cannot understand his words in any other sense than as expressing their persuasion, that the Messiah was to be divine. " But if we produce to them," he says, " these scriptures that I have formerly rehearsed " to you, which expressly shew that the Messiah is both " subject to suffering and the adorable God, they are under " a necessity of acknowledging that these respect Christ; " but they dare to assert, that this (Jesus) is not the Christ. " But that he shall come, and suffer, and reign, and be the " adorable God, they confess; which is truly ridiculous " and foolish, as I shall in like manner shew [†]."

The

[*] Dial. p. 355.

[†] Ας δε αν λεγωμεν αυτοις γραφας, αι διαρρηδην τον Χριστον και παθητον και προσκυνητον και Θεον αποδεικνυουσιν, ας και προανιστορησα υμιν, ταυτας

The doctrine of the ancient Jews with reſpect to the Godhead, and the Meſſiah, if not referred to the teſtimony of the prophets, may be known from the writings of Philo, and from their Paraphraſes. Some of the latter are ſuppoſed to have been written before the birth of Chriſt. Philo flouriſhed, according to our author's own chronology, forty years after this æra. We ſhall conſider his teſtimony firſt, not only as this is the order obſerved by Dr P. in his ſecond work; but as his conceſſions, with reſpect to Philo, may tend to illuſtrate the weakneſs of his reaſoning againſt the doctrine of the Paraphraſts.

Our author, in the Hiſtory of Corruptions, acknow-ledges, that Philo " went before the Chriſtians in the per-" ſonification of the Logos, vol. i. p. 30." But he does not ſay whether this was a real, or only an allegorical per-ſonification. He indeed ſeems to admit that it was real, as it is added; " For he calls this divine Word a *ſecond* " *God."* Perhaps, this proof might be preferred, as ap-parently inſinuating that Philo had no idea of unity of eſ-ſence.

Dr P's words, in their connexion, diſcover an inclination to deprive the friends of the doctrine of the Trinity, of any advantage from the teſtimony of Philo: " For he calls " this divine Word a *ſecond God*, and ſometimes attributes " the creation of the world to this ſecond God, thinking " it below the majeſty of the great God himſelf. He alſo " ſays, that he is neither unbegotten, like God, nor be-" gotten as we are, but the middle between the two " extremes." But ſuppoſing all this to be as our author ſays, what can it avail him? In the words quoted, the pre-exiſtence

---

τας εις Χριſον μεν ειρηſθαι αναγκαζομενοι ſυντιθενται, τυτον δε μη ειναι τον Χριſον, τολμωσι λεγειν —ελευſε·θαι δε και παθειν, και βασιλευσαι, και προσκυνητον γενεσθαι Θεον ομολογουσιν· οπερ γελοιον και ανοητον· ον ομοιως αποδειξα. Dial. p. 294.

exiftence of the Logos is evidently affumed as a firft princi-ple ; whereas Dr P. hath to prove that all the ancient Jews expected that their Meffiah fhould be " no other than a " man like themfelves." But from the writings of Soci-nians, we have had occafion to obferve that, in order to a-void a confeffion of the fupreme deity of Chrift, they will fubmit to any opinion concerning him, however abfurd and contrary to their own fyftem. They will rather join their forces with the Arians, however bitter their con-tentions at times, than *fall under* him, by confeffing that *his throne is for ever and ever.* Like the harlot, the falfe mother, they will prefer a divifion of the child to an ac-knowledgment of the true parent.

But it is at leaft queftionable, if Philo meant as the Doc-tor interprets. According to him, " he attributes the " creation of the world to this fecond God, *thinking* it be-" low the majefty of the great God himfelf *." Here we have an inftance of the great freedom which the Doctor ufes with the words of others. Hath Philo himfelf faid, that he thought it " below the majefty of the great God " to create this world ?" If fo, how does he exprefs him-felf?

In a paffage preferved by Eufebius †, he calls the Lo-gos *a fecond God.* But, as it appears that the ancient Jews underftood the word *Elohim* as fometimes denoting *perfons,* for which reafon, it is thought, they have rendered the plural noun by the fingular Θεος, in the Septuagint ; it has been inferred that Philo, when he called the Logos a *fecond God,* only meant the *fecond perfon* ‡. It cannot be refufed, indeed, that in a variety of paffages he fpeaks of the Logos as inferior to *Him who is.* But when this kind of language occurs,

---

* Hift. Cor. vol. i. p. 30.

† Praepar. Evangel. lib. 7. c. 13. Bedford's Serm. p. 71.

‡ Ibid.

occurs, it may be difficult to prove, that Philo does not view the Logos in a delegated character, entirely different from what belongs to him essentially. For he undoubtedly considers him as both the Son of God, and the Mediator between God and man. Although this manner of expression should be joined with what respects his essence, it may easily be accounted for from the writer's viewing the same person in two lights so very different. Even in the sacred records, we find the language of supremacy, and of subjection, that which is peculiar to God, and that which belongs to man, most intimately connected in the description of him whose name is *Wonderful*.

As a proof of this inferiority attributed by Philo to the Logos, Dr P. quotes that passage in which he is described " as the middle between the two extremes." But had he done Philo the justice to have quoted his words more fully, it would have appeared that he was a special respect to the Logos in his mediatory character. " The Father of " all things," he says, " has bestowed this most admirable " gift upon this Prince of Angels, his most ancient *Logos*, " that he should stand as a mediator to judge between the " creature and the Creator. He therefore intercedes with " him who is immortal, in behalf of mortals. And on the " other hand, he acts the part of an ambassador, being sent " from the supreme King to his subjects. And this gift " he so willingly accepts, as to glory in it, saying, And I " have stood between God and you, being neither unbe- " gotten as God, nor begotten as mortals, but one in the " middle between two extremes, acting the part of an " hostage with both; with the Creator, as a pledge that he " will never be provoked to destroy, or desert the world, " so as to suffer it to run from order into confusion ; and " with creatures, to give them this certain hope, that God, " being reconciled, will never cease to take care of his own " workmanship.

" workmanſhip. For I proclaim peace to the creation
" from that God who removes war, and introduces and
" preſerves peace for ever ·."

Thus his words, when fairly exhibited, appear in a
very different point of view. When he calls the Father
the ſupreme King. he evidently ſpeaks of the Logos in a delegated and aſſumed character Shall we therefore conclude, that he denied his proper deity? With equal propriety may it be inferred, that all who acknowledge Chriſt
as Mediator, deny that he is God. The moſt accurate
human writer may eaſily be repreſented as a heretic, by
culling out a few words without any regard to the connexion, or to the general ſpirit of his work.

But although it ſhould be ſuppoſed that Philo conſidered
the Logos as in ſome reſpect inferior to the Father; nay,
although this could be proved; it would be no ſufficient
evidence that the Jews did not believe the exiſtence of a
plurality of perſons in one nature. For it is well known,
that many who have been zealous for the doctrine of a
Trinity in unity, have had their minds ſo ſtrangely warped
with reſpect to this great myſtery, as to ſpeak of the ſub-
ordination of the Son even as God, of the derivation of
deity from the Father, &c. Underſtanding the language
of Philo with the greateſt ſeverity, it cannot be ſuppoſed
that

---

* Τω δε αρχαγγελω και πρεσβυτατω λογω δωρεαν εξαιρετον εδωκεν οτα
ολα γεννησας πατηρ, ινα μεθοριος ςας, το γενομενον διακρινη τυ πεποιηκοτος.
ο δε αυτος ικετης μεν εςι το θνητυ κηραινοντος αει προς αφθαρτον, πρεσβευ-
της δε τυ ηγεμονος προς το υπηκοον Αγαλλεται δε επι τη δωρεα, και
σεμνυνομενος αυτην εκδιηγειται φασκων, Καγω εισηκειν ανα μεσον κυριυ
και υμων, υτε αγεννητος ως ο Θεος ων, υτε γεννητος ως υμεις. αλλα μεσος
των ακρων, αμφοτεροις ομηρευων· παρα μεν τω φυτευσαντι προς πισιν τυ
μη συμπαν αφανισαι ποτε και απος̔νναι το γενος, ακοσμιαν αντι κοσμυ ελο-
μενον παρα δε τω φυντι, προς ευελπιςιαν τυ μηποτε τον ιλεων Θεον πε-
ριιδειν το ιδιον εργον. εγω γαρ επικηρυκευσομαι τα ειρηναια γενεσει παρα
τυ κωθαιρειν πολεμυς εγνωκοτος ειρηνηφυλακος αει Θευ. Quis rerum divinarum hæres ſit, p. 397.

that he went any further. For he declares the eternity of the Logos in such terms as to oppose him to all creatures. " Moses," he says, " has not likened the rational soul to " any of the things which are created, but has pronounced " it to be the image of that which is divine and invisible; " reckoning it proper that it should be consubstantiated " and conformed to the seal of God, the character of which " is his *eternal* Word.—Therefore it is said that man is " *made after the image of God,* but not after the image of " any creature *."

He asserts the necessary existence of the same divine Person. Addressing himself to others, while speaking of the Logos, he says: " You profess to have the same Father; " not mortal, but immortal, the man of God, who being the " Word of the Eternal, is himself also necessarily immor- " tal †." He evidently ascribes the same eternal and neces- sary existence to the Logos, as to the Father. He declares the absolute perfection and all-sufficiency of his glorious sub- ject. " Unity," he says, " can admit, neither of addition, nor " of subtraction, being the image of God, who alone is " all-sufficient. For other things are by nature vain, and if " there is any solidity in them, it is constricted by the " Word of God. For this is, a bond or glue, compacting " every essence. But he, who connects and conjoins all

" things,

---

* Ο δε μεγας Μωυσης υδενι των γεγονοτων της λογικης ψυχης το ειδος ομοιω, ωνομασεν αλλ' ειπεν αυτην τη θεια και αοραλη εικονα, δοκιμον ειναι νομισας, υσιωθεισαν και τυπωθεισαν σφραγιδι Θευ, ης ο χαρακτηρ εςιν αιδιος λογο —Διο και λεγεται, κατ' εικονα Θευ τον ανθρωπον γεγεννησθαι, υ μην κατ' εικονα τινο, των γεγονοτων. De Plantatione Noe, p. 169.

† Τον αυτον επιγεγραμμενοι πατερα, υ θ ητον; αλλ' αθανατον, αν- θρωπον Θευ, ος τυ αιδιυ λογος ω·, εξ αναγκης και αυτος εςιν αφθαρτος. De Confusione Linguar. p. 255.

I

" things, is perfectly his own completion, and needs no
" other *."

If Philo did not mean to declare that the Logos was of
the *same effence* with the Father, what fenfe can we impofe
on the following affertions? " The Logos is fimilar to no
" fenfible object; but he is the image of God, the moft an-
" cient of all intelligible things, the neareft to him who is
" eftablifhed in truth, there being no line of difference †."
" For his Logos is not made by ftriking of the air (allu-
" ding to the word of man); it is free of all mixture, in-
" corporeal, naked, and differing in no refpect from unity ‡."

He evidently maintains the doctrine of a Trinity. For
he fays, " He who is, is on each fide attended by his
" neareft powers, of which the one is *creative*, and the
" other *kingly*. The creative is God, by which he found-
" ed and adorned the univerfe. The kingly is Lord. It
" is fit that the creature fhould be governed by his Maker.
" Therefore he who is in the middle, being thus attended
" by

---

* Μονας δε υτε προσθηκην, υτε αφαιρεσιν δεχεσθαι πεφυκεν, εικων
υσα τε μονη πληρης Θευ. χαυνα γαρ τα τε αλλα εξ εαυτων, ει δε
τωη και πυκνωθεν ειη, λογω σφιζγεται θειω. κολλα γαρ εστι και δεσμος
ουτος, τα παντα της υσιας εκπεπληρωκως. ο δ' ιερας και συνηφηνας
εκαστα, πληρης αυτος εαυτη κυριως εστιν, υ δεηθεις ετερη τοπαραπαι.
Quis rerum divinarum hæres, p. 396.

† Ο δ', υπερανω τυτων λογος θειος, εις ορατον υκ ηλθεν ιδεαν, ατε
μηδενι των κατ' αισθησιν εμφερης ων, αλλ' αυτος εικων υπαρχων Θευ,
των νοητων απαξαπαντων ο πρεσβυτατος, ο εγγυτατω, μηδενος οντος
μεθοριυ διαττηματος, τυ μονη ο εστιν αψευδως αφιδρυμενος. De Profugis, p. 363.

‡ Ου γαρ εστιν ο λογος αυτω γεγονως αερος πληξις,, αναμιγνυμενος,
αλλω το περαπαν υδενι, αλλα και ασωματος τε, και γυμνος, αδιαφο-
ρων μοναδος. Quod Deus fit immutabilis, p. 238.

" by both his powers, exhibits to the diſcerning mind ſome-
" times the appearance of *one*, and ſometimes of *three* *."

But with reſpect to creation, the ſentiments of Philo aſſume a different aſpect in our author's ſecond work. In
the firſt, he has told us that Philo " attributes the creation
" of the world to the ſecond God, thinking it below the
" majeſty of the great God himſelf." But in the ſecond,
we are informed that " Philo was ſo much a Jew that he
" aſcribed proper creation to God the Father only, and the
" forming of created matter to the Logos †." This is a
ſtrange reverſe of matters, indeed! But the learned gentleman muſt meet with a little indulgence. For here, in the
creation of his own fancy, he gives form to what had been
formerly left in the ſtate of chaos. So little did he underſtand his author, that he miſtook the inſtrument for the
proper agent, and conſidered that as a proof of inferiority,
which is now found to be a ſtanding mark of ſupremacy.

But it is merely doing juſtice to Philo, to inquire if, in
the place referred to, there is any evidence of his denying
proper creation to the Logos. According to Dr P. he expreſſes himſelf in this manner. " He being produced, imi-
" tating his Father, and regarding his patterns, reduced
" things into form ‡." But what our author renders *produced*, ought to be *begotten*. The literal meaning of the
paſſage is, " He, being begotten," or, " He, who is the be-
" gotten, imitating the ways of his Father, and obſerving
                                                  " his

---

* Πατερ μεν των ολων ο μεσος, ος εν ταις ιεραις γραφαις κυριω ονοματι καλειται ο ων· αι δε παρ' εκατερα πρεσβυταται και εγγυταται
τȣ οντος δυναμεις· ων η μεν ποιητικη, η δε βασιλικη προσαγορευεται·
και η μεν ποιητικη Θεος· ταυτη γαρ εθηκε τε και διεκοσμησε το παν· η
δε βασιλικη κυριος. Θεμις γαρ αρχειν και κρατειν το πεποιηκος τȣ γε-
νομενȣ. δορυφορȣμενος εν ο μεσος υφ' εκατερας των δυναμεων, παρεχει
τη ορατικη διανοια, τοτε μεν ενος, τοτε δε τριων φαντασιαν. De Abra-
hamo, p. 287.

† Ear. Opin. vol. ii. p. 14.   ‡ Ibid p. 15.

" his archetypal patterns, produces forms *." Dr P.'s tranflation, in confequence of the word αρχετυπα being overlooked, would naturally lead the reader to fuppofe that the *patterns* meant by Philo were fenfible, that they were fome external works of the Father. Our author could not be a ftranger to the fenfe in which the Jew ufes the term *archetypal*. For he has quoted different paffages in which it occuis, as exprefsly fignifying what is merely intellectual, in contradiftinction to objects of fenfe. Thus he introduces Philo as faying, that " the intelligible and incor-" poreal world is the *archetype* of that which is vifible, con-" fifting of invifible ideas, as this does of vifible bodies †." The ancient writer fuppofes thefe archetypal patterns to be in the Logos himfelf, as he is the image of the Father ‡. Ειδη evidently fignifies fenfible forms or vifible objects, as oppofed to patterns merely ideal. Thus, the whole work of creation is afcribed immediately to the Logos.

Dr P's tranflation makes the language felf-contradictory. For if Philo had meant that the Word merely *reduced* the works of his Father *into form*, it would never have been faid that he " imitated his ways." Had this been the cafe, thefe works muft ftill have been in an undigefted ftate. How could he " obferve the patterns" of the Father, when all things are fuppofed to have been *without form and void?*

Did it feem neceffary, I might mention a great variety of paffages, which clearly prove that Philo afcribes the whole of creation to the Logos. But it may fuffice to refer to a former quotation, in which this matter is fet in the cleareft light. There he afferts that " the creative " power is God, by which he, who is, *founded* and *adorned* " the univerfe."

Vol. I.   B   C H A P.

* Ο γεννηθεις μεντοι μιμυμενος τας τυ πατρος οδυς, προς παραδειγματα αρχετυπα εκεινα βλεπων, εμορφυ ειδη. De Confus. Ling. p. 258.

† Ear. Opin. vol. ii .6.   De Mundi O fi

C H A P. II.

That Philo did not borrow from Plato, in perfonifying the Logos ; and that Plato was not the Inventor of this Doctrine.

" BUT what avails," may it be faid, " the teftimony of
" Philo, as it is known that he was tinctured with Pla-
" tonic philofophy ?" Indeed, this is the fum of Dr P's
objection. " It has been obferved that after the-tranfla-
" tion of the Old Teftament into Greek,—in confequence
" of which the Jewifh religion became better known to
" the Greeks, and efpecially to the philofophers of Alexan-
" dria, the more learned of the Jews had recourfe to an
" allegorical method of interpreting what they found to be
" moft objected to in their facred writings, and by this
" means pretended to find in the books of Mofes, and the
" Prophets, all the great principles of the Greek philofo-
" phy, and efpecially that of Plato which at that time was
" moft in vogue. In this method of interpreting Scripture,
" Philo, a learned Jew of Alexandria, far excelled all who
" had gone before him *."

This objection hath been formerly made, and hath been
fully anfwered by different writers, particularly by the
learned Bp Kidder †. But it is common with the difciples of Socinus to reply to the anfwers given to their objections, merely by bringing them forth anew, with as
much form and importance, as if they had never made their
appearance before. But till they fhew the infufficiency of
anfwers already given, little more is requifite than, after
their own example, although with far more propriety, to
give the fubftance of what hath been advanced by former
writers. According to an ordinary rule, *Affirmanti incum-*

bit

* Hift Cor. vol. i. p. 23.
† Demonftration, Part iii. p. 111. 112.

bit probatio. But there is not a fhadow of evidence offered in fupport of this mighty objeftion. Can one proof be brought from Philo, that he really borrowed the doftrine of a. Trinity, or of the Logos, from Plato? On the contrary, does he not all along fupport thefe doftrines by teftimonies from the Law and the Prophets? He produces no expref-fions from Plato, in fupport of this article of his creed. He would very naturally have adopted this plan in order to fhew the conformity of the one to the other, had he fo ear-neftly wifhed to affimilate the fcriptural to the Platonic doc-trine. To fuppofe that one author hath borrowed from another, merely becaufe of fome general conformity of doc-trine, or fimilarity of particular modes of expreffion, efpe-cially when he exprefsly calls in a third, and owns this as his authority, is unfair; and to affert it, is to beg what ought to be proved.

This exception to the teftimony of Philo would be more plaufible, were he the only Jewifh writer who had ufed fuch expreffions. But it will appear, not only that the Para-phrafts ufed the fame language, but that they had the fame fentiments with Philo. Dr P. indeed, overthrows this ob-jeftion by his own conceffion. He acknowledges that Philo "made a much more fubftantial perfonification of "the divine Logos than any of the proper Platonifts had "done *." Now, as we know the firm perfuafion of the Jews concerning the unity of God, although we fhould fup-pofe one of that nation tinftured with *heathenifh ideas*; his motive for carrying them farther than heathens themfelves is abfolutely inconceivable. Certainly, it is moft natural to think, that he would not have gone the fame lengths with them, unlefs he had been fully convinced that the avowed principles of his nation allowed him to carry thefe ideas as far as he hath aftually done.

The

*Ear. Opin. vol. ii. p. 17.

The objeHion, indeed, feems to fall by its own weight.
It has great appearance of felf-contradiHion. For it is afferted, " that the Jews had recourfe to an allegorical method
" of interpreting what they found to be moft objeHed to in
" their facred writings." But from the conneHion, it certainly muft be inferred that " what was moft objeHed to"
was that which they, in the event, interpreted allegorically,
and what, ccording to this method of interpretation,
contained " all the great principles of the Greek philofo-
" phy, and efpecially that of Plato.". But will our author
pleafe to fhew, how that could be *moft objeHed to*, which
might be interpreted as having the greateft affinity to the
Philofophy which was moft in'vogue? Did the Platonifts
mifunderftand the Scriptures fo far, as efpecially to objeH
to thofe paffages which, when explained by a Jew, ap-
proached moft nearly to their own fyftem? This favours
very much of myftery. The learned Gentleman muft certainly find a more fatisfying reafon for the recourfe which
the Jews are faid to have had " to an allegorical method of
" interpreting." But the faH is ; he wifhes that interpretation to be confidered as *allegorical* which is ftriHly literal ; and is, therefore, under a neceffity of framing a reafon
for the pretended change. Any one who takes the moft
fuperficial view of the writings of Philo muft obferve, that
he not only allegorizes, but that he often obfcures a fubjeH,
abundantly clear of itfelf, by the intemperate ufe of allegory. He frequently indulges this humour in the defcripti-
ons which he gives of the Logos. But we are not thence to
conclude that his very exhibition of him as a perfon was a
mere allegory. On the fame ground might the perfonality of the Father be denied.

But fo far is it from being true that Jewifh writers borrowed from Plato, that there is the greateft reafon to believe
the very reverfe. The DoHor himfelf confeffes, that " as
" Plato

" Plato had travelled into the Eaft, it is probable that he
" there learned the doctrine of divine emanations, and his
" ideas of the origin of this vifible fyftem *.

As it is granted that Plato " travelled into the Eaft," it
is alfo known that he went into Egypt. This is mentioned by Apuleius, a heathen writer and one of his difciples.
Plato, he fays, went thither, " that he might learn the rites
of the prophets †." Numenius the Pythagorean calls Plato " Mofes Atticifing" or " fpeaking Greek‡." Arifto-
bulus, a Jewifh writer, fays ; " It is plain, that Plato follow-
" ed our law, and that he diligently ftudied the feveral
" parts of it ||." Jofephus alfo afferts that Plato efpecially
imitated Mofes §. The fame is affirmed by Chriftian writers. Clemens Alexandrinus obferves, that " Plato was ac-
" quainted with prophecy ;" and that he " derived his phi-
" lofophy from the Jews." He even calls him " the He-
" brew Philofopher ;" afferting that the Greek fages were
generally " thieves, taking the choiceft of their opinions
" from Mofes and the Prophets, without thankful acknow-
" ledgment **." Juftin Martyr declares, that Plato " drew
" many things from the Hebrew rivulets," and that " what-
" foever he faid devoutly of God, or of his worfhip, he ftole
" from the Hebrew Philofophy ††." Theodoret, Joannes
Philoponus, Eufebius, Ambrofe, Auguftin and Tatian affert the fame.

At any rate, is it not far more probable, that Plato borrowed from the Hebrews, than that they borrowed from
him ; as it is certain that he was in Egypt, where many
Jews were fettled ; as we know his great diligence in acqui-

ring

* Hift. Cor. vol. i. p. 28.

† De Dogmat. Platon. ap. Kidder. Part. i. p. 111.

‡ Theodoret. Cur. Graec. Affect. l. ii. ib.

|| Eufeb. Praep. lib. 13. c. 12. ib.   § Lib. 2 cont. Apion.

** Strom. b. i. 5.   †† Apol. 2.

ring knowledge; and as it is otherwife unaccountable whence
he received his notions of a Trinity? Was it from other
Philofophers? From whom did they derive their knowledge of it? Either from imagination, or from tradition.
The firft is improbable, according to the opinion both of the
orthodox, and of Dr P. They grant that this doctrine is
above the line of human reafon. He fuppofes it to be directly contradictory. If fo, is it rational to fuppofe, that
fuch men as Plato, who, it will be granted, in other inftances fpoke in a very fublime manner of the divine nature,
would of themfelves devife a doctrine fo abfurd as this is
faid to be? While all the nations around held fuch a multiplicity of gods, that the Greeks themfelves, fo early as
Hefiod's age, are faid to have had no lefs than thirty thoufand, how can it be accounted for, that Plato, while he in
fome fenfe held the divine Unity, fhould ftumble upon the
number *three?*

Is it faid, that he moft probably had this doctrine from
tradition? Where then had he this tradition? In the Eaft,
furely, whither Plato, and other Philofophers before him, travelled. And whence did it originate? Certainly, from the
remains of primitive Revelation, or from intercourfe with
the Hebrews, whofe facred writings are undoubtedly more
ancient than thofe of any other people. Can it be fuppofed
that Plato travelled into the Eaft for the exprefs purpofe of acquiring knowledge, and never once heard of
thofe moft ancient of all writings; efpecially when the
Jews were at this time difperfed through fo many countries? Is it fuppofable, that if he heard of them, he would
not wifh to learn fomething of their contents? Can we
entertain fuch an opinion of one who was at fo much pains
to be initiated into the Egyptian myfteries? Befides, is it
not certain that other Philofophers before him brought
the fame opinions from the Eaft?

But why fhould we multiply proofs? We have the
confeffion of Plato himfelf, that this Philofophy was not the

fruit of his own reflection, but partly derived from ancient tradition. Nay, he materially acknowledges, that he derived it from the Jews. He says, " This ftory of one and " many (ἰν καὶ πολλὰ) is a tradition which the ancients who " were better, and lived nearer the Gods than we, tranf- " mitted to us *." He afferts, that the fafeft and moft certain way of proving the immortality of the foul, is διὰ λογω θεʊ τινος " by fome divine word or tradition †." He acknowledges, that " the firft inftitution of letters was from the Gods, by certain Barbarians ;" that " he and the reft of " the Greeks received their choiceft traditions and learning " from certain Barbarians more ancient than themfelves ;" and that they " gave a better form to what they thus re- " ceived ‡." He fpeaks of a Phenician fable, refpecting the fraternity " of all men not out of the earth ||;" which undoubtedly refers to the formation of Adam. He alfo mentions " Syrian fables."

It is well known that the Greeks called all other nations Barbarians. Bochart feems juftly to conclude, that Herodotus fpeaks of the Jews under the name of Phenicians. For he fays, that " certain Phenicians came from the coaft " of the Red fea." On this Jofephus makes the following obfervations ; " This writer appears to be certain that the Sy- " rians of Paleftine are circumcifed. Now, the fact is, that " in Paleftine, the Jews only are circumcifed ; and as " he is pofitive in his affertion, what he fays refpecting this " circumftance can refer to no other people §." Xenophon alfo teftifies that the Jews were called Syrians **.

Is it inquired, why Plato did not actually name the Jews? Many reafons might be given ; among which that already

B 4　　　　　　　　mentioned

* Philebus, p 17. ap. Gales Court of the Gentiles, p. 2. b. 3 c. 2.
† Phaedo, p 85. ib.　　　　　‡ Cratylus. 426. ib.
|| De Republ. lib. 3. ib.
§ Vid. Jofeph. cont. Apion. l. i, Bocharti Phaleg. l. 4. c. 34.
** Ap. Gale. part 1. b. 1. c. 4.

mentioned is one. Being neighbours of the Phenicians, who were fo univerfally known by their extenfive commerce, and alfo of the Syrians; they were fpoken of under thefe names which were more familiar to ftrangers. Origen * gives another reafon ; that, becaufe of the pecµliarity of their religion, and feparation from the reft of mankind, the Jews were fo hated by other nations, that Plato might think it impolitic exprefsly to mention their name, left it might expofe the doctrines which he had derived from them to contempt.

But Plato was not the only Philofopher who borrowed from the Jews. Pythagoras undoubtedly did the fame. Hermippus, who writes his life, affirms that he " tranfla: " ted many of the Jewifh Laws into his own Philofophy." Diogenes Laertius fays, that " he went to the Hebrews." The fame is attefted by Strabo and Porphyry, and by Ariftobulus the Jew †. Jofephus alfo afferts, that " many " of the cuftoms of the Jews are incorporated into the " Philofophy of Pythagoras ‡." Clearchus, a difciple of Ariftotle, declares that he faw a Jew, with whom his maſter had often converfed, according to the words which he afcribes to Ariftotle ; " equally to the gratification and " improvement of thofe who could relifh the happinefs of " fuch a converfation ||." It is alfo afferted by various writers, that Pherecydes, who is fuppofed to have been the preceptor of Pythagoras, was much indebted to the Jews.

Socinians ftill feem to fpeak of Plato, as if he had been the firft Philofopher who broached the doctrine of a Trinity. But there is undoubted evidence that it was known to the heathen, many ages before him. His own difciple Plotinus thus expreffes himfelf on this fubject : " That thefe " doctrines are not new, nor of yefterday, but have been
" very

---

* Cont. Celf. lib. 4.   † Gale. p. 2. b. 2. c. 5.

‡ Cont. Apion. lib. 1. || Ibid.

" very anciently delivered, though obfcurely (the difcourfes
" now extant being but explanations of them) appears from
" Plato's own writings ; Parmenides before him having in-
" fifted on them *." Again ; " Parmenides alfo agreed in
" this acknowledgment of a Trinity of divine or archical
" hypoftafes †." As many learned men are of opinion that
the *Tetractys*, by which it is faid, Pythagoras ufed to
fwear, was nothing but the *Tetragrammaton* or name of four
letters, of which he had received fome account from the
Jews ; it is alfo afferted that he held a Trinity of divine
hypoftafes, and therefore fpoke of God fometimes as a
monad, fometimes as a *mind*, and fometimes as the *foul* of
the world ‡. Thence Jamblichus fays in Proclus, that there
" were three Gods alfo praifed by the·Pythagoreans ‖."

It is clear that Orpheus afferted a Trinity, under the
names of Phanes, Uranus and Chronus, one of thefe he called πϱοτογονος Θεος, *the firft begotten God.* Wolfius afferts
from Damafcius, that Orpheus introduced a triform deity §.
" Timotheus the chronographer affirms that Orpheus had
" long ago declared, that all things were made by a co-ef-
" fential or confubftantial Trinity **." He ufes the three
names, *Light, Counfel* and *Life*; and afferts that by thefe
three all things were made. He alfo fpeaks of the Divine
Word, and recommends a fixed adherence to it ††.

There were likewife feveral hints of a Trinity in the
Egyptian doctrines. Jamblichus informs us, that according
to the Hermaic Theology, there was " firft an indivifible
" unity called *Eicton* ; fecondly a perfect Mind, underftand-
" ing himfelf, and converting his cogitations into him-
" felf, called *Emeph*, or *Cneph*; and thirdly, the im-
" mediate

* Plotin. En. 5. b. 1. ap. Cudworth's Intellectual Syftem, p. 546-
† Ibid. 386. ‡ Cudworth, p. 373. ‖ Ibid. 547.
§ Wolf. Excerpt. ex Damafc. Anec. Graec. tom. iii. p. 252.
** Cedrenus ap. Cud. 304. †† Kidder's Demonftration, P. 3. p. 124.

" mediate principle of generation, called by several names
" according to its several powers, as *Phtha*, *Ammon*,
" *Osiris* *." As Cneph was sometimes represented with an
egg coming out of his mouth, Eusebius, on the testimony
of Porphyry, says, that the egg denoted the world, " crea-
" ted by the eternal Logos †."

The Persian *Mithras*, said by his worshippers to be
the father and maker of all things, was commonly called
τριπλασιος *threefold*. Plutarch observes that Oromasdes
" thrice augmented or triplicated himself ‡." In the Oracles ascribed to Zoroaster, it is said that the Father perfec-
ted all things and delivered them to the second Mind, whom
the nations of men commonly take for the first. In a Chal-
daic oracle cited by Proclus, there is mention of a third hy-
postasis under the name of *Psyche*. This, Pletho says, they
also called Arimanius. In one of these Oracles, the paternal Monad πατρικη μονας is said to be enlarged, and to gene-
rate two. Mention is also made of the *Duad* and *Triad*:
and it is asserted that " all things serve these three princi-
ples ||." In another it is said § ; " In all the world there
" shines a Trinity, of which an Unity is the head **."

Plutarch testifies that Zoroaster made a threefold distribution of things ; that he assigned the first and highest rank
of them to Oromasdes, who, in the oracles, is called the
Father ; the lowest to *Arimanes*, and the middle to *Mithras*, who in the same oracles is likewise called the second
Mind ††. That Sanchoniathon, the Phenician, borrows
from the books of Moses, seems undeniable. In his account
of creation, he speaks of the operation of a wind or spirit
on the Chaos. He attributes the production of our first

parents

* Jamblichus de Myster. Aegypt. sec. 8. c. 3. ap. Cud. 354.
† Praep. Evan 1. 3. c. 11. Cud. 352.   ‡ Plutarch de Isid. et Osir. Cud. 287.
|| Kidder, p. 3. 128.
§ Παντι γαρ εν κοσμω λαμπει τριας, ης Μονας αρχει.
** Leslie's Socin. Contr. Dial. 1. p. 43.   †† Plutarch, ubi sup.

parents ·to Colpias and Baau. As *Baau* is undoubtedly the fame word with *Bohu* in the Hebrew text, which we render *void*, *Colpias* is, with the greateft probability, fuppofed to be a compound of thefe three Hebrew words, *Kol Pi Jah*, *The voice of the mouth of the Lord*. Thus he mentions the Lord, the Voice of the mouth of the Lord, and the Spirit *.

Lord Monboddo has obferved, that " at this day the doc-
" trine of the three perfons of the deity in one fubftance is
" an effential part of the creed of the Brahmins," and that,
" they call thefe ·perfons by the fame names that we do,
" *the Father*, *the Son*, and *the Holy Ghoft*. The firft," he
adds, " in their language is *Rama*, the fecond *Vifnou*, and
" the third *Crifna*. This fact is told in a French book,
" written by La Croze, entitled Hiftoire du Chriftianifm
" des Indes, vol. 2. book 4. p. 48. And he relates it
" upon the credit of one Manuel Godhino, a Portugueze,
" who was in India in the year 1663. And I have heard
" the fact attefted by an acquaintance of mine, who had
" been many years in India †." It is undeniable that the
Brahmins hold the doctrine of a Trinity, in a certain fenfe.
The names, however, are expreffed differently by different
writers. The Danifh Miffionaries call the three perfons
Ifuren, *Wifchtnu* and *Biruma*. But it does not appear that
the Brahmins really hold an unity of fubftance. For according to the writers formerly mentioned, they believe in
one fupreme God, above thefe three. Thus they introduce
a Brahmin as faying; " We allow but one primary and
" fovereign Being, and conftantly profefs that the great
" *Triad* of deities acknowledge him for their fovereign
" Lord and Mafter ‡." As they hold, however, that thefe
three

---

* Gale's Court. p 2. b. 1. C 3. Bedford's Sermons, p. 97, 98.
† Origin and Progrefs of Language, vol. v.
‡ Conferences between the Danifh Miffionaries and Malabarian Brahmins, p. 2.

three were produced by him, it is probable that their Tri. nity is a corruption of the original doctrine. They have many inferior deities. But they affert, that they are all the vicegerents of the *Triad* *.

It is not meant to defend the ideas of the different hea. then nations on this fubject, or to affert that they agreed with Chriftians in their doctrine of a Trinity. But thefe things are mentioned, to fhew that this doctrine was much older than Plato ; nay, that there was fomething like a ge. neral notion of a Trinity even among the Gentiles. And we cannot rationally fuppofe that this opinion, in which nations fo remote, both as to time and fituation, agreed, could originate from mere chance. It is much more rea. fonable to think that it fprung from fome ancient tradi. tion. Indeed, Proclus exprefsly declares that it was θεοπα-ραδολης θεολογια, "a Theology of divine tradition," or "reve- " lation." Were it neceffary, it might eafily be proved, that great part of the learning of the heathen was derived, ei- ther from ancient tradition, or from revelation ; and parti- cularly, that their mythology was in general merely a cor- ruption of facred hiftory †.

C H A P.   III.

Of the Perfonality afcribed to the Logos by Philo ; and of the Unitarian Doctrine of Occafional Perfonality.

AS the Doctor finds, even after a re-examination of Philo, that it cannot be denied that he makes the Logos a per- fon, he devifes a new folution of the difficulty, in his Hif-

tory

* Ibid.

† Vid. Bocharti Phaleg et Canaan, Cudworth's Intellectual Syftem, Gale's Court of the Gentiles, Millar's Propagation of Chriftianity, and Banier's Mythology.

tory of Early Opinions. He had formerly left the orthodox to make the moſt of Philo, after ſtigmatiſing him as a
Platoniſt. But having diſcovered, which is more than has
been diſcovered in former ages, that " the Platoniſts them-
" ſelves proceeded no farther than to what may be called
" a ſtrongly figurative perſonification of the divine intel-
"lect ;" he expects to deprive his opponents even of the
little ſervice that Philo might have done them. He formerly obſerved, that " Plato, according to Lactantius, gave
" the name of a *ſecond God*" to the Logos, " ſaying, The
" Lord and Maker of the univerſe, whom we juſtly call
" God, made a ſecond God, *viſible* and *ſenſible* †." However, matters are ſo changed, that the Logos merely " con-
" ſtitutes what they (the Platoniſts) called the intelligible
" world, or the world to be perceived by the mind, and
' *not* by the *ſenſes* ‡."

But, even on this ground, the learned gentleman cannot
agree with himſelf. For in the courſe of forty-eight pages
he quits his *ſecond* theory, and returns to the *firſt ;* becauſe
he finds it more ſuitable to his preſent purpoſe. This is
to ſhew that the Chriſtian fathers " obſtinately held to the
" doctrine of Chriſt being nothing more than the *Logos*, or
" the proper *reaſon, wiſdom,* or *power,* of the Father ;" leſt
they ſhould ſeem to the lower people to introduce *another*
God. He contraſts their conduct with that of the Platoniſts. They, he ſays, " had no difficulty at all on this ac-
" count, as they had no meaſures to keep with unitarians,
" but rather wiſhed to ſtand well with thoſe who held a
" multiplicity of Gods. They, therefore, *never* pretended
" to believe that their *three principles* were *one*, or reſolva-
" ble into one §." Here he is ſo certain of the fact, that
he aſſigns a reaſon for it.

But

But as Plato's " vifible and fenfible being" is for a time metamorphofed into one " not perceived by the fenfes;" Philo's *perfon* now appears to be only an occafional one. The Doctor grants, that " in Philo, we find fomething " more nearly approaching to a real perfonification of the " Logos," than in the writings of the Platonifts. Their Logos, being only " a ftrongly figurative perfonification," is deprived of perfonality altogether. But becaufe Philo " approaches more nearly to a real perfonification," fomething more is allowed to his, as it is a ftep nearer to real exiftence. An occafional exiftence is afcribed to it. " He " did not like them (the Platonifing Chriftians) make a " *permanent intelligent perfon* of the Divine *Logos*, he made " an occafional one of it, making it the vifible medium of " all the communications of God to man, that by which " he both made the world, and alfo converfed with the pa- " triarchs of the Old Teftament *." It is then granted that Philo really made a *perfon* of the Logos. This is fo far good. However, the word *occafional* is thrown in, to deprive this conceffion of all its weight. But hath Philo himfelf faid, that he confidered the Logos as an occafional perfon only? The Doctor does not affert this. He only infers it. Now the premifes, from which he forms fo extraordinary a conclufion, muft certainly be very clear. Hath Philo faid, that this Logos, after being emitted by God is again abforbed? No! Hath he faid, that he hath a perifhable exiftence? The very contrary. For he calls him the " eternal Logos,—of neceffity immortal." What then? Philo, when declaring the faith of the ancient church with refpect to the Logos, happens to exprefs himfelf thus : " This world of ideas has no place but the Di-

　　　　　　　　　　　　　　　　　　　　　" vine

---

* Ear. Opin. vol. ii. p. 3.

" vine Logos which difpofes all things *." The Doctor adds, " In another paffage alfo, fpeaking of the dif-" ferent fignifications of *place*, he fays, that ' one of them ' is the divine Logos, the whole of which God himfelf ' has filled with incorporeal powers.' In this place " the Logos is evidently nothing more than the divine " mind itfelf, or the feat of his ideas †." Although Dr P. could clearly fhew that Philo in fome inftances ufes the term *Logos* as merely fignifying the divine mind, it would not amount to a proof that he never ufes it as the name of a proper perfon. But the connection and ftructure of the firft paffage, afford feveral ftrong prefumptions, that even here a perfon is meant. For as Philo, when elfewhere defcribing the fenfible world, calls it the younger fon of God, as contradiftinguifhed from the Logos, whom he calls the elder ‡, he ufes the fame language here. He alfo afcribes the fame work to the Logos, as in another place to that creative power which, according to his idea, attends him who is ; affirming that he " adorned the univerfe ||." Even here he declares, that the Logos is " the power which " made the world." When he adds that this power " hath " its fource with the true good," he certainly intends to diftinguifh the Logos from the Father. Why does he fpeak of *fource*, unlefs he mean to exprefs perfonal derivation? Can " the divine mind" be faid to have a *fource* in any fenfe. The Doctor certainly mifunderftands that fentence,

in

---

* Ουδ' ο εκ των ιδεων κοσμος αλλον αν εχοι τοπον, η τον θειον λο-γον τον ταυτα διακοσμησαντα· επει τις αν ειη των δυναμεων αυτυ τοπος ἑτερος, ος γενοιτ' αν ικανος, 8 λεγω ωατας, αλλα μιαν ακρατον ην τινυν, δεξασθαι τε και χωρησαι· δυναμις δε και η γοσμοποιητικη, πηγη εχυσα το προς αληθειαν αγαθον.   De Mundi Opificio, p. 3. G.

† Ear. Opin. vol. ii. p. 4.   ‡ Quod Deus fit Immutabilis, p. 232.

|| De Abraham. p. 287.

in which he makes Philo say, " For what other proper
" place can there be to receive, and contain, not only all
" *ideas*, but even a single idea?" In this sentence Philo
does not speak of *ideas*, but of *powers*.

But as our author undoubtedly views both the passages
quoted in the same sense, and the latter, indeed, as most
clearly respecting " the divine mind," by it we may certainly judge of the meaning of the former. From the connexion it evidently appears that Dr P. has grossly mis-
applied it. Giving the different significations of place, Philo says : " It is understood in a threefold sense. First, it
" denotes *space*, which is filled with bodies. Secondly, the
" divine Logos, whom God himself has completely filled
" with incorporeal powers. But in a third sense, God
" himself is called *place*, because he comprehends all, and
" is fully comprehended by none, and because he is his
" own space, containing himself, and filled by himself a-
" lone *." Here he clearly distinguishes God from his Logos ; and therefore, by the latter term does not mean " the
" divine mind itself," but a distinct person from him who
is here called God.

From this passage we also learn, in what sense he says,
" The world of ideas *could have* no other place but the
" divine Logos. For what other place could there be to
" receive and contain, I say not, all his *powers*, but even
" a single one?" He plainly means to exhibit the Logos
as infinite ; and, in contradistinction to every creature, as
                                                    alone

---

* Τριχως δε επινοειται τοπος· απαξ μεν, χωρα υπο σωματος εκ-
πεπληρωμενη. κατα δευτερον δε τροπον, ο θειος λογος, ον εκπεπληρωκεν
ολον δι ολων ασωματοις δυναμεσιν αυτος ο Θεος.—κατα δε τριτον ση-
μαινομενον, αυτος ο θεος καλειται τοπος, τω περιεχειν μεν τα ολα, πε-
ριεχεσθαι δε προς μηδενος απλως,—κ᾽ επειδηπερ αυτος εσι χωρα αυτε
κεχωρηκως εαυτον κ᾽ εμφερομενος μονω εαυτω. De Somniis, p. 447.

alone capable of containing all the ideas, and all the powers of the Father.

Is it any argument againſt Philo, that he calls the Logos " the image of God?" Does not the inſpired writer to the Hebrews do the ſame? *Who is the exprefs image of his perfon,* ch. i. 3. Making allowance for the imperfection of every metaphor uſed on this ſubject, there is not one paſſage produced by the Doctor, but might eaſily be proved to apply to the Logos as a perſon. He ſeems really convinced of this himſelf. And for this reaſon has he produced his new theory of occaſional perfonality.

But have we yet found any thing from which our Author had reaſon to infer, that Philo believed that the Logos was an occaſional perfon? Not a ſhadow of proof. Therefore he calls in the aſſiſtance of his *corps de referve,* his forlorn hope, bold ſuppoſition. " It might be imagined," he ſays, " that the Divine Being, by the emiſſion of this " Logos in ſo ſubſtantial a form, would be deprived of ſome " of his power ; but to this Philo would probably have re- " plied, that this *ſecond God* was only like a lamp lighted at " the original fountain of light, which did not diminiſh its " ſubſtance or ſplendor.—Or he might have ſuppoſed that " the loſs ſuſtained by the emiſſion of the Logos was only " temporary, becauſe he thought that the emiſſion of the " Logos only reſembled the emiſſion of light from the ſun " which was afterwards drawn into its ſource again *." All that this requires is a Spartan anſwer. *Probably! Might !*

A great variety of paſſages might be produced, which clearly prove that, although Philo could have formed the wild idea of occaſional perfonality, he could not have thought of aſcribing it to the Logos, as being totally irreconcileable

Vol. I.   C   concileable

concileable to his other ascriptions. Particularly, as he re-
presents him as the manager of the world, and of all things
in it, and as the vicegerent of God, it is absolutely inconceivable that he could consider him as only occasionally e-
mitted. Illustrating these words, *The Lord is my shepherd*,
he says ; " God governs all this universe as a shepherd go-
" verns his flock, or a king his people ; over-ruling and
" managing the earth, water, air and fire, and whatever
" any of these contains, whether vegetables or animals,
" things mortal or spiritual ; particularly, the ordinances of
" heaven, the revolutions of the sun and moon, and the
" changes and orderly movements of the other stars : all
" these does God govern according to the strictest justice,
" having set over them his righteous Logos, his first begot-
" ten Son, who takes the charge of this sacred flock, as
" the vicegerent of the great king. Therefore it is said,
" *Behold, I send mine Angel before thee, to keep thee in the*
" *way *.*"

Describing the great revolutions of states and empires,
and the changes that take place in the world in general, he
says, " Is it not like a ship tossed hither and thither on the
" waves of the sea, now by prosperous, and then by ad-
" verse winds ? For the Word of God, which the multi-
" tude call Fortune, dances on the globe. Thence, being
" *constantly* in motion through cities, and nations, and coun-
" tries, he supports some with the things that belong to o-
" thers,

---

* Καθαπερ γαρ τινα ποιμηνʼ, γην και υδωρ και αερα και πυρ, και
οσα εν τυτοις, φυτα τε αυ και ζωα, τα μεν θνητα, τα δε θεια· ετι δε
υρανυ φυσιν, και ηλιυ και σεληνης περιοδυς, και των αλλων αστερων τρο-
πας τε αυ και χορειας εναρμονιυς, ως ποιμην και βασιλευς ο θεος αγει
κατα δικην και νομον, προϊσησαμενος τον ορθον αυτυ λογον πρωτογονον υιον, ος την επιμελειαν της ιερας ταυτης αγελης, οιατι μεγαλυ βασι-
λεως υπαρχος διαδεξεται. De Agricultura, p. 152.

" thers, and all with what is provided for all, only chan-
" ging his conduct at different times : that the whole world
" may be managed as one city, according to the beſt form
" of democratical government *."

But why ſhould I multiply evidence? Philo, by a
ſingle ſtroke of his pencil, exhibits his ſubject in ſuch a light,
as muſt for ever expoſe to ridicule the intruded monſter of
occaſional perſonality. When accounting for the duration
of things created, he aſcribes it to their being " framed by
" him who remains, and who is never in any reſpect -
" changed, the divine Logos †.

However, although in the firſt chapter this is only aſſumed as the opinion of Philo, by the time that the Doctor advances ſo far as the ſecond, it is conſidered as proved.
" The principles of Philo have been explained above, viz.
" that the Divine Logos could aſſume *occaſional perſonality*
" to anſwer particular purpoſes, and then be reſtored into
" the Divine Being again ‡." However ſceptical the Doctor
is as to any proof produced againſt his own opinions, there
is no man more eaſy to deal with on this head, when he has
himſelf " particular purpoſes to anſwer." Although it
were granted, as it is not, that, in the paſſages mentioned,
Philo ſpeaks of the Logos in ſuch a manner as will not apply to a perſon ; there would be a manifeſt ſophiſm in the
concluſion. The argument fairly ſtated is plainly this ;

C 2 " He

* Χορευει γαρ εν κυκλω λογος ο θειος, ον οι πολλοι των ανθρωπων ονο-
μαζυσι τυχην · ειτα αει ριων κατα πολεις και εθνη και χωρας, τα αλλων αλ-
λοις, και πασι τα παντων επινεμει, χρονοις αυτο μονον αλλαττοντα παρ'
εκαστοις· ινα ως μια πολεις η οικυμενη πασα την αριςην πολιτειων αγη δη
μοχρατιαν. Lib Quod Deus ſit immutabilis, p. 248

† Μενει γαρ η αυτη ποιοτης, ατε απο μενοντος εκμαχθεισα, και μηδαμη
τριπομενυ, θειυ λογυ. De Profugis, p. 353.

‡ Ibid. p. 45.

" He who occasionally ufes the term *Logos* so as not to de-
" note a perfon, always means that the Logos is an occasi-
" onal perfon:

" But Philo occasionally ufes the term Logos in this
" way :

" Therefore, Philo always means by the Logos an *occa-*
" *sional* perfon only."

Or, more fimply ; " Philo occasionally ufes the word
" *Logos* without reference to a perfon ; *Ergo*, Philo means
" that the Logos is only an occafional perfon." *Probatum
est !*

By this ingenious plan of reafoning, one may make *quid-
libet ex quolibet*. As, in every language, the fame words
admit of various fignifications, one of thefe may be fo oppofed to another as to render all language mere jargon.

But as there is no evidence that in the leaft can fatisfy a
candid enquirer, that fuch an idea as that of occafional perfonality ever entered into the mind of Philo ; how fhall we
account for the Doctor's certainty as to this being the opinion of that ancient writer? Shall we fuppofe that he has
himfelf any partiality for it ? The fuppofition would be
fully as natural as fome of his own, though there were no
other reafon for it, than his extreme anxiety to father fo
fingular an opinion on an author to whom it was never
formerly imputed, and who has in fact given no ground
for the imputation. The Doctor does not mention this
opinion in his Hiftory of Corruptions. But, in confequence of renewed inveftigation, having difcovered that
" Marcellus of Ancyra, and other learned Chriftians, who
" were properly enough ranked among Unitarians," embraced this idea ; and finding that the idea itfelf may be
dignified with the high-founding title of *Philofophical Unitarianifm* **; he, in this treatife, ufhers it in on different occasions.

* Vol. ii. p. 46, 47.

casions. It is, indeed, a very useful notion. For an author, with this philosophical weapon in his hand, may at one blow for ever silence any being, of whatsoever order, who presumptuously rises up as a witness against what are called unitarian principles. It is the very *malleus fidei.*

But where is our author's authority for supposing such a mode of existence? Sure we are, this opinion hath no foundation in the word of God. For *on the seventh day God ended his work*, as to the formation of any new orders of beings. So anxious is Dr P. to reduce the Son of God into the rank of a mere creature, that he will rather unhinge the whole frame and order of creation, than not carry his point. Rather than not deprive him of personality, he will grant a species of it totally unknown to the rule of faith.

He says indeed; " It could not be, that upon this prin-
" ciple, any *new being* was introduced. For a mere *power*
" occasionally emitted, and then taken back again into its
" source, could not come under that description *". But here is downright contradiction ;—a *mere* power, and yet even a temporary personality. If it may be called a being, according to this explanation, it deserves the name of *new* more than any ever heard of before : for there is nothing that bears any resemblance to it, *either in heaven above, or in the earth beneath.* A new being it must be. For every time that it is " emitted," there is a new creation ; in the scale of being, one order, rather a mere *unique* subsists, which, according to the supposition, had no existence before its emission.

But although this idea should have no foundation in scripture, it is *philosophical.* One would think that the ordinary, if not the philosophical, definition of a person were

" as

* Ibid. p. 48.

" an intelligent being, or an individual of any parti-
" cular order of intelligent beings, subsisting by itself."
But how does this correspond to the idea of one " occasion-
" ally emitted from the Divine Being, and drawn into
" him when the purpose for which it hath been emitted is
" answered?" For, according to Marcellus, " the Logos
" was nothing more than a *Divine power*, voluntarily e-
" mitted by the Supreme Being; and though in some sense
" *detached* from himself," yet " entirely dependent on him,
" and taken into himself again at pleasure *." Is a mere
power a *person?* Is a *principle* a *being?* Does such a supposed power possess the essential property of a person, that
of existing *per se*, as distinct from other persons or beings?
Is this philosophical? Of that kind only which is *science
falsely so called, vain deceit, after the traditions of men, and
not after Christ*. But " the thing itself is possible for a
" time †." So is a Centaur, So is a mountain wholly of
gold. Do they therefore exist? Are we to reason from
what is possible to what is real? Here is the wisdom of
God in suffering *the wise*, who *by wisdom know not God*, to
be *taken in their own craftiness*. The doctrine of a plurality
of persons, in one undivided essence, is rejected as a gross
absurdity; blasphemously compared to the ridiculous *Abracadabras* of the heathen ‡; spurned as supposing an im-
possibility. Yet the man who dares to use such language
admits, not only of a power being occasionally converted
into a person, nor merely of a person existing without the
essential distinguishing property of a person, distinct subsistence; but of one person existing in another person. For
the Logos is only " in some sense detached from" the Supreme

---

* Ibid. p. 47.   † Ibid. p. 45.   ‡ Vol. i. p. 53.

preme Being. He is still " nothing more than a Divine
" Power;" but such a power as " it might have been said,
" would have been a person at the creation of the world *."
Those who deny the eternal generation of the Son, maintain an emission of their own, of a temporary kind. Instead of a necessary generation, they hold an occasional e-
mission. With them one essence cannot be common to
more persons than one. Yet one person may be the subject of a multitude of temporary existences.

But, may it be said, is this really Dr Priestley's opinion?
The Doctor, indeed, at times expresses himself mystically, in
conformity to those of whom he writes. He uses language,
which, like the heathen oracles, may be interpreted either
way. He deals greatly in suppositions and probabilities.
And this manner of writing is very convenient. For if
any thing be advanced in the heat of controversy, that is
afterwards found untenable, it can easily be retracted. But
you have as much certainty for this being his opinion, as
he is pleased to give in many other instances. He ascribes
it to " Marcellus, and other learned Christians, who were
" properly enough ranked among Unitarians †." He calls
the doctrine *Philosophical Unitarianism.* He denies that
thus " any new being was introduced ‡." Thus, it is
consistent with learning, with Unitarianism, with Philosophy, with the system of creation. But this is not all. He
expressly says ; " It is even doubtful, whether in some
" cases what are called angels, were any thing more than
" temporary appearances, and no permanent beings ; the
" mere organs of the Deity, used for the purpose of ma-
" king himself known and understood by his creatures ‖."

C 4   Again,

---

* Vol. ii. p. 47.   † Ibid. p. 46.

‡ Ibid. p. 48.   ‖ Vol. i. p. 5.

Again, " God fpake to the Patriarchs either by angels, or " fome temporary appearance, which may fometimes " have been in the form of man *." Certain we are, the Doctor hath not half fo well proved, that this is the opinion of Philo, as that it is his own. But it would not be matter of furprife, although it were afterwards found to be only *occafionally* fo.

Now, if it be granted, that any thing is fo " emitted " from the Supreme Being," as to have a temporary perfonality, to perform the actions of a perfon, to act and fpeak ; call it a divine power, or what you will ; let it be, with unparalleled abfurdity, denied that it is a perfon ; ftill it can go by no other name, it can fuggeft no other idea. Only, it has this fingular property, that it is identified in another perfon. This is a being of fuch a kind, that it may be a perfon at one time, and not at another. " For," Dr P. fays, " On this fcheme, the Logos, it might have " been faid, *would have been* a perfon at the creation " of the world ; and again, when it was employed in the " divine intercourfe with the Patriarchs †." Here is the myftery of Socinianifm ! the *plurality* and *unity* of the fons of Reafon ! Not three perfons in an unity of effence, but according to the number of the heavenly hofts, *ten thoufand times ten thoufand* exifting in one perfon. A participation of the divine nature is denied to the only begotten Son of the Father, while, without any hefitation, all thofe *fons of God*, called *Angels*, are admitted to this honour.

But our author ought ferioufly to confider, that thus he hath virtually declared that he has no objection to the doctrine

trine

---

trine of an occafional plurality. Now, it will be difficult for him to fhow, that what is in the divine nature at one time, may not be at another, nay, is not *always.* For with God there *is no variablenefs.* He ought to confider, that no Trinitarian maintains, that one perfon is properly *detached* from another, far lefs from " the Supreme Being :" and that the great difference between this unitarian plurality and ours, is, that according to the latter, one perfon is effentially in another, (John xiv. 10, 11.) yet fo as to retain diftinction of perfonality ; but according to the former, one perfon is fo in another, as *at times* totally to lofe this. Is the one doctrine more demonftrable from reafon, or from analogy, than the other? It is no contradiction to reafon, that three perfons fhould permanently fubfift in one effence : but it certainly is a contradiction, that the nature, which is plural to-day, fhould be fingular to-morrow.

C H A P. IV.

Of the Doctrine of Philo concerning Angels.—Whether he confidered the Logos as the future Meffiah ?

THE Doctor, having fo well proved, that Philo allows only an occafional perfonality to the Logos, infers, that he afcribes no other kind of perfonality to angels. ' According to Philo,' it is faid, " Angels are nothing more than " this divine Logos ;' fo that he could not confider them as ' having a permanent being.' Speaking of Hagar, he fays, " She was met by an Angel, which is the Logos of God *.' ' Treating of the migration of Abraham, he fays, " He " that

---

* Σημειον δε, το υπανταν αυτη αγγελον θειον λογον, α χρη παρχινεσοντα, &c. De Profugis, p. 352. ap. Auct. 451.

" that follows God muſt of neceſſity make uſe of the at-
" tending *logoi*, which are commonly called angels *." It
clearly ſhews how ſanguine our author is, as to the article
of evidence, that he can make ſuch an inference from the
firſt of theſe paſſages. It may, indeed, be inferred from
it, that in the opinion of Philo, the Word of God might
be called an *angel*, from his being employed as a *meſſenger* : And this is believed by all true Chriſtians. But will
any man, but one determined to force proof where he cannot find it, thence conclude, that according to Philo, every
angel might be called the Word of God ? When that ancient writer calls angels *logoi*, it is evident that he does ſo,
merely in an occaſional way. He indulges himſelf in a
commutation of the names. He calls the Logos an *angel*,
not as if he imagined that he was a creature, for he often
aſſerts the contrary ; but becauſe the Logos acted in the relation of an *angel* or *meſſenger* to him who is unbegotten.
In like manner, he calls the angels *logoi*, not as apprehending that they were eternal and uncreated, like the Logos ;
but, as would ſeem, from their being occaſionally his at-
tendants in his important embaſſies, and being ſometimes
employed in the ſame work, though in an inferior character. Accordingly it is evident, that in the paſſage quoted,
Philo refers to the circumſtance of angels being in company
with the Logos, when he appeared to Abraham at the door
of his tent. For he immediately adds : " Thence it is ſaid
" that Abraham *went forth to bring them on their way* †."
In another place he teaches that God who ſpake to Abraham, on this occaſion, was the Word ‡. He gives no hint that
angels were commonly known by the name of *logoi* ; but
ſays,

---

* Vol. ii. p. 16, 17.

† De Migratione Abraham. p. 324. D. E.

‡ Leg. Allegor. p. 77.

fays, on the contrary, that thofe whom he called *logoi* were commonly called angels; plainly enough intimating, that he was fingular in this ufe of the defignation.

The procefs of our author's reafoning is very uncommon. Philo occafionally ufes the term *logos,* when it does not fignify a perfon; therefore, he confidered the logos as an occafional perfon only. He occafionally calls the angels *logoi*; therefore, he viewed them alfo as merely occafional beings, and as "nothing more than this divine " Logos." But it is truly aftonifhing that Dr P., in order to fupport an abfurd hypothefis, fhould urge the vague and fingular ufe of one term, in direct oppofition to the well known fentiments of the author, as difplayed in a great variety of paffages. Nothing can be more evident, than that Philo confidered angels as permanent beings. Therefore he calls them *animals.* "The firft divifion of ani- " mals," he fays, "is into irrational and rational. But the " rational is again divided into the mortal and immortal " kinds; the mortal that of men, but the immortal that of " difembodied fpirits, which are employed in the air, and " in heaven. Thefe are free of fin, having an immortal " and happy lot *from the beginning*, as not being connected " with the body, the habitation of mifery *." Speaking of the death of Abraham, he fays; " For Abraham ha- " ving left the ftate of mortality, is joined to the people of " God, enjoying immortality, being made like unto the " angels,

---

* Η μεν φυσις των ζωων, εις τε αλογον καί λογικην μοιραν εναντιας αλ-ληλαις ετμηθη το πρωτον· η δε αυ λογικη παλιν, εις τε το φθαρτον και αθα-νατον ειδος, φθαρτον μεν το ανθρωπων, αφθαρτον δε το ψυχων ασωματων, αι κατα τε αερα και υρανον περιπολυσι· κακιας δε αμετοχοι μεν ιισιν αυ-ται, τον ακηρατον κα. ευδαιμονα κληρον εξ αρχης λαχυσαι, και τω συμ-φορ-ς ανηνυτων υκ ενδεθεισαι χωριω σωματι. De Confufione Linguar. p. 270, E. F.

" angels. For the angels are the army of God, incorpo-
" real and bleſſed ſouls *." Does he mean that the ſoul
of Abraham was abſorbed in the divine eſſence?

Our author further objeĉts to the evidence of Philo, that
" he was far from imagining that the Logos had any more
" relation to the Meſſiah, than to any other prophet †."
But perhaps Dr P. has not obſerved that Philo calls him
the Man of God, ſaying, " How can it be that ye ſhould
" not hate war and love peace, who acknowledge one and the
" ſame Father, not mortal but immortal, even the Man of
" God; who, becauſe he is the Word of him who is eter-
" nal, is alſo neceſſarily immortal ‡." When he afterwards calls him " the firſt-begotten and moſt ſacred Word,"
he evidently ſpeaks of him with reſpeĉt to his incarnation
and charaĉter as Meſſiah. For he declares that he is " *the*
" *man* according to the image" of God, and " the Seer
" of Iſrael." The whole paſſage deſerves our attention.
" If any one be not worthy to be called the ſon of God,
" ſtrive to be conformed to his firſt-begotten Word, the
" moſt ancient Angel, exiſting as the Archangel of many
" names. For he is called the Beginning, and the Name
" of God, and the Word, and the Man according to the
" image, and the Seer of Iſrael. Therefore, I have, a
" little above, praiſed the principles of thoſe who ſay, *We*
" *are all the ſons of one man.* For if we are not yet be-
                                                  " come

---

* Δε γαρ Αβρααμ εκλιπων τα θνητα, προστιθεται τω Θεω λαω, καρ-
πυμενος αφθαρσιαν, ισος αγγελοις γεγονως· αγγελοι γαρ ςρατος εισι Θευ,
ασωματοι και ευδαιμονες ψυχαι.   De Sacrificiis Abelis et Caini, p. 101,
102.

† Vol. ii. p. 17.

‡ Επει και πως ουκ εμελλετε φησαιμ' αν, ω γενναιοι, πολεμω μεν
δυσχεραινειν, ειρηνην δε αγαπαν, ενα και τον αυτον επιγεγραμμενοι πατερα υ θνητον, αλλ' αθανατον, ανθρωπον Θευ, ος τυ αιδιυ λογος ων, εξ
αναγκης και αυτος εςιν αφθαρτος.   De Confuſ. p. 255. C.

" come fit to be.called the fons of God, let us be fo at
" leaſt of his eternal Image, the moſt ſacred Word. For
" the Image of God is that moſt ancient Word. And in-
". deed, in many places of the law, the hearers of this Seer
" are alſo called *Sons of Iſrael*, for as much as hearing is
" accounted inferior to ſeeing, and he who is taught always
" holds the ſecond place in relation to him who perceives
" the exact forms of ſubjects without any previous inſtruc-
" tion *." No one can doubt that he ſpeaks of a real
perſon. There is as little reaſon to deny that he aſcribes
divine characters to him, and yet declares him to be a meſſenger. He calls him an *Angel*, and yet *the Name of God*;
a *Man*, and yet *the Beginning*, the *eternal Image*. He evidently views him as the perpetual *Prophet* of the Church,
and the true *Iſrael*. He alſo applies theſe words to the
Logos; *Behold, the man whoſe name is the Branch*, Zech.
vi. 12. rendering them, according to the Septuagint, *whoſe
name is* Ανατολη, the *Riſing Sun*. Juſtin uſes the term
in the ſame ſenſe. I need not ſay that he underſtands it
of Chriſt §.

We

---

* Καν μηδεπω μεντοι τυγχανη τις αξιοχρεως ων υιος θευ προσαγο-
ρευεσθαι, σπυδαζε κοσμεισθαι κατα τον πρωτογονον αυτυ λογον, τον
αγγελον πρεσβυταιον, ως αρχαγγελον πολυωνυμον υπαρχονια. Και
γαρ αρχη, και ονομα θευ, και λογος, και ο καθ' εικονα ανθρωπος, δε
ερων Ισραηλ προσαγορευεται· διο προηχθην ολιγω προτερον επαινισαι
τας αρχας των φασκοντων οτι παντες εσμεν υιοι ενος ανθρωπυ. Και
γαρ ει μηπω ικανοι θευ παιδες νομιζεσθαι γεγοναμεν, αλλα τοι της αιδιυ
εικονος αυτυ λογυ τυ ιερωταιυ. Θευ γαρ εικων, λογος ο πρεσβυτατος.
Και πολλαχου μεντοι της νομοθεσιας υιοι παλιν Ισραηλ καλυνται τυ ο-
ρωντος οι ακυοντες, επειδη μεθ' ορασιν ακοη δευτερειοις τετιμηται, και το
διδασκομενον τυ χωρις υφηγησεως ενεργεις τυποις των υποκειμενων λαμ-
βανοντες αιει δευτερον. De Confuſ. Ling. p. 267.

‡ Dial. p. 327. 334.

We cannot underſtand the following words, without ſuppoſing that Philo believed that the Logos would be incarnate. " There are, as appears to me, two temples of " God ; the one, indeed, is this world, in which the High- " prieſt is his firſt-begotten divine Word. But the other " is the rational ſoul, of which he is Prieſt, who is true " man, of whom the ſenſible image is he, who, according " to the cuſtoms of our fathers, offers up prayers and ſacri- " fices *." Here he undoubtedly views the Jewiſh high-prieſt as merely a type of the Logos in this character.

I have not obſerved, that Philo any where uſes the word *Meſſiah* or *Chriſt*. The neareſt approach that he ſeems to make to this mode of expreſſion, is when applying to the Logos, conſidered in his ſacerdotal character, what is enjoined with reſpect to the manſlayer continuing in the city of refuge till the death of the high-prieſt. On this occaſion, he ſays, that " his head is anointed with oil†." But did not Philo, as well as all the reſt of his nation, expect a Meſſiah? Is it not natural to ſuppoſe, that this moſt inteſeſting ſubject would often engroſs ſo contemplative a mind? Does Philo ſo often find the *Logos* in the Old Teſtament ; and could he diſcern no veſtige of the *Meſſiah?* The difficulty cannot be otherwiſe ſolved, than by ſuppoſing that he meant to deſcribe the Meſſiah under that very name which was ſo familiar to him. His ideas ſeem to have been far more ſpiritual than thoſe of the reſt of his nation who did not believe in Jeſus. Therefore, he might think it improper expreſsly to call the Logos *Meſſiah* ; as

                                                  he

---

* Δυο γαρ, ως εοικεν, ιερα ϑευ, εν μεν οδε ο κοσμος, εν ω και αρχιερευς ο πρωτογονος αυτυ ϑειος λογος ετερον δε λογικη ψυχη, ης ιερευς ο προς αλυϑειαν ανϑρωπος, ου μιμημα αισϑητον ο τας πατριυς ευχας τε και ϑυσιας επιτελων εστιν. De Somniis, p. 463. F.

† Και διοτι την κεφαλην κεχρισται ελαιω. De Profugis, p. 364.

he confidered him efpecially in a fpiritual light, and knew the deep-rooted prejudices of his countrymen in favour of a temporal monarchy. Befides, the term *Logos* was far more fuitable to the bent of his genius. It afforded·him a much more ample field for abftract fpeculation and refined allegory than the other.

But although he does not mention the name, 'we find him afcribing all the fcriptural characters of Meffiah to the Logos. For he defcribes him as an Angel or Meffenger, as a Seer or Prophet, as the true High-prieft who makes atonement, as the Mediator between God and man, as the Governor of the world, as the true Manna, as divine and yet true man, &c. Therefore, he muft either have believed, that he, who was known to the ancient church as the Logos, fhould at length appear as Meffiah ; or that the Logos fhould ceafe to exercife any concern with refpect to the church, and devolve all his work on the Meffiah. We cannot fuppofe the latter, becaufe of the divine and unchangeable attributes which he afcribes to the Logos. We are, therefore, under a neceffity of fuppofing, that he confidered the Logos as the fame perfon who fhould appear as the fon of David. While he not only afcribes to him the neceffary characters of the promifed Meffiah, as including deity, but connects thefe with manhood; it is not conceivable, that he had not fome ideas of the future incarnation of the eternal Word.

I fhall only add, that, as Philo calls the Logos Ἀνατολη, *the rifing Sun*, applying the prophecy of Zechariah to him, chap. vi. 12. the manner in which the paffage has been uniformly explained by his countrymen, affords a ftrong collateral proof, that by the Logos he meant the Meffiah. Many Jewifh writers, who have perfifted in infidelity, have exprefsly applied this language to the latter *. Jonathan

Ben

---

* Martini Pugio Fidei , p. 125. 308. 376. 594.

Ben Uzziel, who, if not cotemporary with Philo, was nearly fo, interprets it in the fame manner: " Behold, the
" man whofe name is Meffiah," &c. Nay, it would appear,
that it was generally expected by the Jews, that the Meffiah would be manifefted under that very name which
Philo gives to the Logos. For it is adopted by Zacharias,
in his fong of praife: *Through the tender mercy of our God,
—the* day-fpring *from on high hath vifited us,* Luke i. 78 *.
The fame word is ufed by the Evangelift, as by Philo.

C H A P. V.

*Of the Senfe in which the Chaldee Paraphrafts ufed the term
Memra.*

OUR author fays in his former work; " We find that
" the Chaldee Paraphrafts of the Old Teftament
" often render *the Word of God,* as if it was a being diftinct
" from God, or fome angel who bore the name of God,
" and acted by deputation fron him. So, however, it has
" been interpreted, though with them it might be
" no more than an idiom of fpeech †." Here Dr P.
fpeaks only in the language of probability. But in his fecond
work matters are ripened into certainty. " With refpect
" to the Jews, it is evident, that in general, they did not
" ufe the term *Logos* in the Platonic fenfe, but as fynony-
" mous to *God,* or the mere token, or fymbol, of the di-
" vine prefence. The Chaldee paraphrafts often ufe the
" word מימרא, *mimra,* which may be tranflated *Logos* or
" *Word.* But that, in the ideas of thefe writers, the word

" of

* Vid. Glaffii Rhetor. Sac. p. 178. Wolfii Cur. in loc.

† Hift. Corrupt. Vol. i.

" of a perſon was merely ſynonymous to *himſelf,* is evi-
" dent from their application of the ſame phraſeology to
" man *."

It was urged by many of thoſe who preceded Dr P. in
the ſame ſyſtem, that the term *memra* ſimply ſignified
ſpeech. The vanity of this pretence has been ſo clearly
demonſtrated †, that he ſeems to leave it to its fate, and
confines himſelf merely to the objection already mentioned.

Some worthy men have undoubtedly gone too far, in
aſſerting that this expreſſion, when uſed by the Paraphraſts,
is *always* to be underſtood of the perſonal Word. It would
ſeem to be ſometimes uſed, as ſimply denoting the mind,
either of God or of man. The ancient Jews, finding that
their ſcriptures afforded undoubted evidence of a plurality
of perſons exiſting in an unity of eſſence, and that action,
ſpeech, coming and walking, are aſcribed to the Word of
Jehovah, would naturally conclude that this name denoted
a perſon. Obſerving alſo, that one divine perſon ſpeaks to
another as begotten of him ; and connecting the character
of *begotten* with the Word, they would naturally enquire,
what might be the reaſon of this deſignation. It would
occur to them, that, as the inward word is produced by the
mind of man, and yet remains in it, the Son is ſo denominated, becauſe he is begotten by the Father, and is eſſentially in him ; and that, as words, when uttered, are the
images and expreſſions of thoſe ideas which the mind at
firſt forms within itſelf, he alſo receives this name, not only
becauſe he is the expreſs image of the Father, but becauſe
all the purpoſes of the Father are both declared by him,
and outwardly accompliſhed, as in the creation of the world,

VOL. I.   D   the

* Earl. Opin. vol. ii. p. 19, 20.

† See Fleming's Chriſtology, vol. i. p. 138. Bedford's Sermons,
p. 290, &c.

the covenant made with their fathers, &c. It being thus necessary to suppose, that all the counsels of the Father were laid in him, which they might also learn from the personality ascribed to *Wisdom*, they would conceive that he was called the Word and Wisdom of the Father, to represent their perfect unity of essence, design and operation.

That they actually formed this opinion, is evident, especially from the language of Philo. Therefore, he describes the Logos from the resemblance of an Architect, forming an idea of a building in his mind, before constructing it. Then, to express the unity of the divine essence and counsels, he adds; " As the preconceived plan of the building " in the mind of the architect has no existence externally, " but is stamped upon the mind of the artist; in like man- " ner, this world of ideas has no place but the divine Logos, " who disposes all things *." This agrees with the account that our Lord gives of himself; *No one knoweth the Father, but the Son.*

Thus conceiving of all the counsels of the Father as formed in and with his Word, is it strange that they should at times recur to the very idea that gave birth to this interpretation,—that of the inward operation of the mind, before outward action or expression? Their personifying the *Memra*, in general, when applied to God, laid them under no necessity of doing so, at least in a proper sense, when they used this expression with respect to man. As little did the simple application of it to man restrict them as to the sense in which they were to apply it to God. For, in all languages, the same words are used in various senses. Socinians have, of all men, least reason to plead this invariable unity of language, as they affirm that those words which are most sacred among all nations, the very names of

God,

---

* De Mundi Opific. Earl. Opin. vol. ii. p. 4.

God, are often applied, without any exception, and without any marks of distinction, to mere creatures. Therefore, by a parity of reason, it might be urged that, because the name JEHOVAH is, according to their theory, sometimes given to a created angel, we are never to understand it in any other sense. Nay, with respect to the very word *Logos*, might it not with equal justness be asserted, that because it sometimes signifies speech, it ought invariably to be understood in this sense? Indeed, it would not only be doing the same justice to the Gospel of John, that is done by Socinians to the Paraphrases, but perhaps as near the real sense as their own interpretation, were a new theorist to plead that, because *logos* in Scripture often signifies *speech*, we were bound to interpret the introduction to that Gospel in this sense; " In the beginning was *speech*," &c.

It has been observed, that the Paraphrasts describe the Word in language analogous to that of the Apostle John, when he says that *the Word was with God.* For they speak of him as " the Word from before the Lord, or which is " before the Lord." Thus Onkelos paraphrases, Gen. xxxi. 22. " And the Word from before the Lord came to La- " ban :" and Exod. xx. 19. " Let not the Word from be- " fore the Lord speak with us, lest we die *." This mode of expression affords the most unquestionable evidence of a personal distinction. Maimonides himself, anxious as he was to obscure all those passages of Scripture that imply a divine plurality, and to conceal every evidence of the Jews having ever held this doctrine, durst not venture so far as Dr P. He had not boldness enough to assert that, with the Chaldee interpreters, the *Word of God* was merely " sy- " nonymous to *God*" himself. He knew that the Targums afforded such unquestionable evidence of the intro-

D 2   duction

---

* Gill on John i. 1.

duction of a diftinct perfon under this defignation, that e-
very one of his countrymen, who was in the leaft acquainted with them, would give him the lie. Therefore, he finds
himfelf reduced to the miferable fhift of pretending that,
when the Paraphrafts fpeak of the Word of the Lord, and
ufe this expreffion where the name of God occurs in the o-
riginal, they mean to defcribe a created angel *.

This objection, however, is by no means new. It has
been hackneyed by writers of the fame perfuafion for
more than a century †. All that it proves, is what we
do not wifh to deny, that the term *memra* does not always
denote the perfonal Word.

But this objection makes its appearance with a very bad
grace, after the Doctor has been obliged to confefs that Philo, a writer of the fame nation, of the fame principles, and
nearly of the fame age, gives a real, although, as is pretended, only an occafional perfonality to the *Logos*. While
this is granted with refpect to Philo, who can believe that
not one of the Paraphrafts, on any occafion, ufes a fynonymous term in the fame fenfe? What would be thought of
any writer in a fucceeding age, who fhould affert that, although Mr Lindfey denied perfonality to the Holy Spirit,
Dr Prieftley, a member of the fame unitarian church, was
always to be underftood in a fenfe directly oppofite; becaufe in fome inftances he had fpoken of the Spirit in language that might imply perfonal agency? Undoubtedly, a-
ny man of fenfe would fay; " It is unnatural to fuppofe,
" that there fhould have been any diverfity of opinion be-
" tween thefe gentlemen on this point; the doctrine of one
                                                    " perfon

---

* *Et fuit Verbum Domini ad me,* &c. Fieri quoque poteft, meo judi-
cio ut Onkelos per vocem *Elohim,* Angelum intellexerit, &c. More Nevochim, par. i. c. 27. p. 33.

† Vid. Deyling. Obfer. Sac. P. i, Obf. 49.

" perfon in deity being the very bafis of their fyftem.
" But let us try, if there be not other expreffions in the
" Doctor's works, which fhew that he entertained fuch i-
" deas of the Spirit as were totally incompatible with per-
" fonality." Let the queftion before us be brought to the
fame iffue. If it fhall appear that the Targumifts afferted
fuch things concerning *the Word of the Lord*, as cannot be
applied to God the Father, and as, at the fame time, imply
real perfonality and divine, perfection; it muft neceffarily
follow that, on thefe occafions, at leaft, they fpake of a perfon, in the divine effence, diftinct from the Father.

They find the Word in the very firft appearance of God
after the fall. That expreffion, *They heard the voice of the
Lord God walking in the garden*, Gen. iii. 8. is rendered,
" They heard the *Word*, &c." All the Targums agree in
this view of the paffage: and that of Jerufalem begins the
next verfe in this manner; " And the Word of the Lord
" God called unto Adam." Another expreffes the meaning of the verfe ftill more copioufly; " They heard the
" voice of the Word of the Lord God walking." It feems
moft natural, indeed, to underftand this language of a perfon. For even the modern Jews cannot deny, that the participle, *walking*, immediately refers to *the voice*, and not to
the Lord God *. *Walking* is undoubtedly the attribute of a
perfon, and not of a mere *voice.* The author of *Tzeror
Hammor* makes this obfervation on the place: " Before
" they finned, they faw the Glory of the bleffed God fpeak-
" ing with *him*," that is, with God; " but after their fin,
" they only heard the Voice walking †." This writer undoubtedly underftood the *Voice* as a diftinct perfon, the

D 3   fame

* Vox enim eft res illa, de qua dicitur, quod ambulaverit in horto.
Maimon. More Nevochim, Par. i. c. 24.

† Sect. Bere fhith. ap. Owen Hebr. vi. i. Exerc. x.

fame whom he before calls the *Glory*. And the latter is one of the perfonal characters of the Meffiah, Ifa. xl. 5. lx 1.

The *Memra* is evidently defcribed as one *fent*. The words of Elijah, 1 Kings xviii. 24. *I will call on the name of the Lord*, &c. are thus paraphrafed by Jonathan; "I will " pray in the Name of the Lord, and he fhall fend his " Word." The Paraphraft could not refer to any meffage from God. For it was not an anfwer by word, but by fire, that Elijah expected. It has never been pre-tended, either by Socinians, or by the orthodox, that God the Father is faid to be fent. If there be but one Divine Perfon, by whom is he fent?

We learn from Gen. xvi. 7. &c. that *the Angel of the Lord found Hagar by a fountain of water*; that he faid, *I will multiply thy feed exceedingly*, and that *fhe called the Name of* JEHOVAH *that fpake to her, Thou God feeft me*. It is evident, that Hagar confidered the perfon who addreffed her as divine. Philo afferts that it was the Word who ap-peared to her *. Jonathan gives the fame view; "She confef-" fed before the Lord JEHOVAH, whofe Word had fpo-" ken to her." With this the Jerufalem Targum agrees: " She confeffed and prayed to the Word of the Lord, who " had appeared to her." It is vain to fay, in the Socinian fenfe, that God himfelf is here meant. For the Paraphrafts muft have known from the text, that the perfon fpoken of is called an Angel. If the Father be meant, how is he cal-led an Angel? We may be told, indeed, that a mere angel often affumes the name, and claims the attributes of JEHO-VAH. But it is not credible that the ancient Jews, who were fo fuperftitioufly tender of the name JEHOVAH, that they would neither pronounce nor write it, left they fhould take it in vain, would ever think of conferring it, or ima-gine

* Καταγιται υπαιτησαντος αγγελȣ, ος εϛι θειος λογος, εις τον δεϛ-ποτικον οικον. De Cherubim, p. 83. C.

gine that it was conferred by God, on a created angel. When, therefore, they call this angel *the Word*, it argues a conviction, that he was both diftinct from the Father, and equal to him. According to the text, he who addreffed Hagar was JEHOVAH, who could multiply her feed ; and yet an Angel. According to the paraphrafes, this Angel was the Word, who was at the fame time the object of prayer. Before Dr P. can fhew that a perfonal Word is not here meant, he muft prove, firft, that God, effentially confidered, may be an Angel or one fent ; and fecondly, that this was the opinion of the Chaldee Paraphrafts. As according to the doctrine afcribed to Philo, this was certainly one of thefe *occafions* on which the Logos was a perfon, the Doctor would alfo need to give his reader a fatisfying reafon why he muft underftand the Paraphrafts, writing on the fame fubject, and ufing the fame mode of expreffion, in fo very different a fenfe.

They defcribe the Word as a *Mediator.* It is faid, Deut. iv. 7. *For what nation is there fo great, who hath God fo nigh unto them as the Lord our God is in all things that we call upon him for?* Jonathan gives the following paraphrafe of the paffage; " God is near in the name of the " Word of the Lord." Again, we find this paraphrafe on Hof. iv. 9. " God will receive the prayer of Ifrael by his " Word, and have mercy upon them, and will make them " by his Word like a beautiful fig-tree." And on Jer. xxix. 14. " I will be fought by you in my Word, and I " will be enquired of through you by my Word *." According to the Jerufalem Targum on Gen. xxi. 33. Abraham, at Beerfheba, " prayed in the name of the Word " of the Lord, the God of the world †." But it is inconceivable, that the Paraphrafts did not here mean to defcribe

D 4

the

---

* See Bedford's Serm. p. 252. 269.
† Ibid. p. 268.

the Word as a Mediator; efpecially as we know that the ancient Jews, when fupplicating God, intreated that he would "look on the face of his Anointed;" and have alfo feen that Philo, nearly cotemporary with fome of the Paraphrafts, exprefsly declared his faith in the Word, as the Mediator between God and man.

They fpeak of *atonement* as made by this *Memra.* On Deut xxxii. 43. Jonathan obferves; "God will atone by " his Word for his land, and for his people, even a people " faved by the Word of the Lord." This exaɕtly corre- fponds with what we have extraɕted from Philo, concern- ing the Word as an High-prieft.

They defcribe the *Memra* as a *Redeemer*, and fometimes as the *Meffiah.* Thefe words, Gen. xlix. 18. *I have wait- ed for thy falvation*, are thus paraphrafed in the Jerufalem Targum; "Our father Jacob faid thus; My foul expeɕts " not the rēdemption of Gideon the fon of Joafh, which is " a temporal falvation; nor the redemption of Samfon, " which is a tranfitory falvation; but the redemption which " thou didft promife fhould come through thy *Memra* to thy " people. This falvation my foul waits for." In the bleffing of Judah, v. 10.——12. particular mention is made of the King Meffiah. It is a ftriking proof that by the *Memra* they meant him who was to appear as the Meffiah, that in the Targum of Jonathan, v. 18. is thus rendered; "Our Fa- " ther Jacob faid, I do not expeɕt the deliverance of Gide- " on the fon of Joafh, which is a temporal falvation; nor " that of Samfon the fon of Manoah, which is a tranfient " falvation. But I expeɕt the redemption of the *Meffiah* " the Son of David, who fhall come to gather to himfelf " the children of Ifrael." It is evident that the one para- phraft has copied from the other: and as the one puts *Meffiah* for *Memra*, it cannot well be denied that they had confidered both terms as denoting the fame perfon.

3

We

We have a remarkable promife, Lev. xxvi. 12. *I will walk among you, and will be your God, and ye shall be my people.* The paffage, viewed in its connection, feems evidently to refer to the great gift of the Meffiah. God promifes, ver. 8. *I will establish my covenant with you.* Even fome of the later Jews underftand this of the new covenant, which God was to make with Ifrael and Judah, foretold by Jeremiah, chap. xxxi. 31. Rabbi Solomon, and the author of *Pesikta,* are mentioned as of this opinion[*]. God alfo declares, ver. 11. *I will set my tabernacle amongst you.* He had already done fo, as to the letter. But this promife evidently has a farther reference. Thence, the ftriking coincidence between it and the words of the Evangelift, has been remarked by interpreters. John fays, *The Word was made flesh, and εσ- κηνωσεν. εν ημιν, tabernacled among us,* chap. i. 14. This is the effence of the promife ; and the very expreffion is remarkably confonant to that of the Septuagint, in the paffage under confideration, Θησω την σκηνην μα εν υμιν.

There is every reafon to think, that the ancient Jews difcerned the Meffiah here. Jonathan gives the following paraphrafe of ver. 12. " I will be your God, and my Word " fhall be unto you God the Redeemer." That expref. fion, ver. 9. *I will have respect unto you,* is rendered by Onkelos ; " I will look upon you in my Word :" and that in ver. 11. *My soul shall not abhor you,* he thus gloffes ; " My " Word fhall not abhor you." The *Memra* is introduced here, without any verbal reference to it in the original, no lefs than thrice in the courfe of four verfes. This certainly argues a ftrong conviction in the mind of the Paraphraft, that the paffage referred to the promifed Deliverer. Socinians themfelves will grant, in words at leaft, that it is only *in* Jefus Chrift that God looks on finful men with complacency.

---

[*] Kidder's Demonftr. par. 3. p. 107.

cency. The Word of God gave the moſt aſtoniſhing proof that he did not abhor his people, when he *tabernacled a-mong* them.

They deſcribe this *Memra* as *only-begotten*, and in this character as the *Creator*. That remarkable verſe, Gen. iii. 22. *The Lord God ſaid, Behold the man is become as one of us*, is paraphraſed in a very ſingular manner : " The Word " of the Lord ſaid, Behold, Adam whom *I have created*, is " the only-begotten in the world, as I am the *only-begotten* " in the higheſt heavens *." The language here aſcribed to the Memra, with what reference to the text avails not in the preſent inquiry, is applicable to a perſon only ; and it will not be pretended by our opponents that it can apply to the *Father*. The perſon intended was believed to be " the " only-begotten Word." How nearly does this language ap-proach to that of inſpiration ! *In the beginning was the Word.—All things were made by him.—We beheld his glory, the glory as of the only-begotten of the Father*, John i. 1. 3. 14.—The word above rendered, *I have created*, is under-ſtood in the ſecond perſon by Glaſſius †. For he reads it, *creaſti*. But it makes no material difference. For in which way ſoever the expreſſion be rendered, it clearly proves the Paraphraſt's belief of the diſtinction of the Word from the Father.

It is not denied that Philo often applies this character of *only-begotten* to the Logos.

If, therefore, the Paraphraſts deſcribe the *Memra* as one ſent, as a Mediator, as one by whom atonement is made, as a Redeemer and the Meſſiah, and as only-begotten ; it is undeniable that they do not mean God the Father. If, notwithſtanding, they aſcribe perſonal and divine characters to the Word, which Dr P. cannot deny, they muſt mean a diſtinct perſon in the divine eſſence.

Many

---

* Targ. Hieroſol. ap. Pfeifferi Theol. Judaic. p. 886.
† Philol. Sacr. lib. i. p. 24.

Many other passages, to the same purpose, might have been quoted from the Targums. But these, we apprehend, are sufficient to satisfy any who are not determined to shut their eyes against evidence.

Mahomet, to whom the Socinians have pleaded kindred *, may surely be sustained as an impartial witness. It was not his object to exalt Jesus Christ. Yet he was so fully convinced, from the writings of the Old Testament, and from the general doctrine of the ancient Jews, that this character belonged to him, that he calls him *the Word of God* †.

Before leaving this part of our subject, we may attend to what Dr P. has objected 'to the evidence, that the Paraphrasts reckoned the Memra and the Messiah the same person. He founds his objection on the words of Jonathan, who says, that " the Messiah and Moses will appear at the " end of the world, the one in the desart, and the other at " Rome, and that the Word, or Logos, will march between " them ‡." Francis Taylor, the first who seems to have objected this as a proof that they did not intend one person by these two names, gives an answer to his own objection. For he adds ; " It is probable, that, as the Jews acknowledge a " twofold Messiah, they might intend to point out the " humble and afflicted one by the name *Messiah*, and the o- " ther, whom they expect as a triumphant conqueror, by " that of *Memra* ||." But these words might be meant merely to signify that, as the dispensation of the Law was under the administration of the *Memra*, that of the latter

day

---

* See their Epistle to Ameth ben Ameth, prefixed to Lefslie's Socin. Controversy.

† Glassii Phil. l. 1. t. 4. f. 3. p. 340.

‡ Vol. iii. p. 46.

|| Apud Pfeifferi Crit. Sacr. cap. 8. qu. 18.

day fhould be fo alfo ; or, that he fhould be the centre of union between the Law and the Gofpel. Thus, it may be viewed as fimilar to that of Philo concerning the fame il-luftrious perfon. When he fays that he is " the middle be-" tween two extremes," God and man, he does not mean to deny his Deity, but to affert his mediatory character. He reprefents him as uniting both. I cannot think that the *Memra* is here meant as a diftinct perfon. For al-though Mofes is fuppofed to ride on one cloud, and the Mef-fiah on another, this is not afferted of the Memra. According to Bafnage, to whom Dr P. refers, the Memra is faid to *walk* or *march*. But Bafnage himfelf refers to Pfeiffer, who quotes the Targumift as fimply faying, " And the Memra " between both *."

But as this feems to be the only paffage of the kind that can be produced, in what way foever it be explained, it is not of fufficient weight in oppofition to a multitude to the con-trary. Inftead of arguing from a fingle paffage in which the writer feems to difcover fome confufion, on a fubject which he could not underftand, while a ftranger to the ac-complifhment of the great promife ; we may rather wonder that, in other places, he expreffes himfelf fo clearly. For we have feen that this very writer accounted the redemp-tion of the Meffiah the fame with that of the *Memra*.

With refpect to the objection, I fhall only add, that al-though we were certain that the Paraphraft meant that the Memra and Meffiah were different perfons, it would be un-fair to judge, by this circumftance, of the meaning of all the other Chaldee interpreters. For it feems evident that the Paraphrafe on the five books of Mofes, afcribed to Jona-than Ben Uzziel, was not written for feveral centuries af-

ter

---

* In fine mundi Mofes e medio deferti exibit, et rex Meffias e medio Romae, alter in nubis unius, alter in alterius culmine equitabit, et verbum Domini inter utrumque. Ibid.

ter his time. For it mentions Conſtantinople and Lombardy *. Now, it is well known that the later Jews in general, in their notions concerning the Meſſiah, have deviated much farther from the faith of Chriſtians, than their predeceſſors. It has been already ſeen, that the Paraphraſts interpret what is ſaid of the *Angel of the Lord* who addreſſed Hagar, of the Word. But this is not a ſolitary inſtance. For they give the ſame account of the Angel who deſtroyed Sodom, of the Angel who went before the Iſraelites in the cloudy pillar, and of him who deſtroyed the Aſſyrians †. While Philo deſcribes the Word as an Angel, they declare *the Angel of the Lord* to be the Word. Thus, it undoubtedly appears that both Philo and the Paraphraſts mean the ſame perſon.

It is well known that many read the words of Eve, on occaſion of the birth of Cain, *I have obtained the man the Lord*, Gen. iv. 1. apprehending that ſhe conſidered this event as the accompliſhment of the promiſe concerning *the ſeed of the woman*. But whatever was the meaning of our common parent, it deſerves our particular attention, that the Paraphraſt renders the whole verſe in the following manner: "And Adam knew his wife Eve, who deſired " *the Angel*; and ſhe conceived and bare Cain, and ſaid I " have obtained a man," or, " the man, *the Angel of the* " *Lord*." As *Jehovah* is the word uſed in the original, we cannot conceive that the interpreter ſhould have given this paraphraſe, had he not known that it was believed by his countrymen, that he who was revealed in ſcripture as the Angel of the Lord was *Jehovah*, or the true God, and alſo that he was to be incarnate as *the Angel of the covenant*, or Meſſiah.

That by the Word the Paraphraſts underſtood the Meſſiah, is evident from their interpretation of theſe words, Pſal.

---

* Prideaux's Connect. Part 2. b. 8. p. 418.

Psal. cx. 1. *The Lord said unto my Lord, Sit thou at my right hand,* &c.　Jonathan renders them, " The Lord said " unto his Word."　Nothing can be more clear, than that the Jews in general, during our Saviour's ministry, understood this passage of the Messiah. Not one of the Pharisees, however much *puzzled,* as our author expresses it, objected to this as the true meaning, Math. xxii. 41.—46.　It is therefore contrary to all the rules of interpretation, to suppose that Jonathan understood the language in a different sense.　It may indeed suit a Socinian intellect, to consider it as the meaning of the Paraphrast, that *Jehovah* spoke to himself; that he desired himself to sit at his own right hand; that he engaged to himself, to make his enemies his footstool; that he sware to himself, that he should be a priest for ever, &c.　For it is natural for those, who are themselves under the empire of folly, to endeavour as far as possible to assimilate every other to themselves.　All this absurdity must follow; if, according to the Socinian hypothesis, by *the Word* the Paraphrasts simply mean *God himself,* that is, the Father, as the only person in Deity.

C H A P. VI.

The Doctrine of the Jews concerning the name Jehovah, *the Angel* Metatron, *and the* Trinity.

" THE Jewish Cabbalists," our author observes, "might " eafily admit that the Messiah might be called *Je-* " *hovah,* without supposing that he was any thing more than " a man, who had no existence before his birth.　That it " must have been the mere *name* and not the *nature* of God, " that the Jews supposed their Messiah to partake of, is all

I

" that

" that can be admitted in the cafe.   Several things in the
" Scriptures are called by the name of Jehovah ; as Jeru-
" falem,—is called *Jehovah our righteoufnefs* ; but this ne-
" ver led the Jews to fuppofe that there were two Jeho-
" vahs, a greater and a lefs *."   It is fo far good that the
Doctor *admits*, that the Jews afcribed the name of God to
the Meffiah.   We fhould not have had fuch a conceffion,
had he not found that there was no evafion.   He afterwards
mentions a Jewifh writer, " who laughs at the pretenfions
" of Chriftians to bring proofs of the Trinity from the cab-
" bala †."   But even the lefs ancient Jews would have
laughed at the Doctor's pretending that they would give the
name *Jehovah* to a mere man.   Maimonides fpeaks the fentiments of the whole nation when he fays ; " The Name of
" four letters has no known etymology ; nor is it communi-
" cated to another.   And there is no doubt that the glori-
" ous name, which, as you know, it is not lawful to utter,
" unlefs in the fanctuary, and by the holy priefts alone in
" their benediction, as alfo by the high priefts on the day of
" atonement ; that, I fay, it refpects fomething in which
" there is no communication between God and man ‡."
Kimchi, explaining thefe words, Ifa. xlii. 8. *Jehovah, that
is my name*, paraphrafes them in this manner ; " That name
" is proper to me."   Thence the Jews are wont to call it

the

---

‡ Sed illum Nomen, cujus literæ funt, *Iod He Vau He*, non habet
etymologiam notam, neque communicatur alteri.   Ac nullum eft du-
bium, quin gloriofum iftud Nomen, quod, ut nofti, non proferre licet,
nifi in Sanctuario, et a facerdotibus Dei fanctis folum in benedictione
facerdotum, ut et a facerdote magno in die jejunii, quin, inquam, do-
ceat de re aliqua, in qua inter Deum et alia, nulla prorfus eft commu-
nicatio, &c. More Nevochim, Pars i. cap. 61.

the proper name of God. The fame writer, on Hof. xii. 5. *Jehovah his memorial*, obferves; " In the name *El*, and *E-lohim*, he communicates with others ; but in this name he " does not communicate with any one." Aben Ezra, on Ex. iii. 14. is at great pains to fhew that this name is proper to God *.

But whatever were the opinion of the Jews, did it oppofe the teftimony of God, it could be of no more weight in the argument, than their rejection of him whom the Father hath fent. God exprefsly teftifies, in many places, that this name is his peculiar : and fhall we refufe to believe him ? He made himfelf known to his people by the name *Jehovah*, to exprefs his nature, and to dftiinguifh him from all whom he called gods, or who were fo called by others. When, therefore, this name was, in compofition, impofed on a place, there could be no danger of its being miftaken by them for God, or being fuppofed to poffefs divine nature ; and thus, no danger of the original defign of this diftinctive name being defeated. But as the idolatry of the world in general confifted in deifying intelligent creatures, had he permitted this name to be given to any fuch, he would have defeated his own defign in the ufe of it, and would himfelf have fignally contributed to idolatry †. When God claims this name to himfelf, it is directly in oppofition to every other nature, to which the folly of mankind might afcribe divinity. *My glory will I not give to another*, Ifa. xlii. 8. This name could not be conferred on a perfon of an inferior nature, without robbing God of his glory, or transferring fome fhare of it to the creature thus denominated.

* Vid. Hoornbeck Socin. Confut. tom. ii. p. 97.

† Guffetii Veritas Salutifera, P. 1. c. 42. p. 312.

denominated.   Whether angel or man, being a fubject ca-
pahle of intellectual and moral perfection, he would be
fuppofed to poffefs fome peculiar excellency, entitling him
to the divine name : and when it was found that this was
conferred by God himfelf, it would be fcarcely poffible to
withhold divine honour, or to believe that it could be dif-
agreeable to him who had conferred it.   But when it was
ufed in compofition, in the names of places, inftead of
having this tendency, it was folely meant to afcribe the
glory to *Jehovah*, who had manifefted himfelf there ; nay, directly tended, in the conftant remembrance of his people, to
appropriate it wholly to him, to the exclufion of every other.

The argument from Jerufalem being called *Jehovah our
righteoufnefs*, is of no weight.   For the natural verfion of
the words is, *And this is he who fhall call her, Jehovah our
Righteoufnefs*, Jer. xxxiii. 16.   The word *call*, in this
place, does not refer either to the name of the Meffiah, or
of Jerufalem ; but to his work of calling her to a participation of New Covenant bleffings.   But although this
name were given to Jerufalem, nothing more could be urged from this circumftance, than from the ufe of thofe compound names already confidered.

Thus, when Dr P. fays, " That it muft have been the
" mere *name*, and not the *nature* of God, that the Jews fuppo-
" fed their Meffiah to partake of ;" he fuppofes them not only to contradict themfelves, but the word of God. The Doctor adds very juftly, concerning the name being given to *feveral things*; " This never led the Jews to fuppofe, that there
" were two Jehovahs, a greater and a lefs." This is the very
thing that has always pinched them in their difputes with the
Chriftians. They know that this name cannot be properly given to another, without acknowledging him to be God. Finding that it is given to the Meffiah, while they oppofe the
doctrine of the Trinity, they know not what to make of it.

Our author's fubfequent reafoning, in reply to the texts quoted by Bifhop Pearfon, and what has been advanced by Mr Taylor of Portfmouth, is both trifling and unfair. " Nothing," he fays, " can be more exprefsly declared " than that there is but one Jehovah ; and in the paffages " quoted by Bifhop Pearfon, there is no intimation of " there being two Jehovahs ; fo that if the Meffiah be Je- " hovah, there muft have been no other being above him, " which Mr Taylor would not fuppofe." No Trinitarian can fuppofe that there is a " Being above" the Meffiah. For the Meffiah is not a diftinct being from God. He is only one perfon in the divine nature, fuftaining a relation different from that which effentially belongs to him. The Father is *above* him, not in a *perfonal*, but only in a *fœderal* refpect. His inferiority, being voluntary, cannot deprive him of his effential dignity. When the Meffiah, there- fore, is called *Jehovah*, it is not as another being than God, but as another perfon than the Father ; originally poffeffing this name in common with him, and invefted with an office which neceffarily fuppofes this. For it is not a name peculiar to one perfon, but expreffive of the undivided nature.

We fhall now confider what the Doctor advances con- cerning the angel Metatron. " The moft," he fays, " that I fhould be difpofed to infer from what the Jewifh " Cabbalifts have faid on the fubject would be, that this " Metatron was fomething fimilar to what Philo reprefents " the *Logos* as being, namely an *efflux of the divinity*, " but no *being* or *perfon*, permanently diftinguifhed from " him." But we have already fhown, that Philo enter- tained no fuch idea. This is the moft that Dr P. is " *dif-* " *pofed* to infer ;" not becaufe he has any folid grounds for fuch an inference, but becaufe he is *unwilling* to make any other, as it would greatly injure his caufe. But as far as

2

we can obferve, he cahnot produce a fingle proof; that any
of the Cabbaliftic writers formed the idea of occafional perfonality.   They had very abfurd ideas concerning angels :
but they were of fuch a nature, as to exclude this fpecies
of abfurdity.   For fome of them apprehended that they
were corporeal *.   They reckoned angels of two kinds,
corruptible and permanent.   Thofe were called *corruptible*,
which were fuppofed to be corporeal, as deriving their exiftence from generation.   So far were they from fuppofing
them to be *emanations* from the divine nature †.   Bafnage,
our author's great authority in Jewifh matters, contradicts
him here.   For, according to his account, the Cabbalifts
affert, that from Metatron all the angels " derive their
" lives, and all other advantages and comforts."

Now, it is difficult to conceive that *he* fhould be the fource
of being to perfons conftantly exifting, and fupport them
in it. who is himfelf only an occafional perfon.   But indeed,
thefe writers exprefsly declare that " he is exalted above
" them all, *continually* beholding the face of God, and
" diftributing to them *every day* bread convenient for
" them ‡."

The Doctor juftly obferves, that there " is little de-
" pendence on the whimfical and uncertain notions of thefe
" Jewifh Cabbalifts §."   But their fingular afcriptions to
the angel Metatron, although they fhould not prove that
they confidered him as the foul of the Meffiah, clearly e-
nough demonftrate that, to their conviction, the Scripture
contained various afcriptions to an angel, which they could
not with propriety interpret of a mere creature.   There-

E 2   fore,

---

* Bafnage Hift. b. iv. c. 9.

† Maimonid. More Nevoch. Par. ii. c. 6.

‡ Bafnage, b. iv. c. 8.   § Vol. iii. p. 45.

fore, they faid that the name of God was in this angel.
Dr P., indeed, quotes Bafnage, as fhewing that this
" means nothing more than that the letters of the word
" *Metatron,* and thofe of *Shadai,* confidered as numerals,
" exprefs the fame number, *viz.* 314." It was natural
for the Cabbalifts, according to their ufual manner, to advert to this circumftance. But we muft attend to their defign. This was to fupport their doctrine of the myftery
of the perfon. For when they found a myftery in a name,
they underftood it as expreffive of a further, and a more
important, myftery. The learned are greatly divided as
to the origin of this name; fome deriving it from the Hebrew, others from the Greek, and others fuppofing it to
be a corruption of the Latin word *Metator,* or of *Mediator.* It feems moft probable, that they adopted the name
as correfponding, in numerals, with *Shadai;* and that this
correfpondence was the reafon of their adopting it, that
thus they might exprefs the character of that angel of
whom it is faid, *My name is in him; Shadai* being one of
the names of God. They do not feem to have inferred
the doctrine from the name, but to have chofen the name
to fuit the doctrine. The former might be fuppofed, if
that of God's name being in this angel, were the only peculiar afcription. But this is far from being the cafe. Even
according to Bafnage, it was he who, by the Jewifh accounts, wreftled with Jacob. Now, thefe writers muft
have known that this angel is exprefsly called *God.*

In the Gemara of Babylon, thefe words are explained;
*Whom fhall he teach knowledge, and whom fhall he make to
underftand doctrine? Them that are weaned,* &c. Ifa. xxviii.
9. This work is firft afcribed to God. Then it is faid;
" But who taught them from the beginning?" that is, as
the paffage is underftood, before the deftruction of the temple. The anfwer is; " If you pleafe, you may fay, Me-
                                        " tatron;

" tatron ; but if you prefer it, *he* hath done both the one
" and the other ;" that is, God hath taught infants both
before and fince that event *. They alfo defcribe Metatron as " the Angel of God's face or prefence ;" and as
performing the funftions of a Mediator. For they fay,
that by him alone we can have accefs to God. They pretend, that " when the tabernacle was erefted in the wil-
" dernefs, another tabernacle was erefted, *viz.* that of the
" child Metatron, whofe name is the fame with the name
" of his God." In this tabernacle, he is faid to " offer the
" fouls of the juft, that he may make expiation for Ifrael
" during the time of his captivity †." When Bafnage is
quoted, as " fhewing that he is the fame with the angel
" Michael," Dr P. might alfo have mentioned that, according to the acknowledgment of the fame author, they
make a God of him ‡. The fame is affertcd by other
writers §. The Talmudifts fay that this Angel " hath
" power to blot out the fins of Ifrael," whence they make
him " the Chancellor of heaven ‖."

From a connefted view of thefe circumftances, it muft
appear, that the later Jewifh writers found themfelves
under a neceffity of afcribing perfeftions to one ,angel,
which properly belong to God only. We may alfo obferve, that their elevation of this angel above all others,
is a proof that they did not believe that the names of Deity
were common even to angels. Their fyftem concerning
Metatron is evidently the beft they could make of thofe

E 3   paffages

---

* Avoda Sara, p. 13. 14.

† Talmud, Chagigah, c. 2. ap. Lampe in Joh. i. 14. Vitringa Obf.
    Sac. l. 1. c. 9.

‡ Hift. b. iv. c. 9.

§ Vid. Wolfii Cur. Phil. in Phil. ii. 9.

‖ Owen on Heb. vol. i. F.x. x. p. 121.

paſſages of ſcripture urged by Chriſtians in proof of a plurality of perſons in the Godhead; while, from their hatred of Chriſtianity, they have generally receded as far as poſſible from this doctrine.

To theſe teſtimonies it may not be improper to ſubjoin the words of R. Moſes Gerundenſis Nehmanni, who wrote about the year 1220. They illuſtrate the ſentiments of ſome of the Jews, even in later times, concerning that Angel to whom divine names are given, and divine operations aſcribed. When explaining Joſh. v. 14. where we have an account of the appearance of one as " Captain of " the Lord's hoſt," he ſays; " This Angel, if we ſpeak ex- " actly, is the Angel-Redeemer, of whom it is written, " *My Name is in him;* that very Angel who ſaid to Jacob, " Gen. xxxi. 13. *I am the God of Bethel;* he of whom " it is ſaid, *And God called to Moſes out of the buſh,* Ex. " iii. 4. He is called an Angel, becauſe he governs the " world. For it is written, Deut. vi. 21. *The Lord brought* " *you up out of Egypt;* and Num. xx. 6. *He ſent his* " *Angel, and brought you out of Egypt.* Beſides it is writ- " ten, Iſa. lxiii. 9: *And the Angel of his Face ſaved them.* " He is that Angel, *viz.* who is the Face of God; of " whom it is ſaid, Ex. xxxiii. 14. *My Face ſhall go, and* " *I will give you reſt.* In fine, he is that Angel of whom " the prophet Malachi ſays, ch. iii. 1. *And the Lord whom* " *ye ſeek ſhall ſuddenly come to his temple, even the Meſ-* " *ſenger of the covenant whom ye delight in.*" Again, he ſays; " Diligently attend to the meaning of theſe words, " *My Face ſhall go before thee.* For Moſes and the " Iſraelites always deſired the chief Angel. But who " this was, they could not truly underſtand. For neither " did they learn it from others, nor could they ſufficiently " attain it by propheſy. But the Face of God ſignifies " God himſelf; which is acknowledged by all interpreters.

" But

" But no one can have the leaft notion of thefe things, un-
" lefs he be truly inftructed in the myfteries of the law."
And again; " *My Face fhall go before you*, that is, the
" Angel of the covenant whom ye defire, in whom my
" Face fhall be feen ; of whom it is faid, *In an acceptable*
" *time have I heard thee : My name is in him : And I will*
" *caufe thee to reft ;* or I will caufe, that he fhall be gentle
" and benign to thee.   Neither fhall he lead thee with
" rigour, but calmly and mercifully *."

The reafon given by this writer for the name Angel,
although true in itfelf, does not clearly exprefs its meaning.
But it contains more than one would apprehend at firft fight.
For when he fays of the perfon fpoken of, that " he is
" called an Angel, becaufe he governs the world;" it is
evident, from the fcriptures quoted in proof of this affertion, that he efpecially intends his government of the
Jewifh church, as a *Saviour*.   He fays that " the Face of
" God fignifies *God himfelf*."   But it is not credible, that
he meant this in our author's fenfe.   He undoubtedly refers to the unity of effence between God and this Angel ;
elfe why would he avoid a particular explanation, leaving
the doctrine as a *myftery ?*   If he meant the fame perfon
with God, there was no myftery, and there could be no
reafon for leaving the fubject abruptly.   But fuppofing him
to mean a plurality in one effence, we difcern a reafon for
his conduct, of fufficient weight with a Jew.   He was
afraid of affording any handle to the Chriftians.

But he explains himfelf more fully in the paffage laft
quoted.   Not having abfolutely afferted the unity of God
and this Angel, he feems to have been lefs on his guard.
By applying the words of Malachi to him whom he calls
the Face of God, it appears that he confidered this perfon
E 4   as

---

* Vid. Poli Synops. in Jofh. v. 14. Owen on the Heb. vol. i.
Ex. x p. 122.

as the future Meffiah.   But it is undeniable, that he viewed
this Angel as a diftinct perfon in the divine effence.   For
although he fays that he is *God himfelf*, he introduces God
as fpeaking to him ; nay, as fpeaking thefe words, which
fome of the more learned Jews underftand, as refpecting
the Meffiah; *In an acceptable time have I heard thee*, Ifa.
xlix. 8.

Even Maimonides, at the very time that he is attempting to fhew that, when we read of God as appearing, we
are to underftand it as meant of a mere angel, quotes the
judgment of Rabbi Chija, although he could not but be
confcious that it oppofed his fyftem.   He gives it every
advantage, by extolling this Rabbi, as " one of their moft
" excellent and greateft wife men."   It refpects what is
faid of Jehovah, as appearing to Abraham, when he faw
three men; and particularly, the folemn addrefs of the
Patriarch to one of the three, *My Lord, if now I have
found grace in thy fight, pafs not away, I pray thee,
from thy fervant*, Gen. xviii. 3.   " Rabbi Chija fays, that
" thefe words of Abraham, were fpoken and directed to
" one, and indeed to the chief one among them.   This I
" leave to thee, as a great fecret deferving thy confidera-
" tion.   He fays the fame thing of what we have in the
" hiftory of Jacob ; *And there wreftled a man with him,*
" &c*."   Why does he roll the burden of this interpretation on Rabbi Chija ?   It has been common with the later
Jews, when they introduced any thing favourable to the
doctrine of a plurality in the Godhead, to give it on the
authority of more ancient writers.   Thus they fkreen
themfelves

---

* R. Chija dicit, quod verba ifta Abrahami; *Domine, fi nunc inveni
gratiam in oculis tuis, ne quæfo, tranfeas a fervo tuo;* quod inquam ifta
verba ad unum, et quidem præcipuum inter illos, dixerit et direxerit;
quod tibi tanquam fecretum magnum, confiderandum relinquo   Idem
dixit de eo quod in hiftoria Jacobi legimus. *Et luctatus eft Vir cum ipfo,*
&c.   More Nevochim, P. 2. cap. 42. p. 310.

themfelves from the charge of herefy; even when they make thofe acknowledgments, which the truth forces from them.   Maimonides, as would feem, mentions this view, from a conviction that the maxim generally adopted by his brethren in later times, concerning God's employing a created Angel, in the *appearances* mentioned, could not bear them out, in the explanation of a variety of paffages.   But he *leaves it as a great fecret,* evidently wifhing to conceal it from the Chriftians.

D. P. feems very certain, that the Jews never entertained any ideas of a Trinity.   Of a great many paffages in their writings, which relate to this doctrine, I fhall mention only a few.   Grotius himfelf, although, as fome of that party have faid, " a Socinian all over," thought fo differently from our author, concerning the Jews, that he has quoted fome of their writers, as calling God three lights, and by the name of Father, Son and Holy Ghoft *.

It has been obferved, that the belief of a plurality is infinuated in the queftions propofed in the Talmud, as to the meaning of that expreffion, Dan. vii. 9. which is rendered in our verfion, *The thrones were caft down,* but underftood by all the Jews, as fignifying that they were *fet up.*   It is inquired, " why the throne, on which the Ancient of days " was to fit, is put in the plural?"   Various anfwers of a trifling kind are given; but the laft is, that " it is blaf- " phemy to fet the creature, on the throne of the Creator, " bleffed for ever."   The following remarkable words form the conclufion; " If any one can folve this difficulty, " let him do it; if not, let him go his way, and not at- " tempt it †."

To the fame purpofe is the converfation between R. Jofhua, the fon of Levi, and Elias, at the mouth of the

cave

---

* Leflie's Socinian Controv. Dial. 1. p. 49.

† Talmud, Ancient Univ. Hift. vol. iii. p. 13.

cave of Rabbi Simeo Ben Jochai, which is recorded in the Talmud. This R. Simeon, with his fon R. Eliezer, are faid to have concealed themfelves in a cave, for twelve years, from fear of the emperor Adrian, and to have written the books of *Zohar* and *Siphri* in this retreat. " Rabbi Jofhua," according to the narrative, " inquired of " Elias, Shall I reach to the future age? He anfwered, If " *that* Lord will. For the divinity was prefent with them. " Jofhua rejoined; I fee only two, but I hear the voice of " three *."

In the ancient work, entitled *Bahir*, it is faid, that " by " the threefold repetition of the term *Jehovah*, we are " taught, that thefe names of the bleffed God, are three " powers, and that every diftinct power is like to each " other, and hath the fame name with it." In the fame work, thefe words, *The Lord reigneth*, Pfa. xciii. 1. are faid to " bear witnefs of the three exiftences, (or fubfift- " ences) in the bleffed Creator. And the whole being " clofed (v. 5.) with *Jehovah*, the peculiar name of God, " intimates that he is the fountain of all, and that from " him are the emanations of all. Thus, in thefe words, " *The Lord reigneth*, there is a great myftery †.

Rabbi Bechai alfo fpeaks of three degrees or excellencies, which are in God. Each of thefe, he fays, is called Glory, and *Panim* or *Perfons*. ‡ For the word is often thus tranflated

in

---

* R. Jehofua filius Levi. reperit Eliam ftantem ad oftium fpeluncæ R. Simeonis ben Jochai; quæfivit ex illo, Perveniamnè in feculum futurum?? Refpondit, Si voluerit ifte Dominus. Aderat enim ipfis fancta Divinitas (Shechinah). Regeffit Jofua; Binos tantum vidi, fed vocem trium audivi. Talmud, cap. ult. Sanhedr. ap. Schickardi Mifhpat Hammelech, cap. 6. p. 187.

† Bedford's Serm. p. 62.

‡ Judæi tres illas Dei proprietates vocant in libro Jetfira חההדיות; id eft Hypoftafes, et in libro Schaare Tzedek פנים הפנימים: id

eft

in the Septuagint. " The firſt degree is the ſupreme Glory,
" the ſecond the middle, and the third the latter Glory.
" And this," it is ſubjoined, " is the myſtery *."

The author of *Zohar* ſays ; " The myſtery of *Elohim* is
" this.   There are three degrees, and every one of theſe
" degrees ſubſiſts by itſelf : and yet all of them are one, and
" knit together in one, nor can one be ſeparated from the
" other †."   Although the Jews induſtriouſly avoid the uſe
of the word *perſon*, Bp. Kidder has obſerved the ſame thing
mentioned by Voiſin, that, in the book *Shaare Tſedek*, theſe
degrees are called *perſons* ‡.   The author of *Zohar* renders Deut. vi. 4. in this manner ; " The Lord (or Jehovah)
" and our God, and the Lord are one."   In his expoſition
of the paſſage, beginning with *Jehovah*, he ſays ; " He
" is the beginning of all things, the Ancient of Ancients,
" the Garden of Roots, and the Perfection of all things ;
" and he is called the *Father*.   The other, or *our God*, is
" the Depth, and the Fountain of Sciences, which proceed
" from that Father, and is called *the Son*.   The other (or
" Lord) he is the *Holy Ghoſt*, who proceeds from them
" both, and is called the Meaſure of the Voice.   He *is*
" *one*; ſo that one concludes with the other, and unites
" them together.   Neither can one be divided from the
" other.   And therefore he ſaith, *Hear, O Iſrael*, that is,
" join together this Father, the Son, and the Holy Ghoſt,
" and make him one eſſence, and one ſubſtance.   For what-
" ſoever is in the one, is in the other.   He hath been the
" whole, he is the whole, and he will be the whole."   Theſe
words are alſo given by Rabbi Markante, which undoubtedly

---

eſt προσωπα five *Perſmas* et *Facies intrinſecas.*   Obſ. I. de Voiſin ad
Martini Pug. p. 406.

* Bedford ibid.   † Kidder's Demonſtr. Part iii. p. 83.

‡ Ibid. p. 85.

edly implies his approbation of them *. Will Dr P. be pleafed to grant, that this is the doctrine of the Trinity? Or could he fubfcribe this Jewifh creed, as purely Unitarian?

Bifhop Kidder gives another extract from the comment of the author of *Zohar*, on the fame paffage. " This is " the *myftery* of him who was before the rocks, and is " united with the *head*, the *ftem*, and the *way*. By *Je-* " *hovah*," the firft Jehovah mentioned Deut. vi. 4. " is " meant the high," or " firft beginning; by the *ftem* is " meant, the ftem fpoken of, Ifa. xi. the ftem of Jeffe; by " *Jehovah*," laft mentioned in the verfe, " is meant the " *way* † " All writers, Jewifh and Chriftian, having viewed the prophefy, Ifa. xi. as refpecting the Meffiah, does it not follow, that this Jew believed in a *divine* Meffiah?

Again, the fame writer fays; " This is the unity of " *Jehovah* the firft, *Elohenu*, *Jehovah*; lo, all of them are " one, and therefore called one; lo, the three names are " as if they were one, and therefore are called one, and " they are one. But by the revelation of the Holy Spirit, " it is made known, and by the fight of the eye, it may " be known, that *thefe three are one.* And this is the " myftery of the voice which is heard; the voice is one, " and there are three things, fire, and fpirit, and water, " and all of them are one, in the myftery of the voice; " and they are but one: fo here, *Jehovah, Elohenu, Je-* " *hovah*, they are one; the three forms, modes, or things, " which are one ‡."

They illuftrate this unity by the three names of the foul of man; " The three powers are all of them one, the
                                                                        " foul

---

* Bedford's Serm. p. 109.   † Demonftr. Part. iii. p. 83.

‡ Zohar in Num. fol. 67. ap. Gill. 1. Joh. v. 7.

" the foul, fpirit, and breath. They are joined as one;
" and they are one: and all is according to the mode of
" the fublime myftery *."

As in the Cabbaliftic tree, there are ten *Sephiroth* or
numbers, the firft is called the chief Crown, and firft Glory,
whofe effence no creature can comprehend; the fecond
is called Wifdom, and the intelligence illuminating, the
Crown of the creation, the Brightnefs of equal Unity, who
is exalted above every head, and the fecond Glory; and
the third, fanctifying Underftanding, the worker and parent of faith. They affert that thefe three firft numbers
are intellectual, and not, like the other feven, *properties* or
attributes †. On the fame fubject it is faid; " Between
" him who produces, and thofe who are produced, there is
" no difference. But he and they are all one, and the fame
" effence; in which, in three points or monads, are form-
" ed *the Crown, Wifdom*, and *Underftanding*: and in thefe
" are comprehended all the reft of the *Sephiroth*, or Nu-
" merations ‡. Rabbi Judah Levi fays; " Behold the my-
" ftery of the numberer, the number, and the numbered.
" In the bofom of God it is one thing; in the bofom of
" man, three: becaufe he weighs with his underftanding,
" and fpeaks with his mouth, and writes with his hand ||."

I fhall only add that, amidft all the zeal of the Jews for
the divine unity, the very manner in which they exprefs
this doctrine implies a conviction of myftery. For it is
one of the articles of their creed, that " God is one by
" an unity peculiar to himfelf," or which hath nothing
" fimilar

* Id. in Exod. fol. 74. ubi fup.

† Sepher Jetzira, R. Menahem, ibid.

‡ Afis Rimonim, cap. 11. ap. Jof. de Voifin, Obf. ad Martini Pug.
Fidei, p 400.

|| Tikkune Zohar, ap. Gill ubi fup.

" fimilar to it *." But if the divine unity neceffarily implies a fubfiftence in one perfon, inftead of being peculiar,
it is juft fuch an unity as belongs to every creature. By
this article, the Jews undoubtedly wifh to diftinguifh the
unity of God from that of all other beings. But the Socinian creed, in this inftance, is evidently framed with an
exprefs defign to affimilate the divine nature to every
other.

CHAP. VII.

Of the Doctrine of the Jews, in exprefs reference to the
MESSIAH, *both at the time of our* SAVIOUR's *appearance,*
and in fucceeding ages.

IT has been already proved, that Philo afcribes real
perfonality to the *Logos*, that he exhibits him as God,
and that he gives him all the fcriptural characters of the
Meffiah. We have alfo feen, that the Paraphrafts defcribed
the fame perfon under the name of *Memra*, reprefenting
him as diftinct from the Father; as his Angel or Meffenger,
and yet truly God; and applying to him that fcriptural
language, which in their time was univerfally allowed to
denote the Meffiah. The opinions of fome later Jews,
concerning the name *Jehovah*, a plurality in the divine
effence, and the Angel whom they call *Metatron*, have
been alfo confidered. Thence it appears, that there is no
juft ground to doubt, that they have ftill had fome traditionary belief with refpect to the doctrine of a Trinity, and that they afcribe to this Angel what they are
confcious belongs only to a divine perfon.

But

---

* Ant. Univ. Hift. vol. iii. p. 13. Stehelin's Tradition of the Jews,
vol. ii. p. 225.

But after all, fome may be apt to fay, that thefe teftimonies are not fo direct as might have been expected in a
cafe of this nature, and that their relation to the Meffiah
is proved only by induction. Although this kind of proof
is all that can be obtained on many important fubjects,
and is of itfelf abundantly fatisfying, when the confequence
is natural; I fhall produce a few paffages from the writings of the Jews, in which they exprefsly declare their fentiments concerning the Meffiah himfelf, or the circumftances of his appearance.

The ideas of the Paraphrafts, with refpect to the Meffiah,
appear from their interpretation of Pfal. xlv. which they
apply to him by name, ver. 3. It is faid on ver. 12. that
" this King fhall defire the beauty of the congregation of -
" Ifrael :" and the reafon is, " For he is thy Lord God,
" and thou fhalt worfhip him *."

It has been already feen, that they underftood Pfal. cx. as
addreffed to the Word, and that not one of the Pharifees
could refufe the juftnefs of our Saviour's interpretation,
when he applied it to the Meffiah. But, even in later
ages, this Pfalm has been underftood in the fame fenfe.
R. Saadias Gaon, when explaining thefe words, Dan. vii.
13. *And lo! one like unto the Son of man, came with the
clouds of heaven,* fays; " This is Meffiah, our righteouf-
" nefs, as it is written, *The Lord faid unto my Lord, Sit
" thou at my right hand,"* &c †. In Midrafch Tehillim,
it is obferved, that thefe words, *Thou art my Son,* Pfa. ii.
are addreffed to the fame perfon, to whom it is faid, *Sit
thou at my right hand‡.*

Indeed, in this Pfalm, the language is not, Jehovah *faid
unto* Jehovah, but *unto Adonai.* According to R. Solomon
Jarchi

---

* See Bedford's Serm. p 383.

† Raimundi Martini Pugio Fidei, p. 398.

‡ Ibid, p. 399.

Jarchi, the name *Adonai* is holy and proper to God. For, commenting on the words of Lot to the Angel who fpoke to him in the perfon of God, Gen. xix. 19. *Oh! not fo, my Lord*, he fays; " Our Doctors have obferved, that this " name *Adonai* is holy, becaufe it is faid of it, *that thou* " *shouldest fave my life.* For he, in whofe power it is, to " kill and make alive, is God *."

Nothing can more clearly prove, that the modern Jews find themfelves as much at a lofs, as their fathers were, to explain the paffage confiftently, without admitting the Deity of the Meffiah, than their having recourfe to the miferable fhift of applying this Pfalm, as well as the fecond, wholly to David, as merely refpecting his fecurity from temporal enemies †. Why have they abandoned the interpretation univerfally admitted by their anceftors, but from a conviction that they cannot grant that it belongs to the Meffiah, in a proper fenfe, to fit on the right hand of God, without granting at the fame time that he is the *fellow* of the Lord of hofts?

In Midrafch Tillim, Pfal. xxiv. 1. *The earth is the Lord's,* &c. is thus explained : " *I am the Lord that maketh all* " *things, that stretched forth the heavens alone, that spreadeth* " *abroad the earth by myself;*" or " *by* him who *is with* " *me,* (Ifa. xliv. 24.) *Who* is this *with me?* David faid " before the bleffed God, fince thou haft created the hea-
" vens

---

* Ibid. p 398.

† Rex David de feipfo compofuit, cum ejus fervi juraffent non permiffuros fefe, ut amplius cum iis in aciem fe conferat, 2 Sam. xxi —Hunc ergo Pfalmum concepit fub perfona fervorum et fubditorum, jurejurando fuo prohibentium eum prodire in aciem ; ficque facienda eft expofitio : Dixit Dominus Domino meo Davidi, fede in domo mea, et in dextram meam ac robur meum fiduciam reponito, dextra enim Domini forti- tudinem exercet. Eft proinde fenfus : Non opus eft ut tu te in bellum procleas, dextra enim Dei pro te pugnat, atque Deus B. ponet inimicos tuos fcabellum pedum tuorum, &c. Chizzouk Emounah, Par. 1. cap. 40.

" vens and the earth by thy Name, I afcribe them to thy
" Name, faying, *The earth is the Lord's.*" But in the
fame work, the Meffiah is faid to be the Name of God :
So on Pfal. xviii. 50. *Magnifying the falvations of his King,
and fhewing mercy to his Meffiah;* " one fcripture faith,
" *Magnifying;* and another, *a tower;* (referring to the
" parallel place, 2 Sam. xxii. 51. *He is a tower of falvation*
" *to his King*). And what is the *tower*, which is made for
" them ? The king Meffiah fhall be as a tower, as it is
" written, Prov. xviii. 10. *The Name of the Lord is a*
" *ftrong tower : thither the righteous runneth, and is fafe*.*"
It has been feen, that, according to Philo, the Logos is the
Name of the Lord.

In Echa Rabbati on Lam. i. 16. we have thefe words;
" What is the name of the king Meffiah ? R. Abba hath
" faid, JEHOVAH is his name ; as it is declared, Jer. xxiii. 6.
" *And this is his name, by which they fhall call him,* JE-
" HOVAH *our Righteoufnefs.* R. Jofhua ben Levi hath faid,
" The BRANCH is his name ; as it is written, Zech. vi. 12.
" *Behold the man whofe name is the* BRANCH. There are
" fome who fay, The *Comforter*, the Son of the mighty
" God ; as it is faid, Lam. i. 16. *Becaufe the Comforter—*
" *is far from me.*——Thofe of the houfe of R. Chaninah
" have faid, his name is *Gracious;* as it is written, Jer.
" xvi. 13. *I will not give the gracious one.* Thofe of the
" houfe of Jannai have faid, *Innon* is his name, Pfal. lxxii.
" 17. *Before the fun fhall his name be filiated.* R. Biba
" hath faid, his name is *Luminous;* as it is declared, Dan.
" ii. 22. *And light fhall dwell* with him †."

They thus explain Pfal. xxi. 1. *The king fhall joy in thy
ftrength,* &c. " R. Nachman hath faid, *Who is this King*

VOL. I. F " of

---

* Martini Pug p 585.

† Ibid. p. 685.

" *of Glory? The Lord of hosts, he is the King of Glory.*
" Our masters have said; No king of flesh and blood is
" invested with his crown. But the holy God will give it
" to the king Messiah; as it is said, (v. 3.) *Thou settest*
" *a crown of pure gold upon his head.* No king of flesh
" and blood is clothed with his purple. And what is it?
" Confession, authority, reverence, praise and glory; as
" it is said, Psal. civ. 1. *Thou art clothed with confession*
" *and majesty.* And of the king Messiah, it is written,
" (Psal. xxi. 5.) *His glory is great in thy salvation.* But
" God hath called Moses by his name; as it is written, *See,*
" *I have made thee a god to Pharaoh,* Ex. vii. 1. and so
" Israel; *I have said ye are gods,* Psa. lxxxii. 6. And he
" calls the king Messiah by his name. JEHOVAH is his
" name. For it is said, Ex. xv. 3. *The Lord is a man of*
" *war,* JEHOVAH *is his name.* And it is written of the
" king Messiah, *This is the name by which they shall call*
" *him,* JEHOVAH *our Righteousness.* Jerusalem also is called
" by his name; *And the name of the city shall be,* JE-
" HOVAH is there, Ezek. xlviii. 35 *."

The Jews cannot refuse that the name JEHOVAH is given
to the Messiah. But from their obduracy, and from their
hatred of the Christian Doctrine, they wish to derogate
from the honour necessarily implied in this ascription, by
referring to the language used with respect to Moses, Israel
and Jerusalem. However, they know abundantly well,
that the name *Elohim* is not like that of *Jehovah,* incommunicable; that, although Jerusalem received this name
as conjoined with another word, this entirely alters the nature of the designation; and that the name is never given,
either simply, or with *toar* †, as the Jews express it, that is,

in-

---

* Midrasch Tehil. ap. Martini Pug. p. 517.

† Vid. Glassii Grammat. Sacr. i. p. 533.

in connexion with fuch a noun as that here fignifying *juft*, to any creature whatfoever. It has already been proved, that, even according to the acknowledgment of Maimonides, the name *Jehovah* is incommunicable.

In Ifa. xxviii. 5. it is faid, *In that day fhall the Lord of hofts be for a crown of glory, and for a diadem of beauty, unto the refidue of his people.* Jonathan renders thefe words; " In that time fhall the Mefliah of the Lord of hofts be for " a crown," &c. For *Jehovah* in the original, he fubftitutes the name of Mefliah. This plainly fhews that he confidered it as the fame privilege to the church, to have the Mefliah for a crown of glory, as to have *Jehovah* himfelf; and of courfe, that he confidered the Mefliah as effentially *Jehovah*. It is well known, that the Jews have fuch a veneration for the Targum of this writer, that they afcribe to it fomething divine. And it may well be fuppofed, that he would not have dared to give fuch a paraphrafe, had it not been generally believed by the Jews of that age, by the more enlightened part at leaft, that the Mefliah fhould be God.

I have formerly quoted a paffage from Juftin Martyr, which clearly proves his full perfuafion, that, in his time, the more learned among the Jews, admitted that the Mefliah fhould be the adorable God *. Now, he afferts this, even after Trypho had endeavoured to draw a veil over this part of their creed. The latter, indeed, notwithftanding all the evidences of obduracy, and of a contentious fpirit, which Juftin lays to his charge, and which undoubtedly appear in the courfe of the difpute, had not effrontery enough to affirm that none of the Jewifh Doctors believed the divinity of the Mefliah. Juftin had afked him, " If it was ac-" knowledged by the Jews, that any other was entitled to

F 2   " adoration,

---

* See above, p. 12.

" adoration, and was Lord and God, befides him who re-
" ceives this name in Scripture, the maker of all, *and the*
" *Meſſiah,* whoſe incarnation the whole tenor of ſcripture
" declares?" Trypho replies; " How can we acknowledge
" this? Since *we have made it a queſtion,* whether there be
" any other befides the Father only *." Had not Trypho
been conſcious that many of his brethren expected a divine Meſſiah, he would never have expreſſed himſelf in this
manner. Nor would Juſtin have aſſerted that they did, after Trypho had attempted to avoid ſo important a conceſſion, had he not been fully perſuaded of the truth of his
allegation.

Some of the later Jews, amidſt all their ſtudied obſcuri-
ty, plainly diſcover a conviction with reſpect to the incarnation of a divine perſon. For theſe words concerning Abraham, *And the Lord appeared to him in the plain of Mam-*
re, Gen. xviii. 1. are thus explained: " This is as if the
" ſcripture had ſaid; *Though afterwards theſe ſhall be*
" *ſurrounded with my ſkin, and out of my fleſh I ſhall ſee*
" *God,"* (Job xix. 26.) The preceding words ſo clearly point out the Meſſiah, that it cannot be ſuppoſed that
theſe interpreters meant to apply them in any other
ſenſe: *For I know that my Kinſman-Redeemer liveth, and*
that he ſhall ſtand up the latter one upon the earth, ver.
25 †.

R. Solomon Jarchi obſerves on this place, that " A-
" braham deſired to ſtand, but God ſaid to him, Sit down.

" For

---

* Καγω ειπον, μη τι αλλον τινα προσκυνητον, και κυριον, και Θεον λεγο-
μινον εν ταις γραφαις νοιετε ειναι, πλην τυ τυτο ποιησαντο; το παν,
παι τυ Χρισυ, ος δια των τοσητων γραφων απεδειχθη υμιν ανθρωπος
γινομενος; και ο Τρυφων, πως τυτο δυναμεθα ειναι ομολογησαι οποτε ει-και
αλλος τις εςι πλην τυ πατρος μονυ, την τοσαυτην ζητησιν εποιησαμεθα;
Dial. p. 293

† Bereſchit ketanna, ap. Martini Pug. p. 571.

" For thou art a ſtriking ſign to thy poſterity. For it
" ſhall come to paſs, that I will ſtand in the counſel of
" the judges; as it is ſaid (Pſal. lxxxii. 1.) *The Lord*
" *ſtandeth in the aſſembly of the gods* *."

In the days of the Meffiah, the Jews expected ſalvation immediately from God, as oppoſed to the *hand* of
man †. According to this view, the Paraphraſts render
Zech. ii. 10. " Sing and rejoice, O church of Zion, be-
" cauſe behold! I will reveal myſelf, and place my di-
" vinity in the midſt of thee, ſaith the Lord: and ma-
" ny nations ſhall join themſelves to the people of the
" Lord in that day, and ye ſhall know that the Lord
" hath ſent me to propheſy unto you." Nothing can be
more evident than that they conſider the ſpeaker as a
divine perſon; and yet as a meſſenger, and as declaring
that he would act the part of a prophet to his church, at
the ſame time that he placed his divinity in the midſt of
her. It deſerves our attention, that ſome of the Jewiſh
writers have explained this paſſage by what is ſaid, chap.
ix. 9. *Behold, thy king cometh unto thee* ‡.

R. Moſes Hadarſchan, after quoting theſe words, Cant.
i. 4. *We will be glad and rejoice in thee*, ſubjoins; " When
" ſhall this be? When the captives ſhall aſcend from hell,
" and the Shechinah (or Divinity) on their head; as it is
" ſaid, Mic. ii. 13. *And their king ſhall paſs before them,*
" *and the Lord on the head of them.*" To the ſame purpoſe
it is ſaid, in Bereſchit rabba on Gen. xliv. 18. " When
" ſhall we rejoice? When the feet of the Divinity ſhall
" ſtand on the mount of Olives; as it is written, Zech. xiv.
" 4. *And his feet ſhall ſtand on that day on the mount of*
" *Olives* ||."

F 3

It

---

* Martin. loc. ſup. cit.   † Grabe Spicileg. vol. i. p. 358.

† Midraſch. Canticor. ap. Martini Pug. p. 512.

‡ Martini Pug. p. 685.   Grabe Spicileg. vol. i. p. 364.

It is very remarkable, that they even fpeak of this e-vent as paft. Thus, in Midrafch Tillim, it is faid, in an-fwer to that queftion from Pfal. x. 1. *Why ftandeft thou afar off, O Lord?* " This is as if it had been faid, *And* " *it came to pafs that, as he cried, they would not hear,* " Zech. vii. 13. R. Jochanan faid; Three years and a " half was the Shechinah ftanding on the mount of Olives, " and crying, *Seek the Lord, while he may be found, call up-* " *on him while he is near,* Ifa. lv. 6.*" It is no lefs remark-able, that they limit the duration of this folemn addrefs from the Divinity, exactly according to the time generally allotted to the perfonal miniftry of the Son of God.

Even Maimonides fays; " Behold, it is explained unto " thee, that our Rabbies were of opinion, that in procefs of " time all the Ifraelites fhould receive another law, as be-" fore, *immediately* from the mouth of the bleffed God † "

Perhaps, it is in this fenfe that we are to underftand the high afcriptions of the Jews to the Meffiah in his pro-phetical character. Abarbanel acknowledges that he fhall be greater than Mofes, and that " thofe things which lie " hid in the hearts of men fhall be clearly known to " him ‡. ' Gerfon fays; " And it fhall come to pafs, that " a certain prophet fhall arife, who fhall *at the fame time* be " a prophet to all the nations of the earth; and this fhall " be the king Meffiah; as it is faid in Midrafch that the " Meffiah fhall be far greater than Mofes §." It is not eafy to account for fuch language on the idea of their being fatisfied in their minds, that he is to be " no other than a " man like themfelves."

To

---

* Martini Pug. p. 661.

† De Fundamentis, lib. iii. c. 19. Bedford, p. 389.

‡ Ad Jef. xi. ap Lampe in Joan. vi. 14.

‖ In Legem, fol. 198. ibid.

To the Meffiah they afcribe the power of taking away fin.
" The purification which the Meffiah will make, fhall be
" for the expiation of fin in general, for deftroying tranf-
" greffion and making an end of fin, which retains man-
" kind under its yoke. For as the firft man was the firft
" who finned, fo Meffiah fhall be the laft, who fhall com-
" pletely take away fin *.

According to this view, are thefe words, Pfal. ii. 12.
Kifs the Son, explained : " This may be illuftrated by a pa-
" rable. A certain King was angry with his fubjects.
" They therefore went, and made his Son their friend, that
" thus they might conciliate the mind of their King. The
" Son departed, and reconciled his Father, as they had re-
" conciled to themfelves the Son. They went to give thanks
" to the King. But the King faid to them : You give
" thanks to me ; but go and offer them to my Son. For
" had it not been for him, I fhould have deftroyed the pro-
" vince †." The introduction of this parable, as an illuftration of the text, is entirely *malapropos*, unlefs it be
meant, not only that the Son reconciles us to the Father, but
that he has a juft claim to the fame honour and worfhip
which are given to the Father.

An ancient tradition is mentioned in Berefchit Rabba
on Gen. xlii. 6. that " ten kings fhould reign from the
" beginning of the world to the end of it ; of whom the
" firft is the Bleffed God, and the laft the Meffiah, accor-
" ding to Pfal. lxxii. 8. Dan. ii. 35. 44. and that in this
" laft king the kingdom fhould return to the Lord the
" rightful owner, and that thus he who was the firft king
" fhould be the laft ‡" It is faid in another work, that

F 4   " the

* Neve Schalom, lib. ix. c. 5. Voifin, Obferv. p. 398.

† Midrafch Tillim ap. Lampe in Joan. i. 18.

‡ Martini Pugio, p 316. Lampe in Joan. i. 50.

" the crown of the bleffed God is not put on him who is
" *man only* : but God hath put it on the bleffed king Mef-
" fiah *." It alfo deferves our attention, that even the
modern Jews, in their commentaries on Gen. i. 2. fay,
that the Spirit of God, that *moved on the face of the waters,*
is the Spirit of the king Meffiah †.

Thus, in direct contrariety to our author's teftimony, the
Jewifh writers oppofe the Meffiah to a mere man. To him
they alfo afcribe the work of raifing the dead; a work, in
their opinion, peculiar to God, at leaft when confidered as
univerfal. Therefore they fay, that there are three keys
" which are not delivered to any deputy, that of life, of rain,
" and of the refurrection of the dead ‡."

Nor is the doctrine of the miraculous conception of the
Meffiah totally loft among them. In the Jerufalem Talmud, it is faid that thefe words Pfal. cx. 3. *From the womb,
from the morning, fhall be the dew of thy youth,* are to be explained by Mic. v. 7. *As a dew from the Lord,—that tar-
rieth not for man, nor waiteth for the fons of men* ||.

On Gen. xxxvii. 22. R. Mofes Hadarfchan declares his
fentiments in thefe words : " The Redeemer, whom I will
" raife up from among you, fhall not have a father, ac-
" cording to Zech. vi. 12. *Behold the man whofe name is
" the* BRANCH, *and he fhall grow up out of his place.* So
" alfo Ifa. liii. 2. *And he fhall grow up before him as a
" tender plant, and as a root out of a dry ground.* So alfo
" David fays of him, Pfal. cx. 3. *From the womb,* &c. In
" fine, it is written, Pfal. ii. 7. *This day I have begotten
" thee* §."

R. Solo-

* Tanchuma, fol. 28. ap. Lampe ibid.

† Berefchit Rabba. Owen on Heb. i. 1. 2.

‡ Gerfon ad Deut. xxxiv. 10. Talmud, &c. ap. Lampe in Joan. v. 21.

|| Obferv. J. de Voifin in Proœm. Martini Pug. Fid: p. 125.

§ Ibid.

R. Solomon Jarchi obferves on Ifa. vii. 14. *Behold, a virgin fhall conceive*, &c. " There are fome who fay that " this was made the fign, becaufe a virgin *fuit non* " *apta generationi* *." Indeed, the moft of their writers underftand the paffage of Hezekiah, or of the fon of the prophet; as the fign of Judah's deliverance. But they do not confine themfelves to this application. In Bemidbar rabah (fect. 4.) the prophecy is viewed as ultimately re-fpecting the Meffiah. For it is faid; " Hezekiah of him. " felf knew the bleffed God. For it is written of him, " ver. 15. *Butter and honey fhall he eat, that he may know* " *to refufe the evil, and choofe the good.* In like manner " hath the king Meffiah known the bleffed God †."

The words of the daughters of Lot, Gen. xix. 34. *That we may preferve feed of our Father*, are thus explained; " R. Tanchuma hath faid; It is not written a *fon*, but " *feed*; that feed, *viz.* which fhall come from another " place, and that is Meffiah ‡."

On Gen. iv. 25. *The Lord hath appointed me another feed,* it is obferved ; " R. Tanchuma, in the name of R. Sa. " muel, hath faid; This is that feed which fhall arife from " another place. And what is that? It is the king Mef- " fiah ||. The fame language is elfewhere afcribed to R. " Nechoniah and R. Jacob the fon of Abbin §."

To the fame purpofe there is a remarkable paffage in Berefchit Rabba; " R. Jofhua the fon of Levi hath faid; " Come and fee that the way of the bleffed God is not " like that of flefh and blood. For flefh and blood wounds
" with

---

* Obferv. J. de Voifin in Proæm. Martini Pug. Fid. p. 125.

† Ibid. p. 124.

‡ Berefchit ketannah ap. Martini Pug. 284.

|| Berefchit Rabba, ibid.

§ Midrafch Ruth, ibid.

" with a knife, and heals with a plaifter. But the
" way of the bleffed God is not of this nature. For he
" heals by the very means by which he wounds. It is
" this that is written, Jer. xxx. 17. *For I will reſtore*
" *health to thee, and will heal thee of thy wounds.* And
" this ſhalt thou find in Joſeph and in Iſrael, when he ſhall
" heal them by the very means by which he hath wound-
" ed them. Did not Iſrael ſin in a virgin? as it is writ-
" ten, Ezek. xxiii. 3. *There they bruiſed the teats of their*
" *virginity.* And they are puniſhed in a virgin; as it is
" ſaid, Lam. v. 11. *They raviſhed the women in Zion, the*
" *virgins in the cities of Judah.* But he will return and
" give comfort by a virgin; as it is declared, Jer. xxxi. 21.
" 22. *Turn again, O virgin of Iſrael; turn again to theſe*
" *thy cities. How long wilt thou go about, O backſliding*
" *daughter? For the Lord hath created a new thing in the*
" *earth, A woman ſhall compaſs a man.* R. Hunah, in the
" name of R. Idi. and R. Joſhua the ſon of Levi, have ſaid;
" This is the king Meſſiah, of whom it is ſaid, Pſal. ii. 7.
" *To day have I begotten thee.* And concerning this Iſaiah
" ſays, (chap. lxii. 1.) *For Zion's ſake will I not hold my*
" *peace,—till the juſt One thereof go forth as brightneſs,* &c.
" And it is this that the ſcripture hath ſaid, Judg. v. 8.
" *God hath choſen new things: then ſhall he conquer the*
" *gates,*" or as otherwiſe tranſlated, " *then ſhall uncleanneſs*
" *be ſubdued* *."

From ſuch paſſages many learned men have, without
any heſitation, inferred that all the Jews, at the time of our
Saviour's appearance, were firmly perſuaded of the divinity of the promiſed Meſſiah. As I would wiſh invariably
to prefer truth to ſyſtem, I muſt acknowledge, that, in my
apprehenſion, the premiſes will not warrant ſo unlimited a
conclusion.

* Martini Pug. p. 284.

conclufion.   To me it appears, that the more learned and in-
quifitive of that age, fuch efpecially as devoted themfelves to
the ftudy of fcripture, were convinced that the Meffiah was
foretold in language expreffive of a divine character.   Even
the Pharifees, who paid far more regard to their own traditions than to the doctrines of revelation, could not refufe
that he was the *Lord* of David ; his Lord, in fo exalted a
fenfe, that the idea feemed totally repugnant to that of his
being his fon.   Their inability to anfwer Jefus feems to
have proceeded, in a great meafure, from their unwillingnefs to acknowledge the juftnefs of his claim of deity.   It
cannot be conceived, that they were ignorant of the current
doctrine with refpect to a perfonal Logos.   But it may well
be fuppofed that, while they knew that the fcripture afcribed to the Meffiah, both the attributes of deity, and the
truth of humanity, their carnal minds could not eafily di-
geft the doctrine of the union of two natures fo infinitely
remote in one perfon.

If the more intelligent Jews did not believe a plurality
in the divine effence, it is an unaccountable circumftance,
that they fhould never object to our Saviour the grofs abfurdity of his doctrine, when they underftood him as declaring that he was the Son of God in a proper fenfe.   If
the idea was totally ftrange to them, how do they fo readily
put this conftruction on his words, *He faid that God was
his Father, making himfelf equal with God?* John v. 18.
x. 33.   It feems very clear, that *the Jews* here referred to
were the rulers, or members of the great Sanhedrim, who
are often defigned in'this manner by the Evangelift John *.
That they connected the character of *the Son of God* with
that of *the Chrift* or *Meffiah,* is alfo evident from their u-
fing the terms as both applicable to the fame perfon, Luke
xxii. 67. 70.

But

* See chap. v. 15, 16. 33. 44. ix. 13. 18. 22.

But while it feems inconceivable, that they had no apprehenfions of the deity of the Meffiah, I am far from fuppofing, that they believed this doctrine in a proper manner.
It appears to have made no impreffion on their minds.
The truth, that they knew, *they held in unrighteoufnefs.*
They *received not the love of it.* They perverted the
cleareft precepts of the law, in order to accommodate them
to their lufts. And we need not be furprifed, though this
great myftery fhould have had little attention from them;
nay, though they fhould have attempted to obliterate it
from their minds. They were wholly bent on a temporal
falvation. Therefore, the idea of a fpiritual Meffiah would
be extremely ungrateful. It would throw a gloom on their
brighteft profpects, and pour its faddening influence on
their moft pleafing hopes of worldly aggrandizement.
Thence, many of them feem determined to reject any one
who fhould appear as the Chrift, how great foever his atteftations; if his character did not correfpond to their carnal
inclinations. It is obfervable, that the chief priefts and
fcribes curtail the prophecy of Micah, concerning the Ruler
of Ifrael. They do not quote that part of it which refpects his eternal exiftence, Mat. ii. 16. Some, it is evident, acted in direct contrariety to their own convictions.
They believed that Jefus was the Chrift. But their faith
had no influence on their practice. They believed this in
the fame manner, as Saul did the future advancement of
the typical David. He *knew well that he fhould furely be
king, and that the kingdom of Ifrael fhould be eftablifhed
in his hand,* 1 Sam. xxiv. 20. Yet fo obdurate was his
heart, that he daily fought the life of the Lord's anointed.
Indeed, that king whom the Lord rejected feems, in this
inftance, to have prefigured thofe judges of Ifrael, who
were alfo rejected of him, becaufe they perfecuted the
glorious Antitype.

But

But they do not feem to have made any formal oppofition to this doctrine, till it appeared that Jefus affumed no other character than that of a fpiritual Saviour. For when the Jews, that is, as we may moft naturally fuppofe, the Sanhedrim fent priefts and Levites from Jerufalem to John Baptift, they were enjoined to demand of him, if he was Elias? John i. 19. 21. Now this queftion is evidently taken from the prophecy of Malachi, ch. iii. 1. in which it is plainly declared, that the Angel of the covenant fhould be *the Lord;* that *Lord* who was to fit at the right hand of God, Pfal. cx. 1. and whom they were to *worfhip,* Pfal. xlv. 11. and alfo that he fhould *come to his temple.* We cannot fuppofe, that they underftood the one part of the prophecy, and totally overlooked the other. Though they had done fo, John's reply muft have brought it to their recollection. For he faid, *I am the voice of one crying in the wildernefs, Prepare ye the way of the Lord,* that is, of JEHOVAH, according to the prophecy to which he refers. It is probable, that thefe very meffengers heard the teftimony of John, on the day following, when he declared the pre-exiftence of Chrift, in the plaineft terms, faying, *He was,* or *exifted before me,* and explained the nature of this pre-exiftence, by *bearing record, that he was the Son of God,* John i. 30. 34. At any rate, as this was uniformly his doctrine, it could not be unknown to the Sanhedrim. For he declared to the Pharifees and Sadducees, that it belonged to Jefus to baptife with the Holy Ghoft, that the church was *his floor,* and that eternal vengeance was his prerogative, Mat. iii. 7. 11. 12.

Whatever ideas the more learned Jews had with refpect to the deity of the Meffiah, they feem to have concealed them from the common people. They *took away the key of knowledge,* Luke xi. 52. It was natural for them to do fo, as a temporal falvation engroffed all
their

their hopes and defires. For the proclamation of a divine Meffiah muft have given a fatal blow to their own authority ; as they were in general fuch carnal men, and fo unlike thofe who were prepared to welcome a fpiritual Deliverer. At this period, they held the poor in the greateft contempt, calling them " the people of the earth," and accounting them *curfed*, John vii. 49. As they knew not the law, their teachers did not wifh to make it known to them. The ignorance of the people was the bafis of their authority.

The doctrine of the divinity of the Meffiah feems to have been nearly loft among the vulgar. Of this the gofpel-hiftory affords various evidences. Even Jofeph and Mary appear to have little acquaintance with it. Although they knew, by immediate revelation, that Jefus was the promifed Meffiah, the proofs of his divinity rather excited admiration than wrought conviction in their minds. When he faid to them, *Wift ye not that I fhould be about my Father's bufinefs? they underftood not the faying*. With refpect, not only to this reply, but to what had been fpoken by the fhepherds, by Simeon, and by Anna, it is declared that Mary *kept all thefe fayings in her heart*, Luke ii. 49. 51.

This doctrine, indeed, feems to have been as unacceptable to fome of the common people, as to thofe of fuperior rank. For when Jefus declared, that he was *the bread that came down from heaven, they murmured at him, faying, Is not this Jefus, the fon of Jofeph?* John vi. 41. 42. But thefe were Galileans, who were more grofsly ignorant than others ; who *fat in darknefs, and in the region of the fhadow of death*, Ifa. ix. 1. 2. It may be fuppofed, that thofe who refided at the fountain of Ifrael, were rather better acquainted with the character of Meffiah. Accordingly, the very objection, that thofe *of Jerufalem* made to Jefus,

I

Jefus,

Jefus, contains a proof that they expected one who fhould be more than man: *We know this man whence he is : but when Chrift cometh, no man knoweth whence he is*, John vii. 27. They could not mean this of the family whence the Meffiah fhould fpring, or of the place of his nativity. For they knew that, as man, he was to be of the family of David, and to be born in Bethlehem, ver. 42. We muft, therefore, be at a lofs for a meaning to thefe words, unlefs we underftand them as expreffing fome apprehenfions of his divinity, ftill remaining even among the common people. Jefus himfelf attefts the truth of their confeffion with refpect to the origin of the Meffiah, only as applying their language to himfelf; *Ye cannot tell whence I come*, chap. viii. 14.

Some of thofe who waited for the confolation of Ifrael, appear to have had far clearer views of the divine character of the Meffiah than others. When Simeon fays, *Mine eyes have feen thy falvation,—the Glory of thy people Ifrael*, Luke ii. 30. 32. he feems to acknowledge Jefus as the true *Shechinah*, the Glory of the Lord. The cloud of glory, which was the immediate token of the divine prefence among them, had been long their diftinguifhing privilege. *To them pertained the glory*, Rom. ix. 4. It is very probable, that the venerable faint refers to that prophetical addrefs to the church, Ifa. lx. 1.—3. *Arife, fhine, for thy light is come, and the Glory of the Lord is rifen upon thee.* He proclaims this Salvation as *prepared before the face of all people.* This is alfo predicted, chap. lx. 5. *The glory of the Lord fhall be revealed, and all flefh fhall fee it together.* Elizabeth calls Mary the Mother of *her Lord*, Luke i. 43. Zechariah alfo acknowledged the Meffiah as *the Higheft*, ver. 76.

But can the darknefs, which in that age involved the minds of the generality of the nation, with regard to the deity of the Meffiah, be a fufficient argument againft this doctrine?

doctrine? Indeed, in has been ftrenuoufly afferted, that it was totally unknown to them. This, however, cannot be believed by any impartial inquirer. But although it were true, muft we thence infer, that God never revealed this doctrine to their forefathers, or that they never believed it? It muft firft be proved that, becaufe the great body of that people expected only a temporal deliverance, Jefus was never foretold as a Saviour from fin, and that he had no claim to this character. The adverfaries of the deity of Chrift ought alfo to deny, that Jefus fhould have been a fuffering Meffiah. For if we are to regulate our faith, concerning his character, by that of the Jews, in one inftance; why not in every other? Such abfolute ftrangers were thofe of that age to the doctrine of the Meffiah's humiliation, that, although they all knew that he was called *the Son of man,* when Jefus fpoke of his being *lifted up,* they cried out, *Who is this Son of man?* as if they had never before heard of the defignation, John xii. 34. All fuch reafoning from the ideas of this people, at or after the time of our Saviour's appearance, muft be of little weight with thofe who know that the myfteries of the kingdom were hid from them; that they were given up to the lufts of their own hearts; that the awful meffage of Ifaiah was fulfilled in them, *Hear ye indeed, but underftand not; fee ye indeed, but perceive not,* &c. (Ifa. vi. 9. 10. Mat. xiii. 14. 15.) and that *they knew not the voices of the prophets which were read every fabbath day,* Acts xiii. 27.

Even the difciples were greatly under the influence of this fpiritual ftupor. Till the moment of our Lord's afcenfion, their minds were ftill warped with the idea of a temporal falvation. When he foretold his paffion, they reckoned it totally incompatible with his character, and an event abfolutely incredible. That very difciple, who gave the moft noble confeffions of the Meffiah, was fo fhocked

at

at the idea, that under the impulfe of the moment he entirely forgot his ftation, and began to rebuke his Lord, Mat. xvi. 21. 22.

It ought to be obferved, however, that, confidering the great privileges of the difciples, we cannot otherwife account for the aftonifhing darknefs of their underftandings, than by turning our thoughts to the fovereign difpenfation of the all-wife God. It is his pleafure, under the Gofpel, to confer peculir honour on the miniftration of the Spirit. As the purchafe of our redemption belonged to the Son, the whole efficacy of his work œconomically depends on the operation of the third Perfon. Thus, the Perfonal miniftry of Jefus had little effect, in the mean time, on the difciples themfelves. For *the Holy Ghoft was not yet given, becaufe that Jefus was not yet glorified,* John vii. 39.

As the opinions of the Jews, at the time of our Saviour's appearance, are not the rule of our faith, as little is it to be regulated by thofe of their fucceffors. It cannot be fuppofed that a people, who rejected the true Meffiah, and who were therefore rejected of God, would become more fpiritual in their apprehenfions. On the contrary, we may naturally imagine that they would wax worfe and worfe. Accordingly, we find the later Jews endeavouring to defend their incredulity, by refufing the application of many fcriptures to the Meffiah, which were thus applied by the unanimous teftimony of their anceftors. There is, however, no reafon to doubt that, in many inftances, they have acted contrary to their own convictions, and have denied doctrines which they unqueftionably believed.

The conduct of Maimonides has been already confidered. Many other proofs of their diffimulation might be produced. But at prefent, I fhall mention only one. It has been feen, that many of the Jewifh writers acknowledge the miraculous conception of the Meffiah. Others, however, attempt to

explain

explain away the meaning of their traditionary language, by pretending that he is to come from Moab, and that in this fenfe he is *the feed that fhall come from another place* *. Rather than feem to favour the Chriftian doctrine, they will transfer the honour of giving the Meffiah to a people ex-cluded from the congregation of the Lord *even to their tenth generation.* The oppofition made by fome to the more fcriptural views of the Meffiah given by others, is no fuf-ficient teft of the ancient faith of the nation. For although thefe are not found in all their writings on this fubject, their being found in any of them is a clear enough indica-tion of the fentiments of their anceftors. For not one of their writers would have borrowed fuch doctrines from the Chriftians.

Our author founds the greateft part of his reafoning con-cerning the *deity* of our Saviour on the opinions of the Jews, at the time of his appearance, or in fucceeding ages. But he ought to remember, that the obfervation which he makes with refpect to the *miraculous conception,* is fully as appli-cable with refpect to the former. " I own, however," he fays, " that the expectations of the Jews (any further than " they have a real foundation in the prophecies) ought not " by any means to determine our judgment in the cafe, fo " as to weigh againft any proper argument that may be al-" leged on the other fide †."

CHAP.

* Yoifin Obf. in Martini Pug. p. 288.

† Ear. Op. vol. iv. p. 12. 13.

C H A P.   VIII.

Of the Faith of the ancient Jews, concerning that Person who is called the Angel of the Lord.

THE doctrine of Philo, of the Paraphrasts, and of some later writers, concerning the divine nature, and the character of Messiah, has been particularly considered. But the most proper and convincing evidence of the faith of the ancient Hebrews, is contained in the scriptures of truth. How little regard soever some may pay to the assertions of uninspired Jewish writers, because of the confusion of their ideas, and their apparent inconsistency; if it appear from the Old Testament, that one Angel is revealed as a divine Person, and was acknowledged in this character by the Church, long before the coming of Christ; it must be granted, either that her members were polytheists, or that their scriptures revealed, and that they believed, a plurality of persons in an unity of essence. We have already considered the ascriptions of the later Jews to the Angel *Metatron :* and it will not appear surprising that they ascribed so much to him, when we attend to what the Holy Ghost reveals concerning him who is called *the Angel of the Lord,* or, as some render the expression, *the Angel-Jehovah.*

Dr P. skips over this ground as lightly as possible. " Fre-" quent mention," he says, " is made in the scriptures of an-" gels, who sometimes speak in the name of God, but then " they are always represented as the creatures and the servants " of God *." Does the Doctor mean to assert that angels in general are permitted to assume *the name of God,* or to speak

---

* Vol. i. p. 5.

in the firſt perſon? It is denied, that this honour is conferred on any angel but one. It is indeed moſt probable,
that in all places of the Old Teſtament where we read of
the Angel of the Lord, the uncreated Angel is meant. Unqueſtionable proofs of this occur in moſt of theſe places.'
When our author ſays of *angels*, that " they are always re-
" preſented as the creatures of God,"· he certainly means to
extend this aſſertion to *every* Angel mentioned in ſcripture. But the falſity of this will appear. For either there
are certain *criteria* by which God may be diſtinctly known
from his creatures, or there are not. The latter cannot be
aſſerted, without impeaching the wiſdom of God, and without ſuppoſing that he hath left mankind a prey to idolatry.
There can be no *criteria* more diſtinctive of God, than thoſe
names, attributes, works and worſhip, which are peculiar to
him. If, therefore, an Angel is revealed, to whom all theſe
belong; we muſt neceſſarily conclude that he is a divine
Perſon, and yet diſtinct from him whoſe Angel he is ſaid to
be. That this is the caſe with reſpect to *the Angel of the
Lord*, appears from many paſſages in the Old Teſtament.

We are informed, Gen. xvi. 9. that he who appeared to
Hagar was the Angel of the Lord. She called him *God*,
and we are aſſured that he was *Jehovah*, ver. 13. " *She called*
" *the Name of the Lord that ſpake unto her, God.*"—Indeed,
this expreſſion, *the Name of the Lord*, may be conſidered as
a perſonal character, ſignifying, not merely that the name
of *Jehovah* was given him, but that it was *in him*, (Ex. xxiii.
21.) as poſſeſſing the ſame nature with the Father. For
we are certain from the teſtimony of Philo, that the ancient
Hebrews knew this Angel, whom they alſo called the Word,
by the deſignation of *the Name of the Lord* *. Hagar did
not call him *God* who ſpake *by* the Angel. But ſhe called
the

---

* Leg. Allegor, lib. ii. p. 76. De Confuf. Linguarum, p. 267.

the Name of the Lord *that spake to her*—God.— She ascribes the *attribute* of omniscience to him. For she called him the *God that saw* her; evidently referring to his testimony, that the Lord had *heard her affliction*, ver. 11. He revealed himself, and she believed in him, as one to whom divine *works* belonged. For *the Angel of the Lord said unto her, I will multiply thy seed exceedingly*, ver. 10. There can be no doubt that he here speaks in his own name; and as little that she understood him in this sense. She gave this Angel divine *worship*. For she addressed him as God, in the language of faith and praise, and in the ascription of divine perfection to him; *Thou God seest me*, ver. 13. She knew no *being*, superior to him, as the all-seeing God. For she said, *Have I also here looked after him that seeth me?* Thus, on occasion of a single appearance only of this Angel, we find all the *criteria* of divinity appropriated to him.

Either Hagar knew that he who spake to her was an Angel, or she did not. If she did, and at the same time believed that he was a creature, she was wilfully guilty of both blasphemy and idolatry. For she gave all that honour to this Angel which she could have given to God himself, had she been perfuaded that he was the speaker. If she did not know that this was an Angel, and according to the Socinian system, a creature; the fault lay wholly in the mode of revelation. God took no care, either for his own glory, or for the salvation of this woman. He communicated his will to her in such a manner as necessarily to betray her into the most fatal mistake.

Again, either this worship was acceptable, or it was not. If it was; God accepted it, either as intentionally addressed to himself through the creature as a medium, or as addressed to the creature mistaken for himself. If the former be true, there can be no objection to the Popish worship of Angels and Saints, or even to the Pagan worship of the heavenly

bodies,

bodies, or of flocks and ftones. For the more learned or ingenious advocates for both have ftill contended, that the worfhip was really addreffed to the Supreme Being, *through* the creatures as his emblems. Indeed, the conduct of Hagar cannot admit of fuch an apology. For there is not the leaft evidence that her worfhip refpected any being, but that to whom it was immediately addreffed. If this worfhip was accepted, as being intentionally addreffed to God, although the creature was miftaken for him; then it does not avail, whether in our worfhip we addrefs the proper object, or not. God will be pleafed even with that worfhip addreffed to the Devil, if he happen to be miftaken for the Supreme Being.

If this worfhip was not acceptable, it is denied that there are any characters by which one may know whether one's worfhip be acceptable or not. Although the worfhip of Hagar had been as good as any ever offered, fhe could fcarcely have had better evidence of its being well pleafing to God. She met with no reproof. On the contrary, the Angel of the Lord afterwards fpoke to her out of heaven, and delivered a meffage of comfort to her. Nor did he in the leaft change his ftyle. For he ftill claimed the work of *making* Ifhmael *a great nation*, ch. xxi. 17. 18.

If this Angel was a creature, he was far lefs concerned for the glory of his Maker than that Angel who appeared to John, Rev. xix. 10. God himfelf was lefs zealous for his glory under the Old Teftament, than he is under the New. In a word, this Angel was an ufurper, and Hagar an idolater.

It was this Angel who *called to Abraham out of heaven, faying* " *Thou haft not withheld thy fon, thine only fon from* " *me,*" ch. xxii. 11. 12. Will our author fay that Abraham meant to offer up his fon to a creature? Or, could there have been a place in *heaven* for any creature, who would

have

have dared to claim this unequalled act of worſhip, as belonging to him? Indeed, the circumſtance of the place
being mentioned, whence this Angel ſpoke, both to Hagar
and to Abraham, is evidently meant to diſtinguiſh him
from created Angels. This of *ſpeaking from heaven* is appropriated to God. He appeals to it as an evidence of his
deity. *The Lord ſaid unto Moſes, Thus ſhalt thou ſay unto
the children of Iſrael, Ye have ſeen that I have talked with
you from heaven*, Ex. xx. 22. Moſes afterwards uſes the
ſame argument, when ſumming up the proofs which Iſrael
had received of JEHOVAH being the only true God: *Out of
heaven he made thee to hear his voice*, Deut. iv. 36. This
circumſtance is ſingled out, as being a proof, both of omniſcience, and of almighty power. Of omniſcience; becauſe *ſpeaking from heaven* is the ſign that God *hears in heaven*, Neh. ix. 27. 28. Of almighty power; becauſe it
ſhews that the *voice* which he *ſends out* is *mighty*, Pſal. lxviii.
33. Thence alſo it appears that no change of place is neceſſary with him to whom this is aſcribed, in order to the
accompliſhment of his will: whereas mere angels muſt
walk to and fro, Zech. i. 10. be literally *ſent forth*, Heb. i.
14. *fly* from heaven to earth, and come to the perſon or
place which their commiſſion reſpects, Dan. ix. 21. 23.

If the ſpeaker on this occaſion was a created Angel, the
proof which ſatisfied him that Abraham truly feared God
was the ſtrangeſt that can be imagined. *Now, he ſaid, I
know that thou feareſt* GOD, *ſeeing thou haſt not withheld
thy ſon, thine only ſon from* ME. He knew that Abraham
was a ſincere worſhipper of the true God, becauſe he was
the moſt daring idolater that had ever appeared in the world.
*The Angel of the Lord called unto Abraham out of hea-
ven the ſecond time, and ſaid, By myſelf have I ſworn, ſaith*
JEHOVAH, *for becauſe thou haſt done this thing, and haſt not
withheld thy ſon, thine only ſon; that in bleſſing I will bleſs*

G 4 *thee,*

thee, &c. ver. 15. 17. Perhaps, it may be faid, that here the Angel only delivers the words of God, becaufe he throws in that expreffion, *faith Jehovah*. But, fiom the words themfelves it is moft natural to conclude, that he ftill fpeaks in his own name; as Abraham's not withholding his fon, is the reafon affigned for the promife of bleffing him. Now, we have feen that the Angel faid, *Thou haft not withheld thy fon from me*: and we muft either fuppofe that the fame *Jehovah* is ftill meant, or that Abraham offered up his fon both to God and to a creature. But the Spirit of infpiration leaves u. at no lofs with refpect to the illuftrious Perfon who fwore. We are affured that this Angel did fo, Judg. ii. 1. as we fhall fee more fully afterwards.

We are informed, Gen. xxxii. 24. that there wreftled a man with Jacob. From Hof. xii. 3. 4. we learn that this was an Angel, and yet God. *By his ftrength he had power with God, yea he had power over the Angel, and prevailed.* It is not meant that, by having-power over a created Angel, he confequentially had power with God. For thus the climax would be deftroyed, and the language ought to have been; "He had power over the Angel, yea, he had power "with God." Both expreffions denote one operation of power. For both refer to the fame *ftrength* as the means. The firft may denote the *nature* with which he had power, as referring to *God* effentially confidered: and the fecond particularly declares the *perfon* with whom he wreftled. This was the *Angel-Jehovah*, or the fecond perfon of the Godhead. That this is the real meaning, is abundantly evident. For, with refpect to this very perfon, it immediately follows, He, *viz.* Jacob, *wept and made fupplication* UNTO HIM. Here we have an Angel, who not only hath the *name* of God, but divine *worfhip* given him. It is equally clear, that it was his prerogative to perform *works* proper to God only. For *he bleffed him there*, Gen. xxxii.

29. We are also affured that this Angel was the God of Bethel, who had there appeared to Jacob. For it is further faid, Hof. xii. 4. *He found him in Bethel, and there he fpake with us* *.

That no doubt may remain who this Angel is, his dignity is yet more fully declared in the following words; *Even* JEHOVAH *God of hofts,* JEHOVAH *is his memorial,* ver. 5. His dignity is declared, in fuch a manner as to confine this name to that nature which he poffeffes. We learn the fame doctrine, indeed, from Gen. xxxi. 11. 13. *The Angel of the Lord fpake,—faying,—I am the God of Bethel, where thou anointedft the pillar, and where thou vowedft the vow* UNTO ME. When this Angel told Jacob that he was *God,* and that very perfon to whom Jacob had formerly directed the moft folemn acts of worfhip; would it ever enter into the mind of the Patriarch, that he who thus fpake to him was a fellow-creature? That he knew him to be an Angel, is undeniable; for we have his own teftimony to this purpofe : and if he confidered him as a creature, inftead of being a faint, he was a grofs idolater. For he not only gave this Angel his faith and worfhip, but afcribed the whole of his falvation, both temporal and eternal, to him as God; trufting in him, and praying to him for all bleffings, when performing his laft duty to his children : *God, before whom my fathers Abraham and Ifaac did walk, the God who fed me all my life long unto this day ; the Angel, who redeemed me from all evil, blefs the lads,* Gen. xlviii. 15. 16. If Jacob was an idolater, his fathers Abraham and Ifaac were the fame. For he declares that this Angel was the God before whom they walked. Nay, he folemnly tranfmitted this idolatry to his pofterity. Now, in this cafe, can we juftify God from the charge of enticing his fervants to idolatry;

* Gen. xxxv. 15.

idolatry; by allowing a meffenger of his, a mere creature, to addrefs them in fuch language, that they could not confider him as any other than God? Nay, on this fuppofition, how can we give any credit to the fcriptures as a divine revelation; fince thefe men are ftill exhibited as true worfhippers?

Let Socinians vainly affert what they pleafe; although Jacob knew this perfon to be an Angel, nay, wreftled with him as a man, he believed in him as the true God. For when he *faw* no one but this Angel, in the likenefs of his own nature, he faid, *I have feen God face to face, and my life is prolonged,* Gen. xxxii. 30. As this Angel affumed the human form, fo far that Jacob could wreftle with him; it is evident that the latter viewed this as a prelude of his actual incarnation for the work of our redemption. For he celebrates this Angel, with whom he had wreftled as a man, as his *Goël,* or *Kinfman-Redeemer*; and prays that, in this very character, he would blefs his pofterity, Gen. xlviii. 16.

The *plain man* Jacob underftood the doctrine of Angels far better than our learned author. He knew that there were many others, who were called Angels. But he acted towards them in a manner entirely different. During that very journey in which the Angel wreftled with him, he was met by a multitude of thefe created fpirits, Gen. xxxii. 1. *Jacob went on his way, and the angels of God met him.* But he offered no libation of tears; he fupplicated no blefing from them; nor did he once endeavour to detain them. Although he acknowledged that Angel, of whom we fpeak, as God; he viewed them only as his *army,* ready to fulfil his command. He named the place, where he wreftled, *Peniel,* from God himfelf; becaufe he had *feen* him. But all the honour conferred on the other, was that of being named from his fervants; as he had no idea that the perfons, whom he *faw* there, could be confidered in any fuperior light. *And when Jacob faw them, he faid, This is God's hoft : and he called the name of that place Mahanaim,* that is, *hofts,* or *armies.* He carefully diftinguifhed thefe *hofts* from the *God of hofts.*

It is immediately after the doctrine concerning angels, quoted above, that **Dr P.** expreffes his doubts " whether, " in fome cafes, angels—were any thing more than tempo- " rary appearances, and no permanent beings; the mere " organs of the deity, ufed for the purpofe of making him- " felf known." He feems confcious that one Angel, at leaft, claims fo much to himfelf, and has fo much afcribed to him in Scripture, that he dares not, as he regards his religious fyftem, leave it on the ground he has taken, *viz.* in afferting that " angels fometimes fpeak in the name of God ;" left the Angel referred to fhould be found to poffefs fuch at- tributes, to perform fuch works, and to receive fuch wor- fhip, as might *feem* to fhew the famenefs of his nature with that of God. He thinks it the fafeft courfe to deny a pro- per being to thofe who are called ,angels, *in fome cafes,* at leaft. Doubtlefs, this is doing the bufinefs at once. The Doctor cuts the knot that he cannot unloofe. He is as well fenced againft any proof of the pre-exiftence of the Son of God, from this quarter, as any ancient Sadducee could have been. For we know that he denies *fpirit* ; and he is very doubtful whether there be fuch a being as an *angel,* (Acts xxiii. 8).

We have formerly confidered his doctrine on this fubject. But as he introduces it on this occafion, we may obferve, that Jacob had no idea that the Angel-Redeemer was an *oc- cafional* perfon. For he afcribes a continued exiftence to him, not only during the whole of his own life, but during that of Abraham, and of Ifaac. For we connot eafily conceive that thefe patriarchs could *walk before* a non-en- tity.

tity. From his language alſo with reſpect to created angels, it ſeems moſt natural to think that he rather viewed
them as a *ſtanding army*, than as a temporary *militia*, raiſed
for the buſineſs of the moment, and to be afterwards ſo
completely *reduced*, that not a veſtige ſhould be left behind.

It ſeems pretty clear that it was the ſame uncreated
Angel who appeared to Balaam; from his declaring that
the way of that prophet was perverſe *before him*; and
commanding him to ſpeak the word that *he ſhould ſpeak* unto him, Num. xxii. 32. 35. We muſt thence conclude that
it was the ſame perſon who afterwards appeared and *ſpake*
to Balaam. On this head he declares that he had heard
the *words of God*, and *ſeen the viſion of the Almighty*, chap.
xxiv. 4. We are informed that *the Spirit of God came upon
him*, ver. 2. Therefore, on this occaſion he acted as *the
Spirit of Chriſt* (1 Pet. i. 11.) immediately communicated
by him, in the character of the *Angel-Jehovah*.

There is no reaſon to doubt that it was the ſame Angel
who appeared to Joſhua, and announced himſelf as *captain
of the hoſt of* JEHOVAH, Joſh. v. 13.—15. He ſtood over
againſt Joſhua *with his ſword drawn in his hand*. His mar-
tial character and appearance exactly correſponded to the
promiſe made to Iſrael concerning him : *If thou ſhalt indeed
obey his voice,—then I will be an enemy unto thine enemies;
and an adverſary unto thine adverſaries. For mine Angel
ſhall go before thee, and bring thee in unto the Amorites*, &c.
and I will cut them off, Exod. xxiii. 22. 23. In the ſame
manner did he appear to Balaam, when he *ſtood in the way
for an adverſary againſt him*, becauſe he was an adverſary
to Iſrael, Num. xxii. 22. 31. 32. and afterwards to David,
when he had ſinned in numbering the people, 1 Chron. xxi.
16. He indeed appeared to Joſhua as a man, as he had
done to Abraham, to Jacob, and as he afterwards did to

Zechariah. But when Joshua understood his function, he
did not hesitate to consider him as divine. For he *fell
on his face to the earth, and did worship.* So far was
the Angel from refusing this worship, that he did not deem
it sufficient. He further required the highest token of religious homage that we have any account of in Scripture.
When Joshua said, *What saith my Lord unto his servant?
the captain of the Lord's host said unto Joshua, Loose thy
shoe from off thy foot, for the place whereon thou standest is
holy,* literally *holiness,* as denoting the highest degree of lo-
cal sanctity. This is the very language which JEHOVAH
spoke to Moses, the predecessor of Joshua, Exod. iii. 5. Under the law, those places were called holy, where God was
pleased to manifest himself, 2 Chron. viii. 11. Can it be supposed that the presence of a creature could communicate
this holiness? However, no reasonable person can imagine
that he who appeared to Joshua was a creature. He is called JEHOVAH ; and he claims the sovereign disposal of human concerns. And JEHOVAH *said unto Joshua, See, I have
given into thine hand Jericho, and the king thereof, and the
mighty men of valour,* chap. vi. 2. It deserves our attention
that the designation which JEHOVAH takes to himself on
this occasion, is that which is frequently given to the Messiah. For what is rendered *Captain* literally signifies *Prince,*
Isa. ix. 6. Dan. x. 21. xii. 1.

This Angel afterwards claimed the work of bringing the
children of Israel out of Egypt, and of conducting them to
the land of promise ; declared that it was he who sware to
their fathers, and that the covenant was his ; and reproved the people for not obeying his voice. *And an Angel,*
or rather, *the Angel of the Lord came up from Gilgal to
Bochim, and said,* I MADE *you to go up out of Egypt, and
have* BROUGHT *you into the land which* I SWARE *unto your
fathers ; and* I SAID, I WILL "NEVER BREAK MY CO-
"VENANT

" VENANT *with you.*—But ye have not OBEYED MY
" VOICE," Judg. ii. 1. 2. Is this Angel " reprefented as a
" creature," or as a mere " fervant of God ?" He undoubtedly refers to the oath of JEHOVAH to Abraham.
Of this the Angel fays, *I fware.* Could the oath of a
mere creature be any fecurity to them ? Or would they be
fuch fools as to think it ? Could a created meffenger prefume to call the covenant his ? Or would a holy creature
daré to fwear *by himfelf ?* But this Angel did. And we
may reft affured that *he fware by himfelf, becaufe he could
fwear by no greater,* by no fuperior *being,* (Heb. vi. 13.)

Socinians vainly endeavour to find a parallel, even in
the conduct of fellow-creatures towards each other. An
earthly Embaffador, indeed, reprefents the perfon of his
prince, is fuppofed to be clothed with his authority, and
fpeaks and acts in his name. But who ever heard of an
Embaffador affuming the very name of his fovereign, or
being honoured with it by others. Would one in this
character be permitted to fay, *I George, I Louis, I Frederic ?*
As the idea is ridiculous, the action would juftly be accounted high treafon. Would the moft illuftrious plenipo-
tentiary, referring to a treaty made by his fovereign with a
neighbouring power, and declaring his fixed refolution to
abide by it, fay, *I will never break my covenant with you ?*
Or, if fent to undutiful fubjects, to remind them of his
mafter's kindnefs and their own ingratitude, would he
prefume to fay, " *I brought you* into this fertile country,
" which you now poffefs, but ye have not obeyed *my voice ?*"
Do not embaffadors, however great their powers, in all
memorials, and deeds of every kind, written or fpoken, ftill
ufe their own names, and diftinguifh themfelves from their
royal mafters? And can we fuppofe that the humble mi-
niflers of the King of Kings may ufe far greater freedom
with his names, attributes, works and honour, than thofe

of

of a petty fellow-worm with his? Satan is the only angel that we read of, who ever claimed the honour due to
God. Socinians, under the pretence of pious zeal for the
glory of the Father, as the One Supreme, rob the Son of
his prerogative. Yet after all, they give it not to the Father, but lavish it among all his angelic hoſt.

This Angel of the Lord alſo appeared to Gideon, Judg.
vi. 12. He is called *Jehovah*, ver. 14. He claims the honour
of ſending Gideon, ſaying, *Have not I ſent thee?* He promiſes his own preſence to him, ver. 16. *And* JEHOVAH *ſaid
unto him, ſurely, I will be with thee.* By a look he communicates ſtrength to Gideon, ver. 14. *And the Lord looked upon him, and ſaid, Go in this thy might.* Gideon addreſſes him as the object of prayer, ver. 17. He had no idea
that this Angel was a creature. For, according to an
ancient traditional notion with reſpect to the viſion of God,
he was afraid that he ſhould die. *And when Gideon perceived that he was an Angel of the Lord, or,* as it may be
read, *the Angel-*JEHOVAH, *Gideon ſaid, Alas, O my Lord*
JEHOVAH; *for becauſe I have ſeen the Angel-*JEHOVAH
face to face, ver. 22. He had aſked a ſign of the Angel;
and he brought fire out of the rock, and conſumed the ſa-
crifice. This was the very ſign to which Elijah afterwards
referred the whole determination of the controverſy between JEHOVAH and Baal, 1 Kings xviii. 24. *The God that
anſwereth by fire, let him be God.* It was by this ſign
that *Gideon perceived that he was the Angel-*JEHOVAH; in
the ſame manner, as on that occaſion, when *the fire of the
Lord fell and conſumed the burnt-ſacrifice.* For, *when all
the people ſaw it, they fell on their faces, and they ſaid,*
JEHOVAH *he is the God,* JEHOVAH *he is the God,* ver. 29.
30. In both inſtances, this was known to be a ſign of the
divine preſence. For thus, at the dedication of the tabernacle,

nacle, God had manifested his presence, power and grace to their fathers, Lev. ix. 24.

The same glorious person appeared to Manoah and his wife, Judg. xiii. 3. 9. While they knew that he was an Angel, they, like Gideon, were afraid that they should die, because they had *seen God*; as they express themselves, ver. 21. 22. When Manoah asked this Angel's name, he said, *It is Wonderful*, ver. 18. It was not the name of him that sent him, but his own, that he thus expressed. This is a striking proof that he was that *Son*, who should be afterwards *given*. For this is one of his names, the word being the same as in Isa. ix. 6. And on this occasion, the propriety of this name was manifested by his conduct, to the conviction of the astonished spectators. For when Manoah had offered a kid unto the Lord, *the Angel did wonderously; and Manoah and his wife looked on*, ver. 19. It is the same person that is said to have done *wonderously*, who declared his name to be *Wonderful*. The one term undoubtedly refers to the other. But he who thus did wonderously was JEHOVAH. Therefore, the offering was made to this Angel as JEHOVAH. For according to the original, the words run thus : He offered *it unto* JEHOVAH, *and he did wonderously*. *It was* undoubtedly of the Angel that the woman said, *If* JEHOVAH *were to kill us, he would not have received a burnt-offering, and a meat-offering at our hands : neither would he have shewed us all these things, nor would as at this time have told us such things as these,* ver. 23. It was the Angel who *received* their offering, who *shewed* and *told* them these things.

Whether Nebuchadnezzar had received any knowledge of the Jewish theology by means of Daniel, or from what might have been said by the three witnesses against his idolatry ; or spake, like the high-priest, by an immediate impulse, without knowing the proper meaning of what he said, faid, or borrowed his ideas from tradition, we cannot pretend to determine.   But the account which he gives of the deliverance of thefe faithful confeffors, is perfectly confonant to the creed of the ancient Jews.   *He faid, Lo, I fee four men loofe, walking in the midft of the fire ;——and the form of the fourth is like the Son of God,* Dan. iii. 25. Afterwards he declares his fentiments concerning this illuftrious Perfon, in thefe words ; *Bleffed be the God of Shadrach,* &c. *who hath fent his Angel and delivered his fervants,* ver. 28.

We have formerly feen that this Angel, when he appeared unto Jofhua, made himfelf known as *Prince of the hoft of the Lord.*   It would feem to be the fame illuftrious Meffenger, who is called *Michael, one,* or rather, *the firft of the chief princes,* Dan. x. 13. *Michael your Prince,* that is, the prince of the people of God, ver. 21. and *Michael the great Prince,* chap. xii. 1. The laft of thefe paffages evidently refers to the Gofpel ftate, and expreffes the whole of that diftinguifhed appearance that he fhould make for the church during this difpenfation.   Either, Michael is he who appears as the Meffiah ; or, in this prophecy, the honour which exclufively belongs to the Meffiah is appropriated to another, and *the world to come* is *put into fubjection* to a mere angel.   The language of the place feems primarily to refpect the incarnation of this *Prince.   And at that time fhall Michael ftand up, the great Prince who ftandeth for,* or *who is fet over, the children of thy people.*   As at the time of the delivery of the prophecy, this Angel is defcribed as fuftaining a peculiar relation to the church, of a permanent nature ; when the fame phrafeology is ufed with refpect to futurity, it muft denote a new and more fignal appearance in this relation.   His appearance in our nature may properly be denominated *ftanding up,* as the correlate of his being *raifed up ;* a phrafe often ufed in this

fenfe,

sense, Deut. xviii. 15. 18. Acts ii. 30. iii. 22. vii. 37. Indeed, the same term is used in different places, to denote the same illustrious event. *In that day there shall be a root of Jesse, who shall stand for an ensign of the people*, Isa. xi. 10. *And he shall stand and feed in the strength of* JEHOVAH, Mic. v. 4. Job expresses the same idea, although a different word is used in the original. *I know that my Redeemer liveth, and that he shall stand up the latter*, or *last one, upon the earth*, chap. xix. 25. The Patriarch declares his persuasion of the present existence of this glorious Person, whom he claims as his Redeemer. But he was also assured that, in a future period, he would, even to the sensible eye, more signally appear in this character, as *the latter one*, who should *redeem* him from all that destruction brought upon him by the former. For this designation may be viewed as equivalent to that used by the Apostle Paul, when he calls Christ *the last Adam*, 1 Cor. xv. 45.

The word rendered *stand up*, occurs often in this prophecy. In all the other passages, it denotes a distinguished appearance in a new situation; either that of kingdoms newly formed, chap. viii. 22. or of individuals assuming the royal character, chap. viii. 23. xi. 2, 3, 4. 7. 20. 21. or acting a new part in this character, chap viii. 25. If it be granted that Christ is meant, when we read of Michael and his angels, Rev. xii. 7. it cannot be supposed that the same name could belong to any other under the Old Testament. The *standing up* of this Prince is represented as succeeded by *a time of trouble, such as never was since there was a nation*. To what period can this so properly refer, as to that which succeeded our Lord's appearing in human nature, when the Jews were so severely punished for their unbelief? Our Lord evidently alludes to these very words, when, in describing the calamities of that people, he says ; *For then shall be great tribulation, such as was not since the*

beginning

beginning of the world to this time, no, nor ever shall be,
Mat. xxiv. 21. That *remnant according to the election of
grace*, Rom. xi. 5. which was saved during the time of
trouble, seems also to be particularly pointed out in the following words of Daniel; *At that time thy people shall be
delivered, every one that shall be found written in the book.*
What our Lord adds concerning these days of trouble corresponds with this declaration: *For the elects sake those
days shall be shortened*, Mat. xxiv. 22.

But how special soever the respect which this prophecy
has to the first age of Christianity, it cannot be confined to
this. For the resurrection is introduced, ver. 2. But as
the gospel dispensation is often prophetically represented
as one day, it is well known that the events belonging to it
are as often exhibited in the closest connexion, without any
regard to distance of time, and that the same language frequently respects very different events ; one mercy or judgment being the presage of another, and being also a partial
accomplishment of a prophecy to be more fully accomplished in future. Of this kind are the predictions of our
Saviour, recorded in Mat. xxiv. some of which must necessarily be viewed as respecting, both his coming to pu-
nish the Jewish nation, and his final coming ; as the awful
visitation of that people was undoubtedly meant as a prelude, and pledge of the certainty, of the last judgment.

However, the character of Michael not being so particularly defined as that of the divine Messenger called the
Angel of the Lord; I do not, in the general argument,
lay any stress on the view which I have ventured to give of
this prophecy.

We have a striking account of this Angel in the prophecy of Zechariah. He appears as a man in the midst
of the church, which is represented as in a low situation.
But even in this character he appears superior to other an-

gels,

gels, chap. i. 8. who are *fent to walk to and fro throughout the earth*, ver. 10. and give an account of the ftate of mat-ters to him as their Lord, ver. 11. He is defcribed as inter-ceding with JEHOVAH, and as fuccefsful in his interceffion, ver. 12. 13. as fent by the Lord of hofts, and yet as himfelf bearing this name, ver. 20. chap. ii. 8. It is obfervable that, throughout this prophecy, the title of *the Angel of the Lord* is appropriated to this one Angel who appears in the like-nefs of human nature.

It may be afterwards fhewn that this was the Angel who appeared to Mofes as the I AM, and who *went before* the children of Ifrael. But fo ftrong is the evidence ari-fing from the paffages already confidered, in fupport of the doctrine of our Saviour's divinity, in connexion with that of his operation as an Angel under the Old Teftament, that it is fcarcely conceivable that any one, who does not reject the Scriptures, fhould refufe the force of it, without wil-fully refifting the teftimony of the Spirit. If this fcriptural proof has not been fairly ftated, let Dr P. point out the fal-lacy, that none may be deceived.

Whatever ideas the Jews may be fuppofed to have generally entertained, at the time of our Saviour's appear-ance ; and whatever have been their opinions fince ; it is evident that when the prophecy of Malachi was deli-vered, they expected a divine Meffenger, one who had both the nature of God, and the office of an *Angel;* that fame Angel who had *faved them all the days of old.* Therefore faith the prophet ; *The Lord, whom ye defire, fhall fuddenly come to his temple, even the Meffenger of the covenant whom ye delight in,* chap. iii. 1. There can be no proper reafon to doubt, that the perfon referred to is the Meffiah. This is granted even by the modern Jews *.

He

* Chizzcuk Emounah, cap. 39.

He was peculiarly the object of their *defire* and *delight*. But our opponents muft either grant that, in the days of Malachi, the Jews defired, delighted in, and of courfe, expected a divine Meffiah; or charge the prophecy with carrying a falfehood in it; nay, one fo palpable, that it could not for a moment efcape any individual of that nation. This muft undoubtedly have been the cafe, had they expected no other Meffiah " than a man like them- " felves." For, although *Adonai* be the word here ufed, it is acknowledged by the Jews, as has been already feen, that it is a name expreffive of divine power *.

CHAP. IX.

Of the Son being revealed in the Old Teftament; as the Word, and Wifdom of God.

HAVING proved, as we hope, to the fatisfaction of the candid, that the ancient Jews believed in a perfonal Word; we proceed to examine the ground of their faith, or to inquire, if there be any evidence that the Meffiah was revealed, in the Scriptures of the Old Teftament, under this character. Many paffages might be mentioned, which it feems moft reafonable to underftand in this fenfe. But we fhall only attend to a few, which cannot with propriety bear any other meaning.

In the thankfgiving which David offered up, after the prophet was fent to inform him of God's acceptance of his intention to build him an houfe, inftead of the action itfelf, he ufes this language; *For thy* WORD'S *fake, and according to thine own heart, haft thou done all thefe things,*

H 3

2 Sam.

* See above, p. 86.

2 Sam. vii. 21. From the expreffion, as it appears in this place, there is no neceffity for fuppofing that David meant the perfonal Word. But the cafe is otherwife, when we turn our eye to the parallel paffage, 1 Chron. xvii. 19. *O Lord, for thy* SERVANT'S, *fake, and according to thine own heart, haft thou done all this greatnefs.* Here the Word of God appears as his fervant. Under this defignation, indeed, was he revealed to the church of Ifrael, Ifa. xlii. 1. *Behold my* SERVANT *whom I uphold.* Some underftand the expreffion, as it is recorded in the Chronicles, as if it were an *ellipfis,* inftead of, " For the fake of the word which " thou haft fpoken to thy fervant." But we apprehend that no other inftance of fuch an ellipfis can be produced. According to this view, in the one place it is the word; in the other the perfon to whom it was fpoken. Thus, there muft be an abfolute change of the fubjeft. If we take the language fimply, without fuppofing an ellipfis, and at the fame time underftand the *word* as denoting the revelation formerly made to David; there is a change of the very *caufe* of the divine operation. For in the former paffage, God is faid to do all this for *his word's* fake, that is, for *his own* fake, for the honour of his faithfulnefs. But according to the latter, it is all done for David's fake: and this language is afcribed to him at the very time that he is difclaiming all merit, and humbly faying, *What am I,— that thou haft brought me hitherto?*

It feems alfo moft natural to underftand 1 Sam. iii. 21. in the fame fenfe: *And the Lord appeared again in Shiloh: for the Lord revealed himfelf to Samuel in Shiloh, by the Word of the Lord.* It is firft declared that the Lord *appeared.* The following claufe is added as an illuftration of the manner of this appearance: *For* JEHOVAH *revealed himfelf by the Word of* JEHOVAH. Literally, he *fhewed himfelf.*

I

self. The expression is singular. As far as I can observe, it is not elsewhere used.

If we look back to Gen. xv. 1. we shall find another passage that cannot well bear a different meaning : *After these things, the Word of the Lord came unto Abram in, or by a vision, saying, Fear not, Abram : I am thy shield.* It is evident that, on this occasion, there was an appearance of the speaker. He *came*, or *was by vision*. Now it is clear from scripture, that the Father never assumed any form. This could not be a creature. For not only is he called *Lord God*, and described as the object of faith, ver. 6. but he expressly announces himself as that JEHOVAH who brought Abram *out of Ur of the Chaldees*, ver. 7. He is God the Judge, ver. 14. and he enters into covenant with Abram, ver. 18.

The Word not only appears, but is also the speaker. *The Word came—saying.* A mere word may be spoken or *said*. But we cannot easily conceive, how it should speak or *say*. This form of expression, indeed, is frequently used in the Old Testament. But no proof can be given, that it is not the personal Word who is meant in all the places where it occurs. The probability lies on the other side; especially when it would be doing violence to the context to understand the expression differently. It cannot be said that *Jehovah* is the substantive agreeing with the participle *saying ;* because the name is here *in statu regiminis*, and therefore under the government of *Dabar*, rendered *the Word*

It does not appear that, in the Hebrew scriptures, the noun *governed*, in the state of construction, is used as the nominative of the verb, or the antecedent of any personal or relative pronoun, to the exclusion of the noun *governing*.

It is this Word that says, *Fear not, Abram ; I am thy shield.* Neither here, nor in most of the passages where the same mode of expression is used, do we find that

H 4   common

common introduction of the divine meſſages, *Thus ſaith the Lord.* If *the Word* be not here underſtood perſonally, no perſon is mentioned. For we have ſeen that the name, *Jehovah,* is ſo connected, that it cannot denote a perſon diſtinctly from *the Word.* The pronoun *I* neceſſarily re- lates to the whole term, *the Word of Jehovah.* We alſo find the ſame character elſewhere aſcribed to the Word, which is here claimed by him : *The Word of Jehovah is tried; he is a buckler,* or *ſhield to all thoſe that truſt in him,* Pſal. xviii. 30. Here the pronoun *he* immediately refers to *the Word of Jehovah.*

There is evidently an interchange of language between this Word and Abram. *And Abram ſaid, Behold, to me thou haſt given no ſeed,* &c. *And behold, the Word of the Lord unto him, ſaying, This ſhall not be thine heir,* ver. 3. 4· *Came,* in our verſion, is a ſupplement. I ſhall only add, that the pronoun *he* occurs again in ver. 5. It is *the Word of Jehovah* of whom it is ſaid; *And he brought him,* viz. Abram, *forth again.*

Hag. ii. 4. 5. has been underſtood by various interpreters as denoting the *Logos.* *I am with you, ſaith the Lord of hoſts, according to the word that I covenanted with you when ye came up out of Egypt, ſo my Spirit remaineth among you: fear ye not.* Thus it is in our verſion. But the tranſlators have marked theſe words, *according to,* as a ſupplement. The introduction of it certainly obſcures the true ſenſe. If we read the paſſage ſimply, without the ſupplement, the particle אֵת, *eth,* may be viewed as demonſtrative ; *I am with you ;—The Word,* &c. But it ſeems more proper to conſider it as a prepoſition ; becauſe the ה *he demonſtrative* is joined with דבר, *dabar.* Thus it may be juſtly tranſ- lated, *with; I am with you,—with the Word,* &c. To make the ſenſe agree with the ſupplement, our tranſlators have rendered the conjunction ו *ve, ſo.* But there is no

occaſion

occasion to deviate from its ordinary meaning which is *and*.
את *eth*, as a preposition, seems to govern רוחי *ruhi*, *my
spirit*, as well as דבר *dabar*, *the Word;—with the Word,—
and with my Spirit remaining in the midst of you*. The
word עמדת, being the participle, most naturally connects
with the preposition. Thus *Jehovah of hosts* declares how
he is present among his people   It is *with* his Word and
Spirit, and by their operation. Thence the passage has
justly been urged as a proof of a Trinity of persons *.

The Word is literally said to have been *cut off*. This is
the original and proper meaning of the expression rendered
covenanted. For it is used only in a secondary sense, to signify the making of a covenant. It is also to be observed,
that generally when it has the latter signification, it is joined
with the word *Berith* †. Now, the Word was typically *cut
off* in their coming out of Egpyt, in the ordinance of the
Passover, which was celebrated on the very night of their
departure. He was *cut off* in all the sacrifices instituted in
the wilderness. But although the ordinary sense were preferred, it would be no objection to our view of the passage.
Junius and Tremellius read; *The Word in whom I covenanted*. For *the law was ordained in the hand of a Mediator*. But though the preposition, *in*, were not supposed to
be included, there could be no impropriety in understanding the language of Christ: for he is *given for a covenant
of the people*, Isa. xlii. 6. xlix. 8. because it is only in him
that God enters into any foederal transaction with sinful creatures. Therefore, he is also called *the Messenger*, or *Angel
of the covenant*, Mal. iii. 1.

Besides

---

* Glassii Phil. Sacr. lib. iii. t. 6. p. 1068.

† I can find one passage only where it is used by itself to denote a foederal transaction, 2 Chron. vii. 18.

Befides the natural and proper meaning of the words, there are feveral things which confirm this view. It ftrictly agrees with the account elfewhere given of the privilege of the ancient Church, Ifa. lxiii. 9. 10. *The Angel of his prefence faved them.---But they rebelled and vexed his Holy Spirit.* Befides, the Meffiah is the great fubject of this meffage of comfort. For it immediately follows; *Yet once, it is a little while,---and I will fhake all nations, aud the defire of all nations fhall come,* Hag. ii. 6. 7. The connexion of thefe words with the preceding affords an unanfwerable proof, that the perfonal Word is meant. For the continued prefence of this *covenanted Word,* is here affigned as one great reafon why they were *not* to *fear.* Now, we are affured from undoubted authority, that the ceremonial law, as long as it continued, was *a yoke of bondage.* But this is not all. The very abolition of that word which was covenanted, or of the covenant confidered as legal, is here promifed as ground of confidence and comfort. For this is the unqueftionable meaning of thefe words, *I will fhake the heavens:* and thus we find them applied, Heb. xii. 26. 27. as denoting the vifible frame of the Church. It is alfo declared, for the further confolation of believers, that this fhould take place in *a little while.* Now, it would be abfurd to fuppofe, that God fhould declare the continuance of a covenant to be matter of comfort, at the very time that, with the fame defign, he promifes its fpeedy abolition.

The Doctor evidently underftands Solomon as merely allegorizing, when he fpeaks of *Wifdom,* Prov. viii *. While Socinians endeavour to evade the force of any argument derived from the ufe of that defignation, *the Word of the Lord,* by afferting that it means *God himfelf;* they find it neceffary to change their ground with refpect to *Wifdom,* which

* Hift. Corrupt. vol. i. p. 24. 30.

which they underſtand as ſignifying a particular attribute of
Deity. But although they ſpeak as if they were the only
people poſſeſſed of reaſon, they give ſuch interpretations of
ſcripture as leave it loaded with abſurdity. For if the wiſe
man celebrates a mere attribute, he expreſſes himſelf in a
manner irreconcileable to the common rules of language.
For this Wiſdom ſays; *Counſel is mine, and found wiſdom,*
ver. 14. It muſt be granted, either that a perſon is meant,
or that an attribute may be the ſubject of an attribute;
nay, that a thing may be predicated of itſelf. Does not
the reader learn a great deal, by being informed that " wiſ-
" dom belongs to wiſdom?" Nor is it much better to ſay,
in this ſenſe, *I have ſtrength.* Is power an attribute of the
attribute of wiſdom? That expreſſion, *I was ſet up from*
everlaſting, ver. 23. can with no propriety apply to a mere
perfection. When underſtood of perſonal Wiſdom, it has a
beautiful and comfortable meaning; as denoting his eternal
ordination to the office of Mediator. In what ſenſe can the
attribut eof wiſdom be ſaid to be *brought forth?* ver. 25.
The language cannot be underſtood of any actual or opera-
tive diſplay of this perfection. It expreſsly excludes ſuch
an idea. For this event is ſaid to have been previous to
creation, that is, before any external manifeſtation of the
divine perfections. It will not be pretended, that this perfection was generated in the divine eſſence. And we cannot think of any view, beſides that ordinarily taken, which
would not do violence, either to the connexion, or to common ſenſe.

This Wiſdom is not only *brought forth,* but *brought up,*
ver. 30. How can we ſuppoſe an attribute to be compared
to a *foſter child?* Place is aſſigned to it; *Then was I by*
him: and affection,—*rejoicing, delights.* An inſpired Evangeliſt, ſpeaking of the ſame Wiſdom, under another character, our opponents themſelves being judges, borrows the
comparifon

comparifon here ufed, expreffing it more fimply ; *The only begotten, who is in the bofom of the Father*, John i. 18 *. Here, indeed, we have the ideas conveyed by both thefe terms, *brought forth*, and *brought up*, exhibited at once. That the language is applicable to a perfon only, may be after-wards proved.

The fame perfon is evidently introduced, chap. i. 20.—32. Wifdom is made to fay, *I will pour out my Spirit unto you*, ver. 23. That a fpirit may have wifdom, can be eafily conceived. But it is to fuppofe a ftrange inverfion, to fay that the attribute of wifdom may give his fpirit, or dif-penfe his influences to others.

Our author endeavours to get rid of this paffage, by com-paring it with others in which the figure of perfonification is employed. " One method of allegorizing," he fays, " which took its rife in the Eaft, was the perfonification of " things without life, of which we have many beautiful " examples in the books of fcripture, as of *wifdom* by So-" lomon, of *the dead* by Ezekiel, and of *fin* and *death* by " the apoftle Paul †."

That this figure is often ufed in fcripture is undeniable. But it will be obferved, that generally the perfonification is not continued long ; and that the fpeaker or writer returns to the proper ftyle. There is not an example of the perfoni-fication of one thing being fo long continued, and including fo many circumftances, any where elfe in fcripture. Be-fides, whatever circumftances are introduced, in the ufe of this figure, juftly apply, at leaft in a metaphorical fenfe, to their fubject. But it has been feen, that things are here afcribed to Wifdom, which, if it be underftood as a per-fection,

---

* Vid. Lampe in loc. Guffetii Comment. in Ling. Ebraic. in voc. אמון·

† Hift. Cor. vol. i. p. 24.

fection, cannot admit of any meaning. It ought alfo to be obferved, that however frequently this figure is ufed, there is no difficulty in knowing that the language muft be under-ftood figuratively. It is fo introduced, as fcarcely to leave the weakeft reader in doubt. But the paffage before us, as Socinians explain it, is entirely different, in this refpect, from every other of the fame kind. For it is undeniable, that almoft all readers and interpreters, ancient or modern, even the moft learned, have viewed this as the defcription of a perfon. Befides, when this figure is introduced in the language of infpiration, it always appears with the greateft propriety and beauty. But the perfonification of the attribute of wifdom, confidering the circumftances already mentioned, would be forced and unnatural.

There is a great difference between this paffage and that referred to in Ezekiel, chap. xxxvii. There we are informed that what is narrated, took place only in vifion. For the whole is explained of the houfe of Ifrael. All that was tranfacted, was an emblem of a fpiritual work. The fervants of the Lord, at his command, prophefy or preach to thofe who are *dead in fins.* The *flefh* and *finews* of a pro-feffion often appear, where there is no fpiritual life. This can only proceed from the *Breath* or *Spirit* of Jehovah, and muft be prayed for by his fervants. Here facts exactly correfpond with emblems.

Sin is perfonified, Rom. vii. and faid to *deceive,* to *work,* to *flay* ; becaufe it is the immediate agent in producing all thefe effects, as diffufing diforder and defilement through the foul. It *deceives.* For all the power of deception pro-ceeds from it. It *works all manner of concupifcence ;* as the operations of various lufts are merely the workings of this general principle. It *flays.* This word is indeed ufed figuratively, with refpect to the mind. But ftill it expreffes what is true in a fpiritual fenfe. Thus it really *flew* Saul,

by

by driving him nearly to deſpair, by *working death* in his ſoul. *Death* is alſo perſonified. But nothing is aſſerted of it, which muſt neceſſarily be underſtood of a real perſon ; as hath been proved with reſpect to Wiſdom.

That apocryphal book, the Wiſdom of Solomon, affords many proofs that the ancient Jews conſidered Wiſdom as a perſon. I ſhall refer to one only. " Wiſdom is the worker " of all things, in whom is an underſtanding ſpirit, holy, " only-begotten, manifold, ſubtle, lively,—quick,—who " cannot be letted,----the breath of the power of God," chap. vii. 22. Theſe things cannot apply to the attribute of wiſdom. For it is here repreſented as the immediate agent in creation, and as what *cannot be letted,* which ex- preſſions more properly belong to power. It is ſaid to *have a ſpirit.* This cannot, with any propriety, be aſſerted of an accident. It is *only-begotten.* To aſſert this of an attri- bute, would be a ridiculous ſtretch of perſonification. When ſaid to be *lively, quick,* &c. it exactly correſponds with the account given, Heb. iv. 12. 13. of that Word *with whom we have to do.* It is called " the breath of the power of " God." This could never be meant by any reaſonable perſon, however much addicted to figurative writing, as a deſcription of the perfection of wiſdom. For the reverſe only could be aſſerted. Power, as an attribute, might, by a ſtrong figure, be denominated " the breath of the *wiſdom* of God ;" as being its expreſſion, and manifeſtation. But the propoſition is abſurd, if inverted ; unleſs it be meant of a perſon, whoſe generation might be expreſſed in this manner.

Wiſdom is evidently introduced, in the New Teſtament, as a perſon. Not to inſiſt on that paſſage, *Wiſdom is juſti- fied of her children,* Mat. xi. 19. there are others about which there cannot reaſonably be any diſpute. Our Sa- viour uſes this language ; *Therefore alſo ſaid the Wiſdom of* *God,*

God, I will fend them prophets and apoftles, Luke xi. 49.
The pronoun *I* evidently refers to *the Wifdom of God* as the
fpeaker.   This Wifdom not only fpeaks, but fends.   Here
there is not a fhadow of reafon for fuppofing a figurative
perfonification.   For Jefus is not delivering a parable or
prophecy.   The whole language of the context is ftrictly
literal.   But the Spirit of God elfewhere gives us a key
for underftanding this language, as ufed in both Teftaments;
by informing us that *the Wifdom of God* is *Chrift,* 1 Cor.
i. 24.

BOOK

A

VINDICATION

OF THE

DOCTRINE of SCRIPTURE, &c.

BOOK II.

THE DOCTRINE OF THE NEW TESTAMENT CONCERNING JESUS CHRIST.

CHAP. I.

The Logos proved to be a Person, from the Introduction to the Gospel of John.

AMONG the many passages in the New Testament which represent the Word as a person, the Introduction to John's Gospel appears with distinguished lustre. Therefore, in every age, the adversaries of the Deity of Christ have laboured to involve it in darkness. The sum of what is maintained by Dr P. seems to consist in these assertions:

I. That John did not mean, by the Logos, a person, but an attribute.

II. That it is almost certain that his design, in writing his Gospel, was to correct those who believed that the Logos was a person.

      III. That

III. That, in the introduction to his Gospel, he alludes to the very same system as in his first Epistle, in which he blames those only who denied the reality of Christ's human nature.

I. Dr. P. asserts, that John did not mean, by the Logos, a person, but an attribute. " The Christian philosophers," he says, " having once got the idea that the Logos might " be interpreted of Christ, proceeded to explain what John " says of the Logos in the introduction of his Gospel, to " mean the same person, in direct opposition to what he " really meant, which was, that the Logos by which all " things were made was not a being distinct from God, " but God himself, being his attribute, his wisdom and " power, dwelling in Christ, speaking and acting by " him *."

This, like the most of our author's positions, rests solely on his own assertion. But although the proof properly belongs to him, I shall endeavour to bring positive proof to the contrary. It might be urged, as an argument of no inconsiderable weight against this assertion, that those who make it cannot produce another instance, from the New Testament, of the word *Logos* being used to signify the *wisdom* or *power* of God as an attribute : whereas it hath been proved, that the correspondent term, in the Hebrew, is so used in the Old, as necessarily to denote a person : and I hope to make it appear that *Logos*, in some other passages, must be understood in the same sense. But I am willing to rest the whole controversy with respect to the meaning of the term as here used, on the evidence arising from the passage itself. For if we attentively consider the Introduction to this Gospel, which includes the first eighteen verses, we shall find almost as many arguments against the Socinian explanation, as there are words.

It

* Hist. Corrupt. vol. i. p. 31.   Earl. Opin. vol. i. p. 68. 181.

It is Dr P.'s profeſſed intention to " labour in the diſ-
" covery and communication of truth *." All who agree
with him, pretend to reduce the doᶜtrines of revelation to
the level of human underſtanding. Thoſe who profeſs to
inſtruᶜt mankind, eſpecially when it is their avowed deſign
to overthrow eſtabliſhed opinions, ought fairly to attend to
every objeᶜtion, and endeavour to ſatisfy every reaſonable
inquirer. I ſhall, therefore, at times take the liberty of
propoſing a queſtion, or of ſtating a difficulty, ariſing from
their interpretations of this paſſage. · For if the friends of
the Unitarian ſyſtem ſincerely wiſh to make converts, they
muſt not, as hath generally been their praᶜtice hitherto,
deal in unſupported aſſertions, or ſtart aſide from the point
of an argument, by propoſing another of their own ; but
fairly meet every objeᶜtion, give it due weight, and plainly
demonſtrate its futility.

To give a diſtinᶜt view of the Evangeliſt's deſign, it may
be the moſt proper plan to conſider the verſes in their order.

Ver. 1. 2. The verb ⲱ, rendered *was*, undoubtedly applies with far more propriety to a perſon than to an ·attri-
bute ; as denoting the eternal and neceſſary exiſtence of the
Word. In this ſenſe it is uſed by the ſame inſpired writer
with refpeᶜt to God the Father, Rev. 1. 4. ὁ ων, *who was*.
Our Lord ſpeaks of himſelf in the ſame language, ver. 8.
I am he ὁ ων, *who was.*

If the Evangeliſt meant to deſcribe an attribute, was it
not prepoſterous and unneceſſary to ſay that it *was in the
beginning*, that it *was with God?* If this be the ſenſe, is
he not chargeable with an unmeaning tautology, when he
adds ; *The ſame was in the beginning with God?* For who
could ſuppoſe that the Divine Being exiſted before his own
wiſdom and power, that the eſſence of God preceded his

I 2   perfections?

---

* Dedication to Hiſt. Cor. p. vij.

perfections ? As it is ordinary with writers to exert all their powers in framing a ftriking introduction ; confidering John merely as a writer, is this paffage in any refpect confonant to the elevation of thought, and propriety of expreffion, evident in every other part of his writings ? Viewing him as infpired, is fuch an unneceffary affertion, efpecially as repeated with the greateft folemnity, worthy of the Spirit of infpiration ?

Indeed, it feems undeniable that, if the Evangelift meant by this term to denote an attribute, there was no occafion whatfoever for the repetition in ver. 2 ; efpecially as the thing afferted contains no proof that this was his meaning. For if it was once underftood that this term fignified merely a divine perfection, inftead of its being neceffary repeatedly to affure the reader, that the attribute of *wifdom* or *power* was with God in the beginning, and not afterwards ac- quired or generated,—a fingle declaration of this would ap- pear fuperfluous. If, then, this affertion is of no avail to prove that an attribute is meant ; if, even fuppofing that it were, fuch a repetition would be unneceffary ; we muft endeavour to difcover fome fufficient reafon for this repeti- tion, which feems to have been introduced by the writer as peculiarly emphatic. The only reafon that can naturally be fuppofed, is, that the Evangelift having afferted that the Word was God, in order to exprefs his proper and fupreme Deity, wifhed to guard every one againft that very error into which our author hath fallen, of concluding, from this expreffion, that there was only one perfon in the divine effence. Therefore he adds ; *The fame was in the begin- ning with God.* It is afcribing a very retrograde motion to the infpired *amanuenfis,* to fay, that after he had fpoken of the Word as an attribute, and pofitively afferted that it was *God himfelf,* he fhould inftantly fly off from this final idea, and in the very next words exhibits his fubject in a loofer form,

as

as only *with* God. But if we view this repetition as defigned to guard the reader againſt ſuppoſing that ſuch an
unity is meant as excludes a plurality of co-equal perſons,
we perceive its force and propriety in a very ſtriking light.
We have the ſubſtance of the three foregoing propoſitions
contained in one; and not merely ſo, but each of theſe
truths exhibited in its proper connexion.

The *demonſtrative* ουτος, rendered *the ſame*, has peculiar
emphaſis. For it does not merely denote the perſon formerly mentioned, but this perſon according to the very deſcription given of him, as *God.*

Thus Baſil explains the paſſage; " That ſame Word,
" which was God, was alſo in the beginning with God *."
Here that term is uſed, which in different places expreſſes
the language of the Father, when pointing out Jeſus Chriſt
as the objeƈt of his love, and of man's faith; particularly,
as diſtinguiſhing him from Moſes and Elias, to whom, it
would ſeem, the three diſciples were inclined to pay more
reſpeƈt than was lawful. Ουτος *This is my beloved Son ;—
hear ye him*, Mat. xvii. 5. alſo iii. 17. The Baptiſt's particular deſignation of Jeſus, when he pointed him out to
others, as it were with the finger, is expreſſed in the ſame
manner; as we learn from ver. 15. 30. 33. 34. of this chapter.

The prepoſition προς, tranſlated *with*, ſeems to be moſt naturally underſtood in the ſenſe of παρα *apud.* Socinians cannot
well objeƈt to this view as it is that of their patron the learned Grotius. This mode of expreſſion is uſed in other parts of
ſcripture, with reſpeƈt to the Son of God; as in Prov. viii.
30. *Then was I by him, as one brought up* WITH *him.* So
Chriſt himſelf prays; *Now, O Father, glorify thou me
with thine own ſelf, with the glory which I had* παρα σεαυτω,

I 3

with

---

* Illud ipſum Verbum, quod Deus erat, in principio quoque erat apud
Deum. Ap. Lampe in loc.

with thee before the world was, chap. xvii. 5. Thus, the propofition προς marks a perfonal diftinction. In the New Teftament, it frequently denotes the prefence of one perfon with
others. In this fenfe our Lord fays; *O faithlefs generation,
how long fhall I be* (προς υμας) *with you?* Mark ix. 19. And
Paul; *Not only when I am prefent* (προς υμας) *with you,* &c.
Gal. iv. 18 [*]. But this term does not feem to be any where
ufed, in the fenfe here impofed on it by Socinians, to exprefs
the refidence of a quality in a fubject, as effential to the fubject in which it refides. Ουτος, *the fame,* being thus connected
with πρ·ς, fhews that the fubject, according to the account
given of him as God, was *with God,* that is, the Father.
The repetition of thefe words, *in the beginning,* as connected with the other affertions, denotes that as God, he was
eternally with God : it being generally granted that *in the
beginning* is an Hebrew idiom for expreffing eternity [†]. For
whatever was in the beginning, before the creation of all
things, muft have eternally exifted. Thence, the Evangelift
declares that the Word *was in the beginning with God,* to
fhew that his exiftence was coeval with that of the Father.

We generally judge of the meaning of a writer in one paffage, from the fenfe in which he ufes the fame language in another, concerning which there is no difpute ; unlefs it appear
that we muft neceffarily underftand the fame terms differently. But it is granted, even by Dr P. [‡], that John, in the introduction to his firft Epiftle, by *the Word of Life* means our Lord
Jefus Chrift. Now in what manner does he exprefs himfelf
there? *What was from the beginning,----concerning the Word
of Life,----declare we unto you* [§]. How analogous this is to the
language

---

[*] Vide Lampe in Joh. i. 2.

[†] Sicut mos eft Hebræis Aeternitatem populariter defcribere. Grot.

[‡] Vol. i. p. 190.

[§] Ο ην απ' αρχης,—περι τυ λογυ της ζωης,—επαγγελομεν υμιν.

language used by the same writer in the introduction to his Gospel, must appear to every reader, whether he wish to perceive it or not. *In the beginning was the Word---In him was Life* *. Αρχη has unquestionably the same meaning in both places. That designation, *the Word of Life,* conveys the very idea expressed in the passage before us, *In him was Life.*

It was pretended by ancient Socinians, that this name was given to Jesus, because he announced the Word of Life †. Dr P. does not refine so, much. He says of the inspired writer; " What could he mean by speaking of " Jesus under the figure of life,—but that he was really *a* " *man* ‡." But then he must also have meant that Christ was *eternally a man.* For he who is called *the Word of Life,* is in ver. 2. said to be *that eternal Life which was with the Father.* This evidently expresses the peculiar reason of the designation, his possessing life essentially and being the fountain of it to all creatures. Thence it is said, chap. v. 11. *This life is in his Son.*

We may, also observe the exact correspondence between these words—*that eternal Life which was with the Father,* and those in the Gospel; *The same was in the beginning with God* ||. For ην εν αρχη and αιωνιον are certainly synonymous expressions.

If it be still urged that, in the introduction to the Gospel, a mere attribute is meant, let the following queries be answered : " To what purpose would it be said that that *was* " *with God,* and *in the beginning with God,* which was God " himself? Who could be ignorant, that the Creator was

I 4

" in

---

* Εν αρχη ην ὁ λογος.—Εν αυτω ζων ην.

† Schlichting in loc.   ‡ Vol. i. ibid.

|| Ητις ην προς τον πατερα, 1 Epist.—Ουτος ην εν αρχη προς τον Θεον, Evang.

" in the beginning of the creation? Who would fay that " the one God was with the one God? Who would oppofe " this one God to the one God, as different?" I have a right to put thefe queftions to the Socinians of this age, as they are the very words of one of their Patriarchs *. Indeed, it is a circumftance extremely unfavourable to the Socinian fyftem, that its fupporters have found it abfolutely neceffary fo often to change their ground, in explaining this remarkable paffage; whereas the friends of the Deity of Chrift have uniformly applied it to him as a divine Perfon. The ancient enemies of the Word rejected the whole Gofpel of John, becaufe it fo directly oppofed their fyftem. Some, in later times, have denied the authenticity of the Introduction; becaufe it fupplied their opponents with unanfwerable arguments. The more modern Socinians, while they have found it beyond their power to difprove its authenticity, have done their utmoft to render it of as little ufe as poffible, by explaining it in oppofition to common fenfe, and to all the ordinary rules of conftruction. Two centuries ago, Socinians applied it to Chrift perfonally confidered: but endeavoured to explain it away, by pretending that the *new* creation was meant. Thofe of this age underftand it of the *old*; but deny that the Word is to be viewed as a Perfon.

Schlichting, indeed, is more fair than many of his fucceffors. For, though not lefs acute than any of them, he fo keenly feels the force of truth, as not only to grant that a Perfon is meant, and that this is Jefus; but he argues with great propriety againft underftanding the paffage of an attribute. " This Word," he fays, " is a Perfon properly fo called, and " that Jefus.—Undoubtedly, all thefe things which John " mentions, *In the beginning*, &c. and what follows, *cannot* " be

---

* Schlichting in loc.

" be afferted but of a Perfon; thence, not of the fpeech of
" God properly fo called, nor of the faculty of fpeaking,
" nor of reafon, nor of power, nor of any other attribute *."

All things were made by him, ver. 3. The fubject of this
affertion is unqueftionably the immediate agent in creation.
But Socinians underftand this language of the attribute of
wifdom. However, if any particular attribute be perfonified, as the more immediate agent in creation, this honour
undoubtedly belongs to *power.* If *wifdom* be figuratively
viewed as an agent, it is more remote than *power*; which,
becaufe of its immediate agency, is often called God's *hand*
and *arm.* A confcioufnefs that their explanation was juftly
liable to this objection, feems to have induced our author,
and fome of his brethren, to include both thefe attributes
in the definition of the *Logos.* Therefore he fays; " The
" Logos was—God himfelf, being his attribute, his wifdom
" and power †." But this definition is evidently a contradiction
in terms. For wifdom and power are not *an attribute.* They
are two diftinct attributes. The very perfons, who are fuch
enemies to a plurality, can foift it in, when occafion ferves,
under the idea of perfect unity. By what figure of fpeech,
or rule of conftruction, from what new difcovery of the
power of numbers, are we to learn that *one* is *two?* Here
is *unity* including *plurality*, in the fame refpect. Yet thefe
are the men who make fo violent an outcry, if a plurality
is faid to fubfift in unity, not in the fame, but in a different
refpect.

When the Doctor publifhed his Hiftory of Corruptions,
he certainly thought that he had rightly apprehended the
meaning of the facred writer. For he informed the public,
that others had " explained what John fays----in direct op-
" pofition

---

† In Joan. chap. i. p. 3.   † Hift. of Cor. vol. i. p. 31.

" pofition to what he *really meant* *." , But the learned gentleman, it would feem, has fince that time fome how or
other got more into the fecrets of the Evangelift.   For he
now affures us, that " the only Logos that he acknowledged,
" was the *power of God*, an attribute of the Father †."
Socinian writers certainly feel greatly at a lofs in explaining this paffage.   They wifh, if poffible, to retain the idea
of *wifdom*; confcious as they are that the ordinary fenfe of
the term *Logos* has moft affinity to this.   But they alfo
know that perfonification more properly belongs to *power*,
as the immediate agent in creation.   They cannot include
both, without lofing the unity of their *Logos*: and when,
as in this inftance, the term is reftricted to the attribute of
power, its natural fenfe is loft, and a new one impofed, for
which they have not the countenance of a fingle paffage of
fcripture.

Had the Evangelift *really meant*, as our author afferts, to
oppofe the Gnoftics only ; would it not have been far more
proper to have declared that all things' were made by *God
himfelf?* For they held that the world was made by one of
their æons.

By the way, we may obferve, in oppofition to thofe who
make the Word to be a created God, and the fecondary
caufe of all other creatures, that δι 'αυτ8, *by him*, cannot be
underftood inftrumentally.   For where no matter pre-exifted,
there could be no inftrument.   If *all things* were made by
him, matter itfelf was a part of his work ; which neceffarily fuppofes him to be a primary agent.   If *without him nothing was made that was made*, it certainly follows that he was
not himfelf made.   For had he been one of the things made,
he muft have received his being without any agency on

his

---

his own part. Thence, it could not have been truly affirmed, that *without him* was *nothing* made.

In him was life, ver. 4. Some apprehend that this clause
is to be restricted by the following, *and this life was the*
light of man; as if the Evangelist meant only that spiritual life which Christ communicates to men *. But it
seems more naural to suppose that, having asserted in the
preceding words, that all things were made by the Logos,
he first shews whence this work belonged to him, by declaring that all life was essentially in him, and then parti-
cularizes one kind of life more immediately in view, as of
consequence proceeding from him. The Word made all
things, because all life was in him as its natural fountain;
and therefore, that which regards the soul of man must in
every age have been derived from him.

But the Socinian view of this verse is attended with un-
surmountable difficulties. We may, indeed, form the idea
of an attribute being personified. But we cannot suppose
that an attribute should not only be viewed as a subject, but
have something ascribed to it in the abstract; especially
when the abstract is not used figuratively, b t properly, as
denoting the real existence of the predicate in its subject.
An attribute of deity might be called a *Word*, or even a
living Word. But scripture affords no example of power
or principle being said to exist, in the abstract, in a mere attribute. Now, whatever this *Word* be, *life* is said to have
been *in* it.

The communication of this life, mentioned in the words
immediately following, shews that life was in the *Logos*, as
its proper subject, source and repository. This further illustrates the gross impropriety of the language, if applied to
an attribute. For it is ascribed as the efficient cause of all
that

* Lampe in loc.

that light of knowledge conferred on man. Here, there would be an accident, not merely perfonified, and exhibited as the fubject of a principle properly refiding in it; but as the proper efficient caufe of another principle refiding in fubjects entirely different. A ftrange jumble of diffonant figures, indeed! as inadequate to fuggeft one juft idea to the mind, as the fortuitous concourfe of atoms, to produce a regular, animated and intelligent fubject.

It ought alfo to be obferved that, even fuppofing the figurative ftyle to have been hitherto ufed, it is dropped here. For had it been carried on, the language would have been, " He was life, and this life," &c. Thefe words, however, *In him was life*, are not figurative, but ftrictly proper; as expreffing the refidence of a power in its own fubject. As the term *light*, here ufed properly, is afterwards introduced as a perfonal defignation, it is a ftrong prefumption that a real perfon is meant. For in fcripture, when any thing is perfonified which is not really a perfon, the figurative ftyle is generally firft ufed, and then the fimple. But here this plan is reverfed.

Ver. 5.----11. That the fame fubject, whether perfon or attribute, is here defigned *the light, that light,* and *the true light,* which is in the introduction called *the word*, will appear from a very flight attention to the context. For there is no interruption in the narrative. When it is faid that all things were *made* by *the Word*, it is added, as the reafon of this declaration, and as the evidence of that power afcribed; *In him was life.* Then light is mentioned, as the immediate effect of this principle of life, and as a further evidence of his being the fource of life, becaufe of his communicating the light of falvation. The mention of Chrift's harbinger, fo far from being an interruption, is a collateral proof of the continuance of the fame fubject. There is, indeed, a change of the defignation. What is firft called
the

the *word*, is afterwards denominated *light*. But this was highly proper, as the ancient Jews not only called their Redeemer the *Word*, but expected him as the *Light*. The prophets gave him this appellation, Ifa. ix. 1. Chrift fpoke of himfelf under the fame character; *I am the light of the world*, chap. viii. 12. xii. 35. &c.

The term εκεινος fhews that there is no change of the fubject. For, according to its ufe, it has evidently a retrofpect to all that has been previoufly faid. The ufe of αυτον alfo, ver. 10. rendered *him*, inftead of αυτο, *it*, which the connection with φως ftrictly required, fhews that the Evangelift has ftill had but one fubject in view. Befides, the fame work is afcribed to the Light, as to the Word; *The world was made by him.*

· There is as little reafon to doubt that our Lord Jefus Chrift is perfonally defigned *the Light*. This appears from the manner in which the light is fpoken of; *that Light*. He is alfo called *that true Light*, becaufe he fully poffeffes all that the expreffion implies; and as contrafted with all the inferior lights which his church hath enjoyed, and immediately with the Baptift. Great was the honour conferred upon John, in being fent to *bear witnefs of that Light*. But this was the moft that could be faid of him: whereas it is given as the great evidence of Jefus being *that true Light*, that he communicates light to others. Even when he acknowledged John to be a *burning and a fhining light*, he ufed a word fignifying a borrowed light, λυχνος*. John is defcribed as *fent from God ;* but he was *fent* as a mere man. He was himfelf *lighted* by him who *lighteth every man*. He was but a *lamp* lighted by a communication from the *true Light*. He *bore witnefs of that light*, only by derivation from him who derives from no other. And he could only *bear witnefs*. He

---

* Chap. v. 35.

He could not favingly illuminate any of his hearers. But Jefus *lighteth every man who cometh into the world*, whether as *fent*, like John, in an extraordinary character, or as coming in the ordinary way; whether the light communicated be that of reafon, or of grace. For he is that *God who commanded the light to fhine out of darknefs*.

The language of the Evangelift concerning John, *He was not that Light*, affords a very ftrong proof that a perfon is meant. For if he had ftill fpoken of an attribute, and been fatisfied that he had ufed terms fully expreffive of his meaning, what good reafon can be given for here informing his reader that he had not the Baptift in his eye? If he had not ftill meant to defcribe a perfon, was not this a very unneceffary parenthefis?

Befides, proper perfonal fubfiftence is afcribed to this *light; He was in the world.* A change of fituation is alfo afferted. This is at any rate afcribed to God improperly, and merely fignifies a difference of manifeftation. But it cannot be afcribed to an attribute, either properly or figuratively.

Property is alfo afcribed to this light; He came to *his own.* But this always fuppofes a perfon, and not an accident.

In a word, this light is faid to have been rejected. *His own received him not.* It cannot be doubted, that this denotes the rejection of Chrift by his own people the Jews. We muft therefore fuppofe, either that the fame perfon is here meant, who is at firft called *the Word*, and of confequence that Chrift *was in the beginning with God;* or, that a new perfon is introduced, without the leaft intimation of any change of the fubject. The confiftency of this with the Evangelift's defign, thofe who affert it may fhew.

It cannot, with any femblance of reafon, be pretended, that the expreffion under confideration fignifies that this

Word,

Word, or *Light,* was rejected, when it afterwards dwelt in the man Jesus. For not only does the structure of the passage shew that it was not an attribute, but a person, that they did not receive; but the same thing is evident from the general tenor of these passages of scripture which declare this rejection; Isa. liii. 3. *He is despised and rejected of men;* ----*he was despised and we esteemed him not.* Therefore he is addressed by the Father as that person *whom man despiseth, and whom the nation abhorreth,* chap. xlix. 7.

Thus, it appears that *the Light* is a Person. Therefore, Jesus being called *the Light, that Light, that true Light;* as it is this very Light of whom it is said, *In him was life;* as he, of whom this is said, is *the Word;* is it not undeniable that Jesus Christ is himself the Word? As there was creating *Life* in the Word, ver. 3. as there was the same in the Light by whom *the world was made,* ver. 10.; and as both these terms denote the same subject, is not Jesus Christ that personal Word by whom the world was made?

Ver. 12. *To as many as received him,* &c. If it be still urged that an attribute is meant in the beginning of the chapter, the same must unquestionably be meant here. For no new subject is introduced, if a new one be introduced at all, till Jesus Christ is expressly mentioned, ver. 17. or at any rate, till the Word is exhibited in a new relation, ver. 14. as *made flesh.* But how can an attribute not only be *received,* but confer power? How can one believe on the name of an attribute? An attribute is itself a name. Thence, the *name* of God often denotes his attributes. But if the Logos be merely an attribute, *believing on the Name* of the Word, is believing on the name of a name. Therefore, the expression is an absolute solecism. It ought to have been, " who believe on *the* Name," or, at any rate, " on the " name of God," that is, on *the Word,* that divine attribute formerly mentioned.

It

It would be vain to reply, that it is the name of Jesus afterwards mentioned. Not to say, that this is contradictory to all the rules of language ; if Christ be personally a mere man, as Socinians assert, it would be believing on a man only. For such an inhabitation of the Word as they pretend, could never make the name of Christ the object of faith ; because he is still supposed to be a creature. But they ought seriously to consider, that believing in *the Word, who was in the beginning with God,* is one thing necessarily implied in the faith here described. For the Evangelist plainly refers to that *name* by which he had already denoted his glorious subject, and by which he elsewhere describes him : *And his Name is called, the Word of God,* Rev. xix. 13. Believers in his Name are, therefore, in ver. 18. said to be *born,* or *begotten not of the will of man, but of God ;* because it is this Word, on whose Name they believe, who *gives them power to become the sons of God.*

Ver. 14. *The Word was made flesh and dwelt among us.* Socinians say that an attribute *was* made flesh, because *it* dwelt in the man Jesus. But this exposition is liable to many weighty objections.

In the plain language of narrative, like that of the whole Gospel history, as far as it relates to facts, can an attribute, because it acted by a man be with propriety said to be therefore *made flesh ?* This is the harshest metaphor ever used, if it does not denote a personal union.

The operation of an attribute by a Person, if this be all that is meant, is nothing new. *The Word* had been often *made flesh* before. This must have been the case, when the prophets were under the direction of the Spirit, which Socinians make to be the *power,* that is, the *Logos* of God. *The Word was made flesh,* though it may be said that it did not *dwell* among men, when the Spirit of the Lord, as a spirit of *strength,* came upon Sampson. If nothing more

be

be meant, there was no occasion for the language of wonder in the prediction of this event. Dr P. is no friend to the doctrine of the miraculous conception. Was it any wonder, then, that *a young woman* should, in the ordinary way, *conceive and bring forth a son?* The birth of John Baptist was more surprising than that of the Saviour. For he was the son of her *who was called barren.* The father was *old,* and the mother *well stricken in years,* Luke i. 18. John was *filled with the Holy Ghost from his mother's womb;* whereas it is denied that Jesus was so till he was thirty years of age. If there was a difference between Jesus and others who were actuated by the Spirit, in degree only; such a difference might make the effects more wonderful, but not the thing itself. For the wonder does not consist in the degree, but in the nature of the operation.

Now, Socinians assert that the *Logos* spoke and acted by the man Jesus, in the same manner as the Spirit operated on the prophets. But when they inform us that he *dwelt* in Jesus, was *united* to him and constantly acted by him; their language necessarily implies that the difference between what was enjoyed by Christ, and by the prophets, was not merely gradual, but essential. For they were under his *influence* only; and this influence was merely occasional. But as the Spirit *rested* on Jesus, the Logos, which according to Socinians, was this spirit, really *dwelt in* him. Now, what was this spirit, power or wisdom, which was united to, and dwelt in Jesus? Our author tells us that it was " God himself *." He also says, that " every Soci- " nian acknowledges, that the Deity of the Father *resided* " in the man Christ †." Thus, they grant a real union of the whole Deity to a human person, while they refuse a personal union or real incarnation. But if the whole Deity

Vol. I.   K   was

---

* Hist. Cor. vol. i. p. 11.   † Preface to Elwall's Trial, p. 4.

was fo *made flesh*, as conftantly to *dwell* in the man Jefus, it has much the appearance of real incarnation, though of a very ftrange kind, that of one perfon in another.

The word εσκηνωσε, *dwelt*, contains an evident allufion to the *Shechinah*, or cloud of glory, which was in the earthly tabernacle. Now, according to the Socinian view of the preceding claufe as fignifying a mere inhabitation, the fecond is tautological. If it was already faid that the word *dwelt in flesh*, there was no occafion for adding that he *dwelt as in a tent, or tabernacle*. This being the proper meaning of εσκηνωσε, the idea was anticipated. For this term is not merely connected with the following words, *among us*; but particularly refers to the manner in which he dwelt. The force of the Evangelift's language, according to the Socinian interpretation, is, " The word dwelt in the man Jefus, and " dwelt as in a tabernacle." Perhaps, it is to evade this objection, that they explain the term εσκηνωσε as denoting a conftant refidence, or abiding fome confiderable time *. But on the contrary, it denotes only a temporary refidence; for a *tent* is oppofed to a permanent habitation. The infpired writer feems to allude to the temporary refidence of the *Shechinah* in the tabernacle, as oppofed to its fixed refidence in the temple; or to the frequent removals of the tabernacle from one place to another, when it was always taken down, whereas God afterwards *chofe a place to put his Name there*, Deut. xii. 5.

And we beheld his glory, the glory as of the only-begotten of the Father. The particle *as* can only be underftood, as denoting either propriety, or famenefs : for none, in our time, will underftand it as expreffive of comparifon.

If viewed as denoting *propriety*, it fignifies that all the glory, which is the prerogative of the only-begotten, appeared in the 'Word made flefh. But if the glory beheld

in

---

* Famil. Illuftr. p. 31.

in the Word was that which became the only-begotten, does not the whole glory of the divine nature effentially belong to him; is not the *only-begotten* perfonally the fame as the *Word?* Socinians indeed, are divided as to the fenfe of the term *only-begotten.* Some underftand it of the miraculous conception. Others, who deny this, affert that it merely fignifies that he was the peculiar object of the Father's love, and fo denominated in the fame fenfe as Ifaac, who was not the only child of Abraham, but the fpecial object of his love.

As to the firft; could the whole glory of the divine nature become one who was at beft a mere man? With refpect to the other; the reafon given by Socinians for that peculiar love, which, according to them, procured to Jefus the appellation of *only-begotten,* is his unequalled holinefs. Now, how did this appear? Was it not in his being *full of grace and truth?* Nay, did it not eminently confift in thefe? Did not his *glory* alfo as really lie in the difplay of thefe perfections, as in the manifeftation of wifdom or power, though it might not ftrike the carnal eye fo much? If then, the glory of the word became Jefus, becaufe he was the object of the Father's peculiar love; if he was fo, becaufe of his holinefs, or grace and truth; if, at the fame time, the glory fpoken of eminently confifted in thefe; did not this glory become him, becaufe he eminently poffeffed it already? Thus, Socinians, by rejecting the true reafon of Chrift being called *the only-begotten,* are reduced to the neceffity of giving a thing as the reafon of itfelf. Is not this as abfurd as to fay, that a man, becaufe he is in *the ftate of a king* is entitled to *royalty;* while it is at the fame time acknowledged, that this is the very thing which conftitutes the regal ftate?

But it is denied that this glory became him, merely becaufe he was the object of the Father's love, if he was a mere man. For it is a divine glory, a real poffeffion of the attri-

butes

butes of Deity. Chrift himfelf claims it as fuch : *All that
the Father hath is mine.* Every believer in Jefus might,
on the fame ground, claim a real communication of divine
perfections. For thu: our Lord fpeaks of the Father's love
to all his people ; *That the world may know that thou haft
loved them, as thou haft loved me,* John xvii. 23. Therefore,
to return to Socinians the objection which we owe them on
this head, Chrift could as little be called the *only-begotten* of
the Father, becaufe of his love, as Ifaac could, according to
them, be called the only fon of Abraham, on another account.
For the Father, in this refpect, has many other fons. The
moft that could be faid of Jefus, in regard to this, is that he is
the firft born among many brethren. Indeed, the objection,
founded on the circumftance of Abraham having many
other children, of itfelf falls to the ground. For Ifaac is notwithftanding called his *only fon,* in a peculiar fenfe. For
when this language was ufed, Ifaac was his only fon by lawful marriage, as well as his only child of promife.

As may denote *famenefs.* In this cafe, the meaning is, that
the glory of the Word made flefh, is effentially the fame as that
of the only-begotten. Of confequence, the *Word* is not an
attribute united to a perfon, but effentially the fame perfon
as the *only-begotten.* Can the Word be effentially different
from him, and the glory effentially the fame, as the proper
glory of a perfon? It is evidently the meaning of the infpired writer, that the glory difplayed by the Word, in human nature, was that very glory which belongs to the eternal Son of God. Thus, he expreffes the identity of the
perfon, notwithftanding the change of manifeftation.

Here, it would be vain to recur to the pretended fenfe of
only-begotten, as denoting the object of peculiar love. Suppofing this to be the meaning, there is a plain, though ftrange,
inverfion of the words. For they ought to have been ;
" We beheld the glory of the only-begotten *as* the glory

3   " of

" of the Word." According to the Socinian hypothesis, as they now stand, what has been all along the subject becomes at once the predicate.

Full of grace and truth. These words suggest several other objections to the Socinian view of this passage. Though it were granted that by the Word we were merely to understand an attribute of deity, or more than one; it could not be proved that *wisdom* or *power* is exclusively, or even especially meant.

For we have no authority for this interpretation, but the assertion of Socinians. And it would be inconsistent with *reason* to assume any thing of this kind as truth, on so slender a foundation. They cannot produce one indisputed proof from the New Testament, of the term-*Logos* being used, as denoting either *wisdom* or *power.*

If we are to distinguish between the divine perfections, with respect to their display in the Mediator and his work, there are others that seem to have a prior claim to either of these. *Love* or *grace* would more naturally occur. For great as was the display of wisdom and power in the mediatory character and work, it was inferior to that of *love.* As it is distinctively declared, that *the Lord delighteth in mercy*, it is natural to imagine that his delight in this attribute would be peculiarly manifested in the work of our salvation. Therefore, especially in reference to the Gospel, it is said that *God is love*, 1 John iv. 8. And this is the only perfection that is spoken of in such peculiar language, as if the very essence of God were resolved into it.

All the manifestations of the wisdom and power of God, by Jesus Christ, must be ascribed to his grace as the spring or principle. For goodness is properly the communicate perfection of deity, to the operation of which we owe all that display of others which brings solace to sinful men.

The attributes of *grace* and *truth* are expresly men-

tioned

tioned by the Spirit of God, in the paffage. They are even repeatedly mentioned; and *grace*, no lefs than four times within the compafs of four verfes. Therefore, it would have been fully as natural to have fixed on one or both of thefe attributes, as fignified by *the Word;* efpecially as we fometimes find the term λογος conftructed with *grace*, λογω της χαριτος, *the word of grace*, Acts xiv. 3. and fometimes with *truth*, λογον της αληθειας, Eph. i. 13. as well as with *wifdom*, 1 Cor. xii. 8. The Gofpel is called *the word of grace*, and *the word of truth*, becaufe the difplay of thefe perfec· tions is its great fubject. It may be afterwards proved, that Chrift himfelf is called *the Word of the grace* of God.

Thefe attributes are exprefsly mentioned as manifefted in Jefus Chrift, during his refidence among men. For whether we connect the expreffion, *full of grace and truth*, with thefe words, *dwelt among us*, or with thofe immediately prece- ding it, *the only-begotten of the Father*, the fenfe is materially the fame. According to the former, he is faid to have ap- peared to men *full of grace and truth*. According to the latter, thefe are attributed to the only-begotten, as what pro- perly became him. Which foever of thefe views be preferred, his glory is defcribed as efpecially confifting in the difplay of thefe perfections. To the fame purpofe the apoftle Peter, when he has defcribed Jefus as *anointed with the Holy Ghoft, and with power*, fums up his character in thefe words, *who went about doing good*, Acts x. 38. as implying that all the difplay of *power* made by him, immediately proceeded from the divine *grace* or *goodnefs*, manifefting itfelf in the whole of his conduct.

Perhaps, it may be faid, that *grace* and *truth* are not men- tioned as divine perfections; but the one as expreffive of the beneficence of the human heart of Jefus, and the other of his conftant integrity. But in what way foever the Word dwelt in Jefus, in thefe perfections confifted the glory fpoken of.

of. The manifestation of these was the evidence of his possessing them. Besides, there is an evident allusion to the common language of the Old Testament, with respect to the displays of divine glory. There *mercy and truth* are said to *meet together*, Psal. lxxxv. 10. and this clearly refers to the display of these attributes in our salvation The Evangelist seems to carry on the allusion to the pillar of cloud and fire, which is called *the glory of the Lord*. It has been thought that this especially represented these two perfections; the fire, the divine *truth*, which is the splendor of his holiness; and the cloud, surrounding the fire, that *grace* which tempers the other, without which it would be to sinners *a consuming fire*. The very word, *full*, shews the continuance of the allusion to this symbolical pillar. We have seen, that the expression εσκηνωσε refers to the literal tabernacle. Now, as this, when the cloud covered it, is said to have been *filled* with the glory of the Lord, Ex. xl. 34, 35. when the Word dwelt in the tabernacle of the human nature, the illustrious Person was *full* of grace and truth. In this consisted his glory: and this glory was *beheld* by his disciples, as the typical glory had formerly been, by the people of Israel [*].

This grace was also, in its influence, communicated to men: *Of his fullness have all we received, and grace for grace*, ver. 16. But none can plead for the communication of the grace of a mere man, who do not hold the doctrine of supererogation.

It may be further observed that when God especially declares or displays his glory, he does not particularly mention his *wisdom* or *power*, but his *grace* and *truth*. Thus, in the remarkable manifestation made to Moses, JEHOVAH *proclaimed the Name of* JEHOVAH,—*The Lord, the Lord God merciful and gracious, long suffering, and abundant in goodness and truth, keeping mercy for thousands, forgiving*

K 4 *iniquity,*

---

[*] Vide Lampe in loc.

iniquity, and tranſgreſſion, and ſin, and that *will by no means clear the guilty,* or *hold it,* that is, ſin, *innocent,* Ex. xxxiv. 5.—7. That expreſſion, *abundant in goodneſs and truth,* is ſtrictly analogous to this, *full of grace and truth.* Every thing contained in this proclamation is included in theſe two. He *keeps mercy,* and *forgives iniquity,* becauſe *abundant in goodneſs ;* and alſo, becauſe *abundant in truth,* as being faithful to his promiſe. He *will not hold ſin innocent,* becauſe *abundant in truth,* even as to his threatening, in which his eſſential honour is as much concerned as in his promiſe. It deſerves to be noticed, that Jehovah made this declaration, expreſsly in anſwer to the earneſt prayer of Moſes, *I beſeech thee, ſhew me thy* glory, chap. xxxiii. 18.

According to the Socinian interpretation, the attributes of *grace* and *truth* muſt be ſuppoſed to be included in *wiſdom* or *power.* The abſurdity of this is evident. For though all the divine attributes, ſtrictly ſpeaking, are God himſelf; yet, when we come to diſtinguiſh them according to our manner of apprehenſion, we cannot ſay that one attribute is another, or includes another. Can we ſuppoſe an inſpired apoſtle to ſay that the attribute, either of *wiſdom,* or of *power,* was *full of* the attributes of *grace and truth ?* And it has been ſeen, that if an attribute be meant in the firſt verſe, the ſame muſt be meant here ; becauſe there has been no change of the ſubject.

But as Socinians are determined to explain the term *Logos* of one or more attributes of God, we may eaſily diſcern their reaſon for overlooking theſe which preſent themſelves in the very paſſage. They could not make them apply ſo well to the work of creation, aſcribed to the Word, in the beginning of the chapter. And little as they grant to *wiſdom* and *power* in the work of redemption, for accompliſhing which the Word was made fleſh, they are reſolved to yield ſtill leſs to *grace* and *truth.* For they reduce the gift

of

of *grace*, in Christ himself, to mere precept and example; and in his work, they destroy its very name, and change it into *debt*. They also make a sacrifice of *truth*, by denying the immutability of the moral law, the truth of the threatening, the eternity of punishment, the necessity of a real atonement; and by refusing that the prophecies and promises were really fulfilled in Christ, and that the types had any proper relation to him.

Ver. 15. *John bare witness of him, saying, This was he of whom I spake, He that cometh after me is preferred before me, for he was before me.* Socinians reject the testimony of John with respect to the dignity of Jesus; pretending that John said that Jesus was *preferred before* him, or admitted to greater honour, because he was more worthy of it. But these words, οτι πρωτος μυ ην, will not admit of this sense. For had this been meant, instead of ην *was*, εστι *is*, ought to have been used, to agree with ερχομενος and γεγονεν, which are both expressive of the present. Nor is this change accidental. For ην occurs again in ver. 30. though the other expression is a little varied. It must therefore signify a priority of existence. That this is the true meaning, undeniably appears from the frequent use of the other term, πρωτος, in the language of the same inspired writer, as denoting the eternal existence of the Son of God. Our Lord employs it, when speaking of himself; *I am* ὁ πρωτος, *the first*, and *the last*, Rev. i. 11 *. If he did not exist before John, the very use of such language with respect to himself would be a certain indication of his being much inferior to the Baptist. For according to the scheme of Socinians, the latter debases himself, even in comparison with a fellow-worm; but Jesus exalts himself, at the unspeakable expence of arrogating the distinctive titles of the Supreme God. Therefore, also, even according to their interpretation, it is

not

---

* See also ver. 17. chap. ii. 8. xxii. 13.

not true, that he " did not hold it for a prey to be as
" God."

When John elfewhere defcribes the decline of his own
honour, and the increafe of his Lord's, he adds, as a fufficient reafon for this; *He that cometh from above, is above all,*
chap. iii. 31. He does not fay, in the future, *fhall be*, as referring to his exaltation, but in the prefent, *is*, as fignifying
that notwithftanding the depth of his humiliation, fo that
no man received his teftimony, ver. 32. he was fuperior to
every creature. The reafon is evident. His fuperiority is
founded on his effential dignity. For John affigns the divine origin of Jefus as the reafon of his being preferred,
not to himfelf only, but to all minifters, to all creatures without exception. To imprefs his hearers the more, he repeats
this declaration in the fame verfe; only fubftituting *from
heaven*, inftead of *from above*.

Ver. 17. *The law was given by Mofes, but grace and truth
came by Jefus Chrift.* *Grace* and *truth* were formerly mentioned as divine perfections, difplayed in him. They are
now confidered as to their effects. The Hebrew believers
were ftill greatly attached to Mofes. Therefore, the Evangelift, having fhewn the fuperiority of Jefus to John the
Baptift, proceeds to illuftrate his fuperiority to the man of
God. He does fo nearly in the fame manner as the infpired
writer to the Hebrews, chap. iii. 5, 6. where he fhews that
Mofes was faithful as a *fervant* only, but Chrift as a *Son
over his own houfe.* When the Evangelift fays, *The law*
εδοθη, *was given by Mofes*, he reprefents him merely as the
inftrument employed by the fupreme Law-giver. When he
adds, *But grace and truth* εγενετο, *were made by Jefus Chrift,*
he clearly exhibits him as the author of all the grace communicated to others, this being *the grace of our Lord Jefus
Chrift*, both purchafed and conferred by him; and as the
author of all the *truth* of the New Teftament, in contra-

ɪ

diftinction

distinction to the shadows of the Old. As the Evangelist uses the same word (εγενετο) which, in ver. 3. expresses the work of the *old* creation, ascribed to the Word; it is evident that he as really ascribes that of the *new* to Jesus Christ, and thus points him out as that very Word by whom *all things were made.*

Ver. 18. *No man hath seen God at any time; the only-begotten, who is in the bosom of the Father, he hath declared him.* The Evangelist, having preferred Christ to Moses, evidently anticipates an objection from the unbelieving Jews. He knew they would reply, that *God spake unto Moses face to face,* Ex. xxxiii. 11. But he asserts that it had never been the privilege of any man to see God with the sensible eye, or fully to comprehend his essence with the intellectual. He seems to allude to what God had said to Moses, when he so earnestly desired to see his glory: *Thou canst not see my face; for no man can see me and live,* ver. 20.

But what the Evangelist denies with respect to every man, with respect to every creature (ȣδεις) without exception, he ascribes to the only-begotten. He does not indeed expressly say, that he had seen God. But he declares this truth no less effectually, by asserting that he *is in the bosom of the Father.* As this phraseology implies the incomprehensible filiation of the Son, it denotes a state of the most intimate union and communion with the Father, as necessarily flowing from this filiation. Human language cannot afford an expression that could more emphatically designate the most perfect ground of knowledge, whether respecting the nature, or the purposes of the Father. / It would almost seem to be contrasted with what God said to Moses; *Thou shalt see my back-parts, but my face shall not be seen,* Ex. xxxiii. 23. The only-begotten, being *in his bosom,* always sees his face.

When

When this language is viewed in connexion with what follows, *He hath declared*, or *acted the part of an interpreter*, it is perfectly evident that John means to afcribe to the only-begotten that vifion of the Father, which he hath denied of every creature; and to infinuate that all the revelation, which he made to the Church, was the confequence of this. He gives the fame teftimony as the Baptift; *What he hath feen,—he teftifieth*, chap. iii. 32. nay, the fame as Jefus himfelf; *I fpeak that which I have feen with my Father*, chap. viii. 38. He introduces a term commonly ufed among the Greeks, to denote the Perfon who interpreted the facred myfteries *. A fimilar character is given by Elihu to the Angel of the covenant, Job xxxiii. 23.—*An angel with him, an interpreter, one among a thoufand.* It is emphatically faid, ἐκεινος, HE *hath declared;* as pointing out the great inferiority of Mofes, confidered as a meffenger between God and the people of Ifrael.

Indeed, it would feem that, in this verfe, the Evangelift reduplicates upon what he has previoufly declared, as fhewing that he has all along had the fame fubject in his eye. When he fays, that the only-begotten is *in the bofom of the Father*, it is equivalent to what he has already faid of him as the *Word*, that he was *with God*. He proclaims his unchangeable exiftence, by afferting that he *is*, or *exifts in the bofom*, &c. For this was literally true of him, even while he was on earth, as to the human nature ; according to his language to Nicodemus, chap. iii. 13.—*The Son of Man, who* IS *in heaven*. What he denies of any creature *at any time*, he attributes to the only-begotten at all times. He ever *exifts* in the bofom of the Father, and therefore he ever *fees* him. When it is added, *he hath declared*, it fhews in what fenfe the Son hath been called *the Word*, and *the Light* : as he hath not only communicated all that external

nal

* Lampe in loc. Not.

nal revelation which the Church enjoys, but effectually *reveals* the Father, so as to illuminate the benighted understanding. In fine, although the Word was *made flesh*, and the *glory* of the only-begotten *beheld* in human nature, it is evidently refused that he was mere *man*, or a mere *creature.* For he is contradistinguished from every *man*, from every creature, however highly favoured.

II. The Doctor also says that John's design, in writing his Gospel, was to correct those who gave a personal subsistence to the Logos. " It is almost certain." he observes, " that " the apostle John had frequently heard this term made use " of in some erroneous representations of the system of " Christianity that were current in his time, and therefore he " might chuse to introduce the same term in its proper sense, " as an attribute of the Deity, or God himself, and not a " distinct being that sprung from him * " What these erroneous representations were, we learn from a preceding passage: " It seems very evident that, in that introduction, the Apo- " stle alludes to the very same system of opinions which he " had censured in his Epistle, the fundamental principle of " which was that, not the Supreme Being himself, but an " emanation from him, to which they gave the name of " *Logos*, and which they supposed to be the Christ, and in " habited the body of Jesus, was the maker of all things, " &c †."

He elsewhere says; " It appears to me highly proba- " ble, that it was in opposition of this doctrine of *æons*, " that John wrote the Introduction to his Gospel, in which " he explains the only proper sense in which the terms " *Logos, only-begotten, life*, &c. of which the Gnostics made " such mysteries, ought to be taken; asserting, more espe- " cially, that the *Logos*, which is spoken of in the scriptures, " and

* Hist. Corrupt. vol. i. p. 12.   † Ibid. p. 11.

" and the only Logos that he acknowledged, was *the power*
" *of God,* an attribute of the Father, and therefore not to
" be diftinguifhed from God himfelf *."

It has been feen that, if John, merely in his own idea,
viewed the Word as an attribute, he was chargeable with
great impropriety in his manner of writing. But if he
meant directly to refute thofe who maintained that the
Word was a Perfon, and to prove that this was no other
than an attribute; every argument, already urged, applies
with redoubled force. If the reafon for " introducing this
" term," was to fhew its proper fenfe, in oppofition to the
Gnoftics, who gave a perfonal fubfiftence to the *Logos ;* certainly, there never was a writer who did lefs to accomplifh
his purpofe, nay, more to defeat it.

If John meant to refute thofe who afcribed perfonality
to the Word, was not the perfonification of his fubject,
even fuppofing that it was meant figuratively, the moft
unfeafonable figure ever ufed, and the moft improper plan
he could have devifed? Was not this the moft likely method, I do not fay, for leaving the fubject ftill in darknefs,
but for encouraging the error ? If a writer of ordinary dif-
cretion found that a mere attribute, in confequence of being perfonified by former writers, came at length to be
viewed as a real perfon, and earneftly wifhed to correct a
miftake fo fatal, as to affect the very object and truth of
all divine worfhip, nay, wrote exprefsly for this end;
might it not reafonably be expected, that, when he entered on his fubject, he would, firft of all, entirely lay afide
the figurative ftyle, and fpeak in the fimpleft language
poffible? Is it not granted that, on the contrary, the Evangelift adopts and continues the language of perfonification ?
Might not one as reafonably hope to extinguifh fire by
pouring oil upon it?

Though

---

* Ear. Op. Vol. i. p. 181.

Though it were granted, that John alluded to the false doctrines of the Gnostics concerning their *æons*, and designed to correct them, it would not follow that he meant to shew that the *Logos*, whom they reckoned among their *æons*, was an attribute. The vanity of this pretence appears from what has been formerly observed. For the apostle would never have said that the *Logos* was *God*, and then that he was *with* God. He must have known that the Gnostics could not have wished a better prop for their fabric. For as they asserted that these *æons* were originally *emanations* from God, in this sense would they most probably explain his language, when he declares that the Logos *was God*. " But then," would they say, " the E-" vangelist still acknowledges the truth of our doctrine. " For he also shews that the Logos existed distinctly, by " adding, *The same was in the beginning with God.* And " he leaves his system in this state ; which he would not" " have done, had he meant to oppose ours, as far as it re-" lates to the distinct existence of the Logos." Indeed, these famous Gnostics, the Valentinians, made the greatest use of this Gospel, in proof of their doctrine *. According to our author's hypothesis with respect to the design of the Evangelist, it will also be somewhat difficult for him to shew, how " an attribute of the Father," in other words, the Father *himself*, could be said to be *only-begotten*, or to be *begotten* in any sense?

If John wished to shew that the Word was merely an attribute, he must have meant that it was *in* God ; and he must also have used a term that would clearly express his idea. If he meant to signify that there was no distinc-

tion

---

* Hi autem qui a Valentino funt, eo, quod est secundum Johannem [Evangelio] plenissime utentes, ad ostensionem conjugationum suarum, &c. Iren. lib. iii. c. 11. f. 7.

tion of perſons in the divine eſſence, would not ɛις, *in,* have been far more proper than προς, *with?*

Does not that repetition, *The ſame was in the beginning with God,* take away all the ſuppoſed force of the preceding aſſertion, *The Word was God?*

If John meant to ſhew that the Logos was not a perſon, was not his conduct very unaccountable, in retaining the perſonification, after changing the deſignation of his ſubject?

Did he not give the greateſt countenance to the very error which, it is ſaid, he meant to oppoſe, by not only perſonifying the Light, but by doing ſo, after he had ſpoken of it without any figure, in theſe words, *The life was the light of men?*

As it is granted that many, in that age, believed that Chriſt was the Word; as the terms *Word* and *Light* denote the ſame ſubject; as it cannot be ſuppoſed that, when this Goſpel was written, any continued to reckon John the Light; if the Evangeliſt meant to ſhew that Jeſus was not the Word, but that this was ſimply an attribute, would it not have been far more natural and proper, to have ſaid that *Jeſus Chriſt* was not *that Light,* than to ſay that this character did not belong to *John?*

Had the Evangeliſt meant to ſhew that the Word was merely an attribute, is it not natural to ſuppoſe that he would have told what particular attribute was intended by this metaphorical term?

Did he mean to ſhew that this was *power?* How, then, inſtead of taking the leaſt notice of this, does he particularly mention two other attributes?

According to the deſign aſcribed to the Evangeliſt, was it not extremely odd, that he ſhould retain the metaphorical name, and the figure of perſonification, in the moſt critical part of his narrative, ſaying; The *Word* was *made fleſh?*

Would

Would it not have answered the pretended purpose far better to have said, " The power of God resided in Jesus " Christ?"

If it was the apostle's design to put those right who had fatally erred from misunderstanding the language of allegory, would not such a simple declaration as the following have been more proper than all that he says? " Jesus Christ is not " that Word of God, by which all things were made. For " the Word is a divine perfection. But Jesus is a mere man, " who owes his being to this Word." Could the Evangelist be excusable, considering the supposed circumstances, in sacrificing perspicuity to figure, or truth to elegance of diction?

If there be any such thing as inspiration, can it be supposed that the Holy Spirit would have suffered the Evangelist to have erred so far from his scope, or to have left men still in the dark about the very subject of his discourse; nay, even while it was his design to reclaim them from the supposed error, would have allowed him to go such lengths for confirming them in it?

But as the Evangelist all along speaks of the Word in language proper to a person, ascribes existence to it, presence with another, creation, the residence of life, communication of light; distinguishes it from a human person mentioned; ascribes to it coming, property, rejection, reception, the grant of power, a name, incarnation, habitation among others, the glory of a person, and fullness of perfections; though there were no other test by which we could judge of the writer's design, than this very introduction, would it not appear to *ordinary* reason, most natural to conclude, that, instead of writing to contradict and convince those who believed that the Word was a Person, he had written expressly to confirm their doctrine?

I shall only add, that the testimony of the ancients with respect to the design of John, in writing his Gospel, is of

no inconfiderable weight. Irenæus declares, that " John
" defigned by his Gofpel to remove that error which was
" fown among men by Cerinthus *." The truth of this
Dr P. admits † : But it is only that he may turn it his own
way. The apoftle wrote to contradict the Gnoftic idea of
the perfonality and pre-exiftence of the Logos. He wrote
in fupport of the Unitarian doctrine. But Jerom declares
that iohn had the Ebionites efpecially in his eye. " Laft
" of all," he fays, " at the requeft of the bifhops of Afia,
" he wrote his Gofpel againft Cerinthus and other heretics,
" and efpecially againft the doctrine of the Ebionites, then
" beginning to appear, who fay that Chrift did not exift be-
" fore Mary ‡." Is it objected that Jerom was too late ?
But the teftimony of Irenæus muft be underftood with the
fame latitude. For, as he fays that John wrote his Gofpel,
that he might " confound and perfuade them (the heretics)
" that one God made all things by his Word," if we receive his teftimony, it muft be underftood according to his
own ideas of the Word. Now, it cannot be refufed that
he ufes this term as denoting a Perfon ‖. If any doubt of
this remain, let his own words be confulted, which at the
fame time exprefs his conviction as to the apoftle's defign
in writing : " John declaring the one God Almighty, and
" the one only-begotten Chrift Jefus, by whom all things
" were made, afferts that this Perfon is the Son of God,
" that this Perfon is the only-begotten, that this is the
                                        " Maker

---

* Lib. iii. c. 11.   † Hift. of Cor. vol. i. p. 12.

‡ Noviffimus omnium fcripfit Evangelium, rogatus ab Afiæ epifcopis
adverfus Cerinthum, aliofque hæreticos, et maxime tunc Ebionitarum
dogma confurgens, qui afferunt Chriftum ante Mariam non fuiffe. Unde
et compulfus eft divinam ejus nativitatem edicere. Catalog. Script. Ec-
clef. in Juan.

‖ Iren. ibid.

" Maker of all things, that this is the true Light who lighteth
" every man, that this is the Maker of the world, that this
" is he who came to his own, that this very Person was
" made flesh, and dwelt among us *.

·Now, though we were at a loss as to John's defign, which
is abundantly evident from his own language, it is hardly
conceivable that Irenæus, the disciple of Polycarp, the disciple of John, could be so far a stranger to it, as to suppose
it to be the very reverse of what it really was. And this
must have been the case, if John wrote to shew that the
Word is merely an *attribute.*

CHAP. II.

Of the Design of the First Epistle of John.

DR PRIESTLEY afferts that John, in his first Epistle, cen-
sures thofe " who believed Chrift to be man only in ap-
" pearance ; and that this was the *only* herefy that gave
" him any alarm †." Our author elsewhere enters into a
particular proof of this. " The doctrine of the Gnostics,"
he says, " concerning the Person of Chrift, was so offenfive
" to him, and it was so much upon his mind, that he begins
" his first Epistle feemingly in a very abrupt manner, with
" the strongest allusions to it. *That which was from the*
" *beginning* ‡," &c. Thus he tries to wreft one of the
L 2					weapons

---

* Τυ γαρ Ιωαννη ενα Θεον παντοκρατερα, και ενα μονογενη Χριϛον Ιησουν
κηρυσσοντος, δι'ȣ τα παντα γεγονεναι λεγει τȣτον υιον Θεȣ τȣτον μονογενη,
τȣτον παντων ποιητην τȣτον φωι αληθινον, φωτιζοντα παντα ⟨ νθρωπον,
τȣτον κοσμȣ ποιητην, τȣτον εις τα ιδια εληλυθοτα, τȣτον αυτον σαρκα
γιγονοτα, και εσκηνωκοτα εν ημιν· Lib. i. c. 1. p, 38.

† Hist. of Corrupt. vol. i. p. 10.   ‡ Earl. Opin. vol. i. p. 190, 191.

weapons of his adverfaries out of their hands, and to turn
it againft the Gnoftics, that he may himfelf evade its ftroke.
Whatever may be thought of his dexterity in handling it,
every one muft admire his boldnefs.

He fays of John; " What could he mean by fpeaking of
" Jefus under the figure of *life*, as a perfon who had been
" *heard, feen*, and even *handled*, fo that they had the evi-
" dence of all their fenfes, but that he was really a man,
" had a real *human body*, and not merely the appearance of
" one; which, it is univerfally allowed, was an opinion that
" was entertained by many perfons in his time *." But he
muft certainly reckon the apoftle a very unfkilful reafoner.
For, if this was his meaning, while he gave a fatal blow to
one falfe doctrine, he fupported another. I need not fay,
that the Gnoftics believed the pre-exiftence of Chrift. The
Doctor grants that John here " fpeaks of Jefus under the
" figure of *life*." He indeed, keeps part of the *figure* behind
the curtain. For John fpeaks of Jefus as *the Word of life:
That which was from the beginning, which we have heard,
which we have feen with our eyes, which we have looked
upon, and our hands have handled of the Word of life*, &c.
But our author elfewhere plainly acknowledges that Chrift
is " called *the Word of God* †;" though fuch an acknowledgment might not have been expedient in this place.
However, *life* is not, in ver. 1. the name of the perfon
fpoken of, but the epithet affixed to the name; the expreffion being equivalent to *the living Word;* but with this difference, that it is more emphatic, as particularly fignifying
that he is the *fountain* of life. There can be no doubt that it
is the fame perfon, who, in this paffage, is called *the Life*,
and *the Word of life*. But if John fpoke of Jefus as *life*,
to fignify " that he was really *a man*, what could he mean
" by

* Earl. Opin. vol. i. p. 190.　　　† Famil. Illuftr. p. 31.

" by ſpeaking of" him as *the Word of life?* It will not be
ſaid, that the *Word* itſelf derived its *life* from the humanity
of Jeſus.   Did the *Word*, that is, according to the Socinian
view, the *power* of God, give this human *life* to Jeſus? Yet
this could not have entitled him to bear its name.

The attempt to impoſe a ſenſe on the term, as here uſed,
different from that in which it occurs in the Goſpel, is vain.
As our opponents cannot deny that the inſpired writer uſes
it in the ſame ſenſe, both here, and in the Revelation; by
what arguments can they prove that, in his Goſpel, he de-
viſes a new one, not only different from the other, but dia-
metrically oppoſite?

But it has been already ſeen, that this expreſſion, *the
Word of life*, is of the ſame import with that uſed in the
Goſpel, concerning the Word, *In him was life.*   But how
was this Word *from the beginning?* Our author, ſurely,
will not underſtand the term αϱχη in one ſenſe here, and in
another when explaining the introduction to the Goſpel;
unleſs he mean to avail himſelf of both the contradictory
expoſitions of Socinians; ſome of whom have underſtood
it of the *beginning of the world*, and others of the *beginning of the Goſpel.*   Indeed, if αϱχη be not uſed in
the ſame ſenſe here, as in the Goſpel, its ſenſe is loſt.
The beginning of the Goſpel cannot be meant; for Jeſus
did not then *begin* to *live*, or to be *really a man*: Nor the
beginning of his human life; for ſurely, the inſpired writer
would never think of declaring with ſo much ſolemnity,
that Jeſus had *really* been a man, from the time of his becoming a man.

The apoſtle, however, in the following verſe, expreſsly
limits the ſenſe of his language.   As the expreſſion, *Was
from the beginning*, is equivalent to that, *In the beginning
was the Word;* he ſhews that he had no other meaning.
Therefore, he employs this ſtriking parentheſis; *For the*

life.

life was manifefted, and we have feen, and bear witnefs, and fhew unto you that eternal life which was with the Father, and was manifefted unto us, ver. 2.   Dr P. endeavours to give a new turn to this verfe, by fubftituting *manifeft* in both places where εφανερωθη occurs ; as if the apoftle had only meant to fay that it was *plainly feen* that Jefus was *really a living man.*   But our verfion expreffes the true fenfe ; as this term is properly ufed to denote the manifef-tation of fomething, which, though it formerly exifted, was hid, or not fo fully known ; or of a perfon, making him-felf known in a new manner.   Not to mention a variety of other inftances, it is thus ufed, 1 Tim. iii. 16. *God was manifefted in the flefh.*   Will our author interpret the term in the fame fenfe there, as in the beginning of John's Epif-tle ? Will he fay, that it fignifies that God was *really* in-carnate ?

But if John meant nothing more than that Jefus was really a man, how does he not merely call him *life,* in the abftract, (a metaphor ufed no where elfe in this fenfe) but *eternal life ?* How does he affert that Jefus *was,* or *exifted with the Father ;* evidently referring to a ftate previous to his being *manifefted unto us ?* Was it the way to confute the Gnoftic doctrine of the pre-exiftence of the Word, to affert the *eternity* of his exiftence ? Was it the moft direct method to prove that Chrift was a real man, and no more, to de-clare that he had no beginning ? By the manifeftation of the *temporal* life of Jefus, that is, of his being *really a man,* how could he be *manifefted* to the difciples as *eternal life ?* Becaufe he had been with them, as having a *real human body* how could they hence learn that he was *that Eternal Life which was with the Father ?* Did this *real human body* eternally exift ? Though the learned gentleman feems to reckon matter *eternal,* it cannot be fuppofed that he will afcribe to it *eternal life.*   An enemy to revelation could not

have

have hit upon a better expedient for expoſing the apoſtle to ridicule. But it muſt be evident to every candid reader, that it is by no means the truth of Chriſt's *human* life that John is ſo anxious to make known, but the real manifeſtation of his *divine*.

Our author, indeed, in order to ſupport his own doctrine, makes an inſpired writer deny his. In his former work he has obſerved, that John, in the introduction to his Goſpel, " affirms that the *Logos* by which all things were made, " was not a being diſtinct from God, but God himſelf, that " is, an attribute of God * ?" Yet, he grants that John, in his epiſtle, calls Jeſus *life ;* and therefore, cannot refuſe that he calls him *the Logos,* or *Word of life.* Was the Word a Perſon, when John wrote his Epiſtle, and had it become a a mere Attribute, by the time that he wrote his Goſpel? This was poſſible, indeed, according to the doctrine of *occaſional perſonality,* which Dr P. calls *philoſophical Unitarianiſm.* But ſurely, however narrow his creed as to *inſpiration,* he will not go ſo far as to ſay, that John retracted, in his Goſpel, what he had written in his Epiſtle ; or that he wrote his Goſpel to *cenſure* the errors which he had himſelf propagated. How, then, did the apoſtle call Jeſus *the Word,* in this Epiſtle, and yet write the introduction to his Goſpel, to ſhew that he was *not the Word,* but that this was God himſelf?

In another reſpect, the apoſtle can be vindicated from ſelf-contradiction, only by ſuppoſing that Dr P. is chargeable with it. For he firſt aſſerts that John, in the introduction to his Goſpel, " explains the *only proper ſenſe* in which " the term—*life*—ought to be taken †." Here our author certainly underſtands it as denoting a divine attribute. Yet, he informs us, in the courſe of a few pages, that, in the Epiſtle, it denotes only the truth of our Saviour's humani-

ty.

* Hiſt. of Cor. vol. i. p. 11.   † Earl. Op. vol. i. p. 181.

ty *. This is a ftriking tranfition, indeed! from an attribute to a perfon,—from a divine attribute to a human perfon.
If the term be ufed in its *only proper fenfe*, when reftricted
as in the Gofpel, to the nature of *God;* how can it, in the
epiftle, fignify nothing more than the exiftence of a *mere
man?*

Dr P. fays; " It is univerfally allowed, that Chrift having
" merely the appearance of a man, was an opinion that
" was entertained by many perfons in his (the Apoftle's)
" time †." This opinion, indeed, has been generally afcribed
to Simon Magus; becaufe, as he pretended that himfelf
was known in Judea as the Chrift, he taught that he fuffered
in appearance only. But as few of thofe called Gnoftics
acknowledged that he was the Chrift, the opinion as to Chrift
having only the appearance of human nature was not generally received by Gnoftics till after the death of John.
Our author informs us that " the Gnoftic teachers, who op-
" pofed the apoftles, were Jews;" and that they " were *in*
" *all refpects* the fame that the Cerinthians are defcribed to
" have been ‡." He at the fame time informs us, that " the
" Cerinthians and Carpocratians believed that Jefus was not
" only a man, born as other men are, but alfo the proper off-
" fpring of Jofeph as well as of Mary ||." If, therefore, John
meant to write againft Gnoftics, it was certainly moft natural for him to level his doctrine againft thofe, of Jewifh
origin, who *oppofed* him and the other *apoftles;* efpecially
as this epiftle feems to have been wrote before the deftruction of Jerufalem, and of confequence, before the Gentile
Gnoftics made any figure. How, then, can it be believed,
that his principal defign in writing, was to cenfure a herefy
not maintained by thofe againft whom he wrote; nay, that
this was " the only herefy that gave him any trouble?"

Dr

---

* Earl. Op. vol. i. p. 190.   † Ibid.   ‡ P. 144. || P. 177.

Dr P. endeavours to confirm his doctrine as to the ſcope of this epiſtle, by quoting chap. iv. ver. 2, 3. *Every ſpirit that confeſſeth that Jeſus Chriſt is come in the fleſh, is of God. And every ſpirit that confeſſeth not that Jeſus Chriſt is come in the fleſh, is not of God: and this is that ſpirit of antichriſt, whereof ye have heard that it ſhould come, and even now already is it in the world.* " *Coming in the fleſh,*" he ſays, " can have no other meaning than *having real fleſh*, which " many of the Gnoſtics ſaid Chriſt had not *." It is rea-ſonable, however, to allow the inſpired writer the liberty of explaining himſelf. After a digreſſion with reſpect to the worldly ſpirit of theſe falſe prophets, he ſhews what he meant by Chriſt's *coming in the fleſh*, ver. 9. *In this was manifeſted the love of God towards us, becauſe that God ſent his only-begotten Son into the world, that we might live through him.* *Coming* and *ſending* are undoubtedly relative terms. *Coming in the fleſh*, ver. 2. correſponds with *ſen-ding into the world*, ver. 9. Suppoſing that " *coming in the* " *fleſh,* can have no other meaning than *having real fleſh,*" it muſt ſtill follow that *ſending into the world* means God's *giving real fleſh.*—To whom? To *his only-begotten Son.* Dr P. will not pretend that Jeſus received this title from his miraculous conception, or the manner in which he *had real fleſh.* I have not obſerved that he any where explains this term. But as he reckons that expreſſion, *the Son of God,* equivalent to *the Chriſt*, it is moſt probable that he has the ſame view of *only-begotten.* But according to him, Jeſus was not the Chriſt till he was *anointed* at his baptiſm. How, then, did God *ſend his only-begotten Son into the world,* that is, *give real fleſh* to him, before he had ſuch a Son ? But it is denied that Jeſus was the *only-begotten,* with reſpect to his *unction* as Meſſiah. For the apoſtle, in this very

                                                                chapter,

* Earl. Op. vol. i. p. 191.

chapter, extends this privilege to all faints. *Ye have an unction from the Holy One, and ye know all things.—The anointing, which ye have received of him abideth in you,* &c. ver. 20. 27. In this fenfe, Jefus could only be called the *firft-begotten.* Nay, if the term *only-begotten* refer merely to the character of *the Chrift,* believers are more properly and ftrictly the fons of God, than their Saviour is. For, although it is in a fpiritual fenfe, they are really *begotten* of God. But whatever the term *only-begotten* includes, muft have been true of Jefus, at leaft at the very time of his miffion into the world; elfe God did not fend his only-begotten Son, but only one who was to be fo in confequence of his miffion.

We are certainly to underftand the doctrine of this epiftle according to the introduction, which, our author himfelf being judge, is a key to the whole. If fo, Chrift was the *only-begotten* in a fenfe truly peculiar, as being *the Word of life, that eternal Life which was with the Father, and was manifefted unto* men, when he was *fent into the world.* Whatever love God might difplay in afterwards making this perfon his Son, in the Socinian fenfe, the love of God could not be *manifefted* in *fending* him if this character did not belong to him before his miffion. If this *fending* refer to temporal life only, how can we *live through him?* If nothing more be meant than his *having real flefh,* Jefus was like the firft man *made a living foul,* but he cannot be *a quickening fpirit.*

The Doctor adds; " *Coming* here cannot imply any pre-
" exiftent ftate; for then the flefh in which he came muft
" have pre-exifted *.*" But this is a mere quibble. For by a parity of reafon, when God fays, *Lo, I come to thee in a thick cloud,* Ex. xix. 9. we cannot believe the pre-exiftence of the glorious Perfon who came in this manner,
without

* Earl. Op. vol, i. p. 191.

without believing that of the cloud alſo. Some think that εν σαρκι is here uſed for εις σαρκα *into the fleſh*, the one being often put for the other *. But though the ordinary ſenſe of the prepoſition be retained, the moſt that the expreſſion *in the fleſh* can ſignify, is the *manner* in which Chriſt *came*. And undoubtedly, a perſon, who has previouſly exiſted, may be ſaid to *come* in a particular manner, without its being neceſſarily ſuppoſed that the *manner* pre-exiſted, as well as the *perſon*.

The learned gentleman is not quite pleaſed with the tranſlation of this paſſage. He ſays; " It might be ren- " dered, that *Jeſus is Chriſt come in the fleſh*." But there is ſtill another verſion fully as natural, *Whoſoever ſhall confeſs Jeſus Chriſt who hath come in the fleſh* †. Thus, the prin- cipal ſubject of confeſſion is not his *coming in the fleſh*, but Jeſus Chriſt himſelf in the whole extent of his character. This agrees better with the apoſtle's illuſtration of this confeſſion in ver. 9, 10. where Jeſus is deſcribed as the *pro- pitiation*, and *the Saviour of the world*; and in ver. 15. where it is peculiarly pointed to the eſſential dignity of his Perſon; *Whoſoever ſhall confeſs that Jeſus is the Son of God, God dwelleth in him.* Had John meant directly to oppoſe the doctrine of an *apparent* humanity, every one muſt ſee that his language would have been far more proper, had he ſaid, *that Jeſus is the Son of man ;* eſpecially as this is the expreſſion ordinarily uſed in ſcripture, to denote his media- tory character. Inſtead of ſaying, *come in the fleſh*, it would have conveyed the apoſtle's idea far more clearly, had he ſpoken of Chriſt's coming *of the fleſh ;* as his lan- guage is accidentally expreſſed by our author, in his Hiſtory of Corruptions ‡.

In

---

* Vid. Glaſſii Rhet. p. 527. Wolfii Cur. Phil. in loc. vol. v.

† This is the tranſlation given of the phraſe by Dr Whitby, before he became Socinian.　　‡ Vol. i. p. 10.

In reply to what had been faid by the learned Dr Horfley, now Bifhop of St David's, that the expreffion *coming in the flefh*, led to the notion of Jefus having " had his choice " of different ways of coming," our author obferves ; " On " the contrary, I think the expreffion fufficiently fimilar to " other Jewifh phrafes, of which we find various examples " in the fcriptures, and that it may be explained by the " phrafe *partaker of flefh and blood*, Heb. ii. 14 *." But the Doctor is very unhappy in his choice of a parallel text. For the very next claufe difproves his allegation. The apoftle ufes the phrafe referred to with refpect to *the children*. Does it therefore follow that the language of John may be explained by it? On the contrary, the infpired writer to the Hebrews varies his language, when he fpeaks of the *Leader of our falvation*. He knew that it would naturally occur, that men were entirely paffive in receiving human nature. Therefore, he ufes an expreffion, with refpect to Chrift, which denotes action : *He took part of the fame.* It is equivalent to that in Phil. ii. 7. *He took upon himfelf the form of a fervant.* As this language can admit only of an active fenfe, it is evident, from the connexion, that it refpects not any thing pofterior to the incarnation of our Lord, but his very affumption of our nature.

Dr P. adds ; " If the word *coming* muft neceffarily mean " *coming from heaven*, and imply a pre-exiftent ftate, John " the Baptift muft have pre-exifted : for our Saviour ufes " that expreffion concerning him, as well as concerning " himfelf, Matt. xi. 18, 19. *John came neither eating nor* " *drinking.—The Son of Man came eating and drinking*, " &c. †" And undoubtedly, the word *coming*, as ufed concerning both, implies pre-exiftence of a certain kind. For it refers to the entrance of both on their public miniftrations,

---

* Earl. Op. vol. i. p. 193.   † Ibid.

ſtrations, or to the manner in which Chriſt and his forerunner ſeverally appeared in a public character. With this limitation, our Lord ſays, ver. 12. *From the days of John until now, the kingdom of heaven ſuffereth violence*; not from the time of his birth, but of the commencement of his miniſtry. Beſides, *coming* is a far more indefinite expreſſion than *coming in the fleſh*; which reſtricts the *coming* to the firſt appearance of the Perſon in human nature, and is never uſed concerning John, or any mere creature. The Doctor is chargeable with a fallacy, when he reaſons on the ground of the ſimple term *coming* being underſtood as if it " ne-" ceſſarily meant *coming from heaven.*"

He further obſerves; " It may alſo be aſſerted, with " more certainty ſtill, concerning all the apoſtles, that they " pre-exiſted; for our Saviour, in his prayer for them, re-" ſpecting their miſſion, makes uſe of the term *world*, which " is not found in 1 John iv. 2. where he ſays, John xvii. 18. " *As thou haſt ſent me into the world, ſo have I alſo ſent* " *them into the world.*" Here the ſophiſm lies in the uſe of the term *pre-exiſted.* Our author tacitly aſſumes, that if the phraſe, *ſending into the world*, imply a pre-exiſtence of any kind, it muſt denote a pre-exiſtence of the ſame kind in both caſes. He ſurely underſtands this languge, with re-ſpect to the apoſtles, as referring to their miſſion in a public character. When our Lord ſays, *I have ſent them into the world*, it neceſſarily implies their pre-exiſtence in a dif-ferent ſtate, as men living in a private ſtation, little known, and not expoſed to any peculiar difficulties and dangers, ſuch as they were now to encounter in the fulfilment of their miſſion. It cannot be pretended that the other ex-preſſion reſpects the commencement of our Saviour's mini-ſtry. For Dr P. has quoted it as correſpondent with that of *coming in the fleſh.* He cannot plead that the phraſe, *ſent into the world*, muſt have the ſame idea affixed to it in

both

both claufes, without granting that Jefus as really *fent* the apoftles *into the world*, that is, that he as really fent them *in flefh*, or gave them human nature, as the Father fent him *in flefh*, or gave him human nature.

He thinks that " it may be afferted, with more certainty ftill concerning all the apoftles that they pre-exifted," be-caufe the term *world* is here ufed, " which is not found in 1 John iv. 2." But our author muft know that the whole phrafe, *fent into the world*, is found in 1 John iv. 9. which, it has been feen, exactly correfponds with the preceding ex-preffion, *come in the flefh*.

If we pay the leaft regard to the meaning of the term *coming*, as ufed with refpect to Chrift in other paffages of the New Teftament, the vanity of our author's affertions muft appear at firft view. It is faid of *the true Light*, that *he came unto his own*, John i. 11. But this *coming* evidently implies pre-exiftence. For it is declared concerning the fame Perfon, in the verfe immediately preceding, *He was in the world;* that is, he exifted in the world, before he came in flefh. If this be not true, what fenfe can be affix-ed to thefe words of Jefus; *I came forth from the Father, and am come into the world: again I leave the world, and go to the Father?* John xvi. 28. Do they not as clearly fig-nify that he exifted with the Father, *before* his coming into the world, as that he fhould exift with the Father, *after* his leaving it? When this term refpects the nativity, it is ufed in fuch a fenfe, that Jefus, *when coming*, or in the very act of entering, *into the world*, could *fay, A body haft thou pre-pared me*, Heb. x. 5.

The true fenfe of the term muft certainly be learned from thofe prophecies, concerning the appearance of the Meffiah, which are recorded in the Old Teftament; and in conformity to thefe muft the language of the New be un-derftood. The Jews were accuftomed to defign the Mef-

fiah ο ερχομενος, *he that cometh*, Matt. xi. 3. They borrowed this language from their fcriptures. For there he is
fometimes fimply defcribed under this character, with a declaration of the certainty of his appearance; as in Hab.
ii. 3. Heb. x. 37. *He that cometh fhall come.* On other occafions, the dignity of the Perfon is declared. He is reprefented as coming with divine Majefty, though in human
form : *Behold,* one *like the Son of man came with the clouds
of heaven,* Dan. vii. 13. His divine nature is often exprefsly declared : *Behold your God fhall come,* Ifa. xxxv. 4.
This expreffion evidently denotes a manifeftation of himfelf entirely different from any that his church had formerly enjoyed. It fignifies a difplay of his glory even
to the eye of fenfe. *They fhall fee the glory of* JEHOVAH,
ver. 2. That his people might not deceive themfelves, he
particularly mentions the figns of his appearance, ver. 5.
*Then the eyes of the blind fhall be opened, and the ears of the
deaf fhall be unftopped,* &c. His work is declared : ver. 4.
He will come and fave you. The converfion of the heathen is metaphorically expreffed, as one great effect of his
coming : *In the wildernefs fhall waters break out,* &c.
Thus, the whole paffage evidently refers to the time of
Meffiah's appearance.

This manifeftation was not to be by means of an inferior
perfon. Therefore it is written, *Say unto the cities of Judah, Behold your God. Behold, the Lord God will come,----
Behold, his reward is with him, and his work before him,*
chap. xl. 9, 10. This illuftrious Perfon is, in chap. lxii. 11.
defcribed in the fame characters, only with a change of defignation : *Behold, thy falvation cometh : Behold, his reward is with him, and his work before him.* He was immediately to difcharge the work of a fhepherd, chap. xl. 11.
He fhall feed his flock like a fhepherd. He was to be preceded by *the voice of one crying in the wildernefs, Prepare*

ye

ye the way of JEHOVAH, ver. 3. Here alfo, we have a prediction of the difplay of his glory, even to the fenfible eye,
ver 5. *And the glory of the Lord fhall be revealed, and all
flefh fhall fee it together, for the mouth of the Lord hath
fpoken it ;* or, as the words may be read, *all flefh fhall fee together, that the mouth of the Lord hath fpoken,* that is, that
JEHOVAH himfelf is the fpeaker ; according to chap. lii. 6.
formerly explained.

The account given of the Meffiah, as *come,* exactly correfponds with thefe prophecies. God was not manifefted
in the human perfon of Jefus ; but *the Son of God was manifefted in the flefh,* that is, in the human nature, 1 John iii.
8. The glory that was beheld, was properly his own. It was
the glory as of the only begotten, John i. 14. When he
wrought miracles, he *manifefted forth his glory,* chap. ii. 11.
When the difciples of John, as fent by their Mafter, faid to
Jefus, *Art thou he that fhould come ?* he referred them to
thefe very works which were foretold by the prophet Ifaiah,
as the figns of the coming of their God : *The blind receive
their fight, and the lame walk,* &c. Matt. xi. 3—5. His
name was called *Jefus,* not becaufe God was to accomplifh
the work of falvation by him as an inferior agent ; but becaufe he was himfelf to *fave his people,* Matt. i. 21. He is
exprefsly called *Salvation,* Acts xiii. 47. He appropriates to
himfelf the language ufed with refpect to the coming of
the church's *God* and *Salvation ; Behold I come,—and my
reward is with me :* and to affure her that it was he who
was foretold as thus coming, he alfo appropriates thefe divine characters which follow in the prophecy of Ifaiah
(chap. xli. 4.) *I am the Firft and the Laft,* Rev. xxii. 12,
13. If Jefus be not that divine Perfon who was to *feed
his flock like a fhepherd,* his followers are chargeable with
blafphemy when they call him the *great* Shepherd of the
fheep, Heb. xiii. 20. and the *chief* Shepherd, 1 Pet. v. 4.

For

For neither of these characters can apply to him, who is infinitely inferior to another invested with this office.

But in what manner soever that expression, *come in the flesh*, be rendered, the sentence of inspiration condemns Unitarians as well as those who denied the truth of Christ's human nature. For according to the plain meaning of the words, he *came in the flesh*, not only as *Jesus*, but as *Christ*. But those who have held the simple humanity, have always denied this. For they do not believe that *Jesus* was *Christ*, that is, *anointed* to the work of salvation, till thirty years after his *coming in the flesh*.

The Doctor asserts that " there is no trace in this epistle " of any more than one heresy." He might as well say, that there is no trace of any more than one *antichrist*. In what sense does John say, chap. ii. 18. that there are *many antichrists?* Whether is it most natural to understand this language of a number of individuals of one heretical class, or of different heresies ? If we are to prefer the former sense, these words, ver. 18. *Ye have heard that antichrist shall come,* must respect one person only.

Our author, indeed, is not very consistent with himself, in his account of the design of the inspired writer. For he informs us that " the denial of the human nature of " Christ was the only heresy that gave him any alarm." Yet he attempts to prove that he was no less alarmed at the denial of Jesus being the Christ. But these were different heresies, though they had one general name. They were even opposed to each other ; so that he, who, in our author's sense, denied that Jesus was the Christ, did so, because he considered Jesus as one Person, and Christ as another.

The Doctor wishes it to appear that John had no respect to Ebionites, in what he says of *false prophets, antichrists,* &c. He particularly quotes chap. ii. 22. *Who is a liar, but he that denieth that Jefus is the Chrift ?* underftanding thefe words of the Gnoftics, who held that *Chrift* was one being, and *Jefus* another *. But the difference between Gnoftics and Ebionites as to the perfon of Chrift, was very trifling. Both the early Gnoftics and they believed that Jefus was a mere man. Both denied the miraculous conception Both held that there was nothing fupernatural about Jefus, till after his baptifm. They agreed in affer-ting that then the *Chrift* defcended upon him, in the form of a dove. By this name the Gnoftics called the Spirit †. Both believed that this defcent was the only fource of the miraculous powers of Jefus. Both denied a perfonal union between the *Logos* and the human nature. Modern Unita-rians wifh it to be believed, that their predeceffors confider-ed the *Logos* or *Spirit*, as a mere power or attribute. But we fhall afterwards fhew that they, as really as the Gnoftics, believed that the *Chrift* pre-exifted. It has been generally thought that the Ebionites extended the name *Chrift* to the man Jefus, whereas the Gnoftics did not. But this opinion feems to have been formed merely from the filence of an-cient writers; as the principles of the Ebionites have not been fo fully explained as thofe of the Gnoftics. Let us, however, fuppofe it to be true that they differed in this re-fpect, can it thence be rationally inferred that the latter were accounted heretics, while the former, notwithftanding their conformity in other refpects, paffed for genuine Chri-ftians ? The Gnoftics believed in him, whom they thus de-fcribed, as the true Meffiah. It is, therefore, inconceivable that John fhould condemn the one, and juftify the other; that he fhould reft the truth of a profeffion of Chriftianity on fo flight a difference.

It is far more natural to think that thefe words, *Who is*

a

* Ibid. p. 199.

† Epiphanii Haer. 28. fect. i. p. 110. Haer. 30. fect. xiv. p. 138.

a liar, &c. reſpect the denial of ſuch a Chriſt as had been promiſed. Now, what was the great character of this Meſſiah? Was it, that at his baptiſm the Spirit ſhould reſt upon him, in which both Gnoſtics and Ebionites agreed? This was the leaſt part of his qualification. The apoſtle explains his meaning in the words immediately following, ſhewing that he eſpecially referred to the eſſence of this Perſon. *He is antichriſt, that denieth the Father and the Son.* Was the Gnoſtic an *antichriſt,* becauſe he did not extend the name *Chriſt* to the man Jeſus? And did the Ebionite deſerve a better name, who denied that Jeſus had any natural father but Joſeph? Such a denial of the *Chriſt,* or *Meſſiah,* is evidently meant, as implies a rejection of the firſt Perſon in the character of a Father, and of the ſecond in that of a Son.

But the Doctor has diſcovered, that even the language uſed with reſpect to the ſonſhip of Chriſt refers to Gnoſtics. As they " maintained," he ſays, " that *Jeſus* and the *Chriſt* " were different perſons, the latter having come from hea- " ven, and being the Son of God, whereas Jeſus was the " Son of man only, the expreſſion of *Jeſus being the Son of* " *God* is as directly oppoſed to the doctrine of the Gnoſtics " as that of *Chriſt coming in the fleſh* *." This is a ſtrange effort of ſophiſtry. The Gnoſtics believed that *Jeſus was the Son of man only.* Therefore, John could not mean to include Ebionites. They believed, forſooth, that Jeſus was the Son of God. But in what ſenſe? Did they ſay that God was *his own Father?* That he was ſo *a Son born,* as to be *the mighty God?* Nothing of this kind is meant. They believed that he was *the Son of God,* becauſe he was *the Chriſt.* For our author aſſerts that theſe are equivalent ex- preſſions †.

There is an evident fallacy in his uſe of that expreſſion,

* Ibid. p 195.   † P. 200.

the Son of God. From the peculiar ſtructure of the ſentence, a ſtranger to Unitarian principles would ſuppoſe, that our author meant that John had extended this language to *Jeſus,* in the ſame ſenſe in which the Gnoſtics confined it to *Chriſt.* Now, he tells us that they conſidered the *Chriſt* as " having " come from heaven," referring to the ſenſe in which they underſtood the term, *Son of God,* as expreſſive of a divine nature. But when he introduces the ſame term, as extended to *Jeſus,* according to that view which he is pleaſed to aſcribe to the apoſtle, he totally changes the ſenſe. It ſignifies no- thing more than what belongs to a mere man, to one who never " came from heaven." As the " Gnoſtics maintain- " ed that *Jeſus* and *Chriſt* were different perſons," they could not conſiſtently call Jeſus *the Son of God,* or ſay that he " had come from heaven." Therefore, they were *falſe prophets, liars, heretics, antichriſts.* But how do Unitarians avoid the ſame characters? They give the compliment of the name to *Jeſus Chriſt;* but deny that he is truly the Son of God, or that he " came from heaven," either as *Jeſus,* or as *Chriſt.* They do not, like theſe heretics the Gnoſtics, believe that *Jeſus only is the Son of man.* In that very ſenſe in which the Gnoſtics uſed this term, they be- lieve nothing more concerning *Jeſus Chriſt.*

It is very evident that, in the paſſage laſt quoted (chap. ii. 22.) the weight of the apoſtle's accuſation lies in this, that the heretics alluded to, denied an eſſential relation be- tween the Father and the Son. They ſo denied the Son, as to exclude themſelves from any intereſt in the Father. Therefore it is added, ver. 23. *Whoſoever denieth the Son, the ſame hath not the Father.* But the denial of the divine nature of Chriſt is a direct attack on the Father, perſonally and paternally viewed. For he is a Father, in a proper ſenſe, ſolely in relation to his only-begotten Son.

3

That

That the apoftle here efpecially refers to the pre-exiftence and deity of the Son, without which he could not be the *Chrift*, appears in the cleareft manner from what follows. It is immediately added; *Let that, therefore, abide in you, which ye have heard from the beginning. If that which ye have heard from the beginning fhall remain in you, ye alfo fhall continue in the Son, and in the Father*, ver. 24. He exhorts them to continue in that doctrine which they had *heard from the beginning.* He feems to point out the nature of this doctrine, by an allufion to the very terms in which he had expreffed it in his introduction : *That which was from the beginning, which we have heard*, &c. Allufions of this kind, even where the fenfe of the terms is varied, are very common with Hebrew writers. Having given the defignation of *eternal life* to the Perfon whom he had thus defcribed, he alludes to this very defignation, by declaring the effect of their continuance in the doctrine concerning him ; *And this is the promife that he hath promifed us, even eternal life*, ver. 25. He then fays ; *Thefe things have I written unto you concerning them that feduce you*, ver. 26. to fhew that the feducers, whom he had chiefly in his eye, were fuch as denied that the Son was *that eternal life which was with the Father.*

In the profecution of the fame defign, after declaring their fecurity for *abiding in him*, as the object of their faith, and exhorting them to the exercife of this grace, he breaks out in the language of admiration at the great honour conferred on Chriftians, in confequence of their union to a divine Perfon. *Behold, what manner of love the Father hath beftowed on us, that we fhould be called the fons of God! Therefore the world knoweth us not, becaufe it knew him not. Beloved, now are we the fons of God; and it doth not yet appear what we fhall be: but we know that, when he fhall appear, we fhall be like him ; for we fhall fee him as he is,* chap. iii. 1, 2. When believers are faid to be the fons of *God*, the fame divine Perfon is meant, whom *the world did not know*, who *fhall appear*, and whom they fhall *fee as he is*. There can be no doubt that the Son is meant; efpecially as it is he who is faid to *appear*, chap. ii. 28. and they who do righteoufnefs are faid to be *born*, or *begotten of him*, ver. 29. They are the fons of *God*,—*who was manifefted to take away our fins*, ver. 5. *who laid down his life for us*, ver. 16.

He alfo declares that Jefus is fo the *Chrift*, as to communicate his *unction* to others; not in the extraordinary gifts of the Spirit alone, but in thofe which are faving, and which are the privilege of all true believers, preferving them from deftructive errors, chap. ii. 20. 27. Therefore, when the apoftle fpeaks of denying that Jefus is *the Chrift*, he means a rejection of him as a divine Perfon, who had power to take away our fins meritorioufly, by laying down his life for us; and efficacioufly, by communicating to us his Spirit.

Dr P. thinks that the paffage, which we have laft confidered, " may explain what Peter meant by *denying the Lord* " *that bought them*, 2 Epif. ii. 1. as it may be fuppofed " that he meant denying *Jefus* to be the *Chrift* *." But the mode of expreffion evidently implies that it was fuch a denial of Chrift as affected the truth of his *purchafe*. It is granted that the Gnoftic doctrine terminated in this. For as they afferted that, at the time of the fuffering of Jefus, the Chrift left him, and afcended into heaven, it neceffarily follows that he had not power to pay the price of our redemption. But did not thofe, equally, at leaft, *deny the Lord that bought them*, who denied that Jefus Chrift was ever more than man, and that he had any power, or indeed, any defign to purchafe the church?

He

* Ibid. p. 200.

He alſo quotes 1 John v. 5. *Who is he that overcometh the world, but he that believeth that Jeſus is the Son of God?* The apoſtle expreſſes himſelf differently, ver. 1. *Whoſoever believeth that Jeſus is the Chriſt, is born of God.* Theſe expreſſions our author accounts equivalent. But the faith here deſcribed is not a faith merely reſpecting his miſſion, but directly terminating upon his Perſon. It hath Chriſt for its proper object. It is *believing on the Son of God,* ver. 10. for *eternal life,* ver. 11. a faith apprehending this life in the Son, as what can be had in him only, ver. 12. It is *believing on the name of the Son of God,* ver. 13 It is a confidence in him as the object, and the hearer, of prayer, as one whoſe will muſt regulate all our petitions, and who in a ſovereign manner grants them when thus regulated. *And this is the confidence that we have in him, that if we aſk any thing according to his will, he heareth us. And if we know that he hear us, whatſoever we aſk, we know that we have the petitions that we deſired of him,* ver. 14, 15. If Jeſus be not the Son of God, as having the ſame nature with his Father, and yet the object of ſuch a faith ; while a plurality of perſons is diſcarded, creature-worſhip is introduced.

The faith meant as effectually excludes Unitarians, as it did Gnoſtics. For one great deſign of this epiſtle is to declare the work of the Son of God. Were it true that the apoſtle had laboured ſo much to prove the truth of his humanity, would he have done it without any proper end? Our Lord aſſumed real human nature, that in this he might obey and ſatisfy for us. Indeed, the doctrine of atonement runs through the whole of this epiſtle. The apoſtle teſtifies that *the blood of Jeſus Chriſt his* (God's) *Son, cleanſeth us from all ſin,* or, to read it more elegantly, according to the Socinian view, *The blood of Jeſus Chriſt the Chriſt cleanſeth us,* &c. chap. i. 7. He proclaims him a *the propitiation for our ſins,* and on this foundation as the *advocate,* chap. 11. 1, 2.

Thence,

Thence, alfo, he declares *the forgivenefs* of fins *for his name's fake*, ver. 12. He teftifies, as has been feen, that God was manifefted for *taking away our fins*, chap. iii. 5. and that he *gave his life for us*, or *in our ftead*, ver. 16. Did God *give his only-begotten Son?* It was *that we might live through him*, that he might *be the propitiation for our fins*, *the Saviour of the world*, chap. iv. 9, 10. 14.

When the apoftle afferts that Jefus *came by water and blood*, chap. v. 6. it undoubtedly implies that he came in real flefh. But this is afferted only in fubferviency to the great end of his affuming our nature. The language feems to be of the fame import with that which John ufes in his Gofpel, chap. xix. 34. But why fuch particularity, if merely to affure us of the truth of the human nature, efpecially as it does not feem to have been denied by many of the Gnoftics when this epiftle was written? But by the ufe of this language he fhews, that the ceremonial law had its completion in Chrift, and that we receive both pardon and fanctification through him. Thus he teftifies that *the fountain* was really *opened for fin, and for uncleannefs.* If we can believe that the water and blood, by which Chrift came, were meant merely to prove the truth of his humanity, we become Gnoftics indeed. We fuppofe the God of the Jews to have been an evil being, who oppreffed his people with an intolerable yoke of bondage, without any advantage, either to themfelves, or to us; who afflicted them, not for their *profit*, but for his *pleafure*.

If it be fuppofed that *the water* refpects the baptifm of Chrift, the doctrine has the fame tendency. The Gnoftics in fome fenfe granted that *the Son of God came by water;* as they faid that the *Logos* defcended on the man Jefus at his baptifm. But, even in that early age, they denied that *the Son of God came by blood*. For they afferted that the Logos left Jefus, when he was about to fuffer. But according

ding

ding to the apoſtle, he *came*, not only as *the Chriſt*, as one *anointed*, but as *Jeſus, who* ſhould, by his death, *ſave his people from their ſins.* He ſays of *the Spirit, the water, and the blood,* that as witneſſes *they agree in one,* ver. 8. becauſe they all teſtify that *eternal life* is *in the Son of God.* The *water*, or his baptiſm, *bears witneſs*, becauſe it ſhews his divine call to the work of ſalvation. The *blood* does the ſame. For it teſtifies the truth of his purchaſe of this bleſſing; as thereby it appears that *he laid down his life for us*, chap. iii. 16. The Spirit agrees with both. For he applies the blood of Chriſt to the ſoul, and witneſſes within believers that they are the ſons of God, making them to *know that they have eternal life*, ver. 13. Therefore, the apoſtle ſays, *He that believeth on the Son of God hath the witneſs in himſelf*, ver. 10. But his doctrine oppoſes Unitarians, ancient and modern, as directly as Gnoſtics; becauſe of their denying the efficacy of his death.

The deity of the Word is expreſsly declared ver. 7. But I ſhall not enter on the proof from this verſe; as the various objections to its authenticity would lead me into too wide a field of controverſy *.

When the apoſtle ſums up this epiſtle, he thus expreſſes the great deſign of it : *Theſe things have I written unto you that believe on the name of the Son of God, that ye may know that ye have eternal life, and that ye may believe on the name of the Son of God*, ver. 13. Thoſe to whom he wrote already *believed on the name of the Son of God.* They did not merely receive the teſtimony which he gave. But they relied *on* him, perſonally conſidered, as a ſure ground of confidence for ſalvation. Nor was this all. They believed that he was the proper Son of God, and relied *on* him in this character. For *believing on the name* undoubtedly de-

notes

---

* See Martin's Critical Diſſertation on this verſe, and his reply to Emlyn.

notes the particular refpect that faith has to its object, according to the *denomination* particularly fpecified.

But as John had previoufly declared that they were expofed to danger from *feducers,* the manner in which he expreffes his defign in writing points out the nature of that heretical doctrine which gave him moft alarm. He wrote *that they might know that they had eternal life.* This clearly implies that the doctrine of the *feducers,* whom he oppofed, tended to deprive them of this 'great and comprehenfive bleffing. It cannot be fuppofed, that he refers to any who directly denied the eternal ftate. Even the Gnoftics, who difbelieved the refurrection of the body, acknowledged the eternal exiftence of the foul. Therefore, they could no more be faid to deny *eternal life,* than thofe in our day who, going to the other extreme, believe the eternal exiftence of the body alone. The apoftle certainly refers to the natural confequence of the doctrine of thofe heretics whom he has in his eye. The connexion of the different parts of the verfe, and of the whole with the context, nay, with the general tenor of the epiftle, determines the nature of their great and leading error. They denied that Jefus Chrift was *the Son of God,* that is, that he was *that eternal life which was with the Father.* They reprefented him as a mere man, who, therefore, could have neither power nor right to communicate *eternal life* to others, becaufe he needed to receive this bleffing for himfelf. They alfo denied the merit of his fufferings, and the whole defign of his *coming by water and blood.*

How might thefe Chriftians *know that they had eternal life?* The apoftle fhews that this *knowledge* naturally flows from faith *on the Son of God.* For he had faid immediately before; *This life is in his Son. He that hath the Son hath life,* ver. 11, 12. They had the Son as the object of their faith. They were united to him, as Godman. Therefore,

they

they might be affured that they had eternal life; becauſe it is *in* him, he being eſſentially the fountain of life, and thence infinitely fit to be the repoſitory of it, as Mediator, in conſequence of purchaſing it by his blood. Thus, if we allow the inſpired apoſtle himſelf to declare his deſign in writing, we may be aſſured that it was eſpecially to eſtabliſh Chriſtians in the faith of theſe two great doctrines, which Unitarians have ſtill denied, the Deity of ·Chriſt, and a real Atonement for ſin, as including the purchaſe of eternal life.

He adds; *And that ye may believe on the name of the Son of God,* aſſigning this as another reaſon for writing. Though they already believed, his writing was not, in this reſpect, vain labour. For as they could only be aſſured of eternal life, in conſequence of believing in Chriſt as *the Son of God,* or a divine Perſon; he ſhews that their continued intereſt in that bleſſing was inſeparably connected with perſeverance in this very faith. They were ſtill to rely *on the Son of God.* It was alſo his deſign to confirm their faith in this reſpect. The connexion between theſe two, *that ye may know,* and *that ye may believe,* ſhews that the degree of their aſſurance as to an intereſt in eternal life would be in proportion to the ſtrength of their faith in Chriſt as *the Son of God,* and reliance on him in this character. For the more firmly that this great doctrine is *believed with the heart,* the more certain we are of the ſecurity of our foundation for eternity. Therefore, as they already conſidered the Son of God as the object of prayer, he proceeds to urge the neceſſity of aſſurance as to the enjoyment of all theſe bleſſings *aſked* of him, *according to his will,* ver. 14, 15. To encourage them ſtill more to perſevere, and to make progreſs in this faith, he declares that their prayers for eternal life, even in behalf of others, would be heard and anſwered by Chriſt; if theſe were the

fruit

fruit of confidence in him as *the Son of God*, ver. 16. *If any man fee his brother fin a fin which is not unto death, he fhall afk, and he fhall give him life for them that fin not unto death.*

What he has obferved with refpect to this fin, leads him to fpeak of that *which is unto death.* Then he declares his own affurance, and that of his brethren, as to prefervation from this fin; their affurance of a fpiritual birth, as oppofed to the miferable ftate of the world; and finally, returning to his principal fubject, he declares their affurance with refpect to the coming of the Son of God in our nature, and an intereft in him, compendioufly expreffing the fubftance of that doctrine which he has delivered concerning him, in the preceding part of the epiftle; *And we know that the Son of God is come, and hath given us an underftanding that we may know him that is true; and we are in him, that is true,* even *in his Son Jefus Chrift. This is the true God, and eternal life,* ver. 20. The firft expreffion in which we have the word αληθινος, *true*, feems to refer to the Father. The fecond may be underftood of the Son, as well as the laft propofition in the verfe. Socinians, indeed, apply the whole to the Father. They plead that the pofition of the article before the words *true God*, fhews that he is meant to whom the name moft perfectly belongs *. But that this name does not as perfectly belong to the Son as to the Father, they have yet to prove. It is well known, however, that the ufe of the article, in conjunction with the word Θεος *God*, is no certain argument. It is fometimes thus ufed to denote the falfe deities of the heathen, Acts vii. 43. xiv. 11, *&c.* Sometimes, the true God is mentioned without the article, Matt. iv. 4. v. 9. Sometimes, the name is given to Chrift with the article, Tit. ii.

13.

---

* Volkel. lib. v. c. 10.

13. Heb. i. 8. ·Socinus himſelf acknowledges that this rule is not univerſal in the Greek language.

Here we have the demonſtrative pronoun ꝗτος *this;* the proper uſe of which is to point out what is preſent, either to the ſenſes, or to the mind. It does not, indeed, invariably refer to what is laſt mentioned, but ſometimes to the principal ſubjeƈt of diſcourſe. But when the principal ſubjeƈt is that laſt mentioned, there can be no doubt as to the reference of the demonſtrative. Now, Chriſt is not only the ſubjeƈt immediately mentioned, but that of the whole epiſtle *.

The Socinian view charges the apoſtle with the moſt unmeaning tautology. For he is not only ſuppoſed to give the Father the denomination of *true* in the two preceding clauſes, but to repeat it a third time. As the truth of his deity is ſaid to be ſtill meant, the third declaration muſt be equivalent to an aſſertion, that " the true God is the true " God." For ꝗτος always reſpeƈts its ſubjeƈt according to the deſcription preceding.

But Socinians not only attempt to tear away the demonſtrative from its proper and natural ſubjeƈt, but entirely to change the ſenſe of the prepoſition εv. They cannot refuſe that theſe words, " We are *in* him that is true," are properly tranſlated. But becauſe the Saviour hath too much honour, if the ſame prepoſition bear this ſenſe in the following clauſe, they contend that ıt ſhould be rendered *by;* as ſignifying that we are united to the true God by his Son †. This prepoſition is uſed, in the New Teſtament, in the ſenſe of δια *by,* in two or three places. But it never occurs in two different ſenſes in the ſame paſſage; and as far as we can obſerve, it is never uſed in this ſenſe by John. It would certainly have been the moſt improper occaſion

he

he could have chofen for ufing a term, which could not exprefs his meaning, unlefs its ordinary and proper fenfe were
rejected, when guarding thofe to whom he wrote againft
idolatry, and according to Socinians, exclufively afferting
the deity of the Father. For, if here underftood in its natural fenfe, it certainly denotes that believers are in the
Son, in the fame refpects in which they are in the Father.

But as they cannot, by all their attempts on this paffage
itfelf, fufficiently obfcure the evidence arifing from it, they
find it neceffary to call in another, as an auxiliary. Thus
Dr P. fays that this language " may be confidered as an allu-
" fion to the words of Chrift addreffed to the Father, and re-
" corded by this very apoftle, John xvii. 3. *This is life eter-*
" *nal that they might know thee, the only true God, and Jefus*
" *Chrift, whom thou haft fent *.*" This exception hath been
often anfwered. But our author does not take the leaft notice of any thing that has been offered in reply.

The very fcripture introduced to prove the exclufion of
Jefus from the character here given him, defeats the defign
of its introduction. For it fhews that *eternal life* does not
confift in the knowledge of the Father only. Therefore,
this, as a perfonal defignation, cannot, in the epiftle, be
meant exclufively of him. Socinus himfelf was fenfible of
this. Therefore he applies it to the Son †.

It is alfo evident, from the handle now made of this text,
that Socinians have changed their ideas of Deity. For the
Polifh divines, while they faid that the true God was here
oppofed to idols, acknowledged that Chrift was a true, and
not an imaginary God ‡. According to this doctrine, there
muft either be more true Gods than one ; or Chrift muft be

one

* Ibid. p. 33.   † Refpons. ad Bujek. cap. 8.

‡ Non diffitemur quidem, Chriftum verum et nequaquam imaginarium
Deum effe. Volkel. l. 5. c. 10. p. 423. ap. Hoornbeck Socin. Confut.
vol. ii. p. 86.   3

one with the Father   But their ſucceſſors deny the Deity of the Son in every ſenſe of the word. What, then, can we think of a faith that changes the very object of worſhip in the courſe of a century or two?

Dr P. adds: " Without this interpretation, theſe two " texts would flatly contradict one another; for how can " the Father be *the only true God,* if the Son be true God " alſo * ?" But even ſuppoſing that John refers to the Son, he does not ſpeak of a *true God* different from him whom Jeſus addreſſes in this character; but of him who is eſſentially the ſame. For our Lord ſays; *I am not alone ; but I and the Father that ſent me,* John viii. 16. *He that hath ſeen me, hath ſeen the Father. Believe me, that I am in the Father, and the Father in me,* chap. xiv. 9. 11. It is evident that our Lord, in his interceſſory prayer, does not contraſt himſelf with the Father, as if he had no claim to the character of *the only true God.* For by the ſame rule of interpretation, it might be denied that the Father is omniſcient, becauſe it is ſaid that the Son *had a name that no one knew but he himſelf,* Rev. xix. 12.

It muſt alſo be obſerved that the character *only* does not belong to the ſubject *thee,* but to the predicate *true God.* For the article τον precedes μονον, diſtinguiſhing the ſubject from the predicate. Thus the expreſſion does not ſignify that *the Father only* is *the true God,* but that *the Father* is *the only true God;* not as oppoſed to the Son, but to all falſe deities †. But it deſerves our attention, that the Socinians, in all their cavils at particular paſſages, as underſtood of the deity of Chriſt, proceed on a *petitio principii,* by ſtill taking it for granted that there cannot be a plurality of perſons, without a plurality of gods. Thence they aſſume it as unqueſtionable, that the Son cannot be called *the only true God,* without denying this character to the Father.

But

---

* Fam. Illuſtr. ibid.   † Vid. Lampe in loc.

But even according to their own expofition of the language of John, they leave too much to Chrift, for a mere man; when they grant that he *gives an underſtanding that we may know him that is true.* For. this does not merely, or even principally, fignify a communication of the outward means of light; but of real internal light. For this is oppofed to the underſtanding as *darkened,* Eph. iv. 18. where the fame word (διανοια) is ufed. It is diſtinct from, and fubfequent to, the work of the Spirit, as giving outward revelation, Eph. i. 18. For how great foever *the light,* without this *the darkneſs* will *not comprehend it,* John, i. 5. God alone can give this *underſtanding,* Eph. i. 18, 19. Heb. viii. 10. x. 16. It is *God who commanded the light to ſhine out of darkneſs,* who *ſhines in our hearts,* 2 Cor. iv. 6.

They alfo grant that Jefus *gives eternal life,* according to John xvii. 2. If fo, he gives God himfelf. For *the* true *God* is *eternal life.* But can a mere creature have the true God at his difpofal?

But however inconfiftent Unitarians are, we may be affured that the infpired writer is confiftent with himfelf. Dr P. cannot refufe that, in his introduction, he gives the character, *Eternal Life,* to the Son. And fhall we fuppofe that he robs him of it, in the conclufion. This would, indeed, be a ftriking inftance of the art of finking. But the apoftle carries his original idea through the epiftle. Thus he fays, chap. ii. 13. *I write unto you, fathers, becauſe ye have known him that is from the beginning.* He repeats the fame great truth, ver. 14. to imprefs it more deeply. There can be no doubt that he alludes to what he had faid in his introduction. For he adds another character which he had there given of the fame glorious Perfon; *I have written unto you, young men, becauſe ye are ſtrong, and the Logos of God abideth in you.* In ver. 20. he calls him *the Holy One.* But this is a peculiar defignation of the true God. In chap.

iii.

iii. 24. he shews that the Son of God *abideth in* him *that keepeth his commandments,* and that it belongs to him to give the Spirit.

The apostle concludes his epistle with these words, *Little children, keep yourselves from idols.* As *the true God* is here opposed to *idols,* it hath been objected that " we have no " instance of this with respect to Christ." Though this were true, it would not prove that he is not God. But the assertion is contrary to fact. For in 1 Cor. viii. 6. he is opposed, equally with the Father, to idols : *To us there is but one God the Father,—and one Lord Jesus Christ.* Here the apostle is directly treating of false gods. These words, Heb. i. 6. *Let all the angels of God worship him,* are generally supposed to be taken from Psal. xcvii. 7. *Worship him all ye gods.* There, the object of worship is directly opposed to *graven images* and *idols.*

It seems to be generally thought that Cerinthus was cotemporary with the apostles. Theodoret has asserted that this heretic urged the worship of angels * : and it has been supposed that Paul opposes his doctrine, Col. ii. 18. Mosheim says that Cerinthus required of his followers, that they should worship the Supreme God in conjunction with the Son †. He does not give his authority for this assertion. But it is probable, from what has been ascribed to this heretic, with respect to the worship of angels. As he undoubtedly considered the Son as inferior to the Father, John might add this exhortation, because those who worshipped Christ, but not as God supreme, really made him an idol. By connecting this exhortation with a declaration of the true Deity of Christ, he shews that he is the object of worship on this foundation only. In this view, his exhortation seems far more natural, than when understood as directed against idol-worship in general, or against the Nicolaitans, who ur-

* Comment. in Epist. Paulin. p. 355. ap. Ittig. de Hæres. p. 52.
† Hist. Cent. 1. part ii. c. 5. vol. i. p. 145.

ged the eating of idolothytes. For he does not once refer to either of thefe in the preceding part of the epiftle.

I fhall only add, that I am much inclined to think that the apoftle, in the ufe of the word αληθινος *true*, ver. 20. primarily refers to the *truth or faithfulnefs* of God, as bearing witnefs concerning his Son. It cannot be refufed that a confiderable part of the chapter relates to this. The apoftle, when fpeaking of the teftimony of the Spirit, ver. 6. had afferted that he is αληθεια *truth*. He had fpoken of *the witnefs of God* as *greater* than that of man, ver. 9. and declared the heinous iniquity of thofe who rejeﬔ it, ver. 10. *He that believeth not God hath made him a liar.* He had particularly declared the great fubjeﬔ of this teftimony, ver. 11. *This is the record, that God hath given to us eternal life, and this life is in his Son.* As in ver. 20. he fpeaks of *the Son* as *eternal life*, it is very natural to think that he would allude to his atteftation in this charaﬔer. This verfe, indeed, feems to be a compend of all that he has faid direﬔly on the fubjeﬔ, from the fifth verfe downward; of the *coming of the Son of God*, ver. 5, 6. of the *veracity* of God the Father as a witnefs, ver. 9—11. of the *union* of believers to Chrift, ver. 12. of his *Deity*, as he is the objeﬔ of faith and of prayer, ver. 13.—15. and of *eternal life* as *in* him, and difpenfed *by* him, ver. 11, 12, 13. 16. Thus, the apoftle fhews whence fome believe the divine record, while others rejeﬔ it, *making God a liar. The Son hath given them an underftanding that they may know him that is true*, that is, that they may know God as *faithful*. By this gift, he unites them to himfelf, as infinitely worthy of their truft. *And we are in him that is true, in his Son Jefus Chrift.* The charaﬔer αληθινος *true*, is familiar with this infpired writer, as denoting the Son. It occurs in the fame form as here, without any fubftantive, Rev. iii. 7. *He that is true;* and chap. xix. 11. *He is called faithful and true;* and he is fo

called

called as *The Word of God*, ver. 13. The apoſtle, having
aſcribed to the Son that *truth* which, in this place, is evidently
appropriated to God as an eſſential perfection, makes a natural tranſition to the univerſal *truth* of his eſſence as God.
He does not change his idea. He only extends it. For
the veracity of God in a fœderal character flows from the
truth of his eſſence. It is becauſe he is God, that he *changes
not*, that he *cannot lie*. The ſecurity of thoſe who are *in*
the Son, with reſpect to *eternal life*, is at the ſame time declared. *This is the true God, and eternal life.*

This view of the paſſage affords a ſtrong collateral proof
of the authenticity of the ſeventh verſe. For the veracity
of the Spirit, as a witneſs, having been already declared,
we have here a declaration of the veracity of the Father,
and of the Word. Thus, we have a particular atteſtation
of the faithfulneſs of each of *the Three that bear record in
heaven.*

C H A P. III.

*Additional Evidence, from the New Teſtament, of Chriſt
being the Logos.*

AS a proof of the juſtneſs of that view which has
been given of the term *Logos*, it may not be improper
to mention ſome other paſſages of the New Teſtament, in
which it evidently occurs in the ſame ſenſe. John, undoubtedly, had a peculiar pleaſure in the uſe of this term.
For, not to mention ſome other places, where, as ſome
apprehend, he uſes it as a perſonal character, there is one,
the application of which adverſaries themſelves cannot deny.
This is Rev. xix. 12, 13.

They

They confider it as an eafy matter to underſtand the meaning of this name. But the Spirit of God certainly leaves it as a myſtery. *He had a name written that no one knew but he himſelf.* Is this name unknown as to the very expreſſion? It will not be faid that this is meant. For the divine expreſſes it in the next verfe, *His name is called, The Word of God.* How, then, is it unknown? Undoubtedly, as to' its full import, and the myſtery contained in it. For it may be underſtood as referring to his ineffable generation, to his being in the Father, and alfo to his official charaĉter, as he is both the Father's Counfellor, and his Interpreter. In whichfoever of thefe lights it be viewed, it exceeds our comprehenfion. There feems to be an allufion to the reply given by this illuſtrious Perfon to Manoah; *Wherefore aſkeſt thou after my Name, feeing it is wonderful?* Judg. xiii. 18. Some apprehend that there is alfo a reference to the words of Agur, Prov. xxx. 4. *What is his Name, and what is his Son's Name, if thou canſt tell*?* Socinians, indeed, evidently think far more of their wifdom, than Agur did of his. For they are not at a lofs to tell the full import of the Name of the Son and Word of God.

It deferves our notice, however, that Dr P. in another work, makes the following acknowledgment: " The rea- " fon why John calls Chriſt *the Word of God,* was probably " his feeing that name or title written upon his thigh, in " the Revelation, which is fuppofed to have been written " before his Gofpel †." He is here fpeaking of the intro- duĉtion to the Gofpel. When thefe *illuſtrations* were pu- bliſhed, he preferred the other fenfe of the term *Logos,* as denoting an attribute. But he was not fo fully fatisfied that it could bear this fenfe only. Elfe, why did he give a reafon, which appeared to him *probable,* for its being ufed as a perfonal charaĉter? He alfo fays, " Chriſt being called

" *the*

---

* Vid. Vitring. in Apoc. xix. 12.   † Famil. Illuſtr. p. 32.

" *the Word of God*, on account of his being in a more emi-
" nent manner commiſſioned to declare the will of God,
" they (ſome Chriſtians in John's time) imagined that he
" was meant in many paſſages of the Old Teſtament, in
" which mention is made of the *Word of God.*" For he
acknowledges, that it is " an opinion which is known to
" have prevailed in his time, that the Spirit which animated
" Chriſt, having pre-exiſted, was that Being who formed this
· " world *."

Here are ſeveral important conceſſions : Firſt, that it was
an opinion which prevailed in the time of John, that Chriſt
pre-exiſted : Secondly, that thoſe who embraced this opinion
believed that, in many paſſages of the Old Teſtament, he
was called the *Word :* Thirdly, that he certainly bears this
name in the New Teſtament : and that John gave him this
name, *probably* becauſe he, in the Revelation, ſaw it written
on his thigh. Now did we uſe the ſame freedom with *pro-*
bability, which our author often does, we would deduce from
it *certain* concluſions. And it would naturally occur ; Firſt,
that the uſe of this term by John, as a perſonal character, was
a confirmation of that prevailing opinion ; Secondly, that he
would uſe it in no other ſenſe than that in which it was revealed to him, as ſuſtained by his Lord, that is, as a perſonal name.

The Doctor however ſays ; " In contradiſtinction to all
" this, the apoſtle here aſſerts, that by the *Word of God*,
" we are not to underſtand any Being diſtinct from God."
What believer in the Trinity ever ſuppoſed this ? *The*
dream be to them that hate our Lord, *and the interpretation*
to his enemies ! But Socinians ſtill falſely aſſume, that a diſtinction of perſons neceſſarily implies a diverſity of being.
With them, this is equivalent to the idea of a perſon diſtinct
from the Father. But if it was John's deſign to ſhew that
the Word was only an attribute, there was not merely a

contra-

* Ibid. p. 31.

contradiſtinction to that " opinion which is known to have
" prevailed," but a *contradiction* to that Revelation with
which he was himſelf favoured. If the Revelation was
written before the Goſpel, how did that which was a Perſon,
when the former was penned, dwindle into a mere attribute
before the date of the latter?

But John is not the only inſpired writer, in the New
Teſtament, who gives this name to Chriſt. Luke ſpeaks of
thoſe who *from the beginning were eye-witneſſes, and miniſters of the Word*, chap. i. 2. In calling them *eye-witneſſes*,
he has evidently the ſame meaning as John, when he ſays;
*That which we have ſeen with our eyes, which we have look-
ed upon,—of the Word of life*, &c. 1 Epiſt. i. 1. How
could they be *eye-witneſſes* of the Word, or *look upon* it, as
preached? The term υπηρεται, rendered *miniſters*, neceſſarily
ſuppoſes a perſonal character in conſtruction with it ; according to its conſtant uſe in the New Teſtament, referring to
the ſuperior who is ſerved, and not to the thing about which
their ſervice is engaged.

In this ſenſe alſo it ſeems to be uſed by Paul, as his language is recorded by the ſame inſpired writer, Acts xx. 32.
*Now, brethren, I commend you to God, and to the Word of
his grace, which is able to build you up, and to give you an
inheritance among all them who are ſanctified.* This language
may be viewed as denoting Chriſt. For he is joined with
God, that is, the Father, in a certain external operation. It
properly belongs to a Perſon, to build up, and to give an
inheritance. The uſe of the term παρατιθεμαι favours this
ſenſe. It denotes the commitment or commendation of a
perſon or thing to the care of another ; as it is uſed, Luke
xxiii. 46. Acts xiv. 23. 1 Pet. iv. 19. The Goſpel is ſaid
to be *commended* or *committed* to men, 2 Tim. ii. 2· but no
where elſe are men ſaid to be commended to it. Chriſt,
may well be called *the Word of* the *grace* of God. For as
the Word made fleſh, he is *full of grace*.

Various

Various reaſons have been given by learned interpreters, for underſtanding the inſpired writer to the Hebrews as ſpeaking of Chriſt, under the character of *the Word of God.* chap. iv. 12, 13. They have argued from his aim in this epiſtle, which was, as far as he lawfully could, to accommodate himſelf to the ideas and modes of expreſſion common amongſt thoſe to whom he wrote. They have alſo urged his ſpecial deſign in introducing the *Logos* here, in what ſenſe ſoever it be underſtood. He evidently means to alarm thoſe to whom he addreſſes himſelf, and, according to the general ſcope of the epiſtle, to illuſtrate the unſpeakable danger of rejecting or departing from Jeſus Chriſt, whom he, in the preceding chapter, calls *the living God.* Now, the propriety of introducing the character under conſideration, appears from the uſe of it elſewhere. For Chriſt is thus denominated, in relation to the judgments which he executes on the enemies of the Goſpel. For when his name is declared to be *The Word of God,* he appears *clothed in a veſture dipped in blood,* and *out of his mouth goeth a ſharp ſword, that with it he ſhould ſmite the nations,* Rev. xix. 13. 15.

The connexion confirms this view. A Perſon is referred to, ver. 13. *Neither is there any creature that is not manifeſt in his ſight : but all things are naked and opened unto the eyes of him with whom we have to do.* That the Perſon referred to is Chriſt, appears from the laſt words of this verſe, προς ον ημιν ο λογος. If, with ſome tranſlators, we render the expreſſion, *of whom our diſcourſe is;* they can be underſtood of him only. For he is the great ſubject of the epiſtle. If, according to our verſion; the inference is the ſame. If we underſtand them as reſpecting the preſent ſtate, they muſt relate to him. For *all power is given* unto him *in heaven, and in earth ;* and he is the immediate object of our faith. If we view them as referring to judgment, and render them, *to whom we muſt give an account,* which many reckon the proper tranſlation ; ſtill they peculiarly reſpect him. For *the Father judgeth no man, but hath committed all judgment to the Son.* Beſides, the relative *his* is cloſely connected with *The Word of God* as its antecedent : and it is unnatural to apply it to any other. Thus the Word is ſaid to be *a diſcerner of the thoughts and intents of the heart,* becauſe *there is not any creature that is not manifeſt in his ſight.* The inference in ver. 14. *Seeing, then, that we have a great High Prieſt,* &c. is thought to confirm this view ; as the argument would be weakened by the intro- duction of a ſubject eſſentially different.

The attributes of this Word are ſtrictly applicable to Chriſt. It is ζων, *living.* This cannot properly be ſaid of the word of revelation itſelf, which is only the mean of the communi- cation of life. But Jeſus claims this character. *I am, ο ζων, the living One,* Rev. i. 18. He is *the Word of life,* 1 John i. 1. a character which Dr P. himſelf can apply to no other. We have ſeen that no other can be meant, when it is ſaid *In him was life.*

This Word is ενεργης, *powerful.* The expreſſion unqueſtion- ably applies with far more propriety to the ſource of divine energy, than to the mere inſtrument of its conveyance. The ſame Word is *ſharper,* or *more penetrating than any two-edged ſword.* It has been ſeen that this very idea is introduced in the deſcription of him whoſe *name is called, The Word of God,* Rev. xix. 13. 15. *Out of his mouth goeth a ſharp ſword.* Nay, Chriſt appropriates this character to himſelf, Iſa. xlix. 2. *He hath made my mouth like a ſharp ſword, and made me a poliſhed ſhaft.* This Word *is a diſ- cerner of the thoughts,* &c. This is elſewhere expreſsly aſſerted of Chriſt. *He knew what was in man.* He declares concerning himſelf ; *All the churches ſhall know that I am he who ſearcheth the reins and hearts,* Rev. ii. 23 *.

C H A P.

---

* Vid. Owen in loc. Glaſſii Philol. l. 1. t. 4. ſ. 3.

C H A P. IV.

The Divinity of Chrift proved from the three firft Gofpels.

OUR author, in his hiftorical works, gives himfelf no trouble with the multiplied proofs of the Divinity of our Saviour, produced from the Gofpel-hiftory. With a fingle touch of his *befom of deftruction*, he fweeps them all away ; as if no one would ever dare to offer any proofs of this doctrine from the Gofpels, or fo much as look into them for this purpofe, after he has told them that none are to be found there. " Jefus Chrift," he fays,—" made no other pre-
" tenfions," than that he was a mere man, " referring all
" his extraordinary power to God his Father :—and it is
" moft evident that the apoftles, and all thofe who converfed
" with our Lord, before and after his refurrection, confider-
" ed him in no other light than fimply as a man approved
" of God by figns and wonders which God did by him *."
—" If we look into the Gofpel-hiftory, we fhall find that
" all that our Saviour himfelf taught, or infinuated, were
" his divine miffion in general, or his being the Meffiah in
" particular, with the doctrine of the refurrection, and that
" of himfelf coming again to raife and judge the world.—
" He never told the difciples, that he had pre-exifted, or
" that he had any thing to do before he came into the
" world †." Again he fays, " If we look into the Gofpels
" and the book of Acts, we fhall find that thofe *fublime*
" *doctrines* (of the pre-exiftence and divinity of Chrift) as
" they (the Fathers) call them, were not taught in an early
" period. For none of the three firft Gofpels make the
" leaft

* Hift. of Cor. vol. i. p. 2.   † Hift. Earl. Op. vol. iii. p. 64.

" leaft mention of any thing in the perfon or nature of
" Chrift, fuperior to thofe of other men *."

The fuppofed filence of the three firft Evangelifts, and
of our Saviour himfelf, on the head of the Divine nature,
conftitutes the foundation of two of the chief *arguments*
urged by Dr P. *againft the divinity and pre-exiftence of
Chrift* †.

We might well be filled with aftonifhment at the audacity of thefe affertions, were not admiration itfelf incapable
of any further exertion, with refpeft to men who have
already gone the length of denying the Lord who bought
us. But as we are not difpofed implicitly to receive the
Doctor's determinations, we fhall inquire, what evidences
of the divinity of Chrift occur in the teftimonies given by
the Evangelifts? and alfo confider his own teftimony to this
purpofe, as recorded by them.

Our author efpecially fixes on the *three firft* Gofpels, as
not " making the *leaft mention* of *any thing*, in the perfon
" or nature of Chrift, fuperior to thofe of other men :" and
thefe, indeed, have not generally been viewed as containing
much evidence in fupport of this doctrine. Therefore,
they demand our particular attention. To avoid repetition,
we fhall view them in connexion.

It is granted, that the primary defign, both of our Lord,
and of his minifters, was to prove his divine miffion, as the
promifed Meffiah. This appears, not only from his difcourfes, but from the diftinct teftimonies given by the Evangelifts. For, this point being once eftablifhed, true faith
would neceffarily infer, that Jefus was juft fuch a Saviour as
the prophets foretold ; a divine Perfon, *Immanuel*, JEHOVAH,
JEHOVAH *our righteoufnefs*, JEHOVAH-ROPHI, JEHOVAH *of
hofts*, &c. With no propriety could he have been acknowledged

* Earl. Opin. vol. iii. p. 158, 159.

† Earl. Opin. vol. i. p. 10. 12. 22.

ledged as the promifed Meffiah, had he not produced the
moft decifive evidences of divinity. For the prophets had
ufed fuch language, as to exclude every one, but a divine
Perfon, from any claim to that character. Accordingly, the
very fame circumftances which proved that he was Meffiah, inconteftably proved that he was *God over all.* For,
although he acted in concurrence with the Father and Spirit,
he neverthelefs acted by his own power. Therefore, he
exprefsly informs his hearers that he could have no claim to
be received as Meffiah, unlefs he performed works properly
divine. John x. 37. *If I do not the works of my Father,*
believe me not. But befides thefe evidences of divinity that
arife from his character as Meffiah, even the three firft Gofpels afford a variety of others, of a diftinct nature, fufficient to fatisfy faith.

Jefus is defcribed as *Immanuel,* or *God with us,* Mat. i.
23. and the Evangelifts were not acquainted with fuch re-
finement of fpeech, as to fuppofe that this fhould mean *a*
mere man with us, however remarkably he might be diftinguifhed by his holinefs. Socinians have not yet dif-
proved the authenticity of this paffage ; though their batteries have been pointed againft it for many centuries.
Dr P. himfelf, in one of his treatifes, grants that it is au-
thentic ; though, fince the publication of that work, he has
clearly renounced the doctrine of the miraculous conception, as having " too much the air of *fable,*" as " an in-
" confiftent and ill-digefted ftory *." But this only verifies what is written concerning fome, that they *wax worfe*
and worfe, deceiving, and being deceived †. Indeed, he makes
fuch a handle of the doctrine, while pretending to acknowledge the authenticity of the paffage, that perhaps it was
the faireft way to reject it entirely. In his *Familiar Illu-*
ftrations, fpeaking of the name *Immanuel,* he fays ; " If
" we

* Earl. Opin. vol. iv. p. 120. 123.
† 2 Tim. iii. 13.

" we confider other inftances of names impofed by the di-
" vine direction in the fcriptures, we fhall find that they
" do not always exprefs any thing characteriftic of the per-
" fon on whom they are impofed, but that they were in-
" tended to be a memorial of fome divine promife or af-
" furance, refpecting things of a public or general con-
" cern *." To this purpofe he mentions the names of Ifaiah's
children *Shearjafhub* and *Maherfhalalhafhbaz*, Ifa. vii. 3.
viii. 1. But the Doctor does not refufe that the name
Immanuel had *fome* relation to the work that Jefus was to
perform. Therefore, it was, at leaft, in fo far " charac-
" teriftic of the perfon." But this can in no fenfe be faid
of the other names referred to. What was to be *done* by
the fons of Ifaiah? He adds; " Of Jerufalem it is faid, *This*
" *is the name wherewith fhe fhall be called, The Lord our*
" *Righteoufnefs,* (Jer. xxxiii. 16.)" But this is not in point.
For the Doctor ought to know that the literal tranflation
of thefe words is, *This* is *he who fhall call her,* or, *He, who*
fhall call her, is *the Lord,* &c.

He further fays; " In like manner the divine Being, by
" appointing Chrift to be called *Emmanuel,* engaged to
" manifeft his own prefence with his people, by protecting
" and bleffing them, and inflicting vengeance on their ene-
" mies and oppreffors. For this prediction was given up-
" on the occafion of an invafion by the Ifraelites and Sy-
" rians." Had this name been impofed upon any child
born in that age, our author might have had fome reafon
for what he fays. But what fecurity could it be to the
people of Judah, on occafion of a prefent invafion, that a
child

.* P. 28. 29. In our progrefs, we fhall frequently refer to this treatife;
becaufe the Doctor himfelf refers *his* reader to it, for " the right under-
" ftanding of thefe particulai texts," often barely mentioned in his hiftory. It would be ungenerous, then, to deprive *ours* of fo fignal a benefit.

child ſhould be born about eight hundred years afterwards, who ſhould receive the name *Immanuel;* if this was all? Had our author been expoſed to ſuch imminent danger, it may be preſumed that he would have reckoned this very poor conſolation. He makes the *ſign* to lie in God's " ap- " pointing Chriſt to be called *Immanuel.*" But neither in the prophecy, nor in the goſpel-hiſtory, have we the ex- preſs appointment of this. name ; but only a prediction of this as the event. Therefore, the ſign did not conſiſt in the appointment of the name ; nor even principally in the name itſelf; but in the miraculous circumſtance of a vir- gin bearing a ſon, and in his really being what the name denoted.

The truth of this appears from various conſiderations. The danger was ſo imminent, that extraordinary ſecurity was requiſite. Judah ſeems to have been, at this time, threatened with a total deſtruction. But the mere appoint- ment of a ſignificative name, our author himſelf being judge, would have been nothing uncommon. The manner in which the ſign was offered, ſhews that it was to be of a miraculous kind : *Aſk thee a ſign of the Lord thy God; aſk it either in the depth, or in the height above,* Iſa. vii. 11. This does not imply a verbal, but a real ſign. That which is promiſed, is made to conſiſt in the two things already mentioned : *A* VIRGIN *ſhall conceive, and bear a Son, and ſhall call his name* IMMANUEL. It is introduced with a note of wonder ; *Behold!* God claims the work as peculiarly his own ; JEHOVAH *himſelf ſhall give you a ſign.* This lan- guage undoubtedly ſignifies, that the very *giving* of this. ſign ſhould be a ſpecial and extraordinary diſplay of divine grace and power. But all theſe things the Doctor finds it moſt expedient to paſs over in ſilence.

As the promiſe of this ſign was to be the great ſupport of the faith of believers, till it ſhould be fulfilled ; as it was of

itſelf

itſelf ȏf ſuch a nature as to ſeem incredible ; it would appear that God gave them an inferior and earthly ſign, in
ſubſerviency to the other, for ſupporting their faith in the
mean time, and encouraging them confidently to expeƈt the
accompliſhment of the prediƈtion. For ver. 16. ſeems to
refer to *Shearjaſhub* : *Before* THIS *child ſhall know to refuſe
the evil, and chooſe the good, the land that thou abhorreſt ſhall
be forefaken of both her kings.* We cannot, otherwiſe, perceive any reaſon why Iſaiah was commanded by God to
take his ſon with him, a mere child, when going to meet
Ahaz. The event alſo verifies this view. For both Pe-
kah and Rezin were ſlain within two years after this declaration *.

That the name *Immanuel* is ſtriƈtly perſonal, appears
from that beautiful apoſtrophe made by JEHOVAH to him
who ſhould be thus denominated : *The Lord ſpake alſo unto
me, ſaying, The ſtretching out of his wings* (the armies of the
king of Aſſyria) *ſhall fill the breadth of thy land, O Immanuel* †. Nay, as God's ſpecial intention in announcing
this extraordinary ſign, was to aſſure his church that the
ſpiritual deliverance ſhe ſhould receive from him at a future
epoch, was her great ſecurity as to a preſent temporal deliverance ; believers, in that age, evidently conſidered it in
this light. Therefore we find them triumphantly bidding
defiance to the hoſtile nations that were leagued for their
deſtruƈtion : *Aſſociate yourſelves, O ye people, and ye ſhall be
broken in pieces ;—for God is with us* *. It would be vain to
ſay, that they refer to him only who had given them the
ſign. For their language clearly reſpeƈts that Deliverer
who was the ſign promiſed. By faith they realiſe it as preſent. They view the illuſtrious Perſonage referred to as
already in the midſt of them. And well might they do ſo.
For he it was, who had ſtill *ſaved them*, who *bare them, and
carried*

<hr />

* 2 Kin. xv. 29. 30. xvi. 9.   † Iſa. viii. 8.   ‡ Ch. viii. 9, 10.

carried them all the days of old. They view him as the Lord of Hofts, who was to be *fanctified in their hearts:* and this Lord of Hofts is that very *Immanuel* who fhould *be for a ftone of ftumbling,* ver. 13, 14. 1 Pet. ii. 8.

That this is properly a perfonal character, further appears from the connexion ftated by the Evangelift between it and the name *Jefus*, Mat. i. 21. 23. As Jofeph was commanded to call him who fhould be born *Jefus*, we are told that *all this was done, that it might be fulfilled which was fpoken by the prophet;—They fhall call his name Immanuel.* We are at the fame time informed, that his name was to be called, *Jefus, becaufe he fhould fave his people from their fins.* Therefore, either the name *Immanuel* denotes the dignity of the perfon, as qualifying him for the work of falvation, or the name *Jefus* does not denote his proper work. The one muft fignify, that he is truly *God with us;* or the other cannot fignify, that he *faves his people from their fins.* The latter cannot be a perfonal character, unlefs the former be fo too. For we are exprefsly affured, that the name *Jefus* was impofed upon him, by divine authority, to verify the prophecy; that is, as equivalent to the name *Immanuel,* and as fhewing that he was *God with—his people,* whom he was to *fave.*

Had the fign confifted in Chrift's being " appointed to be " called Immanuel," as the Doctor afferts, undoubtedly Jofeph, or Mary, would have been exprefsly commanded to give him this name. But inftead of this, the angel fays; *Thou fhalt call his name Jefus.* This indifputably proves, that the fign confifted in the *meaning* of the name, as ftrictly defcriptive of the perfon. Is it inquired; why then is it faid in Ifaiah, *She fhall call his name Immanuel?* The event fhews the import of the expreffion; and that a perfonal verb is here ufed for an imperfonal, which is very common in Scripture. Accordingly, in Matthew we have it; *They fhall call.* The Doctor, indeed, how zealous foever for our tranflation on certain occafions, adopts another reading here, though fupported only by one of Stephen's MSS. and by that of Cambridge *. But this language merely fignifies what the perfon fhould really be ; as, in Scripture, things are often faid to be *called*, when the meaning is, that they *are*, or are *manifefted to be* †. This muft be the fenfe. For there is a ftriking difference between thefe words, *They fhall call his name Immanuel*, and what follows, *She called his name Jefus*, ver. 25. That the name was fully verified in him, will afterwards appear ‡.

The Evangelifts afcribe to our Saviour *knowledge* of the *thoughts* of men. This is evidently quite different from that *difcerning of fpirits*, (1 Cor. xii. 10.) which was one of the extraordinary gifts conferred in the apoftolic age. The latter feems to have been confined, either to doctrines, or to pro- phetic oracles. Thofe, who poffeffed this gift, had a power of judging whether thefe came from God or the devil. The apoftles feem to have ufed the term *fpirit*, not as de- noting the ftate, but the doctrine of men, 1 John iv. 1. This view is offered to Socinians with a good grace, as it is that of their own Grotius. It is alfo approved by Slichting ||. It does not appear, that even the apoftles had the gift of knowing the ftates of men. Though it fhould be urged that we are to underftand the *difcerning of fpirits*, as in- cluding this, it cannot be pretended that they had this pow- er conftantly. They often admitted thofe as believers, whom they afterwards difcovered to be hypocrites. Thus did Peter *perceive*, that Simon, who formerly feemed to believe, was *in the gall of bitternefs*, Acts viii. 23. But however this gift fhould be explained, it is no where faid in the New Teftament, that any of the followers of Jefus

knew

---

* Vid. Pfeifferi Oper. Hebraic. et Exotic. N. T. loc. 2. Pfaffii Var. Lect. cap. 2. p. 205. Vitring. in Ifa. vii. 14.

† Whitby in loc.   ‡ Vid. Pearfon on the Creed, art. 2. p. 129. 130.

|| In loc.   3

knew the thoughts of men. This the Evangeliſts not only aſcribe to him, but they evidently ſpeak of it as a power which, according to their apprehenſion, he conſtantly poſ-ſeſſed *. This is alſo deſcribed as nowiſe the reſult of any ordinary means of information ; for *he needed not that any ſhould teſtify of man*, John ii. 25. or of any ſpiritual com-munication ; but as a power eſſentially belonging to Jeſus. Therefore, he is ſaid to *know in himſelf*, John vi. 61. This knowledge is alſo deſcribed as extending to all men, and to all in man. *He knew all men.----He knew what was in man*, John ii. 24, 25.

Now, the knowledge of the thoughts of man is a divine prerogative. Therefore the Pſalmiſt aſſigns this work to God; *Try me and know my thoughts.* He views it as the ſame with that of ſearching the heart, which has never been ſuppoſed to belong to any creature. For theſe words are added as exegetical of the preceding ; *Search me, O God, and know my heart*, Pſal. cxxxix. 23. The Pſalmiſt makes the ſame aſcription elſewhere, when ſuppoſing the caſe of apoſtacy from God, or ſecret idolatry ; *Shall not God ſearch this out ? for he knoweth the ſecrets of the heart*, Pſal. xliv. 20, 21. This work God expreſsly claims as his own ; *I know—their thoughts*, Iſa. lxvi. 18. Nay, on this head, he puts all crea-tures to defiance ; *Who can know it ? I* JEHOVAH *do ſearch the heart, I try the reins*, Jer. xvii. 9, 10. The faith of the Old Teſtament church correſponded with ſuch declara-tions. Therefore Solomon ſays, in his prayer at the dedi-cation of the Temple; *Thou, even thou only, knoweſt the hearts of all the children of men*, 1 Kin. viii. 39. T e Word of God, as oppoſed to every *creature*, is *a diſcerner of the thoughts and intents of the heart*, Heb. iv. 12, 13. That this is to be underſtood of his perſonal Word, we have elſe-where endeavoured to prove *. What greatly confirms this

---

* Matt. ix. 4. xii. 25. Luke v. 22. vi. 8. ix. 47. xi. 17.

† Chap. iii. p. 185. Sermons on the Heart, vol. ii. p. 319—323.

view, as it alſo ſhews in what ſenſe we are to underſtand
the many teſtimonies of this kind given by the Evangeliſts,
is the expreſs declaration of our Saviour in his exalted ſtate;
" *All the churches ſhall know that I am he who ſearcheth
the reins and hearts*, Rev. ii. 23. This language evidently
excludes any ſuperior kind of knowledge of the heart. If,
therefore, Jeſus does not know it as the Father does, he is
chargeable with that *robbery* which the Spirit of God denies, and which Socinians, in their own way, have all along
attempted to ſhow that he never *thought of.* But the knowledge, claimed by him, is preciſely of the ſame kind with
the Father's. This appears from the *end* propoſed by both
in this work. When JEHOVAH ſays, *I—do ſearch the heart,
I try the reins;* it is *even to give every man according to his
ways*, Jer. xvii. 10. When Jeſus ſays, *All the churches
ſhall know that I am he who ſearcheth the reins and hearts,*
how is it meant that his claim to this divine prerogative
ſhall be *known ?* It is by the perfect adminiſtration of juſtice. For it immediately follows; *And I will give unto
every one of you according to his works*, Rev. ii. 22. Jeſus,
therefore, diſcovers his claim to this character in the ſame
manner with the Father. He muſt, of conſequence, have
the ſame title.

God ſeems to have granted, at times, to thoſe who were
inſpired, a knowledge of the moſt ſecret *words* and *actions*
of men; as an evidence of their miſſion, and for the accompliſhment of his purpoſes of mercy or judgment. This
is evident from the hiſtory of Eliſha, with reſpect to the
king of Syria, and alſo his ſervant Gehazi. But in the
firſt inſtance, his knowledge extended to *the words* only, that were ſpoken in the king's bed-chamber, 2 Kings
vi. 12. As to the ſecond; there was nothing more
than a diſcovery of the language and conduct of Gehazi,
chap. v. 26. Thus, God hath revealed to his ſervants, as
we

we may ſay, only the *overt* acts of men. But he hath always reſerved to himſelf the knowledge of their thoughts. Nor have we an inſtance of any one of his ſervants pretending to judge of the thoughts of men, but by induction from their words or actions.

However, the reaſon of Jeſus knowing the thoughts, as given by Dr P. is his " being appointed the king and judge " of men." Therefore he " has powers given him adapted " to thoſe offices, eſpecially the knowledge of the human " heart, and the prerogative of declaring the forgiveneſs of " ſin.—We ought not therefore," he ſays, " to be ſurprized " at ſuch expreſſions as theſe, Matt. ix. 4. *And Jeſus know-* " *ing their thoughts,* John ii. 25. *He knew what was in* " *man* *." Here Dr P. ſpeaks of Chriſt's being a *king* and *judge,* as if theſe terms denoted different *offices.* As Socinians endeavour to ſink the prieſtly office in the kingly, we need not wonder that they try to make two of the latter. In this, as in many other reſpects, they reſemble the Papiſts, who, having denied that the ſecond precept of the law is diſtinct from the firſt, divide the tenth, to preſerve the number. He alſo ſeems, as far as poſſible, to diminiſh the knowledge belonging to Chriſt. He ſpeaks of " the knowledge " of the human heart." Now, in the common uſe of language, this carries a very different idea from diſcernment of thoughts. A man of ſtrong natural powers and accurate obſervation, with a conſiderable portion of experience, may be ſaid, in a limited ſenſe, to poſſeſs " the knowledge of " the human heart," while no man, in his right reaſon, would ſo much as think of ſaying, that he knew the *thoughts.* But who can blame our learned author? His ſyſtem, ſomewhat different from that of the Baptiſt, neceſſarily requires that not he, but his maſter ſhould *decreaſe.*

But

---

* *Famil. Illuſtr.* p. 22. We may, in another place, attend to what our author advances with reſpect to Chriſt's *declaring* the forgiveneſs of ſins.

But let us examine the force of the reason assigned for this knowledge, whatever be the supposed degree. It was necessary for Jesus, as " appointed the king and judge of " men." It is a power " adapted to these offices." And who can deny it? But pray, good Sir, when was he invested with these offices, and intrusted with this power? If I am not much mistaken, you and your brethren tell us on some occasions, that he received all his honour and power after his resurrection. Something very like this has escaped your own pen. " The reason why Christ was so much di- " stinguished by God the Father, is frequently and fully ex- " pressed in the scriptures, *viz.* his obedience to the will of " God, and especially in his submitting to die for the bene- " fit of mankind * "----" The *power* and *glory* which was " conferred upon Christ are expresly said to be the reward " of his obedience, and to be subsequent to his resurrec- " tion †." But if Jesus was not made a king and judge till after his resurrection, and if the knowledge of the heart be a " power adapted to these *offices*," surely he could have no occasion for it, and no title to it, before. However, if we may believe the Evangelists, Jesus *knew what was in man,* knew *the thoughts,* in his state of humiliation. That event, to which this part of the Gospel-history refers, took place near the commencement of his ministry.

But Socinians are chargeable with wonderful shuffling on this head. When pressed with the passages of scripture which ascribe essential dominion to Jesus, especially if these express the faith of believers after his exaltation, they positively assure us, that all his honour and *godlike* power are the fruit of it. On the other hand, when assailed by arguments taken from what he said and did, or from what the disciples believed, in his state of abasement, they virtually retract the former assurances, and are pleased to in-

form

* Appeal, p. 13, 14. † Famil. Illustr. p. 40, 41.

form us, that he had a great deal of honour and power, even while in *the form of a ſervant*, that is, while purchaſing this very honour and power by his obedience. There ſeems, indeed, to be a ſtudied ambiguity in our author's language; " Chriſt being appointed the *King* and *Judge* of men, *has* " powers given him adapted," &c. But the queſtion is, *Had* he theſe powers, before he was conſtituted King and Judge; or, in other words, before he had any need of them? The faƈt is direƈtly the reverſe of what is pretended by Dr P. Chriſt is appointed the King and Judge of men, becauſe he eſſentially poſſeſſes powers adapted to the work.

There is a continual outcry made by the party, againſt the uſual diſtinƈtion between the, eſſential and mediatory charaƈters of Jeſus; when employed to ſolve the apparent contradiƈtions in the accounts which the ſcriptures give of him. But Socinians find occaſion for a diſtinƈtion far more ſtrange. According to the former, two very different relations are ſuſtained by one Perſon; which is abundantly common among men. But by the latter, the ſame Perſon is ſuppoſed to ſtand in ſituations direƈtly oppoſite, in the ſame nature and relation. It is no contradiƈtion, that Jeſus ſhould be the proper Son of God, in one relation; and true man in another; that, according to the former, he ſhould know all things (John xxi. 17.), and be ignorant of ſome things, according to the latter. But that he ſhould have omniſcience and limited knowledge; the ſtate of a ſervant, and the ſtate of God; no power and honour as a King and Judge, and yet a great portion of both,----in one nature and relation; that he ſhould, at the ſame time, be purchaſing a reward to be had only in conſequence of finiſhing his work, and yet poſſeſſing it; are contradiƈtions of the groſſeſt kind. On this head, at leaſt, there is a palpable defeƈt in the Socinian ſyſtem: and it muſt be new modelled, ere it can be received by men of true reaſon.

O 3

Our

Our author kindly informs us, that " we ought not to be
" furprized at fuch expreffions as thefe, *Jefus knowing their*
" *thoughts,*" &c.   This argues great tendernefs for weak
readers, who might be fo fimple as to apprehend that no
one could know the thoughts but God.   He feems to grant
that there is, apparently at leaft, fome ground for furprize.
The good man is afraid that the furprize, efpecially after all
that he has faid to depreciate the Perfon, fhould hurt, not
us only, but his own beloved fyftem.   But like many *phy-*
ficians of no value, the very means he ufes to prevent, increafe the diforder.   For we are more furprized than ever,
to learn, not only that a fervant obtains great part of his
reward, although the proper confequence of his work, before he has well entered on it ; but that a mere man may
certainly and conftantly *difcern the thoughts and intents of*
the heart.   Had this been told thofe who attended on the
miniftry of Jefus, it would have furprized them more than
any thing he either faid or did.

The Evangelifts reprefent Chrift as the *object* of *faith.*
Thus Matthew applies that prophecy to him ; *In his Name*
fhall the Gentiles truft, chap. xii. 21.   But *trufting in the*
Name of Jefus, is fimply trufting in Jefus himfelf, efpecially
according to the Revelation given of him in the Word ;
juft as *loving the name* of the Lord, and *calling* upon his
name, denote the love and worfhip of God.   But if the
Evangelifts viewed Jefus as the object of faith, they muft
have confidered him as God.   They were no ftrangers to
that awful denunciation, *Curfed be the man that trufteth in*
man ; and they muft have confidered themfelves as lying
under the lafh of it, had they trufted in Jefus, believing him
to be a mere man.   Nay, had this been their idea, they could
never have thought that the prophet Ifaiah fpoke of him.

They alfo reprefent him as the *object* of religious *worfhip.*
Accordingly they inform us, that the wife men came to
worfhip

worſhip him, Matt. ii. 2. The word * uſed cannot be underſtood of civil homage. For univerſally, in the New Teſtament, it denotes ſuch worſhip as belongs to no creature.
When Cornelius worſhipped Peter, the latter ſaid, *Stand
up; I myſelf alſo am a man*, Acts x. 26. In what ſenſe it
is uſed by Matthew, appears from our Lord's reply to Satan;
Thou ſhalt worſhip the Lord thy God, chap. iv. 10. That
this act of adoration, by the wiſe men, was accepted of
God, appears pretty plainly from the peculiar care exerciſed with reſpect to their preſervation from the wrath of
Herod, ver. 12. It is ſcarcely ſuppoſable, that God would
have interpoſed by immediate Revelation, for preſerving
idolaters. Beſides this inſtance of the worſhip of Jeſus,
we have a variety of others recorded †. It is evident, indeed, that he received religious adoration from all his diſciples. For while *he was parted from them,—they worſhipped him*, Luke xxiv. 51, 52. We are aſſured that after his
aſcenſion the diſciples continued their worſhip. This was
ſo well known, that the primitive Chriſtians are denominated by a periphraſis taken from this very circumſtance.
They are deſcribed as thoſe who call on this name (Son of
God) Acts ix. 20, 21. Now, no one can deny that invocation is a ſpecial act of worſhip. By ſome it is reckoned
the higheſt. Therefore, either the Son of God ought to
be worſhipped; or, all the firſt Chriſtians were idolaters.

Could we believe, with Socinians, that this word, when
uſed by the Evangeliſts with reſpect to Chriſt, is to be underſtood in a different ſenſe from that in which it is applied
to the Father, we would be under a neceſſity of concluding,
that the New Teſtament church is not ſufficiently guarded
againſt idolatry, and that the Evangeliſts were very improper perſons for committing the Hiſtory of Jeſus to writing.
For with reſpect to both the worſhip given to God, and

O 4   that

---

* Προσκυνεω.   † See Matt. viii. 2. ix. 18. xx. 20.

that given to Chrift, they ufe the very fame word, without the leaft note of diftinction.

He is held forth, in the Evangelical Hiftory, as the Lord God of the children of Ifrael. Therefore the Angel foretold concerning John Baptift; *Many of the children of Ifrael fhall he turn to the Lord their God.* Who this is, evidently appears from the words that follow; *And he fhall go before him in the fpirit and power of Elias,* Luke i. 16, 17. Now, whomfoever John preceded as an harbinger, he muft have been *the Lord God—of the children of Ifrael.* But it was Jefus whom he preceded, as John himfelf teftifies; *He that cometh after me, is preferred before me,* John i. 27. and again, addreffing his difciples; *Ye yourfelves bear me witnefs that I faid, I am not the Chrift, but that I am fent before him,* John iii. 28. In all the Gofpels, and alfo in the Acts, Chrift is reprefented as that illuftrious Perfonage, whofe forerunner the Baptift was *. On this account, Zacharias calls John *the prophet of the Higheft.* For, fays he, *thou fhalt go before the face of the Lord to prepare his ways,* Luke i. 76. But let any man in his right fenfes fay, If this language would not have been both abfurd and blafphemous, had John been the prophet and harbinger of a mere man?

Indeed, the Lord, whofe way is here faid to be prepared, is JEHOVAH. For the Evangelift Matthew informs us concerning John, that *this is he that was fpoken of by the prophet Efaias, faying, The voice of one crying in the wildernefs, Prepare ye the way of the Lord,* chap. iii. 3. But the word ufed by the prophet, is JEHOVAH, Ifa. xl. 3. Therefore Jefus, who had John for his forerunner, is, and was confidered by the Evangelifts, as JEHOVAH. Now, notwithftanding all the *vain things,* that the people have imagined, in their combination againft the Lord, and his Anointed; as long as the word of God remains, this muft be confidered

---

* Matt. iii. 3. Mar. i. 2, 3. Acts xiii. 24, 25.

fidered as his incommunicable name. All the prefumptuous affertions and filly quibbles of Socinians, can be of no force, with a believing foul, when oppofed to fuch language as this, *I am* JEHOVAH, *that is my name, and my glory will I not give to another*, Ifa. xlii. 8. When the church prays for vengeance on the enemies of God, who have *made a tumult, lifted up the head, and faid, Let us take to ourfelves the houfes of God in poffeffion,* it is for this end, *That men may know that thou, whofe name alone is* JEHOVAH, *art the Moft High over all the earth*, Pfal. lxxxiii. 18. He, therefore, who is *the Higheft* (Luke i. 76.) or *the Moft High*, and who has the name JEHOVAH, is God in the proper fenfe of language ; is God alone, not as excluding the Father and Spirit, but as truly divine, and as oppofed to every creature, however exalted.

Luke informs us, that Jefus was recieved by believers, in his time, as the Lord of hofts. For when recording the teftimony of Simeon, he declares, that he faid to Mary the mother of Jefus ; *Behold, this child is fet for the fall and rifing again of many in Ifrael, and for a fign that fhall be fpoken againft*, chap. ii. 34. Thefe words are taken from the prophecy of Ifaiah, chap. viii. 13, 14, where they are fpoken of JEHOVAH of hofts : *Sanctify the Lord of hofts himfelf ; and let him be your fear, and let him be your dread. And he fhall be for a fanctuary ; but for a ftone of ftumbling and for a rock of offence, to both the houfes of Ifrael. ----And many of them fhall ftumble and fall, and be broken, and be fnared, and be taken.* That Jefus, then, who was *a ftone of ftumbling*, was yet to be the object of religious fear and worfhip, as the omnipotent God, who *doth according to his will in the army of heaven, and among the inhabitants of the earth.* For *the Lord of hofts* is a name expreffing almighty power and univerfal dominion, as well as fovereignty of operation. Simeon, therefore, believed in Jefus as *the Lord*

of

of hoſts. Nor was this deluſive exerciſe. The Evangeliſt informs us, that *the Holy Ghoſt was upon him,* ver. 25. If Simeon was miſtaken, Luke muſt have been ſo too. Indeed, we find the apoſtle Peter alſo conſidering Chriſt as that *ſtone of ſtumbling* foretold by the prophet, 1 Ep. ii. 8. Thoſe, who in our day, oppoſe him as the Son of God, have need diligently to inquire, whether the prophecy be not fulfilled in them.

C H A P. V.

Of our Saviour's Doctrine and Conduct with reſpect to his Divinity.

ANOTHER *argument* urged by Dr P. *againſt the Divinity or Pre-exiſtence of Chriſt,* is founded on his ſuppoſed ſilence on this ſubject. " The manner," he ſays, " in which our Lord ſpeaks of himſelf, and of the power " by which he worked miracles, is inconſiſtent, according " to the common conſtruction of language, with the idea of " his being poſſeſſed of any proper power of his own, more " than other men have *."

What we mean to offer in reply to this argument, will not only ſhow that our Saviour claimed divinity to himſelf, but at the ſame time ſerve as a continued proof of what the Evangeliſts believed concerning him. The Doctor ſtrenuouſly urges the conceſſion of the fathers, that, in the three firſt goſpels, Jeſus is deſcribed merely as man ; and pleads from the ſuppoſed latenefs of the publication of John's goſpel, that, although the divinity of Chriſt were taught in it, the greateſt part of the firſt believers muſt have died without any knowledge of this doctrine. We ſhall therefore

* Earl. Opin. vol. i. p. 13. 14.

fore continue to direct our principal attention to what is narrated by Matthew, Mark, and Luke. And if it appear, that they really believed this doctrine, and taught it in their writings ; the whole of our author's reasoning from inaccurate or disjointed expressions taken from the works of the fathers, really or apparently asserting the contrary, must fall to the ground.

We have already proved that Christ is acknowledged by the Evangelists as the *object of faith.* They also represent him as exhibiting himself in this very character : *Whoso shall offend one of these little ones who believe in me, &c.* Mat. xviii. 6.

He demanded *supreme love* from his followers. *If any man come to me, and hate not his father, and mother, and wife, and children, and brethren, and sisters, yea, and his own life also, he cannot be my disciple,* Luke xiv. 26. that is, every one, who would be his disciple, must love him more than all these ; as we learn from Mat. x. 37. If the love, here demanded, be not supreme, we know not what can come under this description. It is love, that excludes the partnership of every other object. This demand undoubtedly implies all that God claims, as his right, in the first and great commandment; *Thou shalt love the Lord thy God with all thy heart, and with all thy soul, and with all thy mind,* Mat. xxii. 37. The love, here required, is by no means included in that secondary precept, *Thou shalt love thy neighbour as thyself,* ver. 39. For Jesus requires, that a man should comparatively *hate* his nearest and dearest neighbour, *yea, his own life also,* for his sake.

Jesus prescribed his *Name's sake* as the *supreme end* to be proposed by his disciples. This language was quite familiar to the Jews, to whom he addressed himself. But they had been always accustomed to restrict it to God. However frequently this expression occurs in the Old Testament,

we

we do not once read of the *Name's sake* of a creature. It also invariably denotes the supreme motive, reason, or end, whether it be immediately proposed by God or by man. God assigns this as the cause or end of his conduct, in opposition to every other that might be supposed ; *For my Name's sake will I defer mine anger ;---even for mine own sake will I do it.* He mentions this as equivalent to his glory as the highest end. For it immediately follows ; *For how should my Name be polluted? and I will not give my glory to another,* Isa. xlviii. 9. 11. This is described as the end of coming to worship at Jerusalem. Therefore Solomon says ; *Concerning a stranger,---that cometh out of a far country for thy Name's sake ;---when he shall come and pray towards this place; hear thou,* 1 Kin. viii. 41—43. Believers, under that dispensation, are described as suffering on this as the proper ground ; *Your brethren that hated you, that cast you out for my Name's sake, said, Let the Lord be glorified,* Isa. lxvi. 5.

This very language Jesus appropriates to himself, and applies so very particularly in regard to his followers, as to leave no reason to doubt that he wished to be considered as that very Being who spoke to his ancient church by Isaiah. He assures his disciples, that their lot should be the same with that of former believers, and that their blessedness should consist in suffering for his Name's sake. *Blessed are ye, when men shall hate you, and when they shall separate you from their company,—for the Son of man's sake. Rejoice ye in that day,—for in like manner did their fathers unto the prophets,* Luke vi. 22. 23. *Every one that hath forsaken houses, or brethren, or sisters, or father, or mother, or wife, or children, or lands, for my Name's sake, shall receive an hundred fold, and shall inherit everlasting life,* Mat. xix. 29. Christ says to Ananias concerning Saul ; *I will show him how great things he shall suffer for my Name's sake,* Acts ix. 16. Therefore, unless Christ have the same

Name

Name with God, as being of the same nature, he sets up his glory as a new supreme end, and robs God of his prerogative. If this be with the Father's consent, he suffers his Name to be *polluted* and *gives* his *glory to another.*

Not only do the Evangelists, as we have already seen, represent Jesus as the object of religious worship; but Jesus himself chearfully *accepted* the *worship* that was given him. It has been observed, that the word used by them, always in the New Testament, denotes religious adoration. But though it were possible to prove the reverse, it would not affect the argument. For when we read of the worship of Jesus, the circumstances recorded are such as clearly shew, that it was not of a civil, but of a religious kind. It might justly be urged, that, on every occasion, he renounced all the honours of royalty. He refused to be made a king, or even for once to act the part of a judge in civil matters. And can it be thought, that he would receive the highest token of veneration ever given to an earthly sovereign? Even supposing that he knew, that this was meant merely as civil respect, on his own principles he ought to have refused it. For he constantly testified, that his kingdom was *not of this world.* If, therefore, he received this as civil homage, he voluntarily, and in the most effectual manner, confirmed that carnal people in their wild ideas with respect to a temporal kingdom of the Messiah.

But we find that frequently the form of this worship was such, that although he had known that it was meant merely as civil, he could not lawfully have accepted it. Jairus fell at his feet, Mark v. 22. The Syro-phenician woman did the same, ch. vii. 25. His disciples *held him by the feet and worshipped him*, Mat. xxviii. 9. This kind of worship was sometimes given to kings, or their substitutes; but it was unlawful. It was demanded by the kings of Persia. Various reasons have been given why Mordecai

the

the Jew would not bow to Haman ; but the most natural idea is, that he accounted it unlawful. This is the reason assigned by the Jewish historian, who must have been best acquainted with the opinions of his own nation. " Morde- " cai alone," he says, " bowed not to him, such obedience " being against the custom of his country *." Even the more intelligent heathens were shocked at this kind of worship, when offered to man, being persuaded that it was divine. Thus Sueton observes, that " Lucius was the first " who procured that Claudius Cæsar should be adored as " God: for when he returned from Syria, he would not " presume to approach him otherwise than with his head " veiled, and turning himself round, he *fell down before* " *him* †."

This form, then, being used in the idolatrous worship of man, had Jesus been nothing more, he could not have re- ceived it without giving the most express encouragement to idolatry. But we have not a single instance of his testi- fying the least dissatisfaction. No one can doubt, that the Devil demanded religious adoration from him, when he said ; " *All these things will I give thee, if thou wilt fall down and worship me*, Mat. iv. 9. This very worship the wise men gave to Jesus ; for the expression is the same ‡. Nay, this very worship Jesus accepted from Jairus. For, as Mark says, *He fell down*, ch. v. 22. Matthew informs us, that he *worshipped him*, ch. ix. 18 ||. That is, he wor- shipped Jesus by prostration, the very manner in which Je- sus himself, considered as man, worshipped the Father. For

he

---

* Antiq. l. xi. c. 6.

† Idem miri in adulandum ingenii, primus C. Cæsarem adorari ut Deum instituit: cum reversus ex Syria non aliter adire ausus esset, quam capite velato, circumvertenique se, deinde procumbens. In Vitell. cap. 2.

‡ Εαν πεσων προσκυνησης μοι. Mat. iv. 9. Πεσοντες προσεκυνησαν αυτω, ch. ii. 11.

|| Πιπτει προς τ͘υς ποδας αυτ͘ν.—Προσεκυνει αυτω.

he fell on the ground, and prayed, Mark xiv. 35. If Jesus, then, was a mere man, the angel, who refused the worship of John, was more zealous for the glory of God than he. For this was the very way in which John offered to worship this heavenly messenger: *I fell at his feet to worship him* *. But he rejected it with horror, assigning it to God as his exclusive prerogative, saying; *See thou do it not : I am thy fellow-servant ;—Worship God*, Rev. xix. 10. According to the Socinian doctrine, Jesus ought to have done the same. For how much soever he be exalted above believers, he is still their *fellow-servant*, considered in his relation to God. If Jesus had no right to religious adoration, would not Peter have been a better foundation for the church, than he? For when Cornelius *fell down at his feet, and worshipped him*, he *took him up, saying, stand up ; I myself also am a man*, Acts x. 25, 26.

Jesus claimed the glory of the Father as his. What, in one passage he calls the glory of his Father, he, in another, calls his own. *The Son of man shall come in the glory of his Father, with his angels*, Mat. xvi. 27. *When the Son of man shall come in his glory, and all the holy angels with him, then shall he sit upon the throne of his glory*, ch. xxv. 31. In both places he speaks of his coming to judgment. The *glory* is *his*, and the *throne* also. He could never have uttered such language, unless his and the Father's glory were one.

He claimed the church as his property, saying, *Upon this rock will I build my church*, Mat. xvi. 18. But this argument we shall illustrate afterwards.

He asserted his Lordship over the Sabbath. Thus, in reply to the cavils of his enemies, on occasion of his disciples plucking and eating the ears of corn, he said ; *The Son of man is Lord even of the Sabbath-day*, Mat. xii. 8. As this day was consecrated by God, no one could have a right to loose

the

---

* Επεσα εμπροσθεν των ποδων αυτε προσκυνησαι αυτω.

the obligation of the precept, but God himfelf. It would be vain to fay, that Chrift received this right by delegation. For, according to the Socinian fyftem, he was not yet come to his kingdom. At any rate, the lordfhip, here claimed, is evidently unlimited.

C H A P. VI.

Of the Evidence of our Saviour's Divinity, from his Miracles.

JESUS manifefted and maintained his claim to a divine character, by the miracles that he wrought. It is grant-ed, that thefe were more directly meant to prove his divine miffion as Meffiah; and that our Saviour appealed to them in this refpect. But they alfo proved the effential dignity of the Meffenger. The mere working of a miracle, in-deed, will not prove the divinity of the immediate agent. The moft that it can prove, is a miffion from God. It alfo confirms the truth of the doctrine which is·taught. But if the immediate agent of the miracle lays claim to Deity, the truth of his doctrine in this refpect cannot be denied, without a denial of the reality of the miracle.

Jefus wrought miracles in confirmation of his doctrine. Thefe muft have confirmed the whole of his doctrine; or they could not confirm any part of it. He taught that he was the true Meffiah: and it is granted by Socinians, that his claim to this character was incontestably demon-ftrated by his wonderful works. If he alfo taught that he was God, the fame works muft have equally confirmed this branch of his doctrine. But he undoubtedly did fo, by de-claring that he had power to forgive fin: and he appealed to miracles as an evidence of this power. When the man fick of the palfy, was brought to him, *feeing their faith, he said, faid, Son,---thy fins be forgiven thee. But fome of the Scribes faid within themfelves, This man blafphemeth. But he faid, Whether is it eafier to fay, Thy fins be forgiven thee, or to fay, Arife and walk?* He declares, that it is the fame to him to work a miracle, and to forgive fin; both thefe being equally exertions of divine power. Then he adds; *But that ye may know that the Son of Man hath power on earth to forgive fin, (he faid to the fick of the palfy) Arife, take up thy bed, and go into thine own houfe,* Matt. ix. 1.---6. But we propofe to explain this paffage more fully afterwards, as containing a diftinct and peculiar proof of our Saviour's Deity, and of his afferting his claim to it.

But our Lord did not merely claim particular prerogatives of Deity, and prove his title to thefe by his works. He exprefsly afferted his unity of effence with the Father, and appealed to his works as incontrovertibly proving the truth of his doctrine in this refpect. *Though ye believe not me, believe the works: that ye may know that the Father is in me, and I in him,* John x. 38, 39.

This language undoubtedly fignifies, that the Father could as little work, nay exift, without the Son, as the Son without the Father. It fhews in the cleareft manner, in what fenfe he had previoufly faid, *I and my Father are one,* ver. 30. The Father exifts and operates in him: he exifts and operates in the Father: and thus they *are one* in effence and operation.

Now, either the wonderful works of Jefus were not real miracles; or they were decifive proofs of his being God equal with the Father. Socinians will not affert the former. For this would reduce them to the neceffity of entirely denying that Jefus is the Meffiah. They cannot, therefore, evade the force of the latter.

But this proof of the Deity of Chrift, is not the only one which arifes from his wonderful works. Thefe very works afford us evidence of a more direct nature. The manner ‚in which he wrought his miracles, the concomitant circumstances, and the language of the sacred writers who record them, clearly shew, that he acted as a divine Person, that, in various instances, he wished this to appear, and that the inspired historians viewed matters in no other light.

Jesus wrought miracles in *his own Name.* Had he sustained no higher character than that of a servant, he ought to have used the Name of God, if not as necessary for working the miracle, yet for shewing others, by what power, and for what end, it was wrought. In this respect, he ought also to have set an example of self-denial before his followers. But we have not a single instance of his exercising this power, in the Name of God. Therefore, if it was not essentially his own, he acted a most ungrateful and undutiful part; a part,—that, instead of entitling him to honours inconceivably exceeding those conferred on any other servant, shewed, in the clearest light, that he deserved the most severe punishment which injured Omnipotence could inflict. His disciples acted very differently. We have not a single instance of their exercising the power entrusted to them, without an express declaration of dependence. Not one of them performed a miracle in his own name. And it is very remarkable, that they never mention the Name of God, but that of Jesus. They ascribe all their power to him. The seventy disciples returned, saying, *Lord, even the devils are subject to us, through,* or *in thy Name,* Luke x. 17. Jesus restricted his disciples to this manner of operation : *In my Name they shall cast out devils, they shall speak with new tongues,* &c. Nay, he suspended all their delegated power of working miracles upon faith in his Name. He declared all their future miracles to be *signs* that should *follow them that believed,* Mark xvi. 17. Accordingly, the apostles testify the greatest anxiety lest any should

think

think that thefe works were done by their own power, afcribe all their power to their Mafter, and declare that their exercife of it was the immediate fruit of faith in him. Thus, when the multitude marvelled at the cure of the lame man, Peter addreffed them in thefe words, immediately referring to *the Prince of Life ;----And his Name, through faith in his Name, hath made this man strong :----yea, the faith which is by him, hath given him this perfect foundnefs,* Acts iii. 16. Here, they acknowledge him, not only as the Supreme Agent in the miracle, but as both the object, and the author of their faith, which was the mean by which they performed it.

Jefus wrought miracles by his *own power*, as a divine agent. He was, therefore, chargeable with no arrogant affumption, in working them in his own Name. All the power that was neceffary for the performance of the moft wonderful works, refided in him as its proper fubject. Thence, with refpect to the cure effected on the woman who *came in the prefs behind, and touched his garments,* we are informed that *virtue had gone out of him,* Mark v. 27. —30. He was, indeed, *a man approved of God, by miracles, and wonders, and figns, which God did by him,* Acts ii. 22. Thefe were evidences, that he was *anointed with the Holy Ghoft, and with power,* and that *God was with him,* chap. x. 38. But while God was *with* him, as his fervant whom he *upheld*, this was not all. The Father was alfo *in* him, as his own eternal *Son.* Therefore as we have feen, he appeals to his works, as evidences of his equality with the Father. *If I do not the works of my Father,* he fays, *believe me not. But if I do, though ye believe not me, believe the works : that ye may know that the Father is in me, and I in him,* John x. 37, 38. He declares himfelf to be as properly an agent in thefe works, as the Father. *If I do not the works of my Father,* &c.

But

But as the disciples attributed all their works to Jesus, it was by no means an empty compliment. For, in working miracles, they constantly acted by a communication of power from him. He claims the prerogative of conferring this : *I give unto you power to tread upon serpents, and over all the power of the enemy*, Luke x. 19. The inspired writer of the History of the Apostles informs us, that Paul and Barnabas *spake boldly in the Lord, who gave testimony unto the word of his grace, and granted signs and wonders to be done by their hands*, Acts xiv. 3. They appear merely as his instruments. But he who has no physical power of his own, who in all his exertions is no more than the instrument of another, cannot communicate his power to a third person. Far less can he do so, according to his own pleasure. But as there was great variety in the extraordinary gifts conferred by the Head of the church, his disciples ascribed sovereignty to him in the distribution of them : *Unto every one of us is grace given, according to the measure of the gift of Christ. Wherefore he saith, When he ascended, ---he gave gifts unto men*, Eph. iv. 7. 8.

He wrought miracles by a *word* of *command*. On this account, even unbelievers were astonished. When our Lord had cast out an unclean spirit, his hearers were *all amazed, and spake among themselves, saying, What a word is this ? for with authority and power he commandeth the unclean spirits, and they come out*, Luke iv. 36. The Evangelists take particular notice of this circumstance. *He cast out the spirits*, saith Matthew, *with his word*, chap. viii. 16. Thus, he clearly shewed, that he was that very Word who created the worlds. For his almighty *fiat* was all that was necessary. *He spake and it was done.* As, *in the beginning*, he had said, *Let there be light, and there was light*, in the days of his flesh he said, *Be thou clean, and immediately the leprosy was cleansed*, Matt. viii. 3. We have but one instance

of

of any of the followers of Chrift working a miracle in an
authoritative manner.   Paul faid to the fpirit of divination
that poffeffed a certain damfel, *I command thee to come out
of her*, Acts xvi. 18.   Is it faid, that Jefus gave to the
twelve, *power and authority over all devils, and to cure difeafes* (Luke ix. 1.)?   The very manner of expreffion contains a fufficient reply.   For *he gave* them this power;
and it was only to be exercifed in his name, Mark-xvi. 17.
Now, as he, who has no phyfical power of his own, who is
merely the inftrument of another, cannot communicate this
power to a third perfon, and far lefs in a fovereign manner;
leaft of all, can he confer a right to exercife it in his own
name.   Although the former were not impoffible, the latter would be an act of rebellion againft the original and
proper fuperior.   Even in that folitary inftance already
mentioned, Paul is careful to fhew that he did not fpeak
from his own authority.   For he fays; *I command thee, in
the Name of Jefus Chrift, to come out of her.*   Jefus gave his
command abfolutely, without the leaft limitation or reference to any higher agent; Paul, only like a fervant repea-
ting the orders of his Mafter.   So powerful was Chrift's
word of command, that he could not only himfelf fufpend
the laws of nature; but, by directing this word to another,
fubject them to him alfo.   Peter was convinced of this.
He faid, *Lord, if it be thou, bid me*, or rather, *command me
to come unto thee on the water.   And he faid, Come.   And
Peter walked on the water, to go to Jefus.*   But to fhew,
that it was only faith in the power of Chrift, conveyed by
his command, that enabled the difciple to do this, he began
to fink as foon as his faith began to fail, Matt. xiv. 28.—30.
    Jefus difcovered his fupreme authority by the language
of *rebuke*.   When there was a great ftorm, he *rebuked the
wind, and faid unto the fea, Peace, be ftill: and the wind
ceafed, and there was a great calm*, Mark iv. 39.   This word

is never once ufed with refpect to any of the difciples, when
we read of the miracles wrought by them. It carries fuch
an air of majefty with it, as undoubtedly to convey the idea of
divine authority. The action, expreffed by it, feems to have
made this impreffion on thofe who were witneffes. They
appear to have been lefs afraid at the danger itfelf, than at
the manner in which it was removed. *They feared exceedingly, and faid one to another, What manner of Perfon is
this, that even the wind and the fea obey him?* ver. 41. We
cannot conceive, that the infpired writers viewed it in any
other light. For the three former Evangelifts all mention
the circumftance of his rebuking thefe ftormy elements;
and they all ufe the fame word *. Indeed, this language is,
in fcripture, appropriated to God, particularly with refpect
to the fea. *The waters flood above the mountains. At thy
rebuke they fled.*----*He rebuked the Red Sea alfo; and it was
dried up,* Pfal. civ. 6, 7. cvi. 9. The Seventy, in their verfion, ufe the fame word with the Evangelift. Thus, Jefus
fhewed, that it was he who had formerly manifefted his dominion over the watery element, and that this afcription
belonged to him, *Thou ruleft the raging of the fea: when
the waters thereof arife, thou ftilleft them,* Pfal. lxxxix. 9.
For when he rebuked the fea, *there was a great calm.*

He alfo rebuked the devils, when he caft them out, Matt.
xvii. 18. Mark i. 25. The difciples attempted nothing of
this kind. Jefus gave them power to heal. That of rebuking difeafes he referved to himfelf. When the mother
of Peter's wife was *taken with a great fever, he rebuked the
fever, and it left her,* Luke iv. 38, 39.

Our Lord, in his miracles, difplayed *creative* power, and
this extending to the whole of nature. At the power of the
difciples was limited, we find nothing like a creating act
performed by any of them. But he multiplied the loaves.

He

* Ἐπιτιμήσει.

He turned water into wine. When his difciples came to land, *they faw a fire of coals there, and fifh laid thereon, and bread,* John xxi. 9. It was a miracle of this kind that Satan demanded, as a proof of our Saviour's Deity: *If thou be the Son of God, command that thefe ftones be made bread,* Matt. iv. 3. He defires that he would change one body into another, as this was a creating act; and that he would do fo by a word of *command,* as it was in this manner that God created. Jefus not only gave forth his command, but he directed it to dead matter. He fpoke to the clofed ear and to the fettered tongue of the deaf man; and they obeyed his voice. *He faid, Ephphatha, that is, Be opened. And ftraightway his ears were opened, and the ftrings of his tongue were loofed,* Mark vii. 34, 35. The legion of devils acknowledged his abfolute power, when they faid, *Suffer us to go into the herd of fwine.* Jefus himfelf declared it, when he anfwered, *Go,* Matt. viii. 31, 32. It cannot reafonably be alleged, that he had this univerfal authority, becaufe all power was given him in heaven, and in earth. For Socinians deny that he was advanced to this honour, before he had finifhed his obedience. But he difplayed that fovereign authority of which we fpeak, in the very depths of his humiliation. Even when he delivered himfelf up to his enemies, by a fingle word he made the multitude *fall to the ground,* John xviii. 6.

Jefus could communicate his healing power, when the object was at *a diftance,* as well as when at hand. In this way he cured the centurion's fervant. We are told, indeed, concerning Paul, that *from his body were brought unto the fick handkerchiefs or aprons, and the difeafes departed from them,* Acts xix. 12. But here there was the intervention of a fenfible mean, evidently expreffing the inferiority of the fervant to the Mafter. How much more like a divine agent, to effect a cure on a diftant object by a word,

than

than by a handkerchief! The centurion knew that nothing more was neceffary. *Speak .the word only*, he fays, *and my fervant fhall be healed*, Matt. viii. 8.---13. When thefe miracles of the apoftle of the Gentiles are recorded, the Spirit informs us, that *God wrought them by the hands of Paul*, Acts xix. 11. He was merely the inftrument. But this is never faid of Jefus. On the contrary, he extols the faith of the centurion, becaufe it was fo great. Now, what was the object of this faith? The fovereign authority of Chrift. With this the centurion does not compare, but contraft, his own limited power : *I am a man under authority.* He argues from the lefs to the greater.

He declared his mighty works to be the effects of his own *will*. *The Son quickneth whom he will*, John v. 21. The leper, who came to him, in à twofold refpect expreffed his faith in the divine power of Jefus. He worfhipped him ; and he teftified his perfuafion that the exercife of divine power depended on his will. *Lord, if thou wilt, thou canft make me clean.* Jefus approved, both of his worfhip, and of his confeffion. For he faid, *I will, be thou clean*, Matt. viii. 2, 3. In a work afcribed to Juftin Martyr, thefe words are thus viewed : "That the power of the Son "and Holy Ghoft is not inferior to that of the Father, we "learn from the facred writings. But in what manner, "hear the word itfelf. *Whatfoever the Lord pleafed, that* "*did he in heaven, and in earth* *. Thus fpake David con- "cerning the Father. But the Son fhewing this very power "on the leper, fays, *I will, be thou clean*, &c. †"

The wonderful works, performed by Jefus, are exprefsly called *his* own. Thus it is faid, *Many believed in his Name, when they faw* HIS *miracles which he did*, John ii. 23. It has been obferved, that the word θεωρειν is applied, both by facred, and by profane writers, to feeing and diligently con- · fidering

* Pfal. cxxxv. 6.   † Expofitio Fidei, p. 377.

fidering any thing as a divine work. But whatever was the idea of thefe perfons, the infpired apoftle particularly informs the church that the miracles were Chrift's. There is no tautology here. Our Lord did not merely perform thefe miracles, but he performed them as *his*. He did not act as an inftrument. They were his own works. It is indeed furprifing, that the force of this ftriking expreffion has been overlooked by our tranflators *. We have the fame properly rendered, chap. vi. 2. *A great multitude followed him, becaufe they faw* HIS *miracles which he did.* But nò fuch language is ufed concerning the miracles wrought by the apoftles. The Evangelift Mark, even when recording the honourable commiffion given them, guards his readers againft fuppofing that thefe works were theirs. Though performed by them, he afcribes them all to Chrift. *They went forth, and preached every where, the Lord working with them, and confirming the word with figns following,* chap. xvi. 20. The fame Lord is meant, who, in the preceding verfe, is faid to have been *received up into heaven.*

The *end* that Jefus had in view, in working miracles, is a proof of his Deity. He, indeed, defigned to prove the truth of his miffion ; but in connexion with this, his divine nature. He fought not his own glory, becaufe he was in a ftate of humiliation. But he occafionally difplayed fo much of it, as to fhew that his humiliation was voluntary. When he turned the water into wine, *he manifefted forth his glory, and his difciples believed on him,* John ii. 11. When information was fent him of the ficknefs of Lazarus, he faid, *This ficknefs is not unto death, but for the glory of God, that the Son of God might be glorified thereby,* chap. xi. 4. Here he mentions his own glory as the ultimate end in the miracle he had in view. One circumftance, concerning this miracle, deferves our particular attention. Martha, although fhe

* Θεωρθντες αυτου τα σημεια α εποιι.

she believed in him, seems to have thought that he had his miraculous power merely by delegation, and that he could not exert it without prayer to God for his assistance. *I know,* she says, *that even now whatsoever thou wilt ask of God, God will give it thee.* But Jesus, much as he sought the glory of him that sent him, could not seek it at the expence of what essentially belonged to himself. He would work no miracle, till the faith of Martha rose in its exercise. Therefore, he proceeds to shew her that he was himself the fountain of life. All miracles being signs, the work that he was about to perform on Lazarus being especially a sign of his divine power in raising the spiritually dead ; he first instructs her in his character as *the Resurrection and the Life,* as the object of faith in this respect. When Martha seemed to object to the removal of the gravestone, Jesus reproved her in these words, *Said I not unto thee, that if thou wouldest believe, thou shouldest see the glory of God ?* ver. 40. Whether he had expressly uttered this language before, or only refers to the tenor of his discourse, we cannot say. But he had formerly declared himself to be the object of faith as *the Life.* Therefore, the glory to be seen, by means of this faith, must have been his glory. Indeed this is nothing more than what he had declared to his disciples.

In a word, the miracles of Jesus are *recorded* for our use, as evidences of his being a divine Person. John xx. 30, 31. *Many other signs truly did Jesus in the presence of his disciples, which are not written in this book. But these are written, that ye might believe that Jesus is the Son of God ; and that believing, ye might have life through his Name.* That this character, *the Son of God,* respects the divine nature of Christ, I mean afterwards particularly to shew. I shall only observe at present, that the Evangelist here declares, that these signs were written for the express purpose of exhibiting Jesus in such a character, that he might safely
be

be acknowledged as the proper object of faith, and, as such, communicate life to all who believe in him.

Before leaving this point, it may be proper to confider an objection, on which our author feems to lay great ftrefs. It has, indeed, been all along a principal ftrong hold of the party. The Doctor refers to it different times in what he calls *Arguments againft the Divinity of Chrift.* " He al-
" ways fpake of himfelf," he fays, " as receiving his doc-
" trine, and his power from him (God), and again and
" again difclaimed having any power of his own. John v.
" 19. *Then anfwered Jefus and faid unto them, Verily, ve-*
" *rily, I fay unto you, the Son can do nothing of himfelf.*
" Chap. xiv. 10. *The words which I fpeak unto you, I fpeak*
" *not of myfelf, but the Father that dwelleth in me, he doth*
" *the works* *.—There is alfo another confideration which I
" would recommend to thofe who` maintain that Chrift is
" either God, or the Maker of the world under God. It is
" this : The manner in which our Lord fpeaks of himfelf,
" and of the power by which he worked miracles, is incon-
" fiftent, according to the common conftruction of language,
" with the idea of his being poffeffed of any proper power
" of his own, more than other men have †."

It is a ftriking evidence of the perverfenefs of men, that the very language which clearly proves the equality of the Son with the Father, fhould be urged as a proof of his effential inferiority. In reading the New Teftament, it in-
deed deferves our particular and conftant attention, that the great end which Chrift had immediately in view, in his perfonal miniftry, was to demonftrate his divine miffion. This was efpecially neceffary, becaufe he could not otherwife fhew that he was the promifed Meffiah, that he had authority to alter the ftate of the church, and that his doc-
trine was fubftantially the fame with what had been taught

and

* Earl Opin. vol. i. p. 10.   † Ibid. p. 13.

and believed from the beginning. Although as the eternal
Son of God, he was effentially entitled to all thofe acts of worfhip that belong to the Father, yet he was the immediate object of faith, in order to falvation, only as *a Son given **. For,
merely as a Son, he had no connexion with our falvation.
Faith could have no ground to reft on, but his character as the
Son engaged to be our Surety. This was its only *way*. Therefore, his title to the character of Meffiah proved that he was
a Son equal with the Father. I may fay, indeed, that the
proof was reciprocal. The moment that his mediatory character was eftablifhed, it undeniably followed, that he was
the proper Son of God. For no other was promifed; and
his work was fuch, that none but God could perform it.
On the other hand, in proving his character as Meffiah, he
appealed to his doctrine and works. Now, he *fpake the
words of God*, John iii. 34. and did fuch works as fhewed that
the Father was in him, and he in the Father, that he was of
the fame effence with him. Thence it naturally followed,
that he was the true Meffiah. Thus, his mediatory character proved his Deity, and the evidences of his Deity eftablifhed his claim to the character of Mediator.

This being the cafe, it is not furprifing that we fhould
find him ufing many expreffions which include both; and
that, in one fentence, he fhould fpeak of himfelf both as an
inferior and as an equal. The firft paffage referred to by
the learned gentleman, feems to be one of thefe. The generality of orthodox writers have, indeed, confined it entirely to the Deity. In this fenfe Jefus might fay, with the
greateft propriety, *the Son can do nothing of himfelf*, becaufe
he can do nothing *feparately* from the Father, the effence
being the fame. But, as our Lord undeniably fpeaks of himfelf as Mediator in feveral of the following affertions, it
appears that even in this he makes choice of fuch language
as will apply to him, either in his effential, or in his official
character.

* Ifa. ix. 6.

character. This was very natural, indeed. For almoft all the external works of God which have been done by the Son, have been done by him as Mediator, or in relation to his mediatory work. Not merely had the previous difplays of his judicial or of his quickening power this refpect, but all his work of providence fince the fall, and the whole of his conduct towards his ancient church. Therefore, Jefus could not properly defcribe his operation, even as a divine Perfon, in its full extent, had he excluded that delegated character in which he had made all thofe difplays of Deity to the church, with which fhe had formerly been favoured. Be-caufe he fays, *The Son can do nothing of himfelf,* muft we conclude that he meant to deny effential equality with the Father? The words immediately added, *but what he feeth the Father do,* fhew the very contrary. Thefe our author has prudently left out, when quoting this verfe, and framing his argument from it. They undoubtedly reftrict the mean-ing of the preceding declaration, and particularly fhew in what fenfe we are to underftand the expreffion *of himfelf.* The Jews had charged him with Sabbath-breaking, and alfo with making himfelf equal with God. He replies to the charge complexly viewed. He informs them, that he *can do nothing,* even in the difcharge of the mediatory work entrufted to him, inconfiftent with the will of his Father; and that, therefore, in *loofing* the Sabbath, he was not to be viewed as a tranfgreffor, becaufe he did nothing but what *he feeth the Father do* in continuing to work, in the prefer-vation and deliverance of his creatures, on the Sabbath, as well as on other days. As a proof that he cannot oppofe the Father in his operation, he fubjoins; *For what things* SOEVER *he doth* THESE *alfo doth the Son* LIKEWISE, that is, the fame works in all their extent, in the fame manner. He means to affert, that his effential equality with the Fa-ther, proved by abfolute famenefs of operation, precluded

the

the poffibility of his doing any thing, even in the difcharge of his office, that could make him a tranfgreffor. Here we have a clear proof, that his mediatory inferiority is not in the leaft inconfiftent with effential equality. This negative affertion, therefore, inftead of fhewing that his power is limited and derived, proves that is is really divine.

Dr P. entirely miftakes the meaning of the paffage. Our Lord does not fpeak of the *origin*, but of the *exercife* of this power. He does not deny that he had any properly *his own ;* but that he could employ it in oppofition to the Father. For while he refufes that he can do any thing inconfiftent with the will and example of the Father, or with the commandment given him as Mediator ; he at the fame time afferts that he can do (τι) *whatfoever he feeth the Father doing.* And to whom can this language belong, but to a perfon effentially divine ? When he afterwards afferts, that he hath life *in himfelf,* ver. 26. it takes off all the force of the argument drawn from his faying, that he *can do nothing of himfelf.* For if the former expreffion mean any thing, it muft mean that he is poffeffed of proper power of his own, that he has what the Doctor obftinately refufes, extraordinary power inherent in himfelf *. That *the Son can do nothing of himfelf,* but in the manner expreffed, inftead of difproving, as clearly demonftrates, his effential perfection, as when it is faid of God, that he *cannot deny himfelf,* 2 Tim. ii. 13. The unity of the divine effence prevents the former, as well as the latter. The only difference is, that the laft expreffion immediately refpects the perfections, and the other the perfons in the nature of God.

When our Lord ufes the word *feeth,* he feems to choofe a term that refers to, both his mediatory, and his divine character. A fervant, as Jefus was in his mediatory work, hath his eye to the hand of his Mafter. But the nature of the

---

* Famil. Illuftr. p. 22.

the vifion is fuch, as clearly to fhew that no fervant, but one effentially equal, could be capable of it. For it extends to all the operations of the Father, without exception. It hath often been juftly obferved, that fuch expreffions, when ufed with refpect to the Deity, do not fignify the *means* of knowledge, but the *figns* and *evidences* of it *. When it is faid, that the Son *doth whatfoever he feeth the Father doing*, it by no means implies, as Grotius afferts †, that the Son imitates the Father, as a fcholar doth his mafter; or that the Father works firft in order of time, and that the Son works after him : but that being infinitely acquainted with the will of the Father, and being of the fame nature, he performs the felf-fame works. *Seeing*, here, is the fame with divine omnifcience ‡. *Hearing* is in this very fenfe afcribed to the Holy Spirit ; *Whatfoever he fhall hear, that fhall he fpeak*, John xvi. 13. Whether he be viewed as a Perfon, or, according to Socinians, merely as a perfection, *hearing* muft be underftood as the evidence of infinite knowledge. In the fame fenfe our Lord declares concerning himfelf, John iii. 11. *We fpeak that we do know, and teftify that we have feen :* where *feeing* is exegetical of *knowing ;* only, as fome apprehend, expreffive of the peculiar manner of knowing, by intuition. For he *hath feen the Father.* He recommends himfelf as *the faithful and true witnefs*, by referring to ocular demonftration and perfonal acquaintance, which, as connected with integrity, are accounted the beft qualifications of a witnefs among men. He does not teftify from report, but from what he hath *feen.* Nor, like a falfe witnefs, does he declare what he is ignorant of, but what he *knows* infinitely well. This language is evidently ufed after the manner of men. But it muft be underftood without the idea of that imperfection neceffarily attached

to

---

* Vid. Owen on the Spirit, p. 162. † In loc.

‡ Vid. Glaffii Phil. Sac. l. 5 t. 1. c. 7. p. 1574.

to human knowledge. It is said with respect to God absolutely considered ; *The Lord looked down from heaven upon the children of men, to see if there were any that did understand, and seek God,* Psal. xiv. 2. But shall we thence infer, that God can know nothing, without the use of those means employed by man ?

Dr P. also quotes John xiv. 10. as a proof that Jesus has neither doctrine nor power of his own. He indeed says, *The words which I speak unto you, I speak not of myself; but the Father that dwelleth in me, he doth the works.* But if the connexion and design of this language be fairly considered, it will appear that Socinians have no great reason to boast of their argument from it. Our Lord does not express himself in this manner, because the disciples were giving him too much honour, but because they gave him too little. Jesus having said, *If ye had known me, ye should have known my Father also : and from henceforth ye know him, and have seen him ;* Philip takes occasion to say, *Lord, shew us the Father, and it sufficeth us.* He most probably wished to see the Person, or some visible likeness of the Father. But Jesus reproves him for his ignorance : *Have I been so long time with you, and hast thou not known me, Philip ? He that hath seen Me, hath seen the Father : And how sayest thou then, Shew us the Father ?* Our Lord says, *He that hath seen Me, hath seen the Father;* because he is *the express image of his Person.* I am bold to aver, that had these words been uttered by the most holy man that ever existed, they would have been blasphemy. For supposing that Jesus was perfectly holy as man, and no more, it was impossible that all the divine perfections could be seen in him. Those especially that are most distinguishing, as being incommunicable, must have been totally hid. How could the proper eternity of God be seen in him, who had no existence before he was born in Bethlehem ? His immensity, in a man confined

confined to a particu'ar fpot? His omnifcience, in one whofe knowledge was limited? Or his incomprehenfibility, in a Perfon whofe nature was as fully underftood by the difciples as their own? No fingle perfection could be fully feen, unlefs finite can contain and difplay that which is infinite.

But' to fhew that he afferted unity of effence with the Father, he adds this queftion; *Believeft thou not, that I am in the Father, and the Father in me?* Then he declares; that in giving this teftimony concerning his own effential dignity, he no more acted independently of the authority of God, than in any other part of his doctrine; but only faithfully difcharged his office as Mediator. *The words that I fpeak unto you, I fpeak not of myfelf.* As a proof that his teftimony was true, he appeals to his works. *But the Father that dwelleth in me, he doth the works.* By this appeal, he does not mean to declare, that they merely proved the truth of his doctrine in general, but that they particularly eftablifhed that which he prefently afferted, his famenefs of nature with the Father; fhewing that the Father conftantly dwelt in him, not only by his Spirit, with refpect to office, but effentially. Thence, the works done by him, in fupport of his claim to Deity, were as much the Father's as his; and were, therefore, to be viewed as the Father's confirmation of Chrift's doctrine on this head.

To guard his difciples againft the poffibility of miftaking his meaning, he repeats what he had already advanced, demanding their faith. *Believe that I am in the Father, and the Father in me.* He mentions himfelf in the firft place, becaufe the point to be proved was his own effential dignity, of which fome of his difciples were not fufficiently convinced. For they had no doubt of his being the Meffiah, and could never imagine that his works were performed by any power but that of God. Then he illuftrates his equality with the Father, by fhewing the efficacy of faith in him as its proper object, in producing works such as his, and greater, as to their spiritual effects, in consequence of the effusion of the Spirit, ver. 12. He also proves that his power is the same with the Father's, in hearing and answering prayer : *Whatsoever ye ask in my Name, that will I do.* Nay, he repeats this declaration, the more to impress them with a sense of his essential dignity : *If ye shall ask any thing in my Name, I will do it*, ver. 13, 14.

Thus, we have a striking proof of the presumption of Socinians, in their perversion of this passage. For it contains the clearest evidence that the Son is of the same essence with the Father. But our author will admit nothing as a proof of the Trinity, but what would destroy the unity, or overthrow the work of mediation. Unless it appear that the Son can act separately from the Father, or, at least without regard to his will, he insists that he is a mere man. In his application of these passages, he fully verifies his own observations. By attending only to some " particular expres-" sions, and neglecting, or *wholly overlooking* others, the " strangest and most unaccountable opinions may be ascrib-" ed to writers. Nay, without considering the relation that " particular expressions bear to others, and to the tenor of " the whole work, sentiments the very reverse of those " which the writers meant to inculcate may be ascribed to " them *."

But Dr P. is not done with this objection. He illustrates it in the following manner : If Christ " was the " Maker of the world, and if, in the creation of it, he ex-" erted no power but what properly *belonged to himself*, and " what was as much *his own*, as the power of *speaking*, or " *walking* belongs to man (though depending ultimately " upon that supreme Power, in which we all live, and move, " and have our being) he could not, with any propriety,
" and

* Earl. Op. vol. i. p. 2.

" and without knowing that he muſt be miſunderſtood, have
" ſaid that *of himſelf he could do nothing*, that *the words*
" *which he ſpake were not his own*, and that *the Father*
" *within him did the works* *."

Did this power belong to Chriſt alone, the Doctor's inference would be juſt.   But power may *properly* belong to
one, although not excluſively.   Thus Chriſt as " the Maker
" of the world," and as " exerting no power but what pro-
" perly *belonged to himſelf*," might ſay with propriety " that
" *of himſelf he could do nothing.*"   His language might have
been liable to miſinterpretation, had he ſaid nothing more
than what our author is pleaſed to quote.   But he *knew* that
he could *not* be *miſunderſtood* by any who were not determined to wreſt his words; as he added ;—*but whatſoever he
ſeeth the Father doing.*   For this expreſſion muſt have convinced his hearers, that he claimed an operation as extenſive
as the Father's.   The deſign and connexion of the other
paſſage as clearly ſhew that he could not be miſunderſtood
by his diſciples.

The reſemblance uſed by the learned writer is certainly
ill-choſen.   For he could not be " the Maker of the world,"
whoſe power did not more *properly belong to himſelf*, than
the power of ſpeaking or walking to man.   For the creature is dependent on God his Maker for the whole of his
power.   But this cannot be ſaid of the Son.   For he doth
all the works of the Father ομοιως, *in the ſame manner*, John
v. 19.   I ſhould alſo think, that a man " depends on that
" ſupreme Power in which we all live, and move, and have
" our being," not merely *ultimately*, but *immediately*.   Unleſs, it can be proved, that we can ſpeak without breathing,
every exertion of this faculty muſt proceed from Him who
giveth to all, not merely the principle of *life*, but *breath*,
and all things.   If it be allowed that *walking* is one ſpecies

Q 2   of

* Ibid. p. 14.

of motion; undoubtedly, in the exerciſe of this power alſo, we muſt immediately depend on Him *in* whom we *move*.

C H A P. VII.

Of the Proof of our Saviour's Divine Nature, from his forgiving Sin.

JESUS claimed the prerogative of conferring forgive-neſs. Even Socinians will not refuſe that the proper exerciſe of this power belongs to God only. But Dr P. when illuſtrating our Saviour's language to the paralytic man, Matt. ix. 2. expreſſes himſelf in this manner: " Chriſt " being appointed the *King* and *Judge* of men, had power " given him adapted to theſe offices, eſpecially the know- " ledge of the human heart, and the prerogative of declaring " the forgiveneſs of ſin, which always accompanies the re- " gal authority; but being aſſiſted by divine wiſdom and " diſcernment, as well as by divine power in the exerciſe of " this high office, it is, in fact, the ſame thing as the judg- " ment and mercy of God diſplayed by the inſtrumentality " of Jeſus Chriſt *." His ideas concerning the knowledge of the heart, we have already conſidered. He confines our Saviour's prerogative to that of merely *declaring* the for-giveneſs of ſin. Jeſus indeed ſaid to the man ſick of the palſy, *Thy ſins be forgiven thee.* This is all that the Doc-tor quotes. But even this is more than a mere declaration of forgiveneſs. The ſcribes underſtood it as a claim of power actually to forgive. For they ſaid, *This man blaſ-phemeth.* Chriſt ſpoke the ſame words to the woman who had been a ſinner : and his hearers put the ſame conſtruction on them,

* Famil. Illuſtr. p. 22,

them. *Then they that sat at meat with him, began to say among themselves, Who is this that forgiveth sins also?* Luke vii. 48, 49. We have no reason to think, that, in either of these instances, they misunderstood him. For with respect to the former, he expressed his meaning still more clearly, addressing himself to those who inwardly accused him of blasphemy ; *That ye may know that the Son of man hath power on earth to forgive sins* (*he saith to the sick of the palsy*) *Arise, take up thy bed*, &c. He wrought a miracle expressly for the purpose of shewing them, that he had power, not merely to declare the forgiveness of sins, but actually to forgive them. An inspired apostle ascribes the same power to Jesus; nay, speaks of this as the common faith : *As Christ forgave you, so also do ye*, Col. iii. 13.

Some Socinians have been more liberal to Jesus, than our author seems disposed to be. They have acknowledged, that he really had power given him to forgive sin, in consequence of his exaltation. But our Lord Jesus, who is *the only wise God*, foreseeing the impiety of his adversaries, hath provided an antidote. For he claimed this power, and wrought a miracle to prove that he really possessed it, in his state of humiliation. *That ye may know*, he says, *that the Son of man hath power* ON EARTH *to forgive sins*, &c. Therefore, if any deny this important truth, they do not err for want of means. They *may* know it, if they do not wilfully resist the clearest evidence.

But I am rather at a loss to know what the Doctor means by saying, that " the prerogative of declaring the forgive-" ness of sin *always* accompanies the regal authority." It cannot be supposed that he refers to the royal prerogative of extending mercy to condemned malefactors, *of forgiving sin* against the state. For this is more than he grants to the Saviour. Besides, it has not been *universally* accounted a necessary accompaniment of regal authority. Does he mean the

right

right of merely *declaring* this forgivenefs? But how can this be a natural concomitant of royalty, without the right of actually forgiving? We have not heard of any prince pluming himfelf on the poffeffion of " this high office," as our author calls it. Did he talk to a temporal monarch, of his " prerogative of declaring the forgivenefs of fin ;" he would certainly apprehend that the good man miftook him for *His Holinefs*. The only thing that could make him he-fitate, would be the meannefs of the afcription, which even the *Servant of the fervants of Jefus* would reckon an infult to his dignity.

But according to the nature of the expreffion, without infifting on its aukward fingularity, evidently meant to ferve the prefent purpofe, the prerogative of the *King of kings* muft be unfpeakably inferior to that of many earthly potentates, who have the right of actually forgiving crimes againft the ftate. But our author exhibits the King of Zion as a mere herald. He referves no other honour for him than that of proclamation. However, this declaratory func-tion may be greater than we apprehend. For Jefus is " af-" fifted" not only " by divine wifdom and difcernment," but " by divine power," in the exercife of " this high of-" fice." Whatever ufe the Doctor may fuppofe for the former, I cannot conceive what he has to do with the latter. One would not think, that the mere intimation of a fentence required much power. But here we have a parcel of *great fwelling words* heaped together, to hide the mere nothing that is left in point of fact; like the many pompous titles of a prince without power, and without dominions.

The Doctor's magic lanthorn, entirely different in its con-ftruction from thofe generally ufed, having the power of re-ducing its object almoft to nothing ; he gives a very necef-fary caution to the wondering fpectators. " We ought not " to be *furprifed*," he fays, " at fuch expreffions as this,

     " *Thy*

" *Thy fins be forgiven thee.*" He has certainly fomething
in view that may remove our aftonifhment. Here it is.
" The multitude who faw Chrift exerting a miraculous
" power upon this occafion, and heard him exprefs himfelf in
" this manner, had no idea of his claiming any extraordinary
" power, as *naturally inherent in himfelf*; for it is faid, ver. 8.
" that *when the multitude faw it, they marvelled and glorified*
" *God, who had given fuch power unto men.*" The whole
force of our author's argument is ; " Good Chriftian people,
" there is not the leaft reafon for your wondering that Jefus,
" a mere man, God's fervant, fulfilling that obedience necef-
" fary for his own falvation, fhould not only know the
" thoughts of men, but declare that he had *power to forgive*
" fins ;—*as* the *unbelieving* Jews themfelves did not thence
" conclude that he was a divine Perfon." But the very
Jews were *furprifed*. They *marvelled*. Yes ; " but they
" had no idea of his claiming any extraordinary power as
" *inherent in himfelf.*" If our author has compared this account with that given by the other Evangelifts, which is
not quite improbable, he muft know that the multitude had
no proper ground for entertaining fuch an idea. For it
does not appear, that they heard our Lord's difcourfe. Very
few, indeed, could hear it. For at this time he was in a
houfe, and the croud was fo great that thofe who brought
the paralytic man had to uncover the roof and let him
down from it, Mark ii. 1.—4. But it would have injured
the Doctor's argument, to have referred to this circumftance. At what, then, did the *multitude marvel?* Certainly, at what they *faw*. This is the very language of
that Gofpel quoted by our author. They faw a man carried in on a bed, himfelf walk out, carrying his bed : and
*when they faw, they marvelled, and glorified God, who had
given fuch power unto men*. The miracle, of itfelf, proved
nothing more than a communication of divine power. They

were not acquainted with the ground on which our Lord declared it to be wrought.

But although the multitude " had no idea of his claiming " any extraordinary power, as *inherent in himfelf*," becaufe they had not an opportunity of hearing the claim; it is evident that thofe had who did hear it. The Doctor himfelf fays; " The Scribes and Pharifees, indeed, faid within " themfelves, *This man blafphemeth*, ver. 3." Now, it is probable, that they were almoft the only perfons who had an opportunity of making this reflection. As they always loved the chief feats, we cannot fuppofe that they would be ftanding without, while the vulgar were feated within. Accordingly, we learn that while there was not *room* for the multitude, " not fo much as about the door, certain of " the Scribes were fitting there," that is, in the houfe, Mark ii. 2. 6. Nay, *there were Pharifees and doctors of the law fitting by, which were come out of every town of Galilee, and Judea and Jerufalem*, Luke v. 17. Such a band moft probably filled the houfe. Thus, it would appear that the *idea* was *entertained* by all who had an opportunity of hearing our Lord's difcourfe. They faid, *This man blafphemeth*. And had fome modern *Doctors* been fitting with them, they muft, according to their principles, have joined in the charge.

But we are told, that " the Jews called it *blafphemy*, to " pretend to be the Chrift *." The proof brought to fupport this affertion, we may confider afterwards. But can Dr P. really believe, that thefe Scribes, Pharifees, and Doctors of the law, charged our Lord with blafphemy, on this occafion, becaufe he feemed to claim the character of Meffiah? For the honour of his *reafon*, whatever elfe fhould fuffer in the caufe, we muft fcorn the idea. Could the carnal Jews apprehend, that Jefus pretended to be the Chrift,

by

* Ibid.

by " declaring the forgivenefs of fin?" Did " this high of-
" fice" correfpond with their notions of the Meffiah? Did
they not expect one, whofe work had no refpect whatfoever
to fin, a temporal prince to fubdue their outward enemies?
Or, will our author avail himfelf of his doctrine as to
" regal authority?" Will he choofe to fay, that they charged him with blafphemy, becaufe he claimed that *declaratory*
power, " which always accompanies" it? But did not Dr
P. know, when writing this, that two other Evangelifts exprefsly give, as the reafon of this accufation, that Jefus
claimed what was ftill acknowledged by Jews as the peculiar prerogative of Deity, the power of forgiving fins?
*Why doth this man thus fpeak blafphemies? Who can for-
give fins but God only?* Mark ii. 7. *Who is this that fpeaketh blafphemies? Who can forgive fins but God alone?* Luke
v. 21. Is there one word concerning Chrift or Meffiah
here? while, according to the Doctor's ftrange affertion,
their queftion ought to have been, " *Who can forgive fins*
" *but the Meffiah only?*" Is there any unprejudiced man,
who can doubt that the laft words of thefe cavillers contain
the reafon of the preceding accufation? or, that it was recorded by the Evangelifts with this view? Thefe very Pharifees and Doctors would have blufhed at fuch difingenuity.
Is this the man who is *confident that he is a guide of the
blind, a light of them who are in darknefs, an inftructer of
the foolifh, a teacher of babes?* For all the noife made by
Socinians about *reafon*, one would think that they confidered it as appropriated to a particular herefiarch; and that
the only *reafon*, required of his difciples, were implicitly
to receive his teftimony, even when, as in this inftance, directly contrary to that of the Spirit of infpiration. This
is the *reafon* of an Unitarian, to believe that when the Jews
exprefsly charge our Saviour with blafphemy, for claiming
what themfelves fay, belongs to God alone, they only mean

to

to accuse him of pretending to be a *mere man :* as this, we are told, is the higheſt notion they entertained of the promiſed Meſſiah.

C H A P. VIII.

That Jeſus declared his Deity by calling himſelf the I AM.

THAT God revealed himſelf by this name to his an-
cient people, our opponents cannot deny. When he appeared to Moſes in the buſh, and gave him a commiſſion to the Iſraelites, Moſes inquired how he ſhould anſwer that queſtion, which they would naturally propoſe, *What is his Name ? And God ſaid unto Moſes,* I AM THAT I AM: *and thus ſhalt thou ſay unto the children of Iſrael,* I AM *hath ſent me unto you,* Ex. iii. 14. In his ſubſequent revelations, eſpecially in theſe by the prophet Iſaiah, he often uſed this name, by which he had ſo early made himſelf known. It certainly denotes the eternal, neceſſary, immutable and incomprehenſible exiſtence of God. If it appear, that Jeſus revealed himſelf under this deſignation, in its proper meaning, as applied to God in the Old Teſtament, and that the faith of his diſciples terminated on him in this reſpect; no reaſonable doubt can remain, that he is *God over all,* and that he was acknowledged as ſuch by thoſe whom he employed to publiſh his doctrine to others.

We learn from one of " the three firſt Goſpels," that he promiſed his preſence to his diſciples, by appropriating to himſelf this divine title : *Where two or three are gathered together in my Name, there* AM I *in the midſt of them,* Matt. xviii. 20. It is acknowledged by Dr. P. that this is a " paſ-
" ſage which ſeems to ſuppoſe the omnipreſence of Chriſt *."

This

* Famil. Illuſtr. p. 26.

This is a confiderable conceffion. For thus it is granted, that the great Prophet, whom his people were to *hear in all things, feemed* at leaft to claim divine perfection. If this did not really belong to him, he muft have been unfit for his office, fince he did not abftain from *all appearance of evil**, of the greateft evil, the robbery of making himfelf equal with God. He could not, therefore, be a proper perfon for being heard *in all things*.

" But," out author adds, " if we confider the whole of " this paffage, in which our Lord is fpeaking of the great " power of which his difciples would be poffeffed, and efpe- " cially of the efficacy of their prayers, we fhall be fatisfied " that he could only mean, by this form of expreffion, to " reprefent their power with God, when they were affem- " bled as his difciples, and prayed fo as became his difciples, " to be the fame as his own power with God ; and God " heard him always." The whole that Dr P. feems to wifh, in explaining this verfe, is to deprive Jefus of his glory. If he can accomplifh this, he cares not by w$_h$at means ; nor does he give himfelf any trouble whether he make fenfe of the paffage or not. He will give all this power to the difciples, if he can withhold it from their Mafter. For " this " form of expreffion," he fays, " reprefents *their* power with " God." Or if he leave any to him, it is no more than they poffefs. In this refpect, he will not even allow the *preeminence* to him, to whom the Holy Ghoft afcribes it *in all things*, Col. i. 18. According to this doctrine, any ordinary Chriftian can pray as effectually as Jefus Chrift. But this clearly fhows, how little account we are to make of the highfounding words which Socinians ufe concerning the Saviour. They refemble the falutations of the foldiers, before they crucified him. Do they acknowledge him to be " the Son " of God, his dear Son, the chief of his Sons, the interced-
" ing

* 1 Thef. v. 22.

" ing High Priest, the one Mediator?" But, as the wise man says, *Let us hear the conclusion of the whole matter.* The power of any Christian, praying in a proper manner, is " the same as his power with God."

But as if Dr P. had been conscious that he was palming a sense upon the text that it could not bear; when describing the circumstances in which the intercession of the disciples is as powerful as that of Christ's, he finds it necessary to use some circumlocution :—" When they were assembled " as his disciples, and prayed as became his disciples." What part of his text does this refer to? why, surely, to that expression, *in my Name.* But our author wisely keeps it in the shade, as it must have spoiled the whole picture. For the lowest sense that can be put upon this phrase must imply, that he is in *some* respect superior to them ; else why use his Name at all? Their own would do as well. But if, when thus " assembled as his disciples, and praying as be- " comes them," that is, *gathered together in his Name*, their prayers are so effectual, they must have still less occasion for his being *in the midst of* them. And how is he *in the midst of* them? That the Doctor leaves to the reader himself to discover. Although we could believe the blasphemous absurdity, that their power with God is as great as his; we could never suppose this to be meant by that expression, *there am I in the midst of them.* For this language, as used in Scripture, always respects the presence of a Person *. If his presence be still necessary, one would think that they had also some occasion for his *power.*

But as Jesus does not help them in prayer, we need not wonder that he does not *hear* them. For the Doctor adds ; " That our Lord could not intend to speak of himself as " *the God who heareth prayer,* is evident from his speaking " of the Father, in this very place, as the person who was

3   " to

---

* Vid. Hoornbeck Socin. Confutat. tom. 1. p. 150.

" to grant their petitions, ver. 19. *Again I say unto you,*
" *that if two of you shall agree on earth, as touching any*
" *thing, it shall be done for them, of my Father who is in*
" *heaven* *." But this is begging what the Doctor has yet
to prove, that becaufe the Father is God, the Son cannot
be fo. It is granted, that, according to the œconomy of redemption, the gift of all bleffings is primarily afcribed to
the Father. But they all come immediately from Chrift.
For the Father hath *given all things into his hand.* Therefore our Lord informs them, how every bleffing proceeds
from the Father. It is by his own prefence. Inftead of
there being any contradiction between ver. 19. and that immediately under confideration, according to the fenfe in
which we view it, there is the moft perfect harmony. In the
former, our Lord merely declares the efficacy of focial prayer.
But, in the latter, he proceeds to fhew the only way in
which it is effectual. It muft be in his name, that is, from
a regard to his authority, and in the exercife of faith in him.
Now, how a mere man can be the object of faith, let the
Doctor fhew at his leifure : and this may be the more difficult, as Socinians are very fhy of allowing this honour to
God himfelf. But befides, the prefence of Chrift is promifed to the difciples, as their fecurity for the gift of the
bleffing prayed for. And how a mere man in heaven can
be always prefent with two or three on earth, fo as to be
really *in the midft of them*, is another difficulty which it belongs to our author to folve. The connexion of the two
verfes undeniably fhews, that the whole efficacy of the
prayers of his people depends, not merely on their praying
in his Name, but on their enjoying his prefence. *It fhall
be done for them.* FOR, *where two or three,* &c.

It would be natural to fuppofe that he who anfwered prayer, fhould alfo hear it. But we know that Jefus anfwers the

prayers

* Fam. Illuftr. ib.

prayers of his people. For he fays, John xiv. 13, 14. *What-foever ye fhall afk in my Name, that will I do, that the Father may be glorified in the Son. If ye fhall afk any thing in my Name, I will do it.* This paffage explains the other. It fhows how Chrift is *in the midft of* his praying people. It is to do what they afk in his Name. Thus *the Father is glorified in the Son,* becaufe the bleffing afked is given, by the Son as Mediator, from the Father, œconomically confidered as the fountain of all grace.

There are feveral things in thefe words, which fhew that Chrift claims the honour of Deity. He not only fuppofes his followers to be congregated in his Name, (language never ufed of a creature) ; but he fays, *There am I ;* evidently intimating, that he is prefent wherever this is the cafe. We cannot believe this, without believing that he is every where prefent. Here he ufes that mode of fpeaking appropriated by God to himfelf, under the Old Teftament. Εχει ειμι exactly correfponds with '‎אֲנִי שָׁם, *There am I,* Ifa. xlviii. 16. Although our author cannot perceive that " Chrift intends to fpeak of himfelf as *the God that heareth* " *prayer,*" this phrafe muft have been familiar to a Jewifh ear. For it is the very language ufed by God, when he reveals himfelf in this character : *Then fhalt thou call, and the Lord fhall anfwer ; thou fhalt cry, and he fhall fay,* HERE I AM, Ifa. lviii. 9.

They could be no lefs acquainted with the expreffion connected with it,—*in the midft of them.* For in a great variety of places in the Old Teftament, God had thus declared his prefence with his people, and his protection of them, his readinefs to hear and to help them. When they were in the wildernefs, next to their total deftruction, the greateft judgment he could threaten was this, *I will not go up in the midft of them,* Ex. xxxiii. 3. Afterwards he faid to them, *The Lord thy God walketh in the midft of thy camp, to deli-*

ver thee, and to give up thine enemies before thee, Deut. xxiii.
14. Here he immediately refers to the vifible tokens of
his prefence in the tabernacle of the congregation, which was
in the midft of the camp, and which prefigured his *taberna-
cling* in flefh *among* his people, (John i. 14.) From this very
confideration, that *God is in the midft of her,* the church affures herfelf that *God fhall help her, and that right early,*
Pfal. xlvi. 5. This was her confolation amidft her greateft
calamities : *Yet thou, O Lord, art in the midft of us, and we
are called by thy Name,* Jer. xiv. 9. We need not obferve,
that there is a ftriking conformity between this paffage and
the words of our Saviour.

. But this language does not merely refpect God's typical
prefence amongft his people. It fometimes exprefsly regards
the glorious Antitype. Therefore, when it is faid, *God is in
the midft of her,* the church evidently refers to *Immanuel;*
for fhe adds, *The Lord of hofts is* WITH US, Pfal. xlvi. 7.
This is declared to be the fong of Zion in the gofpel day ;
Great is the Holy One of Ifrael in the midft of thee, Ifa.
xii. 6. Concerning the fame period it is faid ; *The
King of Ifrael, even* JEHOVAH, *is in the midft of thee;
thou fhalt not fee evil any more,* Zeph. iii. 15. And again,
Ye fhall praife the NAME *of the Lord your God :—and ye
fhall know that I am in the midft of Ifrael, and that I am
the Lord your God, and none elfe,* Joel ii. 27. The proof
given of this is fo remarkable, that the difciples muft
have underftood, when the Spirit was poured down, at leaft,
that Chrift was the glorious Perfon who fpoke by Joel. For
it immediately follows ; *And it fhall come to pafs that I will
pour out my Spirit upon all flefh ; and your fons and your
daughters fhall prophefy,* ver. 28 *.—Thus, the difciples
being Jews, accuftomed to this language, could not but underftand

---

* Compared with Acts ii. 16.—18.

derstand our Lord as promising his continual presence with them, as really as the divine presence had been enjoyed under the Old Testament; and indeed in that more excellent way foretold with respect to the New.

The Doctor also quotes Matt. xxviii. 20. *Lo, I am with you always, even unto the end of the world;* and makes a feeble attempt to shew that these words convey no idea of power that may not belong to a mere creature. " Christ," he says, " who is constituted *head over all things* to his church, " undoubtedly takes care of its interests, and attends to " whatever concerns his disciples; and *being with* a person, " and *taking care* of him are, in the language of scripture; " equivalent expressions. See Gen. xxi. 20. 22. xxviii 15. " xxxix. 2 *." This is very true. But the Doctor forgets to tell his reader, that in the passages referred to, this *being with* a Person denotes *God's taking care* of him; and that it is a care extending to all places where the Person may be, Gen. xxviii. 15. and to all actions, chap. xxi. 22. Now, this is all that we assert; with this difference only, that what is spoken, in the places cited, of an individual, is here promised to a collective body in succession.

Dr P. adds; " Besides, Christ having a near relation to " this earth, may even be *personally present* with his disci- " ples when they little think of it." I need not say, that by " being personally present," he means the presence of his human nature only. Now, after this position, our author will find it very difficult to maintain his ground against the church of Rome. He is more nearly allied to her than he imagines. I should wish to know how he is pleased to dispose of such a passage as this? *He shall send Jesus Christ, —whom the heaven must receive, until the times of restitution of all things,* Acts iii. 20, 21. I might also refer to that, *Though we have known Christ after the flesh, yet now henceforth*

* Famil. Illustr. p. 26.

henceforth know we him no more, 2 Cor. v. 16. But the Doctor has his anfwer ready. Chrift may know his difciples *after the flefh,* or according to the human nature, when they do not know him in this way, that is, " when they little " think of it." Our author feems to differ much from the glorious Perfon of whom he thus fpeaks, who faid to his hearers, *The flefh profiteth nothing,* John vi. 63. But the promife can be of little fervice to Dr P. even according to his own explanation. For it is not matter of faith with him, but only of probability : " Chrift—*may* be perfonally " prefent." After this, however, he may fpare his ridicule at the doctrine of *Tranfubftantiation.* For if Chrift may be prefent as to his human nature, when his difciples " lit- " tle think of it:" that is, when they have no fenfible evi- dence of his prefence, it will be difficult for the Doctor to prove, that he may not be prefent, as to his real body and blood, when his difciples can fee, and feel, and tafte nothing but bread and wine.

Thus, both Papifts and Socinians hold a real bodily prefence : and they perfectly agree in this important point, that Jefus may be really prefent, without fenfible figns. He who believes this, has already fwallowed the moft unpalata- ble morfel in the doctrine of tranfubftantiation. For, ac- cording to the confeffion of Roman Catholics themfelves, great as the miracle of the converfion of the wafer into the body and blood of Chrift is, that of his being thus really prefent, without any evidence to the fenfes, is far more amazing and ftupenduous *.

But the Doctor does not therefore affert the omnipre- fence of Chrift. He has difcovered that the difciples can do without this. " It is by no means neceffary," he fays, " that he be perfonally prefent every where at the fame " time." I fufpected that matters would have this end, al-

* Moore's View of Society and Manners in Italy, Let. 64.

though the Doctor begun with informing us, that " Chrift
" attends to whatever concerns his difciples." What is to
become of thofe poor creatures, with whom he does not
happen to be perfonally prefent, in the time of their neceffity? How does he attend to their concerns? Let us hear
our author. " It is by no means neceffary,—fince God may
" communicate to him a power of knowing diftant events, cf
" which he appeared to be poffeffed when Lazarus was
" fick." But, pray, what does the power of knowing diftant events fignify, without ·the power of affifting every
believer? If but one be neglected, the work of the Mediator is imperfect. And if he is not every where prefent,
either myriads muft be neglected ; or it remains to be proved, that the neceffities of Chriftians are fo difpofed, that
every one can wait till it come to his turn to be relieved.
If Jefus has only the " power of knowing diftant events,"
without that of fuccouring every individual, would he not
be as well without it? Such a power can be of very little
advantage to *the multitude of them who believe :* and it muft
rather give pain, than pleafure, to the poffeffor ; becaufe
he muft feel himfelf in the fituation of one who knows the
mifery of a beloved friend, but by reafon'of diftance, or
multiplicity of engagements, can be of no fervice to him.
How can he be *head over all things*, who can attend to fome
things only? When on fome emergency, he happens to be
on earth, if a greater occur, and the cry reach to heaven,
what is to be done?· Is the work performed by another ?
Then, the unity of the divine adminiftration is deftroyed ;
and fomething is taken out of his hand, *into* whofe *hand all
things* have been *given.* But how could *all power* be *given
unto him*, who has only *fome* power ; nay, rather knowledge
than power? The Doctor, indeed, ferioufly gives as ridiculous a defcription of him whom he calls his Saviour, as
Elijah ironically gave of Baal. His difciples will need to·

. . *cry*

cry aloud; for peradventure their Lord *is on a journey,*
1 Kings xviii. 27.

But after all, our author is not certain, whether God
really communicates this " power of knowing diftant events"
to Jefus, or whether he had this " when Lazarus was fick :"
His faith is of a very doubtful kind. It ftill refts in *may
be's* and *appearances.* " He *may* communicate.—He *ap-
" peared* to be poffeffed." The only thing of which the
Doctor feems certain, is, that, even in his *fuppofitions,* he
does not grant too much honour to the Redeemer. " This
" is *certainly,*" he fays, " no greater power than God may
" communicate to any of his creatures." Pray, do take care,
Sir, that nothing more be afcribed to the Son of God, than
may be given to *any creature,* however low in the fcale of
being. You certainly *do God fervice,* in doing all in your
power *againft the name of Jefus of Nazareth.* Whatever
be your error, it is not that of *honouring the Son as the
Father.*

But it gives our author no trouble, that his comment is a
flat denial of the text. Jefus fays to his difciples, *Lo, I am
with you* ALWAYS. Dr P. fays, that he is with them *at
times* only. Jefus gives his difciples reafon to believe. that
they conftantly need his prefence. " Nay," fays the Doctor, " this is by no means neceffary." Jefus affures them,
that *all power is given unto him in heaven, and in earth,*
which, one would think, implied divine power. Our author is perfuaded, that Jefus is deftitute of the moft neceffary power, that of being every where prefent, in order to
relieve his difciples : and is not certain, if he has even that
of knowing their neceffities. Of this alone he is *certain,*
that Jefus has *no* power given him that *may* not be " com-
" municated to *any* creature" in heaven, or in earth.

Having illuftrated the futility of Dr P.'s expofition, it
may be proper to obferve a few things concerning this pro-

mife. There is a remarkable correfpondence between it and what we have in Hag. i. 13. *I am with you, faith the Lord.* The Evangelift ufes the very words of the Seventy, with no variation, but that of arrangement. The Greek fairly expreffes the force of that phrafeology in the Hebrew, by which God ftill denotes his own prefence in the church. We have the fame promife, with an important enlargement, addreffed to Zerubbabel and Jofhua, chap. ii. 4, 5. *Be ftrong and work, for I am with you, faith the Lord of hofts, with the Word that I covenanted with you, when ye came out of Egypt ; and my Spirit remaining among you.* This we have elfewhere fhewn to be the literal tranflation of the paffage *. Now, either thefe words, *I am with you,* fpoken by Chrift to his difciples, have the fame meaning as when delivered by Haggai, as the meffage of JEHOVAH ; or, the fervants of the Lord, in gofpel times, have lefs encouragement than thofe whom he called to *work,* under the law.

The promife evidently imports a conftant uninterrupted prefence : *I am with you all days,* or *at all times.* There is not only the ufe of that fingular and emphatic expreffion, εγω ειμι, *I am,* correfponding with the language of God under the Old Teftament ; but the prefent and future are at once connected : *I am with you—to the end of the world.* We have no example of the ufe of this language, but by a divine Perfon. Thus God expreffes his immutable exiftence, by joining the prefent, fometimes with the paft, and fometimes with the future ; fignifying, that how much foever the creature may change, there is no change with him. *From the time that it was, there I am,* Ifa. xlviii. 16. *Even to your old age I am he,* chap. xlvi. 4. If Jefus be not God, he at leaft affumes his peculiar language. But he is, indeed, *the fame yefterday, to-day, and for ever,* Heb. xiii. 8.

Befides, he introduces this promife with a note of admiration,

---

* See above, p. 120, &c.

ration, *Lo !* This is the very manner in which God foretold that he would announce himfelf to his church in the
laft times.   There is one prophecy that may well carry terror to the heart of a Socinian.   *My Name continually
every day is blafphemed.   Therefore, my people fhall know
my Name; therefore they fhall know, in that day, that I am
he that doth fpeak, Behold, it is I;* or, rather, without the
fupplement, *Behold,* or, *Lo, I,* Ifa. lii. 6.   This feems to be
pointed out as the very language that the God of Ifrael
would utter, in the Gofpel difpenfation, as difcovering himfelf to his people.   For he is introduced as fpeaking with
refpect to the Gentiles, chap. lxv. 1.   *I faid, Behold me, Behold me.*   With fully as much propriety it may be read,
Behold, I. For the word is the fame in the Hebrew as in
chap. lii. 6. and, in the Septuagint, it is tranflated in the
very language ufed by the Evangelift Matthew, in recording the words of Jefus, Ιδε ειμι.   The expreffion feems to
fignify that this glorious *Speaker* was clearly to unfold his
own excellency, that he was *one who fhould bear witnefs of
himfelf,* John viii. 18.   When the woman of Samaria faid,
I know that Meffias cometh, Jefus anfwered her in the very
language of God by the prophet; *I, that fpeak unto thee,
am* *.   And, truly, all his genuine difciples know that it is
he that doth fpeak thefe comfortable words, *Lo, I am with
you.*   It is worthy of our notice, that immediately after
that remarkable declaration in Ifaiah, there follows a very
pathetic defcription of the fervants of Chrift who were to
go forth preaching the Gofpel, *beginning at Jerufalem.*—
*How beautiful upon the mountains are the feet of him that
bringeth good tidings, that publifheth peace, that bringeth good tidings of good, that publifheth falvation, that
faith unto Zion, Thy God reigneth,* ver. 7 †. as if *the Spirit*

R 3   *of*

* Εγω ειμι, ο λαλων σοι. John iv. 26. Ifa. lii. 6. according to the Septuagint, is, Εγω ειμι αυτος ο λαλων.

† Vid. Heidegger. Hiftor. Patriarch. vol. i. Exer. iii. f. 12.

of Chrift would *teftify before hand* the very circumftances in which he fhould exprefsly utter the language under confideration, to his fervants, *Go ye, and teach all nations,—and lo, I am with you ;* and that all their ftrength for that work, and comfort in it, depended on this declaration.

I fhall only add, that Jefus appropriates this divine language to himfelf, at the very time that he commanded the difciples to baptize all nations *in his Name,* as well as in that of the Father and Spirit. The force of this command may be afterwards illuftrated.

On other occafions, our Lord fpeaks of himfelf in the fame ftyle. He faid to the Jews, *If ye believe not that I am, ye fhall die in your fins,* John viii. 24. He evidently fpeaks in this manner, with refpect to his divine origin, which he declared to be unknown to the Jews, ver. 14. *Ye cannot tell whence I come.* Now, he could not have faid this in truth, had he had no higher origin than his birth of Mary. For with this they were all acquainted, Matt. xiii. 55. He had faid, *I am not alone, but I and the Father that fent me,* ver. 16. language which we cannot conceive to be applicable, in any fenfe, to a creature. He had declared that they did not know his Father, and that if they had known him, they would have known his Father alfo, ver. 19. He had faid, as in the verfe immediately preceding, *I am from above.* That this directly refpects his origin, we learn from the ufe of the fame language by John Baptift; who contrafts his own *earthly* origin with his, who, being *from above,* muft of neceffity be *above all,* chap. iii. 31. In the clofe of this difcourfe, our Lord ufes that remarkable expreffion, *Before Abraham was, I am,* ver. 58. It is clear that he proclaims himfelf to be a divine Perfon. For when Abraham is fpoken of, the verb γινομαι is ufed. But ειμι is introduced to exprefs the exiftence of the Saviour. The firft properly denotes fuch a being as implies beginning, and refers to

birth

birth or creation. But the other is always uſed, when ſelf-exiſtence is meant. The ſame diſtinction is here obſerved, as in the introduction to this Goſpel. Whereas the Evangeliſt ſays, *In the beginning* ην, *was the Word*, the exiſtence of all creatures is very differently expreſſed; *All things* εγενετο, *were made by him*. Thus our Lord oppoſes his own eternal *exiſtence* to the *making*, or, which is the ſame, to the *birth* of Abraham. He alſo ſpeaks of his own exiſtence in the preſent time, while that of Abraham is expreſſed in the paſt: *Before Abraham was made*, or, *born*, *I am*. Thus, he oppoſes the immutability of his exiſtence to the changeable nature of the creature. Here there ſeems to be a tacit, though ſtriking reply to their own teſtimony concerning Abraham and the prophets, ver. 53. *Art thou greater than our father Abraham, who is dead? And the prophets are dead.* It was a full anſwer to the queſtion ſubjoined, WHOM *makeſt thou thyſelf?* It is as if he had ſaid, " By your own " confeſſion, the moſt that can be ſaid of Abraham, is, that " he *was*; but, in every period of time, it may juſtly be " ſaid of me, that *I am*." Theſe words muſt be viewed in their connexion with the awful declaration he had formerly made, ver. 24. *If ye believe not that I am, ye ſhall die in your ſins.* They were ſo to believe this, as to be aſſured in their minds that he exiſted before Abraham. This faith alone could preſerve them from condemnation.

To ſay, that this is a mere *enallage*, is ridiculous. For we cannot ſuppoſe ſo unuſual a change of the preſent for the paſt, without a very peculiar reaſon. Some have pretended, that our Lord here ſpeaks of his being *before Abraham*, as to the decree. But it has been juſtly urged in reply, that the word ειμι *am*, when uſed abſolutely, denotes *actual* exiſtence, and that this is confirmed by the uſe of the pronoun εγω, *I;* that there is nothing in the context to ſhew that the language of our Saviour is not to be underſtood abſolutely; that, as the queſtion propoſed by the Jews reſpected his perſonal exiſtence, whether he had *ſeen Abraham*, if his anſwer did not alſo reſpect this, it was not in point; and that, as it was our Lord's deſign to ſhew that he was older than Abraham, if he only declared, that he was fore-ordained in the purpoſe of God, before Abraham's birth, it proved nothing; becauſe, in the ſame ſenſe, every one of his hearers might have claimed a priority *.

To ſuppoſe that Jeſus meant to evade a direct anſwer to their queſtion, is to do him the greateſt injury. It is to charge him with the profanation of a ſolemn oath. For he prefaces his declaration with theſe words, *Amen, amen*; which he never uſes, but on the moſt important occaſions and intereſting ſubjects. For this was the Jewiſh mode of ſwearing; and as uſed by him, expreſſes his moſt ſolemn teſtimony, as *the Amen, the faithful and true witneſs*. Here alſo we find him expreſſing himſelf in language never employed, either by prophets, or by apoſtles; *Verily, verily, I* SAY *unto you*. The prophets had always exhibited God as the ſpeaker. Their common introduction was, *Thus ſaith the Lord*. The apoſtles never delivered a meſſage in their own name. But Jeſus ſtill expreſſed himſelf in this manner.

The vanity of another Socinian ſubterfuge, that our Lord means to aſſert his exiſtence, before Abraham *was made,* —*the father of many nations*, has been fully illuſtrated by Dr Whitby, in his expoſition of this paſſage. But it is ſo egregiouſly mean, that the Jews themſelves, though, for the honour of their father Abraham, they had inclined to torture our Saviour's language, would have bluſhed to have uſed it.

Dr P. gives another view of theſe words. " The mean-" ing of this paſſage," he ſays, " clearly is, that Abraham " *foreſaw* the day of Chriſt, and that Chriſt was the ſubject

of

---

* Vide Lampe in loc.

" of prophecy before the times of Abraham *." It is sometimes of great ufe, in a bad caufe, for a man to feem confident of its. goodnefs. But matters are not quite fo *clear* as
the Doctor apprehends. For the queftion, to which this
was the anfwer, was not, " Hath Abraham feen thee ?" but,
Haft thou feen Abraham? And furely, there is a confiderable difference between the two. What Abraham faw, was
the day of Chrift. But if Chrift's reply has any relation
to the queftion, or any meaning; what he faw, was Abraham *himfelf*. The learned gentleman, in his view, blends
two things totally different. The Jews feem to have at
firft mifunderftood our Saviour, when he faid, *Abraham
faw my day*; as if he had afferted, that he had feen Abraham's day. Therefore they faid, *Thou art not yet fifty
years old, and haft thou feen Abraham?* But Jefus, in his
reply, fhews them that what they inferred by miftake, was
true in itfelf. Had he faid, " Before Abraham was, I *was*,"
it would have been lefs ridiculous to have explained it of
his being " the fubject of prophecy." But what does our
author make of that expreffion, *I am?* However, though
it had been, *I was*, the fenfe impofed by him would ftill be
extremely unnatural. What would the Jews have thought
of John Baptift, had he told them that he was before Jeremiah, fecretly meaning that he had been prophefied of by
Ifaiah? If the learned writer have no *clearer* illuftrations
of fcripture to offer to the public, for the honour of the
word of God, and for the credit of his own underftanding,
which perhaps weighs as much with him, he had better
confine himfelf to ftudies that feem more fuitable to his
genius.

He adds; " This faying of our Lord is illuftrated by
" what the author of the epiftle to the Hebrews fays con-
" cerning all the ancient worthies, *viz.* that they *all died in*
" *faith,*

---

* Famil. Illuftr. p. 40.

" *faith, not having received the promifes, but having feen*
" *them afar off* In this manner, therefore, Abraham faw
" the day of Chrift." This quotation, indeed, illuftrates
the *firft* " faying of our Lord,"—*He faw it, and was glad.*
But what comes of the *fecond ? Before Abraham was, I am.*
Though Abraham faw the day of Chrift *afar off,* what is
this to the purpofe of Chrift's feeing Abraham, though he
did not feem to be *fifty years old ?*

*Dr Priefley's objection to the argument from the ufe of thc
title,* I A M, *confidered.*

THE only notice that our author directly takes of this
remarkable expreffion, is in the following obfervation. " As to thofe who think that our Lord meant to in-
" timate that he was truly and properly God becaufe he
" ufed that expreffion *I am,* by which the true God announ-
" ced himfelf to Mofes, they will perhaps be fenfible how
" little ftrefs is to be laid upon it, when they are informed,
" that, though the fame phrafe occurs very often in the
" hiftory of Chrift, our tranflators themfelves in every place
" excepting this, render it by *I am he,* that is, I am the
" Chrift. It is ufed in this fenfe in the 24th verfe of this
" Chapter, *If ye believe not that I am he, ye fhall die in
" your fins.* And again in the 28th verfe, *When ye fhall
" (have) lift up the Son of man, then fhall ye know that I
" am he* *." This, then, is the mighty proof of " the
" little ftrefs to be laid upon it,"—the authority of a tranflation. Can this be the fame perfon, who, in the page immediately preceding, quarrels with the tranflation of that
expreffion in Phil. ii. 6. rendered *equal with God. Quantum*

* Famil. Illuftr. p. 41.

tum mutatus ab illo? But this gentleman can, either contradict our venerable translators point-blank, or argue from
their version, as if they had been infpired; juft as it fuits
the prefent purpofe. It is evident, however, that they wifh
the reader to obferve, that the pronoun *he* is a fupplement,
as it is inferted in different characters from the reft of the
verfe. The Doctor is miftaken, when he afferts that " our
" tranflators, in every place, excepting this, render the ex-
" preffion, *I am he.*" For in three different places, it is rendered, *It is I.* When Jefus came walking on the waters,
it was thus he rebuked the fear of the difciples; *Be not
afraid* εγω ειμι, literally, *I am*, Matt. xiv. 27. Mark vi. 50.
John vi. 20. Here he evidently utters the language in which
God was wont to addrefs their fathers; *Fear not, I am
with thee*, Ifa. xli. 10. He declares himfelf to be a Perfon
of fuch dignity and power that his prefence ought to remove all unbelieving fear.

Dr P. cannot refufe, that " the true God announced him-
" felf to Mofes" by that expreffion which our Lord ufes.
The learned Whitby, before he became Socinian, underftood this language as relating to the Deity of Chrift. Finding, however, that it is mentioned as an expreffion common with the *falfe Chrifts* he offers the following folution
of the difficulty. " As for the phrafe, εγω ειμι, *I am*, let it
" be noted, that in the other Evangelifts it is only ufed to
" fignify what the *falfe Chrifts* would fay, and fo can have
" no other import than *I am the Chrift;* but in this Gofpel
" it feems to fignify, *I am the Son of God;* for he that faith
" *I am, &c* *."

But I am willing to give all its force to Dr P.'s objection,
and to admit that, whenever Chrift ufes this expreffion, it
refpects him even as Meffiah. Yet I muft refufe the Doctor's inference, that therefore it " does not mean the eternal
" God."

* Paraph. on John viii. 58.

" God." For the only Meffiah exhibited in fcripture, is *God manifefted in the flefh.* The *miffion* of the Son is always affumed, by Socinians, as a fufficient objection to his equality with the Father. But as they allow that JEHOVAH ufes this language in the Old Teftament, if it appear that he ufes it in the character of one *fent*, it muft follow that the objection receives a full anfwer from God himfelf.

It may certainly be laid down as a firft principle, that he who fpoke to Mofes was the true God. For the Doctor has acknowledged that " the true God announced himfelf " to Mofes by that expreffion *I am."* But the Holy Spirit informs us, that he who fpoke in this manner was an Angel : *The Angel of the Lord appeared unto him in a flame of fire, out of the midft of a bufh*, Ex. iii. 2. It cannot be faid that, although an Angel appeared, it was JEHOVAH himfelf who fpoke. For the glorious Speaker commands Mofes to fay : JEHOVAH *the God of your fathers, the God of Abraham, of Ifaac, and of Jacob, appeared unto me*, ver. 16. The Perfon that *fpoke*, was the fame that *appeared* unto Mofes ; and he who appeared, was *the God of Abraham.* Mofes was fully convinced of this. For *he was afraid to look upon God*, ver. 6. Socinians, by refufing that this Angel was a divine Perfon, produce that very objection which Mofes expected to meet with from the ignorant and ftubborn Ifraelites. *They will fay*, JEHOVAH *hath not appeared unto thee*, chap. iv. 1. But that he might be able to make an effectual reply to it, God gives him the power of working miracles, adding as the reafon of the gift ;----*that they may believe that* JEHOVAH, *the God of their fathers, hath appeared unto thee*, ver. 5.

It is well known, that the Septuagint was commonly ufed among the Jews, at the time that the New Teftament was wrote. Now, it deferves our particular attention, that our Lord adopts that very phrafeology concerning himfelf, Rev.

i. 8; that is ufed by the Seventy to exprefs the language in
" which the true God announced himfelf to Mofes." In both
places we have that expreffion, Εγω ειμι ο ων. But Jefus,
knowing that this was the very language by which the Jews
denoted the true and felf-exiftent God, if this charaɛter does
not belong to him, intrenched on the honours of Deity, by
arrogating them to himfelf. I need not take time to fhew
that Jefus is the fpeaker in Rev. i. 8. This is undeniable
from his claiming the fame charaɛters with thofe unqueftionably claimed by him ver. 11. 17. chap. ii. 8. xxii. 13.

An Angel was afterwards promifed as the leader of Ifrael.
God faid; *Behold, I fend an Angel before thee, to keep thee
in the way, and to bring thee unto the place which I have promifed.* By way of diftinɛtion, God calls him *his* Angel;
Mine Angel fhall go before thee, Ex. xxiii. 20. 23. From
the account given of this Angel, in the book of Exodus, we
might fafely conclude that it was he who appeared to Mofes,
and revealed himfelf as the I AM. The work affigned
him was that of bringing Ifrael into the place which God
had prepared. But the Angel who appeared to Mofes in a
flame of fire claimed this work as his: *I am come down----
to bring them up into a good land,* chap. iii. 8. vi. 8. The
charaɛters given him are divine: *My Name is in him,* chap.
xxiii. 21. His *voice* is fpoken of as the fame with God's,
ver. 22. chap. xix. 5:

But we have clear evidence from fcripture, that the Angel promifed was he who appeared unto Mofes. For Stephen declares concerning this Prophet, that *God fent him
a ruler and deliverer by the hand of the Angel who appeared
to him in the bufh,* Aɛts vii. 35. This does not merely fignify that God employed this Angel in the miffion of Mofes;
but that Mofes was *in the hand* of this Angel, as long as he
fuftained the charaɛters mentioned, that is, as long as he was
in the church in the wildernefs. Therefore, when it is

afterwards faid, *This is he that was in the church in the wil-*
dernefs, with the Angel who fpake to him in the mount Sinai,
ver. 38. though the latter . expreffion may more immediately refpect the delivering of the law, yet it may be extended
to the revelation formerly made to Mofes by this Angel in
the fame mountain. For concerning this Stephen had faid;
There appeared to him in the wildernefs of mount Sinai, an
Angel of the Lord in a flame of fire in a bufh, ver. 30. Although it fhould be urged, that the giving of .the law alone
is meant, ftill it would follow, that he who *fpake to Mofes,*
face to face, as God, fuftained a delegated character; and
that this was the faith of true Ifraelites in the days of Stephen.

It is evident that both Mofes and the Ifraelites confidered
the Angel, who was promifed them, as divine. When they
provoked God by worfhipping the golden calf, he threatened that he would *not go up in the midft of them,* Exod.
xxxiii. 3. The reafon of the interceffion of Mofes, and of
the mourning of the people, was not that God had formerly
promifed his own prefence, but now that of an Angel only;
nor that he had formerly promifed the uncreated Angel,
but now a created one. For he had never engaged to give
them his prefence, otherwife than by *fending* an Angel.
With this both Mofes and Ifrael were fatisfied, accounting
it the divine prefence. But ftill there was an important difference. God had formerly promifed this Angel to *keep*
them in the way, and to *bring* them to Canaan. All that
he now promifes is, that he fhall *go before* them, to drive
out their enemies. He leaves the work of *leading* them, and
of *bringing* them into that land, on Mofes himfelf, Exod.
xxxii 34. refufing to *go up in the midft of them,* in the
perfon of this Angel. Therefore Mofes addreffes God
in the following terms; *See, thou fayeft unto me, Bring up*
this people, and thou haft not let me know whom thou wilt
fend

fend with me, chap. xxxiii. 12. Nothing can be more plain, than that Mofes had ftill underftood the original promife, as fignifying that the people of God were to enjoy his prefence immediately, and yet by one *fent*.

His language is very emphatic ; *Thou haft not let me know* אֵת אֲשֶׁר, the perfon *whom thou wilt fend*. We have the fame expreffion, Gen. xliv. 1. *He commanded*, אֵת אֲשֶׁר, literally, *the* —— *who was over his houfe*, that is, as we render it, *the fteward of his houfe*. The Lord anfwered; *My prefence fhall go*, ver 14. The term here ufed is plainly a perfonal defignation, denoting that Angel whom God had promifed, before the people offended him. For this illuftrious Meffenger is elfewhere called *the Angel of his prefence*, or *face*, Ifa. lxiii. 9. But, in the perfon of this Angel, the people of God were to enjoy his own *prefence*. For this promife was merely a renovation of that formerly made, *I will fend an Angel before thee, to keep thee*, &c. and the latter was equivalent to his faying, that he would *go up in the midft of them*, Exod. xxxiii. 3. The fame expreffion is elfewhere ufed, to denote the perfonal prefence of a creature: *I counfel—that thou go up to battle in thine own perfon*, literally, *that thy prefence go up*, 2 Sam. xvii. 11.

This divine Meffenger might be called the *prefence* or *face* of God, or *the Angel of his face*, for different reafons. He might receive thefe defignations, becaufe of his going before Ifrael in the appearance of a pillar of cloud and fire. For as a man is known by his face, God made known the truth of his prefence in the camp of Ifrael by this fymbol. Indeed, it would feem to be in this fenfe only that Mofes fpeaks of God being feen by his people *face to face. They have heard*, fays he of the heathen nations, *that thou Lord art among this people, and that thou Lord art feen face to face, and that thy cloud ftandeth over them*, &c. Num. xiv. 14. Deut. v. 4. They faw him *face to face*, no other way than

by

by *his cloud ftanding over them.* For they faw no fimilitude, Deut. iv. 12. 15. He might alfo be thus denominated,
becaufe in him the divine perfections were difplayed, God's
Name being *in him.* This language certainly fignifies, that
there was an intimacy between this Angel and him who
fent him, to which no other was admitted. Befides, it would
appear that the Deity never affumed any vifible appearance,
but in the perfon of this Angel, John v. 37. Perhaps, we
may add as another reafon, that all the grace of God was
communicated to his people through him, Numb. vi. 25.
Pfal. lxxx. 7. Ifa. lxiii. 9. That divine perfon, who appeared to Abraham in the likenefs of human nature, feems to
be called the *Face* of God. The two Angels who attended
him, inform Lot that the cry of Sodom was *waxen great
before the face of* JEHOVAH, Gen. xix. 13. It was the fame
glorious Perfon whom Lot intreated, in whofe fight he found
grace, who was merciful to him, ver. 19. and accepted him
in his prayer, ver. 21. and who, as JEHOVAH, *rained fire
and brimftone from* JEHOVAH, on the cities of the plain,
ver 24. It needs not feem ftrange, that Mofes was fo ear-
neft to have this Angel, called *the Face* of God, to go with
him : as it appears that he was the object of his worfhip.
For what we have rendered, *Mofes befought the Lord his
God*, literally is, *Mofes befought the Face of* JEHOVAH *his
God*, Exod. xxxii. 11. And he did fo at the very time
that God threatened to withdraw his face.

Did this Angel appear in the pillar of cloud and fire ? The
Branch of JEHOVAH is promifed to the Church, under the
New Teftament, as a pillar of the fame kind, Ifa. iv. 2. 5.
And we know that the Son is *the brightnefs of glory*, Heb.
i. 3. Did this Angel *go before* the Church? Jefus is given
as *a Leader to the people*, Ifa. lv. 4. God faid, *Behold, I fend
an Angel before thee,—to bring thee into the place which I have
prepared*, Exod. xxiii. 20. Jefus appropriates this work to
himfelf,

himſelf, with reſpect to that better Canaan of which the
other was merely a type. *I go to prepare a place for you.—*
I will come again, and receive you unto myſelf, John xiv. 2, 3.
When God ſays, *My Face ſhall go,* he adds, *and I will give*
you reſt. This is the very work of our Lord Jeſus. He
ſays, *I will give you reſt.* And his reſt is unſpeakably ſuperior to that given by the typical Jeſus, Heb. iv. 8. It is
reſt for the ſoul, Matt. xi. 28, 29. Were the divine perfections diſplayed in that Angel? And is not Jeſus *the image*
of the inviſible God, the expreſs image of the Father's *perſon?*
Was the Angel of God's preſence admitted to peculiar intimacy with him? And is not *the only-begotten* ſtill *in the boſom*
of the Father? John i. 18. Was all the grace of God communicated through him? We know that God is propitious
to us, only as he *looks on the face of* his *Meſſiah,* Pſal. lxxxiv.
9. The greateſt token of his reconciliation to Iſrael was
his promiſing that his *Face* ſhould *go:* and the greateſt token
of his love to the New Teſtament Church, is the uninterrupted preſence of Jeſus *to the end of the world.* For *he is*
our peace. In a word, the whole adminiſtration of the
Church, from the fall till the appearance of the Meſſiah,
was committed to this Angel. For *the Angel of his face* or
preſence ſaved them: in his love, and in his pity he redeemed
them; and he bare them, and carried them all the days of old.
But this was the Son of God. For, not only is this his proper work under the goſpel; but it is granted even by Socinians, that, in the laſt propheſy of th' Old Teſtament, he is
deſcribed as *the Angel of the covenant, whom* his people *de-*
lighted in, Mal. iii. 1. Now, they knew no other under
this character, than that Angel who ſware unto Abraham,
and who claimed the covenant as his, Judg. ii. 1. In the
ſame paſſage he ſeems to be called *the Face of the Lord.*
For it is foretold with reſpect to John his harbinger; *Be-*
hold, I ſend my Meſſenger, and he ſhall prepare the way be-

fore me, literally, *before my Face.* This language is retained by Zacharias, when prophetically addreſſing his ſon;
Thou ſhalt go before the Face of the Lord *. It was promiſed concerning this Angel, that he ſhould *ſuddenly come
to his temple.* And he did come ſuddenly. For Jeſus,
on his firſt viſit to this holy place, after the commencement of his miniſtry, expelled all who defiled it, John ii. 13.
None of them could *abide the day of his coming*, or *ſtand
when he appeared*, Mal. iii. 2.

Thus, we have a key to the true meaning of a great
variety of paſſages, in which we read of the *Face* of God,
of the *ſhining* or *lifting up* of his *countenance ;* and of the
many prayers of the ancient church for this bleſſing. As
the language of believers, or at leaſt, as that of *the Spirit of
Chriſt*, and as *written for our inſtruction*, they undoubtedly
refer to the incarnation of the Son of God. Particularly,
in the eightieth Pſalm, there is a frequent repetition of this
prayer, *Cauſe thy Face to ſhine :* as expreſſing the great object in view ; and in the cloſe, the church expreſsly declares
who is meant by this deſignation, and what is the bleſſing
intreated in theſe words. She refers to the Meſſiah under
another character : *Let thy hand be upon the man of thy
right hand, upon the Son of man, whom thou madeſt ſtrong
for thyſelf*, ver. 17.

It is highly probable, that the ſame glorious Meſſenger
is called God's *Way.* For Moſes having ſaid, *Thou haſt not
let me know the* Perſon *whom thou wilt ſend*, immediately
adds, *Make me to know thy way*, Ex. xxxiii. 12, 13. He
ſubſtitutes this expreſſion in the room of that blank which
he had left in his complaint, and places before it the ſame
demonſtrative and emphatic particle : *Thou haſt not let
me know* אֲשֶׁר אֶת, *the* Perſon *whom thou wilt ſend.----
Make me to know* אֶת דרכך, as it may be rendered, *that
thy*

---

* Προ προσωπȣ μȣ, Septuag. Προ προσωπȣ τȣ Κυριȣ, Luke i. 76.

thy way. That Angel, who is the *Face* of JEHOVAH, might by a beautiful figure be alſo called his *Way,* becauſe of the office allotted to him, which was to *lead* the Iſraelites, and to *keep them in the way.* For *the Lord went before them in the pillar of cloud, to lead them the way,* Ex. xiii. 21. We know that Jeſus ſuſtains the double character of a *Leader* and a *Way;* nay, that he is a *Way* poſſeſſed of ſuch virtue, that *the wayfaring men, though fools, ſhall not err therein,* Iſa. xxxv. 8. He expreſsly calls himſelf *the Way:* and it can ſcarcely be ſuppoſed that he does ſo without a reference to the typical pillar, and to that conducting Angel whoſe ſymbol it was; eſpecially as he takes this deſignation at the very time that he apparently alludes to the work of this Meſſenger, in *bringing* ancient Iſrael *to the place prepared for them. I go,* he ſays, *to prepare a place for you.----I am the Way,* John xiv. 2. 6. Moſes ſaid, *Make me to know thy Way, that I may know thee, and that I may find grace in thy ſight.* Jeſus ſays to his diſciples, *I am the Way.----No man cometh unto the Father, but by me. If ye had known me, ye ſhould have known my Father alſo,* ver. 6, 7 *.

S 2   But

---

* A variety of paſſages in the Old Teſtament might be mentioned, in which the term *way* ſeems to denote a perſon. *As for God, his Way is perfect, the Word of the Lord is tried; he is a buckler to all thoſe that truſt in him,* Pſal. xviii. 30. That the Meſſiah is here called God's Way, would appear from the following clauſe. For according to the natural conſtruction of the original, it is *the Word of* JEHOVAH who is *a buckler.* Pſalm lxvii. evidently refers to the Goſpel diſpenſation; as it reſpects the converſion of the Gentiles. The Pſalmiſt firſt prays that God would cauſe his *Face* to ſhine. Here we have the very term which God uſes, when he ſays, *My preſence ſhall go.* He then declares the end for which he craves this bleſſing; *that thy Way may be known upon earth, thy ſaving health among all people,* ver. 2. Now, *the ſaving health* of God can be *known* only through him who is *the Way.* Indeed, that very word is here rendered *ſaving health,* which in many other places is tranſlated *ſalvation,* particularly in Iſa. xlix. 6. where it confeſſedly denotes

Jeſus

But as this particular view is not immediately connected with the argument, I fhall proceed to confider fome other paffages in which the divine Name I AM is given to One fent. ·

It occurs in this fenfe in Ifa. xlviii. 16. formerly referred to ; *Come ye near unto' me, hear ye this : I have not fpoken in fecret from the beginning, from the time that it was there am I, and now the Lord God and his Spirit hath fent me *.* The Speaker declares that he is One *fent* and yet the felf-exiftent God, whofe *hand laid the foundation of the earth,* ver. 13. and the *Goel* or *Kinfman-Redeemer* of Ifrael, ver. 17. a defignation which can only belong to *the Word made flefh.* He not only defcribes himfelf as fent, but proclaims his miffion in the character of a *Speaker.* This, we know, is an eminent branch of the office of Meffiah. He even appropriates all the Revelations made to the church, from her firft exiftence, as immediately his †. He declares the publicity

Jefus our *Way.* It is prophefied concerning the Gofpel church ; *Thy teachers fhall not be removed into a corner any more, but thine eyes fhall fee thy teachers. And thine ears fhall bear a word behind thee, faying, This is the Way, walk ye in it,* chap. xxx. 20, 21. It is undoubtedly the work of the fervants of Chrift to point him out as *the Way* The teachers of the church, in primitive times, were thus employed They exhorted the difciples, as they had *received Chrift Jefus the Lord, fo to walk in him,* Col ii 6. And they could only *walk in him,* as having *received* him as their *Way.* It is promifed ; *An highway fhall be there, and a way, and it fhall be called the way of holinefs,* Ifa. xxxv. 8. Now, *the way into the holieft is through the blood of Jefus ;* and it is *confecrated,* Heb. x. 20. fo as to appear to be indeed *the way of holinefs.* The Lord faid by another prophet, *Where is the good way? and walk therein, and ye fhall find reft for your fouls,* Jer vi. 16 This is juft what he promifed, when Mofes defired to know his Way. *My Face fhall go, and I will give you reft* And we have feen that this is what Jefus promifes, when inviting finners to himfelf, Matt. xi. 28, 29.

* The words may be read with equal juftice to the original. *The Lord God hath fent me and his Spirit.*

† Vid. Heidegger. Hift. Patriarch. Part I. Exerc. iii. f. 12, &c.

blicity of theſe, the more to aggravate their incredulity. This very language does the Meſſenger of the covenant apply to himſelf : *I ſpake openly to the world----and in ſecret have I ſaid nothing,* John xviii. 20 *.

Although εγω ειμι had been ſtill rendered *I am he,* it would have expreſſed no more than what is often particularly declared, in the language of prophecy, concerning this illuſtrious Meſſenger, who is the I AM. For the ſame perſon ſays, Iſa. xliii. 13. *I am he :* and he connects this with the following characters, *I am the firſt and the laſt.* Theſe he urges, in addreſſing his church, as affording the moſt powerful argument againſt fear, chap. xliv. 6.---8. *I am the firſt and the laſt.---Fear ye not.* Now, theſe very characters does Jeſus appropriate to himſelf, and apply in the ſame manner, Rev. i. 17. *Fear not, I am the firſt and the laſt.* In the prophecy of Iſaiah, this language is given as that of JEHOVAH, the King and Redeemer of Iſrael ; beſides whom there is no God : *Thus ſaith* JEHOVAH, *the King of Iſrael, and his Redeemer,* JEHOVAH *of hoſts, I am the firſt and the laſt, and beſides me there is no God.* Therefore, either Jeſus is a divine Perſon, or he was chargeable with robbery in aſſuming theſe characters. Either, it was he who, under the Old Teſtament, uttered this language, and who was the King and Redeemer of Iſrael ; or, the Goſpel church, in her privileges, is infinitely inferior to the Jewiſh. For Jeſus is her King and Redeemer. Either, theſe characters are uſed with ſuch peculiarity as to denote that they belong to God only, and that there is no God beſides that Being to whom they are immediately aſcribed ; or they have no meaning, as here introduced. If the former be true, Jeſus muſt be truly God : for they belong to him.

This expreſſion, *I am he,* is ſo evidently uſed as emphatically

tically

---

* Εν κρυπτω ελαλησα υδεν. This is nearly the ſame with the verſion of the Seventy, Ουκ εν κρυφη λελαληκα.

tically denoting God, that many learned men have confidered the pronoun הוא as one of his names *. It ſeems
eſpecially to denote the immutability of the divine nature,
as in Pſalm. cii. 27. *But thou art the ſame*, or *thou art* HE.
Its emphaſis is ſometimes particularly expreſſed in the
Greek, and applied to our Lord, as in Heb. i. 12. Συ δε ο
αυτος ει; and chap. xiii. 8. *Jeſus Chriſt*, ο αυτος, *the ſame*,
yeſterday, &c. Had this been written in Hebrew, we may
be aſſured from the tranſlation of Pſal. cii. 27. according to
the Septuagint, that it would have been הוא

The ſame emphatic expreſſion is uſed in another paſſage,
formerly referred to, Iſa. lii. 6. *They ſhall know, in that*
day, that I am he that doth ſpeak, or *he, the Speaker*. We
have ſeen that this belongs to Jeſus. Here he is evidently declared in his character as *Meſſiah*. For it is Jeſus who ſpoke
on earth, Heb. ii. 3. and who now *ſpeaketh from heaven*,
chap. xii. 25. Our Lord's language, even with reſpect to
thoſe falſe Chriſts who ſhould appear, is ſo remarkable, that
we are under the neceſſity of believing, that the ancient
Jews underſtood the words of the prophet, *that I am he*, of
the Meſſiah, and as expreſſing the very manner in which he
would announce himſelf. Thus our Lord ſays, *Many ſhall*
come in my Name, ſaying, οτι εγω ειμι, *that I am*, Luke
xxi. 8. This is a literal tranſlation of the expreſſion in
Iſaiah †; nay, the very terms in which it is tranſlated by
the Seventy. In that ſolemn declaration, *When ye have*
lift up the Son of man, then ſhall ye know that I AM HE, *and*
that I do nothing of myſelf, but as my Father hath taught me, I
SPEAK *theſe things*, our Lord ſeems to repeat the very words
of the prophecy; *They ſhall know in that day, that* I AM
HE *that doth* SPEAK ‡. It is alſo ſaid, *My people ſhall know*
                                                 my

---

* Vid. Pfeifferi Dif. Script. Loc. Cent. 4. 1. 23.

† כ אני הוא י

‡ Τοτε γνωσεσθε οτι εγω ειμι, και—ταυτα λαλω, John viii. 28. Γνω-
σεται ο λαος μυ το ονομα μυ εν τη ημερα εκεινη, οτι εγω ειμι ο λαλων.
Septuag.

my Name. What is this Name? *The Speaker*. This is the very defignation given him, Heb. xii. 25. τον λαλαντα.

I fhall only add a proof that the ancient Jews, while they underftood the title I AM as proper to God, applied it to the Meffiah. Mofes, in his laft fong, introduces JEHO-VAH as faying; *See now that I, even I am he, and there is no God with me : I kill, and I make alive ; I wound, and I heal: neither is there any that can deliver out of my hand,* Deut. xxxii. 39. This text is thus rendered by Jonathan ; " When the Word of the Lord fhall be manifefted t, re-" deem his people, he fhall fay to all people : See now, that " I am he, who am, who have been, and who fhall be," the very language of our Saviour, Rev. i. 8. " and there is no " other God befides me. I in my revenge do kill, and I do " thoroughly make alive my people of the houfe of Ifrael, " and I do heal them in the latter days." As this bleffing has been referred to *the latter days*, by which the Jews ftill underftand the time of the Meffiah's appearance, it has been juftly inferred that it is he who is here called the Word.

It is undeniable that the name JEHOVAH is equivalent to that of I AM. Therefore, when God had, under the latter defignation, given to Mofes his commiffion, he repeats it in this manner; *Thus fhalt thou fay unto the children of Ifrael,* JEHOVAH, *the God of your fathers,—hath fent me unto you,* Ex. iii. 15. And again; *Wherefore fay unto the children of Ifrael, I am* JEHOVAH, chap. vi. 6. Of confequence, all the arguments formerly brought to prove that the name JEHOVAH is properly given to one in the character of an Angel, with equal force of evidence demonftrate his title to the name I AM.

That one is revealed as JEHOVAH who *fends*, and another as JEHOVAH who is *fent*, is as certain as any truth contained in the facred volume. For *thus faith* JEHOVAH *of hofts, After the glory hath he* SENT *me unto the nations*

S 4   *that*

that fpoiled you ; for he that toucheth you, toucheth the apple of his eye. For behold, I will fhake mine hand upon them, and they fhall be a fpoil to their fervants : and ye fhall know that JEHOVAH *of hofts hath* SENT *me. Sing and rejoice, O daughter of Zion : for lo, I* COME, *and I will* DWELL *in the midft of thee, faith* JEHOVAH. *And many nations fhall be joined to* JEHOVAH *in that day, and fhall be* MY *people : and I will* DWELL *in the midft of thee, and thou fhalt know that* JEHOVAH *of hofts hath* SENT *me unto thee,* Zach. ii. 8.—11. This paffage evidently refpects the Gofpel difpenfation. For *many nations* are to be *joined to the Lord.* It is equally clear that the Speaker is JEHOVAH, and yet *fent ;* that he who is thus *fent* by JEHOVAH, is the avenger of God's peo-ple, *comes* undoubtedly in his incarnation, and *dwells in the midft* of them *, as JEHOVAH ; that they are *his* people; and that they know both that he *is* JEHOVAH, and that he is *fent* by JEHOVAH. If this be not the obvious meaning of the paffage, I, in the name of all who love our Lord Jefus Chrift, challenge Dr P. to fhew what other it can bear.

From the preceding obfervations, and alfo from what we have formerly feen, when inquiring into that character, *the Angel of the Lord,* it appears that this glorious Meffenger, even under the Old Teftament, performed all the work proper to the Meffiah, and afcribed to Jefus under the New, as far as the circumftances of that difpenfation would admit of it. Did the Meffiah come in our nature ? This Angel often came in the likenefs of it, and was at times fuppofed to be truly man Gen. xxxii. 24. Judg. xiii. 16. Did Jefus declare that he was fent, and yet equal with the Father ?

This

---

* So ftriking is the refemblance between the language of the Evan-gelift John, and that of the prophecy, efpecially as rendered in the Sep-tuagint that we can fcarcely fuppofe that he did not mean to allude to it Εσκηνωσιν εν ημιν, John i. 14 Κατασκηνωσω εν μισω σν, Sept. Both expreffions properly fignify *dwelling as in a tabernacle.*

This Angel did the fame, Zech. ii. 11. Did the Son of God become *one* with thofe whom he was to *fanctify?* Heb. ii. 11. The character of a *Kinfman-Redeemer* to his peo le was fuftained by this Angel, Gen. xlviii. 16. Was it the w rk of Jefus to reveal the whole will of God to the church? The fame work was performed by this Angel, before the coming of the Meffiah. Is Chrift promifed to the Gofpel church as *the Angel of the covenant*, nay, as himfelf *the covenant of the people?* Ifa. xlii. 6. It was this Angel who made the fame covenant with Abraham and his feed, Judg. ii. 1. It has been feen that the character of a *Leader* belongs equally to both. Is the one *the Captain of our falvation?* Heb. ii. 10. The other was *Captain of the hofts of the Lord,* Jofh. v. 14. Is Jefus a Saviour? The An-gel of God's prefence faved his ancient people. Is *the grace of our Lord Jefus exceeding abundant?* The fame grace was confpicuous in this glorious Perfon. For *in his love, and in his pity* he redeemed them, Ifa. lxiii. 9. Does it belong to Chrift to forgive fin? Acts v. 31. The fame was the pre-rogative of this Angel. For he faid to Jofhua the high prieft, *I have caufed thine iniquity to pafs from thee,* Zech. iii. 4. Are Chriftians *accepted in the Beloved?* It was this Angel who rendered the facrifice of ancient believers acceptable, Judg. vi. 21. Is it the work of the Meffiah to intercede for his church? The fame office was fuftained by this An-gel. He prayed for Jofhua, that he might be delivered from Satan, Zech. iii. 2. juft as our Lord did for Peter, Luke xxii. 32. Does it belong to Jefus effectually to *blefs* his people, in *turning them from their iniquities?* Acts iii. 26. The fame work was claimed by the Angel of JE-HOVAH. For he faid to Abraham, *In bleffing I will blefs thee,* Gen. xxii. 17. and he bleffed Jacob in the very place where he prefented his fupplication, chap. xxxii. 29.

Is Jefus the Deliverer of his people? Rom. xi. 26. No wife

wiſe inferior was the character of this Angel. For he was celebrated as *encamping around them that feared him*, and *delivering them*, Pſal. xxxiv. 7. Had the Meſſiah a right to ſend forth meſſengers in his Name, to preach the goſpel to others? It was the Angel of the Lord who ſent Moſes to the Iſraelites in Egypt, Ex. iii. 2. 14. and other prophets to their poſterity, 1 Chro. xxi. 18. Did Jeſus communicate the Spirit to church members? This glorious Meſſenger, in former times, *put his Spirit in them*, Iſa. lxiii. 11. Is the whole adminiſtration of providence in the hand of Chriſt? Equally important was the truſt of this Angel, Gen. xxi. 18. xxii. 17. Are angels employed by Jeſus, as his miniſters, for making known his will, Rev. xxii. 16. and for accompliſhing the purpoſes, both of providence and grace? Heb. i. 14. They occupied the ſame ſtation under the Angel of JEHOVAH, Zech. ii. 3, 4. i. 11. vi 8. Does Jeſus *ſmite the nations* with his *ſharp ſword*, and *rule them with a rod of iron?* Rev. xix. 15. He carries on the ſame work with that Angel of the Lord who ſmote the Aſſyrians, Iſa. xxxvii. 36. Does our Saviour viſit his church with afflictive diſpenſations becauſe of ſin, and *kill her children with death?* Rev. ii. 22, 23. The ſame Angel appeared *with a drawn ſword in his hand*, and ſmote the Iſraelites, ſo that David was *afraid becauſe of the ſword of the Angel of the Lord*, 1 Chro. xxi. 14.—16. 30. Both Jeſus and this Angel claim that divine character, I AM. Jeſus being repreſented as *ſpeaking from heaven*, Heb. xii. 25. he appears in the ſame light with this Angel who *called* to Hagar, and to Abraham, *out of heaven*, Gen. xxi. 17. xxii. 11. 15. Is it Jeſus whom we muſt now *hear?* The Iſraelites were under the ſame obligation with reſpect to this Angel, Ex. xxiii. 21. Is there no eſcape, if we turn away from him that ſpeaketh from heaven? Heb. xii. 25. Concerning this Angel it was declared, *He will*

not

not pardon your tranfgreffions. If, therefore, Jefus be not effentially the fame as this Angel, the unity of the church is loft. The patriarchs and their pofterity had one Saviour; and Chriftians have another. We are not bleffed with faithful Abraham, nor are we under the fame covenant. But as the fcripture affures us that the whole adminiftration of the ancient church was committed to this Angel, we have, as has formerly been feen, the fame inconteftable evidence of the identity of this Angel and the Meffiah *.

Our author obferves that " it even appears to have been " the great object of the Jewifh religion, as contained in " the books of Mofes, to preferve in-the world the worfhip " of the one true God, notwithftanding the univerfal ten- " dency to polytheifm among all nations in the early ages †." Therefore, it may naturally be imagined that God, in his infinite wifdom, would ufe the moft proper means for attaining this end; particularly, that if he made himfelf known under certain defignations, he would either confine all thefe entirely to himfelf, or if not all, yet fome of them, efpecially fuch as might be expreffive of his effence ; and that, if he ever ufed any of the reft in fpeaking of creatures, he would ufe them evidently in an inferior fenfe. That he has acted in this very manner, is evident from the revelation which he gave to his peculiar people. Here we find him not only applying to himfelf, with a ftriking peculiarity, fome of thofe defignations which are occafionally given to creatures ; but appropriating others, as abfolutely incommunicable to them in any fenfe whatfoever.

All idolatry confifts in giving that glory to the creature which belongs to the Creator. One great fource of this, efpecially to the more ignorant part of mankind, has been the miftaking of the creature for the Creator. It muft, therefore, be fuppofed that, if God hath ever employed

mere

---

* See p. 273, 274.   † Ear. Opin. vol. iii. p. 2.

mere creatures as inftruments in delivering his will to their fellow-creatures, he hath, in the profecution of his great end, ufed the moft effectual means to prevent the objects of the Revelation from apprehending that they immediately heard the voice of God. We can fuppofe no mean fo obvious, nor one that would fo directly tend to prevent this miftake, as that of prohibiting thofe whom he employed from perfonating their great employer, ufing any of his names as if they might occafionally be given to them, or expreffing themfelves in fuch terms as might lead the hearers to imagine that God himfelf was the immediate Speaker. If, on the contrary, this neceffary precaution hath been neglected; if God hath permitted a creature to fay to his fellow, I am JEHOVAH, I AM THAT I AM; if he hath alfo directed thofe who were under the Spirit of infpiration, to record thefe Revelations in this very manner; fo far hath he been from ufing thofe means that were moft confiftent with infinite wifdom, for the prevention of idolatry, that we cannot conceive that he could have taken more direct or effectual methods for eftablifhing it, although this had been his avowed defign in the whole of that Revelation contained in the Old Teftament. Could I believe all that is fuppofed, and all this muft be believed by every one who denies the Supreme Deity of the Son, the God of Abraham fhould never be my God.

C H A P. X.

Of the Caution which fome Fathers are faid to afcribe to the Apoftles, in divulging the Doctrine of the Divinity of Chrift; and of the abfolute filence afcribed to them, on this fubject, by Dr Prieftley.

OUR author, in his firft work on this fubject, endeavoured to prove, that the primitive church was

known to be *properly* Unitarian, from the conduct of Athanafius in afcribing to the Apoftles " great caution in di-
" vulging the doctrine of the proper divinity of Chrift *."
It was replied by Dr Horfley, that Athanafius, in the paffage referred to, fpeaks of unbelieving Jews only, and commends the wifdom of the apoftles in chufing the moft proper method of inftruction †. A great deal has been advanced on both fides, in the progrefs of this controverfy :
and it muft appear, to any impartial reader, that Dr Horfley has eftablifhed his point.   But as our author has that
peculiar happinefs of not being eafily put out of conceit
with any thing he has once advanced, this is again brought
forward in due form, in his large work.

I do not mean properly to enter into the queftion with
refpect to the difputed paffage, as it has been fo fully agi-
tated already ; and would have faid nothing on the fubject,
had it not feemed a piece of juftice to Athanafius, and to
the truth, to produce a few extracts from his writings, which
plainly fhew that he had a very different opinion of the
conduct of the apoftles from that afcribed to him, and
which, as far as I can recollect, have not been introduced
in the courfe of the difpute.   This may be the more proper, as, according to Dr P. " the teftimony of Athanafius,
" on account of his known orthodoxy, and of courfe, his
" unwillingnefs to make any needlefs conceffions to his ad-
" verfaries, may be thought to have more weight than any
" other ‡".

For the fake of thofe who have not feen what has been
already publifhed on this fubject, it may be previoufly neceffary to quote the paffage which has occafioned fo much
litigation.   I fhall give it according to our author's verfion:
" Will they affirm, that the apoftles held the doctrine of
                                                            " Arius,

---

* Hift. of Cor. vol. i. p. 12.
† Charge, &c. p. 20.—25.   ‡ Vol. iii. p. 86.

" Arius, becaufe they fay that Chrift was a man of Naza-
" reth, and fuffered on the crofs? or becaufe they ufed thefe
" words, were the apoftles of opinion that Chrift was only
" a man, and nothing elfe? By no means : this is not to be
" imagined. But this they did as wife mafter-builders,
" and ftewards of the myfteries of God ; and they had this
" good reafcn for it. For the Jews of that age, being de-
" ceived themfelves, and having deceived the Gentiles,
" thought that Chrift was a mere man, only that he came
" of the feed of David, refembling other defcendants of
" David, and did not believe either that he was God, or
" that the Word was made flefh. On this account, the
" bleffed apoftles, with great prudence, in the firft place,
" taught what related to the humanity of our Saviour to
" the Jews, that having fully perfuaded them, from his mi-
" raculous works, that Chrift was come, they might after-
" wards bring them to the belief of his divinity, fhewing
" that his works were not thofe of a man, but of God.
" For example, Peter having faid that Chrift was a man
" who had fuffered, immediately added, *He is the Prince of*
" *life.* In the Gofpel, he confeffes, *Thou art the Chrift,*
" *the Son of the living God;* and in his Epiftle, he calls
" him *the Bifhop of fouls* *."

Dr

---

* Ουδεν γαρ αυτοις ατολμητον· οτι και αυτοι οι αποσολοι τα Αρεια
εφρονεν· ανθρωπον γαρ αυτον απο Ναζαρετ, και παθητον τον Χρισον
απαγγελλουσιν, εκεινων τοινυν τοιαυτα φανταζομενων, αρ' επειδη τοις
ρημασι τετοις εχρησαντο, μονον ανθρωπον ηδεισαν τον Χρισον οι αποσολοι, και πλεον ουδεν ; μη γινοιτο· ουκ εστιν ουδε εις ουν ποτε τετο λα-
βειν· αλλα και τετο ως αρχιτεκτονες σοφοι, και οικονομοι μυστηριων
Θεου πεποιηκασι, και την αιτιαν εχουσιν ευλογον· επειδη γαρ οι τοτε
Ιουδαιοι πλανηθεντες, και πλανησαντες Ελληνας, ενομιζον τον Χριστον
ψιλον ανθρωπον, μονον εκ σπερματ☉· Δαβιδ αχρεσθαι, καθ' ομοιοτη-
τα των εκ τε Δαβιδ αλλων γινωμενων τεκνων· ουτι δε Θεον αυτον, ουδε

Dr P. endeavours to fhew that Athanafius not only meant
" the believing Jews, but them *principally* * ; that he did
" not think that the apoftles had preached the doctrine of
" the divinity of Chrift with much effect † ; that he muft
" be underftood to fay, that the Jewifh converts, while
" (through the caution of the apoftles) they were ignorant
" of the divinity of Chrift, preached the Gofpel in that
" ftate to the Gentiles ‡ ;" and ' that Athanafius muft have
" fuppofed that both the Jewifh and Gentile churches were
" Unitarian in the time of the apoftles ||." His mode of pro-
bation is very fingular. He objects to the proofs which Athanafius gives of the Apoftles having preached the divinity of Chrift, as not fufficiently *diftinct* §. Then, for the
fupport of his objection, he makes a leap from the *opinion*
of Athanafius to the *intention* of the apoftle Peter; afferting, that " in this fpeech he could not *mean* to allude to"
the divinity of our Saviour ¶. The plain meaning of this
is ; *Athanafius* could not believe that the Apoftles preached
this doctrine in a clear or diftinct manner, becaufe " the in-
" ftances he produces" are not fo *diftinct* as to prove it to
the conviction of *Dr Prieftley*.

Athanafius, in illuftrating the harmony of the Apoftles in
the declaration of this doctrine, mentions an expreffion ufed

by

οτι λογ☉ σαρξ εγενετο επιστευον. τατα ενεκα, μετα πολλης της συ-
νεσεως οι μακαριοι αποττολοι τα ανθρωπινα τα σωτηρ☉ εξηγαντο πρω-
τον τοις Ιαδαιοις, ινα ολως πεισαντες αυτας, εκ των φαινομενων και
γενομενων σημειων, εληλυθεναι τον Χριστον, λοιπον και εις τα περι της
θεοτητ☉ αυτα πιστιν αυτας αναγαγωσιν, δεικνυντες οτι τα γενομενα
εργα ακ εστιν ανθρωπα, αλλα Θεα. αμελει Πιτρ☉ ο λεγων ανδρα παθητον τον Χριστον, ευθ☉ συνηπτεν, Ου-☉ αρχηγ☉ της ζωης εστιν, &c.
De Sententia Dionyfii, Op. vol. i. p. 553, 554.

* Ear. Opin. vol. iii. p 90.	† Ibid. p. 95.	‡ Ibid. p. 97.
|| Ibid. 96.	§ Ibid. p. 93.	¶ Ibid. p. 94.

by Paul in his difcourfe at Athens. Therefore, our author wifhes it to appear that, according to the ancient writers, the *apoftolical referve* on this head continued till about the year 53. I am aftonifhed that Dr P. can venture fuch an infinuation. For nothing can be more evident than that Athanafius reprefents the apoftle Peter as proceeding to the doctrine of the divinity, as foon as he had fully proved that Jefus was the Chrift, nay, as proving it by the fame arguments. For, according to the venerable Father, the apoftle having fhewn that Chrift was come, by his miracles, he λοιπον και in *the reft* of his difcourfe proved " that the works " done were not thofe of a man, but of God." Why does Athanafius fubjoin, " for example, Peter having faid that " Chrift was a man who had fuffered, *immediately* added, " *He is the Prince of Life*," unlefs he means this as an *example* of Peter's preaching the divinity of Chrift as well as his humanity, preaching it in the very fame difcourfe, preaching the humanity in fuch a manner as *immediately* to guard the honour of the divinity?

I might quote many paffages from the writings of Athanafius, in which his fentiments, with refpect to the conduct of the apoftles and the faith of the whole church, appear directly oppofite to thofe imputed to him by Dr P. But two or three may fuffice. Illuftrating the doctrine of the Trinity, he fays ; " We fee that this was the tradition, and the " doctrine, and the faith of the church univerfal from the " beginning, which our Lord himfelf delivered, which the " apoftles preached, and which the fathers preferved. For " in this is the church *founded*, and he who falls from it, " neither can be a Chriftian, nor deferves the name of a " Chriftian.—That this is the very faith of the church, " they (the enemies of the Trinity) may learn from the " commiffion which our Lord gave to his apoftles, when " fending them forth. He commanded them to lay this

I   " foundation

" foundation in the church, faying; *Go ye, and teach all*
" *nations, baptizing them into the Name of the Father, of*
" *the Son, and of the Holy Ghoft.* But the apoftles, going
" forth, taught in this very manner : and this is the doc-
" trine which is preached throughout the whole church un-
" der heaven. The church, therefore, having this foun-
" dation of the faith, let them tell us, if it be a Trinity *."
Defcribing the errors of Marcellus and Paulus Samofatenus,
he fays; " Had they been actuated by any regard to the
" future, had they believed the coming and the judgment
" of God, or had they been afraid of punifhment, they
" would have acceded to the faith, believed the Gofpels,
" and liftened to the apoftles, rather than to human rea-
" fonings. For the apoftles, going forth, ftraightway with
" the moft perfect harmony preached that Chrift was the
" Son of God, that he was born in Bethlehem of the feed
" of David according to the flefh, that he was made like
" unto men, and crucified for men under Pontius Pilate.
" They declared that the fame Perfon was God and man,
" the Son of God and the Son of man from heaven and
" from earth, impaffible and paffible, and that he was no
                                                    " other

---

* Ιδωμεν δε ομως και πρὸ τυτοις, και αυτην την εξ αρχης παρα-
δοσιν, και διδασκαλιαν, και πιςιν της καθολικης εκκλησιας, ην ο μεν
Κυριὸ εδωκεν, οι δε Αποςολοι εκηρυξαν, και οι πατερες εφυλαξαν· εν
ταυτη γαρ η εκκλησια τεθεμελιωται· και ο ταυτης εκπιπτων, ετ' αν
ειη, ετ' αν λεγοι το Χριςιανὸ·——και οτι αυτη η πιςις η της εκκλησιας εςι, μαθητωσαν, πως ο μεν Κυριὸ, αποςιλλων τυς Αποςτο-
λυς, παρηγγειλε τυτον θεμελιον τιθεναι τη εκκλησια λεγων, Πορευθεν-
τες, μαθητευσατε παντα τα εθνα· βαπτιζοντες αυτυς εις το ονομα τυ
Πατρὸ, και τυ Υιυ, και τυ Αγιυ Πνευματὸ· οι δε Αποςτολοι πο-
ρευθεντες, ετως εδιδαξαν. Και τυτο εςτιν εις πασαν την υπ' ερανον εκ-
κλησιαν το κηρυγμα· εκεν τυτο εχυσης της εκκλησιας το θεμελιον της
πιςτεως, &c. Ad Serapion, vol. i. p. 202, 203.

" other, not two perfons, not two *hypoſtaſes*, not two ob-
" jects of adoration *."

Not only does Athanaſius give this account of the preaching of the apoſtles in general, but he elſewhere explains
that very diſcourſe of Peter, to which the paſſage quoted
by Dr P. refers. On this occaſion, however, the worthy
Father has not Dionyſius to vindicate from the charge of
hereſy in what he had advanced in oppoſition to the Sabel-
lians, (whom Athanaſius often repreſents as the Jews of
that age,) and therefore, he does not find it neceſſary to
borrow an argument from the *prudence* of the apoſtles in
their manner of addreſſing the literal Jews, the predeceſſors
of theſe heretics in unbelief. We may therefore conclude,
that he is capable of judging more coolly concerning the
conduct of the apoſtles. He is ſo very particular, that having quoted theſe words, *He hath made him both Lord and
Chriſt*, Acts ii. 36 †; he gives a long paraphraſe of them,
in connexion with the reſt of Peter's diſcourſe. " Peter,"
he ſays, " having learned theſe things from Chriſt (con-
" cerning his divinity and humanity) in both reſpects cor-
" rects the Jews," ſaying ; ' O ye Jews, the holy ſcriptures
' declare

---

* Ει γαρ προσεδοκων το μελλον, ει Θεɤ επιδημιαν και κρισιν επιστευον, ει κολασιν εφοβɤντο, τη πιστει προσηρχοντο, ευαγίελιοις ε-
πειθοντο και Αποστολοις ηκολɤθɤν μαλλον η λογισμοις ανθρωπινοις.
Χριστον γαρ ευθεως εκηρɤξαν εξελθοντες οι Αποστολοι συμφωνως και
ακολɤθως τον υιον τɤ Θεɤ, τɤτον εν Βηθλεεμ γενηθεντα εκ σπερματɤ·
Δαβιδ κατα σαρκα, τον ομοιωθεντα ανθρωποις, και σταυρωθεντα υπερ
ανθρωπων επι Ποντιɤ Πιλατɤ, αυτον ειπον Θεον, αυτον ανθρωπον, αυτον ειπον υιον Θεɤ, αυτον υιον ανθρωπɤ, αυτον εξ ɤρανɤ, αυτον απο
γης, αυτον απαθη, αυτον παθητον, ɤκ αλλον, ɤ προσωπα δυο, ɤχ
υποστασɤς, ɤ προσκυνησɤς δυο. Unum eſſe Chriſtum, Opera,
vol. i. p. 666.

† Cont. Arianos Orat. iii. Op. vol. i. p. 382.

:' declare that Chrift fhall come ; and you account him a
' mere man, as one of the defcendants of David.   But the
' fcriptures do not point him out in this light, but rather
' declare him to be Lord and God, and immortal, and
' the Prince of life.'   Then he makes Peter introduce thefe
words, *The Lord faid unto my Lord,* &c. and the language
of David concerning the refurrection of Chrift, and afterwards proceed in this manner ; ' If you therefore can prove
' that a perfon of this defcription has already come, and
' can demonftrate that he is God, then with propriety may
' you oppofe us.—Moreover, the figns which he exhibited,
' prove that he was God incarnate, that he was life itfelf,
' and the Lord of death.—After we were unwilling to
' know God by his Word, and to ferve our natural Lord
' the Word of God, it pleafed God to fhew his own divine
' power in man, and to draw all men to himfelf.   But to
' have done this by mere man would have been unbeco-
' ming ; left we having a man for our Lord, fhould have be-
' come worfhippers of man.   Therefore, on this account the
' Word himfelf was made flefh, and the Father hath called
' him Jefus, and thus *made him Lord and Chrift* ; that, as
' in the Name of Jefus every knee boweth, fo we fhould
' know him as King, and Lord, and at the fame time the
' Son, and through him know the Father.'   " Therefore,
" the greateft part of the Jews who heard thefe things were
" convinced, and afterwards acknowledged the Chrift *."

T 2   A

---

* Ο τοινυν Πετρ©· μαθων ταυτα παρα τε σωτηρ©·, κατ᾽ αμφοτε-
ρα διορθμεν©· τες Ιεδαιες, φησιν· ω Ιεδαιοι, Χριστον ερχεσθαι, καταγ[ελλεσιν αι θειαι γραφαι, και υμεις μεν ψιλον ανθρωπον αυτον,
ως ενα των εκ τε Δαβιδ νομιζετε, τα δε γεγραμμενα περι αυτε ε τοιε-
τον αυτον, οιον υμεις λεγετε, σημαινεσιν· αλλο μαλλον Κυριον και
Θεον, και αθανατον, και χορηγον ζωης καταγ[ελλεσιν.——ει μεν εν
δυνασθε ειπειν, ως ελθοντ©· προτερον τετε, και δυνασθε δειξαι, Θεον
αυτον

A little after he says concerning the language of Peter;
" When he spoke these things, he was by no means silent
" with respect to the eternal and paternal deity of the
" Son; as he had already observed, that he had *shed forth*
" *the Spirit* on us. But to bestow the Spirit in a sovereign
" manner, is not the work of a creature, but the preroga-
" tive of God *." In another place, he observes even
concerning

αυτον ειναι, αφ' ων εποιησε σημειων και τερατων, εικοτως ημιν διαμα-
χεσθε.——και παλιν, αφειλεν ο Θεος, το δε και τοιαυτα σημεια ποιησαι αυτον, οια γεγονε, δεικνυσι, Θεον ειναι τον εν σωματι· και αυτον
ειναι την ζωην, και Κυριον τε θανατε.——επειδη εκ ηθελησαμεν δια
τε λογε αυτε επιγνωναι τον Θεον, και δελευσαι τω φυσει δεσποτη η-
μων τω λογω τε Θεε, ηυδοκησεν ο Θεος, εν ανθρωπω δειξαι την εαυτε
κυριοτητα· και παντας ελκυσαι προς εαυτον· δι' ανθρωπε δε ψιλε τετο ποιησαι απρεπες ην· ινα μη ανθρωπον Κυριον εχοντες, ανθρωπο λα-
τραι γενομεθα· δια τετο ο λογος σαρξ εγενετο· και εκαλεσε το ονομα
αυτε Ιησουν, και ουτως εποιησεν αυτον Κυριον και Χριστον ο Πατηρ·——
ιν' εν το ονοματι Ιησου, ον υμεις εσταυρωσατε, ωσπερ παν γονυ καμ-
πτει, ουτως και Κυριον και βασιλεα αυτον τε τον υιον επιγινωσκωμεν,
και δι' αυτε τον πατερα. Ιουδαιων μεν ουν οι πλειστοι ταυτα ακε-
οντες, ενετραπησαν και λοιπον επιγνωσαν τον Χριστον. Ibid. p. 386,
387.—With the same propriety may we infer from this passage, that, according to Athanasius, these Jews did not *acknowledge* the Christ for a considerable time *after* they were
converted, as it is inferred from the other, that, in the opinion of this Father, the Apostles did not divulge the doctrine
of the divinity of Jesus for a considerable time after explaining the doctrine of the Messiah. If, in the one case, he
means that they confessed Christ immediately upon their
conversion, the same intimate connexion must be meant in
the other. For λοιπον is the term used in both places. If
there be any difference, it is in favour of the other place.
For there Athanasius also introduces ευθυς.

---

* Και γαρ ταυτα λεγων, εκ εσιωπησε περι της αιδιε και πατρι-
κης θεοτητος τε υιε· αλλα και προειρηκως ην· οτι το πνευμα εξεχεεν

εφ'

concerning thefe words, *Jeſus, a man declared by God in the midſt of you,* ver. 22. " What is faid by the bleffed Peter " proclaims the right and fincere doctrine of the Deity of " the only-begotten, not feparating the perfon of God the " Word from the man born of the Virgin †."

From thefe paffages let the reader judge, if Dr P. can reafonably perfift in afferting that in the opinion of Athanafius, neither the apoftles preached, nor the primitive Chriftians believed the divinity of our Saviour.

The Doctor, with the fame defign, adds a variety of paffages from the writings of Chryfoftom and other fathers who lived in later ages. But it would ferve no good purpofe to follow him through this labyrinth. Although it were unqueftionably true, that all the fathers, whom he has quoted, were perfuaded that the apoftles were cautious in divulging the doctrine of the divinity of Chrift, becaufe of the prejudices of *believing* Jews, would we thence be under a neceffity of concluding that the primitive church was ignorant of the Deity of Chrift, or that the apoftles never preached this doctrine ? The confequence would, indeed, be neceffary, were the opinions of the fathers the rule of our faith. But, bleffed be God, we have the fcriptures of truth : and we are as much bound to fearch them for ourfelves, as they were. If we find this precious doctrine in the oracles of God ; it does not concern us, what was the opinion of pious, but fallible men. As far as circumftances correfpond, the divine Spirit fpeaks as directly

T 3

to

εφ' ημας· το δε μετ' εξυσιας διδοναι το πνευμα, 8 κτισματ☉, οιδε ποιηματος εςιν· αλλα Θεϋ δωρον. Ibid. p. 388.

† Το τοινυν λεγομενον υπο τϋ μακαριϋ Πετρϋ, ορθην και ειλικρινη την θεοτητα , μονογενους κηρυσσει· 8 την υποςασιν χωριζων τϋ Θεου λογϋ απο τϋ εκ Μαριας ανθρωπϋ. Contra Arianos Oratio V. Op. vol. i. p. 546.

to us, as he did to thofe to whom the fcriptures were immediately addreffed.

Dr P. does not, however, entirely reft his proof, with
refpect to the conduct of the apoftles, on the opinion of
the fathers. He afferts that, " if we look into the book
" of Acts, we fhall find that thefe *fublime doctrines (of the*
" *pre-exiftence and divinity* of Chrift) were not taught in an
" early period.—All the preaching of Chrift," he fays, " of
" which we have an account in the book of Acts, is that,
" Jefus was the Meffiah, whofe divine miffion was confirmed
" by miracles, efpecially that of his own refurrection, and
" by the gift of the Spirit *." But it is evident that almoft
all the difcourfes, recorded in the Acts, were addreffed to
Jews who did not believe ; and many of them were the
firft addreffes made to fuch. This, then, is the force of Dr
P.'s argument : " The apoftles, in their firft difcourfes to
" thofe Jews who rejected Chrift as a deceiver, did not
" clearly declare his Deity to them : therefore, they never
" gave any inftructions, on this fubject, to thofe who did
" believe." He, who can fee the force of this fort of reafoning, will fwallow any thing.

Even fuppofing the truth of our author's affertion, it
would not be more difficult for us to affign a reafon for the
conduct of the apoftles, than for him (on his own principle,
that Jefus claimed no higher character than that of a human
Meffiah), to fhew, in a fatisfactory manner, why he fo frequently charged his difciples to *tell no man* who he was.

Though it were granted that, in the whole book of Acts,
there was not one direct declaration of the Deity of Chrift;
yet on the ground of that fact already mentioned, that almoft all the difcourfes, which are there recorded, were addreffed to unbelievers, it might be fhewn that it could not
thence be juftly inferred, that the apoftles never preached
this doctrine, or that the firft Chriftians did not believe it.

I

I fhall not argue from the example of the great Prophet himfelf, who faid even to thofe difciples, who had attended him during the whole of his perfonal miniftry, *I have many things to tell you, but ye cannot now bear them;* nor from that prudence enjoined on them, when he faid, *Be ye wife as ferpents;* nor from the conduct of one apoftle, who wifely availed himfelf of the difputes between the Pharifees and Sadducees. The argument founded on the prudence of the apoftles, may have been carried too far on the one hand; and it has certainly been unjuftly interpreted on the other.

While we maintain that the difciples of Jefus believed and taught his Deity, their conduct in efpecially infifting, in the difcourfes referred to, on his mediatory character, may be fufficiently vindicated, from a variety of confiderations.

How ardently foever they wifhed to convince the unbelieving Jews of his divinity, they could not have chofen a more proper method than that which they adopted. The eye of the mind bears a ftriking refemblance to that of the body. Did natural light, in all its fplendor, at once burft upon the bodily eye, it would produce a temporary fufpenfion of its powers. Were this continued, it would foon deftroy the vifual faculty. But the God of nature hath wifely ordained the gradual diffufion of light. The fame order is preferved with refpect to the mind. In every fcience there are firft principles, the knowledge of which is primarily neceffary. If thefe be difregarded, the mind, inftead of receiving inftruction, is ftupified. Before the coming of Chrift, God dealt with his church as in an infantile ftate, imparting knowledge only by degrees, and extending his inftructions, juft as fhe was able to receive them. Under the New Teftament, he hath provided *milk for babes*, as well as *ftrong meat* for them whofe *fenfes* are *exercifed*. The Spirit teaches us that the firft principles muft be known,

before

before there can be any progress towards perfection. Our Lord told his hearers of *earthly things*, before he would tell them of those that were heavenly, (John iii. 12). Therefore, it was moſt natural and proper for his apoſtles, primarily to inform their hearers of thoſe *earthly things* which pertained to their Lord, as reſpecting his human nature. This was, indeed, the *foot* of that *ladder* by which they were to aſcend.

No reaſoning can be more concluſive, or more convincing, than that which proceeds on the conceſſions, or previous convictions of thoſe with whom we argue. This method the apoſtles obſerved. There is a ſaying of Peter, the ſound of which is ſo pleaſing to our author, that he loſes no opportunity of introducing it. He gives it a place almoſt in every work on this ſubject, large or ſmall. " The apo- " ſtles," he ſays, " and all who converſed with our Lord, " before and after his reſurrection, conſidered him in no " other light than ſimply as *a man approved of God, by* "*ſigns and wonders which God did by him,* Acts ii. 22 *." But it is evident that Dr P. either wilfully or ignorantly, has never attended to the proper deſign and real force of this language. The apoſtle Peter does not, in theſe words, give a ſummary of *the common faith.* But he particularly mentions the humanity of Chriſt, becauſe he was about to ſpeak of his ſufferings, death and reſurrection, and wiſhed to convince his hearers of their guilt in crucifying him, even from what themſelves believed. Had he ſaid ; " Jeſus, " the eternal Son of God, equal with the Father,—him be- " ing delivered,—ye have taken, and by wicked hands " have crucified and ſlain, and he hath riſen from the dead," they would perhaps have conſidered his language as a proof of their former charge, that theſe men were *full of new wine,* ver. 13. The apparent contradictions would moſt probably have prevented their giving him a further hearing. But

---

* Hiſt. of Corrupt vol. i. p. 2. Ear. Op. vol. i. p. 11. vol. iii. p. 210. 434. Appeal, p. 16. General View, p. 13. &c. &c.

But he proceeds with them on grounds which they could not deny. While they believed that Jefus was a man, they could not refufe that he had the moft extraordinary atteftations. Therefore he fays; " Ye men of Ifrael, hear " thefe words; Jefus of Nazareth, a man approved of God " *among you,* by miracles, and wonders, and figns, which " God did by him in the midft of you, *as ye yourfelves alfo* " *know;* him being delivered,—ye have taken, and by " wicked hands have crucified and flain ; whom God hath " raifed up." It is remarkable that, in all the places where we have met with this paffage, as quoted by our author, he does not once give the twenty fecond verfe fully. He generally throws out thefe words, which mark the true defign of the apoftle, as containing his appeal to the knowledge of the Jews themfelves. He calls Jefus *a man,* juft as he calls him *Jefus of Nazareth;* in both cafes, accommodating his language to their apprehenfions. From the mode of expreffion, there is no more reafon to infer that he accounted Jefus a mere man, than that he confidered Nazareth as the place of his nativity, becaufe he ufes that phrafeology which was common with the Jews, on this falfe fuppofition.

He fays that Jefus was *approved of God.* But this phrafe does not convey the full or proper meaning of ἀποδεδειγμενον. It is, *pointed out* in the plaineft manner, *fet forth* or *demonftrated by God to,* or *among you,* (1 Cor. iv. 9.). Had the apoftle meant, as he is underftood by Socinians, to affure his hearers that Jefus was a mere man, he would have expreffed himfelf very differently. He does not, in this place, particularly fpecify what Jefus was *demonftrated* to be. He either leaves a blank, which he was afterwards to fill up in the progrefs of his difcourfe ; or infinuates that the wonderful works, performed by him, moft clearly proved his title to all that honour which they knew he

had

had claimed, and for claiming which, they had condemned him, that of being the proper Son of God.

The infpired hiftorian Mofes calls thofe *three men*, Gen. xviij. 2. to none of whom this charaĉter really belonged. For two of them were angels, and the other was JEHOVAH. Why, then, does he call them men? Becaufe they appeared as fuch; and becaufe Abraham, at firft, confidered them in no other light. In the fame fenfe, he who wreftled with Jacob is called *a man*, Gen. xxxii. 24. although he had power to blefs him, ver. 26. 29. and was truly God, If thefe might be called *men*, who had nothing more than the *appearance* of human nature; much more he, of whom it is granted that he was truly man. If JEHOVAH himfelf might receive this defignation, becaufe he affumed merely the likenefs of our nature; it can be no argument againft his being God, of whom it is believed that he affumed this nature in reality. Indeed, both Mofes and Peter fpeak of the fame glorious Perfon.

The apoftle's addrefs is a ftriking example of the argument *ad hominem*. It is as if he had faid, " To confider " Jefus merely as he appeared to you in human nature, you " cannot deny that he was a great and extraordinary per- " fon, and that he had the higheft atteftation poffible. " Therefore, when you crucified him, it muft have been " *with wicked hands*." His faying that God *did* thefe things *by him*, is no proof that he confidered Jefus as a mere man. For though the works which our Saviour performed, in all their circumftances, were a full demonftration of his Deity; yet the particular relation in which he performed them, was that of a fervant. Dr P. can derive no advantage from this language, unlefs he beg the queftion. For the warmeft friend of the Deity of Chrift affents to the words in their proper meaning, as truly as he. There was the greateft propriety in faying, that *God* did thefe things *by him*,

                                                        becaufe

becaufe the Jews had impioufly afcribed his moft illuftrious works to Belzebub.

But it cannot be proved that the affertion, that *God did* thefe things *by him*, as *man*, excludes his divinity. For *all the fulnefs of the godhead dwells in him bodily.* The human nature of Chrift was the medium of the manifeftation of divine power. It is univerfally allowed by the orthodox, that our Saviour, even in his exalted ftate, *received* and *receives gifts in the man*, Pfal. lxviii. 18. *God* alfo *raifed* him *up.* But can our author prove that this general defignation of the Deity excludes *God* the Son? Did he not declare that he had *power to lay down his life, and to take it again*?

Little as Athanafius, according to our author's teftimony, could find in favour of the divinity of Chrift in the apoftle's difcourfe, he found fomething even here. For, explaining this verfe, he fays; "From thefe figns and mi-"racles which the Lord did, he was demonftrated to be, " not a mere man, but God incarnate *." I am not fure, but the language might be properly rendered, *which God in the midft of you did by him*; as expreffive of that antitypical dwelling as in a tabernacle, of that real incarnation of a divine Perfon, fo long and fo frequently promifed to the church, in terms precifely of the fame import. It deferves our notice, that the promife in Joel, which the apoftle illuftrates as the fubject of his difcourfe, is immediately preceded by another, expreffive of God's dwelling *in the midft* of his church, chap. ii. 27 †.

Thofe conclufions, to which the mind is neceffarily led, as the refult of its own principles, or of its previous convictions and operations, have peculiar energy. Here were many

---

* Απο γαρ των σημειων και ων εποιει θαυμασιων ο Κυριος, απεδει- χθη υχ' απλως ανθρωπος, αλλα Θεος ων εν σωματι. Contra Arianos Orat. iii. Opera, vol. i. p. 383.

† See alfo chap. iii. 17.

many witneſſes, ſolemnly teſtifying that *God* had *raiſed up* that very Perſon whom the Jews had crucified. The Holy Spirit evidently atteſted theſe witneſſes by the miraculous gift of tongues. Therefore, as ſoon as their hearers were convinced of the truth of their teſtimony, they would conclude within themſelves, that Jeſus had ſuffered unjuſtly. They would inſtantly recollect the ground of his condemnation by their Sanhedrim. This, they knew, was his own teſtimony, that he was *the Son of God.* Finding that his character was vindicated, in ſo extraordinary a manner, they muſt immediately have inferred the truth of that teſtimony, and concluded that he was the Son of God, in that very ſenſe according to which he was ſuppoſed to be chargeable with blaſphemy, *as making himſelf equal with God*, and aſſerting his title to ſit at the right hand of power.

In that age, God condeſcended to call the attention of carnal men, by evidence addreſſed to their ſenſes; confirming divine truths by miracles, which were *a ſign to them who believed not,* 1 Cor. xiv. 22. It was, therefore, moſt natural for his ambaſſadors, *firſt* to appeal to theſe facts which had been ſubjected to the ſenſes of men; and to deduce from them all thoſe inferences that were native, as clearing the way for the reception of doctrines truly more *ſublime.*

Some of theſe diſcourſes recorded in the Acts were delivered in ſuch circumſtances, that the diſciples could not avoid this method, or at leaſt, could not obſerve any other ſo proper. When *cloven tongues, like as of fire, ſat on each of them*, and *every man heard them ſpeak in his own language;* they were under a neceſſity of accounting for theſe aſtoniſhing circumſtances, in reply to the inquiries of ſome, and to the ridicule of others, Acts ii. 12, 13. They could not anſwer that queſtion, *What meaneth this?* without declaring that it was the work of Jeſus. They could not

erſuade

perfuade their countrymen, that it was his work, without proclaiming his refurrection and glory. They could not proclaim thefe, without referring to his death, and criminating thofe who had crucified him. They could not convince them of their guilt in crucifying him, fo directly, as by proving that he was the true Meffiah. For it was only a part of their guilt, that they had rejected the Son of God. This formally confifted in their rejecting him in the moft endearing character which he could fuftain, that of the promifed Deliverer. As all their national hopes, defires and longings centered here, the apoftles could not touch any other ftring that poffeffed fuch univerfal influence. Indeed, they could not fhew that the effufion of the Spirit was the work of Jefus, without immediately defcribing him as Meffiah. For all the promifes of the gift of the Spirit referred to the time of his appearance: and it was not immediately as the Son of God, but as Mediator, that he had *fhed forth that which they heard and faw.* It was as being himfelf the *Chrift,* the *Anointed,* that he communicated this anointing to others. As King of Zion, on occafion of his triumphant entry into his palace, he diftributed gifts to men, and proclaimed pardon *even to the rebellious.* From him as the head of the body, exalted in *human nature,* did thefe influences defcend on the members. It would, therefore, have been highly improper to have paffed over his mediatory character, the more immediate caufe of all this, in order to prove his divine nature, which was the more remote; efpecially as the remote caufe could not be believed, without a previous conviction with refpect to the immediate.

The fame obfervation will apply to the addrefs of the apoftles to the council, when they were interrogated in regard to their healing the impotent man, Acts iv. 5.—12. The rulers faid; " By what power, or by what name have

" ye

" ye done this?" The apoftles replied; " If we this day
" be examined of the good deed done to the impotent man,
" by what means he is made whole; Be it known unto
" you all,—That by the name of Jefus Chrift of Naza-
" reth, whom ye crucified, whom God raifed from the
" dead, even by him doth this man ftand here before you
" whole." They declare that the cure was effected in
confequence of the exaltation of Jefus as Mediator, of his
being *raifed*, and *becoming the head of the corner*, ver. 12.
And this was, undoubtedly, the moft proper courfe that
the apoftles could take, in the firft inftance at leaft. For
their miraculous powers proceeding from him as Mediator,
every time that thefe were exercifed, there was a renewed
vindication of his character, and a new evidence of the
great guilt of his perfecutors.

It was as neceffary to believe the real humanity of
Chrift, as the truth of his divinity. For without the one,
men could receive no benefit from the other. The works
afcribed to him, as properly his own, are fo great, that, to
reafon, it feems fully as difficult to believe that he was
truly man, as that he was the Son of God. Had not the
apoftles guarded againft this extreme, the Jews who, from
their writings, were fo well acquainted with the intervention of angels, might have fallen into that error, which
fo generally prevailed in fucceeding ages, of fuppofing that
Chrift had only the appearance of humanity, and that he
only feemed to fuffer, to die, to rife again, and to afcend.
His own difciples, both before and after his death, when
they faw him fufpend the ordinary laws of nature, were
under the temporary influence of this error. When they
beheld him *walking on the fea, they were troubled, faying,
It is a Spirit*, Matth. xiv. 26. When, after his refurrection,
he *ftood in the midft of them, the doors being fhut, they were
terrified and affrighted, and fuppofed that they had feen a*
2   *Spirit,*

Spirit, Luke xxiv. 37. The Holy Ghoſt, who afterwards ſpoke by them, not only guarded their immediate hearers againſt this error; but, foreſeeing its future prevalence, provided the church with a ſufficient antidote.

It was neceſſary that the diſciples ſhould eſpecially declare the divine miſſion of Jeſus as the Meſſiah; becauſe in this character he wrought ſalvation. It was only as *ſent* by the Father, that he could be the Saviour, as his *ſervant* and *elect,* that he was to receive the Spirit and *bring forth judgment to the Gentiles,* Iſa. xlii. 1. The knowledge of Jeſus as the eternal Son of God, could, of itſelf, have been of no real advantage to ſinful men. Therefore, before his coming, his divinity was ſtill revealed in the moſt intimate connexion with his mediatory character. Did the Father teſtify to the Iſraelites, that his Name was *in him?* He, at the ſame time, revealed him as an *Angel* or *Meſſenger,* commanding them to *obey his voice.* When he was declared to be a begotten Son, and exhibited as the object of faith, he was alſo proclaimed King over Zion. That character, *the mighty God,* is given him in connexion with others expreſſive of his office. When his *goings forth* are ſaid to have been *from of old, from everlaſting,* he is at the ſame time deſcribed as *the Ruler of Iſrael,* who ſhould *come forth* out of Bethlehem.

Thus, alſo, the apoſtles took the moſt proper plan for combating the prejudices of the Jews. We have heard a great deal concerning their firm perſuaſion that the Meſſiah was to be a mere man. It is granted on both ſides, that the doctrine of the *reſurrection* was denied by many of this people. Perſons of this deſcription could have no fear of God, and, of conſequence, no reſpect to Jeſus, although declared to be divine. But a conviction of the truth of this doctrine, as examplified in him when once produced in their minds, would be a mean of awakening them to con-

cern

cern about their eternal interefts. There was another prejudice, fully as powerful and prevalent among them, as
any of the former. This was in favour of a falvation
merely of a *temporal* nature. While this remained, the
proclamation of a divine Saviour would be defpifed. But,
as the refurrection of Jefus proved that he was the true
Meffiah; his previous fufferings, and his entrance into
glory, would convince thofe who did not reject the former
evidence, that he came to accomplifh a fpiritual falvation.
By ftriking againft the prejudices laft mentioned, the a-
poftles *laid the axe to the root of the tree.* Although it
were certain, that the Jews of that age generally believed
that the Meffiah was to be no more than man; while we
know the doctrine of fcripture, and the faith of their pro-
genitors, we muft be perfuaded that the great reafon of
their delufion in this refpect, was their having loft all fpiritual apprehenfions of his work and kingdom.

The method, adopted by the apoftles, feems to have
been confonant to that of God himfelf, in making known
to his people the character of Jefus. He firft gave them
the moft abundant, and the moft fatisfactory evidence of
the dignity of the Perfon whom he fent. This confifted in
his own teftimony from heaven, in the teftimony of John
the Baptift, in that of Jefus himfelf, and in that alfo of his
works, to which he often appealed as undeniable proofs of
his divinity. Thence the apoftle John demonftrates that, although *his own received him not,* it was not for want of evidence. For he fays; *We beheld his glory, the glory as of
the only-begotten of the Father.* In the introduction to his
firft epiftle, he alfo fhews that *the Word of life* was moft
clearly *manifefted.* But God had another, and a final, evidence in referve for them. This, indeed, more immediately referred to the *mediatory character* of Jefus. It was
no other than *the fign of the prophet Jonas.* Need we
wonder,

wonder, then, that the apoftles fhould efpecially infift on his refurrection ?. They could not prove, or even mention this, without afferting his humanity. They generally af-cribe the work to God. But this was alfo proper. For it was a direct proof of the innocence of Jefus, tending to remove the prejudices of the Jews againft him as an im-poftor, and a blafphemer. It was alfo a certain demonftra-tion of the perfection of his mediatory work. While the apoftles afcribed the refurrection to God, they denied it to Jefus *as man* only; but, as has been feen, did not exclude the fecond Perfon of the Trinity, any more than the firft or third.

The mediatorial character of Jefus was that fpecial point of teftimony with which he entrufted his fervants. If they clearly and fully declared this, the primary end of their miffion, efpecially as refpecting their countrymen, was fulfilled. It being once eftablifhed that Jefus was that illu-ftrious Perfon foretold, the Jews were referred to more an-cient, and, to them, more inconteftable proofs, as to his effential dignity. Thefe were their own fcriptures. To thefe our Lord himfelf had appealed, when proving his equality with the Father. He had accufed his hearers of difbelieving the teftimony of Mofes, becaufe they rejected his : *Had ye believed Mofes,* he fays, *ye would have believed me,* John. v. 46. The fame method was obferved by his fervants. To mention one inftance only ; it is evidently the defign of Stephen, to prove that the prophet foretold by Mofes was that Angel who declared that he was the God of Abraham, of Ifaac, and of Jacob, Acts vii. 30, 31, 32. 37, 38.

It was not the principal work of the apoftles to pro-claim the effential dignity of the promifed Meffiah. This had been done in the cleareft manner, in the promifes and

predictions refpecting his appearance. Nor was it the immediate end of their miffion, to unfold the nature of the
mediatory office, the perfonal qualifications neceffary for
the difcharge of it, the means by which the work of the
Mediator was to be accomplifhed, or the evidences of its
actual completion. All this was alfo done to their hands.
The great defign of the law, and of the writings of the
prophets, being to teftify of Chrift in thefe refpects; had
the apoftles directly entered on this work, their conduct
would have contained a reflection on *the Spirit of prophecy,*
as if it had not been *the teftimony of Jefus.* They were efpecially to identify the Perfon *of whom Mofes, in the law, and
the prophets, did write.* For this is indifpenfably neceffary
in all evidence that has a perfonal refpect. They were to
fhew that this very Jefus, whom the Jews had crucified, was
he. For, after the coming of the Meffiah, how juft foever
the abftract notions that men might entertain concerning his
revealed character, if they denied that Jefus was the perfon, notwithftanding their having fufficient means of information, they expofed themfelves to the danger of *dying in
their fins.* The apoftles were to identify the Perfon, by
fhewing that all thofe fenfible evidences of the accomplifhment of the work of mediation, which had been promifed
in the fcriptures, were verified in Jefus; particularly in his
wonderful works, his great humiliation, his fufferings to the
death, his refurrection, afcenfion, and effufion of the Spirit.

That this was their more immediate work, is evident
from what our Lord fays to them with refpect to the end
of their miffion: *I fent you to reap that whereon ye beftowed
no labour: Other men laboured, and ye are entered into their
labours,* John iv. 38. He refers not only to his own and
the Baptift's labours, but to thofe of all the prophets. He
reprefents them as fowers, and the apoftles as reapers:

Herein

Herein is that faying true, One foweth, and another reapeth,
ver. 37. The prophets had the laborious work of *plowing
up the fallow ground ;* of fowing, among a carnal people,
the precious doctrine concerning the Perfon and Office of
the Saviour. The apoftles are faid, like reapers, to *enter
into their labours ;* becaufe their principal work was to declare that Jefus was that Meffiah fo particularly defigned by
the prophets, to produce fufficient evidence of this, and thus
to reap the fruits of their labours in the converfion of multitudes. The primitive church underftood our Saviour's
words in this very fenfe. Thus they are explained by
Irenæus. " Who are thefe who *laboured ?*—This is evi-
" dently to be underftood of the patriarchs and prophets,
" who alfo prefigured our faith, and differminated in the
" earth the doctrine of the coming of the Son of God, de-
" claring *who* and *what manner of perfon* he fhould be ;
" that their fucceffors, who feared the Lord, might readily
" acknowledge the coming of Chrift, being inftructed by
" the prophets." This he illuftrates, firft by the conduct
of Jofeph, in retaining Mary, after being informed that fhe
was with child of the Holy Ghoft ; then, by the fudden
converfion of the Eunuch. " On this account," he fays,
" Philip, when he found the Eunuch of the Queen of E-
" thiopia reading thefe things which are written, eafily
" perfuaded him to believe that the perfon fpoken of was
" Chrift, who was crucified under Pontius Pilate, and fuffer-
" ed whatever the prophets foretold ; and that he was that
" Son of God who gives eternal life to men. And as
" foon as he had baptized him, he departed from him. For
" nothing befides was wanting to him who was before in-
" ftructed by the prophets. He was not ignorant of God
" the Father :—but only of the *advent* of the Son of God,
" which being foon made acquainted with, he went on his

" way

" way rejoicing, and became a preacher of the coming of
" Chrift in Ethiopia. On this account alfo, the apoftles,
" when gathering the loft fheep of the houfe of Ifrael, and
" addreffing them from the fcriptures, fhewed that Jefus,
" who was crucified, was the Son of the living God, and
" perfuaded great multitudes *."

They were to prove the mediatory character of Jefus,
efpecially from that *fenfible* evidence with which they had
been favoured, not for their own fakes only, but for the
behoof of others. What they had *feen with their eyes, and
looked upon, and heard, and handled of the living Word*, they
were to *déclare* to others. Therefore, they are called *eye-
witneffes of the Word*, Luke i. 2. When defcribed in this
character, the death and refurrection of Jefus, with remiffion
of fins through his blood, are fometimes mentioned as the
principal articles of their teftimony, chap. xxiv. 46.—48.
*Thus it behoved Chrift to fuffer, and to rife from the dead
the third day, and that repentance and remiffion of fins fhould
be preached in his name.—And ye are his witneffes of thefe
things* †. It is fometimes extended to all the circumftances
of his life, as well as of his death, refurrection and glory,
Acts x. 39. 42. On other occafions, the refurrection alone
is mentioned, as if it had been the only article of their teftimony ; becaufe it was the great evidence of the perfection
of his character, including all the reft. Therefore, when
the vacancy in the facred college was to be fupplied, the
definition of an apoftle is fimply given in thefe words ; *One
muft be ordained to be a witnefs with us of the refurrection*,
Acts i. 22.

It may be faid, that ' if Jefus was truly God, it would
" have tended more directly to illuftrate his dignity, had the
" apoftles

" apoftles plainly declared that he rofe from the dead by
" his own power." But the doctrine of the refurrection,
urged in this manner, would not have fo properly confirmed that of remiffion of fins through his blood. The a-
poftles were bound efpecially to declare, that he was *raifed*
again for our juftification, that his refurrection was the great
evidence of the perfection of his obedience and fufferings as
our Surety, and of the acceptance of his work by God the
Father, acting as Judge. When preaching the doctrine of
falvation, it was neceffary for them to adhere to the œco-
nomy. For they could preach it on no other ground. And
even in adhering to this, they had abundant opportunity of
declaring the dignity of the Perfon.

But the apoftles were not the only witneffes of thefe
things. The Spirit of God concurred in this teftimony.
Now, he is fpoken of as a joint witnefs with them : *We are*
his witneffes ;—and fo alfo is the Holy Ghoft, Acts v. 32.
Elfewhere, he is reprefented as a fuperior witnefs, confirming their teftimony, and attefting themfelves : *God alfo*
bearing them witnefs with figns, and wonders,—and gifts of
the Holy Ghoft, Heb. ii. 4. By his miraculous gifts, he attefted them as faithful witneffes. His own teftimony concerning Jefus efpecially refpected the perfection of his work
as Mediator, his glory and power as exalted in human nature. As fent to the church, he is *the Spirit of Chrift*,
1 Pet. i. 11. that is, of the Meffiah. As Jefus is called *the*
Chrift, becaufe he was *anointed* by the Spirit ; the latter is
called *the Spirit of Chrift*, becaufe he is communicated by
him in his mediatory character. We muft, therefore, fuppofe that it is more directly his work, under the New Teftament difpenfation, to teftify of Jefus, in this very refpect.
When it is faid, John vii. 39. that *the Holy Spirit was not*
yet given, becaufe that Jefus was not yet glorified ; it is
plainly intimated that the effufion of the Spirit was the

great

great evidence and teſtimony of the glory of Jeſus as Mediator. To the ſame purpoſe is the language of Peter,
Acts ii. 33. *Therefore being by the right hand of God exalted,—he hath ſhed forth this which ye now ſee and hear.*
Afterwards, he appeals to the effuſion of the Spirit; as the
external evidence of the exaltation of Jeſus as a Prince,
and a Saviour, ver. 36. THEREFORE, *let all the houſe of
Iſrael know aſſuredly, that God hath made that ſame Jeſus
both Lord and Chriſt.* As *the Spirit of Chriſt teſtified be-
fore-hand the ſufferings of Chriſt, and the glory that ſhould
follow ;* after both, he teſtified the ſatisfactory nature of the
one, and the certainty of the other.

It being, therefore, peculiarly incumbent on the apoſtles,
to declare the reſurrection and the glory of Chriſt, with the
gift of the Holy Spirit to him, that he might communicate
it to others ; it is evident that they could not give their
teſtimony in a proper manner, without aſcribing theſe
things to God. For as the reſurrection reſpected a part of
the humanity of Jeſus, the glory that followed eſpecially
terminated on this nature. The apoſtles could not in ſtrict
propriety of language diſtinctly ſpeak of his divine nature
as ſuffering, dying, riſing again, and being glorified. Beſides it is granted, on all hands, that Jeſus, as Mediator, was
the Father's ſervant. Therefore the gift of the reward
muſt be aſcribed to the Father. For it was a judicial act,
in conſequence of that work which the Mediator had
finiſhed.

The propriety of their conduct will yet further appear,
from the natural and neceſſary conſequence of a belief of
the mediatory character of Jeſus. The attention of their
hearers was firſt arreſted by a declaration of the reſurrection and glory of that very Perſon whom they had crucified. They could not diſbelieve theſe things, becauſe they
were not merely atteſted by men of unexceptionable cha-
raſters,

racters, but by the Spirit of God.   For they not only *saw*
the ancient and well known symbol of the Divine presence
abiding on each of the apostles, which would most probably
bring to their recollection the testimony of the Baptist,
that he who came after him should *baptize* them *with fire,*
as the sensible emblem of the baptism of the Holy Ghost :
but they *heard* unlearned men addressing every man in his
own language.   Therefore, unless they shut their eyes and
stopped their ears, they could not deny the presence and
operation of the Spirit, or doubt that he confirmed the testimony of the speakers.   As soon as they were assured of
the truth of the facts attested, they would naturally inquire
into the extent of the character of Jesus.   Thus, also, their
minds would be prepared for receiving information.   This
mode of instruction *a posteriori* is far better calculated for
the generality of minds, than that *a priori.*   The apostles
themselves learned the meaning of Christ's sayings, and the
dignity of his Person, most fully from the event.   Not till
after his resurrection, did they understand that, when he
said, *Destroy this temple,* &c. he spake of the temple of his
body, and that the literal temple was only a type of this.
When, as that King who brought salvation, he entered in
humble triumph into Jerusalem, and was hailed by the
multitude as he that came in the Name of the Lord ; *these
things understood not his disciples at the first : but when
Jesus was glorified, then remembered they that these things
were written of him, and that they had done these things
unto him,* John xii. 16.

We have already seen, that those who received the
testimony of the apostles, must have considered the resurrection of Jesus as a Divine vindication from the charge of
blasphemy, on the ground of which he was condemned ;
and of course, as a convincing evidence of the truth of that
testimony, which he sealed with his blood.   Therefore, al-

though

though it did not appear, from the compendious history of the Acts, that the apostles formally deduced this conclusion, we might be assured that they had it ultimately in their view. We might even suppose, that they particularly expressed it, on various occasions. For we know that they were uniform in their doctrine. And we find one of them expressly testifying, in another place, that Jesus was *declared to be the Son of God with power,—by the resurrection from the dead*, Rom. i. 4. that is, he was powerfully exculpated from the unjust sentence of his adversaries, when they condemned him for blasphemy against God, because he called himself his *Son*.

When the apostles spoke of Jesus as having ascended, as having received the promise of the Spirit, and as bestowing such precious gifts as repentance and remission ; the Jews must necessarily have inferred, that he was exhibited as a divine Person. If they believed that he had such power and glory, they must also have believed his Deity. For their own prophetical writings declared that it was *God* who should thus *ascend*, and *receive gifts*, Psal. lxviii. 18. When they knew that Jesus was exalted to give, even to his murderers, they could not but conclude that this was he who was described as *the God of their salvation,* who should receive gifts even *for the rebellious* *. The very idea of his having power to forgive sins, would, according to their own principles, satisfy them that he was truly divine. For it was a received maxim with them, how silly foever it may appear to their more enlightened friends the Socinians, that *no one could forgive sins but God only*. In a word, they could not believe that Jesus would judge the world, without either believing that he was a divine Person, or re-

nouncing

---

* Indeed, by an attribution of what strictly belongs to one nature to the whole person, it is expressly declared that *God was—received up into glory*, 1 Tim. iii. 16.

nouncing that article of their Creed, fo long received as matter of infpiration, that *God* was *Judge himfelf*, Pfal. 1: 6.

Hitherto, I have fpoken of *means* only ; God, in the general tenor of his operations, as regularly employing thefe, as if the fuccefs wholly depended on them ; and it being incumbent on his fervants to obferve the fame method. But when it is confidered, that the apoftolical addreffes were accompanied, not merely by the outward and extraordinary operations of the Spirit, but, to all who believed, by thofe that were inward and efficacious ; the argument acquires additional force. They would be led to form the conclufions already mentioned, not merely by the dictates of reafon, and from the neceffary connexion of the truths which they newly embraced with thofe formerly believed ; but efpecially by that Spirit of truth, who was promifed to *lead into all truth*, and whofe fpecial work was to teftify of Jefus.

C H A P. XI.

Proofs from the Book of Acts, that the Apoftles taught the Doctrine of the Divinity of Chrift.

IT has been feen, that the apoftles fulfilled the primary end of their miffion, in preaching that Jefus was the Mefliah ; and that the evidence by which they proved this doctrine, was fuch as neceffarily implied that he was a divine Perfon. But this is not all. From their difcourfes, recorded in the Acts, and from other circumftances there narrated, it appears that they not only believed this doctrine, but taught it, even in addreffing unbelievers.

The

· The prayer for direction in the choice of an apoſtle, in room of Judas, would ſeem to have been addreſſed to Jeſus, as the ſearcher of hearts, chap. i. 24. Not only is he generally diſtinguiſhed, in the New Teſtament, as *Lord;* but this deſignation is, in ver. 21. joined with that of Jeſus. The language is ; *Thou, Lord, who knoweſt the hearts of all men, ſhew whether of theſe two thou haſt choſen.* Now, it cannot be refuſed, that the choice of an apoſtle properly belonged to the Head of the Church; and that this was a right which he claimed and exerciſed, while on earth. Therefore it is ſaid, ver. 2. that he *gave commandments unto the apoſtles whom* HE *had choſen.* But if he was not the object of this prayer, though he choſe all the reſt, he had no hand in the choice of Matthias. On this ſuppoſition, a ſtrange contradiction muſt be admitted, that his honours and privileges were diminiſhed by his exaltation. The very end of the choice was, that one might *take part of this miniſtry and apoſtleſhip.* But if Jeſus did not chooſe him, how could he be *an Apoſtle of Jeſus,* that is, *one ſent by* him?

The language uſed in this prayer, is perfectly applicable to the Saviour. For he declares, that *all the churches ſhall know that it is he who ſearcheth the reins and hearts,* Rev. ii. 23. Can we ſuppoſe, then, that he ſhould either deprive himſelf or be deprived of this firſt opportunity, after his aſcenſion, of diſplaying his omniſcience and ſovereignty, or of one ſo important?

Nor was it uncommon for his diſciples to addreſs him as the hearer of prayer. For we learn from the next chapter, that Peter, when *filled with the Holy Ghoſt,* (ver. 4.). applied the prophecy of Joel to Jeſus, as the object of invocation, ver. 21. *And it ſhall come to paſs, that whoſoever ſhall call on the name of the Lord, ſhall be ſaved.* Now, theſe words evidently reſpect our Saviour. For that *great and*

and notable day of the Lord, mentioned in the preceding
verfe, is the fame which is elfewhere denominated *the day
of the Lord Jefus,* 1 Cor. v. 5. 2 Cor. i. 14. But there can
be no reafonable doubt, that the prophecy refpects him as
the object of invocation. For another apoftle exprefsly applies it to *the Lord Jefus,* Rom. x. 9.—13. It is remarkable
that thefe words are immediately introductory to that language, of which our author has made fuch a handle; *Jefus
of Nazareth, a man approved of God,* &c.

The apoftle Peter, even while fpeaking of Jefus as Mediator, throws in a declaration ftrongly expreffive of his
Deity: *Whom God hath raifed up, having loofed the pains
of death, becaufe it was not poffible that he could be holden of
it,* ver. 24. He does not mean that the refurrection of Jefus,
as accomplifhed by God, was the reafon why he could not
be holden of death; as if the power of God, effecting this
refurrection, were oppofed to the power of death. For
then he ought to have faid; " It was not poffible that he
" could be holden of death, becaufe God raifed him up."
But it is directly the reverfe; *God raifed him up,—becaufe
he could not be holden of death.*" Indeed, God the Father,
in the character of Judge, gave him this acquittal, becaufe
of the perfection of his facrifice. But had Peter meant
nothing more, he would moft probably have faid,—" be-
" caufe it was not *juft,*" &c. Thus, it would have been,
ουκ ην δικαιον. But inftead of this, it is ουκ ην δυνατον. This
expreffes the natural dignity of the Perfon. Another word
is added, which conveys the fame idea,—κρατεισθαι. The
literal fenfe of the expreffion is; " becaufe it was not pof-
" fible that he fhould be retained under its *power.* Could
an infpired apoftle apply this language to a mere man, how
innocent foever? Does it not neceffarily imply that the
Perfon defcribed is effentially *the Prince of Life?*

When declaring the faith of David, that *of the fruit*
. . . *of*

*of his loins,—*God *would raife up Chrift,* the apoftle throws in this important parenthefis, *according to the flefh,* ver. 30. If Jefus hath no other nature than the human, is not this as abfurd a reftriction as ever was ufed?

In the procefs of his difcourfe, he obferves that Jefus, *being by the right hand of God exalted, and having received of the Father the promife of the Spirit, had fhed forth that which they faw and heard,* ver. 33. Dr Horfley has remarked that here " the three Perfons are diftinctly men- " tioned in a manner which implies the divinity of each ;" and that the expreffion τ8 πατρος, *of the Father,* in which we have " the fubftantive with the article prefixed, denotes " a perfon, whofe character it is to be the Father ;" pater- nity being " the property which individuates the Perfon *." There feems alfo to be fomething peculiar in the introduc- tion of the effential Name *God,* before that of thefe perfonal defignations, *the Father,* and *the Holy Ghoft.* We cannot think of a reafon for this peculiarity, unlefs it denote that, although according to the œconomy of our redemption, the exaltation of Jefus is more immediately afcribed to the Father, this is not to be underftood exclufively. For here it feems to be afcribed to the *right hand* or *power of God* effentially confidered. Indeed, the divine power of the Son as really appeared in his refurrection and afcenfion, as that of the Father. He was not merely *raifed up.* He *rofe again†.* He was not merely *exalted.* He *afcended.* He *entered into his reft.*

But the laft part of the verfe contains a ftriking proof of the Deity of Chrift. *He hath fhed forth this which ye now fee and hear.* I need not fay, that the apoftle means the miraculous operation of the Spirit. But the effufion of the Spirit is never attributed to one confeffedly a mere

man.

---

* Letters to Dr Prieftley, p. 101.

† Rom. xiv. 9. 1 Cor. xv. 4. 12. 2 Cor. v. 15. 1 Thef. iv. 14.

man. Indeed it is faid that, *through laying on of the a-*
poftles hands, the Holy Ghoft was given, chap. viii. 18. But
what an important difference is there in the language!
They are not faid to *give*, or to *fhed forth* the Spirit, either
in his gifts, or in his graces. There is a referve for a divine donor. They were mere inftruments, whofe work it
was to preach the word, to baptize with water, and to obferve the outward fymbol of the impofition of hands. But
God alone could make the means effectual. It is declared,
that he *fheds on us abundantly the renewing of the Holy*
Ghoft δια, through Jefus Chrift, Tit. iii. 5, 6. But though
the fame prepofition is ufed in both places, it is in very different fenfes. In the firft, it is not fo much as faid, that the
Spirit was given *through the apoftles*. It is connected with
the mean ufed by them as inftruments. For the impofition
of hands was accompanied with prayer. *They prayed for*
them, that they might receive the Holy Ghoft, chap. viii. 15.
In the other paffage, it denotes, not the inftrumental, but
the meritorious caufe. We are faid to be renewed *through*
Jefus Chrift; but it is as *our Saviour*, who by his infinite
merit hath purchafed the influences of the Spirit. For
Jefus, that he might fanctify the people,—fuffered without
the gate, Heb. xiii. 12.

As the apoftles were mere inftruments, they ftill acknowledged this. For they not only prayed for the influences
of the Spirit, but afcribed all the communications of thefe
to Jefus. Thus Ananias faid to Saul; *The Lord, even Jefus*
—hath fent me, that thou mighteft—be filled with the Holy
Ghoft, chap. ix. 17. They reprefented the Spirit as communicated to others, not by them, as if the power had been
theirs; but in the fame manner in which he was communicated to them. Thus Peter teftifies concerning the Gentiles; *As I began to fpeak, the Holy Ghoft fell on them, as*
on us at the beginning, chap. xi. 15. On this occafion, there

was

was not even the impofition of hands. The preaching of
the word was the only mean: and the Spirit was given, at
the very commencement of Peter's difcourfe, that it might
appear to be wholly a divine work.

This fpiritual baptifm is the very circumftance fingled
out by John the Baptift, as the great external evidence of
the fuperiority of Jefus: *I indeed baptize you with water ;
but one mightier than I cometh, the latchet of whofe fhoes I
am not worthy to unloofe : he fhall baptize you with the
Holy Ghoft and with fire*, Luke iii. 16· This evidence
of fuperiority is, indeed, of an official kind: as the language denotes the unfpeakably fuperior nature of his baptifm. But when John referred his hearers to *fenfible* evidence, it was neceffary that he fhould fpecify an act of Jefus
as Mediator. For all that he did among men was in this
character. However, it feems to be ultimately refolved
into his effential dignity. Therefore, he is faid to be ισχυ-
ροτερος, *mightier*. John declares this to be a prefent attribute of Jefus: *He* IS *mightier*. The effential power was
prefent, although the effect was future ; *He* SHALL *baptize*.
The debafing language, which John ufes concerning himfelf, alfo fhews that he was convinced of an effential, as
well as of an official, diftinction. For if Jefus was merely
a meffenger, John being the fame, though the former be
fuppofed to have been much fuperior to the latter, being
equally fervants of one infinitely fuperior to both, it is inconceivable that John fhould have declared, that he was
unworthy to do the meaneft office to Jefus, even to unloofe
the latchet of his fhoe. He was not fo much of a courtier
as to fpeak in this ftyle. He would have been chargeable
with a grofs falfehood. For the greateft diftinction in rank
that can be fuppofed to fubfift between two fervants of the
fame mafter, cannot fo far debafe the one, as to render him
unworthy to perform the meaneft office to the other. Indeed,

deed, from the Baptiſt's teſtimony, as recorded, John i. 15.
it is clear, that he conſidered the eſſential dignity of Jeſus as
the foundation of his preference to himſelf with reſpect to office. This may be elſewhere illuſtrated.

The effuſion of the Spirit muſt be viewed as a certain
proof of the Deity of Chriſt, by all who believe that the
Spirit is a Perſon. But although, according to the Socinian
hypotheſis, he ſhould be conſidered as only the *power* or
virtue of the Divine Being, more would be aſcribed to Jeſus
than can belong to a creature. To ſuppoſe that almighty
power may reſide in a finite ſubject, is contrary, not to
theology alone, but to ſound philoſophy. For nothing can
be received in a proper ſenſe, which exceeds the powers of
the recipient. But *all power is given* to Chriſt, *in heaven,
and in earth.*

There is no occaſion, however, for abſtract reaſoning.
The paſſage, in its connexion, clearly ſhews that Peter
meant to exhibit Jeſus as a divine Perſon. For his language concerning the gift of the Spirit evidently refers to
what he had declared in the introduction. All the inter-
mediate part of his diſcourſe ſeems deſigned to ſhew, how
he could attribute this power of giving the Spirit to one
clothed with human nature. He ſays, ver. 16, 17. *This
is that which was ſpoken by the prophet Joel, and it ſhall
come to paſs in the laſt days, (ſaith God) I will pour out
my Spirit upon all fleſh,* &c. He firſt aſcribes the work to
God ; *ſaith God, I will pour.* Then he aſcribes it to Jeſus ;
He hath ſhed forth this. The ſame verb is uſed in both
places. Could any Jew doubt that he who εξεχεε *ſhed* or
poured out, (ver. 33.) was eſſentially the ſame, who in
ver. 17. is made to ſay, εκχεω, *I will pour out ?*

What has been ſaid clearly ſhews that this work could
not be performed by Chriſt as a mere inſtrument. Beſides,
the very language excludes this view. As the Hebrew
word,

word, correfpondent to that here ufed, implies the idea of copioufnefs, the metaphor being taken from the effufion of water from the clouds, (Ifa. xliv. 3.) it feems alfo to allude to the divine nature of the work ; God alone being the Father of the rain. To whomfoever thefe words, *I will pour out,* apply, the Spirit which he communicates is his own. For it follows ;—*Of my Spirit.* Now, if Chrift be not God, the Holy Spirit could not be called *his.* But we know that he is exprefsly faid to be *the Spirit of Chrift,* 1 Pet. i. 11. And Chrift himfelf fays, *I will fend him unto you ;*—a mode of fpeaking which muft have difcovered the moft impious arrogance in any creature.

Again, as this Spirit *divideth* of his *gifts and graces unto every man feverally* as he *will,* 1 Cor. xii. 11. either Chrift does not participate in this fovereignty of operation, or he does. If he does not, he cannot with the leaft propriety be faid to *fhed forth* the Spirit. If he does, then he poffeffes divine fovereignty. For if it be abfurdly refufed that, in the paffage referred to, the Spirit is fpoken of as a Perfon, in order to make fenfe of the words, it will be neceffary to fuppofe that the Father is meant, whofe *power* he is faid to be ; becaufe fovereignty is the attribute of a perfon only.

Chrift being faid to be *exalted,* and at the fame time, to have *poured out* the Spirit, it is evident that thofe who heard this difcourfe muft either have fuppofed that the fpeaker afferted the ubiquity of Chrift's human nature, or believed that he poffeffed a nature infinitely fuperior to that to which exaltation is properly afcribed.

In a word, the apoftle refers to Pfal. cx. 1. *The Lord faid unto my Lord.* It is granted that David calls the Meffiah *his Lord.* This is a term denoting dominion, and a right to worfhip; as he acknowledges, concerning the fame glorious Perfon, Pfal. xlv. 11. *He is thy Lord, and worfhip worſhip thou him.* But how could David be ſubject to Chriſt as *his* Lord, if he had no exiſtence before he became *his Son ?*

Peter concludes his diſcourſe with theſe remarkable words ; *Therefore, let all the houſe of Iſrael know aſſuredly, that God hath made that ſame Jeſus, whom ye have crucified, both Lord and Chriſt,* ver. 36. that is, the Father hath judicially *conſtituted* him *Lord and Chriſt,* in human nature ; and by this effuſion of the Spirit hath manifeſted that he really poſſeſſes all the dignity and power which theſe titles imply. He declares that Jeſus is *Lord ;* giving him a character expreſſive, not of eſſence, but of authority ; yet, as we have ſeen, of ſuch authority as entitles the poſſeſſor to divine worſhip. Was it, therefore, poſſible for the Jews to hear this, without being perſuaded that the apoſtle meant to deſcribe Jeſus as a Divine Perſon ? Indeed, the preceding words, *Sit thou at my right hand,* can be. underſtood in no other ſenſe than as a call to the Son, in our nature, to a participation in all the glory of the Father. For *the Man whoſe name is the Branch,* not only *builds the temple of the Lord,* but *bears the glory,* and *ſits and rules upon his throne,* that is, the throne of JEHOVAH. That they are deſcribed as equal in power, and in glory, is evident from what immediately follows ; *And the counſel of peace ſhall be between them both,* Zech. vi. 12, 13 [*].

In a ſubſequent diſcourſe of the ſame apoſtle, on occaſion of the curing of the lame man, he exhibits Jeſus not only as Meſſiah, and particularly as the prophet whom Moſes foretold, chap. iii. 22. but as the *Son* of *God,* ver. 13. In what ſenſe he gives him this deſignation, appears from the words that follow ; *But ye denied the Holy One, and the Juſt,* *—and killed the Prince of Life,* ver. 14, 15. Now, the meaning of theſe expreſſions, as underſtood by his hearers,

VOL. I. X muſt

[*] Vid. Vitring. Obſerv. Sac. lib. 2. c. 5.

muft be determined from the manner in which they had
been applied in their own fcriptures. Had Peter called
Jefus *the Holy One of God*, it might have been faid that the
Jews acknowledged this as a defignation of the Meffiah ;
without affixing to it the idea of Deity ; becaufe, as ufed
in the Old Teftament, it feems to refpect him in his official
character. But the queftion is, how did they underftand this
exclufive language, *the Holy One*, as there ufed ? When Job
fays, *I have not concealed the words of the Holy One*, chap.
vi. 10. could he be underftood as fpeaking of any other
than God ? When the prophet fings, *The Holy One came
from mount Paran*, could there be any doubt that the fame
glorious Perfon was meant, of whom it is faid in the claufe
immediately preceding, *God came from Teman?* Hab. iii. 3.
When they heard this language, Ifa. xl. 25. *To whom then
will ye liken me, or fhall I be equal? faith the Holy One;*
could they hefitate to underftand it as uttered by JEHOVAH,
and as an exprefs claim of the exclufive poffeffion of perfect holinefs ? Had not God ftill revealed himfelf to his ancient people, as *the Holy One in the midft of* them ? Hof.
xi. 9. During the whole of the old difpenfation, was he
not acknowledged by the Church under this exclufive character, expreffed in connexion with that mutual relation
which fubfifted between them in regard to his infinite holinefs ? Is it not for this reafon, that he is fo often celebrated
as *the Holy One of Ifrael?* Therefore, could the Jews hear
this well-known, this diftinctive character of the true God
applied to Jefus, without fuppofing that his difciples afcribed Deity to him, and even held him forth as that very
God whom their fathers had worfhipped ? Or could the difciples of Jefus give him this character, without the leaft
caution or reftriction, and not be guilty of blafphemy, were
he a mere man ? Would the believing Jews have received
their

their teftimony without the flighteft cenfure, if they had not been perfwaded that Jefus was truly God?

The Jews knew that there was none *righteous* but their God. They knew that, in the revelations which he had made of himfelf, he had often exclufively claimed this cha-racter. They could not be ignorant that, in a way of emi-nence, it belonged to God only. They could form no idea of *fongs from the uttermoft part of the earth, even glory to the righteous*, Ifa. xxiv. 16. but as directed to JEHOVAH, the only object of worfhip. Therefore, when they heard the apoftles proclaiming Jefus, not only as *the Holy One*, put as *the Juft*, they could not credit their teftimony, without believing his Deity. Can it be fuppofed that he who, while on earth, would not receive the title of *good Mafter*, without fhewing that this was properly an attri-bute of the Divine nature alone, would be fo changed, in confequence of his exaltation, as to fuffer his fervants to apply to him the attributes of Deity, not merely without limitation, but κατ' εξοχην, in a way of eminence? Thofe who deny that he is God, muft fuppofe a fhocking abfur-dity, indeed; that he communicated the Spirit to his dif-ciples, for the purpofe of robbing the Father of his effential honour.

The believing Jews would not be ftartled at this lan-guage. They had not underftood their own fcriptures, if they did not formerly know that a Divine Perfon was pro-mifed as Meffiah: and at any rate, the Spirit would now inftruct them in this. They could not attentively read the prophecy of Zechariah, chap. ix. 9. concerning that *King* who was to come to them, without obferving that the two great characters of their God were afcribed to him. For as Zechariah proclaims the King of Zion as *juft and ha-ving falvation*, or *a Saviour;* this is the very language in which God had revealed himfelf to his people, Ifa. xlv. 21.

X 2 *A*

A juſt God, and a Saviour. In the former paſſage, indeed, the name *God* is not mentioned. But they could not conſiſtently underſtand it of a mere creature; becauſe the demonſtrative pronoun is uſed in that form which marks the ſuper-eminent ſenſe in which the attributes belong to the Perſon deſcribed; *Juſt and having ſalvation* HE. This ſeems to be equivalent to the additional language in Iſaiah, *There is none beſide me.* The form of the'expreſſion is preciſely the ſame as that in Deut. xxxii. 4. *Juſt and right* HE; where Moſes evidently deſcribes the incomparable rectitude of the divine nature.

There is a beautiful contraſt ſtated in the language of the Apoſtle. One man is not oppoſed to another. But the⸴*Holy and Juſt One,* to *a man a murderer* *. The antitheſis is double. Wickedneſs is oppoſed to righteouſneſs, and man to God. It would have been dreadful, had they merely preferred a wicked to a juſt man. But in this conſiſted their tranſcendent iniquity, that they preferred *a man,* and one who had forfeited all claim to the character of *holy* and *juſt,* to him who poſſeſſes theſe perfections abſolutely and eſſentially. They rejected the great gift of divine grace, (Rom. viii. 32.) and *deſired, that as an act of grace, a murderer ſhould be given unto them* †.

But the Apoſtle does not only call Jeſus *the Holy One,* and *the Juſt,* but *the Prince of Life.* He undoubtedly intends this as a Divine character. It denotes ſuch a principality as can be aſcribed to him alone who is the *author* of any thing. Thus it is uſed by the apoſtle of the Gentiles, when he ſpeaks of *the Captain,* or rather, *the Author of our ſalvation, as made perfect through ſuffering,* Heb. ii. 10. and when he deſigns Jeſus *the author of our faith,* chap. xii. 2. In this ſenſe it is alſo uſed by profane writers ‡.

When

---

* Ανδρα γονεα. † Χαρισθηται.

‡ The heathen were wont to celebrate their Supreme God as the author

thor

When the apoftle fays, *Ye have put to death the Prince of Life*, if this character did not belong to Jefus before he was crucified, not only is the antithefis falfe, but that which is mentioned as the great conftituent of their guilt had no exiftence. The apoftles indeed declare, on another occafion, that God had *exalted him, with his right hand, a Prince and a Saviour*, chap. v. 31. But this by no means fignifies that he received thefe characters in confequence of his exaltation; but only, that thus they were glorioufly acknowledged by the Father as previoufly belonging to Jefus. For when *the Prince of Life* is faid to be *killed*, the language implies that he was both *a Prince and a Saviour*, before his death. For thefe expreffions are fynonymous; the latter being a Hebraifm, fimply fignifying that he is *the Prince of Salvation*, that is, *of life*. His fuftaining this character feems to be mentioned as alfo the reafon of his refurrection, (*whom God hath raifed from the dead*) in the fame fenfe in which the apoftle had faid, on a former occafion, that *it was not poffible that he fhould be holden* of death. For in his refurrection, he not only obtained a judicial difcharge as Mediator, but was manifefted to be *the Son of God with power*, as being effentially *the Author of Life*.

The Jews were accuftomed to adore God as their *life*, as *the ftrength* of it, who *held their fouls in life*, and to confefs that *the fountain of life* was with him *. Therefore, when

X 3   the

thor of nature, becaufe they fuppofed that all things owed their being to him. Thus Cleanthes, in his hymn addreffed to Jupiter, fays,

Ζευς φυσεως αρχηγε—

Εκ σε γαρ γενος εσμεν.

Thus it appears that they ufed the term, not as fignifying a communicated authority, but an original and independent power of beftowing life †.

† See Burgh's Inquiry, p. 130.

* Pfal. xxvii. 1. lxvi. 9. xxxvi. 9.

the apoftles declared that Jefus was the *Prince* and *Author of Life*, the language being equivalent to their own, they could not receive their teftimony, without believing that he was that *fountain of Life* they had ftill adored, that he had *life in himfelf*, and that as a Prince he beftowed it, in a fovereign manner on whomfoever he pleafed.

The apoftle, having declared the dignity of the Perfon, proceeds to vindicate his claim to the honour of that work in which he and his brethren were the immediate agents: *And his Name—hath made this man ftrong.* Peter, who was a Jew, addreffing himfelf to Jews, fpoke in their own idiom. This was a phrafeology with which they were perfectly acquainted. God had ftill ufed it in thofe revelations which he had made of himfelf to their forefathers. It was more ancient than their exiftence as a nation †. By the *name* of God, the pofterity of Abraham were wont to underftand God himfelf, efpecially with refpect to his revealed character, and as oppofed to the falfe apprehenfions and unauthorized worfhip of thofe nations to whom he had not made himfelf known. Sometimes, it denoted all the divine perfections; and at other times, it had a particular refpect to one. To the *Name* of God this people were accuftomed to direct all their faith, love and worfhip; and to afcribe all their protection, deliverance and falvation; confidering this as the fame with directing or afcribing thefe to God himfelf. To this they ufed to attribute the miracles wrought in behalf of their fathers. They knew that his *Name* was *great in might*, Jer. x. 6. and interpreted his wondrous works as declaring that it was *near*, Pfal. lxxv. 1. Therefore, when they were told by this plain fifherman, that the *Name* of Jefus had made the lame man whole, they would entertain no other idea than that he meant to give him a divine character.

Was

† Ex. vi. 3.

. Was there any Jew who might be apt to fuppofe that this unlettered preacher introduced a new idiom; and improperly afcribed miraculous virtue to this name, without meaning to reprefent the Perfon as the principal efficient caufe of the miracle? The apoftle provides an antidote againft this mifapprehenfion, by alfo mentioning the inftrumental caufe: *His Name,* THROUGH FAITH *in his Name, hath made this man ftrong.* The multitude could not fuppofe that Peter fpoke of two inftruments; of the *Name* itfelf as one, and of *faith* in it as another. Far lefs could they imagine that a mere inftrument could be the object of faith. For *faith in a name* could convey to them no other idea than that of an act of worfhip directed to a divine Perfon. They not only knew the Name of the Lord as the object of faith * : but that it had been prophefied concerning the Saviour, according to the tranflation then generally ufed, *In his Name fhall the Gentiles truft,* Ifa. xlii. 4. And they did not dare to fpeak in this manner of the name of any creature.

Is it faid, that the Name of Jefus is here expreffive of *power,* and that this language is ufed for preventing the miftake that the more ignorant might be apt to fall into, as though the apoftles by their *own power had made this man to walk,* ver. 12 ? Still it is evident, that the Jews could not underftand Peter as fpeaking of any power not effentially belonging to Jefus; becaufe the whole effect of *making* the man *ftrong* is afcribed to the Name of Jefus, as the principal efficient caufe; while this very Name is alfo reprefented as the object of faith, the inftrumental.

They could not apprehend that the apoftle meant to give no greater honour to Jefus, than that of being the medium which faith employed in its operation. For, to fhew that h. is its proper object, and alfo the author of that miracle produced by

X 4   its

its inftrumentality, he is further exhibited as the author of that faith which terminated on himfelf : *Yea, the faith which is* BY HIM *hath given him this perfect foundnefs.* For δια here undoubtedly denotes the principal efficient caufe, as it is often ufed *. Thus Jefus is proclaimed as the author, both of the miracle, and of the mean by which it was effected. To him is the whole work afcribed. Nay, faith *in* him as its proper object, and *by* him as its author, is reprefented as fo powerful, that the effect is inftrumentally attributed to it : *Faith—hath given him perfect foundnefs.* Such language would have been highly improper, had not Peter meant to defcribe its object as divine. Had not this been the cafe, the apoftles, while anxious to guard the multitude againft afcribing too much honour to themfelves, would have directed their eye to the Father. But while they declare that it was not their *own power* that effected the miracle, they afcribe it entirely to *the Author of Life.* While they deny that it was the fruit of their *holinefs ;* they give all the glory to *the Holy One and the Juft.*

Thus, they fhew that Jefus had difcovered himfelf to be *the Author,* not only of natural *life,* by the external cure ; but of that which is fpiritual, *fulfilling the work of faith* in the heart. The faith in Jefus, which they avow, muft have been very different from that of a Socinian. Indeed, it may be prefumed, that the faith of the latter, though he had lived in the apoftolic age, would never have been the mean of fuch a cure. It would have been too remote a caufe for producing fuch an effect. For a Socinian faith in the Name of Jefus is, at beft, merely one inftrument in fubordination to another. But from what we have feen, it may be fairly concluded, that thofe who received the teftimony of the apoftles, were perfuaded that Jefus was that

Meffenger,

---

† Rom. xi. 36. Gal. i. 1. 2 Tim. i. 14. Heb. ii. 10. ix. 14.

Meffenger, of whom the Father had faid, *My Name is him,* Ex. xxxiii. 21.

Even after Peter had declared that Jefus was that Prophet whom Mofes foretold, left his hearers fhould imagine that this was the higheft honour that belonged to him, he returns to his former fubject, and concludes this addrefs by a declaration of his divine power: *Unto you firft, God having raifed up his Son Jefus, fent him to blefs you, in turning away every one of you from your iniquities,* chap. iii. 26. The Jews ufed to fpeak of one man as blefling another, by wifhing or praying that he might be blefled. But they had no apprehenfion that this of itfelf could be effectual. They knew that God alone could blefs, by truly conferring good, or delivering from evil. They knew that the man was blefled, whofe *fin* was *covered,* and *in whofe fpirit* was *no guile,* Pfal. xxxii. 1, 2. But they were alfo affured that it was the divine prerogative thus to *turn from iniquity.* Thence the whole church of Ifrael, under the name of Ephraim, is reprefented as concurring in this language; *Turn thou me, and I fhall be turned; for thou art the Lord my God,* Jer. xxxi. 18. Ephraim acknowledges the inutility of all external means without this efficacious operation; *Thou haft chaftifed me, and I was chaftifed, as a bullock unaccuftomed to the yoke.* Therefore, it was a part of the folemn worfhip of the church to fupplicate this very blefling. And fhe did fo, with reiterated acknowledgments, that her falvation depended on the exercife of the converting power of the *Lord God of hofts,* Pfal. lxxx. 3. 7. 19.

Had the Jews been fimply told that Jefus was fent to *blefs* them, they might have fuppofed it to be meant that, like their high prieft, he would fupplicate God for bleflings, in their behalf. But it being declared that he was fent to blefs them in *turning* them from inquity; as this language denoted an efficacious blefling, of the moft important kind,

they

they could not believe the apoftolical report, without being perfuaded that he who fhould thus blefs them was *God, even their own God*, whom their fathers had fo long expected for this gracious purpofe, and who, when he' fhould come to blefs them, was to *make all the nations glad, judge the people righteoufly, and govern the nations upon earth*, Pfal. lxvii. 4. 6.

When the apoftles were brought before the Sanhedrim, to give an account of their conduct in healing the impotent man, the following queftion was put to them ; *By what power, or by what name have ye done this?* chap. iv. 7. Without any hefitation, and with one voice, they give the very fame account of the miracle as they had given to the multitude ; declaring that it was *by the Name of Jefus*, ver. 10. They do not in the leaft qualify their language, as they certainly would have done, had they confidered him as an agent effentially inferior. Indeed, as if they faid too little in afcribing this temporal deliverance wholly to him, they amplify their afcription, by extending it to falvation of every kind ; *And there is not falvation in any other*, ver. 12. The Jews knew that their God had claimed falvation as his prerogative, as equally incommunicable with his diftinctive name, and as dependent on that abfolute perfection which this name implied. For he had faid, *I, even I am* JEHOVAH, *and befide me there is no Saviour*, Ifa. xliii. 11. Can it, therefore, be fuppofed that they could hear the apoftles affert, that there was not falvation *in* any other, without fuppofing that they believed him to be JEHOVAH? Or can we imagine, that thefe holy men would be fo carelefs about the peculiar rights of Deity, if they had not believed that Jefus was the God of their falvation? They knew that God had not only expreffed the unity of the Saviour as emph· ically as the unity of the Godhead, but that he had joined them as infeparable ; becaufe cause he who acknowledges any Saviour but God, really denies the unity of his essence, by assigning his work to the creature. Thus, those who call themselves *Unitarians,* have no title to the name. For in their pretended zeal for the unity of God, they sacrifice the unity of the Saviour. That they may exclude the Son of God from the divine nature, they admit mere man into a divine office.

But the apostles prove that *there is not salvation in any other,* by the following argument ; *For there is not another name under heaven, given among men, in which* (δει) *we must be saved.* If Jesus be a mere creature, it was *necessary* for them to know the name of JEHOVAH as the great efficient cause of salvation, as well as the name of Jesus, which could only be the instrument. It was *necessary for* them *to be saved in* this superior name. If Christ be a creature, it was an impious falsehood, that there was *not another name given* for salvation. For God had revealed his own name to his people, as the object of their trust. He had pointed out *the Name of* JEHOVAH as *a strong tower into* which *the righteous* should *run,* and be *safe,* Prov. xviii. 10. The apostles can be vindicated from the charge of being false witnesses only by supposing that they considered the *name of Jesus,* as implying that of JEHOVAH. They knew, indeed, that this was the fact ; that he was called *Jesus,* as being according to the meaning of the word in Hebrew, *the salvation of* JEHOVAH, or JEHOVAH *the* SAVIOUR.

If the *power* of Jesus be merely delegated, all their anxiety to denude themselves of any share of the glory, was vain. For they still left it with a creature ; and were, therefore, as far from giving it to the rightful owner, as if they had kept it to themselves. Their conduct, indeed, bore a more threatening aspect to the honours of Deity, than if they had done so. For others would be more in danger of worshipping their glorified Master, than them.

When brought before the council a fecond time, they thus vindicate their conduct in teaching in the name of Jefus ; *Him hath God exalted with his right hand, a Prince and a Saviour to give repentance to Ifrael, and forgivenefs of fins*, chap. v. 31. It is evident that fuch power is afcribed to Chrift, as cannot belong to any creature. We have feen that the whole church of Ifrael is introduced as acknowledging that converfion, iffuing in true repentance; is a divine work. Thofe who were really convinced of fin, would be affured that this was the effect of the power of God. The moft obdurate could not fuppofe that one man could *give repentance* to another. When they heard the apoftles afcribe to Jefus, not the gift of *repentance* only, but of *forgivenefs* alfo, they could not but think that they gave him that honour which their church had always appropriated to God. Even the unbelieving Jews were perfuaded that *no one could forgive fins but God only*. The priefts and Sadducees, who had imprifoned the apoftles, ver. 17. would not be fo favourable in their conftruction as to fuppofe, that they meant that Jefus had merely the power of *declaring forgivenefs*. They could not have perceived the propriety of afferting that he was *exalted* for this end. For it muft naturally have occurred to them, that he could have done this work far better on earth. And they would not fuppofe that there were any in heaven that needed fuch a declaration. The Sadducees, indeed, were more *rational* believers, than to imagine that there could be a heaven of *fpirits*.

That Stephen preached the fame doctrine, is evident from the account which he gives of the vifion at Mount Sinai, Acts vii. 3c. For he declares that it was an *Angel of the Lord*, who appeared in the bufh and faid, *I am the God of Abraham*. He means no created angel. For no Jew of that age would have afcribed fuch language to a

creature. Besides, he exprefsly calls this Angel *the Lord,*
or JEHOVAH, ver. 33. Had he believed that there was
but one Perfon in the divine effence, he could not have
thought of calling him an 'angel or *meffenger.* For by
whom could he be *fent?* But he ufes that language which
was well known to his fathers. They believed that the
Angel of the divine prefence, the Angel of the covenant,
was JEHOVAH. He evidently defcribes him as that Angel
who gave the law by the miniftration of other angels in
the character of his fervants ; and who directed the church
in the wildernefs, ver. 38.

That the protomartyr had Jefus in his eye, in the whole
of his narrative, appears from his giving him that title of
divine perfection formerly explained. He calls him *the
Juft One,* ver. 52. This is alfo undeniable, from his addreffing Jefus as the object of worfhip. He would have re-
coiled with horror from fuch impiety, had he not believed
that Jefus was the *God of Abraham. They ftoned Stephen
calling upon God, and faying, Lord Jefus, receive my fpirit,*
ver. 59.

Dr P. obferves, that " the word *God* is not in the origi-
" nal, as our tranflators have fignified, by their directing it
". to be printed in the Italic character : fo that this text by
" no means fignifies that Stephen acknowledged Chrift to
" be God, but only informs us that Stephen addreffed him-
" felf to Chrift, whom he had juft feen in perfon, in a ftate
" of great exaltation and glory *." The word *God* is,
indeed, a fupplement. But the want of it, in the original,
inftead of proving that Stephen did not acknowledge
Chrift to be God, is a more unexceptionable proof that he
did, than if it had been ufed by the infpired hiftorian. For,
in this cafe, the adverfaries of the Deity of Chrift would
have urged that an important diftinction was ftated between
the

* Famil. Illuftr. p. 37.

the refpect which the protomartyr paid to God, and that which he paid to Jefus.

The Doctor is determined, if poffible, to fhew that Stephen, though he did *addrefs*, that is, *worfhip* Jefus, did not confider him as God. He quotes thefe words : *He, being full of the Holy Ghoft, looked ftedfaftly into heaven, and faw the glory of God, and Jefus ftanding on the right hand of God ; and faid, Behold I fee the heavens opened, and the Son of man ftanding on the right hand of God*, ver. 55, 56. Then he obferves, " This very language clearly implies " that he confidered the *Son of man*, and *God*, as diftinct " perfons." This may be admitted, if properly explained. For the term *God* often denotes the Father, although not as confining the Godhead to him. But our author undoubtedly means, that Stephen excludes the Son by the ufe of this word. If, in his fenfe, the martyr *confidered* them as diftinct Perfons, it muft have been becaufe he *faw* them as diftinct. For the only ground that Dr P. has for declaring what Stephen confidered, is Stephen's own declaration as to what he *faw*. It muft follow therefore, that God has a bodily right hand ; and that Stephen faw this with the natural eye, as diftinctly as the human nature of Jefus.

Although Socinians and Materialifts may not ftartle at this inference, the more fober part of mankind will underftand the language as metaphorical, and as containing an allufion to the tokens of dignity among men. Stephen fpeaks of *the Son of man* as *at the right hand of God*, to denote the exaltation of the human nature, in union to the divine. For whatfoever *the glory of God* is, Jefus is defcribed as a partaker of it. The Jews did not underftand Stephen's language as Dr P. does. They unanimoufly confidered it as blafphemy againft God. Therefore, *they ftopped their ears, and ran upon him with one accord*. When he declared that Jefus was the Meffiah, and accufed them

as

as his murderers, they bore with him. When he proceeded to accuse them of having *always refifted the Holy Ghoft*, and of breaking the law given them; they vented their indignation, only by gnafhing on him with their teeth. But they were accuftomed to affix fuch a meaning to the language under confideration, that they could not hear him a moment longer. They caft him out of the city, as one whofe blood would defile it, becaufe of his fuppofed blafphemy; according to the divine ordinance with refpect to this crime, Lev. xxiv. 14. They put him to death alfo in the manner appointed. For the blafphemer was to be ftoned by all the congregation, ver. 16. as well as the perfon who enticed to the worfhip of other gods, Deut. xiii. 6.—10. They probably thought that he was guilty of both thefe crimes.

But though they had formerly been in any hefitation as to the evidence of his guilt, they could be in none afterwards. For he perfifted in his fuppofed crime, during the very execution of the fentence. *They ftoned Stephen, calling upon* Jefus. Dr P. informs us, however, that " the " word which is here, and in 1 Cor. i. 2. rendered to *call* " *upon*, is far from being appropriated to *invocation*, as pe- " culiar to the divine Being. It is the fame word that is " rendered to *appeal to*, as when Paul appeals to Cæfar *." Some of our author's predeceffors have denied that Stephen did invoke our Saviour; afferting that his words fhould be rendered, *Lord of Jefus*. But our author finds that this ground is not tenable. Therefore, he acknowledges that Jefus is the object of this addrefs. But he endeavours to evade the confequence of this confeffion; firft, by fhewing that religious invocation is not here meant; and fecondly, by gallantly refifting the force of fome other texts, which according to our tranflation, oppofe this view. As to the firft, it would feem that his mind was by no means diftracted by a variety of evidence. For he refers only to

2   thofe

* Ibid.

thoſe places in which the word ſignifies an. *appeal*. But does he ſeriouſly think that Paul *appealed to* . Cæſar in the ſame ſenſe in which Stephen *called upon* Jeſus? Did Paul *commend his ſpirit into the hands* of the Roman Emperor? I aſk the Doctor's pardon. He may perhaps ſuppoſe that he did, when he ventured his *body* in Cæſar's hands.

But he adds, that the ſame word " is uſed when a perſon " is ſaid to be *called* by any particular name; as Judas " *called* Iſcariot, &c. There can be no doubt, therefore, " but that it has the ſame meaning· both in 1 Cor. i. 2. " and alſo in Acts ix. 21. *Is not this he that deſtroyed them* " *who called on this name in Jeruſalem?* that is, all who " called·themſelves *Chriſtians*. It is ſo rendered, Jam. ii. " 7. *Do they not blaſpheme the worthy Name by which ye* " *are called?* or, as it is ·more exactly rendered, *which is* " *called*, or impoſed, *upon you?* that is, by which ye are " diſtinguiſhed." But becauſe this word *ſometimes* ſimply ſignifies to *call* or *denominate*, muſt it *always* bear this ſenſe? It is indeed queſtionable, whether the expreſſion in James does not reſpect the ſolemn invocation of this name in baptiſm. At any rate, a gentleman who has taught Greek ought to pay ſome regard to the conſtruction. And undoubtedly the language of James, and alſo that in Acts xv. 17. is· very different from what we have in 1 Cor. i. 1. and Acts ix. 21. When it ſignifies, *called upon you*, it is. ονομα το επικληθεν εφ' υμας. But can our author produce any example of ſuch an expreſſion as τοις επικαλυμενοις το ονομα, having the ſame meaning? Both the Seventy, and the wri-ters of the New Teſtament, uſe the expreſſions differently, the former in a *paſſive*, and the latter in an *active* ſenſe.

The reaſon aſſigned by Dr P. for refuſing to underſtand theſe words, 1 Cor. i. 1. *With all who in every place. call upon the Name of our Lord Jeſus Chriſt*, as ſignifying that. adoration " which is due to the one living and true God,"

is

is a ftriking proof of the audacity of error. That this is
not meant " is evident," he fays, " from the very next
" words ; *Grace be unto you, and peace, from God our Fa-*
" *ther, and from the Lord Jefus Chrift ;* where Chrift is
" evidently fpoken of as diftinct from God *." Becaufe
Chrift is not mentioned as the fame Perfon with the Father,
who, in the New Teftament, is more generally diftinguifhed
by the name *God,* therefore he is not the object of adoration ; though in the very words from which the pretended
proof is derived, *grace* is prayed for from him, as directly
as from the Father. It will be difficult for our author to
prove, that Acts ix. 21. refers to the difciples being called
Chriftians ; as it appears that they were not known by this
name for fome confiderable time after the event narrated in
that paffage, chap. xi. 26.

But notwithftanding the laborious attempts of Socinians,
to avert the force of the argument arifing from the ufe of
this term, there are fome paffages, in which it occurs, that,
as far as I know, they have not dared to meddle with ; as
2 Tim. ii. 22. Rom. x. 13, 14. When Paul fpeaks of thofe
επικαλεμενων, *that call on the Lord out of a pure heart ;* when
he quotes thefe words from Joel, *Whofoever fhall call upon
the Name of the Lord, fhall be faved ;* the fenfe is fo reftricted by the connexion, that they cannot deny that divine
worfhip is meant. This, then, is the proper queftion ; if the
invocation, granted in the cafe of Stephen, can be underftood in any fenfe, but as " peculiar to the divine Being ?"

As Dr P. admits that the protomartyr did *invoke* Jefus,
we would wifh to know for what end he did it, if he did
not mean to *worfhip* him ? Stephen himfelf does not leave
us at a lofs as to his defign. For this was the fubftance of
his addrefs, *Lord Jefus, receive my fpirit.* Did he *turn to*
him as only one *of the Saints* † ? If he did, was not the

Vol. I. Y cloſing

---

* Ibid. † Job. v. 1.

cloſing act of his life an act of abominable idolatry? Did he not acknowledge Jeſus as one that had *power over the ſpirit?* And does not this belong to God only? Our author ſeems to inſinuate, that the " great exaltation and glory" of Chriſt might be Stephen's apology. But will a Proteſtant maintain that any creature, in the eternal ſtate, may be lawfully called upon in any ſenſe? If Jeſus be not God as well as man, the diſciple made a far worſe choice than his maſter, who, as man, commended his ſpirit into the hands of his Father. But it is evident, that Stephen ſurrendered his ſpirit to Jeſus as *Lord, both of the dead, and of the li- ving.*

He alſo addreſſed Jeſus as the God of pardoning mercy. For *he kneeled down, and cried with a loud voice, Lord, lay not this ſin to their charge,* ver. 60. There is, undoubtedly, no change of the object of invocation. Stephen ſtill ad- dreſſes *the ſame Lord over all,* who *is rich unto all that call upon him,* Rom. x. 12.

This paſſage has ſtill been very puzzling to Socinians : and their perplexity muſt continue, if they adhere to their principles, till awfully removed by a diſcovery of *the Son of man on the right hand of power.* Even Dr P.'s embar- raſſment on this ſubject appears, not only from what we have ſeen, but from what he ſays in his Hiſtory of Opinions. " To conclude, as ſome have done, from the ſingle caſe of " Stephen, that all Chriſtians are authorized to pray to " Chriſt, is like concluding that all matter has a tendency " to go upwards, becauſe a needle will do ſo when a mag- " net is held over it. When they ſhall be in the ſame cir- " cumſtances with Stephen, having their minds ſtrongly " impreſſed with a viſion of Chriſt ſitting at the right hand " of God, they may then, perhaps, be authorized to ad- " dreſs themſelves to him as he did ; but the whole tenor

I   " of

" of the fcriptures proves that otherwife we have no autho-
" rity at all for any fuch practice *."

I know of none who conclude, that Jefus is the object of
worfhip from the *fingle* cafe of Stephen. All who believe
that Stephen worfhipped him, are as fully perfuaded that
he was *called upon* by all primitive Chriftians. But although we had no other exprefs inftance, that of Stephen,
all circumftances confidered, would be unexceptionable as
an example. The conclufion from this cafe would not be
quite fo abfurd as that to which it is compared by Dr P.
It would only be " like concluding that" *every needle*, or
" all matter" of the *fame kind*, would go upwards, if a
magnet of fufficient power were held over it.

But the fimilitude implies another obvious fallacy ;—that
Jefus can have an attractive influence on none of his difciples, like that exemplified in the cafe of Stephen, unlefs
they difcern him with the bodily eye. They are all compofed of fuch inert *matter*, that they cannot afcend to him
in adoration, unlefs the attractive power affect their fenfes.
A fenfible difcovery of the very matter of the body of
Chrift, not an apprehenfion of *his majefty* by faith, is the
only *probable* authority for worfhip. After this, our author, inftead of ridiculing the doctrine of the Trinity, ought
to fpeak refpectfully even of the abfurd doctrine of Tranfubftantiation. For he who can fuppofe that knowing Chrift
after the flefh, is that which tends moft to exalt our ideas of
him, and *perhaps* authorizes adoration, ought to be tender
of thofe who practically indulge themfelves in the pleafing
illufion. The true church of Chrift hath hitherto believed
that *the flefh profiteth nothing*. But it would feem that fhe
hath been grievoufly miftaken. For a view of this " may
" authorize Chriftians to addrefs themfelves to" Jefus as
Stephen did ; that is, to make him the object of prayer. As

Y 2   for

---

* Vol. i. p. 47.

for thofe poor fouls *who have not feen, and yet have believed,* the *Lord Jefus* can be no magnet to them. They know, by faith in the Divine word, that the Son of man *ftandeth* on *the right hand of God.* Their faith difcerns him within the vail. By this fpiritual eye they *fee the King in his beauty.* And though they have *not feen* him with the bodily eye, *yet believing,* they may *rejoice,* even *with joy unfpeakable and full of glory, receiving the end of their faith, the falvation of their fouls,* (1 Pet. i. 8, 9.) , But it would be venturing a great deal too far, to commend their fpirits to him. They do not *fenfibly* difcern him *at the right hand of God :* and how can they *otherwife* be certain that he is there? Without this fpecies of affurance, according to our author, they would pray at random. Thus, inftead of a *rational* fyftem of religion, we have a *material* one, nearly as grofs as that of the church of Rome.

He feems alfo to fupport her doctrine in another refpect. He fuppofes that fuch a vifion may perhaps authorize an addrefs to Chrift, " although the whole tenor of the fcrip- " ture proves that *otherwife* we have no authority at all for " any fuch practice." On the very fame ground may the worfhip of faints and angels be vindicated. For the only meaning that our author's words can bear, is, that the whole tenor of fcripture proves that we have no authority for any fuch practice, *but in the cafe* of feeing Jefus with the bodily eye. If, therefore, one fhould happen to fee an angel, or one of the glorified faints, as the difciples faw Mofes and Elias, the heavenly vifion *may perhaps authorize* worfhip.

The abfurdity of fuppofing an *occafional* object of wor-fhip, is perfectly confonant to the *philofophical Unitarianifm* of *occafional perfonality.* It completes the fyftem. He who has been, or who might have been, occafionally a divine Perfon, may, doubtlefs, be occafionally an object of worfhip. According to Dr P.'s conceffion, when all the

2

faints fhall fee Jefus *as he is*, it may perhaps authorize them *all* to addrefs themfelves to him as Stephen did. If fo, it may be the fafeft courfe to try the fame exercife in this life. The worfhip of heaven cannot well be idolatry on earth. Thofe who will not bow the knee to Jefus now, muft do it very aukwardly when he comes in his glory.

Dr P. has overlooked the circumftance which properly renders the conduct of Stephen a fufficient example for univerfal imitation. We are not to fuppofe that the good man was in a pious reverie. For, according to the teftimony of infpiration, he was *full of the Holy Ghoft.*

We may fafely conclude, that Philip, the Evangelift, preached the divinity of Chrift. For the confeffion of the Eunuch refpected this doctrine ; *I believe that Jefus Chrift is the Son of God*, chap. viii. 37. This cannot be underftood as merely an acknowledgment of Jefus as Meffiah. For the term *Chrift* being ftrictly expreffive of this character, the Eunuch's confeffion would, in this cafe, be the mereft folecifm ; " I believe that Jefus, the Meffiah, is the Mef-" fiah." Unlefs Philip had preached Jefus, not merely as Meffiah, but as a Divine Perfon, there would have been no propriety in the confeffion. For we muft underftand it as reduplicating on the doctrine previoufly delivered.

Indeed, though we have no fummary of Philip's difcourfe, it is evident that he could not give a confiftent view of the paffage from which he *preached Jefus*, without proclaiming his divinity. For as thefe words, ver. 33. *Who fhall declare his generation ?* undoubtedly denote his endlefs life, as the Father of a feed that *no man can number*, they neceffarily imply divine power and glory. For how can a mere man really create again, and give fpiritual life to thofe who are *dead in trefpaffes and fins ?* How could the *taking away* of *his life* be the caufe of life to them, were he not

in

in another refpect *the, Fountain of Life?* How could he act the part of, a Father, to thofe whom he could not fo much as *number?*

. The converfion of Paul has been juftly viewed as a ftriking proof of the truth of Chriftianity. The account given of it affords as convincing evidence of the divinity of Jefus. It is evident that Paul, when he heard the voice from heaven, confidered it as that of a Divine Perfon. But he feems at a lofs to know how he fhould be perfecuting him. *He faid, Who art thou, Lord?* chap. ix. 5. When he found that it was Jefus who fpoke to him, he did not change his addrefs, or acknowledge his miftake. To this very Jefus does he direct his prayer : and this expreffes the language of abfolute fubmiffion to his will : *He, trembling and aftonifhed, faid, Lord, what wilt thou have me to do?* ver. 6.

., Ananias alfo, when he received a command to go to Paul, in like manner addreffes himfelf to Jefus : *Lord, I have heard by many of this man, &c.* ver. 13. That he confidered Chrift as fpeaking to him, and therefore directed his reply to the fame Perfon, is evident from his faying to Paul, ver. 17. *The Lord, (even Jefus that appeared to thee in the way as thou cameft), hath fent me.* The fame difciple fpeaks of all the faints as Chrift's ;—*thy faints,* ver. 13. And there was not one of them who would have reckoned it an honour to be the property of a mere man. He defcribes them all as worfhippers of Jefus, ver. 14. *He hath authority—to bind all that call on thy name.* The genuine fenfe of this expreffion appears from the prefent conduct of Ananias, one of the perfons thus defcribed. Jefus is alfo introduced, as declaring that Paul was a *chofen veffel unto him.* And furely, fuch language does not become any creature. One great defign of the miffion of Ananias is, that, by his inftrumentality, Jefus might communicate the

Holy

Holy Ghoft to Paul, ver. 17. *Jefus hath fent me, that thou mighteft—be filled with the Holy Ghoft.*

If the worfhip of Chrift be idolatry, Paul, it muft be acknowledged, was provided with a very bad fpiritual director. For Ananias undoubtedly exhorts him to pray to Jefus. *Wafh away thy fins*, he fays, *calling on the Name of the Lord*, chap. xxii. 16. That Jefus is meant, cannot reafonably be refufed. For he is the perfon laft mentioned, as *that juft One* whom Paul was to *fee, the voice of* whofe *mouth* he fhould *hear*, and whofe *witnefs* he fhould *be unto all men*, ver. 14, 15. This is alfo evident from the connexion of thefe words, *Wafh away thy fins.* They undoubtedly refer to baptifm. For it is faid immediately before; *Arife, and be baptifed.* It was in this ordinance that he was to *call on the Name of the Lord*, by devoting himfelf to him, apprehending the merit of his blood, and imploring the communication of his Spirit.

Would Paul believe that Jefus could make him an inftrument in enlightening the underftandings, and changing the hearts of finners, and in delivering them from the power of Satan? Would he believe that Jefus could give them pardon and glory, that he was the object of faith, and that faith in him could be the mean of fanctification? Would he confide in him for deliverance from the heathen; or even fubmit to receive a commiffion from him:—and yet confider him as a mere man? But Paul affures Agrippa that Jefus faid to him; *I have appeared unto thee for this purpofe, to make thee a minifter, and a witnefs;—delivering thee from the Gentiles, unto whom now I fend thee; to open their eyes, and to turn them from darknefs to light, and from the power of Satan unto God, that they may receive forgivenefs of fins, and inheritance among them which are fanctified by faith which is in me*, chap. xxvi. 16.—18.

Did not Paul, immediately after his converfion, teftify his full conviction of the divinity of Jefus? *Straightway he*

preached

preached Chrift in the *fynagogues, · that he is the Son of God*, chap. ix. 20. It would be ridiculous to explain this language as fignifying, that Paul merely proclaimed the chara&er of Jefus as Meffiah. This he alfo did. *For, he confounded the Jews which dwelt at Damafcus, proving that this is the very Chrift*, ver. 22. But here we have only one branch of his do&rine. It included another, dif-tin& from this, but not lefs important. For, as the lan-guage may be literally read, *He preached the Chrift*, or *Meffiah, that this is the Son of God*. Would it be worthy of an infpired hiftorian to fay; "He preached the Mef-"fiah, that he is the Meffiah?" That the firft expreffion, τον Χριϛον, *the Chrift*, is to be underftood as particularly re-ferring to Jefus in his official chara&er, is evident from the manner in which it is ufed elfewhere, in regard to the preaching of Paul. For, when addreffing the Theffalonians, he *opened and alleged that this Jefus, whom I preach unto you, is* ο Χριϛος, *the Chrift*, chap. xvii. 3.

Did not Paul, through life, offer the facrifice of praife to Jefus as God, for the honour he had put on him, and the ftrength he had given him? We have his own teftimony. *I thank Chrift Jefus our Lord, who hath enabled me, for that he counted me worthy, putting me into the miniftry; who was before a blafphemer*, &c. Does he not afcribe his converfion wholly to the mercy, grace and power of Jefus? *But I obtained mercy;—and the grace of our Lord was ex-ceeding abundant, with faith and love which is in Chrift Jefus*, 1 Tim. i. 12.—14. If Paul viewed him as a mere man, did he not blafpheme God? Did he not proftitute the attributes of Deity, by afcribing them to Jefus?

When the fame apoftle would give a pattern of preach-ing to thofe who were themfelves bifhops, he exhorts them to *feed the church of God, which he had purchafed with his own blood*, chap. xx. 28. The enemies of the Deity of Chrift cannot agree among themfelves, with re-
fpe&

fpect to this text. Some of the Polifh Socinians acknowledge that the original word is Θεος, and pretend that this
defignation is given to Chrift *officially;* or that God the
Father is meant, and that the blood of Chrift is called *his,*
becaufe of the intimate union between them, notwithftanding diverfity of effence *.

Dr P. is not fo liberal in his conceffions. " In the moft
" ancient manufcripts," he fays, " this text is, *Feed the*
" *church of the Lord,* which generally fignifies Chrift †."
By the way we may obferve that, although our author here
grants that the term *Lord* has *generally* this meaning, when
he defcends to particulars, there are a great many excep-
tions. It can never *fignify Chrift,* however ftrong the collateral evidence, where it can fignify any thing unfriendly
to the Socinian fyftem. Of this we have a ftriking proof
in the paragraph immediately preceding, where that paffage
is introduced, *And thou, Lord, in the beginning haft laid,*
&c. Heb. i. 10. Though there can be no connexion in the
apoftle's reafoning, if thefe words refer not to Chrift, yet
they muft be underftood of the Father alone.

Only three manufcripts are mentioned as reading *the*
Lord; while all the reft, fome of which are reckoned of
at leaft equal authority, give the language according to our
verfion. A few of thefe join *the Lord* with *God.* But
this makes no difference as to the fenfe, but rather confirms
the ordinary reading. It deferves attention, that *the church*
of the Lord is a phrafe never ufed in the New Teftament;
whereas we often read of *the church of God.*

But even fuppofing that the true reading were, *the church*
of the Lord, as refpecting Chrift, the paffage would ftill afford a ftriking proof of his Deity. For it is undeniable
that the church is *God's* (1 Cor. i. 2. x. 32. xi. 22, &c.)
that it is as much his property as a man's houfe is his, to

the

* Vid. Catech. Racov.   † Famil. Illuft. p. 36.

the exclufion of every other proprietor. Therefore we read of *the houfe of God, which is the church of the living God* (1 Tim. iii. 15). But if the church be alfo *Chrift's*, if it be *his own houfe;* it muft neceffarily follow that he is *the living God,* (Heb. iii. 6. 12.)

Our author adds; " Alfo in fome copies it is, *which " he purchafed with blood;* that is, the blood of his " Son." He evidently ftumbles on this ftone. For when he tells us, that " *the Lord* generally fignifies Chrift," it might be fuppofed that he would adhere to this fenfe of the paffage, as fupported by "the moft ancient manufcripts." But the very next fentence is at war with it. The perfon is changed. The term *Lord* is applied to the Father. It avails not, it would feem, though all the members of a text fhould contradict each other, if the whole be preferved from contributing any thing to the doctrine of Immanuel.

He further obferves that " as the *blood of God* is a phrafe " which occurs no where elfe in the fcriptures, we ought " to be exceedingly cautious how we admit fuch an expref- " fion." It would be more honeft and confiftent to fay, that, as the Bible contains fuch a doctrine, as that *the man, the fellow of* JEHOVAH, could be *fmitten,* we " ought to be " exceedingly cautious how we admit fuch a *book.*"

A very fage obfervation brings up the rear : " If Chrift " was God, his blood could not be his blood as God, but as " man." Can our author prove that God could not unite to his own perfect and impaffible nature one infinitely inferior; or that, in this cafe, what properly belonged to the inferior nature, could not be afcribed to the perfon, as denomi- nated from the fuperior ?

A

VINDICATION

OF THE

DOCTRINE OF SCRIPTURE, &c.

BOOK III.

OF THE EVIDENCE OF THE DEITY OF CHRIST, FROM THE USE OF THAT EXPRESSION, THE SON OF GOD.

AS the Evangelifts, in a great variety of paffages, call Jefus *the Son of God*, I once thought of illuftrating this character among the proofs of his Divinity from the three firft gofpels. But this argument opening a wide field, it feemed more proper to view it diftinctly. Nor could it appear in that luftre of evidence which naturally belongs to it, were not fome attention paid to the ufe of this expreffion by other infpired writers. But when this ftriking phrafeology is viewed in connexion with thofe variou ideas which are combined with it in the language of infpiration, like the rays of li,ht concentrated in one point, its force is greatly increafed, and all the objections of adverfaries are *as a thread of tow when it toucheth the fire.*

That

That I may, as far as poffible, do juftice to the fubject, I fhall inquire, how this character was underftood by faints under the Old Teftament; in what fenfe it was proclaimed by the Father; how it was interpreted by holy angels, by devils, and by the enemies of Chrift; what ideas it conveyed, as expreffed by Jefus himfelf; what fenfe believers affixed to it during his abode on earth; and how it was applied to him by the apoftles and others, after his afcenfion.

It may be previoufly obferved, that when Chrift is called *the Son*, without any addition, it is to be underftood in the fame fenfe as when he is more particularly denominated *the Son of God*.

C H A P. I.

Of the Faith of Saints under the Old Teftament; and of the Teftimony of the Father, and of holy Angels, concerning Chrift as the Son of God.

BELIEVERS under the Old Teftament knew the Meffiah as a Son begotten of the Father; as it is faid, Pfal. ii. 7. *Thou art my Son, this day have I begotten thee.* They confidered this as a proper generation, and as implying unity of effence. For they embraced this Son as the object of their faith, and were affured of the bleffednefs of all who did fo. Thus it is faid, ver. 12. *Kifs ye the Son, left he be angry, and ye perifh from the way; when his wrath is kindled but a little: bleffed are all they that put their truft in him.* They could not have this affurance, without believing his Deity. For they were taught by the fame authority, that *curfed is the man that trufteth in man*, Jer. xvii. 5.

They

They knew that this *confidence* was that which belongs to God alone, Iſa. xlviii. 2. 1. 10. They were perſuaded that, if they refuſed to *receive* and *rely* on him as the proper object of their faith, they ſubjected themſelves to eternal miſery ; they would *periſh from the way.* Can any one, therefore, who candidly conſiders their faith in the Meſſiah, as here declared, aſſert of the Jews without diſtinction, that they never expected " any other than a man " like themſelves* ?"

Solomon introduces the Wiſdom of God as giving this teſtimony to the ſons of men ; *When there were no depths, I was brought forth.—Before the mountains were ſettled, before the hills was I brought forth*, Prov. viii. 24, 25. That this can only be underſtood as the language of a perſon, has been elſewhere proved. To the ſame purpoſe is the faith of the church expreſſed by Micah : *Whoſe goings forth have been from of old, from everlaſting*, chap. v. 2.

Long before the incarnation, the church knew this glorious Perſon as *in the boſom of the Father*, as *the Son of his love*; according to that divine teſtimony; *Then was I by him, as one brought up with him*, or *as a foſter-ſon, and I was daily his delight*, Prov. viii. 30. They believed in him as the *Counſellor*, Iſa. ix. 6.

They acknowledged him as a Son whoſe nature was ineffable. Therefore Agur ſaith ; *What is his Son's Name, if thou canſt tell?* Prov. xxx. 4. *Name* muſt be underſtood in the ſame ſenſe here, as in the clauſe immediately preceding, where it is uſed with reſpect to the Father. Now, they knew his name ; but not the full import of it, as expreſſing his incomprehenſible nature. They believed that the nature of the Son was as incomprehenſible as that of the Father. Therefore are theſe two queſtions joined, with a note of defiance equally applicable to both ; *What is his Name, or his Son's Name, if thou canſt tell?*

They

---

* Hiſt. of Corrupt. vol. i. p. 2.

They knew that the *Son given* fhould be *the Mighty God;* and *the Father of Eternity*, Ifa.ix.6. JEHOVAH had called thofe *gods, to whom his word came.* But his ancient people were affured that he had never given this appellation of *the Mighty God* to any of the fons of men, or of *the Father of Eternity* to man who is as grafs. But our author fays; " Thefe titles may not exprefs what Chrift is, but what " God will manifeft himfelf to be in him, and by him; fo " that, in the difpenfation of the gofpel, God, the wife and " benevolent author of it, will appear to be a *Wonderful* " *Counfellor, the Everlafting Father, and the Prince of* " *Peace* *." This is a proof of the great pains which this Gentleman takes to make that *crooked,* which God hath made *ftraight.* If the holy Scripture muft be interpreted in this way, in order to the attainment of its true meaning; it were far better entirely to renounce it. For at this rate, it cannot rationally be fuppofed to be given by God as a rule of faith, as well as of manners, not to the learned only, but to the illiterate, who always conftitute by far the greateft part of mankind. This plan of interpretation directly tends to bewilder the mind in an endlefs labyrinth. It gives the lie to that very fyftem which it is meant to fupport. For while Reafon is made the teft of divine Truth, it muft alfo be fuppofed that Truth is obvious to Reafon, as being revealed in language intelligible to the bulk of mankind. For this end, it muft be ufed according to its common acceptation. But while the avowed defign of what is called *rational theology* is to relieve men from thofe fetters of implicit faith, in which, it is pretended, they are ftill held by all but Socinian teachers; its real tendency is only to give a change of fetters. Though a particular verfion of Scripture be excellent, new light may be thrown on various paffages, by attention to the original languages.

But

---

* Famil. Illuftr. p. 29.

But if it is only fuch an acquaintance with thefe as will en-able us to twift them into all the forms within the compafs of fancy, that can either fecure us in a doctrine fundamen-tal in religion, or deliver us from one deftructive to it, the mafs of mankind muft ftill depend on their teachers.

Our author indeed fays, in the preface to thefe Illuftrations;
" To thofe who lived in the times in which thefe books
" were publifhed, they were no doubt very intelligible;
" the language in which they were written, and the cuftoms
" to which they allude, being perfectly known to them.
" But what was eafy to them, a long courfe of time has
" rendered extremely difficult to us.—In this ftate of
" things, the *ignorant* and *unlearned* are very liable to *wreft*
" *the fcriptures*, as the apoftle Peter fays they ever have
" done." But how dark foever fome paffages may be, which allude to cuftoms now unknown, it was indifpenfably requifite.that all things, neceffary to falvation, fhould be re-vealed in language intelligible to all, in every age and na-tion, who come to the word as *new-born babes*. To fup-pofe the contrary, is to impeach the wifdom of God. For *whatever was written aforetime, was written for our learn-ing*. It is not the darknefs of dead languages, nor igno-rance of ancient cuftoms, that renders the fcripture unintel-ligible; but *the wifdom of this world, leaning to our own underftanding*, and not *trufting in the Lord with all our heart* for the gift of that Spirit who is promifed to *lead into all truth*. In the words referred to by our author, Peter does not fpeak of the *unlearned* only, as *wrefting the fcriptures to their own deftruction*, but alfo of the *unftable*, who, as he has already faid, *having known the way of righteoufnefs, turn from the holy commandment delivered unto them;—bring in damnable herefies, denying the Lord who bought them, and bring upon themfelves fwift deftruction*.

Our

Our author is a living proof that his plan of interpreting scripture throws the mind into a state of scepticism as to any determinate meaning. For, in his interpretation of this remarkable prophecy, he clearly shows the perplexity of his mind. " These titles *may not* express what Christ " is," &c. Those who have wrote on Sacred Philology have been at great pains to instruct the world in the meaning of this phrase, *His name shall be called*, and of others of the same kind; informing us that they signify what one shall really be, or what he shall appear to be. But these writers, with all their mighty learning, have been only laborious triflers. Frequently as it occurs to our author, they have never once attended to this beautiful figure of speech, by which the name of a son is expressive, not of what he is himself, but of what his Father is. For all the cramp terms in Rhetoric, there is not one for this. It is to be hoped that our author, when next he has occasion to treat of this figure, will favour us with a distinctive name for it, that henceforth, for the benefit of posterity, it may be inserted in all the rhetorical systems. So important a discovery, indeed, deserves a place in his own *Lectures on Oratory and Criticism.*

But it happens rather unluckily for his theory, that the name is prefaced with this declaration, *The government shall be upon his shoulder.* Now, it cannot be refused that this respects the Son, who is mentioned immediately before, and signifies that he is to bear the whole weight of it. Therefore, it must be very strange, if not one of all the following characters expresses what this Governor himself should be. His government is particularly described in the next verse : and is there not a single word concerning his Person ? It is also unfavourable to our author, that one of these names is elsewhere assumed by the Son. For it has been proved, that it was he who said to Manoah, *Why askest thou thus*

after

after my name, seeing it is Wonderful, Jud. xiii. 18. It is also certain that these names were not actually imposed upon
Jesus, which Dr P.'s theory necessarily requires. Therefore they can only be viewed as expressing his real character.

But the Doctor is armed *cap-a-pie* against any such
argument. " If this name," he says, " be supposed to
" characterize Christ himself, it will by no means fa-
" vour the common doctrine of the Trinity." We have
a very sage reason, indeed :—" because it will " make
" him to be the Father, or the first person, and not
" the Son, or the second person." He evidently grants
that these words may be viewed as characterizing Christ,
both here, and afterwards when he shews in what sense
they will apply to him. But the very idea of the doctrine of the Trinity puts him so much off his guard,
that he produces an objection which strikes as directly a-
gainst his own application of the passage to our Saviour,
as against ours. " It will make him to be the *Father.*"
If so, why should Dr P. take the trouble to shew how
these words will apply to the *Son*. For if his objection be
just, they cannot apply to him in any sense.

But what is the foundation of this weighty objection?
Christ is called *The Everlasting Father*. The amount of
this reasoning is, that he who is a Son in one respect, cannot
be a Father in any other. But still, the character will apply to the Son, without infringing on the peculiar property
of the Father. He may be called *the Father of Eternity*,
which is the literal translation, as being *the Author of Eternal Salvation*, Heb. v. 9. in the same manner as it is said,
Hath the rain a father? Job xxxviii. 28. respecting its
cause or first principle. Or, he may be thus denominated, as being the *father*, or founder, of that new age or dispensation, which is to *endure as long as the sun and moon;*
the *second Adam*, the father of that *seed* which *shall endure*

for ever. Thus we read of *the everlasting kingdom of our Lord and Saviour Jesus Christ,* 2 Pet. i. 11. According to either of these views, this character is strictly connected and properly agrees with that immediately added, *the Prince of Peace.* For *peace* is the sum of our salvation, and the comprehensive blessing of the Messiah's kingdom *.

But if the passage must be applied in this way, our author consoles himself with the pleasing idea, that it shall be very little to the honour of his Master. "Besides," he says, " whatever powers and dignities are to be possessed by Christ, it " is sufficiently insinuated in this place, that he does not " hold them *independent* and *underived;* since he himself, " and all the blessings that he bestows, are said to be *given,* " that is, by God; and at the conclusion of the prophecy, " in the next verse, it is said, that *the zeal of the Lord of* " *Hosts will perform this.*" Christ himself is indeed said to be *given.* As Mediator, he is the *gift of God.* But he is not *given* by the Father exclusively. He gave *himself for us:* and he gives himself to us in the Gospel. What a mournful abuse is it of this *unspeakable gift,* thence, to form such humiliating inferences concerning him !

However, though the Son himself is said to be *given,* how does our author prove, that " it is sufficiently intimated " in this place that whatever powers and dignities are pof- " fessed by him—he does not hold them *independent* and *un-* " *derived?*" He cannot establish this from what follows, *The zeal, &c.* For he has not yet proved, That the Son himself is not the *Lord of Hosts.* To confine this character to the Father, is to beg the question; a species of *proof* very common with Socinians. Here he is not supported by the ancient Jews. For the Chaldee Paraphrast renders this last expression, *This shall be done by the Word of the Lord of Hosts.*

But

* Vid. Vitring. in loc,

But this remarkable passage is not yet sufficiently mangled. Our author must give it another stroke, a finishing one, that it may never again rise up as a witness against his system. "I would also observe," he says, and certainly it is worthy of observation, more than any thing that plodding critics have ever observed before, " that that " part of the title on which the greatest stress has been laid, " may be rendered *the mighty God my Father for ever*, or " *the mighty God is my Father for ever*." But how will this correspond with what seems to be our author's favourite application of the passage,—to the Father himself? The plain language of such a plan of interpretation is, " Let the " Scripture mean any thing, or nothing at all, if it do not " hurt my system, or *favour the common doctrine of the " Trinity*." Our author does not generally trouble himself with criticism. But when he happens to strike on this key, what a glorious discovery does he give of his philological talents! Your Leufdens and Lightfoots, your Vitringas and Lowths, never favoured the world with any thing like this. The luminous idea of a *patronymic* being here introduced, seems to have been reserved for him.

The later Jews have laboured much to wrest this passage out of the hands of Christians: but they never thought of this happy device. That learned Dutchman, who was at such pains to make the Old Testament a dead letter, wisely thought of reading the preceding words, *The Counsellor of the mighty God*, as applicable to Hezekiah. But he had not invention enough, to make any thing tolerable of those that follow. The Chaldee Paraphrast was so ignorant of the original, that he renders this expression, *The God of wonderful counsel.*

But the *sleight*, the μεθοδεια, as the Apostle calls it (Eph. iv. 14.) in this new translation, lies wholly in the proper management of a small matter, indeed, of a mere *Jod*. As

the

the Hebrew word is *abi*, and not *ab*, our author boldly concludes that it fignifies *my father*. It would be paying too
fmall a compliment to the learned writer, to fuppofe that
he did not know, that this is the ordinary form of the word,
when it occurs, as here, in conftruction with another; of
which there are many inftances. Therefore, according to
this mode of interpretation, inftead of, " The fame is *the*
" father," we ought to read, " The fame is *my* father of
" the children of Ammon unto this day," Gen. xix. 38.
Thus Mofes muft be underftood as faying, Jabal " was *my*
" father of fuch as dwell in tents," and Jubal " was *my* fa-
" ther of all fuch as handle the harp," Gen. iv. 20, 21. We
will alfo have " Kifh *my* father of Saul," 1 Sam. ix. 3. *&c.*
&c. The fubftantive verb *is*, in our author's verfion, is entirely a fupplement of his own. His view is totally repugnant to the punctuation. *Abi* has a different vowel point,
when it fignifies *my father*. The accents are directly a-
gainft it. Though thefe fhould be confidered as of human
invention, yet in the prefent cafe they prove, at leaft, that
the Jews have never dreamed of fuch an interpretation as
our author's.

He fays that this view " is exactly agreeable to many de-
" clarations of the Scripture concerning Chrift, and his
" ufual title of *the Son of God;* and that to this the angel,
" in his falutation of Mary, might probably allude, when
" he faid, Luke i. 32. *He fhall be great, and fhall be called*
" *the Son of the Higheft*." Many things are agreeable to
each other, which are not *exactly* fo. When this is the
cafe, there is no variation, either in fubftance, or in circumftances. Where language is thus fpoken of, it is fuppofed
that there is no difference even in terms. One would
therefore expect, after our author's affertion, that he would
produce a few of many paffages in which God is called *the*
Mighty God the Father of Chrift, or his *Father for ever.*

I   But

But if the learned gentleman diſcover a faint reſemblance, favourable to his purpoſe, with him it is enough to conſtitute an *exact agreement*.

Even ſuppoſing that the angel alluded to this paſſage, inſtead of proving that theſe titles do not belong to Chriſt, it would afford a ſtrong preſumption that they do. For when he ſpeaks of him as *the Son of the Higheſt*, it is certainly in a reſpect different from that in which he mentions *David* as *his father*. I ſhall only add, that were our author's mode of conſtruction admitted, a Trinitarian might urge, with fully as much appearance of reaſon, that the name, *My Father for ever*, or *My everlaſting Father*, denoted in what ſenſe God is the Father of this Son, *viz.* by *eternal* generation.

Indeed, his eternal generation, and therefore his eſſential unity with the Father, was celebrated by the ancient Jews as the foundation of his mediatory truſt. They believed that it was becauſe the Father had *begotten* him, that he would *give* him *the heathen for his inheritance, and the uttermoſt ends of the earth for his poſſeſſion*, Pſal. ii. 7, 8. It was becauſe his *goings forth* had been *from of old, from everlaſting*, that they expected that he ſhould *come forth*, in his temporal incarnation, *to be Ruler in Iſrael*, Mic. v. 2.

We are informed by our author, indeed, that this latter paſſage " may be underſtood concerning the promiſes of " God, in which the coming of Chriſt was ſignified to man- " kind from the beginning of the world;" and that " the " Chaldee Paraphraſt renders it, *whoſe Name was foretold* " *of old* *." But it is to no purpoſe to tell us how an expreſſion *may be* underſtood, while no regard is paid to the ſcope and connexion, or to the ordinary ſenſe of language; and while no reaſons are given in ſupport of the interpretation. A lively fancy, when thus allowed to drive on

with

* Famil. Illuſtr. p. 41.

with loofe reins, may make any thing even of the language of infpiration. The ingenious Bifhop of Avranches
imagined that he alone had difcovered the true meaning of
Ifa. viii. 1. when he underftood the command given to the
prophet, to *write concerning Maherfhalalhafhbaz,* as refpecting that parental act, over which the Holy Scripture, in its
manner of expreffion, often draws the modeft veil of meta-
phor*.

Dr P. cannot produce a fingle inftance of the word rendered *goings forth* †, being ufed to denote the work of God
in promifing or predicting future events. But its root ‡ is
often ufed to fignify a natural birth, or a literal origin.
Thus, of Cafluhim it is faid, *Out of whom came Philiflim,*
Gen. x. 14. *Naked,* fays Job, *came I out of my mother's
womb,* Job i. 21. In this fenfe it is ufed, 2 Kin. xx. 18.
Of thy fons that fhall iffue from thee, &c. ‖. When metaphorically ufed to denote the proceffion of words, the *going forth*
is attributed to the words themfelves, and not to the perfon
fpeaking, or of whom they are fpoken, as muft be the cafe
here, according to our author's view §.

But we need go no farther than the claufe immediately
preceding, where the root is ufed to exprefs a real nativity ; *Out of thee fhall he come forth.* It is unnatural to
fuppofe that the fame word, radically viewed, is ufed in
its ordinary fenfe in the firft claufe, and in another, in which
it no where elfe occurs, in the fecond. Befides, by this
interpretation, the antithefis evidently ftated between a
temporal and an eternal egrefs, is loft.

Dr P. mentions the fenfe given to thefe words, in the
Chaldee paraphrafe, as favourable to his view. But he
has no claim to the benefit of it, in a fingle inftance, when

he

---

* Demonftrat. Evangel. Prop. 7. fect. 15.

† יצא　　　‡ מוצאות

‖ See alfo 2 Sam. vii. 12. 1 Chron. ii. 53. Ifa. xi. 1. &c.

§ See Pfal. lxxxix. 34. Jer. xvii. 16. xliv. 17.

he pays so little regard to its general testimony with respect
to the Memra.   However, though he is willing to wrest a
weapon out of the hand of an adversary, it is to his own
hurt.   For the words of the paraphrase will not bear his
translation.   They do not signify, *Whose name was foretold of old;* but, *Whose name is spoken from eternity, from
the days of the hidden age* *.   In this double expression respecting eternity, the Paraphrast indeed retains the very
words of the original, only expressing them in the Chaldee
manner.

   Dr P.'s view labours under various insurmountable difficulties.   The egress of a promise is not only a very different thing from that of a person; but a promise made
" from the beginning of the world" can never be the same
with a person *going forth from eternity.*   The beginning of
the world has always been considered by Christians as the
beginning of time.   But though before this there was nothing save eternity, time and eternity are two things as different as the mind of man can conceive.   Both the words
here used denote eternity.   That rendered *from of old* †,
is indeed sometimes used to denote a remote æra within the
compass of time.   But it often signifies eternity in the most
proper sense.   It is the attribute of God himself, Deut.
xxxiii. 27. *The Eternal God is thy refuge.*   It expresses his
existence without beginning: *He that abideth of old*, Psal.
lv. 19.   It is the word used by Habakkuk, chap. i. 12. *Art
thou not from everlasting?* We find it in the language of Wisdom, the eternity of which is acknowledged by our opponents, though they refuse its personality : *The Lord possessed
me*—BEFORE *his works of old.*   The priority claimed is
evidently that of eternal existence.   For it immediately
follows ; *I was set up from everlasting*, Prov. viii. 22, 23.
In conformity to this, the language of Micah may be ren-

                    Z 4   dered,

* קדמ· †   שטיה אמיר מלקדמין מיומי עלמא׃

dered, *Whose goings forth have been, from the beginning.*—
not " of the world" indeed, but that beginning afcribed to
Wifdom, of the fame date with eternity, as the terms are fynonymous ; *I was fet up from* EVERLASTING, *from the* BE-
GINNING, *or ever the earth was.* The other word * rendered
from everlafting, is derived from a verb which fignifies *to
hide,* as efpecially denoting duration of a hidden and unknown
kind. Though ufed, in various places, in a limited fenfe, it
moft frequently fignifies abfolute eternity. It is the ftrongeft
expreffion employed in fcripture to denote the eternity of
God himfelf, Pfal. xc. 2. If we can ever be certain that it
is ufed in this fenfe, we muft be fo, when it is joined, as in
the paffage under confideration, with another word of the
fame meaning. Thus it occurs in the place already quoted,
Prov. viii. 22, 23. with refpect to the fenfe of which, as
denoting eternity, there is no difpute. There it is connected with קֶדֶם. Becaufe *days* are here joined with *eternity,*
it is no prefumption that we are to underftand the language
of time. For the fame mode of fpeech is ufed by Wifdom,
in the place referred to ; *I was day by day his delight.*

But although the proof arifing from the words themfelves
were lefs ftriking, there would be fufficient   from
the context, that the perfon defcribed had an exiftenc prior
to his nativity in Bethlehem. In the next words, he is
pointed out as the Judge and Ruler of God's people at the
very time that this prophecy was delivered. For a judicial
act is afcribed to him : *He will give them up,* ver. 3. The
pronoun relates to him only, who is before denomiated *the
Judge of Ifrael,* who was to be *fmitten with a rod upon the
cheek,* ver. 1. and the *Ruler in Ifrael,* ver. 2 ; and who is
mentioned, in the following part of this verfe, in relation

                                            to

---

* עוֹלָם *olam.* This would feem to be the origin of the Latin *olim* ;
efpecially as this refembles the Hebrew word in denoting, both the paft,
and the future.

to *his brethren.* They were to be *given up* to adverſity, *till ſhe who travailed brought forth,* that is, till the Meſſiah ſhould *come forth out of* Bethlehem-Ephratah. The futurity of this great event is mentioned as the very reaſon of the continuance of their calamity : *Therefore will he give them up till,* &c. For God, would have his church to look forward to the incarnation of a Divine Perſon as the foundation of her hope ; and to learn by experience what ſhe had ſo long refuſed to learn by precept, that all her temporal deliverances, amidſt deſerved wrath, were only for the ſake of *Immanuel,* had an immediate reſpect to his coming, and prefigured that ſpiritual ſalvation which he alone could give.

Thus, it was revealed to the Jewiſh church, that he who was then her *Judge* ſhould, as a Kinſman-Redeemer, join *the remnant of his brethren,* even of the Gentile nations, *to the children of Iſrael,* ver. 4. that he ſhould appear to them as a Divine Shepherd, who ſhould *ſtand and feed them in the ſtrength of the Lord, and in the majeſty of the Name of the Lord his God,* ver. 5. as poſſeſſed of the eſſential dignity of the divine nature ; and that it was this illuſtrious Perſon, *whoſe goings forth had been from of old, from everlaſting,* who ſhould give them reconciliation with God, and deliverance from all adverſity. For it is added, ver. 6. *And this ſhall be the peace, when the Aſſyrians ſhall come into our land.*

In what ſenſe we are to underſtand this character, appears from the teſtimony of God the Father: *This is my beloved Son, in whom I am well pleaſed,* Matt. iii. 17. Our author will not pretend that Chriſt is called *the Son of God,* becauſe of his miraculous conception. With as little propriety can it be ſaid, that he receives this name becauſe of the perfection of his obedience. For though his life was hitherto blameleſs, he was only entering on his proper trial,

passing

paffing from a life of retirement to his public miniftry, engaging in various conflicts with temptation, and expofing himfelf to the malice of the world. It had not yet appeared how he would conduct himfelf in fuch trying circumftances. It is, therefore, entirely prepofterous to fuppofe that he fhould receive this diftinguifhing character, before he had proved his title to it. According to this view, it ought to have been, *This will be my beloved Son,* &c. The very for· mation of the language implies that he is a Son, abftractly from the idea of the Father's love. Literally it is, *This is that my Son, that Beloved.* If we confider the firft expreffion as merely fignifying God's peculiar love to him, exclufive of the idea of a proper fonfhip, we charge the Divine Speaker with an unmeaning tautology.

It has been feen, that this character is not equivalent to that of *the Chrift ;* and the fame will more fully appear in the courfe of this inquiry.

When this teftimony was repeated at the transfiguration, it was with this important addition ; *Hear ye him,* Matt. xvii. 5. It cannot be fuppofed as the defign of the Divine Speaker, that Jefus fhould only have the fame honour that his people had given to former meffengers. For the Son is here oppofed to all who had gone before him ; who are reprefented in their different characters, by the two illuftrious perfons prefent. Thefe words are, indeed, the Father's reply to the foolifh propofal of the bewildered difciples, of making three tabernacles, and thus giving the fame honour to Mofes and Elias, as to Jefus. But they are commanded to *hear him,* as greater than Mofes, the inftrumental giver of the law, and as greater than Elias, who was called the reftorer of it. Nor is the argument, enforcing this command, taken from the fuperiority of his doctrine and difpenfation ; but from the fuperior dignity of the Perfon, as being the Son of God effentially confidered. The very

word

word uſed to expreſs the command, confirms th¡s view. For it often occurs in ſcripture, as denoting the whole of that homage we owe to God, with reſpeſt to the revelation he hath given us : *Obſerve and hear all theſe words which I command thee,* Deut. xii. 28. *And the people ſaid unto Jo-ſhua, The Lord our God will we ſerve, and his voice will we obey,* literally, *hear,* Joſh. xxiv. 24. *If ye will not hear,—to give glory to my Name, I will even ſend a curſe upon you,* Mal. ii. 2. *He that is of God, heareth God's words,* John viii. 47.

How this language was underſtood by holy Angels, appears from the addreſs of Gabriel to the Virgin. *The Holy Ghoſt ſhall come upon thee, and the power of the Higheſt ſhall overſhadow thee : therefore alſo that Holy Thing which ſhall be born of thee ſhall be called the Son of God,* Luke i. 35. Socinians have generally explained theſe words as ſignifying, that Jeſus is the Son of God, becauſe of his miraculous conception. But it is not ſaid, that therefore he ſhall *be,* but only that he ſhall be *called,* the Son of God. Nor is he ſo *called,* as if he derived his ſonſhip from his miraculous conception, but becauſe this was a glorious manifeſtation of it. That this is the ſenſe, is evident from the connexion. As theſe words are an anſwer to Mary's queſtion, *How ſhall this be, ſeeing I know not a man ?* the Angel undoubtedly alludes to the prophecy of Iſaiah; *Behold, a Virgin ſhall conceive, and bear a Son, and ſhall call his Name Immanuel,* chap. vii. 14. He informs Mary, that this *ſign* ſhould be fulfilled in her. " Therefore," he ſays, " by this extraordinary circumſtance, it ſhall be clearly " manifeſted that he, who ſhall be born of thee, is indeed " the Son of God, who has been ſo long promiſed to his " Church in the charaſter of a Divine Saviour *." Per-ſons

* Vid. Hoornbeck Socin. Confutat. Vol. ii. p. 37, 38. Biſterfield cont. Crell. p. 303.

fons and things are, in fcripture, frequently faid to be *called* by any particular defignation, when it is fimply meant, that it fhall undoubtedly appear that they really *are* what the defignation imports. Thus it is faid, *He that is left in Zion— fhall be called holy;* that is, he fhall evidently appear to *be holy.* For this is to be accomplifhed, *When the Lord fhall have wafhed away the filth of the daughter of Zion,* Ifa. iv. 3, 4. But we need go no farther than the prophecy to which the Angel refers. There it is faid, *Thou fhalt call his Name Immanuel.* Now, the meaning plainly is, that he, thus miraculoufly conceived, fhall appear to be *God with us.* For Mary did not give him this name, nor did he ordinarily receive it from others. His miraculous conception was the primary evidence of his being *God* MANIFEST *in the flefh,* 1 Tim. iii. 16. It may be further obferved, that that the particle διο, rendered *therefore,* does not neceffarily point out the caufe of Chrift's filiation. For according to its frequent fignification, it fimply denotes the *confequence* of his miraculous conception.

It is remarkable, that the angel fpeaks of that which fhould be born of the Virgin, as a *Holy Thing.* This is not the language ordinarily ufed to denote a perfon. It evidently expreffes his conviction that Mary fhould be the mother of Jefus, only *according to the flefh* or human nature, which had no fubfiftence by itfelf. Language of the fame kind is employed by the angel who appeared to Jofeph : *That which is conceived of her is of the Holy Ghoft,* Matt. i. 20. When Gabriel fays that *even,* or *alfo that Holy Thing* fhould *be called the Son of God;* he declares that, in confequence of its perfonal union to the divine nature, it fhould be evident that this name belonged to the whole Perfon of the Mediator. But the language at the fame time clearly imports, that this name fhould by no means be wholly engroffed by the human nature.

The

The angel undoubtedly knew that, in this instance, that which was to be *born of a woman* should be *clean* *, because of the essential purity of the Person to which it was to be united. We may be assured, indeed, that he who was *in all things made like unto his brethren*, sin excepted, would have been assimilated to them in respect of his conception, had not his infinite holiness precluded the possibility of his becoming literally *the Son of man*. For thus he must have born *the image of the earthy*.

According to the judgment of many interpreters, both ancient and modern, by *the power of the Highest overshadowing* the virgin, we are to understand the second Person of the adorable Trinity as, by his own agency, *taking part of* our nature †. If this be the case, the angel gives the most satisfying reason why *even* this nature should not be excluded from the honour of the name under consideration, although properly belonging only to the Divine. For in consequence of this ineffable assumption, they are indissolubly united in one person. It deserves our attention, that, although the influences of the Spirit are sometimes denominated *power* ‡, this term is not used any where else as a personal designation of the Spirit himself. But as the second Person seems, in the Old Testament, to be designed *the arm of the Lord*, Isa. li. 9. liii. 1. which is a synonymous phrase; in the New, he is expressly said to be *the power of God*, 1 Cor. i. 24.

C H A P. II.

Of the Testimony of Devils, and of the Enemies of Christ.

IT may not be improper to inquire, in what sense this designation was understood by fallen angels. Satan

seems

---

* Job xv. 14. xxv. 4.   † Vid. Wolfii Cur. in loc.   ‡ Luke xxiv. 49.

feems to have founded his temptation on that ftriking teftimony given by the Father. And he loft no time in trying the claim that Jefus had to this character. For *then was Jefus led up of the spirit into the wilderness, to be tempted of the Devil,* Matt. iv. 1. Scarcely had that voice been uttered, *This is my beloved Son,* ere Jefus heard another, faying ; *If thou be the Son of God, command that thefe ftones be made bread,* ver. 3. The tempter evidently interpreted this defignation as implying *creating* power, not merely in its effects, in the change of the very fubftance of things, but in the manner of operation, by a mere word of *command.* Whatever Socinians do, Satan feems to have underftood this character, as denoting that the Perfon to whom it belonged was that *Word of* JEHOVAH, who *spake, and it was done,* who *commanded, and it ftood faft,* Pfal. xxxiii. 6. 9.

All the judicial power afcribed to Chrift is confidered by Socinians as the fruit of his obedience, and as conferred after his work was finifhed. But the devils themfelves knew that, even in the days of his humiliation, he had power to torment them. The idea of this power they connect with his Sonfhip. Therefore Legion faid ; *What have we to do with thee, Jefus, thou Son of God ? Art thou come hither to torment us before the time ?* Matt. viii. 29. This multitude of unclean fpirits acknowledged his *abfolute* authority over them and all creatures. *They befought him, that he would not command them to go out into the deep. They befought him, that he would fuffer them to enter into the fwine,* Luke viii. 31, 32. In this gofpel they are made to addrefs him as *Son of God moft High ;* and they evidently confidered him as heir of all his Majefty and Power. It was becaufe he was Lord of the whole earth, that he had a right to deprive the Gadarenes of their property, in granting the requeft of the hellifh legion.

The devils were at times fo overwhelmed with a fenfe

2 of

of his majesty, as practically to shew that they reckoned him a Son entitled to the same homage with his Father. For *unclean spirits, when they saw him, fell down before him, and cried, saying, Thou art the Son of God,* Mark iii. 11. We are informed, in the same Gospel, that Legion, *when he saw Jesus afar off, ran and worshipped him,* chap. v. 6. They acknowledged him to be a Son of the same nature with his Father. Therefore, they addressed him as *the Holy One of God,* Mark i. 24. Luke iv. 34. When they call him *the Holy One,* they acknowledge him to be supremely and essentially holy, as opposed to all creatures: For thus the essential holiness of the Divine Nature is often expressed in the Old Testament. When they call him *the Holy One of God,* they use an expression of the same import with the *the Son of God;* denoting our Saviour's relation to the first Person as his Father, a relation of so peculiar a kind, that it not only excludes every other from any claim to partnership, but implies the possession of all that holiness which is essential to the Father.

These proofs may be of use to others. But they must be lost on those who are confirmed in our author's sentiments. For he denies that our Saviour was really tempted by the Devil; and agrees with some modern infidels, in asserting that the Demoniacs were merely lunatics [*]. All this is meant to persuade the world, that *there is neither angel nor spirit.*

The Enemies of Jesus understood his claim of Sonship in such a sense, as on this ground to accuse him of blasphemy. It was by no means their idea, that by simply calling God *his Father,* or himself *the Son of God,* he was guilty of this crime. For the Jews arrogated this honour to themselves upon very slight grounds : *We be not born of fornication ;*

[*] Institutes, vol. ii. p. 436.

fornication; we have one Father even God, John viii. 41. They knew that to them *belonged the adoption.* But they were convinced that Jeſus claimed this honour, in ſuch a ſenſe as neceſſarily bore that he was equal with God. And it was from the connexion of his diſcourſe, that they learned his peculiar meaning. They perſecuted, and ſought to ſlay him, becauſe he had healed a man on the ſabbath-day, John v. 16. But his vindication provoked them a great deal more than the action itſelf. *Jeſus anſwered them, My Father worketh hitherto, and I work,* ver. 17. Dr P. views, or pretends to view, theſe words as an excuſe for healing on the ſabbath : " By way of apology, he ſays, *My " Father worketh hitherto,* that is, in the courſe of his provi-·" dence on the ſabbath, as well as on other days ; *and I work,* " that is, on the ſabbath-day alſo. Upon this the Phariſees " are more enraged, *becauſe he called God his Father, and " becauſe he made himſelf* (not *equal with God,* as we render " it, but) *like unto · God,* aſſuming ſo much of his preroga-" tive, as to claim the privilege of working on the ſabbath-·" day *."

This cannot with any propriety be called an *apology.* For it was an expreſs vindication. But it could be neither, unleſs Jeſus uſed the word *hitherto* as applying to his own work, in the ſame ſenſe as to the Father's. God's working on the Sabbath could be no reaſon why a mere man ſhould do ſo. Far leſs could ſuch a reaſon be given by our Saviour. God's continuing thus to work could prove as little ; unleſs Jeſus meant that his work was coeval with the Father's, as being the very ſame. Our Lord's argument evidently conſiſts in this, that he had the ſame right to work on the Sabbath, as the Father, becauſe he was e-qually a divine Perſon ; which appeared from the ſameneſs of the date and duration of his operation. The whole force

of

* Famil. Illuſtr. p. 24.

of the argument lies in the equality of the perfons. Without this, it hath none. The Jews juftly underftood Jefus as
declaring that, though the Father had refted on the Sabbath
from his work of creation, he *hitherto, even until now, or to
this hour,* as the expreffion is elfewhere rendered. (1 John
ii. 9. 1 Cor. viii. 7.) on the Sabbath, as well as on other
days, carried on his work of providence, in the prefervation
of his creatures; and alfo, that he wrought in conjunction with the Father; and had done fo *hitherto,* from the
foundation of the world.

The Doctor endeavours to draw off the attention of the
reader from the true nature of our Saviour's claim, and
from the true reafon of the rage of the Pharifees. He reduces the former to a claim of mere refemblance; and he
divides the latter into two diftinct reafons. " The Phari-
" fees were more enraged," he fays, " *becaufe* he called
" God his Father, *and becaufe* he made himfelf *like* unto
" God." There is a ftroke of Socinian *prieftcraft* here.
The learned gentleman muft know, that the Evangelift
gives both thefe reafons as one: *Therefore the Jews fought
the more to kill him, becaufe he not only had broken the fabbath, but faid alfo that God was his Father, making himfelf
equal with God,* ver. 18. The laft words may be viewed
as their inference from what Jefus had faid, as expreffed in
thofe immediately preceding. But to make a diftinct reafon of them, favours too much of the *cunning craftinefs* of
thofe who *lie in wait to deceive.* However, our author
wifhes in this manner to avert the force of Chrift's calling
God his Father, in that fenfe in which, according to the
natural connexion of the words, the Jews evidently underftood his language; and to make way for his new verfion
of the word *ισον.* He wifhes it to appear, that Chrift's
calling God his Father, was not at all the reafon of their
concluding that he claimed even fo much as *likenefs* to him;

but that this was wholly founded on these words, *I work.*
But if his claim of Sonship suggested no idea either of
equality, or of resemblance, how is it mentioned as in any
respect a reason of their rage? The Doctor, in his explanation, wisely passes over this reason. He also discovers great
address in dividing the true reason. For as the Evangelist
has left it, our author's new translation of ἴσον must have
appeared very aukwardly: " The Jews sought, &c. be-
" cause he—said also that God was his Father, making
" himself *like* unto God."

But truth needs none of these arts. The reason why
the Jews sought *the more* to kill him, as given by John, is
simply this; because *he said that God was his own Father,
making himself equal with God.* The thing that increased
the rage of his enemies, was the manner in which he
claimed this relation. For he did not merely call God his
Father, or abstractly speak of his own work; but he spoke
of his relation to God in such terms, and in so intimate a connexion with his work, as clearly to shew that he wished it
to be confidered as the same with God's, and that he called
God his *proper* Father *.

Had the Jews understood our Saviour as meaning that
God was his Father merely in a metaphorical sense, they
would not have quarrelled with him. For they asserted
the same concerning themselves. But it is the very hinge
of the accusation, that he called God his *proper* Father.
This is so well known to be the native force of the word
ἴδιος, that it scarcely requires particular illustration. This
term is used more generally to denote property of any
kind, as when it is said, John i. 11. *He came to his own,
and his own received him not.* But more strictly, it signifies
the closest degree of relation. Thus it intimates that Simon was the brother-german of Andrew, John i. 42. *He*

first

: * Πατερα ιδιον ελεγε τον Θεον.

first findeth his own brother Simon. Every one is commanded to have *his own* wife, 1 Cor. vii. 2 *. But neither could our Lord call God his *proper* Father, nor could the Jews underſtand his words in this ſenſe, unleſs he meant that God was his *natural* Father. Socinians have never been able to produce a ſingle inſtance of one being called the *proper* father of another, but as implying this idea. Till our author prove that proper and improper, literal and metaphorical, are the ſame, he cannot ſhew that this term, expreſsly uſed for the ſake of diſtinction, denotes a relation of that very kind which it is meant to exclude. But as he who is a proper Son, is begotten of his Father; Jeſus, being the proper Son of God, muſt of neceſſity be ſo begotten. This being the meaning of the word ιδιον, the ridiculouſneſs of our author's ſubterfuge appears at firſt view; He " ſaid alſo that God was *his proper* Father, making " himſelf *like* unto God."

That the Jews underſtood our Lord as claiming a natural relation, farther appears from their inference from his words. They could never conceive that he made himſelf *equal with God*, by calling himſelf his Son metaphorically, or by aſſerting that as God had continued in his work of providence from the beginning of the world, he had been ſtill engaged in a work of a different kind, from the beginning of his miniſtry. The ancient diſciples of Socinus granted that ισον ſignified equality; pretending that the Jews miſunderſtood our Saviour's meaning. Their ſucceſſors, however, are become ſo much better acquainted with the Greek language, as to find that the word muſt be rendered *like*. But our author has not produced a ſingle example of its being uſed in this ſenſe. The attempt would have been vain. For in the New Teſtament, it invariably ſignifies *equality*: and it is conſtantly uſed by profane

fane

---

* Vid. Lampe in John i. 42. Owen Vindic. Evang. p. 168.

fane writers in the fame fenfe. We need not trouble the reader with proofs of what cannot be denied; but fhall fubmit the decifion of this point to a judge whom our author cannot reafonably object to. This is no other than Dr P. himfelf. We have his judgment recorded in the fame work, at no great diftance from what we have quoted, when explaining Phil. ii. 5. " The proper rendering of " this text," he fays, " is, *Who being in the form of God,* " *did not think that being* EQUAL *to God,* or a ftate of equa- " lity with God, *was a thing to be fiezed.* This makes the " whole paffage perfectly juft and coherent, *&c* *." If it fignify *equality* there, *a ftate of equality;* if, according to this view, the *whole* paffage is *perfectly juft;* let our author be kind enough to give us a reafon, why it is not rightly tranflated in the paffage under confideration.

But let us fee how the Jews are foothed, after being fo much enraged by a claim of mere *refemblance* to God. Indeed, the Doctor's cure is as bad as his difeafe. He adds; " To fhew them that he meant nothing arrogant in " what he faid, and that this privilege was given him by " God, he immediately replies,—*The Son can do nothing of* " *himfelf,* &c." If the Jews confidered a claim of mere *likenefs* to God as arrogant, our Lord's reply could never *fhew them* that it was not. For it did not avail to his enemies, on what he pretended to found his claim. The claim itfelf, however viewed, was the ground of their of- fence. They would readily believe that a man, who made fuch a claim, would devife fome excufe for it. The Doctor ought to prove, elfe his chain is broken, that Jefus never pre- tended even likenefs to God, as " affuming any part of his " prerogative." But on the contrary, he grants that our Lord maintained his claim, fuch as it is reprefented.

What Dr P. intends, when he fpeaks of our Lord
" meaning

---

* Famil. Illuft, p. 39.

" meaning nothing arrogant," I cannot well conceive. For he admits that he "; affumed fo much of God's prerogative, " as to claim the privilege of working on the fabbath-day, " as well as God." All the difference between him and the Jews, is that, according to him, this affumption was not by ufurpation, but in confequence of a divine gift. But fo tender is he of the character of Jefus, when there is no occafion for his fervices, that, in order to fkreen it, he fuppofes an abfolute impoffibility, *viz.* that God had given to a mere man fo much of his prerogative, as to work on the fabbath-day, as well as himfelf. But if this be God's *prerogative*, how can he, without *denying himfelf*, give it to a creature? An enthroned worm cannot part with what is called his prerogative, without virtually dethroning himfelf. But in order to avoid an acknowledgment of Chrift's effential dignity, our author makes him claim, as a creature, what God cannot give. He afcribes real *arrogance* to the lowly Jefus, in attempting, on his principles, to exculpate him from the appearance of it.

After all, he fails in his proof. He pretends that our Saviour " fhews that he meant nothing arrogant." To illuftrate this, he was to prove that " the privilege of work- " ing on the fabbath-day was given to him by God." Therefore he refers to ver. 19 *The Son can do nothing of himfelf, but what he feeth the Father do; for whatfoever things he doth, thefe alfo doth the Son likewife.* But our Lord, inftead of lowering his claim here, or fhewing that the Jews underftood it in too high a fenfe, advances it. Inftead of proving a right merely to work on the fabbath, he afferts his right and power to do *all* the works of the Father, in the fame manner with him; without uttering one word concerning the fuppofed gift of a privilege of working on fabbath. Our author adds, indeed: " He then proceeds " to reprefent all his extraordinary power as the gift of his

" Father.

" Father." The Doctor, doubtleſs, wiſhes it to appear that Jeſus eſtabliſhed the particular claim by a general proof. But he reduces the argument of Jeſus to nothing, by making it prove too much. He was to prove that he was not chargeable with arrogance in aſſerting *likeneſs* to God, in working on ſabbath, becauſe God had given him this privilege. According to our author, he proves this, by " re-" preſenting *all his* extraordinary power as the gift of his " Father." But this is not a fair ſtate of our Saviour's proof. For he in fact declares his right to do *all* the works proper to the Father, in the ſame manner with him. Nay, he aſſerts his agency in the very ſame works. A ſtrange apology, indeed, from the mouth of a *mere man.*

Thus, notwithſtanding all that Dr P. advances, the Jews clearly underſtood Jeſus as making himſelf *equal* with God, by claiming a ſameneſs of operation, as proceeding from ſameneſs of nature. The folly of pretending that they conſidered him as claiming *likeneſs* only, if any doubt yet remains, will inſtantly appear to any one who will take the trouble to compare the paſſage with what is ſaid, chap. x. 33. where we have the ſame accuſation renewed ; *Thou, being a man, makeſt thyſelf God.* Indeed, in the paſſage which has been conſidered, we have not only the conſtruction which the Jews put on our Saviour's words ; but the juſtneſs of it is admitted by the Evangeliſt. For he evidently relates it as matter of fact, that Jeſus had not only *looſed* the ſabbath, as the word properly means, but *called* God his own Father, making himſelf equal with God.

Had the Jews put an unjuſt ſenſe on our Saviour's words, it cannot be denied that it was indiſpenſably incumbent on him to correct their miſtake. If he left them in it, he did not do juſtice to his own character ; he did not uſe proper means for the information, either of his enemies, or of his diſciples ; nay, he did not vindicate the eſſential honour of

his

his Father. If they rejected him, becaufe of a fuppofed declaration of equality with the Father, while he meant nothing of this nature ; the blame of this rejection lay on him. His filence muft have been their excufe. Nor was this all. As on this very account, they fought to kill him, he did not properly regard the fixth precept of the law, by ufing all lawful means for the prefervation of his own life. He alfo run a great rifk of feeming to feal an impious falfe-hood with his blood. All thefe, it muft be granted, would have been inconfiftent with the character of the Meffiah.

But our Lord, inftead of fhewing them that they put a falfe fenfe on his words, vindicates them according to the very fenfe in which they were underftood by the Jews. He premifes his vindication with a repetition of that very claim which was the ground of offence ; *The Son.* Then he particularly defcribes the nature and manner of his ope-ration. *The Son can do nothing of himfelf, but what he feeth the Father do,* &c. Thefe words are quoted, indeed, by our author, as a proof that Jefus did not mean to claim equality with the Father. But it has been already proved that, whether they be underftood of him as *the Son of God,* or as *Mediator,* they exprefs a power of doing all the works proper to God *. This undeniably appears from what is immediately added ; *For what things foever he* (the Father) *doth, thefe alfo doth the Son likewife.* One, merely an imitator of God, might be faid to do fomethings *like* unto him. But no man in his fenfes would affert that he could do *all.* However, Jefus does not fay that he works *like* the Father. He afcribes the fame *extent* to his opera-tion,—*what things foever* ; whether they be works of crea-tion, of providence, or of redemption. He claims equa-lity, as to *manner.* *Thefe alfo doth the Son* LIKEWISE. The laft adverb, ομοιως, evidently differs in its meaning

A a 4   from

---

* See above, p. 235—240.

from και, rendered *also*; as denoting that the Son works in the same manner as the Father. He difplays the fame divine Power, Majefty, and Sovereignty; as he fhews in the following verfes. But he does not merely claim the fame extent and manner of operation. He afferts an abfolute famenefs of works; THESE *also doth the Son.*

If any further evidence be neceffary; that the Jews underftood our Lord of fuch a Sonfhip as implied an exiftence prior to h.s incarnation, will appear from their conftruction of his words, when he faid, *Before Abraham was, I am,* John viii. 38, 39. They undoubtedly confidered this as a renewal of his former claim. For *then took they up ftones to caft at him.* It is evident, both from the words themfelves, and from their connexion, that they as little miftook his meaning here. But this paffage has been formerly explained.

The Jews renewed the charge of blafphemy, when our Lord faid, *I and my Father are one,* John x. 30. From the connexion, it is evident that he made this declaration with refpect to unity of effence. For he had immediately afferted unity of power. He had declared concerning his fheep, *I give unto them eternal life, and they fhall never perifh, neither fhall any pluck them out of my hand,* ver. 28. Then their fecurity is further declared; *My Father, who gave them me, is greater than all, and none fhall be able to pluck them out of my Father's hand,* ver. 29. Dr P. indeed, makes fhort work with this paffage: " At the very time," we are told, " that our Lord fays that he and the Father " are one, and in the very fentence preceding it, he fays " that his Father is *greater than all.* But how can the Fa- " ther be greater than all, if there was any other, who was " fo much *one* with him, as to be, in all refpects, *equal* to " him * ?" But we might eafily retort the queftion, and

leave

* Appeal, p. 14.

leave matters on the fame footing on either fide. How could the Son be *one* with the Father, if the Father be *greater than all*, in the Socinian fenfe? For thus there cannot be any other who is *equal* to him, in any refpect. We have certainly as good a right to underftand the unity to the exclufion of the fuperiority fuppofed, as they have to underftand the fuperiority afferted, to the exclufion of a proper unity.

But a candid reader will eafily perceive that when Jefus, after afferting that the Father was *greater than all*, immediately adds, *I and my Father are one*, he does fo, not merely as claiming the fame power with his Father, in preferving his fheep, but as teftifying, in the cleareft manner, that he did not include himfelf among the *all* formerly mentioned. This expreffion evidently refers to thofe only who would attempt to *pluck them out of* the Father's hand. And who would imagine that Chrift fhould be one of them? It would naturally occur to his hearers, that he afferted *unity* with the Father as to that very *greatnefs* of *power* afcribed to him in the preceding words. That declaration, *I and my Father are one*, is undoubtedly added as an exception with refpect to himfelf, in the fame fenfe with what is faid, 1 Cor. xv. 27. The apoftle having obferved that *all things are put under him*, viz. Chrift, adds, *It is manifeft that he is excepted who did put all things under him*. In the fame manner may it be faid; when it is declared, that *the Father is greater than all*, it is manifeft that he is excepted who is *one* with the Father, whofe works are the fame as the Father's, and who fays of himfelf ver. 38. *The Father is in me, and I in him.*

But Dr P. explains this language in the following manner: " That is, we are one in defign and intereft *." Even this view cannot be rationally admitted, without granting unity of effence. For the words certainly exprefs perfect unity;

as

---

* Famil. Illuftr p 23.

as immediately respecting the preservation of believers, which is a divine work. And how can it be supposed that the will of a mere creature, yet exposed to temptation, and *not free from a bias of passion, drawing contrary to duty,* as Socinians speak of our Lord in the days of his flesh, could be so perfectly conformed to that of the Creator, that they might be said to be *one?*

The Doctor adds, " But whatever be the union between " the Father and the Son, it is of such a kind that his dif- " ciples are capable of it with respect to them both ; for " in his prayer for his disciples, he says, John xvii. 20.— " *That they all may be one, as thou, Father, art in me, and I* " *in thee, that they also may be one in us.—And the glory* " *which thou gavest me, I have given them that they may be* " *one, even as we are one,"* &c.

Socinians tell us, at times, that *as* does not denote equality, but resemblance. It is necessary, however, to forget this distinction here. For at all events this passage must be employed to destroy the force of another. But we find the particle *as* used a little before, ver. 18. *AS thou hast sent them into the world, even so have I also sent them into the world.* Will they say that a mere man had the same power in sending the apostles, as the Supreme God in sending him ?

There seems to be a shuffle in that expression, " His dif- " ciples are capable of it." Should it be inquired, " Are " ordinary Christians advanced to as great nearness to God " as Christ himself?" it might be replied ; " All that has " been said, is that they are *capable* of it, as possessing the " same nature." But our Lord does not declare what they are *capable* of, but what they shall all certainly attain. For he speaks of the certain effect of his work. Will our author then say, that all believers attain as perfect an union with the Father, as their Lord, " whatever be the union" between

between the Father and him? Do not Socinians grant that Jefus is fo united to the Father, that all divine wifdom and power are in him? Is it true of believers, that God *giveth not the Spirit by meafure unto them?* Have they *all power in heaven. and in earth?* We are commanded to be *merciful as our Father in heaven is merciful.* Shall it therefore be inferred, that man is *capable of* infinite mercy?

The objection receives no fupport from thefe words: *And the glory which thou gaveft me, I have given them,* &c. For here our Lord fpeaks of that glory which the Father had given him in truft, to beftow on his apoftles and other followers; efpecially that of the knowledge of his *name,* mentioned, ver. 6. and of his *word,* ver. 8. and of a divine miffion, ver. 18.: But this glory he contrafts with what was properly his own, what he had with the Father before the foundation of the world, ver. 5. This he defcribes as incommunicable, as what could only be *beheld* by them; *That they may behold my glory,* ver. 24.

It may be difficult to fhew how John xiv. 10. can be underftood as immediately denoting unity, as to either defign, or intereft. To fuppofe that Jefus fhould fay, " I am " *in* the Father *in defign,* or *in intereft;* and the Father is ' *in* me, *in defign,* or *in intereft,*" is to fuppofe a mode of fpeaking unknown to Scripture, and unexampled in any language.

Our author, in his Notes on the Dialogue between Flekwick and a monk, obferves, that the texts referred to by the former, in reply to an argument from Chrift's claim of unity, " are fufficient to fhew, that Chrift and the Father " might, with propriety and force, be faid to be *one,* with- " out underftanding it to mean, that they were one God, " or one being*." The texts are Acts iv. 32. " The " multitude of them that believed, were of *one heart,* and " of *one foul.*" Gal. iii. 28. " There is neither Jew nor " Greek,

* P. 8.

" Greek,—bond nor free,—male nor female : for ye are
" all *one* in Chrift Jefus." Eph. v. 31. " They two ſhall
" be *one fleſh.*" But theſe paſſages only ſhew, that different perſons may be ſaid to be *one* in different reſpects.
And who ever denied this? They prove nothing as to the
point in hand. The firſt gives us a ſubſtantive joined with
the adjective, which ſhews that the ſenſe is limited to
affection. The meaning of the ſecond appears from the
context, which ſhews that *one new man,* or *one body,* is
meant. For this unity is oppoſed to difference with reſpect
to *nation, rank,* or *ſex.* When man and wife are ſaid to
be *one,* we are expreſsly informed of the meaning, by the
addition of the word *fleſh.* He muſt have very *carnal*
ideas of divine things, who would call in the aſſiſtance of
this text, to illuſtrate the union between the Father and
the Son.

Believers may be ſaid to be *one ſoul, one body ;* and huſ-
band and wife to be *one fleſh.* But none of theſe expreſſions
can prove that the Father and Son are *not* one in eſſence.
It is evident that when this term is uſed, its meaning is to
be learned, either from the ſubſtantive joined with it, as li-
miting the unity in that reſpect particularly mentioned, or
from the connection. But when the term itſelf is uſed
ſubſtantively, it certainly intimates the moſt perfect and
unlimited unity; eſpecially if the context confirm this
ſenſe. If men are not ſtrangers to *Reaſon,* they will exerciſe it in deducing the native concluſion from certain premiſes. In other words, they will be capable of *reaſoning ;*
which is only the exertion of this faculty. But to tear an
expreſſion away from thoſe moſt cloſely connected with it,
and to conjoin it with others that have no greater affinity
t an ſameneſs of ſound, ſhews, either a prodigious want of
that power which is the ſource of reaſoning, or the wilful
perverſion of it.

Nothing can be more clear, than that the idea which the
context

context more immediately fuggefts, is that of unity as to *power.* It is well known that, in the language both of facred and of profane writers, this is metaphorically reprefented by the *hand.* Now, our Lord having ufed this term, with refpect both to himfelf, and to the Father, and in both expreffions having declared the fecurity of his people, to fhew that he did not claim more than what belonged to him, adds; *I and my Father are one,* that is, *one thing, one effence.* He gives this as the reafon why he had fpoken of his *hand* or *power* as an equal fecurity with that of the Father.

The very ftructure of the language, unlefs it denote famenefs of effence, is unbecoming the moft exalted creature. Was it deemed a proof of treafonable arrogance in the prime minifter of an earthly fovereign, to preface his difpatches with *Ego et rex meus* * ? And fhall a mere man, becaufe he is the fervant of God, be permitted to fay, *I and my Father,* without incurring the charge of treafon againft the Moft High?

It is undeniable that, on this occafion, as well as on the former, the Jews were perfuaded that Jefus claimed equality with the Father. For they not only threatened to ftone him, but affigned his fuppofed blafphemy as the reafon; urging, as a proof of this crime, that he had appropriated to himfelf the honours of deity. Nothing can be more clearly expreffed: *For a good work we ftone thee not; but for blafphemy, and becaufe that thou, being a man, makeft thyfelf God,* ver. 33. Now, the argument is the fame as in the former cafe. If Jefus knew that even thofe who were the primary objects of his miffion, *his own* to whom *he came,* underftood his language as an exprefs claim of deity, and did not ufe every mean to convince them of the contrary; either they believed nothing but what he declared, and therefore he is God in the proper fenfe of the term;

* I and my king.

term ; or he could have no right to the character of Meſſiah. If the former be not true, the latter neceſſarily follows from the premiſes. For it cannot be denied that he
knew this to be the conſtruction which they put on his
words. But if he knew that it was falſe, and did not endeavour to rectify their miſtake, he did not act a faithful
part, either to God, or to man. Let us inquire, then, if,
when they charged him with *making himſelf God,* he refuſed or refuted the charge as a groſs calumny? For undoubtedly, this is the part that any honeſt and conſcien-
tious man would have acted, when falſely accuſed on a ſubject of ſuch magnitude.

But he does not ſo much as give up with theſe terms,
that gave them ſo much offence. This a good and wiſe
man certainly would have done, had he uſed them only
metaphorically, and had it been poſſible to expreſs his
meaning as clearly and juſtly without them. Had they
miſtaken him, the moſt natural reply was; " Ye cannot
" juſtly ſay that *I make myſelf God,* by declaring that *I and*
" *my Father are one,* when I have already informed you,
" that *my Father is greater than all.*" This would have been
far more natural and convincing than an appeal to the inferior ſenſe of the name *God,* as underſtood by Socinians;
and unſpeakably preferable to a reference to his works as
thoſe of the Father, and as requiring their *faith* in his teſtimony, in that very reſpect in which, it is ſaid, they miſtook
his meaning.

Our Lord, however, ſtill calls God *his Father,* and himſelf *the Son of God.* He vindicates that truth, for declaring
which they accuſed him of blaſphemy. He proves that
he is *the Son of God,* according to the conſtruction of his adverſaries, as being *God,* firſt, by an argument from the leſs
to the greater. *If he called them gods, unto whom the word of*
God came, and the ſcripture cannot be broken; ſay ye of him,
whom the Father hath ſanctified, and ſent into the world,
Thou

Thou blafphemeft ; *becaufe I faid, I am the Son of God,* ver.
35, 36. He refers to the rulers of Ifrael, who, in Pfal. lxxxii.
are called *gods*. He mentions it as a mark of their inferiority, that *the word of God came* to them. If this refpect
the word of revelation ; it *came* to them as bound by its
authority, and limited in the exercife of that very office, in
regard to which they were called *gods*, by the exprefs command of God Supreme, whom they were to confult for direction, and whofe orders they were to fulfil as his deputies.
To them, in this point of view, he oppofes himfelf as *fanctified and fent by the Father*. The fanctification meant is
evidently fomething previous to his miffion. He was thus
fanctified, as from eternity fet apart, in the council of peace,
for the work of our redemption. He was *fent* as *fanctified*.
Therefore, he exifted before his incarnation. He was alfo
fanctified, and fent by God as his *Father*. Therefore, he
is not a Son in confequence of either his fanctification, or
his miffion. Both thefe phrafes evidently refer to the
greatnefs of the work entrufted to him, the fame that he
had already fpoken of. He was confecrated and fent by
the Father, that, in human nature, he might difcharge that
office, ftill appropriated to God, of being the *Shepherd of
fouls*, ver. 1.—28.

But it is highly probable, that our Lord here fpeaks of
himfelf as the perfonal *Logos*. The whole of that revelation, formerly given to the church, proceeded from him in
this character. In the Pfalm referred to, he feems to be
the immediate fpeaker. This view is moft agreeable to
the order and conftruction of the words. For the relative
term, *ον*, tranflated *him whom*, feems naturally to refer to
ο λογος τȣ Θεȣ as its antecedent. Indeed, the words may be
literally rendered, according to their order : *If he called
them gods, to whom that Logos of God came, (and the fcripture cannot be broken) whom the Father hath fanctified and
fent into the world, fay ye, Thou blafphemeft, becaufe I faid,*

I am the Son of God? I have obſerved only one inſtance of
the relative in the accuſative, as connected with λεγω, ſignifying *of whom.* It is in chap. viii. 54. But it does not,
with equal propriety, bear the ſame ſenſe here. For the
accuſation, as repeated by Chriſt, being expreſſed in the
ſecond perſon, it would have been more natural, had the
dative been uſed; Say ye *to* him, *Thou blaſphemeſt?* According to this view, we have a ſatisfactory reaſon for the
circumſtance, of *the Word of God coming* to theſe Judges,
being ſingled out in preference to every other, by which
their inferiority might have been expreſſed. In the Ethi-
opic verſion, to which great antiquity is aſcribed, this ſenſe
is given to the paſſage : " If he called them gods, to whom
" God appeared, the Word of God was with them," &c.
This view increaſes the force of the argument : " If thoſe
" are called gods, to whom the Logos came, as having
" authority over them, ſetting them apart to the office
" of judging, and giving them ſo diſtinguiſhed a deſig-
" nation, merely as prefiguring his own character and
" work ; (and what is typically declared in ſcripture muſt
" have its full completion in the Antitype :) when this
" very perſon comes to you in human nature, as ſet
" apart, and ſent by the Father for accompliſhing the di-
" vine work of ſaving ſinners, do ye charge him with blaſ-
" phemy, becauſe he claims that ſonſhip in a proper ſenſe,
" which they could claim only in a metaphorical ; and ap-
" propriates the *truth* of that deity, which was aſcribed to
" them only, according to the *ſhadow.*"

Dr P,, ſpeaking of the inferior ſenſe of the term *God,* as
given to Moſes, ſays : " There can be no danger of our
" miſtaking the ſenſe of ſuch phraſes as theſe ; or if it were
" poſſible, our Lord himſelf has ſufficiently guarded againſt
" any miſconſtruction of them when applied to himſelf, by
" the explanation he has given of them ; informing us,
" that, if, in the language of ſcripture, *they are called gods*

I   *to*

" *to whom the word of God came*, (though, in fact, they
" were no other than mere men), he could not be guilty
" of blafphemy in calling himfelf only *the Son of God* *."
This particle *only* evidently implies that, in Dr P.'s idea,
our Lord takes a lower title to himfelf than what was given to rulers.   But, on the contrary, he calls himfelf *the
Son of God*, in contradiftinction to all who, in an inferior
fenfe, were *called gods*, and *fons of the moft High*; thus
expreffing unity of effence with the Father.   For he evidently ufes this language as equivalent to what he had formerly faid, when he called God his Father, in fo peculiar
a manner that the Jews underftood him as claiming deity.
For, though he refutes the charge of blafphemy, he does
not refufe that he *made himfelf God.*   He refutes the
charge, indeed, from a confideration which neceffarily implies his ineffable fuperiority to all creatures.   It is evident,
that the Jews were fully fatisfied that the filiation which he
claimed could, in no fenfe, belong to a creature.   For they
found their accufation on the circumftance of his being
a man, ver. 33.   Our Lord does not merely vindicate his
claim, but proceeds to eftablifh it in all the extent in which
it was underftood by his enemies.   He proves his unity of
effence with the Father from the famenefs of his operation.

Before confidering this proof, we may advert to what
our author adds concerning the former : " Now," he fays,
" if Chrift had been confcious to himfelf that he was the
" *true and very God*, and that it was of the utmoft confe-
" quence to mankind that they fhould regard him in that
" light, this was certainly a proper time for him to have
" declared himfelf, and not to have put his hearers off with
" fuch an apology as this †."   Though Jefus had ufed the
very terms mentioned, Socinians would have devifed fome
plan for evading their force.   For when he is exprefsly

---

* Appeal, p. 14.   † Ibid.

called *the true God,* they boldly refuſe that he is the ſubject ſpoken of. It was certainly moſt proper for our Lord to retain the ſame kind of language that he had formerly uſed. For, not only was this the foundation of the charge of blaſphemy, and therefore underſtood by the Jews as containing a claim of deity; but it exhibited this claim in the moſt proper light. Had he ſimply declared that he was *the true God,* his malicious opponents would have inferred that he meant to dethrone the Father. But by retaining the idea of Sonſhip, he not only aſſerted his real deity, but his diſtinct perſonality. This more immediately belonged to his work of revealing the Father. Nor could he exhibit himſelf as one *ſent,* without referring to another perſon as ſending him. Indeed, the proof which he ſubjoined, from his works, was a more inconteſtible evidence of his claiming real deity, than any ſimple declaration could have been. For though the names of God had been given to mere men, it had never been ſuppoſed that any, who were thus dignified, could perform divine works.

As the former argument depended on teſtimony, he now refers to ſenſible evidence : *If I do not the works of my Father, believe me not. But if I do, though ye believe not me, believe the works ; that ye may know and believe that the Father is in me, and I in him,* ver. 37, 38. So far from ſhewing them that they miſtook his meaning, or from denying that he was *the Son of God* in their ſenſe of the expreſſion, and *made himſelf God ;* he proceeds to prove his unity of eſſence with the Father, from the ſameneſs of his operation ; and, on this ground, he requires their faith as to the unity declared. This is the very doctrine that he had formerly taught, when he ſaid, ver. 30. *I and the Father are one.* This concluding appeal to his works, in the proof and vindication of that claim of unity with the Father, which was the foundation of the diſpute, inconteſtably demonſtrates that he did not mean unity

- of

of defign, but of power.   His enemies, inftead of being convinced that they had miftaken his meaning, were fo confirmed by what he had faid, that they immediately *fought
to take him*. But he, inftead of fhewing that they ftill mifunderftood his language, as, had this been the cafe, he certainly ought to have done, *efcaped out of their hand*,
ver. 39.

. As the Jews had been fo often enraged at Jefus, during
his miniftry, becaufe he *made himfelf God;* as on this account they had frequently fought to put him to death ;
when his *hour was come*, his condemnation' proceeded on
this very ground. The council, notwithftanding various
attempts, not having found falfe witnefs againft him ; the
high prieft, by virtue of that authority committed to him,
in matters of great importance, efpecially when proof
could be obtained in no other way, proceeded to adminifter an oath *. The inftituted form was that of adjuration ; and the pannel was to anfwer *Amen*, as a token of
his affent to the *oath and curfe*. Accordingly, the high
prieft addreffed Jefus in thefe words ; *I adjure thee by the
living God, that thou tell us whether thou be the Chrift, the
Son of God?* Jefus replied, *Thou haft faid*, Matt. xxvi.
63, 64. Thus, according to the Hebrew idiom, he declared
that he was. It was only the folemnity of the oath that
made him break filence. According to the law, when in
this manner he *heard the voice of fwearing*, he was bound
to utter the truth, Lev. v. 1. On two former occafions,
when accufed of blafphemy, though an oath was not formally tendered, he, as *the Amen*, folemnly afferted the
truth of his deity, in the very words required by the law
of adjuration †. On this occafion, it appeared to the Sanhedrim, that they had all the evidence that was neceffary.

B b 2   *The*

* Num. v. 18.—22.

† John v. 19. viii. 58. Vid. Vitring. Obf. Sacr. lib. 3. c. i. fect. 5. 6.

*The high prieſt rent his clothes, ſaying, He hath ſpoken blaſ-
phemy. What further need have we of witneſſes? behold
now, ye have heard his blaſphemy. What think ye? They
anſwered and ſaid, He is guilty of death,* ver. 65. 67. They
unanimouſly agreed in this verdict, Mark xiv. 64.

Becauſe the Jews connected theſe characters, *the Son of
God,* and *the Chriſt,* Socinians pretend that nothing more is
meant by the former, than by the latter; and that the Jews
conſidered this title, *the Son of God,* as belonging to the
Meſſiah, while they expected no other than a mere man.
Let us hear Dr P. on this point: " The Jews called it
" blaſphemy to pretend to be the Chriſt ; for when the
" high prieſt ſolemnly adjured our Lord,—that he would
" tell him *whether he was the Chriſt, the Son of God,* and
" our Lord expreſsly replies that he was the Chriſt, *then the
" high prieſt rent his clothes, ſaying, He hath ſpoken blaſ-
" phemy *.*" Our Lord's reply is the only thing offered as
proof. But Dr P. gives it quite a different turn from what
it has, as rehearſed by the plain Evangeliſt : " our Lord
" expreſsly replies that he was the Chriſt." One who did
not conſult the paſſage, would naturally ſuppoſe that our
Saviour had replied to the firſt part of the queſtion only ; or,
that he had *expreſsly* ſaid, " I am the Chriſt." But his anſwer, being a ſimple affirmative, applied to the laſt, equally
with the firſt part of the queſtion. Becauſe the Doctor
imagines that theſe terms, *the Chriſt,* and *the Son of God,* are
ſynonymous, it is going rather too far to ſay, that " our Lord
" expreſsly replies that he was *the Chriſt.*" But he is ſtill
bolder in another place. For he gives this as our Saviour's
only anſwer: " He confeſſed that he was the Chriſt *only.*"
This we ſhall attend to afterwards.

From an impartial conſideration of what is related in
the goſpel-hiſtory, and of the opinions of the Jews, as recorded in their own writings, it will clearly appear, that
there

* Famil. Illuſtr. p. 22.

there is not the leaft ground for what is afferted by Socinians, that with that people, the terms in queftion were fynonymous, and that our Lord was condemned for claiming
a chara&er, which, in their apprehenfion, belonged to a
mere man.   Indeed, it does not appear that the Jews were
accuftomed, in fpeaking of a perfon invefted with an office,
to give him two denominations, in connexion, merely expreffive of his official chara&er.   But it was very common
with them to conne&t th: name of the office with, an appellation expreffing the natural defcent of the perfon.   Of this
we have many inftances.   We read of *Jofiah, fon of Ammon, king*, Jer. i. 1. of *Zerubbabel, the fon of Shealtiel,
governor ; Jofhua, the fon of Jofedech, the high-prieft*, Hag.
i. 1. of *Joah, the fon of Afaph, the record r*, 2 Kings xviii.
18. 37. Ifa. xxxvi. 3. *&c. &c.*

The high prieft evidently marks a diftin&ion between
thefe chara&ers.   He ufes them, indeed, as both applicable
to one perfon.   But he evidently introduces the latter, as
expreffing a relation different from that expreffed by the
former : *Tell us, if thou be the Chrift, the Son of God.*   If
he does not, is not the laft expreffion a mere tautology ?   If
he referred merely to office, was not the term *Chrift* fufficient ?   Or would it not have been more natural to have added, *the Son of David ?*   For, undoubtedly, the Meffiah, in
his official chara&er, was more generally known by this
defignation*.   Is it not highly unreafonable to fuppofe that,
on this occafion, no idea of divinity was affixed to that cha-
ra&er, *the Son of God*, when, as formerly ufed by our Saviour, it had been always underftood by the Jews, as expreffing a claim of equality with God ?   It is evident that
the high prieft, in his queftion, refers to the fecond Pfalm.
For there is no other paffage, in which the two chara&ers
are conjoined.   Was it unknown to him, to the great coun-

* Matt. ix. 27. xv. 22. xx. 30. 31. Mark. x. 47. 48. Luke xviii. 38,
39, &c. &c.

.cil, or to the Jews in general, that, in this Pſalm, the Son is exhibited as the objeᵓt of that fear, faith and reliance which the ſcripture uniformly appropriates to God?

But our author endeavours to anticipate this objeᵓtion to his theory : " If Chriſt," he ſays, " had not ſatisfied the " Jews that he did not mean to make himſelf equal with " God, would they not have produced it againſt him at his " trial, when he was condemned as a blaſphemer, becauſe " he confeſſed that he was the Chriſt only * ?" When was it that he thus *ſatisfied* them? Was it when *they took up ſtones to caſt at him?* John viii. 59. Was it when they ſought to take him, after explaining the ſenſe in which he called God his Father? chap. x. 39. Does Dr P. really believe that the malicious enemies of Jeſus, who ſought falſe witneſs againſt him, were ſo candid that, though ſecretly *ſatisfied* that he did not lay claim to equality with God, they would not have taken advantage of his words, could they have found witneſſes to agree in their teſtimony? But whence is our author aſſured that they did not produce this charge againſt Jeſus? Does he know all the *things* that the *many falſe witneſſes* uttered? Is he certain, that this is not one of the articles on which their witneſs did not agree together? It is plain, indeed, that this is the very point on which they wiſhed to make him his own ac- cuſer. Thence it is highly probable, that they had pre- viouſly in vain tried every other method of proving it. They unqueſtionably conſidered his declaration in the very ſame light in which his doᵓtrine had formerly appeared. For they gave it the ſame name of *blaſphemy.*

Dr P. elſewhere propoſes another queſtion, which ſhews how much he is at a loſs for argument : " If the high " prieſt expreſſed his horror by rending his cloaths, on " Jeſus avowing himſelf to be the Meſſiah, what would he " have done if he had heard or ſuſpeᵓted, that he had made

" any

* Obſervations added to Elwall's Trial. p. 20.

" any higher pretenfions * ?" What more could he have
done? It is queftioned, if .it was lawful for the high prieft
to rend his clothes on any occafion. Could he have devifed a worfe name than *blafphemy*; or thought of a more
cruel or ignominious punifhment than crucifixion ?

The generality of the Jews, indeed, had loft all fpiritual
apprehenfions of the work of the Meffiah. Therefore, it
cannot be fuppofed that they entertained juft or confiftent
ideas concerning his filiation. But ftill their minds feem to
have been embarraffed by the fcriptural language that exhibited him as *the Son of God.* Of this we have already
produced various proofs.

It may be further obferved, that our Lord, when he made
the folemn confeffion under confideration, at the fame time
claimed the honours of deity. For he faid ; *Hereafter fhall
ye fee the Son of man fitting on the right hand of Power,
and coming in the clouds of heaven,* Matt. xxvi. 64. He claimed divine honour in a twofold refpect ; firft, by declaring
that he fhould *fit on the right hand of Power.* According to the Jews, fitting on the right hand of a Sovereign denoted communion in empire. *Power* was a term
which they frequently ufed to denote God himfelf. Thence
fitting at the right hand of Power, is the fame as fitting
at the right hand of God. But this implies communion
in power and majefty. Therefore, the infpired writer
to the Hebrews might juftly urge the effential dignity of
Jefus from this confideration : *But to which of the angels
faid he at any time, Sit on my right hand ?* chap. i. 13.

That this implies communion in power, and therefore,
unity of effence, is evident from the prophecy of Zechariah concerning the *Man whofe name is the Branch,* chap. vi.
12, 13. to which our Lord might allude †. Alfo, in the
Revelation, the throne of God and the Lamb is fpoken of

B b 4   as

as one, chap. xxii. 3. That the Jews could affix no other meaning to the language of our Saviour, than what we have given, is evident from the hiſtory of the martyrdom of Stephen, Acts vii. 55.—57.

Jeſus alſo claimed divine honour, when he ſaid ; *Ye ſhall ſee the Son of man—coming in the clouds of heaven.* Theſe words moſt naturally refer to the final judgment. This kind of language was well-known to the Jews, as expreſſive of the Divine Preſence and Majeſty. It is often uſed in the New Teſtament concerning the Meſſiah ; moſt probably in alluſion to the manner in which God manifeſted himſelf of old, at the giving of the law. He ſaid to Moſes ; *Lo I come to thee in a thick cloud, that the people may hear when I ſpeak with thee, and believe thee for ever,* Ex. xix. 9. He was pleaſed to fix on this as the token of his preſence. Thence Solomon expreſſes himſelf in this manner, *The Lord ſaid that he would dwell in the thick darkneſs,* 1 Kings viii. 12. Accordingly, we find that the appearance of the cloud was the ſign of the deſcent of JEHOVAH, both in the deſert, and in the land of promiſe, Ex. xxxiv. 5. ; 1 Kings viii. 10. Its overſhadowing the mercy-ſeat was the ſymbol of the perpetual preſence of God, firſt in the tabernacle, and afterwards in the temple. And a ſtriking ſymbol it was. For God's dominion over the clouds is an unqueſtionable evidence of his almighty power *. Therefore it is ſaid, *Aſcribe ye ſtrength unto God:—his ſtrength is in the clouds,* Pſal. lxviii. 34. When the law was given from Mount Sinai, the clouds were alſo uſed as inſtruments for the diſplay of his incomprehenſible Majeſty. Thence Moſes afterwards reminds the tribes, that when the Lord ſpake to them, *the mountain burnt with fire unto the midſt of heaven, with darkneſs, clouds and thick darkneſs,* Deut. iv. 11. To this awful manifeſtation the Iſraelites might

* Vid. Maimonid. More Nevochim, par. 1. cap. 79.

might afterwards refer; when in deſcribing the deſcent of their God, they repreſent *his pavilion round about him* as *thick clouds of the ſkies*, Pſal. xviii. 11. and ſpeak of him as *riding on a cloud*, Iſa. xix. 1. For this deſcription is appropriated to God; and it denotes that he makes the clouds, either his covering, or his chariot, as it is expreſſed Pſal. civ. 3. or both. Accordingly, the language of our Saviour may be underſtood with the ſame latitude. For while, according to Mark, he ſhall come *with* the clouds*, chap. xiv. 62. the expreſſion uſed by Matthew† may be rendered either *in* or *upon the clouds;* though the laſt is moſt literal. In the uſe of this language, our Lord evidently refers to thoſe prophecies in which he is deſcribed as *coming with the clouds of heaven,* and as ſurrounded with *clouds and darkneſs,* Dan. vii. 13. Pſal. xcvii. 2. The laſt of theſe paſſages indeed, is intimately connected with that command given to all the angels to *worſhip him*, ver. 7. It is inconceivable, that the meek and lowly Jeſus ſhould ſpeak of himſelf, or that in both Teſtaments he ſhould be deſcribed by the Spirit of inſpiration, in language appropriated to the Divine Being; unleſs, in his coming as Meſſiah, he really came to his church as that *God* whom ſhe had ſo long *waited for* in the character of a Saviour, Iſa. xxv. 9. Therefore, when it is ſaid that our Lord ſhall *come with clouds*, it denotes that, in his coming, he ſhall ſo diſplay his glorious majeſty, almighty power, and tremendous vengeance againſt his adverſaries, as inconteſtably to prove that he is *God himſelf.*

It is univerſally admitted that, in the interpretation of ſcripture, when any thing is more compendiouſly expreſſed in one paſſage, it is to be underſtood according to the fuller account given in another. Therefore, we are to underſtand what is ſaid by Matthew, concerning our Lord's trial

before

---

* Μετα των νιφιλων.   † Επι των νιφιλων.

before the Sanhedrim, according to the more circumstantial narrative of Luke. From the latter we learn, that what is thrown together by the two first Evangelists, was the subject of two distinct interrogations. It would appear that the first simply was, *Art thou the Christ?* Luke xxii. 67. To this Jesus replied, *If I tell you, you will not believe. And if I also ask you, you will not answer me.* However, as he acknowledged the obligation of the oath, he added; *Hereafter shall the Son of man sit on the right hand of Power;* or, as these words are more fully expressed elsewhere, *Hereafter shall ye see, &c.* They could not but understand this as a declaration of his being the Messiah. For both ancient and modern Jews apply that character, *the Son of man,* and the passage in Daniel to which our Lord refers, to the Messiah *. Although he acknowledged that he was *the Christ,* and appropriated to himself these honours which were foretold as belonging to him, they did not yet proceed to charge him with blasphemy. They consider all this merely as presumptive evidence, and wish for something more direct as to the full extent of his pretensions. Therefore, *then said they all, Art thou then the Son of God?* If they considered this expression as of the same meaning with the other, the question was absurd. For he had already acknowledged that he was *the Son of man,* that is, *the Christ.* But they seem to understand it very differently. For as soon as he acknowledged that he was *the Son of God,* they unanimously found him guilty of blasphemy. Thus, there seems to be no good reason to doubt that the Jews affixed an idea of dignity to this designation, which did not, in their apprehension, belong to either of the former.

There is something very singular in their change of the term. They do not say, *Art thou then the Christ,* or *the*

Son

---

* Zohar in Gen. Bemidbar, &c. See Gill on the place. Chizzouk Emounah, Par. 1. cap. 41.

Son of man? which would have been moft natural, had all
the phrafes been fynonymous; but, *Art thou then the Son of
God?* As he claimed fuch fignal honours, they wifhed to
know if he claimed them as a divine perfon.

If " the Jews called it blafphemy to pretend to be *the
" Chrift,"* why did they never exhibit this charge againft
Jefus, when he claimed this charaćter, without the other?
Why did they ordain that thofe fhould be only *put out of
the fynagogue, who fhould confefs that he was the Chrift?*
John ix. 22. Why did they not call fuch a confeffion
blafphemy? Why did not the Scribes and Pharifees in this
manner take advantage of Jefus calling himfelf *the Chrift,*
when he provoked their rage by expofing their wicked-
nefs? Mat. xxiii. 8. 10. Why did they not charge the
apoftles with this crime? For if it was blafphemy to pretend to be the Chrift, it muft have been blafphemy to acknowledge a pretender in this charaćter.

If any additional evidence be reckoned neceffary, we are
fupplied with it in the account given of our Lord's arraign-
ment at the bar of Pilate. The Jews, fuppofing, perhaps,
that a heathen would pay no regard to a charge of blafphemy, accufed Jefus of fedition, in faying that he was
himfelf Chrift a king. But Pilate acquitted him: *Ye have
brought,* he fays, *this man unto me, as one that perverteth the
people: and behold, I, having examined him before you, have
found no fault in this man, touching thofe things whereof ye
accufe him,* Luke xxiii. 2. 14. This account correfponds
with what we have in the Gofpel of John, chap. xviii.
29.—40. But, in the following chapter, he adds what had
been omitted by the other Evangelifts. After Pilate, upon
a fecond examination, had acquitted Jefus, his enemies
found it neceffary to difclofe that accufation, on the ground
of which they had themfelves already condemned him.
We have a law, fay they, *and by our law he ought to die,*

becaufe

because he made himself the Son of God, chap. xix. 7. What impreſſion did this new crimination make on the Roman Governor? *When Pilate therefore heard that ſaying, he was the more afraid.* Our Saviour's acknowledgment of his *official* character, as *king of the Jews,* (one of the well-known titles of the Meſſiah expected by that people), made little impreſſion on him. He knew that Jeſus called himſelf *Chriſt* or *Meſſiah,* Mat. xxvii. 17. 22. Luke xxiii. 2. But now he ſeems to Pilate to be accuſed as claiming a *perſonal* dignity, which he had not formerly heard of. That even this heathen underſtood the language of the Jews in this ſenſe, is evident. For *Pilate went again into the judgment-ſeat,* and propoſed a queſtion plainly implying that, in his apprehenſion, theſe words, *he made himſelf the Son of God,* did not reſpect any pretended *office,* but his *origin.* He *ſaith unto Jeſus,* WHENCE *art thou?—From thenceforth,* it is ſaid, *Pilate ſought to releaſe him,* ver. 12. He had done ſo before. But now he renews his endeavours with far greater earneſtneſs. And nothing overbalanced his fear, occaſioned by this diſcovery, but the more immediate danger of being himſelf accuſed to Cæſar.

Now, to what law did the Jews refer, when they exhibited this new charge? Certainly, to that reſpecting blaſphemy, Lev. xxiv. 10.—16. For their own language limits the reference;—*becauſe he made himſelf the Son of God.* They plainly allude to the ground of his condemnation by their council. There is not the leaſt evidence that the ancient Jews gave the name of blaſphemy to falſe prophecy. They might charge a falſe prophet with blaſphemy, if he uttered any thing of this nature. But they diſtinguiſhed the crimes.

It has been ſeen that, when Jeſus formerly declared that he was *the Son of God,* he was accuſed of blaſphemy; and that he was thus accuſed, becauſe he ſeemed to the Jews to

make

make himfelf God, although, as they imagined, no more than
a man, John x. 33. Now, as he was condemned by the Sanhedrim for this very claim, as on the fame ground they
urged his condemnation by Pilate; unlefs Dr P. can produce pofitive proof, that this expreffion, *the Son of God*,
was latterly underftood, by the enemies of Jefus, in a fenfe
totally different from what they formerly put on it; and
that, although the reafon why they formerly charged him
with blafphemy, was his *making himfelf God*, they had fo
ftrangely changed their ideas of this crime as to find him guilty of it, becaufe he claimed an office merely *human*;—
every impartial perfon muft conclude that Jefus was condemned by the Jews, becaufe he *faid that God was his
own Father, making himfelf equal with God.*

But although it were true that *the Son of God*, and *the
Chrift*, were fynonymous expreffions; as Jefus knew that
the Jews had formerly, and even on different occafions,
underftood the firft of thefe, when ufed by him, as implying a claim of fupreme Deity, and that after all his explanations they perfifted in their opinion; if, when under oath,
and about to feal his teftimony with his blood, he did not
ufe every means for convincing them that he claimed nothing more than a human character, he did not do juftice
to himfelf, he did not act a faithful part, either to his
enemies, or to his friends, nor did he guard his church a-
gainft the dreadful crime of idolatry.

In a word, as it has been already feen that Jefus, when
accufed of blafphemy on this head, perfifted in his claim
of Sonfhip, in that very fenfe in which the Jews underftood him, and proved that he was *the Son of God* from
his doing the fame works with the Father; if he be not
the Son of God by nature, as being a divine Perfon, he was
juftly condemned as a blafphemer.

Before leaving this part of the fubject, I may obferve

2 that

that even the Centurion, who fuperintended the crucifixion
of our Saviour, immediately upon his death expreffed a
full conviction of his being the Son of God. We are informed by Luke, indeed, that he faid; *Certainly this was
a righteous man,* chap. xxiii. 47. But we are not thence to
conclude, that he meant, or that he faid, nothing more than
that Jefus was innocent of the crime for which he had been
condemned. It muft previoufly be proved, not only that
the Chrift, and *the Son of God,* are fynonymous expreffions;
but that *the Son of God,* and *a righteous man,* are fo too.
For the Centurion faid; *Truly this was the Son of God,* or
as the words may be rendered, *This was truly the Son of
God,* Matt. xxvii. 54. Matters being fo ordered by the
Spirit of infpiration, that what is not fo fully recorded in
one gofpel, is to be learned from another; from a comparifon of the different accounts of Matthew and Luke,
it is moft natural to conclude, that the Centurion at firft expreffed his perfuafion of our Saviour's innocence; and then,
perhaps in confequence of the reflections of *thofe that were
with him,* declared his conviction of the divinity of the
fufferer. The circumftances that induced him to this confeffion, were not fuch as could have been expected, although
a mere man had fuffered wrongfully. *The earthquake, and
the things that were done,* viz. the preternatural darknefs,
the rending of the rocks, and opening of graves, are mentioned by Matthew. But the circumftance peculiarly marked, as making the ftrongeft impreffion on the Centurion,
is the proof which Jefus gave of his being in full ftrength
in the very article of death. This officer, who moft probably had feen many executions of the fame kind, had
always obferved that the ftrength of the fufferer was gra-
dually wafted, fo that before expiring he was incapable of
the leaft exertion. But when he faw that Jefus *fo cried out,*
that is, as previoufly expreffed, *with a loud voice, and gave*

up

up the ghoft, he, faid, *Truly this man was the Son of God,*
Mark xv. 39. As Jefus expired, while his natural ftrength
was unabated, the Centurion feems to have concluded that
his death was a voluntary act, and not the effect of his fufferings.

—

C H A P. III.

Of the Teftimony of Jefus himfelf, concerning his Sonfhip.

WE fhould now inquire, in what fenfe our Lord himfelf called God his Father, or claimed the relation
of a Son. What belongs to this head has been in a great
meafure anticipated on the laft. The gofpel-hiftory, however, affords various proofs of the meaning and extent of
this claim, diftinct from thofe already illuftrated.

1. Jefus reprefents himfelf as a Son, and as beloved of
the Father, *before* his *miffion.* Thus, in the parable of the
vineyard, he fays ; *Having yet therefore one Son, his well-*
beloved, he fent him alfo unto them, Mark xii. 6. Parabo-
lical hiftory, indeed, does not, in all its circumftances, admit of a ftrict interpretation. But this is abfolutely neceffary with refpect to thofe which conftitute the proper fubject of the parable. Now, as the fubject of that referred
to, is, the infinite love of God manifefted to his ancient
people, notwithftanding their continued unworthinefs, in
fending his Son to them ; and the greatnefs of their guilt
in rejecting him ; unlefs it be underftood that God had a
Son, an only Son, who was the object of his love, and
effentially his heir, before he was fent, there is not the leaft
propriety in the parable. The diftinction between him
and the fervants is loft. The great evidence of the love
of the lord of the vineyard, in fending this *one fon, his*

I   *well-*

well-beloved, disappears. We can perceive no. juft reafon
for afcribing to God, after the manner of man, a rational
ground of hope, that the hufbandmen would' *reverence* this
laft meffenger, notwithftanding their rejection of all who
preceded him. In a word, if the Son be not effentially
fuperior to all the other meffengers, that confideration, which
the parable feems defigned to point out, as conftituting the
great guilt of thefe hufbandmen, and as expofing them to divine vengeance more than any thing they had formerly done,
is found to be a mere illufion.

2. He reveals himfelf as a Son *incomprehenfible* to all
creatures. *No one knoweth the Son but the Father*, Mat. xi.
27. Did we confider thefe words as refpecting the *degree*
of knowledge, they would illuftrate the imperfection of
that of the moft eminent faints. But they efpecially refer
to the *kind* of knowledge. Paul, much as he knew of the
love of Chrift, declares that it *paffeth knowledge*, Eph. iii.
19. Our Saviour's language alfo particularly denotes the
incomprehenfiblenefs of the object. Therefore it is thus
expreffed in Luke, *No one knoweth* who *the Son is, but the
Father*, chap. x. 22. His effence is a myftery to every creature. His mode of fubfiftence, as the Son, is equally a
myftery. Had he been merely Jefus the fon of Mary, or
had he been the fon of Jofeph, as many perfuade themfelves; would not his prefumption have been unparalleled,
in fpeaking in this manner?

3. Our Lord declares that he is a Son who perfectly
knows the *nature* of the Father. *No one knoweth the Father, fave the Son*, Mat. xi. 27. This may be viewed in
connection with what is faid, John i. 18. *No one hath feen
God at any time : the only begotten—hath declared* him, or,
hath acted the part of an interpreter. Thefe expreffions, as ·
well as that already confidered, refpect, not merely the degree, but the very nature of the knowledge. The language

guage excludes all creatures, angels as well as men; They may have fome imperfect ideas of the Father. But ουδεις *no one*, no creature of any order, *hath feen God.* All others know him by reflection from his works, or by revelation. The Son alone knows 'him by intuition; being intimately acquainted with his nature, perfections, purpofes and operations. Whatever juft apprehenfions we have of the Father, are from the Son: *No one knoweth the Father, fave he to whomfoever the Son will reveal him.* Our Saviour's language does not merely deny a perfect knowledge of the Father, but any true knowledge of him, except in this way; efpecially as it is recorded by Luke, *No one knoweth* WHO *the Father is*, &c. chap. x. 22. We have the fame declaration elfewhere; *Not that any one hath feen the Father, fave he who is of God*, that is, by eternal generation, *he hath feen the Father*, John vi. 46. Our Lord does not merely affert, that he knows the Father in a way different from that of every other, but that he knows him as perfectly as he is known by the Father: *As the Father knoweth me, even fo know I the Father*, John x. 15. In what manner foever the Father knows the Son, thefe words, as well as thofe formerly mentioned, neceffarily imply that in the felf-fame manner the Son knows the Father. Otherwife our Lord hath expreffed himfelf fo as to expofe his difciples to the moft dangerous error. Indeed, this perfect knowledge of the Father is mentioned by Jefus as the foundation and evidence of his perfect knowledge of his fheep, ver. 14. How could he know who were the objects of the Father's eternal love, how could he diftinguifh them in all places whither they were fcattered, and gather them in all their fucceffive generations, efpecially as they conftitute a *multitude which no man can number*, unlefs he perfectly knew the Father; or, in other words, unlefs his knowledge were infinite? If, then, Jefus declared that there was

ſo wide a difference between his knowledge and that of e-
very other, that he knew the Father as perfectly as he was
known by him ; he, in the moſt ſtriking manner, exhibited
himſelf as a Son partaking of the ſame divine nature.

⋅ 4. Jeſus claims the honour of being a Son who *doth all
the works* of his Father.   This we have already ſeen in general, when conſidering his reply to the charge of blaſphemy.   For he ſays ; *What things ſoever the Father doth,
theſe alſo doth the Son likewiſe,* John v. 19.   But though a
general declaration of this would be a ſufficient ground for
faith, our Lord is pleaſed to deſcend to particulars.   He
proclaims his power to communicate life to the dead :
*For as the Father raiſeth up the dead and quickeneth them,
even ſo the Son quickeneth,* ver. 21.   Now, it is *God who
quickeneth the dead,* Rom. iv. 17.   *Unto God the Lord belong
the iſſues from death,* Pſal. lxviii. 20.   Jeſus alſo claims the
work of judgment.   *For the Father judgeth no man, but
hath committed all judgment unto the Son,* John v. 22.   Whether we underſtand theſe words of the final judgment,
which is evidently meant, ver. 27. or of the ſeparation
which he makes, by the goſpel, of his ſheep from the reſt
of the world ; the argument is the ſame.   If Jeſus be
judge, either his ſentence is definitive, or it is not.   If definitive, he is the Supreme Judge, and therefore God.   For
he is undoubtedly ſupreme, from whoſe ſentence there lies
no appeal.   If not ; *all judgment is* not *committed* to the Son.
That is not true which Jeſus hath ſaid, *The Father judgeth
no man.*   For he muſt judge thoſe who complain of error
in the judgment of a creature.   There muſt be two judges ;
the one human, the other divine : whereas, the ſcripture
uniformly ſpeaks of one only.   It alſo follows, that the
day of the Lord Jeſus is not *the laſt day.*   Juſtice requires
that there ſhould be another trial.

But it cannot be ſaid with any ſemblance of reaſon, that

a mere man acts as the delegate of God, in the work of judgment. He would be totally unfit for it. How could he know, not only all the words and 'actions, but all the thoughts of men? Although a mere man should be suppofed to have a communicated knowledge of the heart; yet this being limited and gradual, as all communications to a creature muft be, could not qualify him for being Judge of the world. For he who is fo, muft know all things at once, and be able, by one intuitive glance, certainly to diftinguifh the goats from the fheep. Socinians, therefore, while they afcribe all judgment to the Son, involuntarily afcribe deity to him. For what they grant neceffarily fuppofes omnifcience.

But indeed, God hath precluded himfelf, by his own word, from employing a mere creature, how well qualified foever he be fuppofed, in the work of judgment. *God is the judge,* Pfal. lxxv. 7. *The dead, fmall and great, ftand before God,* Rev. xx. 12. *God is judge himfelf,* Pfal. l. 6. Therefore, it cannot be faid, that Jefus acts as a mere inftrument. In this cafe, he would not deferve the name of Judge. But we have a decifive proof of the truth of what is afferted, from the end for which judgment is committed to him. It is, *that all men fhould honour the Son, even as they honour the Father,* ver. 23. This language neceffarily denotes all that honour which belongs to the Father; as may be afterwards demonftrated. But if fo, how irrational is it to imagine that one fhould be employed merely as a deputy for this end! When men employ fubftitutes, is it not rather for maintaining their own honour? But if a prince fhould refign the whole exercife of judgment into the hands of another, with this exprefs declaration that he was to have the fame honour as himfelf, and that this was the very defign of the refignation, would not every one juftly infer, that it was his will that the other fhould be confidered as his equal?

If theſe words be underſtood of that gracious diſtinction which our Lord makes, as to all whom the Father hath given him, by means of the Goſpel; ſtill they demonſtrate his deity. For, as has been ſeen on the laſt proof, he alone is qualified for this work, who perfectly knows the purpoſes of the Father; and no one can thus know him, unleſs he be of the ſame eſſence.

The work accompliſhed in this ſeparation, is itſelf divine. Thus Jeſus deſcribes it; *The hour—now is, when the dead ſhall hear the voice of the Son of God: and they that hear ſhall live,* ver. 25. The quickening of dead ſouls is meant; as it is elſewhere ſaid, *You hath he quickened, who were dead in treſpaſſes and ſins,* Eph. ii. 1. But this is as really the work of God as raiſing thoſe who are literally dead: and the alluſion evidently ſuppoſes this. It is *God who commanded the light to ſhine out of darkneſs, who ſhines in our hearts.* The Goſpel is employed as the mean. But of itſelf it is totally inadequate to the end. Indeed, it is committed to men for this very purpoſe, that the work may appear to be God's. *But we have this treaſure in earthen veſſels, that the excellency of the power may be of God, and not of us,* 2 Cor. iv. 6, 7. When faith is wrought in the heart, it is by *an exceeding greatneſs of power,* which has no parallel, ſave that which God the Father *wrought in Chriſt, when he raiſed him again from the dead,* Eph. i. 19, 20. God appeals to this ſpiritual reſurrection as a convincing proof of his infinite power: *Ye ſhall know that I am the Lord,* or JEHOVAH, *when I have opened your graves,—and ſhall put my Spirit in you,* Ezek. xxxvii. 13, 14. Now, Jeſus aſſures us, that all this is effected by his voice. It gives life: and this life is communicated by him, not as an inſtrument, but as a primary agent. Therefore he adds, as the reaſon of his claiming this power: *For as the Father hath life in him-*
ſelf:

self: so hath he given to the Son to have life in himself, ver. 26.

'These words have been generally understood, as referring only to the deity of Christ, and as expressing what has been called *the communication of the divine essence* to him. But, in my apprehension, this language, as it has not the sanction of scripture, conveys an idea inconsistent with the general tenor of its doctrine. It seems very plain, that Jesus here speaks of himself immediately with respect to his mediatory character. Every where else, when language of this kind is used, it denotes dispensation. This gift is also mentioned in the closest connexion with that of judgment, which evidently respects him as Mediator. For it immediately follows ; *And hath given him authority to execute judgment also, because he is the Son of man,* ver. 27

But whatever difference there may be in the immediate application of the words, they necessarily imply, that *the Son hath life* as really in himself as its fountain, and as completely in his power, *as the Father.* Whatever the phrase, *in himself,* signifies in the one case, it must signify in the other. The mode of expression gives no countenance to the absurd doctrine of a derived deity. For it is not said that the Father *hath given life to the Son, that he might have it in himself;* but that he hath *given* to the Son that he might *have life in himself.* The term εδωκε *given,* does not seem to refer to the *life* itself, but to the manner of *having* it. The Father hath conceded to the Son, that he should *have, hold,* or *possess* this life, in his whole person as Godman, and that in this character he should confer it on others. This could only be by an act of concession or dispensation. For, though the life itself essentially belongs to the Son, as to the divine nature, equally with the Father ; yet he hath no right to hold this life in human nature, or sovereignly to dispense it in an inferior character,

without

without a grant on the part of the Father, to whom he hath voluntarily subjected himself.

. What our Lord afferts is simply this, that the Father hath granted to him that, in a new relation, he should hold and communicate that life which properly belongs to him as the Son. It is vain for Socinians to pretend that Jefus here speaks of himfelf as *the Son of man* in their fenfe, that is, as a mere man. For this very grant neceffarily fuppofes the fupreme Deity of its object. Were Jefus a mere man he might *have life.* But with no propriety could it be faid, that he had *life in himfelf.* Unlefs he were God as well as man, how could he have it *as the Father hath ?*

5. It hath been already obferved, that our Lord, in reafoning with the Jews, claims the fame *manner* of working with the Father. This requires a little more attention. If *the Son quickeneth whom he will,* John v. 21. he hath this power, either by donation, or effentially. He cannot, as a mere creature, have this power by donation. For, to fuppofe that God would confer on a creature the power of acting fovereignly, would be to fuppofe that he renounced his own Deity. For a creature, vefted with power to act entirely according to his own pleafure, would be no longer dependent and accountable; the idea of fubmiffion to the will of a fuperior being neceffarily implied in that of dependence, and dependence being the foundation of refponfibility. Therefore, a fovereign and independent creature, is a contradiction in terms. But if this right effentially belong to the Son, he is true God. For fovereignty is an unalienable prerogative of deity. *Our God hath done whatfoever he pleafed ;—faying, I will do all my pleafure,* Pfal. cxv. 3. Ifa. xlvi. 10. *None can ftay his hand, or fay unto him, What doft thou?* Dan. iv. 35. But if the Son be effentially diftinct from the Father, he may fay

untq

unto him, *What dost thou?* For he is equally sovereign with the Father. He quickeneth *even so* as the Father doth. Therefore, we must either suppose the existence of two distinct independent principles, or grant that the Father and Son are essentially one.

Indeed, the Son quickens those only whom the Father hath given him, John xvii. 2. But this affords no proof that the will of the Son is not equally sovereign with that of the Father; but, on the contrary, shew that it is, by demonstrating a perfect identity of will. For, as nothing in one part of scripture can disprove the truth of what is plainly taught in another; the one declaration is not to be viewed in opposition to the other, but both must be understood in their connection. If, therefore, *the Son quickeneth whom he will, even as* the Father; and at the same time quickeneth those only whom the Father wills to be quickened; the reason must be, that Father and Son have essentially one will. To say, that *the Son quickeneth whom he will*, because, as a creature, his will is perfectly subjected to that of God, would be to make the Holy Scripture a mere play of words. For in this case, it would have been shameless arrogance in a servant to have spoken of his own will. His language ought to have been; " As the Father quickeneth, " so the Son quickeneth whom *the Father* will." Were a subject, because he implicitly obeyed his lord, to say that he did whatsoever himself pleased; especially if, in this respect, he should compare his own conduct with his; saying, " As " my lord taxes, condemns, and pardons, even so I tax, " condemn, and pardon whom I will;" would not his sovereign account him, either a madman, or a traitor?

6. Jesus exhibits himself as a Son entitled to the *same honour* with the Father *The Father hath committed all judgment to the Son: that all men should honour the Son, even as they honour the Father,* John v. 22. 23. Socinians have

been

been greatly ftumbled as to this point. They do not merely contradict each other : but there are various in-ftances of the fame writer contradicting himfelf. Socinus, and the moft of his followers in Poland, maintained that the Son was to be worfhipped, even as the Father. But the generality of their fucceffors have denied this ; finding the impoffibility of giving any plaufible reply to the argu-ments of their opponents in proof of the deity of Chrift, while themfelves grant that he is entitled to the worfhip of God Supreme.   Dr P. fays of the text under confideration, that *even as* fignifies *as well as* the Father; adding, " The " fame word is ufed where it can have no other fenfe, in " John xvii. 23. *And haft loved them as thou haft loved me ;* " that is, not in the fame degree, but *likewife* *." But where is the proof that this particle can have no other fenfe? Is our author's affertion fufficient? How can he, according to his principles, fhew that the degree of the Father's love to believers is not the fame as of that to Jefus? Certainly, this affertion is not in a ftate of the moft perfect concord with what we have in the Illuftration im-mediately preceding, that, " whatever be the union between " the Father and the Son, his difciples are capable of it " with refpect to them both." But how *capable*, if pre-vented by an inferior degree of love on the part of God? However, it rather favours of abfurdity, to fpeak of degrees with refpect to the love, or any perfection of the divine nature.   All his love muft be allowed to be infinite ; un-lefs our author pleafe to avail himfelf of a doctrine which Socinians have been long charged with, that this is more than can be afferted of God himfelf. But if any fhould choofe to fay, that Jefus does not *here* fpeak of the love of the Father to him as his eternal Son, but as Head of the Church, in which refpect he and all the members are viewed as one Chrift (1 Cor. xii. 12.); the Doctor could

not

---

* Famil Illuftr. p. 24.

not conſiſtently objeƈt to the explanation, or eaſily prove a difference as to the degree of love.

But, though it were admitted that *as* denotes *likeneſs* only, with reſpeƈt to love, nothing more could be inferred, than that the word καθως does not *always* point out *equality*; which no one ever thought of aſſerting.   When uſed as to ſubjeƈts different in nature, it ſignifies reſemblance only. But, with reſpeƈt to thoſe of the ſame nature, it denotes perfeƈt equality.   Now, it is evidently uſed in this ſenſe here.   For, as we have already proved, our Lord has previouſly aſſerted, in the ſtrongeſt terms, his unity of eſſence with the Father, as manifeſted by unity of power and operation *.

After quoting theſe words, *He that honoureth not the Son, honoureth not the Father who ſent him*, the Doƈtor ſays; " This very laſt clauſe ſufficiently ſhews that the honour " to which Chriſt is entitled is not on account of what he " is, or has, *of himſelf*, but on account of what he derives " from God, as his ambaſſador †."   This clauſe, indeed, proves that he has ſuch a miſſion as does not derogate in the leaſt from his eſſential dignity, that he comes veſted with all the majeſty of the divine nature. But it can never prove, that he derives his title to this honour from his miſſion.   Were a ſovereign to ſend his own ſon, the partner of his throne, on an embaſſy of peace to rebels, informing them that, if they did not honour the illuſtrious ambaſſador, they did not honour himſelf who ſent him ; it would be ſtrange reaſoning thence to infer, that the prince was entitled to no honour but what he derived from his charaƈter as an ambaſſador.   This is, indeed, the amount of our author's reaſoning.   But Jeſus is not merely ſent, but ſent as a Son.   The work aſſigned him is particularly deſcribed,

not

* Vid. Glaſſii Philol. lib. iii. t. 5. can. 27. p. 1010, 1011.

† Famil. Illuſtr. p. 24, 25.

not as the foundation, but as the evidence of that honour to which he is entitled. Did the Father mean that the Son should be honoured only in an inferior degree, he would assign him work suited to an inferior nature only ; his performance of which would be no temptation to give that honour to the ambassador, which is supposed to belong to him alone who sends. But the work committed to the Son is proper to God only. It is his essential prerogative to quicken the dead, Rom. iv. 17. to judge the world, Psal. l. 6. to give eternal life, Psal. lxviii. 20. If, therefore, it be the express design of the Father, in committing certain work to the Son, to be performed by him in our nature, that he be honoured, in consequence of it, according to the nature of the work, which is undoubtedly the plain meaning of our Saviour's language; if, at the same time, the Father send him to do the same kind of work with himself, and in the same manner, nay, the self-same work, ver. 19. 21.; we justly conclude, that it must be the will of the Father, that he should have the same kind and degree of honour.

Had Jesus meant to inform his hearers, that his mission was the only foundation of his title to honour, he certainly would have used these terms which were not liable to mistake, as evidently referring to his official character only. But as he retains that very language which had been understood by them with respect to essence, it clearly shews that he proclaimed this as the proper foundation of his title. By connecting his delegated with his essential character, and also with that of the Father, in these words, *He that honoureth not the Son, honoureth not the Father who hath* SENT *him,* he tacitly assigns the reason of his original dignity being denied; his humiliation being the great obstacle to the carnal mind. Thus, he also shews the great aggravation of the guilt of those who for this reason reject him.

him. For the work, for which he was ſent, contains an illuſtrious proof of his ſupreme Deity; and the rejection of him as *a Son given*, is a denial, not only of the authority, but of the very eſſence of the Father, and therefore, of all true worſhip.

If the Son be not honoured as truly God, the *authority* of the Father is denied. For when he ſent his Son, it was that he might be *reverenced* in this character; and that men, convinced by his divine works, might give him the ſame honour with the Father. The *eſſence* of the Father is alſo denied. For then only is he honoured as a Father, when it is acknowledged that, according to the preceding deſcription, he hath a *proper* Son, who works in the ſame *manner*, with the ſame *extent* and *duration*, who indeed performs the very ſame works with himſelf. If, in all our profeſſed adoration, we confeſs not this eſſential dignity, we do not worſhip the true God, but an idol. If we approach not to him by ſuch a Son as our *way*, we cannot *come to the Father*.

Unleſs *all that honour* be meant, which belongs to the Father, we can ſee no good reaſon for his committing *all judgment* to the Son. A partial truſt would have been abundantly ſufficient for inſuring an inferior degree of honour. But why does our author ſpeak of *degree?* When he quotes John xvii. 23. and explains καθως as there ſignifying a different degree of love, it would appear to be his meaning that the term ſhould have the ſame ſenſe in the paſſage before us. If, therefore, the honour due to the Son differ from that of the Father, in degree only, the Son muſt be entitled to divine honour. But how ſhall this honour be denominated? Is it λατρεια or δκλεια?

However, as Dr P. elſewhere ſpends a ſection in endeavouring to prove that Jeſus is not the object of prayer, it is moſt natural to ſuppoſe that he has quoted John xvii. 23.

becauſe

becaufe he could difcover no other way of avoiding the force of καθως. He could not explain it, as there ufed, of a love differing in *kind*, without acknowledging a difference of effence between Chrift and his difciples. He applies it to the point in hand, either without obferving, or without wifhing that his reader fhould obferve, the total change of the fenfe. For, if the title of Jefus be founded folely on his character as an ambaffador, the honour muft differ in *kind*. The one is the honour due to God; the other that due to a creature. If fo, how is the fame word ufed in fo clofe a connexion, and even repeatedly? How has the fpirit of infpiration left no antidote againft idolatry? If the one honour effentially differ-from the other, how is that which belongs to the Son to be defined?

As our author denies the worfhip of Jefus, he forfakes his predeceffors as idolaters. Of Socinus he fays, that " he diftinguifhed himfelf fo much in difcovering the original " doctrine of the proper humanity of Chrift, as to give occa- " fion to all who now hold that doctrine to be called by his " name *." But had it been in the power of that herefiarch to have given Dr P.'s character, it would not have been fo favourable. He would have faid; " You have rightly judged " that, in my eftimation, it is very probable, that he who " does not incline, or who does not dare, to pray to our Lord " Jefus Chrift, fcarcely deferves the name of a Chriftian : " with this difference however, that it is not *fcarcely*, but " that there is no room for this referve; and that this does " not appear to me merely *probable*, but that I am fully " perfuaded of it." For thefe are his very words, when giving his judgment of one who fhould deny divine worfhip to Jefus †. The Racovian Catechifm, compofed by Smalcius,

---

* Hift. of Corrupt. vol. i. p. 271.

† Recte igitur exiftimafti, mihi quoque verifimile videri, eum qui Dominum Iefum Chriftum invocare non vult, aut non audet, vix Chriftiani

cius, which may be confidered as the confeffion of the Polifh Socinians, exhibits the fame judgment. " *Q.* What
" do you think of thofe who do not call upon Chrift; nor
" think that he ought to be invoked? *A.* I reckon that
" they are not Chriftians, fince in reality they have not
" Chrift *." Nor were thefe vain words. For, when Fran-
cis David denied the worfhip of Chrift, Socinus and his
followers rejected him as a vile heretic; and carried matters fo far, as to pay no regard to him while perifhing in
prifon.

Thus, it appears that the belief of this article was, with
them, not merely a term of communion, but of fuch importance that they accounted it a profanation of the Chriftian name, to give it to any who held the contrary.
Here, then, is an event among profeffed Chriftians, at
which heathens would have blufhed. *Hath a nation changed their gods, which are yet no gods* †? But the Socinian
church hath done fo. Once, fhe worfhipped a God by nature, and another by office. Now, fhe hath renounced the latter, acknowledging that this worfhip was idolatry. While
vainly pretending that fhe alone holds the unity of God,
fhe hath evidently loft her own.

7. Jefus reveals himfelf as a Son in fo peculiar and exalted a fenfe, that the *glory* arifing from the *works* proper
to God, is common to him with the Father. Thus, when
the difciples told him that Lazarus was fick, he replied ;
*This ficknefs is not unto death, but for the glory of
God, that the Son of God may be glorified thereby*, John.
xi. 4. It is the evident meaning of thefe words, that God
had permitted this affliction for his own glory, and would
fo.

tiani nomine dignum effe: nifi quod non modo vix, fed ne vix quidem,
et non modo verifimile id mihi videtur, fed perfuafiffimum mihi eft. Refpons. ad Nemojevium, Ep. i.

    * De Præcept. Chrifti, cap. i. ap. Owen's Vindic. p. 404.
    † Jer. ii. 11.

so over-rule it, that this end should be gained by a striking display of divine power in the resurrection of Lazarus. But the mode of expression clearly declares that
the glory of the Father, and of the Son, is one. Perhaps,
it may be said, that our Saviour means to teach, that all the
glory, which immediately redounded to him from his miraculous works, was designed ultimately to accrue to the
Father; as it is pretended that he did these works merely
by a delegated power. But the very structure of the words
repels this objection. For then they ought to have been
thus disposed; " This sickness is—for the glory of the Son
of God, that God might be glorified thereby." Did a
mere servant say, " I do this work for the glory of my
" master, that I may be glorified thereby," would not
every one, who heard him, conclude, that he proposed his
own glory as the proper and ultimate end of his work ?

Thus it appears, that *the glory of God* is not assigned as
the ultimate, but as the general end; and that *the glory of
the Son of God* is not mentioned in subordination to the
other, but as that end more especially in view. This is
confirmed by the manner in which our Lord designs himself on this occasion. He seldom expressly calls himself
the Son of God. But he does so here; as intimating that
by his miraculous works, he was glorified *as* the Son of
God, *powerfully declared* to be of the same essence with
the Father;; and also, that when thus glorified, God, essentially considered, was glorified, not ultimately and deriva-
tively, but immediately and directly.

8. He reveals himself as a Son who is equally the object of *faith* with the Father. Thus he saith to Nicodemus; *He that believeth not is condemned already; because
he hath not believed in the Name of the only begotten Son of
God,* John iii. 18. The *Name* of Christ often signifies Christ
himself, in the same manner as this language is used concerning

cerning God. As all the names of the Hebrews were fig-
nificative, God, in addreffing that people, very frequently,
adopts this phrafeology, to denote that manifeftation which
he had made of himfelf, by particular defignations, defcrip-.
tive of his attributes or works. Therefore, *believing in the.
Name* of Chrift, fignifies faith in him, according to his re-.
vealed character. This is to be underftood, fometimes more.
generally, and fometimes more particularly. When any.
fpecial character of Jefus is mentioned, it is moft natural to.
think that faith in his name is to be viewed as, in this.
inftance, efpecially operating with refpect to that character. Thus, when we read of *believing in the Name of
the only begotten Son of God*, it naturally fuggefts the idea
of faith in Chrift, *as* the Son of God, *as* a begotten
Son, *as* only-begotten, and *as* of the fame nature with the.
Father. Unlefs particular expreffions are to be underftood
with this particularity, it is vain to fay, as almoft every.
writer has done on the fubject, that the Name of God or
Chrift refpects the revealed character, or in other words, the.
fcriptural defignation of either.

Socinians endeavour to refift the force of this argument,
by diftinguifhing between the primary, and the fecondary,
object of faith. They make the Father the primary object, as being the firft and fupreme caufe of falvation; and
the Son the fecondary, as being only the inftrumental caufe.
They affert that faith in the Father terminates in him as
its ultimate caufe; but that faith in the Son does not ter-
minate in him, but by him is directed to God as its proper
object; as it is faid that *by him we believe in God that
raifed him up from the dead*, 1 Pet. i. 21 *. We grant indeed, that faith immediately refpects Jefus Chrift as Mediator; and that it is by him as its author, and alfo as its
glorious medium, that it terminates on God the Father.
God, effentially confidered, is originally the proper object

of

---

* Socin. cont. Viek. cap. 4.

of faith. But the infinite moral diſtance between him and the ſinner renders the intervention of a Mediator neceſſary. Otherwiſe, God, being *a conſuming fire,* could never be the objeĉt of ſaving faith to any tranſgreſſor. It reſpeĉts the Mediator as our *way;* not as if he were eſſentially inferior to the Father, but becauſe he has become œconomically nearer to us; not becauſe he is unworthy to be its ſupreme objeĉt, but becauſe it could never reach this objeĉt without him. The very circumſtance of his being the immediate objeĉt, is a certain proof of his being the objeĉt of faith in a proper ſenſe. Faith could not reſpeĉt Chriſt even as Mediator, did not his official charaĉter and work neceſſarily ſuppoſe deity. For it reſpeĉts him, in this charaĉter, as re-vealing all that we can know concerning the nature, per-feĉtions, purpoſes and gracious operations of its ultimate objeĉt; and as claiming faith on the ground of his own teſtimony.

Even that faith which terminates on the Father, does not reſpeĉt him excluſively, or as if he were the only divine perſon entitled to it. For it terminates on him, becauſe he, under a federal charaĉter, ſuſtains the honour of offend-ed deity. This order of faith flows entirely from œco-nomy, and from mutual conſent among the adorable per-ſons; the mode of worſhip being regulated according to the mode of operation in the work of redemption. That very faith, which terminates on the Father in his federal charaĉter, as really reſpeĉts the Son and Spirit eſſentially conſidered.

It has been obſerved in reply, that we can no more infer the deity of Chriſt from his being repreſented as the ob-jeĉt of faith, than that of Moſes, or of the prophets, from the ſame circumſtance; as they, in an improper ſenſe, are ſaid to have been *believed,* Ex. xiv. 31. 2 Chron. xx. 20. Faith, as direĉted towards God, is undoubtedly the higheſt

aĉt

act of worſhip; including a variety of inward and ſpiritual acts of the moſt exalted kind. If it appear that, in this view, it reſpects our Lord Jeſus Chriſt, it muſt follow that he is its object in a ſenſe totally different from that in which we are to underſtand what is ſaid of Moſes or the prophets.

But Jeſus ſpeaks of himſelf as the object which faith embraces, through the inſtrumentality of others, John xvii. 20. It muſt therefore, be abſurd to ſuppoſe that he is himſelf a mere inſtrument. Neither Moſes, nor the prophets, exhibited their teſtimony as the foundation of faith. They ſtill referred to divine authority; prefacing their declarations with a *Thus ſaith the Lord.* But Jeſus ſpeaks in his own name, and requires faith in his teſtimony, on the ground of his own authority, John iv. 41. xiv. 11. Therefore, he ordinarily ſpeaks with the greateſt poſſible ſolemnity, in the firſt perſon; *Amen, Amen, I ſay unto you.* True faith, as we have ſeen, fixes on the very Name of the Son of God, as every way worthy to be its proper object. It is a ſubjection of the whole ſoul to him; a captivation of every thought to the obedience of Chriſt, 2 Cor. x. 5. a ſubmiſſion of our will to his, Pſal. xlv. 5. cx. 3. an acknowledgment of his ſovereign authority over conſcience, Mat. xxviii. 20. and a recognizance of his right to ſupreme affection, Luke xiv. 26. Faith is a *fleeing for refuge* to him as *the hope ſet before us,* Heb. vi. 18. a firm perſuaſion of his *ability to ſave to the uttermoſt,* chap. vii. 25. and alſo of the ſovereignty and ſufficiency of his *grace* for this end, Acts xv. 11. 1 Tim. i. 14.—16. It is a *reſt* of ſoul on him, Mat. xi. 28, 29. and an unbounded *confidence* in him, Eph. i. 12, 13. Mat. xii. 21. Faith reſpects Jeſus as its *author* and *finiſher,* Heb. xii. 1. as the very ſpring and ſupport of ſpiritual life, Gal. ii. 20. and as the giver of eternal, John x. 28. It is a commitment of the ſoul to him,

Acts vii. 59. and this cannot be *in well-doing,* unleſs he be *a faithful Creator,* 1 Pet. iv. 19. In a word, it is a ſurrender of the whole perſon to him as his property, and a conſtant propoſal of his glory as the ſupreme end, whether in life, or in death, 2 Cor. viii. 5. Rom. xiv. 8. Phil. i. 20. Let any man in his ſenſes judge, if there be a creature, either in heaven, or in earth, worthy of ſuch a faith?

9. Jeſus reveals himſelf as a Son who hath the ſame *name,* and therefore the ſame eſſence, and a right to the ſame honour, with the Father. For he commands his apoſtles to *baptize in the name of the Father, and of the Son, and of the Holy Ghoſt,* Mat. xxviii. 19. Theſe words have been underſtood in a great variety of ſenſes. But they can admit of no ſenſe, that does not imply the deity of all the three Perſons mentioned. Are they not all invoked in the ordinance of baptiſm? This, then, is a ſolemn act of worſhip, of which the Son is as directly the object as the Father. Does baptiſm denote a conſecration or dedication of the perſon to Father, Son, and Spirit? And is not the perſon baptized as really devoted to the Son, as to the Father and Spirit? If not, the New Teſtament Church is ſo ill-regulated, that, even in her moſt ſolemn ordinances, there is no guard againſt idolatry. Is baptiſm a ſolemn initiation into a profeſſion of faith in the Father, Son and Holy Ghoſt? And is there any thing in the command itſelf, or in the circumſtances connected with it, containing the moſt diſtant inſinuation, that the Son is not as properly the object of faith as the Father or Spirit? Is it his having the whole *power* of the godhead committed to him as Mediator? ver. 18. But if this be the caſe, is he not worthy of the ſame faith with the Father? Is it meant that *all nations* ſhould be turned from the worſhip of them who *by nature are no gods,* to be made the diſciples of a mere man? ver. 19. Is their faith to produce univerſal obedience? And is it,

never-

neverthelefs, faith in a man like themfelves? Is the *pre-fence* of a mere man all the encouragement of the fervants of Jefus, in all their labours and fufferings? Or, can a mere man be prefent with them at all times, and in all places? ver. 20.

Baptizing in, or rather, *into the name of the Father,* &c. cannot fignify the mere mention of thefe *defignations* by which the adorable Perfons are diftinguifhed from each other. The *name* is evidently fomething in which they all agree. For it is fpoken of as one *. It is natural to think that, if our Lord had not meant to exhibit his effence as the fame with that of the Father, he would have repeated thefe words, *into the name.* He obferves this method, where there is unfpeakably lefs danger of miftake. De-claring his work as Mediator, he fays; *I will write upon him* το ονομα, *the name of my God, and* το ονομα, *the name of the city of my God,* Rev. iii. 12.

This manner of fpeaking, with refpect to the divine effence, is not new. It perfectly agrees with the lan-guage of the Father under the Old Teftament. When he promifed to fend an angel before his people, he faid; *Be-ware of him, and obey his voice, provoke him not: for he will not pardon your tranfgreffions; for my name is in him,* Ex. xxiii. 20. 21. Had a mere delegation of autho-rity been meant, it would have been more properly ex-preffed, " He comes" or " acts in my Name," or " My " Name is *on* him." But the language cannot with pro-priety convey any idea but that of identity of effence. It does not denote any thing external or adventitious, but fomething internal and effential. For it literally is, *My*

Name

---

* Baptizate gentes in Nomine Patris, et Filii, et Spiritus Sancti. In Nomine dixit, non in Nominibus. Non ergo aliud nomen Patris, aliud nomen Filii, aliud nomen Spiritus Sancti, quam unus Deus. Ambrof. de Sp. Sanct. lib. i. c. 4.

Name is in his inward part. Besides, these words contain a reason for what is declared immediately before ; *He will not pardon your transgressions.* Now, this declaration, in its connexion, leads us to the sense in which we are here to understand the *Name* of God. The divine perfection of justice is ascribed to this Angel ; and in this respect God's *Name* is said to be *in* him. The language evidently directs us to that solemn proclamation which JEHOVAH made of his *Name*, as *the Lord God,—who will by no means clear,* the guilty, or as it may be read, *hold it,* that is, *sin, innocent,* chap. xxxiv. 5. 7. What was this but a proclamation of his nature? When, therefore, he says of this Angel, *He will not pardon,—for my Name is in him,* he assures the Israelites that, although this glorious Person appeared as his Messenger, he was to be viewed by them in the same light with himself, as essentially possessing all that this name denotes ; and particularly, as that God *to whom vengeance belongeth,* Deut. xxxii. 35. Thus they were taught that every offence against this Angel was as heinous, as if immediately committed against the Father who sent him. Thus also, in these words we have, first, a reason assigned for the care to be exercised by the Israelites left they should provoke this Angel : FOR *he will not pardon your transgressions :* and then, a declaration of the reason of his not pardoning ; FOR *my Name is* IN *him.*

In reply to the argument from the form of baptism enjoined by our Lord, it has been urged by Socinians, that Paul says of the Israelites that they *were all baptized into Moses,* 1 Cor. x. 2. But, in the same epistle, he proposes this question ; *Were ye baptized into the name of Paul?* chap. i. 13. He evidently marks an important distinction between the two expressions. By comparing the command of Christ with the words of his apostle, it appears that the latter expression denotes a solemn profession of faith in the

Person

Perfon into whofe name we are baptized, and of dependence upon him for falvation; efpecially as the Apoftle
joins this queftion with another, *Was Paul crucified for
you?* At any rate, we know that the honour thus conferred on Mofes was merely typical. For *the law was
given in the hand of a Mediator*, Gal. iii. 19. Therefore,
it might as well be faid that the rock, whofe waters fupplied the Ifraelites, was equally honourable with Chrift the
antitype, and equally worthy of faith, as that Mofes and
Chrift are equal in the other refpect. For, becaufe of the
typical relation, the water is called *fpiritual drink;* and it
is faid of *the rock* itfelf, that it *was Chrift*, 1 Cor. x. 4.
Were the Ifraelites *baptized into Mofes?* Yet, even in this
inftance, he was confidered merely as *a fervant, for a teftimony of thofe things which were to be fpoken after*, or as
prefiguring him who is *a Son over his own houfe*, Heb.
iii. 5, 6.

We may here attend to what Dr P. fays with refpect to
the adminiftration of this ordinance. He gives it as his
opinion, that fome of the ancient Unitarians baptized in
the name of Chrift only. " The form of baptifm," he
fays, " fuppofed to be prefcribed in the Gofpel of Matthew,
" *viz. in the name of the Father, the Son, and the Holy
" Ghoft*, and the *trine immerfion* which was ufed along with
" it, contributed very much to eftablifh the doctrine of the
" Trinity. It was natural enough, therefore, for the Unita-
" rians to oppofe this fuperftition by difcontinuing the prac-
" tice; though it is probable that the cuftom itfelf was an
" innovation. That it was not in ufe from the beginning,
" is pretty evident from their being no trace of it in the
" New Teftament, though we are not able to fay at what
" time it began *."—" The form of baptifm," he fays,
" *fuppofed* to have been prefcribed." And who can fuppofe any thing elfe, without virtually charging the Evan-

gelift

* Ear. Opin. vol. iii p. 439.

gelift with inexcufable inaccuracy in his narrative? Perhaps, it would be doing lefs injuftice to the infpired writer,
to ferve the conclufion of his Gofpel in the fame manner
as the introduction,—by a vigorous effort to lop it off at
once. One Unitarian, indeed, has given fo clear a teftimony
to the force of the argument arifing from this paffage, as
to venture a fufpicion that it has been added from the apocryphal *Gofpel according to the Egyptians* *. As our author
advances fo boldly, it would not be at all furprifing, though
we were totd in the courfe of a few years, that a very ancient manufcript had been found, which wanted the whole
of this paffage.

A man who brings down his Saviour to a level with
himfelf, will at times fhew that he pays more regard to his
own judgment, than to his authority. The learned Gentleman will not admit that this was prefcribed as a form,
becaufe " it contributed much to eftablifh the doctrine of
" the Trinity." But if Jefus prefcribed a form tending to
eftablifh this doctrine, either he defigned that it fhould do
fo, or that it fhould not. If the former; the doctrine muft
be true. If the latter; he did not fufficiently guard his
church againft idolatry.

Is it faid, that it remains to be proved that this form
was really prefcribed? It muft be acknowledged, that there
may be confiderable difficulty in *proving* this. For fome
things are fo very evident, that it is not only an infult on
human reafon to attempt to prove them, but fcarcely poffible to do it; becaufe they are more evident at firft fight,
than the moft laboured proof can make them. It cannot
well be doubted, that we have here a command. One thing
that it refpects is *teaching*, or *making difciples of all nations.*
Dr P. can have no objection to this, if it be not underftood in connexion with the doctrine of the Trinity. For
                                                    he

---

* Anonym. ap. Sandium, p. 115. Wolfii Cur. Phil. in loc.

he hopes that, " in due time," what he calls *true religion* will be received " by thoſe who are ignorant of its nature, " whether living in Chriſtian countries, or among Maho- " metans and Heathens *." But I wonder how he has claſ- ſed Mahometans with Heathens ; as the former are *witneſ- ſes* for the unity of God, and far nearer *true religion* than the Trinitarian Greeks who live *among* them.

The command alſo includes baptiſm. This ſeems to be enjoined, as that ordinance by which thoſe who are *taught,* or *made diſciples,* are openly received into the church : *Make diſciples of all nations, baptizing them.* This, then, being the ſign by which perſons are admitted, it is natural to think that it has ſome definite form ; and equally ſo, that the ordinance itſelf being enjoined, the form would not be omitted. Theſe words, *In the name,* &c. immediate- ly following the command reſpecting the ordinance itſelf, muſt either be *ſuppoſed* to expreſs that form moſt agreeable to him who inſtituted the ordinance, and obligatory on all his followers ; or we muſt conclude, that he left every one to follow the way of his own heart. Even Dr P. will ſcarcely plead for the latter. We muſt, therefore, believe that this was the very form preſcribed ; eſpecially as there is no preſcription of any other.

But Dr P. obſerves, that " we have no trace of this " practice in the New Teſtament." But even ſuppoſing that this were true, it would be of as little weight, in op- poſition to an expreſs command, as, in law, evidence mere- ly negative, when oppoſed to that of a poſitive and direct nature. However, by the time that our author has got to the end of the chapter, matters are ſomewhat riper. For there we are informed, that " the apoſtles baptized in the " name of Chriſt only †." That they baptized in the name of Chriſt is not denied. But to ſay that they baptized in his name *only,* is begging what ought to be proved.

D d 4 But

* Dedic. to Hiſt. Cor. p. v.   † P. 444.

But the learned Gentleman is the most happy historian that ever lifted the pen. For facts grow to him like fruits to an husbandman. What, in the beginning of a chapter, peeps into sight, only as the feeble vernal shoot of a supposition, after advancing through the different stages of mere peradventure, of being probable, very probable, most probable, more than probable, almost certain, by the time he has got to the end of it, appears in the state of maturity, as an unquestionable fact. Whatsoever threatens to overwhelm it, whether scripture or reason, by the help of a new supposition or probability, it still keeps up its head; like the rice on the fertile banks of the Ganges, which, though the river has risen far above it at evening, is sure to be uppermost against morning. Although it hath been long a maxim, *Ex nihilo nihil fit;* it seems to be otherwise with our author. For, in his luxuriant soil, proof merely negative may be transformed into positive.

But let us inquire, if the apostles really baptized in the name of Jesus only. We cannot suppose that they did so, without previously supposing, either that they did not believe that our Saviour had prescribed a particular form; or, that they preferred one of their own to his. The former is incredible. For if there ever was a form prescribed by any master, we have one here. That to be observed in the celebration of the Lord's Supper is not more definite. Dr P. has virtually declared the only reason of his hesitation. Did it not " contribute very much to establish " the doctrine of the Trinity," we should never have heard of the least difficulty about the institution. Shall we, therefore, suppose that the apostles preferred one of their own ? But we cannot do so, without charging them with the most daring disobedience. If capable of it in this instance, surely, they were most unfit persons for fulfilling the order immediately connected with this form; which is,

indeed,

indeed, merely a continuation of the same solemn charge ;, *Teaching them to observe* ALL *things* WHATSOEVER *I have commanded you.* As the former injunction is immediately seconded by this, and such universality and strictness required ; can any rational person for a moment suppose, that the apostles would reckon themselves at liberty to neglect the observation of that very form which was so positively enforced ? Had they been possessed, indeed, by the presumptuous spirit of some modern apostles, that can make so free with the words of God, they might have been supposed capable of such conduct. But they had learned to deny themselves, as well as to follow Jesus. Before they pretended to teach others, themselves *became as little children.*

The language used, in the Acts, with respect to this ordinance, is that this or that person was *baptized in the name of the Lord, in the name of the Lord Jesus,* or *in the name of Jesus Christ.* This variety shews, that the inspired historian did not mean to mention the particular form observed in administering baptism, but only the fact with respect to the initiation of certain persons. It would appear totally unnecessary to Luke, particularly to specify a form known to every church member, when simply narrating the reception of converts.

Is it not often simply said that this or that person was *baptized,* without the mention of any divine name ? Shall we therefore infer, that the administrator mentioned none ? Or, shall we conclude, that the proper form of administrating the Lord's Supper is by *breaking of bread* only, because the inspired historian, when speaking of it, makes no mention of *wine* * ?

When it is said of any, that they were *baptized in,* or *into the name of the Lord,* it denotes that they were initiated into a profession of his name, declaring their faith in

him

* Acts ii. 42. 46. xx. 7.

him as a divine Saviour. Now, there was a peculiar propriety in mentioning their reception in this manner. For
the moſt of thoſe referred to were either Jews or proſe-
lytes: and the doctrine of ſalvation through that Jeſus
who was crucified, was their great ſtumbling block. Nor
was it otherwiſe with the Gentiles.

Although this language does not expreſs the form, it expreſſes the ſpirit and deſign of the ordinance. For as our
Saviour is referred to in his mediatory character, there is
a virtual reference to the whole Trinity, as engaged in our
ſalvation, and as adored in this ſolemn act. For we know
him as our *Lord Jeſus Chriſt*, only as *the Son*, ſent by *the
Father*, to procure that ſpiritual baptiſm ſignified by the
external rite; and as ſending *the Holy Ghoſt* for this end.
Therefore, when perſons are ſaid to be baptized in his
name, he is never deſigned by his eſſential character, as
the Son, but always by one derived from his mediatory
function.

Indeed, independently of other evidence, we have a
ſtrong preſumption with reſpect to the uſe of this form
from the language of Paul to thoſe diſciples at Epheſus,
who, when aſked if they had received the Holy Ghoſt, informed him that they had not ſo much as *heard whether
there was any Holy Ghoſt*, that is, any effuſion; for John
himſelf had aſſured them of the baptiſm of the Spirit.
Paul replied; *Unto*, or rather, *Into what then were ye baptized?* Acts xix. 1.—3. The εις τι here ſeems plainly
to refer to the words of inſtitution, εις το ονομα—τ8 Αγι8
Πνευματος. It is juſt as if he had ſaid, " Were ye not bap-
" tized in the name of the Holy Ghoſt; and how can ye
" be ignorant of his effuſion."

But although it were certain that the firſt diſciples baptized in the name of Chriſt *only*, it could not ſerve the
purpoſe of Socinians. For they adminiſtered this ordi-

2　　　　　　　　　　　　　　　　　nance,

nance, as including a folemn act of worſhip, the object of which was Jeſus. Therefore ſaid Ananias to Saul; *Ariſe, and be baptized, and waſh away thy ſins, calling on the name of the Lord,* Acts xxii. 16. Now, *the Lord,* thus ſolemnly invoked as the object of worſhip, can be no other than he in whoſe name the convert was baptized : and this, it is granted, was *the Lord Jeſus.*

Thus, our author, in his zeal againſt the Trinity, has evidently overſhot the mark. For baptiſm being an act of worſhip, implying, not merely invocation, as expreſſed in the counſel of Ananias, but a ſolemn profeſſion of faith in him who is *called upon,* and a dedication of the whole perſon to him ; if the mode of expreſſion uſed in the Acts, could afford any argument in favour of the worſhip of one perſon only, it would go wholly to prove that this perſon was our Lord Jeſus. Dr P. therefore, in his pretended proof, has miſtaken the perſon. For, if he has done any thing, he has proved that, in this inſtance, the apoſtles *worſhipped* Chriſt *only.* However, all that can be juſtly inferred from the language of Luke is, that he conſidered *the name* of the Father, Son and Holy Ghoſt as *one.*

Our author's preſumption muſt be aſtoniſhing to thoſe who *tremble at* the *word* of God, when he adds ; " It is to " be hoped that the Unitarians of the preſent age will imi- " tate their predeceſſors, by baptizing, as the apoſtles did, " in the name of Chriſt only, without the *invocation* of " the Father, Son and Holy Ghoſt, or expreſſing what they " apprehend to be the real meaning of that phraſeology *." For here he not only aſſumes what he has not proved, with reſpect to the apoſtles ; but encourages others, either entirely to renounce the form preſcribed by the King of Zion, or to make additions to it : as if it were dangerous to uſe our Saviour's words without our own explication. He avows his reſolution either to *take away from the words of*
the

the book, or to *add unto the things* contained in it : and he
can be no ſtranger to the threatened conſequence of either.
What ſhall we think of his conſiſtency in admitting that
there is an act of *invocation,* that is, of *worſhip,* in baptiſm ; even while propoſing to make Jeſus the only object
of it ?

On the whole, what eſtimate can we form of a Socinian faith, when we find that its ſubjects avowedly reject
that very language of our Lord, which, according to their
own acknowledgment, " contributes very much to the
" eſtabliſhment of the doctrine of the Trinity,"—upon the
ſlender ground of a pretended doubt, whether it was intended as the preſcription of a form ; while they cannot
prove the contrary ; and while the proof of the doctrine,
ariſing from the words, is the ſame, whether it was thus intended, or not ?

10. Our Lord declares that he is the *only-begotten Son* of
God, John iii. 16. 18. This can bear no other meaning, than
that he is a Son of the ſame nature with the Father.
Other ſons of God are ſaid to be *begotten* of him improperly and metaphorically. But when Chriſt is called *only-
begotten,* it implies that he is *the Son of God* excluſively,
and therefore in the proper ſenſe of the term, as denoting
an eternal and incomprehenſible generation in the divine
eſſence. The connexion of our Lord's diſcourſe ſhews that
identity of nature is meant. He aſſures us that he is *given*
in this character ; *God—gave his only begotten Son,* ver. 16.
How ridiculous, then, to ſay, that he derives the deſignation from ſomething poſterior to this gift ? In ſo important
a light does he exhibit his filiation, that the rejection of
him in this character appears as if it were the only cauſe
of the condemnation of thoſe who enjoy the Goſpel : *He
that believeth not is condemned already ; becauſe he hath not
believed in the name of the only-begotten Son of God,* ver. 18.

In

In this character does he reveal nimself, as illuftrating the right that he had to fay to Nicodemus ; *We fpeak that we do know, and teftify that we have feen*, ver. 11. As the *only-begotten*, he *knew* all that he teftified by perfeft *vifion* of the nature and purpofes of the Father. He had already declared that he *came down from heaven,* ver. 13. and to fhew that he was chargeable with no prefumption in this declaration, he proclaims his eternal Sonfhip. When he fpeaks to Nicodemus of *telling* him *of heavenly things*, he at the fame time informs him that he alone was qualified to do fo, becaufe of his defcent from heaven. Having declared what muft have appeared a paradox to this ruler, that *the Son of man*, even while he fpake to him, *was in heaven ;* he fhews that this was true of that Perfon who appeared to the eye of fenfe merely as *the Son of man*, becaufe he was alfo *the only-begotten Son of God*, ver. 13. 16. Nothing can be more evident, than that what our Lord fays concerning God's *fending his Son into the world,* ver. 17. muft be underftood as fignifying that he indeed *came down from heaven,* ver. 11. otherwife, the whole difcourfe is a mafs of abfurdity.

To the fame purpofe, the beloved difciple defcribes him as *the only-begottten who is in the bofom of the Father,* John i. 18. This denotes not only the infinite love of the Father to the Son, but unity of effence. There is an evident allufion to the love of a father to his own child : and thus Wifdom fays, *I was by him, as one brought up*, Prov. viii. 30 *. His being *in the bofom* of the Father is clearly mentioned as the evidence of his filiation. The allufion is undoubtedly to earthly things. Now, no one will fay, that a man becomes a Father, by carrying a child in his bofom ; but will reverfe the matter, concluding, from this peculiar evidence of love, that the child is really his. Efpecially were it faid, " There is the fon in the bofom of the fa-
" ther ;

---

* Vid. Lampe in loc.

" ther ;" would any one doubt that the mode of expreſſion
preſuppoſed paternity ? According to the language of inſpiration, the Son muſt, in the order of nature, be viewed
as begotten, and the firſt perſon of the Trinity as a Father,
before the former be conſidered as *in the boſom* of the latter. "The *glory,* therefore, that the diſciples *beheld,* was
that *of the only-begotten of the Father,* who had exiſted
from eternity *with God,* being himſelf *God* *. He is ſo begotten, as to be oppoſed to all the adopted ſons of God, who
derive all their *privilege* from him, by *believing in his
Name,* as *the only-begotten Son of God* †.

Many are the cavils of Socinians againſt this ſenſe of the
expreſſion; ſome aſſerting that Chriſt is called *the only-begotten,* becauſe of his miraculous conception ; others becauſe of his reſurrection ; ſome confining it to the Father's
great love to him ; and others, to that glory to which he is
advanced as King of Zion. While one writer pleaſes himſelf with one of theſe views, another finds it neceſſary to
claſs them altogether, that variety may, if poſſible, ſupply
the want of ſolidity. But as Dr P. ſeems carefully to
avoid giving any particular view of this appellation, it
is unneceſſary to trouble the reader with replies to objections, in which the Doctor may refuſe that he has any
concern.

C H A P.   IV.

*Of the Faith of the Diſciples concerning the Sonſhip of Jeſus,
during his Abode on Earth.*

WE are now to inquire, in what ſenſe the diſciples underſtood this character, while Jeſus was with them
as to his human nature.

The

---

* Ver. 14. compared with ver. 1.   † Chap. i. 12. 14. iii. 18.

The teftimony given by Peter deferves our particular attention, as it exprefies the faith of the twelve : *We believe, and are fure, that thou art that Chrift, the Son of the living God*, John vi. 69.   He acknowledges that Jefus is the Son of God in fo peculiar a fenfe, that he effentially poffefies all that life which belongs to the Father.   For this confeffion muft be viewed in connection with what the apoftle had faid immediately before ; *Thou haft the words of eternal life*, ver. 68.   He does not mean that Jefus merely declared the doctrine of eternal life, or gave fuch inftructions as were neceffary for attaining it ; but that he had power to communicate this life by *the words* which he fpake : For his language evidently reduplicates on the teftimony which our Lord had given concerning himfelf, ver. 63. *The words that I fpeak unto you, they are—life*.   How were they *life?* Becaufe he that *believeth on the Son hath everlafting life*, ver. 47. or, as he exprefies the fame truth metaphorically ; *He that eateth me, even he fhall live by me*, ver. 57.

From the frequent connection of thefe terms, *the Chrift*, and *the Son of God*, it has been urged that they are perfectly fynonymous.   But certainly, it would be far more natural to infer from this circumftance, that the latter denotes fome peculiar excellency, which although fuppofed by the former, is not exprefled by it.   If they be fynonymous, they are extremely ill difpofed.   For if that expreffion, *the Son of God*, in its higheft fenfe be applicable to a creature ; Peter ought to have faid, " We are fure that thou " art that Son of God, the Chrift."   For according to the Socinian hypothefis, that character the *Son of God*, was far more general than the other, and more likely to be underftood in the ordinary fenfe.   The Jews often ufed it as applicable to every individual of their nation ; whereas they confined the term *Chrift* to thofe who were *anointed* to the

office

office of priefthood or of royalty. However, as Peter expreffes himfelf, it muft appear to every. candid reader, that
he meant to define the fenfe affixed .to the firft character,
that Chrift, by the fecond, *that Son of God.*

He firft declares that Jefus is the *Chrift*, being, convinced that he was that illuftrious Perfon pointed out by the
prophets as the Lord's anointed to the work of falvation.
With this he conjoins his.other character, becaufe no one
was to be the *anointed* of JEHOVAH, but he to whom he
had faid, *Thou art my Son; this day have I begotten thee,*
Pf. ii. 2. 7. As he is denominated *that Chrift*, to diftinguifh him from all the *anointed* prophets, priefts and kings,
who prefigured him : fo *that Son*, to diftinguifh from believers, whom he makes fons by adoption; from all the Jews,
who, becaufe of their lawful defcent from Abraham, faid
that God was their father, John viii. 41. and to whom, in
a national refpect, *belonged the adoption*; from angels, who,
by creation, are the *fons of God*; and from thofe rulers
who received this name in a typical fenfe

If Peter meant only that Jefus was the Meffiah, his confeffion did not furpafs that of the carnal Jews, with whom
our Saviour had the preceding difcourfe. For they faid,
*This is of a truth that prophet that fhould come into the
world*, ver. 14. As an evidence of their perfuafion that
he was the Meffiah, they would have *come and taken him
by force to make him a king*, ver. 15. Is it faid, that they
feem to have changed their ideas, when Chrift more fully
declared his doctrine? It is granted. But what doctrine
gave them fuch offence? Was it not that of his divinity?
Did they forfake him as unworthy to be acknowledged as
the Meffiah? It was on the very fame ground on which pretended Unitarians would have proceeded. To thefe unbelieving Jews it was an *hard* and indigeftible *faying*, that he
came down from heaven. We are, indeed, to underftand the

I

teftimony

teftimony of the twelve, in connexion with the tenor of
the preceding difcourfe. It was a voluntary confeffion, a-
rifing from the defign of our Saviour's doctrine: and it
has no beauty nor propriety, unlefs viewed in this relation.
When they declare their affurance that he was *that Chrift,
that Son of the living God*, it directly refpects what Jefus
had again and again teftified concerning himfelf, that he
was *that bread which came down from heaven*, ver. 32, 33. 50,
51. 58. and therefore the antitype of the manna; and without any metaphor, that *he came down from* heaven, ver. 38.
and that he was there *before*, ver. 62. He who denies
that this is the fenfe, while he means to facrifice to reafon,
really makes a facrifice of it.

This noble confeffion was again made by the fame Apoftle, in reply to that queftion, propofed by Jefus to his difciples; *Whom do men fay that I the Son of man am?* Mat.
xvi. 13. 16. The ufe of τινα, rendered *whom*, fhews that
Jefus inquires as to their opinion of his *Perfon* and effence.
They evidently underftand it thus. For, although their
anfwer implies that Jefus was not generally fuppofed to be
more than a prophet, it is evident that it does not efpecially refpect the fentiments of the multitude with regard to
his *office*, but their various ideas as to the fpecification of
the *Perfon*: *Some fay, John the Baptift, fome Elias, and
others Jeremias, or one of the prophets*, ver. 14. Then he
demands their own fentiments: *But whom fay ye that I
am?* We cannot imagine that our Lord wifhed to know if
they fimply believed that he was the Meffiah. His former words may be viewed, either, according to our verfion,
as one queftion; or, according to the punctuation of fome
copies, as two; *Whom do men fay that I am? The Son of
man?* that is, " Is this what they fay?" But which foever
of thefe be preferred, it is evident that the difciples contraft this character, *the Son of God*, with that of Jefus con-

fidered merely as to his office. For it cannot be fuppofed, that they were at a lofs to know, that the other defignation, *the Son of man,* which Chrift fo frequently ufed, refpected him, not merely as in human nature, but according to its application in their fcriptures, as the Meffiah in this nature. Had they viewed him as a mere man, they would have ex-preffed this in their reply. For, as has been feen, the que-ftion itfelf required an anfwer refpecting his nature, and they underftood it in this light.

But they contraft this character, *the Son of God,* with that mentioned by himfelf, *the Son of man;* plainly de-claring, that they afcribe to him a nature fuperior to the human. Our Lord evidently underftands their confeffion in this fenfe. For, he replies; *Bleffed art thou, Simon Barjona: for flefh and blood hath not revealed it unto thee, but my Father who is in heaven,* ver. 17. Here our Lord contrafts Peter's human origin as the *fon of Jonas,* with his own as the *Son of God.* He refers to his carnal defcent, in the words *flefh and blood,* in contradiftinction to his own incomprehenfible filiation expreffed in what follows;----*my Father who is in heaven.* He declares the bleffednefs of Simon, in knowing fo important a truth; efpecially as his natural defcent could not be the fource of fuch a perfuafion as he had, but a gracious communication from the Father of Chrift, who alone knoweth the Son, and therefore can alone reveal him. Jefus teftifies fuch peculiar fatisfaction with this confeffion, that on account of it, he gives Simon the furname of *Peter;* and in allufion to the meaning, as well as to the occafion of impofing this name, he fubjoins this declaration with refpect to the foundation of his church; *And on this rock will I build my church;* intending, either his own perfon, as Godman, or the doctrine concerning it, which feems to be elfewhere called *the pillar, and the ground of truth,* 1 Tim. iii. 15 *.

Mark

Vid. Witf. in Symbol. Ex. 2. f. 10.

Mark gives this confeſſion in theſe words, *Thou art the Chriſt,* chap. viii. 29. and Luke, *The Chriſt of God,* chap. ix. 20. Thence Socinians contend that the other expreſſion added by Matthew, is ſtriſtly ſynonymous. Were the argument their own, they would think it a-ſufficient anſwer to ſuch an objeſtion, that in ſome copies the word ὑιος, *ſon,* is found in Luke, and *the Son of God,* in Mark; and that the verſion of Ulphilas, to which great antiquity is aſcribed, gives the confeſſion as fully in Luke's Goſpel *, as we find it in Matthew.

But there is no neceſſity for claiming the aid of theſe variations. The term *Chriſt* ſuppoſes that the perſon to whom it belongs is *the Son of God.* Now, it ſeemed ſufficient to Mark and Luke to give the ſubſtance of the confeſſion; as they knew no other Chriſt than the only begotten Son of the Father. If Mark rehearſes this confeſſion more briefly than other two evangeliſts, he gives his own as fully as Peter had done. And he ſets it at *the head of the book,* as an inſcription expreſſive of the perſonal dignity of his ſubjeſt; that every reader might know who it was to whom he gave the deſignation of *Chriſt* throughout the whole :—*The beginning of the goſpel of Jeſus Chriſt the Son of God,* chap. i. 1. Conſidering the conciſeneſs of his plan, the laſt expreſſion muſt appear to Socinians an unaccountable tautology.

It is granted, that the term, *Son of God,* denotes the ſame perſon as *the Chriſt.* But muſt it neceſſarily follow, that it conveys preciſely the ſame idea? One perſon was *the ſon of Jeſſe,* and *the king of Iſrael.* Will any one, therefore, conclude that theſe expreſſions were ſynonymous? Did not the one denote origin; and the other, office? One Evangeliſt gives the inſcription on the croſs, in theſe words, *Jeſus the King of the Jews;* and another ſimply, *The King of the Jews.* Are we therefore to infer,

                                                            that

* Thu is Chriſtus ſunus Coths.

that thefe expreffions, *Jefus*, and *King of the Jews*, have exactly the fame meaning? Undoubtedly, all that is intended, is to relate the fubftance of the infcription. And what good reafon can be given, why this fhould not alfo be the cafe with refpect to the confeffion of the difciples? By the words, " Thou art *that* Chrift," or " *that* Chrift of God," Mark and Luke exprefs an acknowledgment of him, as that very anointed, who, in the Old Teftament, was declared to be the *begotten Son* of God.

2. We may now attend to the confeffion of Nathanael, who, it is generally thought was the fame perfon elfewhere called Bartholomew, one of the twelve. He faid unto Jefus, *Rabbi, thou art the Son of God, thou art the King of Ifrael*, John i. 49. He acknowledged him to be the Son of God, as poffeffing omnifcience. For his conviction of our Saviour's claim to that character, arofe from the difplay which he had made of this perfection in thefe words; *Before that Philip called thee, when thou waft under the fig-tree, I faw thee*, ver. 48. What was the particular engagement of Nathanael, at the time and place referred to, does not appear. But his reply befpeaks the fulleft affurance, that no eye faw him but that of omnifcience. It is highly probable, that his religious exercife was itfelf of fo peculiar a nature, that the very recollection of it ftruck his mind in the moft forcible manner. Whatever it was, it feems, from the connexion of the paffage, to have been a proof of the juftnefs of that high character given him by Jefus; *Behold, an Ifraelite indeed!* The reply of Nathanael, alfo, fhews a confcioufnefs that his conduct on that occafion demonftrated the truth of the honourable teftimony now given him.

From the queftion propofed by Nathanael in confequence of this teftimony, it appears that at firft he was at a lofs to know how this ftranger fhould be acquainted with his cha-

racter.

racter. Wishing to discover the source of his intelligence, he says; *Whence knowest thou me?* He was certain that it was not from personal intercourse. For he had never heretofore seen Jesus. Perhaps, he might for a moment suppose that it was by report. But as soon as our Lord replied, Nathanael was fully convinced of the omniscience of the speaker. Then he could safely apply to him the language of the Psalmist; *Thou understandest my thought afar off. Thou compassest my path,* &c. Psal. cxxxix. 2, &c.

The faith of Nathanael was not merely rational. It was supernatural. For he came to Jesus under the influence of a strong national prejudice. He despised him before he had seen him. *Can any good thing,* he says, *come out of Nazareth?* ver. 46. As he did not once suppose that Jesus could know, by human means, what had passed *under the fig-tree;* as he was also under the power of that prejudice already mentioned; had not his faith been of divine operation, he would most probably, like many others, have ascribed the superior powers of Jesus to magic. But at once, all his objections are silenced, and he breaks out in this glorious confession; *Thou art the Son of God.*

It is evident, that Nathanael uses this language as denoting a proper filiation. For Jesus mentions the proof which himself had given of divine knowledge as the immediate ground of this Israelite's faith: *Because I said unto thee, I saw thee under the fig-tree, believest thou?* ver. 50. Now, this was no otherwise a ground of Nathanael's faith in Christ, as Messiah, than as it was a clear demonstration of his deity. The faith of this good man did not operate as that of many other believers seems to have done. From the demonstrations of Jesus being the Messiah, they concluded that he was the Son of God; ascending from the less to the greater. But Nathanael concludes, that he is the Messiah, from the satisfying evidence which he gave of

his

his being the Son of God, equal in perfection with the Father. In this very order are the articles of his confeffion difpofed. Nor is his immediate confeffion of Jefus in this character, confidering the ground of it, a contemptible proof that thofe, who *waited for the confolation of Ifrael,* expected a divine Saviour.

3. John, the harbinger of Jefus, gives him this character, as denoting his *eternal exiftence,* and his *power* to *confer the Holy Ghoft.* *I faw,* he fays, *and bare record, that this is the Son of God,* John i. 34. The fenfe in which he ufed this language, muft be learned from what he had previoufly *faid,* and from what he *faw.* He had faid to his difciples; *After me cometh a man, who is preferred before me, for he was before me,* ver. 30. Whereas the Evangelift, in this chapter, calls the Baptift himfelf ανθρωπος, the term ανηρ is ufed to exprefs the defignation which he gave to Jefus. It feems to correfpond to אִישׁ in Hebrew, which, it is well known, is frequently oppofed to אָדָם; the one denoting an excellent or exalted perfon, and the other expreffing meannefs or infirmity. Ανηρ is alfo often ufed by profane writers, to denote ftrength, magnanimity, or excellence. Thus Homer,

Ανερες εϛε, φιλοι, μνησασθε δε θεριδος αλκης.　IL. Θ. 174.

Sometimes they exprefsly oppofe ανδρες to ανθρωποι. Ανδρες και εκ ετι ανθρωποι μονον νομιζομενοι. Xenoph. in Hieron. Thus it is alfo ufed by Herodotus; Πολλοι ανθρωποι, ολιγοι δε ανδρες, In Polymn. It occurs in the fame fenfe in the New Teftament, in its derivative ανδριζεσθε, *Quit yourfelves like men,* 1 Cor. xvi. 13.

But what requires our particular attention is, that John exprefsly afferts the pre-exiftence of Jefus as the reafon of his being preferred before him: *For he was before me.* In the manner of expreffion, we have that diftinction which

the

the evangelist still preserves between an eternal, and a limited, existence; expressing the former always by *ην*. For with respect to human nativity, John was indeed *before* Jesus. But this declaration has been already explained *.

The harbinger calls his Lord *the Son of God*, in relation also to what he *saw*, as the emblem of personal dignity : *He that sent me to baptize with water, the same said unto me, Upon whom thou shalt see the Spirit descending, and remaining on him, the same is he who baptizeth with the Holy Ghost*, ver. 33. The visible descent of the Spirit, and his resting on Jesus, was to John the proof of his being that illustrious Person who had power to communicate the gifts and graces of the Spirit : and this power was to him so satisfying a proof of deity, that he immediately *bare record that this is the*, or more literally, *that Son of God*, ver. 34. He evidently refers to the testimony of the Father concerning him, *This is my beloved Son*; and perhaps to his own previous testimony with respect to priority of existence.

The Baptist could not mean merely to declare that Jesus was the *Christ*, or one *anointed*. The account which he gives of the character of that person in whom this sign was to be fulfilled, as this character was divinely expressed to him, and of his own inference from it, precludes this idea. For as the term *Christ* is passive, had Jesus been pointed out merely in this respect, the language ought to have been, *The same is he who is baptized*. It, indeed, belongs to the Messiah, as he is described in scripture, to *anoint* or *baptize with the Holy Ghost*. But this belongs to him, only as his office presupposes a character originally divine.

To these words, *with the Holy Ghost*, the Evangelists Matthew and Luke subjoin, *and with fire*, Mat. iii. 11. Luke iii. 16. While we have here a prediction of what

E e 4   should

* See above, p. 144.

fhould be the external fymbol of the effufion of the Spirit on the difciples, (Acts ii. 3.), there is undoubtedly a reference to fomething, under the Old Teftament, of a typical nature. Some apprehend, that there is an allufion to the cloud in which the Ifraelites are faid to have been *baptized into Mofes*. It was not only a *pillar of cloud* for refrefhing them, but *of fire* for giving light, and as a pledge of the deftruction of their enemies. Thus, it may be viewed as a ftriking figure of the operations of the Spirit, who not only refrefhes the fouls of all true Ifraelites, but confumes their fpiritual foes *. Others think that there is a reference to what was done, in vifion, to the prophet Ifaiah. His lips were touched with a live coal, as a token of the removal of his iniquity, chap. vi. 6, 7. †.

But to which foever of thefe the allufion is, the words contain a proof of the deity of the perfon to whom they apply. Is the pillar of cloud and fire referred to? Then, an Almighty agent is intended. *For I*, faith JEHOVAH, *will be unto her a wall of fire round about*, Zech. ii. 5. Is the fymbol of Ifaiah's purification alluded to? The inference is the fame. For it is JEHOVAH who *wafhes away the filth of the daughter of Zion,—by the fpirit of burning*, Ifa. iv. 4. Our Lord is faid to *baptize with fire*, which is of a moft fubtile and penetrating nature, to denote the divine energy and efficacy of his work on the heart.

Jefus is here exhibited as that Wifdom who had faid to his church of old; *I will pour out my fpirit unto you*, Prov. i. 23. as that JEHOVAH who had promifed; *I will pour out my fpirit upon all flefh*, Joel ii. 28. For the ufe of water in baptifm is an emblem of this divine effufion: and the work is exprefsly afcribed to our Saviour, with the application of this very promife laft mentioned; *He hath fhed forth this which ye now fee and hear*, Acts ii. 16, 17. 33.

The

---

* Vid. Lampe in Joan i. 33.　　† See Owen on the Spirit, p. 54.

The work itfelf is a clear proof of his deity. It is to *baptize with, pour out,* or *fhed forth the Holy Ghoft.* Now, even according to the Socinian fyftem, which exhibits the Spirit as merely the *virtue* or *power* of God, this work of effufion certainly far tranfcends the rank or power that can rationally be fuppofed to belong, on any account whatfoever, to a mere creature. The poffeffor muft firft have *an arm like God,* and be able to *thunder with a voice like him.* It is to fupppofe a far ftranger myftery than that of the Trinity itfelf, to imagine a mere man capable of exercifing all the power of God, and of difpenfing all his gifts and graces, with all that unfpeakable variety, and that unerring exactnefs which is requifite in the government of the church.

He who *baptizeth with the Holy Ghoft,* difpenfes his gifts and graces according to his own pleafure. Thence we read of *the meafure of the gift of Chrift,* Eph. iv. 7. *The Son quickeneth whom he will,* John v. 21. and therefore regulates all the means neceffary for this end, in a fovereign manner. The Apoftles afcribe the whole of their fuccefs to Jefus, and refolve the different degrees of it into the fovereignty of his will: *Who then is Paul, and who is Apollos, but minifters by whom ye believed, even as the Lord gave to every man?* 1 Cor. iii. 5. The Holy Spirit is faid to be *the Spirit of the Son,* Gal. iv. 6. The language ufed in the paffage under confideration implies a conftancy of power, and therefore, a fovereignty of operation. *The fame is he who* BAPTIZETH. It is obferved that this is the fame as if it were faid, " This is the *baptizer* with the Holy Ghoft." But the fame fovereignty is afcribed to the Spirit : *All thefe worketh that one and the felf-fame Spirit, dividing to every man feverally as he will,* 1 Cor. xii. 11. Now, thefe things cannot be true, unlefs Jefus be really the Son of God, and fo his will and that of the Spirit be effentially one.

In

In this very light does the Baptift contraft Jefus with, himfelf, as difplaying, in the cleareft manner, his own un-fpeakable inferiority. The antithefis is more diftinctly ftated in Luke, (iii. 16.), *I indeed baptize you with water; but—he fhall baptize you with the Holy Ghoft, and with fire.* John could only adminifter the ordinance of baptifm *unto repentance*; as a fymbolical confeffion of this, and as a mean and feal of divine inftitution. But Jefus, faith he, *fhall baptize you with the Holy Ghoft, &c.* he fhall really purify the inward man. But this is a work peculiar to God. It is *God who purifieth the heart*, Acts xv. 9. And he only can do fo; for he alone *knoweth* it, ver. 8. The fuperior nature of this baptifm is the proof that John gives of Jefus being *mightier* than himfelf.

It may be faid, that " although John could baptize with " water only, the Holy Ghoft not being yet given, the " honour afcribed to Jefus was conferred on his followers, " who communicated the Spirit by the impofition of their " hands." But it is never once faid of any fervant of Chrift, how eminent foever, that he *baptized with* the Holy Ghoft. The difciples could pretend to nothing more than *baptizing in* or *into* his name. But it has been already proved that, in the communication of the Spirit, they were ufed merely as inftruments *.

The afcription of this fpiritual baptifm to Jefus is inti-mately connected with other characters of deity. For the Baptift immediately adds; *Whofe fan is in his hand, and he will thoroughly purge his floor, and gather his wheat into his garner; but he will burn up the chaff with unquenchable fire.* Mat. iii. 12. A real propriety in the church is here afcribed to Jefus. It is called *his floor*. But the church is *the houfe of the living God*. It is *God's hufbandry*. Thefe different expreffions convey the fame idea. Will any one fay, then, that the church is as really the property of a

mere

* See above, p. 316, 317.

mere man, as of *the living* God?—Divine justice is represented as essential to Jesus. For it is not said that God's
fan, or sieve, is in Christ's hand, but his own; *whose fan, &c.*
—Omniscience is virtually ascribed to him. For he is said
to perform a work which necessarily implies this perfection:
He shall thoroughly purge his floor.—Believers are described
as peculiarly his property; and how could this be, if he
were not their God? They are *his wheat.*—Heaven itself
is *his garner*, Luke iii. 17.—To him is the eternal punishment of the wicked, as well as the beatification of the
righteous, ascribed: He will *gather his wheat—but the chaff
he will burn with fire unquenchable.* But this work is the
divine prerogative. *God himself is judge.* It is *our God,
before* whom *a fire shall devour*, Psal. l. 3. 6. It is God,
who shall *rain on the wicked fire and brimstone*, Psal. xi. 6.
In *the hand of* JEHOVAH is that *cup*, of which *the wine is
red.* He it is who *poureth out of the same*, Psal. lxxv. 8.
There is only *one Lawgiver, who is able to save, and to destroy*, Jam. iv. 12. None but a divine Person could be fit
for this awful work. Only the omniscient God could certainly discern between the chaff and the wheat. My God!
I appeal from the judgment of a man like myself. By thy
decision only will I stand. So small is the grain of *precious
seed* in this heart, that, were I to be judged by the most
discerning creature, he would be in danger of sweeping it
away with the chaff.

4. The confession of Martha corresponds with those
which we have already considered. She professed her faith
in Jesus, as that Son of God who was himself *the Life*, and
who could sovereignly communicate life to others. Before
our Lord entered into discourse with her, she believed that,
by his presence, he could have prevented the death of Lazarus. For this was her salutation; *Lord, if thou hadst
been here, my brother had not died*, John xi. 21. She at the

2 fame

fame time expreffes her conviction of the conftant efficacy
of his interceffion : *But I know, that even now whatfoever*
thou wilt afk of God, God will give it thee, ver. 22.   She
feemed to confine her ideas of the power of Jefus to bodily
prefence, to divine donation, and to the prevalence of his
prayers.   Therefore, before he would give her any difplay
of his power, he accounts it neceffary to enlarge and ele-
vate her ideas concerning it.   In order to this, he declares
his mediatory character, in fuch terms as neceffarily imply
his original and effential dignity : *I am the refurrection,*
and the life.   He alfo fhews that faith is the mean of deriving life from him, and that he is himfelf the proper object of it : *He that believeth in me, though he were dead, yet*
fhall he live, ver. 25.   Then he declares the eternity of this
life; informing Martha that it is perpetuated by union to
him, and by a conftant life of faith in him : *And whofo-*
ever liveth and believeth in me, fhall never die.   In addition
to this, not for his own information, but for her inftruction,
and for exciting her to the more vigorous exercife of faith,
he propofes the following queftion; *Believeft thou this?*
ver. 26.   She teftifies her affent in thefe words, *Yea, Lord;*
acknowledging his dominion over her faith ; and alfo fub-
joining a more particular confeffion of it : *I believe that*
thou art the Chrift, the Son of God, who fhould come into the
world.   She firft declares her perfuafion of the fovereign
power of Jefus ; and then her faith with refpect to, not only his official character, but his effential dignity and pre-
exiftence.   The connexion between the fimple affirmative
and the following confeffion, fhews that, in her apprehenfion, believing in him, not merely as *the Chrift,* but as *the*
Son of God, was equivalent to a perfuafion of his being *the*
fountain of life,—and having power to communicate, and
to continue it to eternity.   Her faith rifes in its exercife,
and extends in its views, in confequence of the teftimony

of

of *the author and finiſher of faith.* He gave her the moſt convincing evidence of the truth of what he teſtified, with reſpeᢗt to himſelf as *the reſurreᢗion and the life,* by a renewed communication of life to her ſoul. While he ſpoke, he ſhewed, by the operation of his Spirit, that his words were *ſpirit and life.*

If it did not appear to Jeſus that Martha at firſt entertained ideas unworthy of his dignity, why did he exhibit himſelf in a ſuperior point of view? But while ſhe confined all his power to donation, did ſhe not believe that he could obtain any thing from God by prayer? Did ſhe not, therefore, think as highly of him as Socinians do? Is there one of them who believes that Jeſus, in the proper ſenſe of language, is *the Life,* as having it *in himſelf,* and as having a right to communicate it in a ſovereign manner to others?

That Jeſus performed the miracle recorded in this chapter, to confirm the faith of Martha and the reſt of the diſciples in himſelf as a divine Perſon, is evident, not only from what has been obſerved, but from the end which he expreſsly propoſed in this work. It has been formerly ſeen, that he exhibited the glory of *the Son of God* as the ſupreme and ultimate end; ſaying to the twelve, *This ſickneſs is—for the glory of God, that the Son of God may be glorified thereby* *. The Son of God was glorified, becauſe it appeared in a very ſtriking manner, by this miracle, that he is that *God who quickeneth the dead,* and who is the objeᢗ of faith in this characᢗer, Rom. iv. 17. that he hath not merely power to give life, but that he is *the life.* This was *the glory of God* which Martha was to *ſee,* if ſhe continued to *believe;* as our Lord reminds her, when her faith began to decline in its exerciſe, from a conſideration of natural obſtacles, ver. 40.

5. The

* See above, p. 413, 414.

5. The difciples confefs their Mafter in this charaĉter, as expreffive of his *power over nature,* and of his *right* to religious *worfhip.* On occafion of their deliverance from a ftorm, a clufter of miracles is prefented to view. They fee Jefus walking on the waters. At his word, Peter does the fame. When Jefus enters into the fhip, the wind ceafes at once, though boifterous the moment before; and the fhip, which was in the midft of the fea, is *immediately at the land whither they went,* Mat. xiv. 24—33. John vi. 21. Therefore, with one voice, they fay unto him, *Truly thou art the Son of God.* It cannot reafonably be doubted, that they gave him this charaĉter, as fignifying their perfuafion that he was a divine Perfon. For all the concomitant circumftances fhew, in the cleareft manner, that they formed no other opinion. The difciples knew that God alone could fufpend the laws of nature. They could not, indeed, be ignorant, that he had occafionally employed men as his inftruments in this work. But they could never imagine that any man could communicate this power to another; and far lefs, that he could communicate it in an authoritative and abfolute way. They had been witneffes, however, of Jefus doing fo. While they hefitated whether it were he, whom they faw walking on the fea, or a fpirit; Peter propofed this teft of the truth of what his Mafter had faid; *Lord, if it be thou, bid me come unto thee on the water.* He not only gives him a name, in its full fenfe, denoting univerfal dominion; but expreffes his perfuafion that Jefus could extend the fame power, in its effeĉts, to him alfo, and that he could accomplifh this by a word. He craves, that this glorious operator would give forth his word of authority, faying, *Command me to come.* For the word κελευω always denotes authority, and fometimes that which is abfolute and definitive. Thus it is ufed, Mat. xxvii. 64. with refpeĉt to the power of Pilate, the Roman Governor, over

his

his ſoldiers ; *Command that the ſepulchre be made ſure.* In the ſame chapter in which we have an account of the mi_racles under conſideration, it expreſſes the authority of He_rod ; *He commanded* the head of John *to be given her*, ver. 9. It is evident that, as ſoon as Peter received the command from his Lord, he conſidered it as *the word of a king*, and as conveying *power.* For he *came down out of the ſhip.* His faith reſted on the authoritative word of Jeſus. Thus he gave him the honour that belongs to God only.

It was genuine faith. For it was the mean of his ſup_port on the watery element. *He walked on the water.* When he began to ſink, Chriſt does not reprove him for truſting in the word of a man like himſelf; which he cer_tainly would have done, had this been the caſe. But he charges him with truſting too little, and ſharply reproves him for doubting. Now, what did Peter doubt? Unque_ſtionably, the power of Chriſt's word of command. There_fore, our Saviour blames his diſciple for doubting that, which it had been his ſin to have truſted, had jeſus been a mere man. He reproves him for what, on this ſuppoſition, muſt have been his duty ; becauſe it is written, *Curſed be the man that truſteth in man.*

Thoſe who were in the ſhip acknowledged, in conſequence of what they had ſeen, that Jeſus was *truly the Son of God.* The word αληθως, rendered *truly*, often denotes the cer_tainty of that evidence by which the truth of any thing is demonſtrated. But it is alſo uſed to ſignify the truth of a thing itſelf, with reſpect to its eſſence. The latter ſeems to be the ſenſe here. It is equivalent to their ſaying ; " Thou art the true," or " proper Son of God." They could have no other meaning. They not only witneſſed the divine power of his word ; but expreſsly declared their conviction of this, by joining adoration with their confeſ_ſion. They were aſſured that God *alone treadeth upon the waves of the sea*, (Job ix. 8.). Therefore, they *worshipped him, saying, Of a truth thou art the Son of God.* That the term used denotes religious worship, we have elsewhere proved

It also appears that the man born blind, whom Jesus restored to sight, had such a faith in him as the Son of God, especially in consequence of having *the eyes of his understanding enlightened,* as to account him entitled to religious adoration. For when *Jesus said unto him, Dost thou believe on the Son of God ?* on the ground of Christ's testimony, that it was he who spoke to him, he replied ; *Lord, I believe. And he worshipped him,* John ix. 35—38.

C H A P. V.

Of the Use of this Expression by the Apostles and others, after the Ascension of Jesus.

WE are now to shew in what sense this character, *the Son of God,* was given to Jesus, after his ascension. He had promised to send the Holy Ghost, to *lead* the disciples *into all truth.* He was accordingly shed forth on the day of Pentecost. It is of importance to observe the consequence of this effusion. For we are under a necessity of believing, that any former mistakes would henceforth be rectified, and that what they understood imperfectly would be clearly revealed. But, instead of affording any evidence that they had formerly understood the term under consideration in too high a sense, they confirm that very sense in which it has been explained, both in their discourses, and in their writings.

1. That they used it in a different sense from that of either of these expressions, *Jesus* and *Christ,* has been already proved

ved

ved from the subject of Paul's preaching, Acts ix. 20. and from the Eunuch's confession, chap. viii. 37.

2. They ascribe to our Lord a sonship entirely different from that of *adoption*. *God sent forth his Son, made of a woman, made under the law,—that we might receive the adoption of sons,* Gal. iv. 4, 5. According to Socinians, this ought to have been ; " God adopted one, as a Son, to " whom he had no essential relation, that we might receive " the same privilege." For it seems to be now the gene-ral doctrine of these writers, that jesus receives this desig-nation in the same respect as all believers, only with some little difference as to the degree of honour. They agree that it is as really adoption with respect to Christ, as with respect to Christians. For they do not apprehend that, by nature, they are more alienated from God, than he was. But they oppose the inspired Apostle. For while he a-scribes the privilege of adoption, as conferred on those who were morally alienated, to the work of redemption as its immediate cause ; he traces it up to the love of God in sending a *Son*, nay, to the dignity of the person sent, as being *his* Son. If there be any propriety in the Apostle's language, Jesus was the Son of God, before he performed any part of that work, by which, according to Socinians, he entitled himself to this dignity. He was not merely the Son of God, after he had obeyed, or in obeying the law ; but as *sent forth*, as assuming our nature, as submitting to the law. The honour of sonship, to be procured for others, is evidently connected with a dignity (to which it bore some resemblance) proper to the glorious agent, before he entered on the work of purchase. Did not this character, as applied to Jesus, denote a state of existence essentially superior to human birth and legal subjection, there would be something ridiculous in the language here used. What-ever Socinians may make of that phrase, *made of a woman,*

it muſt be hard for them to ſhew that God could have a Son, who ſhould be a mere creature, and yet *above* the law.

3. Jeſus is exhibited as the Son of God, in a ſenſe ſuperior to that in which he is the *Son of David.* This appears from the queſtion which he propoſed to the Phariſees; *What think ye of Chriſt? whoſe ſon is he?* When they anſwered, *Of David,* he immediately replies, *How then doth David in ſpirit call him Lord?—If David call him Lord, how is he his Son?* Mat. xxii. 41.—45. The full deſign of this queſtion we learn from an Apoſtle of Jeſus Chriſt. It was undoubtedly meant to expreſs this important doctrine, that, although *made of the ſeed of David according to the fleſh,* he was alſo *the Son of God according to the ſpirit of holineſs,* or his divine nature, Rom. i. 3, 4. Is there not a contraſt evidently ſtated here? And where can it lie, if it be not between the human, and the divine nature of Chriſt? If he be called *the Son of David,* to which the Apoſtle's language, is equivalent, *according to the fleſh;* unqueſtionably, he is not called *the Son of God* in the ſame reſpect. If the former character engroſs all that pertains to his *fleſh,* or human nature; the latter muſt refer to ſomething entirely different.

Socinians reply, that the word in this paſſage rendered *declared,* ſignifies *conſtituted.* But this ſenſe of οριϲθεντος would deſtroy the antitheſis evidently ſtated between *the fleſh* and *the ſpirit of holineſs.* It is confidently aſſerted that οριζω is never uſed, either in the New Teſtament or elſewhere, as ſignifying to *declare.* But the contrary may eaſily be evinced. It ſeems moſt natural to underſtand it in this ſenſe, Acts xvii. 31. *He hath appointed a day, in the which he will judge the world in righteouſneſs by that man whom he hath declared, &c.* The context requires this view. For with thoſe *times of ignorance which God winked*

at

at, the Apostle contrasts that, in which he speaks, as a time of far greater light. He proves that it is so, from this very circumstance of God *declaring* or *manifesting* Jesus Christ, by his resurrection, as qualified for the work of judging the world. It seems also to be used in this sense, ver. 26. *He hath determined the times before appointed.* If we do not understand it of *declaring*, the language is tautological.

It is considerably in favour of this as the meaning, that, in the Old Testament, God so frequently appeals to this power of *declaring* future events, as a proof of his deity, in opposition to the idols of the heathen *. One would almost think that, in the passage last mentioned, there was a reference to the words of God by the prophet ; *Who, as I,— shall declare it, and set it in order for me, since I appointed the ancient people, and the things that are coming, and shall come ? let them shew unto them ?* Isa. xliv. 7.

This word is used by profane writers to denote such a declaration as implies an accurate and logical definition †. Therefore, here it does not simply signify that Jesus was *declared* to be the Son of God ; but that, by his resurrection, he was strictly and accurately *defined* to be his Son, in such a sense as could apply to no other ‡, and so clearly, that none but those who were wilfully blind could refuse the justness of the character, as applied to him in its proper meaning.

He was thus *declared* εν δυναμει, as existing in the power of God, as essentially possessing omnipotence ||. For this is often the sense of the word, rendered *power*, when used absolutely §. We are not to understand that expression,

the

---

* Isa. xli. 22. xlii. 9. xliii. 9.

† Vid. Scapul. Lexic. in verb. Wolfii Cur. in loc.

‡ Wits. in Symbol. Ex. 7. f. 12.

|| Vid. Owen, Vindic. p. 174.

§ Mat. vi. 13. xxvi. 64. Rom. i. 20.

the spirit of holiness, as denoting the third person of the
adorable Trinity. For it is immediately contrasted with
the human nature of Christ. *According to the spirit* is the
counterpart of that, *according to the flesh.* The former expression must, therefore, denote something in respect of
which Jesus is *the Son of God*, as opposed to his being *the
Son of David.* This can only be his divine nature, which
seems to receive the same denomination elsewhere. Thus
it is said, that *he was put to death in the flesh, but quickened
by the Spirit,* 1 Pet. iii. 18. It would appear that, in the
same sense, he is said to have *offered himself without spot
unto God, through the eternal Spirit,* Heb. ix. 14. We have
this very contrast distinctly stated by the same inspired
writer, 1 Tim. iii. 16. *God was manifest in the flesh, justified in the spirit.* As *the flesh* here undoubtedly denotes
the humanity of Christ, it is most natural to understand
the Spirit, as denoting his divinity. When the eternal Son
appeared in *the flesh,* his enemies denied that he was God.
But he was *justified* in his claim of deity, not only by the
infinite purity *, but by the infinite power of this nature,
especially as displayed in his rising again from the dead.

The divine nature of Christ may be called *the spirit of
holiness*, as he is himself designed *the most holy,* or *the holy
of holies,* Dan. ix. 24. In this passage of Daniel, as Came-
ro observes, *the holy of holies* is the subject, and *anointing*
the attribute †. But it will not be refused, that this anointing denotes the work of the Holy Ghost, with respect to
Jesus in his mediatory character. Therefore, he is *anointed,*
who was, before, *the most holy.* Thus, the latter expression
must refer to his divine nature.

There is the greatest propriety in ascribing the resurrection of Jesus to his own power. Sometimes, indeed, it
is

* Athanas. de Incarnatione Verbi Dei, Opera, vol. i. p. 592.
† Opera. p. 28.

is attributed to the Father; becaufe it was the judicial acquittal of Jefus from all the demands of the law that he had
been *made under*, and the glorious evidence of the perfection
of his facrifice.   But Jefus alfo claims this honour to himfelf,
as a demonftration of his effential power and glory.   *Deftroy this temple*, he fays, *and in three days I will raife it up*,
John ii. 19.   *Therefore doth my Father love me, becaufe I
lay down my life, that I might take it again.*   This could be
no proper reafon of the Father's love, unlefs the Son had a
fovereign authority over his own life.   To fhew that this
is his meaning, he adds; *No one* (ȣδειϛ) *taketh it from me,
but I lay it down of* ꭑꬼⅰⅰⅰⅰ *: I have power to lay it down,
and I have power to take it again*, John x. 17, 18.   He indeed fubjoins; *This commandment have I received of my
Father.*   But this no ways refpects the origin of his *power*,
but the reafon of his exercifing it, (in the ftate of a fervant voluntarily affumed) in his dying and rifing again.   " If
" Chrift had done no more in the refurrection, than lifted
" up his body, when it was revived, he had done that
" which any other perfon might have done, and fo had
" not declared himfelf to be the Son of God with power *."
His refurrection, therefore, muft have been fo owing to his
own *power*, as infallibly to demonftrate that he was the
Son of God, of the fame effence and perfection with the
Father.

But what is the real import of the Socinian doctrine from
this paffage? It neceffarily fuppofes, that Jefus was made
the Chrift, in fome unknown nature, entirely different from
the human, which is here called *the flefh*.   It makes the
Apoftle fay, that Jefus, by his refurrection, was *made* or
conftituted the Son of God in power, that is, a Saviour completely qualified for the great work entrufted to him;
while all the circumftances attending his refurrection

* Pearfon on the Creed, Art. 5. p. 258.

clearly shew that he could not save himself, that he had no power whatsoever, that he was merely passive in this work. According to this luminous view, the greatest display of his weakness contained the most illustrious evidence of his strength.

4. He is described as a Son, whose *obedience* implied unspeakable *condescension. Though he were a Son, yet learned he obedience by the things which he suffered,* Heb. v. 8. In the preceding context, the inspired writer proves that Jesus did not take the honour of the priesthood to himself, but was lawfully called. Having mentioned it as a qualification requisite in an high priest, that he can *have compassion,* ver. 2. as being himself *compassed with infirmity* ; he shews that Jesus was subject to sinless infirmity, by speaking of *the days of his flesh,* and of his severe sufferings during this period ; and he declares that, by these sufferings, he experimentally *learned* all the difficulty of *obedience,* and therefore, from his own experience, *learned* to *have compassion.* Foreseeing an objection from what he had already advanced, chap. i. 2. &c. iii. 6. concerning the essential glory of Christ as the *Son* of God, he boldly meets it. *Though he were a Son,* in so peculiar a sense as to be *the brightness of glory, &c. yet learned he obedience.* The Apostle does not particularly answer the objection, knowing that it is vain to think of satisfying those who can *reply against* God. He had already said enough to satisfy every sincere believer, by shewing that *in all things it behoved him to be made like unto his brethren,* chap. ii. 17. He had proved that this was necessary for the very end referred to,—that Jesus might be a *merciful* high priest, that he might *learn* the difficulty of *obedience.*

Did the Apostle mean, that Jesus procured the honour of filiation, or of being " chief among the sons of God," in the same kind ; there would not be the least propriety in

the

the exception. For the whole force of it lies in the fuppofition, that his fonfhip naturally elevated him above the
neceffity of obedience. This exception, indeed, would imply the groffeft impropriety. For his obedience muft be
confidered as his title to this honour. If Jefus be an adopted Son, the language is, in every point of view, ridiculous.
Was it any thing ftrange for an adopted Son to learn obedience, or to learn it even by fuffering? Had not Abraham, and Mofes, and Job done fo? Or was any thing fo
directly the duty of fuch a fon, as to learn obedience to his
father?

We muft, therefore, underftand the infpired writer as
fpeaking of a fon, who was *made under a law*, which originally had no claim of obedience from him. If it fhould
be faid that the term *Son* is here to be underftood as equivalent to *Mediator*, then the force of the reafoning would
be; " Though he was Mediator, yet he was Mediator."
For his work in this character was comprehended in that
very obedience here defcribed *.

5. He is declared to be a Son, the *miffion* of whom was
the greateft manifeftation of the Father's *love*. *God* so
loved the world that he GAVE *his only begotten Son*, John
iii. 16. *In this was manifefted the love of God toward us,*
becaufe that God SENT *his only begotten Son into the world,*
that we might live through him, 1 John iv. 9. It is granted
that the miffion of the Son is expreffed as the greateft evidence of love, in connexion with the illuftrious end in view,
his being a *propitiation*. But fuch peculiar ftrefs is laid on
the very *fending* of this perfon, as to convey the idea of
his effential dignity. The delivering of one man to death,
for the benefit of others, would have been no uncommon
evidence of love from him, who had already given men for
his church, and people for her life; Egypt for her ranfom,
Ethiopia and Seba for her, Ifa. xliii. 3, 4. How fmall a
gift

* Vid. Cameron. Oper, p. 2.

gift for him, before whom *the nations are as the drop of a bucket and the small dust of the balance!* But suppofing that God had given no greater ranfom ; how could his love be fo fignally manifefted by the gift? Was it fo great a matter to *fend* a mere man *into the world* of men?

6. He is a Son poffeffed of *power* to *deftroy Satan,* and manifefted for this end. *For this purpofe the Son of God was manifefted, that he might deftroy the works of the Devil,* 1 John iii. 8. The fame truth is otherwife expreffed, ver. 5. *Ye know that he was manifefted to take away our fins.* Satan, being *the ruler of the darknefs of this world,* muft be ftronger than mere man. Indeed, the language ufed by John implies, that no one had been able to deftroy Satan's works, before the appearance of the Son of God. Even he could not do fo, but by *taking away our fins.* That this denotes a real deliverance from the guilt and dominion of fin, is clear, not only from the language here ufed, but from the general tenor of fcriptural doctrine. *The ftrong man* could be *fpoiled,* only by the *ftronger,* Luke xi. 22. And he fpoiled him, when *he himfelf bare our fins in his own body on the tree.—For this purpofe the Son of God was manifefted.* This language, if it mean any thing, certainly implies an exiftence, as *the Son of God,* previous to his manifeftation in this character. How could the Son of God be manifefted, had he not been the Son of God before this manifeftation?

Dr P. when confidering a text in which the fame term is ufed, 1 Tim. iii. 16. *God was manifeft in the flefh,* informs us that " it is literally true, that God was manifeft " in the flefh of Chrift," meaning that the perfections of God, were " confpicuous in him *." But the Apoftle's language does not merely imply that the perfections of the Father were manifeft in Chrift ; but that his own were ma-

nifefted

* Famil. Illuftr. p. 38, 39.

nifested as divine. Whatever these words signify, *God*
εφανερωθη, *was manifest in the flesh,* is contained in the following, *The Son of God* εφανερωθη, *was manifested.* All the
difference is, that in the latter phrase the manifestation is
restricted to a person.

" It was with the greatest propriety," our author observes,
" that our Lord said, John viii. 19. *If ye had known me, ye*
" *would have known my Father also,* the wisdom and power
" of God being conspicuous in him *." But why *wisdom* and
power only? Why do Socinians, even on their own principles, as to the manifestation of God, confine it to these two
perfections? Are these the only perfections of the divine nature? This they will not assert. But it would seem, they were
the only perfections manifested in Jesus. If so, God was not
manifested in him. He could not say, with any propriety,
If ye had known me, ye should have known my Father also.
For, even among men, a person is not known by one or
two features in his character. The whole must be viewed.
Much more is this necessary with respect to God, the
knowledge of whom is infinitely more difficult.

But the Doctor adds; " They who will have this text
" to be a proof of the Godhead of Christ, must suppose
" him to be the *Father,* or the first Person in the Trinity,
" and not the *Son,* or the second." What a silly sophism!
The text must prove more than is meant, that, if possible,
it may prove nothing. It is evidently meant to declare a
sameness of nature and perfections. But because this is
more than is wished, it must prove a sameness of person.
Had Dr P. attended to the particle *also,* which marks a
distinction of persons, he must have blushed at his own reasoning.

7. He is a Son that could be the *Saviour* of lost man.
The Father sent the Son to be the Saviour of the world,
1 John iv. 14. But God claims the work of salvation as

his

т

* Ibid.

his prerogative:¹ *I, even I, am* JEHOVAH; *and beside me there is no Saviour,* Ifa. xliii: 11. Nay, he refers to his work of falvation as the proof of his deity : - *There is no God elfe befide me, a juft God, and a Saviour ; there is none befide me,* Ifa. xlv. 21. *Thou fhalt know no God but me,* FOR there is no *Saviour befide me,* Hof. xiii. 4. It is vain to fay, that God employed a man as his inftrument in the work of falvation. For while his language excludes the idea of the delegation of this work to a creature, we certainly know that, whatever the work of falvation was, 'Jefus was not employed as an inftrument. For he fays, *Mine own arm brought falvation unto me,* Ifa. lxiii. 5. If a mere man, this language was rebellion againft God. He had ftill taught his people that it would be *vaunting themfelves againft him,* if they fhould *fay, Mine own hand hath faved me,* Judg. vii. 2. But Jefus *his own felf bare our fins,* 1 Pet. ii. 24. *By himfelf he purged our fins,* Heb. i. 3. And undoubtedly this language denotes fupreme agency in the new creation, as much as that refpecting the old ; *I am* JEHOVAH,----*that ftretcheth forth the heavens* ALONE, *and fpreadeth abroad the earth* BY MYSELF, Ifa. xliv. 24.

But the miffion of a Saviour is not what John principally urges in this paffage. It is the miffion of *the Son of God* for accomplifhing the work of falvation. This he declares to be the great matter of the conviction and teftimony of the minifters of Jefus : *We have feen, and do teftify, that the Father fent the Son.* This is clearly the fcope. For the Apoftle's immediate fubject is brotherly love. This he recommends, not principally from the confideration of God giving a Saviour, but from that of the Father fending his Son in this character. Therefore, he immediately adds a declaration of the neceffity and bleffednefs of confeffing Jefus as a Divine Perfon : *Whofoever fhall con-*

fefs that Jefus is the Son of God, God dwelleth in him, and he in God, ver. 15.

8. He is a Son, who could be *appointed*, or *conftituted* ● *heir of all things*, Heb. i. 2. When this language is ufed, our Lord is undoubtedly pointed out in his mediatorial cha. racter: for in this refpect alone could he receive an ap. pointment. But the appointment is fuch, as not merely to imply real poffeffion, but fo extenfive a poffeffion as is totally incompatible with the ftate of a creature. *All things*, faith Chrift, *are delivered unto me of my Father*, Mat. xi. 27. *All power is given unto me in heaven and in earth*, chap. xxviii. 18. He is *Lord, both of the dead and of the living*, Rom. xiv. 9. Angels and devils, faints and finners, are under his dominion. The management of the church is wholly in his hand. All gifts and graces are at his difpofal. Glory itfelf muft be conferred by him. All the kingdoms of this world are put under his feet. Uni- verfal nature acknowledges his fovereignty. All judgment, whether in the prefent ftate or at the laft day, is committed to him, John v. 22. And is a mere man, is any creature, capable of fuch a truft?

" It muft be fo;" replies the Socinian, " For the infpi- " red writer affures us that all this power is delegated." Let us hear our author. " It is plain from this paffage," he fays, " that whatever Chrift is, he is by divine appoint- " ment;—*whom he appointed heir of all things* ●. But Socinians are refolved to reckon it abfurd, that a perfon, to whom divine powers effentially belong, fhould on a- ny account whatfoever voluntarily fubmit to an appoint- ment to difcharge thefe in an inferior nature affumed by him : while they find no difficulty in conceiving, that one effentially poffeffing no other powers than the human fhould be exalted to the full exercife of thofe that are di- vine.

* Famil. Illuftr. p. 35.

vine. They refuse to believe that he, who *was in the form of God*, could *take on himself the form of a servant*. But they find it perfectly easy to believe, however strange the inversion, that he who is essentially *in the form of a servant*, may take on himself the *form of God*.

It may be said, that " great as the powers are, which the " ·scripture ascribes to Jesus, there is nothing inconceivable " in their being possessed by a mere man; if God, to " whom all things are possible, be pleased to communicate " them." But nothing is possible to God, which implies a denial of his own nature. Sound reason can never admit the creation of a God, or the deification of a man, into the list of possibilities. It rejects the idea of either, as a-theistical. For he who can deny or dethrone himself, is not God.

But in the context, the Apostle clearly shews, that the essential dignity of the Son is the primary foundation of his mediatory honour and trust, as *heir of all things*. For he immediately declares his glory as Creator ; and having said, that *he sat down on the right hand of the Majesty on high*, proceeds to assign the following reason for this peculiar exaltation : *Being made so much better than the angels, as he hath by inheritance obtained a more excellent name than they*, ver. 4. This is generally understood as wholly referring to the mediatory state of Jesus ; and not without apparent ground, as there is a repetition of the allusion to an earthly inheritance. But it seems more natural to understand the last reference as expressive of the essential dignity of Jesus. Thus the apostle declares, that Jesus as far excels angels, even in his mediatory character, as he does in that name which he essentially inherits *. And what is this? We are immediately informed, that he is called the Son, and the *first-begotten*, ver. 5, 6. whereas these exalted

creatures

---

* This is certainly the proper force of τοσυτω and οσω in connexion.

creatures are, in their higheft character, only *meffengers* and *minifters*, ver. 7. He is *begotten*; but they are *made*. Although there is a repeated allufion to an inheritance, yet the language is different. In the firft inftance, the Son is faid to be *appointed* or *conftituted heir* : but in the fecond, it is fimply affirmed that he κεκληρονομηκεν, *hath inherited a more excellent name.* The infpired writer feems to exhibit the Son, firft as an appointed, and then as a natural heir ; as he means to fhew that the latter is the foundation of the former. In this view, his language exactly correfponds with the teftimony of the Baptift, *He that cometh after me is preferred before me, for he was before me,* John i. 15.

9. Jefus is fo the Son of God, that he could be the *Creator. God hath fpoken by the Son, whom he appointed heir of all things, by whom alfo he made the worlds,* Heb. i. 1, 2. Dr P. obferves, that " the doctrine of Chrift having made the " world, is not expreffed by any of the apoftles in a man- " ner fo definite and clear, or fo repeatedly, as its magni- " tude naturally required. For the paffages in their wri- " tings from which it has been inferred that they held this " opinion, are very few *." Will our author pleafe to in- form us, how many paffages would have been neceffary, as a proper foundation for faith, on a fubject of this kind? He grants that there are four which are underftood in this fenfe. And thefe, if clear, are as good as four hundred. But this is the rub. They " are by no means clear and " exprefs to the purpofe. Had this doctrine," he fays, " been true, being of fo extraordinary a nature, and fo " much unlike to any thing that Jews or Chriftians " had been taught before, it would, no doubt, when it was " firft promulgated, have been delivered with the greateft " diftinctnefs, fo as to leave no uncertainty with refpect to " it †." But our author begs one queftion in order to prove another.

---

another. He takes it for granted, that the Jews had no idea that the world was made by the perfonal Word of God. That this doctrine was believed by them, has been already'fhewn. Therefore, every argument that proved the pre-exiftence of Jefus as the perfonal Logos, was a proof of his being the Creator. Befides, the whole doctrine of the apoftles, concerning the new creation, which they afcribed to him, was a more direct and feafonable il-luftration of his deity, than any other could have been. For during a long fucceffion of ages, the Jews had been taught to expect this as a divine work; and it was emi-nently the work of that age in which the apoftles wrote. I may add, that this work was not fimply predicted as divine; but ftill appealed to by Jehovah, as the great proof of the truth of that revelation which he had given of him-felf, and as bearing fuch characters as would infallibly de-monftrate the fupreme deity of the immediate agent.

With refpect to the language of the epiftle, our author obferves, that " in this paffage it is evident, that it was not " the object of the writer to make an exprefs affertion " concerning the making of the world by Chrift, fo as to " exhibit it as an article of any confequence. He was af-" ferting fomething elfe : and what he does fay on the fub-" ject is only one incidental circumftance, among feveral o-" thers *." Our author cannot deny, however much in-clined to it, that the *affertion* is *exprefs*. But he makes a feeble attempt to get free of it, by pretending that it is not exhibited as an article of any confequence. Why then has it a place in the language of infpiration? Is any thing of no confequence, that *the Spirit faith unto the churches?* He interprets the language, as we fhall afterwards fee, with refpect to the *new* creation. What then is the amount of his objection? That the whole of Chrift's work, even as to falvation, is of no confequence. For furely, the fenfe

in

---

* Ear. Op. Vol. I. p. 67.

in which this *article* is underftood cannot alter its importance.   This, it feems, muft be judged of entirely by the
manner of its introduction.   And it is introduced merely
as an *incidental circumftance.*   If the affertion be of no
confequence with refpect to the *old,* it can be of as little
with refpect to the *new* creation.   It is equally incidental
as to either.   Whatever thefe *worlds* be, nothing more is
faid of the *making* of them.   What is the plain meaning
of this, but that it is not of any confequence to the church
whether Chrift *made the worlds* in any fenfe ; that is,
whether he was a Saviour or not?   Here, indeed, we
have a very honeft acknowledgment of the genuine fpirit
of the Socinian doctrine.

He adds ; " Befides, nothing is here faid, or intimated,
" about Chrift making the *material* worlds, for it is only
" faid that he made the *ages* (αιωνας) and the *all things*
" here mentioned evidently means all things relating to a
" particular object, *viz.* the miffion of Chrift, and not all
" the works of nature *."   But it is to beg the queftion a
fecond time, to fay that by *all things* we are to underftand
only *fome things.*   Although αιωνας were meant in our author's fenfe, this term could not limit the preceding declaration, but only denote a part of the *all things* previoufly
mentioned.   The Doctor gives his view of the phrafe more
clearly in another place.   By *ages* he underftands " the
" prefent difpenfation of God's government over mankind,
" which is eftablifhed by the gofpel, the adminiftration of
" which is committed to the Son †."

But if the *ages* mean a *difpenfation* only, and if the *all*
things are to be reftricted by this fenfe, Jefus is not an *heir,*
but merely a fteward.   So far is he from being *heir of all*
things, that he is not heir of any thing.   This frivolous
exception hath been removed an hundred times already:
It hath been fhewn, that the term αιων is never ufed abfolutely,

lutely, as denoting the gofpel-ftate; but that, in this fenfe, it is always connected with fome other term, as μελλων, chap. vi. 5.; and that this difpenfation is no where faid to be *made.* The fcope of the writer alfo oppofes this fenfe. For, having afferted that the Son is appointed heir, he proceeds to illuftrate the propriety of this difpenfation, by declaring his creative power. He was fully qualified to be heir of all, who had given being to all. Befides, he goes on to affert that the Son *upholdeth all things.* This declaration exactly correfponds with what has been already mentioned. He alone can uphold, who hath created.

It is certainly neceffary for Dr P. to fhew how a fingle difpenfation can be called *the ages.* If the mere ftate of the church or world were meant by this term, it would undoubtedly include the Jewifh, as well as the Chriftian, difpenfation. The fucceffion of *ages to come* cannot help our author. For the language refpects the paft, and not the future : *He made.* I fhall only add, that the fame word occurs in this epiftle, where there can be no doubt that the firft creation is meant : *Through faith we underftand that* (τας αιωνας) *the worlds were framed by the word of God,* chap. xi. 3.

The fame work is afcribed to the Son in another paffage ;—*Who is the image of the invifible God, the firft-born of every creature. For by him were all things created, that are in heaven, and that are in earth, vifible and invifible, whether they be thrones or dominions, or principalities, or powers: all things were created by him, and for him ; and he is before all things, and by him all things confift ; and he is the head of the body, the church,* &c. Col. i. 15. 16. " On " this paffage," according to our author, " it is obvious to " remark, that the things which Chrift is faid to have " made are not the heavens or the earth, but fome things " that were *in* the heavens, and *in* the earth *." If he
                                                                                                    made

made all the inhabitants, it is natural to fuppofe that he made the habitations alfo. But by *all things that are*, Dr P. underftands only *fome* things that *were*, in heaven and in earth. For the mode of expreffion leaves the reader uncertain, whether he means that they are ftill there, or not. " Thefe," he fays, " were not natural objects, fuch " as ftars or planets, trees or animals, *&c.* but the creation, " or eftablifhment, of fuch things as *thrones* or *dominions*." There feems to be ftill an abfolute chaos in our author's brain, with refpect to this fubject. He can find nothing *incidental* here. But the doctrine is by no means *definite and clear.* He can fafely tell you what thefe things are not ; but though they are *all things in heaven and in earth*, he cannot venture to fay what they are. They are, indeed, " fuch things as *thrones* and *dominions*." But he fo great- ly venerates *fuch things* as thefe, that he dares not at- tempt to defcribe them. Does he really mean, that *all things*, whether in heaven or in earth, are *thrones* and *do- minions*, or fuch things as thefe ? No. He only means that thefe are the only things that are *created*, that is, eftablifh- ed. For this, he adds, may " therefore be naturally inter- " preted as referring to fome exercife of that *power in* " *heaven and in earth*, which Chrift fays was given to him " after his refurrection." He fuppofes fo at leaft, from the fimilarity of found. For he will not attempt to give the fenfe. He is quite a ftranger to this *exercife*, though by the Apoftle called a *creation*, and extended to *all things*. The reader will therefore pleafe to confider it as ob- *vious*, that by *all things* he ought to underftand *fome* only ; and by the *creation* of *all* things, the *eftablifhment* of fome things, or at leaft, *fome exercife* that may peradventure bear this name. But he muft beware of afking, what this crea- tion or eftablifhment is. For our author can hardly ha- zard a conjecture as to the things faid, or fuppofed, to be establifhed. One thing, however, he can venture to affert; that the making of a *tree* is too great a work for the Saviour.

But his ideas on this fubject do not feem to have been fo dark, when engaged in *illuftrating* fome paffages of fcripture. " By creation," he fays, " we are to underftand " the *new creation*, or *renovation*, in which fenfe the fame " word is ufed by the Apoftle, Eph. ii. 10. *We are his* "*workmanfhip, created in Chrift Jefus unto good works.* " So great a change is produced in the world, in the tem- " pers and conduct of men by the gofpel, that both the " terms' *creation* and *regeneration* are made ufe of to ex- " prefs it *."

We are far from wifhing to deny, that the change effected by the gofpel is called a *creation*. But, of all men, Socinians plead this application of the term with the worft grace. For they afcribe fo little agency to Jefus, in the work of the new creation, as to bring difcredit on the Spirit of infpiration for ufing fo emphatic a term. Did they underftand it in its proper fenfe, when applied to the gofpel; did they really afcribe to the Son of God that *exceeding greatnefs of power* required in the new creation; they could not hefitate to acknowledge his fupreme agency in the old.

Dr P. refers to feveral paffages of fcripture, in order to prove that the effect of the gofpel is called a new creation. But where this is the cafe, there is undoubted evidence, and generally from the ufe of diftinctive terms, that the new is meant. This is undeniable as to all the paffages referred to. In Eph. ii. 10. we read of a *new* man ; in 2 Cor. v. 17. of a *new* creature; in Ifa. lxv. 17. of a *new* heaven, and a *new* earth. But in the paffage immediately under confideration, creation is fpoken of abfolutely.

The

* Fam. Illuft. p. 43.

The Doctor, indeed, seems to be conscious that, according to his system, the use of this term, with respect to the gospel, may appear somewhat unnatural. Therefore, he is at pains to provide an apology for the language of the Holy Ghost. But some may be apt to think that the business is " worse for mending." " We shall see less *harsh-* " *ness*, he says, in this figure (for it seems, it is *harsh* at " best) when we consider that what is called the *Mosaic* " *creation* was probably similar to this ; since for any thing " we know, it was only the *re-making* or *re-conſtituting* " of the world, out of a former chaos." Whether this doctrine affords any inlet to Deism, or to something worse, let the Chriſtian reader judge. It has hitherto been thought by the *weaker* part of mankind, that creation, in the ſtrict ſenſe of the word, was the *calling of things that be not, as though they were;* and that God created the heavens, and the earth, *in the beginning.* On the ground of our author's ſuppoſition, it may with equal propriety be denied that the world had any beginning. For an Atheiſt might ſay to him ; " If you grant that what is called the *Mosaic cre-* " *ation* was not the origin of all things, what other will " you fix on ? Your pretended revelation forſakes you, from " the moment that you renounce the Mosaic æra." Whatever Dr P. *knows* with reſpect to this creation, the church of Chriſt has ſtill known, and *underſtood, through faith*, that the worlds were *ſo* framed by the word of God, *that things which are ſeen were not made of things which do appear*, Heb. xi. 3. and therefore not of any pre-exiſtent chaos. For this could not have been inviſible. This framing of the worlds muſt neceſſarily be that deſcribed by Moſes. For it could not otherwiſe be underſtood *through faith :* becauſe faith reaches no farther than a divine teſtimony. But in our enlightened age, even ſome who profeſs Chriſtianity reckon it far more ſafe to truſt to the pe-

netrating

netrating eye of philofophy, than to the feeble eye of faith.

Our author, however, will find it hard to fupport his hypothefis, as to the meaning of the paffage before us, even with the aid of atheiftical fuppofition. For the connexion of the Apoftle's language clearly fhews, that he here fpeaks of the firft creation. He afferts that God's *dear Son* is *the firft begotten of all creation.* Whether we view this phrafe as fignifying that he was begotten before all creatures, and thus as expreffive of his effential dignity; or as denoting his mediatorial authority over all, by an allufion to the right of primogeniture; the inference is the fame. For it immediately follows; *For by him were all things created.* Is it inquired, why the Son is faid to be begotten before all creatures? The reafon is, *Becaufe* (οτι) *by him all things were created.* Or, why he is Lord of all. The anfwer is the fame. He has an original and effential right to this dignity. His right of dominion is evidently confidered as commenfurate with his agency in creation : and the latter is mentioned as the primary foundation of the former. This manner of reafoning was perfectly familiar to God's ancient church : *The earth is the Lord's, and the fullnefs thereof; the world and they that dwell therein.* For *he hath founded it,----and eftablifhed it,* Pfal. xxiv. 1, 2.

The extent of the work afcribed to the Son, clearly fhews that the firft creation is meant. *By him, all things were created, that are in heaven, and that are in earth, vifible or invifible.* But Dr P. informs us, that " when all " things are faid to be created by Chrift,----nothing can be " meant but fuch things as can properly come under his " government as the Meffiah, and be fubfervient to him " in the conduct of it, including probably the *vifible* powers " and kingdoms of this world, and the *invifible* adminiftra- " tion of angels *." But this is evidently putting darknefs

for

* Ibid.

for light. For nothing can be more plain, than that the
Apostle's language respects neither the visible nor invisible *administration* of the powers mentioned, but the
visible and invisible *ministers themselves;* not their subser-
viency to the kingdom of the Messiah, but their very existence. The Doctor wishes it to appear, that the language of
this place does not respect *persons*, but only the stations occupied by them. But the same terms, in other passages,
undoubtedly denote persons, and can bear no other meaning.
Is it the angelic model of government in the abstract that
the same Apostle intends, when he declares that *the manifold Wisdom of God* is *made known to the principalities and
powers in heavenly places?* Eph. iii. 10. When he says, *We
wrestle—against principalities and powers*, does he not mean
the *rulers* themselves, *the rulers of the darkness of this
world?* vi. 12. Or can his language bear any other sense,
when he tells us, in that very epistle in which he ascribes
the creation of these to Christ, that he *spoiled principalities
and powers*, and *made a shew of them openly?* chap. ii. 15.
It was common with the ancient Jewish writers to call the
angels, or at least one order of them, *thrones* *. Gill's
view of the passage seems very natural. " The Apostle's
" sense is, that the *angels*, the invisible inhabitants of the up-
" per world, are all created by Christ, let them be called by
" what name they will, that the Jews, or the false teachers,
" or any sort of heretics of those times thought fit to give
" them, whether they called them *thrones*, or *dominions*,
" &c †."

It seems to have been customary with the Jews, at the
time that the Apostle wrote, to distinguish all created things
in the way he does in this passage. What he ascribes to
Christ with respect to creation, Philo ascribes to *the Lord the
Archangel* with respect to government. " For it must be
" understood," he says, " that as a charioteer, or as a pilot,

" lie

* Sepher Jetzira Zikhone Zohar, &c. see Gill on the place.   † Ibid.

" he who is presides over bodies and souls, and every li-
" ving thing, over minds and angels, over earth, air and
" heaven, over sensible powers, over invisible natures, over
" all things unseen and seen *."

But although the term *all* were limited to " such things
" as can properly come under Christ's government as the
" Messiah ;" if the language of this passage denote the *new
creation*, or *renovation*, our author's view is clogged with
absurdity. For it must follow that all *such things* were
created anew. Therefore, as devils themselves are subjected to this government, they must be considered as *re-
made*, that is, *renewed* by Christ Jesus.

" And therefore," our author adds, " the Apostle, with
" great propriety concludes and sums up the whole of
" Christ's authority, by saying that *he is the head of the
" body the church.*" Why " with great propriety ?". Because, forsooth, " nothing can be meant," but what our modern divine thinks *proper*. According to his plan of interpretation, " Christ's authority would, indeed, be easily
" summed up ;" and there could be no security that it
would not soon come to a *conclusion*. But before our author can shew that, in his sense, " the Apostle sums up
" the whole of Christ's authority," he must prove that
thrones and dominions, principalities and powers, are a part
of Christ's *body the church.* However, instead of *summing
up*, the Apostle evidently proceeds to another subject.

In the three preceding verses, he has declared the essential glory of the Saviour : For it seems most natural to understand that expression, *the first born of every creature*, of

2   his

---

* Εμηνυε δε το οναρ, εςηριγμενον επι της κλιμακος τον αρχαγγελον
κυριον: υπερανω γαρ ως αρματος ηνιοχον, η νεως κυβερνητην, υποληπτεον ισα-
σθαι το ον, επι σωματων, επι ψυχων, επι θρεμματων, επι λογων, επι αγγε-
λων, επι γης, επ᾽ αερος, επ᾽ υρανυ, επ᾽ αισθητων δυναμεων, επ᾽ αορατων φυ-
σεων, οσαπερ, αθιατα και θιατα. De Somniis, p. 457.

his pre-exiftence. Now, he illuftrates the glory of Chrift as Mediator. He firft declares his authority in general, as reaching to every creature; then more particularly, as refpecting the fubjects of the new creation.

That the Apoftle makes a tranfition from the divine to the mediatory character of Jefus, is evident from various confiderations. In the preceding verfe, he had afferted the priority of Chrift to all creatures: *And he is before all things* *. Dr P. however, denies that this is the fenfe. " *Before*," he fays, " often fignifies before in point of *rank*, " and *pre-eminence*, and not in point of *time*; fo that when " Chrift is faid to be *before all things*, the meaning is, that " he is the *chief*, or *moft excellent* of all." For this we have only our author's bare affertion. He does not produce a fingle paffage in proof of it; and, as would feem, for a very good reafon : for we do not know of one that could be tortured into this form. Obferve, how well his view agrees with the tenor of the paffage. For, according to it, there is the clofeft connexion between the feventeenth and eighteenth verfes; as both refpecting the fame fubject. *He is before all things* in point of *pre-eminence*,—*that in all things he might have the pre-eminence.*

The afcription of providence to the Son, in the preceding verfe, is another proof that the Apoftle changes his fubject. *By him*, he fays, *all things confift*, ver. 17. The Doctor remarks on this claufe; " When it is faid that *in* " *him all things confift*, we are to underftand that in him " all things are *completed*, and compacted; fince the Chri- " ftian difpenfation is the laft, completing one great and re- " gular fcheme of revelation, continually advancing from " the more imperfect to the more perfect †." But the *all things* here mentioned, muft be the fame as in ver. 16. Thefe our author has underftood to be " the powers and " kingdoms of this world, and the adminiftration of angels."

G g 4   I

* Ver. 17.   † Ibid.

I would wilh to know, how the kingdoms of this world are " completed and compacted" *in* the Son of God. It has been feen that devils are among the *things invifible.* It may, therefore, be alfo neceffary to inform us, how they receive their *completion* in him.

The change of fubject is further evident from the new character introduced by the Apoftle, ver. 18. *The firft begotten from the dead.* He contrafts this character of Jefus as Mediator with what he had afcribed to him as the Son,----*the firft begotten of all creation,* ver. 15. If the fubject be the fame, the Apoftle is chargeable with a vain repetition, when he fpeaks of Chrift's *reconciling all things to himfelf, whether they be things in earth, or things in heaven,* ver. 19. For the term *reconciling* properly de-notes the work of the *new creation*; and according to Dr P.'s view, muft convey the fame idea as that in ver. 16. *By him were all things created, that are in heaven, and that are in earth.*

If this paffage does not refpect creation in a literal fenfe, it will fcarcely be poffible to fix on any other, referring to this work, which may not, by the fame lawlefs ingenuity, be wrefted from its natural meaning. The Doctor has materially acknowledged this, and given us a cue. When it is faid, *In the beginning God created the heavens and the earth,* he who pleafes may underftand this language as meaning nothing more than that they were *re-made, re-conftituted,* or *new-modelled.* By the way, I fhould like to know, if *all the hoft of them* (Gen. ii. 1.) are to be confi-dered as the fubjects of a fimilar renovation.

But Dr P., even according to his ftrange interpretation, ftill grants too much to the Son of God. He is under a neceffity of acknowledging that *all things were made for him* as Meffiah [*]. But that of being the final caufe of any of the works of God, is too great an honour for any creature.

This

---

[*] Ver. 16.

This belongs to God only. For he hath *made all things for himfelf. For his pleafure they are, and were, created.* Therefore, he, who is the Meffiah, muft be a divine Perfon: otherwife, God *gives his glory to another.*

10. Jefus is declared to be a Son who *is the brightnefs of glory, and the exprefs image of his* Father's *perfon*, Heb. i. 3. It being the great defign of the infpired writer to the Hebrews, to turn the attention of that people from the type to the antitype; in the firft expreffion, he feems to allude to the cloud of glory which covered the mercy-feat. This was the principal fymbol of the prefence of God in his church, the vifible manifeftation of his glory. Therefore the Godman is, with peculiar propriety, called *the brightnefs of glory.* Thus, the Jews are taught that he is the true Shechinah, who had formerly dwelt, in a typical manner, among his people, manifefting to them the glory of the divine nature, in its relation to a work of grace.

He is alfo defigned *the exprefs image of his*, that is, the Father's *perfon.* Whatever be the particular allufion here, the language denotes that Jefus effentially poffeffes all divine perfections; and that he manifefts all thefe to men. He is fo *the image of the invifible God*, Col. i. 15. that *the light of the knowledge of the glory of God* is in his *face* or perfon, 2 Cor. iv. 6. Dr P. afferts that all thefe expreffions "allude to the divine power and wifdom which were "difplayed in" Chrift, "when he was on earth, but more "efpecially now that he is afcended into heaven. At the "fame time," he fays, "Chrift being called only the *image* "of God, is a fufficient intimation that he is not God him-"felf *." The laft affertion is true in the fcriptural fenfe. The Son is not the Father. But it has formerly been feen, that the term *God* is often ufed diftinctively, to denote the firft Perfon; as the term *Lord*, to denote the fecond. Therefore, it may be faid with equal propriety, that God is not the *Lord*, becaufe Chrift is fo. But

* Famil. Illuftr. p. 23.

But the Doctor adds; " Indeed, if this expreffion was " to be allowed to be any proof of the divinity of Chrift, " it would follow that Adam was God." This is one of thefe *hard fpeeches* which the Lord will judge. It is not only impious, but futile. Our author pretends to found this obfervation on thefe words, Gen. i. 26, 27. *God made man in his own image, and after his likenefs.* But this language concerning Adam, is very different from that ufed with refpect to our Lord. Adam was formed *in* the image of God. Chrift is the image of God. Adam was *made,* Chrift *begotten.* Adam is fpoken of as the image of an image ; Chrift, as the image of a Perfon.

Socinians themfelves virtually grant the vanity of what is alleged by the Doctor. For while they confine the divine image, in which man was created, to dominion over the creatures, they find it neceffary to enlarge their ideas with refpect to Chrift. They acknowledge that " divine " power and wifdom were difplayed in him." The image of God, as communicated to Adam, efpecially confifted in knowledge, righteoufnefs and holinefs, Col. iii. 10. Eph. iv. 24. But Jefus is *the exprefs image of* the Father's *perfon,* as poffeffing all perfection. For if Jefus hath not all divine perfection, he is falfely called the *character* of a divine perfon. If he hath, he is himfelf God ; or that queftion can no longer be propofed, *To whom will ye liken me, and make me equal, and compare me, that we may be like ?* Ifa. xlvi. 5. For in this cafe, a creature might be God's equal, to whom he might be ftrictly likened.

But the language ufed in the paffage before us cannot apply to any creature, however exalted. For, in the firft place, the glory here meant is undoubtedly that of God. Now, he, who is *the brightnefs of glory,* muft poffefs all that glory which is effential to him whom he reprefents. This expreffion does not fignify a reflection, or fecondary

manifeftation

manifeftation of a borrowed fplendor, but that very
fplendor which belongs to the glorious objeft; as that
of the fun, who is feen by his own light. Secondly,
Whofoever is *the exprefs image* of a perfon, muft reprefent
the nature and all the perfeftions of that perfon. We
have no right to confine the language to " power and
" wifdom," or any particular attribute. For it has no limitation. It is generally thought that the term χαφακτηϱ
refers to the impreffion made by a feal on wax *. When
the impreffion is fair, every line is *charafterized.* Thus,
he who is the *exprefs image* of a divine perfon, muft have
every effential perfeftion of God; eternity, immenfity, immutability, omnifcience, *&c.* as well as wifdom and power.
Unlefs this be the cafe, we cannot conceive that Jefus could
fay, without the moft unparalleled prefumption and hlaf-
phemy; *He that hath feen me, hath feen the Father,* John
xiv. 9. Thirdly, This image muft *perfonally* reprefent
him whofe image he is. We cannot form the idea of one
perfon being the *exprefs image of another,* where the image
is of a different fpecies from the perfon who is reprefented.
It would be abfurd to fay, that a man is the *exprefs image*
of the perfon of an angel; becaufe they are not perfons of
the fame order. Much more abfurd muft it be to fay, that
a man is the *exprefs image* of the *Perfon* of God; becaufe
the one is infinitely removed from the other.

11. Jefus receives this defignation, as implying his effential and univerfal dominion in the kingdom of *providence.*
*God—hath fpoken by the Son----who upholdeth all things by
the word of his power,* Heb. i. 1.—3. Dr P. informs us,
that this is " God's power †." It is fo indeed; but not in
his fenfe, as excluding the Son. Here our author feems to
follow Grotius. But the conftruftion excludes this view;
the relative *his* naturally referring to the perfon *upholding.*
But let us fuppofe, for a moment, that the Doftor's interpretation

pretation is juft.' What would follow? That Jefus is a creature? By no means. For it is admitted that he is the immediate agent in providence. Can a creature have omnipotence in truft? Can he even utter the *word* of almighty *power?* Can he fo *command,* that all things fhall *ftand faft?* It is fully as ridiculous to fuppofe that a creature can *uphold by the word of* God's *power,* as that he can *create* by the fame means. For the language here ufed evidently refers to the divine power exerted in creation; and denotes that the work of providence is merely a continued exertion of this power, in the fame manner, Pfal. xxxiii. 9. cxlviii. 5. But according to the fuppofition, a creature muft not only be entrufted with omnipotence, but poffeffed of omniprefence. For this *upholding* extends to *all things.* However, it has been already proved that *the worlds,* faid to be made by him, are the material worlds. Therefore, the *all things* here mentioned muft be underftood with the fame latitude.

The language of this place is of the fame import with that in Col. i. 15. *By him all things confift.* This has been formerly vindicated from our author's glofs. Nothing more is here afcribed to Jefus, than what he claims as his prerogative, when he fays; *My Father worketh hitherto, and I work,* John v. 17. This we have alfo feen, can fignify nothing but a continued famenefs of operation.

12. He is exhibited as the Son of God in fo peculiar a fenfe, as to be entitled to the *worfhip* of the moft exalted creatures: *When he bringeth in the firft begotten into the world, he faith, And let all the angels of God worfhip him,* Heb. i. 6. Dr P., without a fingle reflection on this text, endeavours, in a circuitous manner, to invalidate the argument drawn from it, in proof of the deity of the Son. After quoting it, he adds a number of paffages from the gofpel-hiftory, which refer to the worfhip of Chrift, fubjoin-

I

ing this remark; ". But the very circumftances in which
" this worfhip was paid to Chrift, fufficiently prove that
" divine worfhip was not intended *."

The firft circumftance mentioned is, that " it is well
" known that the Jews had no expectation of any other
" perfon than a man for their Mefliah." This is a very
ufeful circumftance to our learned author. It is ready on
all occafions. Does he combat an argument from eccle-
.fiaftical hiftory, in fupport of our Saviour's divinity? Is it
proved that the firft believers adored the Son? He tells
you that this is impoffible ; becaufe the Jews believed that
the Mefliah would be a mere man. Is it an argument
from fcripture? It receives the fame anfwer. Here he oppofes it to the teftimony of the Holy Spirit refpecting an
exprefs precept. This is its force : " God commanded his
" very angels to worfhip the Son. But he undoubtedly
" meant that they fhould regulate their homage, according
" to the ideas of that people who nationally rejected and
" crucified him as a blafphemer." Though the Doctor's
affertion were true, it might with equal propriety be urged,
that we are not to believe in Jefus as a *fpiritual* Mefliah,
becaufe the generality of the Jews did not expect one in
this character. But it has been proved that thofe who
waited for the confolation of Ifrael, expected a divine Saviour. It has been often faid, that we cannot form a juft
idea of a man's character, without hearing what his enemies
fay of him. And it muft be |acknowledged that Dr P.
feems difpofed rigidly to obferve this rule, in judging of
him whom he calls Mafter.

But let us attend to another circumftance : " When Ni-
" codemus was convinced of the miraculous power of Jefus,
" he concluded, not that he was *God,* but that he muft
" have been *impowered by God;* for he fays, John iii. 2.—
                " *No*

---

* Ibid. p. 27.

" *No man can do these miracles,—except God be with him.*"
The Doctor has already examined Christ's enemies on the
point. The second witness he summons, is one whom Jesus
himself hath declared incompetent, as being ignorant, and
yet in unbelief, ver. 10—12. But, perhaps, our author
has a partiality for this *master of Israel,* as he discovered
such philosophical antipathy to the doctrine of regeneration.

It is mentioned as another " well-known" circumstance,
" that the Greek word, which, in the above mentioned
" passages, is rendered *worship,* is frequently used to ex-
" press a very high degree of respect, but such as may be
" lawfully paid to men of a proper character and rank;
" and indeed," it is said, " our word *worship,* though now
" appropriated to that worship which is due to God only,
" was formerly used with greater latitude, and even in our
" translation of the Bible; as when a servant, in one of our
" Saviour's parables, is said to have fallen down and *wor-*
" *shipped* his master, saying, *Have patience with me, and I*
" *will pay thee all;* where certainly divine worship could
" not be meant." The Doctor artfully blends the signification of the Greek word with the ancient use of the English. This he seems to do, because of his scarcity of evidence from the original. But what has the meaning of an
English word to do with that of a Greek one? Can the
use of a word in one language prove its determinate sense
in another? The only instance from the New Testament,
which seems to have occurred as a proof that προσκυνεω *fre-*
quently signifies civil homage, is that in Mat. xviii. 26.
Our translators certainly did right in rendering it *worship-*
ped. Though this were a true history, it would not prove
what Dr P. wishes. For many a one, from fear, from
fashion, or from interest, has given religious worship to a
mere man. But it must be remembered, that this is a parable:

rable: and it is a _well known_ rule, that parables and alle-
gories are not to be interpreted as if, in every circumftance,
they correfponded to facts. But, indeed, it feems moft
natural to think that, in this parable, our Lord reprefents
the worfhip givèn to him who _can forgive fin._

Dr P. is fo much at a lofs for proofs on this fubject, that
he borrows one from the book of Common Prayer. " It
" is alfo an evidence," he fays, " of this ufe of the word,
" that in our marriage fervice, the man is directed to fay
" to the woman, _With my body I thee worfhip_; and the
" terms _worfhip_, and _worfhipful_, are ftill applied to feveral
" of our magiftrates, and bodies of men." But I cannot
perceive the meaning of all this; unlefs our author means
to do ferioufly, what a facetious divine did in jeft, when he
attempted to prove that all languages were derived from
the Englifh. It would be neceffary for the Doctor, indeed,
to carry the matter a ftep farther, by fhewing, that the
fenfe of words in other languages is to be ftrictly regulated
by that of thofe which moft nearly correfpond to them in
ours. As he has referred his reader to the Marriage Ser-
vice, he ought to have explained the paffage, that it
might be known what kind or degree of _worfhip_ he means.
He fhould alfo have told us, if προσκυνεω is generally to be
underftood as merely fignifying fuch a degree of refpect as
is due to a Juftice of Peace, or to a Common Council; and
if he thinks that nothing more is intended in the command
addreffed to angels. It may, indeed, be fuppofed by fome,
that fuch creatures as thofe referred to, meet with more
worfhip from their dependents, than Socinians allow to
their Lord and Saviour. For they are often the _objects_ of
prayer.

The argument derived from the occafional ufe of this
word in the Septuagint, is of no weight, when oppofed to
pofitive evidence from the language of infpiration.

There

There are several circumstances worthy of attention on the other side. It has been formerly proved that the passages referred to by the Doctor, in which Christ is said to be worshipped, are all to be understood of religious adoration *. As far as I can observe, there is not one place, in the New Testament, which can be understood otherwise. If religious worship be not meant in this passage, the end by no means corresponds to the solemnity of the action. For those who were appointed to be *ministring spirits* to all *the heirs,* could not be supposed to be deficient in *respect* to *the author of salvation.* But when we understand the term of religious homage, we perceive great propriety in the solemn injunction. Thus it appears, that the incarnation of the Son, by which he was *made a little lower than the angels,* was to be no obstacle to the continuance of their adoration.

This passage is generally supposed to refer to Psal. xcvii. 7. *Worship him, all ye gods:* especially as this name seems to be sometimes given to angels. There can be no doubt that the command there respects religious worship. For the person meant, who is undoubtedly the Messiah, is directly opposed, as the proper object of worship, to those false deities mentioned immediately before; *Confounded be all they that serve graven images, that boast themselves of idols.* If we attend to the connexion in which the command is introduced by the inspired writer, there can be no reason to doubt that it respects religious worship. For, as hath been proved, he has previously declared that the Son is the God of nature, and of providence. We have formerly seen in what sense angels themselves understood the worship expressed by this term, and of course, the sense in which they must have understood the command. When the Divine fell down at the feet of one of these pure spirits,

---

* See above, p, 214, 215.

rits, προσκυνσαι αυτω, to give him the " very high degree of " refpeⱦ," which this word denotes, he inftantly replied; *See, thou do it not,* τω Θεω προσκυνησον, *worfhip God,* Rev. xix. 10.

We are certain that angels obey this command in the fulleft fenfe of the word. For the fame infpired writer teftifies, that he heard *every creature in heaven, faying, Bleffing, and honour, and glory, and power be unto him that fitteth on the throne, and unto the Lamb for ever and ever,* Rev. v. 13. How he can be a partner in the higheft adoration, who is not of the fame effence with the Father, let Socinians explain.

13. He is defcribed as a Son who has an effential right to the name of *God,* in the full fenfe of the word. *Unto the Son he faith, Thy throne, O God, is for ever and ever,* Heb. i. 8. Socinians feem to be confcious that this name, when ufed abfolutely and reftriⱦed to an individual, as it is here, invariably denotes the true God. Therefore they endeavour to avert the force of the argument from this paffage, by objeⱦing to the tranflation. Some of their more ancient writers, indeed, among whom was Biddle, had fo much honefty as to acknowledge that the Son is here called God †. But Dr P. is not difpofed to make fuch a conceffion. He obferves that the paffage " may be " rendered, *God is thy throne for ever and ever*; that is, " God will eftablifh the authority of Chrift till time fhall " be no more *." This idea feems to have been firft thrown out by Erafmus; though he was not fatisfied that it was juft. However, it was eagerly laid hold of by Grotius and Enjedinus, as expreffing the true fenfe of the place. But this view is liable to feveral important objeⱦions. It is contrary to the meaning of the Hebrew; as far as ancient interpreters, whether Jews or Greeks, can be confi-

* Biddle's Catechifm.   † Famil. Illuftr. p. 35.

dered as judges. According to the Targum, *God* is in the vocative. In the Septuagint, it is rendered in the fame manner, as in the Greek of the, New Teftament. The Doctor's ancient Unitarian friend, Aquila, whofe learning he greatly commends, feems never to have thought that it could bear any other fenfe than that given in our verfion. There can be no difpute as to the meaning of his language *.

This view is inconfiftent with the preceding context, in which the Son is defcribed as the Creator and Preferver of all things, and as the object of worfhip; and therefore, as God equal with the Father. It alfo changes the natural fubject. This ought to be the *throne* of the Son, as contrafted with the *minifterial* ftation of angels, which is the fubject of the preceding verfe; nay, fuch a throne as can belong to him alone who is effentially *God*, in contradiftinction to the miniftry of thofe who are mere *creatures*, and who were *made* for the purpofe of this miniftry: Of *the angels he faith, Who maketh his angels,* or *meffengers fpirits.—But unto the Son, Thy throne, O God, &c.* But according to the Socinian verfion, *God* is the fubject; not as oppofed to *angels*, but as oppofed to the *Son.* The honour is carried away from the Son to the Father, in direct oppofition to the evident defign of the infpired writer. Nor is this interpretation fupported by the claufe immediately following in the clofeft connexion; *The fceptre of thy kingdom is a right fceptre.* Socinians ought to fhew, how God is the *fceptre*, as well as the *throne* of Chrift's kingdom; elfe we are left to fuppofe that although it has a divine foundation, the adminiftration is merely human.

But they cannot produce a fingle example from fcripture of the ufe of fuch language. God is often claimed by his people as their *rock*, their *refuge*, their *high tower :* but it is no where faid that he is the *throne* of his creature. The

idea,

---

* Ο θρονος σȣ, Θεε, εις αιωνα και ετι.

idea, indeed, is abfurd. When he is called a *rock, &c.* it is confiftent with his dignity : for fuch expreffions denote that defence which is afforded by the ftronger to the weaker. But the Sovereign is certainly greater than his *throne.* Thus, the enemies of the Son, in attempting to prove that he is effentially inferior to the Father, make the Father inferior to the Son. However, they wifh to fupply the word *eftablifh.* I will not fay, that this is to fuppofe a ftrong figure without any neceffity. For with them the neceffity is as great as that of providing a crutch for the lame. But it is evidently to fuppofe a mode of fpeaking to be found no where elfe ; and inftead of explaining the text to make one of their own.

The Doctor adds ; " From this paffage nothing can be " more plain, than that, whatever authority belongs to " Chrift, he has a fuperior from whom he derives it ; *God,* " *even thy God, has anointed thee.* This could never have " been faid of the one true God, whofe being and power are " underived." It is granted that this is not immediately faid of him as God, but as God-man or Mediator. It is no objection to his being addreffed as *God,* that the fubject of the addrefs is his mediatory exaltation. For while the official character of Jefus requires the deity of the perfon as its foundation, it cannot poffibly imply any forfeiture of his effential right. The glory of the God-head is difplayed in human nature. Socinians, however, have laid it down as a firft principle in their fyftem, that although God may communicate his effential perfections to a mere creature, he cannot affume the creature into union with himfelf, and thus ftand in a relation different from what effentially belongs to him. God may *deny,* but he cannot *humble himfelf.* But it is impoffible for them to prove, that he who is inferior to the Father in one relation, may not be his equal in another. If this appear from fcripture, we are bound to believe it :

H h 2   and

and there can be no objection to this being the doctrine of the paffage, but that Socinians are determined to reject this doctrine, however clear the evidence.

But that Jefus is here addreffed as a divine Perfon, is undeniable from the quotation immediately following ; *And thou, Lord, in the beginning, haft laid the foundation of the earth, and the heavens are the work of thy hands. They fhall perifh, but thou remaineft, &c.* ver. 10.—12.   Our learned author is much at a lofs what to make of thefe words.   He tries them firft in one way, then in another, and at length hazards a conjecture as to a third. "In ver. "10, 11, 12." he fays, "the apoftle quotes an addrefs to "God, as the great Creator and everlafting Ruler of the "univerfe, but without any hint of its being applied to "Chrift *."   But as if this were carrying the matter rather too far, it being undeniable that the preceding context contains fome *hints* concerning him, the Doctor advances a ftep farther.   But he advances with great caution, as treading on dangerous ground. "This quotation was *probably* "made with a view to exprefs the great honour conferred "on Chrift, on account of the dignity of the perfon who "conferred it."   But this is rather a round-about way of expreffing honour, and far from being ufual with the concife and energetic writer of this epiftle.   Had this been his defign, it might have been as natural a plan to have told what the honour was.   Some may be apt to doubt too, whether one, writing to Hebrews, and having already told them that the honour referred to was conferred by God, *who fpake to their fathers by the prophets,* could give them a better idea of its greatnefs, by telling them that this God was "the Creator and Ruler of the univerfe."   An Hebrew would certainly have reckoned this a very poor compliment to his own underftanding, and a fufficient proof of the weaknefs of his who thus addreffed them.

But,

* Ibid.

But, according to Dr P. the *probability* of this appears from evidence. " *For* it immediately follows, ver. 13. " *But to which of the angels faid he,* that is, the great " being to whom this defcription belongs, *Sit thou on my* " *right hand,* &c." But this is evidently to be viewed as a diftinct proof from the former. Our author artfully tries to throw the emphafis on the pronoun *he ;* whereas every impartial reader muft obferve that it refts upon thefe words, *which of the angels.* For the infpired writer is not abftractly illuftrating the dignity of *him* who faid this ; nor does he mean to infer the dignity of the perfon to whom this was faid, from fo remote a confideration as the greatnefs of the fpeaker. But he illuftrates this in a direct manner, by denying the honour of fuch an addrefs to any of the angels, how exalted foever. Therefore he immediately afferts that they are *all*, without exception, *miniftring fpirits,* not merely to the King of Zion, but to his fubjects : evidently inferring from this confideration, that they could never receive a call to that honour referved for their Lord. He *fits* as a Sovereign. He *fits on* God's *right hand,* as being effentially his *fellow.* But they are *all fent forth* as fervants.

After all, the Doctor advances a little ; as if confcious that he muft grant fomething more, however reluctantly, unlefs he would feem to trifle with his text. " Or fince " this quotation from the Pfalmift," he fays, " defcribes a " perpetuity of empire in God, it may be intended to in-" timate a perpetuity of empire in Chrift, who holds his " authority from God, and who muft hold it, unlefs God be " unable to fupport it." Still very cautious. It *may—in-timate.* But it cannot even intimate fo much. If thefe words properly refpect the empire of God, they can prove nothing as to the perpetuity of the government of the Meffiah. Did we fuppofe that he were a mere man, and had we no better fecurity for the perpetuity of his empire, than the perpetuity of the divine; we could not be more certain of the continuance of his, than of any human government. For *the powers that be are* alfo *of God.* Yet they are fubject to change. The quotation muft be viewed by itfelf, as refting on its own foundation: and if it proves nothing directly as to the dignity of the Perfon who is Meffiah, or as to the nature of his kingdom, it proves nothing at all. But though this fhould be the cafe, it is no more than what we may expect. For our author, who feems to think that even *the fpirits of the* Apoftles *are fubject unto* him, affures us that Paul, the reputed writer of this epiftle, " often reafons inconclufively, and therefore----" without any particular infpiration *."

' Indeed, he feems to be at pains to make the Apoftle reafon *inconclufively.* For if the reafoning of the paffage, according to the Doctor's interpretation, could prove any thing, it would prove unfpeakably more than he would choofe to admit. If the defcription of " a perpetuity of " empire in God," be any *intimation* of " a perpetuity of " empire in Chrift," it muft certainly intimate that the empire of Chrift fhall continue as long as the empire of God, as long as God is not " unable to fupport it." Now, Dr P. will not refufe that the divine empire is ftrictly eternal. But how will this agree with what he has faid in explaining the preceding quotation? All the perpetuity that he afcribes to the empire of Chrift, is the " eftablifh-" ment of his authority till time fhall be no more."

But notwithftanding all the fhuffling modes of interpretation that may be devifed, it is clear from the connexion that the infpired writer applies the language of the Pfalm to our Lord. Socinians themfelves acknowledge that he is the fubject of the preceding quotations, however ftrangely they explain them. It is alfo evident from the introductory particle και, *And.* There is no correfpondent word,
either

either in the Hebrew, or in the Septuagint. It undoubtedly fignifies that the quotation following is to be applied in
the fame manner as the preceding; and refers to the beginning of ver. 8. *But unto the Son he faith.* To every
unprejudiced reader, it muft convey the fame idea as if that
introduction had been formally repeated.

14. Jefus is a Son in fo peculiar a fenfe that the *church*
is declared to be *his building* and *property.* In the fame
epiftle, chap. iii. a comparifon is inftituted between Mofes
and Chrift. The defign of the Apoftle is to prove the fuperiority of the latter. He fhews that there is as great a
difference between the one and the other, as between the
houfe and the builder of it : *For* ουτος, *this perfon was truly
worthy of more glory than Mofes, in as much as he who
hath builded the houfe, hath more honour than the houfe,*
ver. 3. He fhews that Mofes was merely a fervant in the
houfe of God, but *Chrift a Son over his own houfe,* ver.
5, 6. Chrift, by difpenfation, was alfo a fervant. In this
refpect, he is faid to have been *faithful.* But his fidelity
was not that of a natural inferior. *He was faithful as a Son.*
He was not merely *in* the houfe, like Mofes; but *over* it :
and not *over* it, like one advanced to an honour that did
not originally belong to him ; but *over* it, *as his own houfe,*
his natural property. But how can the church be the property of Chrift, unlefs he be God?

Indeed, the Apoftle proves the deity of our Saviour,
from his work of building the church. *For every houfe is
builded by fome one ; but he that built all things is God,*
ver. 5. It is clear that Chrift is here meant. For he is
immediately fpoken of as the builder; and as, on this very
account, fuperior in glory to Mofes. It feems to be juftly
obferved by the learned Owen, that τα παντα is put for
ταυτα παντα, *all thefe things* that the Apoftle is prefently
treating of. That the expreffion refpects the church, is

evident

evident from the ufe of the word κατασκευω formerly ap‑
plied to the building of the houfe, and no where ufed in
fcripture to denote the creation of all things. Unlefs
Chrift be meant as the builder, ver. 4. the connexion and
force of the argument are loft. For it is not the Apoftle's
defign to compare Mofes with God abfolutely confidered,
but to compare him with God-man *. At any rate, it is
undeniable from ver. 3. that the work of building the
church belongs to Chrift, in a fenfe in which it cannot be
afcribed to any mere fervant. Now, the church is *God's
building*, 1 Cor. iii. 9. Therefore, Chrift is God.

In a word, he is a Son, the faith and knowledge of whom
give *perfection* to our nature. Therefore the Apoftle fays;
—*Till we all come in the unity of the faith, and of the know‑
ledge of the Son of God, unto a perfect man*, Eph. iv. 13.
This conftitutes the perfection of the whole myftical body
of Chrift. Either the Socinian expects an higher perfec‑
tion than what is here defcribed; or, according to his ideas,
his higheft perfection confifts in believing in and knowing
a mere man. But the true Chriftian expects fomething un‑
fpeakably greater. He is fatisfied that, in knowing the
Son more perfectly, he fhall *be filled with all the fulnefs of
God*. But he is alfo affured that, although his attainments
in this refpect will far exceed the prefent, he fhall be eter‑
nally loft in the greatnefs of the fubject. Therefore the
Apoftle, in the preceding chapter, afcribes incomprehen‑
fibility to the Saviour, when fpeaking with refpect to one
perfection only: *That ye—may be able to comprehend with
all faints, what is the breadth, and length, and depth, and
height; and to know the love of Chrift, which paffeth know‑
ledge, that ye might be filled with all the fulnefs of God*,
ver. 17.—19. He fpeaks of the love of Chrift in the fame
terms in which Zophar defcribes the divine nature. The
Apoftle,

* Vide Owen in loc. Cameron. Opera, p. 30. Prælect. in Matth.

Apoftle, indeed, feems to copy his figurative language : *Canft thou by fearching find out God ? canft thou find out the Almighty unto perfection ? It is as high as heaven, what canft thou do ? deeper than hell, what canft thou know ? The meafure thereof is longer than the earth, and broader than the fea*, Job. xi. 7.—9.

Before leaving this fubject, we may attend to an obfervation made by Dr P. which he feems to confider as a fufficient reply to every argument that may be urged from the ufe of this character as applied to our Saviour. Referring to the argument from thefe paffages that exhibit Chrift as the *image* of God, he fays ; " It is with as little " appearance of reafon that Chrift is argued to be very and " eternal God, becaufe he is ftyled *the Son of God;* for all " Chriftians have the fame appellation, I John iii. 2. *Now* " *are we the Sons of God* *."

This reply affords a ftriking proof of the ftrange inconfiftency of Socinians. For it is advanced by the Doctor, after he has granted that Jefus is called *the Son of God* in a peculiar fenfe, as being *the Chrift*, and endeavoured to fhew that thefe terms are perfectly fynonymous *. But as if he queftioned whether this ground were tenable, he eventually refufes that peculiarity formerly granted, and fecures a more extenfive foundation for his batteries againft the truth. One would almoft think that a Socinian would give you leave to make of *his Saviour* what you pleafe, if you do not plead for his deity. But if Jefus be called *the Son of God* in the fame fenfe as all Chriftians, he cannot be thus diftinguifhed as Meffiah. If fo, will the learned writer be pleafed to inform us, what was the meaning of our Lord's teftimony, when he affented to the high-prieft's adjuration ? Do not profeffors of Chriftianity, who *handle the word of God* in this manner, expofe themfelves to the

attacks

---

‡ Fam. Illuftr. p. 23.   † Ibid. p. 22.

attacks of infidels? Might not a Deist say, with great ap.
pearance of reason; " You first inform us, that your Ma.
" ster is called *the Son of God* as being *the Christ*, that is,
" he receives this name in a peculiar sense; nay, that he
" confirmed this sense of the expression by solemn oath,
" Then you assure us that all Christians have the same
" appellation. Either you must believe that every Chri-
" stian is a Messiah, or you believe in none at all."

But to say that all Christians are called *the sons of God*,
proves nothing; unless it can be proved that they receive
this character in the same sense in which it is given to Jesus.
But not even the same language is used. Are they *all*
called God's *proper sons*, his *only begotten sons?* With far
more propriety might it be said that, because all believers
are called *the servants of Christ*, Eph. vi. 6. none receive
this name peculiarly and distinctively, as ministers of the
gospel, Jude ver. 1. Because magistrates and idols are called
gods, by a parity of reason the polytheist might deny that
the scripture maintains the divine unity. He might plead
that it favours heathenism, and that JEHOVAH is a deity in
common with others. For his being called *the true God,
the living God, the one God*, might with equal propriety be
of as little account with him, as Christ's being called God's
only and *only begotten Son* is with a Socinian.

But there is sufficient evidence from the connexion of
that very passage quoted by our author, that, while the
Apostle uses this character by way of resemblance, he
marks a very important distinction. Such a Son is Jesus,
that all other sons receive their *anointing*, not merely by,
but *from* him, and must continue in him in the same respects as in the Father, 1 John ii. 20. 24.; that whosoever
denieth him hath not the Father, ver. 22.; that all other
sons must appear before him as their judge, and are begotten of him as their father; ver. 28, 29. Such is the essential

tial dignity of this Son, that it is an ineffable wonder of
love that any of Adam's family fhould be honoured with
the fame defignation; chap. iii. 1.　He is a Son manifefted
for the very purpofe of taking away the fins of others, and
deftroying the works of the devil, ver. 5. 8. and who pre-
ferves all that are united to him from falling into condemnation, ver. 6.　After all this, had any one faid to the
Apoftle; " You do not mean that this title denotes any
" effential fuperiority in Jefus to us, for we alfo are *all the*
" *fons of God*;" there is every reafon to believe that he
would have pronounced him a baftard, and not a fon.

Dr P. fubjoins; " We are called not only the *children*, but
" *the heirs of God, and joint heirs with Chrift*," Rom. viii.
17. But as the perfons who are thus denominated have
been once under *the law of fin and death*, ver. 2. and *enmity
againft God*, ver. 7. the paffage cannot prove what the
Doctor wifhes.　Becaufe a rebel was mercifully pardoned
by his fovereign, and even admitted to a participation of
the honour belonging to him whom the king acknowledged as *his own fon, his proper fon*, (ver. 3. 32.) would any
one therefore plead that the pardoned rebel was as truly
and properly the king's fon as the other?

To as little purpofe is it urged that " Adam is more
" efpecially called *the Son of God*, Luke iii. 38." For it
is undeniable that he receives this character, becaufe he was
created after the image of God.　But Chrift is thus denominated, becaufe he is the very *image of the invifible God,
the exprefs image of* the Father's *perfon*; not created, but
begotten.　We are alfo told that " Ephraim is called *his*
" *dear Son*," Jer. xxxi. 20.　But there is no connexion
here.　For it is well known that the Ifraelites, (who were
often called *Ephraim*, to diftinguifh them from the kingdom of Judah) received this character, becaufe of their external

ternal relation to God as his peculiar people.　Here it may
have a fpecial refpeÆt to their repentance foretold in the
preceding verfes.　But can Dr P. really mean that this defignation, as denoting the Saviour, is to be underftood in
no higher a fenfe than when applied to thofe who have
previoufly been *as a bullock unaccuftomed to the yoke,* and
who have *borne the reproach of their youth?* ver. 19, 2c.

B O O K

VINDICATION

OF THE

DOCTRINE of SCRIPTURE, &c.

BOOK IV.

OF DOCTOR PRIESTLEY's ARGUMENTS AGAINST THE DIVINITY OF CHRIST.

C H A P. I.

The first Argument, from what is supposed to be the general Tenor of the Scriptures, considered.

THE Doctor prefaces his objections by a very just observation. "An impartial person," he says, "may "easily satisfy himself, that the writers of the books of "scripture held the doctrine of *one God*, and that they were "understood to do so by those persons for whose use the "books were written *." Here in words at least we perfectly agree with our author. But the foundation of the

* Vol. i. p. 3, 4.

Socinian fyftem is laid in the affumption of two falfehoods, as if they had been proved to be indifputable truths; firft, that thofe who hold the doctrine of the Trinity believe in more Gods than one; and fecondly, that *one God* muft of neceffity be *one perfon* only. The charge of polytheifm, however, belongs not to Trinitarians, but to their oppo-nents, who afcribe the perfections and prerogatives of the one God to angels, and to a mere man. It muft be obvi-ous to every impartial reader, that on thefe falfe grounds the whole of Dr P.'s reafoning againft the divinity of our Saviour proceeds.

He grants that the plural number " is made ufe of, when " God is reprefented as faying, Gen. i. 26. *Let us make* " *man.*" " But," he adds, " that this is mere phrafeology, " is evident from its being faid immediately after, in the " fingular number, ver. 27. *God created man in his own* " *image,* fo that the creator was ftill one *being *.*" A plu-rality of perfons in an unity of *being*, is all that we plead for. But nothing will pleafe a Socinian, as a proof of a plurality of perfons, that would not prove a plurality of *beings*, that is, of *gods*. He alfo refers to thefe words, Gen. xi. 7. *God faid, Let us go down, and there confound their language.* His reply to the argument for a plurality from this paffage, is equally fage. " But we find, in the very " next verfe, that it was one being only who actually ef-" fected this." And what Trinitarian ever afferted the contrary? That kind of fpeaking or writing cannot juftly be dignified with the name of *argument*, that proves what has never been doubted by the adverfe party. The Doc-tor ought to have proved, not that one being was the agent in both inftances; but that a fingle perfon is meant, when the plural number is ufed, and that he did not addrefs any other perfon, but *himfelf*.

Our author goes on in the fame important demonftration.

" In

* Ibid. p. 4.

" In all the intercourfe of God, with Adam, Noah, and the
" other patriarchs, no mention is made of more than one be-
" ing who addreffed them under that character. The name
" by which he is diftinguifhed is fometimes *Jehovah*, and at
" other times *the God of Abraham*, &c." He might alfo have
mentioned that he who calls himfelf *the God of Abraham*,
is called *the Angel of Jehovah.* But this would have given
him the trouble of formally anfwering an objection, which,
as has been already feen, he wifely paffes over as lightly as
poffible, when brought in by him, as if merely *en paffant.*
A wife man will not raife a ghoft, which he is not fure that
he can lay.

As a proof of the unity of God, in the Socinian fenfe,
the Doctor refers to Deut. vi. 4. But it has been formerly proved that the ancient Jews, however ftedfaftly
they maintained the doctrine of the divine unity, explained
this paffage of a plurality of perfons *.

" The Meffiah," he fays, " is *fuppofed* to be announced
" to our firft parents under the title of *the feed of the wo-*
" *man*, Gen. iii. 15 †." We hope, the Doctor does not
fuppofe any thing elfe: however unpalatable this expreffion may be to him, now that he has difcovered that the
fcriptural doctrine of the miraculous conception has the
marks of a " ftory inconfiftent and ill-digefted." But he
has found out a method of getting rid of this fingular expreffion : " The phrafe *born of woman*, which is," he fays,
" of the fame import, is always in fcripture fynonymous to
" *man*." It is exprefsly denied that the phrafe *born of wo-*
man is of the fame import with *the feed of the woman.*
There are other paffages which contain language of the
fame import: but it is always fo guarded as to fhew that
an extraordinary, and even an unparalleled event is meant.
Thus it is faid, Jer. xxxi. 22. *The Lord hath created a new
thing in the earth, A woman fhall compafs a man.* But was
it

* See above, p. 74.—76.   † Vol. i. p. 8.

it *a new thing in the earth*, for a man to be *born of a wo-man?* It was a fign that JEHOVAH *himfelf* was to *give*, that *a virgin* fhould *conceive*, and *bear a fon*, Ifa. vii. 14. If Jefus received his human nature in the ordinary way, the Apoftle Paul is chargeable with a mere affectation of fin-gularity, without the leaft reafon, when he fays that *God fent forth his Son made of a woman*, Gal. iv. 3. One of thefe very texts on which the Doctor leans, for the fupport of his affertion with refpect to the confonancy of the phrafes mentioned, proves to him a broken reed which pierces into the very heart of his argument. This is Job xxv. 4. *How can he be clean that is born of a woman?* Becaufe no one *born of a woman*, according to the ordinary courfe of na-ture, can be *clean;* it was neceffary that our high-prieft fhould be *feparate from finners* in his very conception, and therefore that he fhould be *made of a woman*.

Dr P. quotes Deut. xviii. 18. *I will raife them up a pro-phet, from among their brethren*, &c. adding, with an air of triumph ; " Here is nothing like a fecond perfon in the " Trinity, a perfon equal to the Father, but a mere pro-" phet, delivering in the name of God, whatever he is or-" dered fo to do *." This kind of reafoning would be va-lid, if the friends of the deity of Chrift refufed that he fuftained any other character than that of a divine perfon. But on no other fuppofition does it deferve an anfwer. Much in the fame manner, might thofe, who never faw David till he was afcending Mount Olivet, weeping, with his head uncovered, and bare-foot, fay ; " Here is nothing " like the King of Ifrael." Jefus fays to his difciples, *Lo, I am among you as one that ferveth.* With equal propriety might it be argued from thefe words, that he conld be in no refpect fuperior to the difciples, becaufe *here is nothing like* fuperiority. Our author ought to give his argument its due weight. For the words of God by Mofes will equally

prove

prove that Jeſus was not to be a prieſt or a king, as that he
was not to be a divine perſon ; becauſe he is not *here* mentioned under any of theſe characters. But this is not to
give *arguments from the tenor of ſcripture*, but from detached paſſages, and even without regard to the principal
deſign of theſe.

It is not fact, that here we have " nothing—but a mere
" prophet." It would, indeed, be of no avail to us, were
the Saviour revealed in his divine nature only. We would
utter the ſame language as the Iſraelites, when God ſpoke
to them immediately. They were ſo afraid of his majeſty that they ſaid, *Let not God ſpeak with us, leſt we die,*
Ex. xx. 19. They wiſhed for one, in their own nature,
to mediate between God and them. They propoſed Moſes : and God declared his aſſent. But it is evident that
he was accepted merely as a temporary mediator, and as a
type of one unſpeakably fitter for the work. For it was
on this very occaſion, of the people expreſſing their deſire
of a Mediator, that the prophecy under conſideration was
delivered. In the choice of the occaſion, God ſhewed
them, that, in complying with their propoſal, he uſed
Moſes merely as a type. Therefore, he directed their
principal attention to the Antitype, at the very time that
it would have been moſt neceſſary to have confined their
attention to Moſes, had he not been employed in an inferior character. Moſes himſelf, well aſſured of his own inferiority, does not fail to remind the Iſraelites of the circumſtance mentioned. *The Lord thy God will raiſe up unto*
thee a prophet, from the midſt of thee, of thy brethren, like
unto me, unto him ye ſhall hearken. ACCORDING TO ALL
THAT THOU DESIREDST *of the Lord thy God in Horeb, in*
the day of the aſſembly, ſaying, Let me not hear again the
voice of the Lord my God, neither let me ſee this great fire
any more that I die not. And the Lord ſaid unto me, They

have well spoken that which they have spoken. I will raise them up a prophet, &c. The promise of a future revelation of the divine will could have brought no confolation to the affrighted and dejected Ifraelites, had they not been affured that it fhould be made by one in human nature. It was impoffible, indeed, that he could otherwife accomplifh the work of mediation. It was neceffary that he fhould be *taken from among men*, Heb. v. 1. But he is not revealed as " a mere prophet." His prophetical character, according to which he was to fpeak the words of God, is mentioned as one branch only of his mediatorial office.

The Doctor afferts that Jefus is here exhibited as a *mere* prophet, moft probably, becaufe he is faid to be *like unto* Mofes. But the word ufed in the original does not fignify fo perfect a fimilitude as admits of no difference. It by no means implies that the perfons or things compared agree in all circumftances. It is enough, if they agree in one or more refpects in which the comparifon is ftated. Nor is it neceffary, that there fhould be an exact fimilarity with refpect to degree. This may be greater or lefs. Sometimes it denotes likenefs, where the perfon or thing compared falls fhort of that with which it is compared ; as in Joel ii. 3. *The land is* AS *the garden of Eden* ; Lam. ii. 13. *Thy breach is great* LIKE *the fea.* Ὡς, the Greek word which correfponds to it, is ufed in the fame manner in the New Teftament. Mat. v. 48. *Be ye perfect* AS *your Father in heaven is perfect.* In other places, it marks fuch a likenefs, that the thing compared exceeds the other. Pfal. ciii. 13. LIKE AS *a father pitieth his children, the Lord pitieth them that fear him.* But it is undeniable, that his compaffion infinitely tranfcends that of any earthly parent *.

Thus, when Chrift is compared to Mofes, it is not meant that they agree in all refpects. Nor will it follow that the former

---

* Vid. Guffetii Comment. in L. Ebraic. in lit. ב.

former does not ſurpaſs the latter, even in thoſe reſpects in which the compariſon is inſtituted.   Therefore, when God ſays to Moſes, *I will raiſe up a prophet—like unto thee,* the expreſſion properly is, *as thou art.*   In the New Teſtament, in both the places where this prediction is quoted, the words are ſo rendered as to ſhew that this is their real meaning : Acts iii. 22. vii. 37. *A prophet ſhall the Lord your God raiſe up unto you of your brethren,* ως εμε, *as he raiſed up me.*   The compariſon is ſtated between Moſes and the Meſſiah, with reſpect to the circumſtance of the latter being a prophet, related to thoſe to whom he ſhould be ſent, as poſſeſſing the ſame nature with them : which was the very conſolation that Iſrael *deſired.*   But it by no means follows that they were equal, as to either perſonal or official dignity.   For thus the prophecy would not have been verified in Jeſus.   For as he is here compared, he is elſewhere contraſted with Moſes, John i. 17, 18.   *The law was given by Moſes, but grace and truth came by Jeſus Chriſt.*   They are not merely oppoſed as to what came by each, but, as we have formerly ſhewn, with reſpect to the very manner of its coming.   *The law was* GIVEN *by Moſes, but grace and truth,* εγενετο, *were* MADE *by Jeſus Chriſt.*   But they are further contraſted.   For it immediately follows ; *No man hath ſeen God at any time.*   This ſeems to be ſpoken with a ſpecial reference to Moſes, as ſhewing that when it is ſaid that God ſpake with him *face to face,* Ex. xxxiii. 11. it ſignifies that he was admitted to greater nearneſs than any other *mere* prophet, but not that he really ſaw God himſelf, or had a proper and full diſplay of his glory *.

That this prophecy declares ſuch a *likeneſs* as admits of great ſuperiority, is evident from its intention, nay, from the very phraſeology.   For when it is ſaid, *Unto him ye*

ſhall

---

* See above, p. 155, 156.

fhall hearken, the church is prepared for a total change of the difpenfation, and informed that fhe fhall then be loofed from Mofes, and fubjected to the authority of Chrift. It is remarkable, that Maimonides explains the following declaration, *Whofoever will not hearken unto my words which he fhall fpeak in my Name, I will require it of him*, by the the language of God refpecting his Angel, Ex. xxiii. 21. *Beware of him, and obey his voice ; for my Name is in him :* although he views the prophet as diftinct from that Angel *.

Chrift is evidently compared with Mofes, as the antitype with the type ; fo as to illuftrate the great fuperiority of the former. Mofes, indeed, is not the only pattern to which this prophet is likened. Another is mentioned in the fame paffage. This is *all* the *defire* of Ifrael. It would appear that this is principally in view, in the likenefs expreffed. For when Mofes has faid, *A Prophet fhall the Lord your God raife up,—like unto me*, he immediately adds, as if the comparifon were too weak, *like unto all that thou haft defired*. For the fame term, denoting refemblance, is ufed in both claufes. It feems to have the fame meaning, as if he had faid ; " God will not merely give you a pro " phet like unto me, but correfpondent to the utmoft " extent of your defires, as expreffed by you on that me " morable day when you wifhed no more to hear the ap " palling voice, or to fee the awful fire of the divine Ma " jefty." God himfelf teftifies peculiar approbation of their language, not becaufe they had propofed Mofes as their Mediator, but becaufe they difplayed a conviction of their abfolute need of one, to convince them of which was the great end of the Law, as being only *a fchoolmafter to bring them to Chrift*. He teftifies his approbation, becaufe it was his fpecial intention, in the whole of that difpenfation, to fhew them the neceffity of fuch a Mediator as

could

More Nevochim, Par. 2. c. 34.

could really remove from them that *great fire* of the divine indignation. Therefore, he gracioufly lays hold of this opportunity of directing their principal attention to Jefus, as that Mediator who alone could *grant them according to their heart, and fulfil all their counfel;* as is faid of *the Name* of the God of Jacob, Pfal. xx. 4. To the primary occa- fion of this prediction, there is a beautiful allufion, joined with a declaration of its accomplifhment, Heb. xii. 18—24. *Ye are not come unto the mount—that burned with fire,— and the voice of words, which they that heard, intreated that the word fhould not be fpoken to them any more;—but ye are come—to Jefus the Mediator of the new covenant, and to the blood of fprinkling.* Therefore, with great propriety it is added, in reference to the ftrict charge concerning this prophet; *See that ye refufe not him that fpeaketh.*

I fhall only add, that while Dr P. denies the deity of Chrift, becaufe it is not mentioned in this prophecy, a Jewifh friend, to whom he frequently appeals, directly re- verfes the matter, although from a fimilar mifapprehenfion of the comparifon. He denies that it can apply to Jefus at all, becaufe he declared himfelf to be God *.

The Doctor further obferves; " By Ifaiah, who writes " more diftinctly concerning the Mefliah than any of the " preceding prophets, his fufferings and death are men- " tioned, chap. liii. Daniel alfo fpeaks of him as to *be cut* " *off*, chap. ix. 26. But furely thefe are characters of *a* " *man*, and not thofe of *a God* †." Undoubtedly, fuffer- ings and death are predicted of him as man; becaufe it was only the human nature that could fuffer. But it will not thence follow that he is not God, unlefs it can be fhewn that thefe are the greateft lines in his character. But both Ifaiah and Daniel, in thefe very paflages, fhew that it was

I i 3   *not*

---

* Nizzachon ap. Owen on Heb. Vol. 1. Ex. 9. p. 99.
† Vol. 1. p. 9.

not for himself that he fuffered and was *cut off*, and that his fufferings had fuch efficacy as cannot be afcribed to thofe of a mere man. For *with his ſtripes we are healed*, Iſa. liii. 5. and in confequence of this, *who ſhall declare his generation?* ver. 8. Becaufe of his bearing their iniquities, he *juſtifies many*, ver. 11. He, who is thus the *Redeemer* of his church, is *the holy One of Iſrael, the God of the whole earth*, whofe name is JEHOVAH *of hoſts*, chap. liv 5. The Angel, in the revelation made to Daniel, fpeaks of the Meffiah or *Anointed*, as *the moſt Holy* previous to his unction. For he was to be *anointed*, or conſtituted *Meſſiah* in our nature, by the gifts of the Spirit, as being already, in his divine nature, *the moſt Holy*, Dan. ix. 24. In being *cut off*, he was to *finiſh tranſgreſſion, make an end of ſins, make reconciliation for iniquity, and bring in everlaſting righteouſneſs*. But perhaps, the real reafon why our author fo obſtinately denies the divine nature of Chriſt, is that he does not perceive the neceſſity of that divine work afcribed to him.

As the Doctor proceeds to illuſtrate the confonancy of the Jewiſh ideas to the prophecies concerning Chriſt, we might have looked for a proof, that although they expected a mere man, they were fully fatisfied that he ſhould be a *ſuffering* Meffiah. But feeble as our author's fyſtem is, it is at war with itfelf. For he immediately adds; " Accordingly, it " appears in the hiſtory of our Saviour, that the Jews of " his time expected that their Meffiah would be a *prince* " and a *conqueror*, like David, from whom he was to be " defcended." What means this *accordingly?* If it mean any thing, it muſt denote that the expectations of the Jews were *according to* the predictions of Iſaiah and Daniel. And how is this proved? Both thefe prophets, in the paffages referred to, defcribed a *ſuffering* Meffiah, a *prince* indeed, but who ſhould be *cut off*. Therefore, the faith of the Jews was perfectly confonant to the revelation, and is

a

a proper pattern for us : becaufe they expected a *prince* and a *conqueror*, that is, a prince, who inftead of being himfelf *cut off*, fhould only *cut off* others. The force of this curious reafoning plainly is, that, like the Jews, we fhould not only deny the *divine*, but the *fuffering* character of the Meffiah.

It is next objected, that " Chrift himfelf always prayed " to this one God as his God and Father * The whole ftrength of this objection lies in a denial of the poffibility of a divine perfon acting the part of a Mediator. For if the Son, in confequence of a voluntary fubftitution in our ftead, affumed human nature, he, in that nature, as a public perfon, owed all thofe duties to which we are bound by the law, as far as they could be performed by one free from perfonal fin, and among the reft, that of prayer. The work of obedience is afcribed to the whole perfon of the Mediator, becaufe of the hypoftatical union : but ftrictly it belonged to the human nature only. As in this nature alone he could fuffer ; this only, in proper language, could be the fubject of faith, hope, and the other graces that became him in fulfilling all righteoufnefs. Prayer is afcribed to the one Mediator. But it was not properly the act of the divine nature, but of the human, fubfifting in his one perfon. Therefore, he did not pray to the *one God*, as excluding his own divine nature ; but either to the Father, œconomically confidered as fuftaining the honour of deity in the work of redemption ; or to God effentially confidered, as including each divine perfon. Thus the Meffiah is addreffed as God, with refpect to his effential dignity, at the very time that God is faid to be his God as Mediator, Pfal. xlv. 6.—8. *Thy throne, O God, is for ever and ever.— God, even thy God, hath anointed thee with the oil of gladnefs.* What is fubjoined, with refpect to Chrift's doctrine

I i 4 and

* Ibid. p. 10.

and power, we have fully confidered in another part of this work.

The Doctor afferts that " the Apoftles, to the lateft pe-
" riod of their writing,—reprefent the Father as the one
" true God, and Chrift as a man the fervant of God who
" raifed him from the dead, and gave him all the power
" of which he is poffeffed, as the reward of his obedience*."
In proof of this bold affertion, he refers to Acts ii. 22.
which we have elfewhere confidered. He alfo quotes,
1 Tim. ii. 5. and Heb. ii. 9. in fupport of his doctrine.
But when it is faid, *There is one God, and one Mediator between God and men, the man Chrift Jefus*, it is not meant
to confine the deity to the Father, or to affert that the Mediator is mere man. For the evident defign of the paffage
is to exhibit God, not in his effential, but in his oeconomi-
cal character, as *our Saviour*, ver. 3. and to fhew that it is
his will that fome of all orders of men, (ver. 2.) fhould be
faved and come to the knowledge of the truth, ver. 4. Therefore, he points out the only way of being *faved*, and that
truth which it is indifpenfably neceffary to *know*. This is
the way of mediation, which he fhews is neceffarily one,
by reafon of the unity of the divine nature. For we cannot fuppofe that there are more ways of mediation than
one, without fuppofing, as the heathen did, a multiplicity
of gods, who muft be appeafed one in one way, and another in another. As the moft convincing proof of it being
the *will* of God *to fave* men, it is declared that a Mediator
is provided in their own nature. In this refpect it hath never been denied that he is inferior. But muft it thence be
inferred that he is nothing more than man? The work
afcribed to him, in the words immediately following, proves
the contrary. For he *gave himfelf a ranfom for all*. But
had he been a mere creature, he could have had no power to
give himfelf for others, and his gift would have been of no
avail.

---

* Ibid. p. 10.

avail. For the utmoſt that a creature can do, he owes to the law for himſelf.

Becauſe it is ſaid, 1 Cor. viii. 6. *To us there is but—one Lord Jeſus Chriſt*, it might with equal propriety be argued that the Father is excluded from all *dominion*, as that the Son is here excluded from deity, becauſe it is ſaid, *There is one God.* It is as eaſy to conceive that the Son ſhould be God in one reſpect, and the Mediator between God and men in another, as that God ſhould *reconcile us to himſelf*, 2 Cor. v. 18. which language undoubtedly ſignifies that he employs means for this end ; that although the offended party, he acts the part of a conciliator.

As to Heb. ii. 9. Chriſt was indeed *made a little lower than the angels.* But it is vain for our author to believe this, while he rejects the deſcription given of him in the preceding chapter, as infinitely higher than the angels, by virtue of his eternal Sonſhip. However, although he ſhould pay as little regard to the firſt chapter of this epiſtle as he does to the firſt chapter of Luke, the very paſſage quoted might convince him, that the perſon ſpoken of previouſly exiſted in a higher character. For it is declared that he was MADE *a little lower*,—FOR *the ſuffering of death.* Now, Dr P. muſt grant either that God's great end in *making* man, is to ſubject him to ſuffering and death ; or that Jeſus, as eſſentially poſſeſſing a higher nature, was, by an extraordinary act, clothed with the human, for a ſpecial end, in the accompliſhment of which he had no equal. And what was this ? It is declared in the very verſe referred to,—*that he by the grace of God ſhould taſte death for every man.*

The Doctor inquires, " Why was not the doctrine of the *trinity* taught as explicitly, and in as definite a man-" ner in the New Teſtament at leaſt, as the doctrine of " the *divine unity* is taught in both the Old and New Teſ-
" taments,

" taments, if it be a truth *?" The great defign of God, in both Teftaments, is to declare his nature and perfections, not abftractly, but as manifefted in his operations, and efpe-cially in the work of our redemption. If, therefore, names, attributes, works and worfhip, proper to God only, are afcribed to diftinct perfons, although one or more of thefe be generally defcribed as fent, it is fufficiently clear that they muft be divine. If notwithftanding thefe effen-tial characters, we deny their deity becaufe of their oeco-nomical relations, our guilt is greatly aggravated. For we refufe to know God in the moft amiable, benevolent and ufeful character in which he could difcover himfelf. The perfonal Wifdom of God, to degrade whom it is our author's great work, gives a fhort but ftriking reply to fuch queftions: *All the words of my mouth are—plain to him that underftandeth.* And again, *A fcorner feeketh wifdom, and findeth it not: but knowledge is eafy to him that underftand-eth*, Prov. viii. 8, 9.; xiv. 6.

Dr P. adds, " Why is the doctrine of the unity always " delivered in fo unguarded a manner, and without any " *exception* in favour of a Trinity, to prevent any miftake " with refpect to it, as is always now done in our orthodox " catechifms, creeds, and difcourfes on the fubject?" God hath not thought fit to lay down a connected fyftem of truth. He requires it as an act of homage which we owe to him, that we fearch the fcriptures, and compare fpiritual things with fpiritual, that we may difcern his will. This holds with refpect to all the doctrines of revelation. But, indeed, in fome texts the doctrine of a Trinity in unity is as clearly declared as ever it was in any human creed. But what does this avail? Either the plain meaning of words is denied; or by the help of a manufcript or two, we are entirely deprived of the text. The inftitu-tion of Baptifm, which is a folemn act of worfhip, con-

tains

* Ibid. p. 12.

tains as *unguarded* a declaration of the *Trinity*, to ufe the Doctor's own language, as any one respecting the *unity*. As thefe orthodox creeds, &c. contain the faith of by far the greateft part of Chriftians, they clearly fhew that, according to the common fenfe of the Chriftian world, the doctrine of a Trinity of perfons is as plainly declared as that of unity of effence.

Our author, in different parts of his work, appeals to Deut. vi. 4. undoubtedly confidering it as one of the moft *guarded* expreffions of the *unity*. But will he be pleafed to inform us, why in this paffage two divine names are introduced, and one of thefe twice ; why *Jehovah* is faid to be *one Jehovah ;* when the Doctor muft be confcious that the unity, according to his view of it, would have been better guarded, had *Jehovah* been faid to be *one perfon*, or fimply *one ;* and why one of the names is given in the *plural*, when this circumftance evidently tends, in the moft direct manner, to convey the idea of *plurality ?* If, as is allowed on all hands, one great defign of the Jewifh difpenfation was to preferve the doctrine of the divine unity, amidft the corruption of furrounding heathens ; if, as is equally certain, the Jews themfelves were greatly addicted to idolatry, and eager to embrace the flighteft pretence for polytheifm ; can any fatisfactory reafon be imagined for the frequent ufe of this plural expreffion, and efpecially in the proclamation of the unity, without fuppofing a neceffity for it from the nature of God, as implying a plurality in unity ? Have we not every reafon to believe that, otherwife, it would have been carefully avoided on every occafion, and efpecially on this ; left it might prove a fnare, or be pleaded as a pretence, if not for the worfhip of *more Jehovahs,* at leaft for the worfhip of *more perfons* than one, that is, according to the Socinian hypothefis, of *more Gods ?*

The Doctor feems determined, like his worthy friends

the

the Jews, to charge Jefus with the character of a *deceiver*, considering the manner in which he expreffed himfelf, if he entertained the idea of equality with the Father. His words, indeed, fill the mind with horror. " It would " be a fhocking abufe of language," he fays, " and would " warrant any kind of *deception* and *impofition*, if Chrift " could be fuppofed to fay, that *his Father was greater* " *than he* *, and yet fecretly mean his *human nature* only, " while his divine nature was at the fame time, fully equal " to that of the Father †." Our author does not feem well acquainted with the very principles that he oppofes. For it is not faid that Chrift means his *human nature only*, but his mediatory character in general. He could not be faid *fecretly* to mean this, unlefs he had never made himfelf known to his difciples in any higher character. Believing his equality with the Father as God, we could not charge him with a *fecret* meaning, not to mention the blafphemous idea of *deception*, although he had not here proclaimed his fuperior nature ; as he had done it on many former occafions. But indeed he had particularly declared this equality in the preceding difcourfe. He had reproved Philip and the other difciples, becaufe they had not fufficiently clear ideas of it ; and taught them, not only that *the Father was in him*, but *he in the Father*, and that in feeing him, they had *feen the Father*, ver. 9.—14. He had referred them to the great event of the effufion of the Spirit, for a more diftinct knowledge and ftedfaft faith of this important truth, ver. 20. *At that day ye fhall know that I am in my Father.* But as the occafion of thefe declarations, was his telling them that he was to *go* from them ; as this expreffion ftumbled their minds, becaufe it feemed inconfiftent with what he had already faid, and to imply inferiority, he at length proceeds to fhow that his *going to the Father*

2   .   was

---

* John xiv. 28.   † Ibid. p. 15.

was really in an inferior character, as his mediatory fervant, and their forerunner.   Is there any fecret *meaning* here? Not thofe who believe, but thofe who deny the deity of Chrift, afcribe a fecret meaning to him.   For when he fays that the *Son of man hath power to forgive fins*, our author maintains he could only mean that he had power to *declare* forgivenefs.   When he fays, *Where two or three are gathered together in my Name, there am I in the midft of them*, Dr P. afferts, that he could only mean to reprefent the power of the difciples with God.   When Jefus teftifies that he was *before* Abraham, we are affured that " his " meaning clearly is, that Abraham *forefaw*, and of confe. " quence, was *before* him *." When he fays, *I and the Father are one*, we are taught that his meaning was, that they were *one* in intention only ; not in power, in purpofe, in effence, or in any of thefe refpects which the term moft naturally im- plies, efpecially according to its connexion, and in which it was underftood by thofe who heard him.

The Doctor's reafoning from the conduct of the apoftles, as narrated in the Acts, has been formerly examined.   He exhibits the fame argument in another form.   " Leaft of all " would Chrift have been confidered as a man in *reafoning*, " and *argumentation*, though his external appearance fhould " have fo far put men off their guard, as to have led them " to give him that appellation.   Had the Apoftle Paul con- " fidered Chrift as being any thing more than a man, with " refpect to his nature, he could never have urged with the " leaft propriety or effect, that, *as by man came death, fo by* " *man came alfo the refurrection of the dead* †.   For it " might have been unanfwerably replied, This is not the " cafe ; for indeed, by man comes death, but not by man, " but by *God* or the *Creator of man*, under God, comes " the refurrection of the dead ‡."   No one who underftood the defign of the Apoftle's reafoning - although fully per-

fuaded

* Famil. Illuftr. p. 22. 26. 42.   † Cor. xv. 21.   ‡ Vol. i. p. 19.

fuaded of the divinity of our Saviour, would have given fuch an ánfwer. For in thefe words, the Apoftle does not mean to declare by what *power* the refurrection is accomplished, but in what *manner* this blefling is conveyed to us, and the *certainty* of this conveyance. For the whole preceding argument, 1 Cor. xv. 4.—20. is defigned to fhew that the refurrection of Chrift is the great proof of this doctrine. Therefore, the different appearances he made, after his refurrection, are particularly enumerated. In what fenfe it is faid, *By man came the refurrection*, is undeniable from the verfe immediately preceding; *But now is Chrift rifen from the dead, and become the firft fruits of them that flept;* and alfo from the verfe immediately following: *But every man in his own order, Chrift the firft fruits*, &c. It would have been no *unanfwerable* argument to the Apoftle's affertion, fuppofing him to have believed the divinity of Chrift, to have faid, that the refurrection came not *by man*, but *by God;* unlefs the Apoftle had denied the reality of Chrift's human nature. For the truth of his divinity can be no argument againft the truth of his humanity.

When, in the fame chapter, the Apoftle proceeds to declare the *power* by which the refurrection is accomplished, although he afcribes it to Chrift, he fpeaks of him in different terms. He calls him a *quickening fpirit*, ver. 45. becaufe he raifes the dead; and *the Lord from heaven*, ver. 47.

The Doctor thus proceeds in his reafoning: " It muft " ftrike every one who gives the leaft attention to the " phrafeology of the New Teftament, that the terms *Chrift* " and *God*, are perpetually ufed in contradiftinction to each " other, as much as *God* and *man;* and if we attend ever " fo little to the theory of language, and the natural ufe of " words, we fhall be fatisfied that this would not have been " the cafe, if the former could have been predicated of the " latter,

" latter, that is, if Chrift had been God." *Chrift* and *God*
are ufed as diftinct terms ; but not in-contradiftinction, as
denoting diverfity of nature, far lefs as contradiftinguifhed
in the degree afferted. For if this were the cafe, not one
of thefe terms would ever be applied to both perfons ; nor
would the work denoted by either, as effential to that perfon to whom the term belongs, be afcribed to the other. It
is not faid that the Father is ever called *Chrift*. But it is
evident that Chrift is often called *God. The Word was
God.—Thy throne, O God, is for ever and ever.* That Jefus
is meant in both places, hath been already proved. The
very term *Chrift*, although a name of office, implies that
the perfon to whom it belongs is effentially divine. For he
is *anointed* with the Spirit *without meafure.* And can this
be afferted of a creature ? He is anointed as *the moft Holy*,
Dan. ix. 24. And can this defignation belong to a man
naturally as much expofed to fin as we are ? He is anointed, as the begotten Son of God, Pfal. ii. Therefore, to fay
that " the terms *Chrift* and *God* are as much contradiftin-
" guifhed as *God* and *man*," is to *imagine a vain thing, in
plotting againft the Lord and his Anointed.* Only fubftitute
the word *man* for *Chrift* in many places of the New Teftament, and obferve what a *pleafant* effect it will have, as
to the faith and confolation of Chriftians ! *Baptifing them
in the name of the Father*, that is, of God, *and of* A MAN,
and of the Holy Ghoft.—The grace of MAN, *and the love of
God, be with you. Paul, an Apoftle, not of men, neither by
man, but by* A MERE MAN, *and God the Father*, &c.

He further obferves : " We fay *the prince and the king*,
" becaufe the prince is not the king." This is true in human concerns. But it does not apply here. For royalty is
as effential to the Son as to the Father. He is *the fellow of*
JEHOVAH *of hofts.* If he had not been really in the ftate of
God, how could he have *emptied himfelf?* Can a perfon

empty

empty himfelf of that which he never poffeffed; nay, from which he hath ftill been infinitely removed? This analogical argument goes beyond the mark. If it prove any thing, it proves that Chrift is *not a king*. Does our author really mean to affert this? It would only be a completion of his work. I do not wonder that thofe who fay, *How can this man fave us?* fhould be unwilling to fubmit to his *government*. This kind of language reminds one of the ungracious reply of the churlifh Nabal, concerning the type; *Who is David? and who is the fon of Jeffe? there be many fervants now a-days that break away every man from his mafter*, I Sam. xxv. 10.

Paul indeed " fays that the church at Corinth was *Chrift's*, " and that Chrift is *God's*." But it will not follow, that " he could have no idea of Chrift being God, in any proper " fenfe of the word." For in this affertion the Doctor ftill fuppofes what he has not proved, that it is impoffible for him who *humbleth himfelf to behold the things that are done in heaven, and on earth*, to humble himfelf fo far as to *take upon him the form of a fervant*. The Apoftle had certainly no idea that the church was a *man's*.

C H A P. II.

An examination of the Argument againft the Divinity of Chrift, from the pretended Difficulty of tracing the Time when it was firft divulged.

THE Doctor's nicely-conftructed chain of reafoning from the fuppofable *furprife*, and *doubt*, and *hefitation*, and *fpeculation*, and *debate*, which muft have been occafioned by the firft preaching of the divinity of the Son *,

fall*

* Ibid. p. 23, 24.

falls entirely to pieces, in confequence of what has been
formerly proved, that the ancient Jews believed a plurality
of perfons in the divine effence, and that the firft preachers
of the Gofpel really exhibited Jefus as a divine perfon.

He further afferts, that " it cannot be faid that John Bap-
" tift preached any fuch doctrine *." But that this was the
great article of his teftimony concerning Jefus, we have
alfo fhewn.

On the fame fubject of our Saviour's deity he propofes
this queftion ; " If it had ever been known to Peter, can we
" fuppofe that he could have denied him as he did † ?" Might
not any infidel plead as ftrongly, from this circumftance,
againft Chrift being the Meffiah? Might it not be faid,
Had Peter believed he was the Saviour of the world, and
as himfelf afterwards declares, that there was *not falvation
in any other*, " can we fuppofe that he would have denied
" him as he did?" It is not eafy to fay, how far a perfon
may go under the power of temptation. Our author himfelf, as he informs us, was once " a Trinitarian, and prayed
" confcientioufly to the three perfons without diftinction,—
" in the ferious fimplicity of his heart,—impreffed with a
" full perfuafion that all the three perfons were fully equal
" in all divine attributes ‡." Doubtlefs, he then thought
that his perfuafion was founded on as good a ground as any
that Peter could have, the word of God *who cannot lie :*
and had any one told him that he would afterwards *deny*
the fecond Perfon, and do his utmoft to prove that he was
a mere man, he might have been apt to reply, with the
fame Peter, *Lord, though all men fhould be offended becaufe
of thee, yet will I never be offended ;* or, in the words of Ha-
zael to the prophet, *Is thy fervant a dog, that he fhould do
this great thing ?* 2 Kin. viii. 13. We would rejoice to

Vol. I.   K k   hear

* Vol. I. p. 25.   † Ibid. p. 27.   ‡ Ibid. p. 41.

hear that, like Peter, our author had alfo *wept bitterly* becaufe of his denial.

He endeavours, by a very curious *manœuvre*, to avert
the force of the confeffion of Thomas. " If it be fuppofed,"
he fays, " that Thomas was acquainted with this moft ex-
" traordinary part of his Mafter's character, which led him
" to cry, *My Lord and my God**, when he was con-
" vinced of his refurrection, as he was not one of the *three*
" who had been entrufted with any *fecrets*, it muft have
" been known to all the *twelve*, and to Judas Ifcariot among
" the reft. And fuppofe him to have known, and to have
" believed, that Jefus was his *God* and *Maker*, was it pof-
" fible for him, or for any man, to have formed a delibe-
" rate purpofe to betray him ;—or if he had only heard of
" the pretenfion, and had not believed it, would he not
" have made, fome advantage of that impofition, and have
" made the difcovery of this, as well as of every thing elfe
" that he knew to his prejudice ? †" Some things are fo
weak as fcarcely to deferve, or even to admit of an anfwer.
One inference, however, natively occurs from the reafoning both in this, and in the preceding quotation ;—that the
doctrine of Socinians, according to their own confeffion,
tends greatly to relax the influence of faith in Chrift, and
to render the adherence of the foul to him extremely feeble.
It muft necessarily make men bad martyrs ; ftill prefenting
a temptation to apoftacy. For our author does not feem
to think it near fo great a crime to deny *Chrift*, as to deny
God. The moft that can be faid in favour of fuffering for
the Saviour, is, that it is *daring to die for a good man*.

It was certainly as poffible for Judas to betray his God,
as his Saviour. He could have done neither, had he really
believed the truth, either of Chrift's divinity, or of his mediatory character. But whatever faith he had, was dead.

He

---

* John xx. 28.   † Ibid. p. 27, 28.

He had no *God* but *Mammon*. He fought no *falvation*, but
what came from *the bag*. Befides, Satan had *entered into
his heart*. With the fame propriety, therefore, might it be
afked, " Is it poffible for Satan to carry on a conftant war
" againft God, to whom he, as a creature, owes his being?"
But, perhaps, the Doctor may decline to meet me on this
ground, as the exiftence of the devil feems to be no article
in his creed. It is queftionable, if he believes him to be even
an *occafional* being. " Whatever," he fays, " is afcribed
" to this being will appear, if we confider the circumftan-
" ces of the feveral narrations, to be derived from nothing
" but the irregular paffions of men, which are, of them-
" felves, a caufe adequate to the effect *." Like the defcription of *Wifdom* in the book of Proverbs, all is *allegory!*
But does not the learned Gentleman deferve our thanks
for his generofity ? As he bereaves us of that gracious Angel who is able to *fave*, he endeavours to rid us of that
evil one who has been generally viewed as the inftrument
in *punifhing*.

   As little, furely, can be inferred, againft the deity of
Chrift, from the filence of Judas on this article, as againft
his Meffiahfhip ; becaufe we have no evidence that he cri-
minated our Saviour with refpect to this. Such filly negative evidence, from the treafon or filence of one difciple,
can be no argument againft the exprefs teftimony of another. The amount of this reafoning is ; " Becaufe we
" know the treafon of a falfe difciple, we muft reject the
" confeffion of a true one. Becaufe Judas fays nothing with
" refpect to the divinity of Chrift, we are not to believe
" Thomas in what he does fay."

   I fhall only add that the perfect harmony between the
reafoning of Dr P. on this occafion, and that of the infidel
Jew in Celfus, muft ftrike every one who is acquainted

K k 2

with

---

* Inftitutes of Nat. and Rev. Relig Vol. 2. p. 434.

with the work of Origen in reply to him. Their arrows, equally pointed against divine truth, are so much alike, that one would think they had been drawn from the same quiver. " How can we reckon him God," does he say, " who " —was basely taken, being betrayed by those whom he " called his disciples?—Did it become him who was ac- " counted the Saviour, and the Son of God most high, and " his messenger, to be betrayed and delivered up by his " familiar friends," &c *. There is this difference, however, that the *heathen* philosopher had penetration enough to observe that the argument was of equal force against Jesus being the Messiah, and therefore, against the whole of the Christian revelation.

The Doctor, in another work, comes a little closer to the point. Of the words of Thomas he says; " This is an " abrupt exclamation, and no connected sentence at all, and " seems to have proceeded from a conviction, suddenly pro- " duced in the Apostle's mind, that he who stood before " him was, indeed, his Lord and Master raised to life by " the power of God. The resurrection of Christ and the " power of God, had so near a connexion, that a convic- " tion of the one could not but be attended with an ac- " knowledgment of the other †." When he calls the con- fession of Thomas " an abrupt exclamation," he insinuates nearly the same thing with those who have supposed the language of the Apostle to be equivalent to one of these un- meaning and irreverent addresses, so commonly made, in our time, to the Majesty of heaven; such as, *God bless me*! *Good God*! &c. "His words evidently express admiration and surprise, perhaps immediately excited by the discovery Jesus made of his having-heard his language to the disciples, although not present as to his human nature; nor, as Tho- mas might be fully assured, informed by them, none of them

* Origen cont. Celf. lib. 2. p. 62.   † Famil. Illustr. p. 33.

them having feen Jefus fince Thomas had proclaimed his obftinacy in unbelief. According to this fuppofition, the confeffion of Thomas was, as to its immediate occafion, fimilar to that of Nathanael, when Jefus declared that he had feen him under the fig-tree, John i. 48, 49.: although both muft be ultimately referred to the divine power of Jefus influencing the heart. For *no man can fay that Jefus is the Lord, but by the Holy Ghoft.*

The words of Thomas form as *connected a fentence* as the occafion required. It is connected in its parts. For the particle *and* connects the firft part of the addrefs with the fecond ; neceffarily referring both to one perfon. It is connected with what our Lord had faid. For the Spirit declares it to be the anfwer of Thomas ; *Then Thomas anfwered.* The whole is addreffed to Jefus : *Thomas anfwered and faid unto him.* It muft be admitted that the whole fentence was addreffed to Chrift, or denied that any of it was fo. For, if there be any meaning in language, thefe words, *faid unto him,* muft denote that Jefus is the object of the laft, as well as of the firft part of the addrefs. He not only *anfwered and faid unto him, My Lord ;* but he *anfwered and faid unto him, My God.* Little connexion as our author finds in thefe words, he takes care not to ftrengthen it by his explanation. To fay that Thomas referred to the power of *God,* is introducing a new fubject without the flighteft ground from the paffage ; nay, in direct oppofition to the very language of infpiration. Here we beg leave to remind the author of his own words : " There is no ufe in language, " nor any guard againft deception, if fuch liberties as thefe " are to be allowed *."

He proceeds to reafon in this manner : " If the doctrine " of the divinity of Chrift had been actually preached by " the Apoftles, and the Jewifh converts in general had

K k 3

" adopted

* Vol. I. p. 15.

" adopted it, it could not but have been well known to the
" unbelieving Jews. And would they, who were at that
" time, and have been ever fince, fo exceedingly zealous
" with refpect to the doctrine of the divine unity, not have
" taken the alarm, and have urged this objection to Chrifti-
" anity, as teaching the belief of more Gods than one, in
" the Apoftolic age? And yet no trace of any thing of
" this nature can be perceived in the whole hiftory of the
" book of Acts, or any where elfe in the New Teftament*."
But all this reafoning proceeds on a fuppofition, the falfity
of which we have already proved, that the Jews had no
notion of a plurality of divine perfons. We have feen that,
during Chrift's miniftrations, they often accufed him as a
blafphemer, for *making himfelf equal with God*, by calling
God *his own Father* ; and that at length they condemned
him on this very ground. Such a conftruction of our Saviour's language could never have occurred to them, had
they not had fome idea of God having a *proper Son*, equal
with himfelf. They could not therefore accufe the Apoftles
on this head, without criminating the national, traditionary
and revealed faith. We know that bitter enemies lay hold
of every expreffion that can by any means be conftructed
to the prejudice of thofe whom they oppofe. But " it could
" not but have been well known to the unbelieving Jews,"
that the Apoftles afcribed the *pouring out of the Spirit* to
Jefus, Acts ii. 17. 23. that they proclaimed *falvation* to
thofe who *called on his name*, ver. 21. afferted that it was
not poffible that he could be holden of death, ver. 24. defcribed him as *Lord*, and as *fitting at the right hand* of JE-
HOVAH, ver. 34. as the object of faith, ver. 38. as *the holy
One, the juft One, the Author of life,* chap. iii. 14, 15. afcribed infinite *power* to his *Name*, ver. 16. and declared his
power to *blefs* them, in *turning every one of them from their*
iniquities,

---

* Ibid. p. 29, 30.

iniquities, ver. 26. They had affirmed to the very rulers, that there was *not salvation in any other*, chap. iv. 12. and that it belonged to him to *give repentance and forgiveneſs*, chap. v. 31. &c *. The leaſt that can be ſuppoſed, is, that their enemies were convinced, that they aſcribed to Jeſus thoſe characters which their church and nation had always aſcribed to the true God. When, therefore, we do not find the leaſt reflection on theſe doctrines as blaſ-phemy, the argument is much ſtronger againſt the Doctor than for him. 'For it is impoſſible to conceive, that they ſhould not have exhibited this charge againſt the Apoſtles, had they not been ſecretly convinced that they aſcribed no more to Jeſus than what their own ſcriptures aſcribed to the Angel of the covenant. Therefore, they do not venture to blame the miniſters of Jeſus for giving too much honour to the Son of God, whom they proclaimed as the Meſſiah; but for teaching that a man, whom they had crucified, was he: juſt as they had accuſed and condemned Jeſus, not for ſaying, as they underſtood his language, that the Father had a *proper* Son, equal with himſelf; but becauſe he, *being a man*, and as they apprehended, nothing more, made him-ſelf equal with God.

It may be thought that this does not remove the diffi-culty, becauſe, as the Doctor obſerves, " as ſoon as ever " the Jews had any pretence for it, we find them ſufficient-" ly quick and vehement in urging this their great objec-" tion to Chriſtianity." This was not originally their great objection; for as we have ſeen, they had ſufficient pretence for it from the beginning of the Baptiſt's miniſtry. They may now make this pretence. But they did not at firſt reject Jeſus, becauſe too much was aſcribed to him in a ſpiritual reſpect, but becauſe too little was aſcribed to him in a carnal. The Spirit of God expreſsly informs us

K k 4   that

---

* See above, Book II. chap. 11.

that the *ſtumbling-block* of *the Jews* was *the croſs*. Their unbelief was, foretold as what would turn on this very hinge. *He ſhall grow up—as a root out of a dry ground: he hath no form nor comelineſs; and when we ſhall ſee him, there is no beauty that we ſhould deſire him. He is deſpiſed and rejected of men,* Iſa. liii. 2, 3. The want of external *form,* that is, of worldly greatneſs, is evidently aſſigned as the reaſon of rejection. While our Lord was on earth, they never objected to the application of theſe words to the Meſſiah; *The Lord ſaid unto my Lord, Sit thou at my right hand.*

But it is undeniable that, ſince the rejection of that people by God, they have become far darker in all their apprehenſions with reſpect to revealed truth; and finding that the Chriſtians argued from their conceſſions and interpretations of Scripture, have either renounced or obſcured ſome of their more ancient doctrines. We need not wonder that this ſhould be the caſe in regard to the doctrine of a plurality, when it is undeniable that many paſſages, which their more ancient interpreters applied to the Meſſiah, have, in later times, from their hatred of Chriſtianity, been almoſt univerſally denied to have any ſuch meaning. To refer to that only which has been quoted above from Pſal. cx.; had it not been the eſtabliſhed opinion of the Jews, during our Saviour's abode on earth, that theſe words reſpected the Meſſiah, we cannot conceive that the Phariſees ſhould have been ſo *puzzled,* as our author ſays, to give a proper anſwer. Yet by the time that Juſtin Martyr wrote, they had ſo accommodated their religious ſyſtem to their neceſſities, that it was generally denied that this paſſage had any ſuch reference. For he aſſerts, in his Dialogue with a Jew, that the Rabbies " preſumed to apply it to " Hezekiah *."

An

---

* Dial p. 409.

An obfervation brings up the rear of this fection, which, according to the firft principles laid down by the Doctor himfelf, gives an unlucky ftroke to the whole of the foregoing hypothefis : " It is really fomething extraordinary," he fays, " that this opinion,. that Chrift was the medium of " all the divine commnuications to mankind under the " Old Teftament Difpenfation, fhould have been *fo readily* " *received*, and have *fpread .fo generally as it did among* " Chriftians, when it not only. has no countenance from " Scripture, but is exprefsly contradicted by the author of " the epiftle to the Hebrews *." Were the laft part of this affertion true, or in other words, were there any truth in what Dr P. has taken fo much trouble to prove, that fuch an idea was never entertained before, or in, the apoftolic age ; the circumftance mentioned would be *really extraordinary*. For, as the Chriftian church received all her doctrines by means of Jewifh converts, who are fuppofed to have been fuch firm believers in the divine *unity*, according to the Socinian fenfe ; fhe muft have been as fully. eftablifhed in the belief of the mere humanity of Jefus, as in that of his being Meffiah. Now, let our author apply his own principles. As all the firft Chriftians firmly believed that their Meffiah was a mere man, that there was but one perfon in the divine effence, and that any other doctrine was heathenifh polytheifm and idolatry ; " the doctrine of Chrift's having had any exift- " ence or fphere of action, before he came into the world " (as that of his having been *the medium of all divine com-* " *munications* to the patriarchs, and efpecially the doctrine " of his being equal to God the Father himfelf) muft have " been *new* and *extraordinary* doctrines,—muft have been " firft heard with great *furprife*, probably received with " fome *doubt* and *hefitation*, and could not but excite much " *fpeculation*

* Vol. i. p. 34.

" *speculation* and *debate* :" for " thefe are *always* the con-
" fequences of the promulgation of new and extraordinary
" opinions, the minds of men not having been previoufly
" prepared to receive them *." Yet our author acknowledges that this very opinion, " that Chrift was *the medium*
" *of all divine communications* to mankind, during the Old
" Teftament, this *new* and *extraordinary* doctrine, was
" *readily received*, and *fpread generally among Chriftians.*"
This is *really fomething extraordinary*, and muft undoubtedly be confidered as not entirely reconcileable to the
Doctor's *twelfth* Maxim of Hiftorical Criticifm ; that
" great changes in opinion are not ufually made of a fud-
" den, and *never* by great bodies of men †." The Doctor
may alfo pleafe to apply the fixteenth Maxim, which although not meant to be applied in this manner, anfwers as
well as if it had been framed for the purpofe. " When a
" time is given, in which any very remarkable and in-
" terefting opinion was not believed by a certain clafs of
" people, and another time in which the belief of it was
" *general*, the introduction of fuch an opinion may always
" be known by the effects which it will produce upon the
" minds, and in the conduct of men ; by the *alarm* which
" it will give to fome, and the defence of it by others. 'If,
" therefore, *no alarm was given*, and no defence of it was
" made within any particular period, it may be concluded
" that the introduction of it did not take place within that
" period ‡."

But he leaves this circumftance juft as *extraordinary* as
he found it. And for a very good reafon. It is a bar in
his way, which he may overleap, but cannot remove. He
perceives, that it is impoffible to account for this fact, even
when he has the choice of his principles. It directly oppofes them. It is, indeed, abfolutely incredible, that the
doctrine

* Ibid. p. 23, 24.   † Vol. iv. p. 300.   ‡ Ibid. p. 301, 302.

doctrine referred to fhould have been fo *generally received* in the fecond century, unlefs it had really been the doctrine of the firft.

: Thus, *the Difficulty of tracing the time in which the doctrine of the Divinity of Chrift was firft divulged,* inftead of being an *argument* which, as our author fays, " concludes " very ftrongly againft" the truth of this doctrine, eventually proves an infurmountable objection to the truth of his own. That it was *divulged* fome time or other, cannot be denied. But as he cannot difcern any of thefe appearances which " are *always* the confequence of the promulgation of a new " and extraordinary doctrine ;" it muft follow, that even at the time that he fixes for its promulgation, it was not accounted either *new* or *extraordinary*.

But infolvable as he finds this difficulty upon philofophical, hiftorical, or critical principles, the good man tries it by thofe of Scripture. This is fomewhat out of his ordinary line ; as he very feldom prefers faith to philofophy. But fuch a deviation might be neceffary on an *extraordinary* occafion. Although he reckons the *reafoning* of the Apoftle Paul often *inconclufive*, he is willing to be indebted to him, when he finds that his own is more fo. He is fatisfied that this doctrine " is exprefsly contradicted by the " author of the epiftle to the Hebrews, in Heb. i. 1. *God* " *who at fundry times, and in divers manners, fpake in time* " *paft unto the fathers by the prophets, has in thefe laft days* " *fpoken unto us by his Son.* Again, chap. ii. 2, 3. *If the* " *word fpoken by* angels *was ftedfaft, &c. how fhall we* " *efcape, if we neglect fo great falvation ; which at the firft* " *began to be fpoken by the Lord.* What can be more " evident," does he fay, " than that the writer of this " epiftle had no idea of God having fpoken to mankind " by his Son before the time of the gofpel * ?" The Doctor, by introducing the firft paffage as oppofed to the orthodox fyftem,

* Vol. i. 35.

fyftem, fhews how little he attends even to its firft principles. It is fuppofed, indeed, that all the appearances,
made by God, under the Old Teftament, were in the fecond Perfon; and affirmed that the Spirit who was in the
prophets acted as *the Spirit of Chrift,* being fent by him.
But we know of none who have fuppofed that, in thefe
refpects, the Son acted abfolutely, or merely as the fecond
Perfon. As the order of operation correfponds to the
order of fubfiftence, this holds not only in all the effential,
but in all the œconomical works of God. The contrivance
of redemption, and the miffion of the fecond Perfon, as
Mediator, being immediately afcribed to the Father, all the
communications that have been made to the church, are
viewed as revelations of what is primarily, though not exclufively, *his* will. Therefore, when it is urged that the
fecond Perfon appeared under the Old Teftament, it is
always underftood that he acted as the Meffenger of the
Father, in confequence of his own voluntary engagement
in the everlafting covenant.

It is granted that the Father is meant, in this place, by
the term *God.* But when it is faid that he *fpake by the
prophets,* it is not the intention of the infpired writer to
deny that the Son acted the part of a fœderal Meffenger
between the Father and the prophets, in communicating
his will to them by his Spirit. For the only oppofition
here ftated, is between thofe who *immediately* communicated the will of God under the different difpenfations.
The Father is faid to have fpoken, under the Old Teftament, *by the prophets;* becaufe they were the immediate
inftruments of delivering his will to the church. But it
is declared that, *in thefe laft times he hath fpoken—by the
Son;* becaufe the *great falvation began to be fpoken by the
Lord* himfelf.

By

By a parity of reafon, our author might plead that this language, *fpake by the prophets,* " fhews that " the writer " had no idea that God on any occafion fpake to mankind" by any other inftruments than the prophets, " before the " time of the gofpel." But the very text brought in as another proof of the Doctor's affertion, fhews that others were employed. For the law is called *the word fpoken by an-gels,* becaufe of their being ufed as inftruments in producing the lightenings, thunderings, earthquake, found of a trum-pet, and voice of words in which it was expreffed. Thence this law is faid to have been *ordained by angels,* and *given by the difpofition of angels.* But God the Father did not employ them immediately. The Son acted as *Angel of the covenant,* ufing them as miniftring fpirits between him-felf and the people of Ifrael. In this fenfe alone can we underftand what is faid by Stephen, when giving an ac-count of Mofes ; *This is he who was in the church in the wildernefs, with the Angel who fpake to him in the Mount Sinai,* Acts vii. 38. This, as we have formerly proved, could be no other than that Angel who afterwards infor-med the Ifraelites that he had fworn unto their fathers, faying, *I will never break my covenant with you,* Judg. ii. 1. This was a divine Perfon, although in the character of a meffenger ; the very fame who was afterwards *made flefh.* For he who afcended is the fame who defcended on Mount Sinai, and was there in the midft of his angelic hofts, Pfal. lxviii. 17, 18. But our author is not entirely fatisfied ; notwithftanding the abundant fupply borrowed from an infpired writer, when analogical reafoning, hiftorical criti-cifm, and fuppofition itfelf have failed him. He ventures another throw at the old game ; and it is his laft. " To " the Jews, however," he fays, " the Arian doctrine muft " have been more *novel* than that of the orthodox Chri-" ftians in the time of Juftin Martyr, and therefore, would

3   " probably

" probably have been received with more furprize." The
Doctor has found himfelf under a neceffity of acknowledging that the promulgation of the orthodox fyftem was
not attended with any of thefe circumftances, which " are
" *always* the confequence of a new and extraordinary doc-
" trine," and he attempts to account for this *extraordinary*
fact, by afferting that, as the orthodox fyftem preceded the
Arian, it would not be fo *furprizing*, that is, fo obnoxious
to the Jews as the latter would have been.

But I cannot perceive that he has any ground for this
affertion. Not only does Dr P. himfelf confider, but he
endeavours to fhew that the Jews " confider three perfons
" as three Gods, and that this tritheifm fhocks them *."
While, therefore, it is granted that, in the time of Juftin
Martyr, the Son was held to be a diftinct perfon from the
Father; according to the principles afcribed to the Jews,
they muft have confidered him as a *diftinct God*, as much as
the idol of the Arians. Indeed, it would feem that, according to the Doctor's own account of the Jewifh faith, the
Arian doctrine would have occafioned *lefs* furprize. For
he has formerly afferted that " angels fpeak in the name of
" God †;" and he doubtlefs adopts this opinion as perfectly
agreeable to the Jewifh theology. It is alfo mentioned as
a Jewifh idea, that " God fpake to angels, when he faid,
" *Let us make man* ‡." If therefore, according to them,
angels might be of God's counfel in the work of creation,
and fpeak in the name, nay, as reprefenting the very perfon of *Jehovah*, while the divine unity remained uninjured;
it could only be carrying the matter a little farther to fuppofe a fupereminent angel, or even a fuperangelic being to
be created by God, and to be employed as his inftrument
in creating the reft of his works. Our author does not
reckon even the latter fuppofition repugnant to reafon, or
inimical to the divine unity. For " God," he fays, " *might*
" *have*

* Vol. iii. p. 37. † Vol. i. p 5. ‡ Vol. iii. p. 27.

" *have* created one being of such extraordinary power, as
" should make it unneceſſary for him to exert any more
" creative power; ſo that all that remained of creation
" might be delegated to that great derived being *." Now,
if our author, in perfect conſiſtence with Unitarian principles, can form ſuch a ſuppoſition, he cannot refuſe that the
Jews, referred to, might have done the ſame; unleſs he
means to grant that he has not ſuch ſtrict ideas of divine
unity as they had.

C H A P. III.

*A conſideration of the Argument againſt the Divinity of
Chriſt from his not being the Object of Prayer.*

" OUR Saviour himſelf," Dr P. obſerves, " always
" prayed to his Father, and with as much humility
" and reſignation as the moſt dependent being in the uni-
" verſe could poſſibly do; always addreſſing him as *his*
" *Father*, or the author of his being; and he directs his diſ-
" ciples to pray to the ſame Great Being, *whom only*, he
" ſays, *we ought to ſerve* †." We have already ſpoken of
Chriſt's praying. But we would wiſh to know from the
learned Gentleman, if ſuch language as that, *Father, I will*,
(John xvii. 24.) become " the moſt dependent being in the
" univerſe?" Jeſus indeed addreſſes God as *his Father:*
and it may be admitted that God the Father was the author of his human nature. For it is written, *A body haſt
thou prepared me.* But this did not exclude the divine
agency of the ſecond Perſon; elſe it never could have been
ſaid, that he *took upon him the form of a ſervant*, Phil.
ii. 7. that *he himſelf took part of fleſh and blood*, Heb. ii.
14. that *he took on him the ſeed of Abraham*, ver. 16. But
he

* Vol. i. p. 57.   † Ibid. p. 36.

he feems efpecially to call God *his Father*, to exprefs his faith in God as *well pleafed with him* in his Mediatory cha. racter, *for his righteoufnefs fake*, and *in* him with all his fpiritual feed. For when it is foretold that the Meffiah fhall addrefs God as *his Father*, this character is connected with others expreffive of a fœderal relation : *He fhall cry unto me, Thou art my Father, my God, and the rock of my falvation*, Pfal. lxxxix. 26.

This paragraph ends with fomething very like a fallacy ; —" *whom only*, he fays, *we ought to ferve.*" According to the connexion of the fentence, *the Father* is the fubject re. ferred to by the pronoun *whom*. Thence, one who would take the words upon Dr P.'s quotation, would infer that Jefus had faid, *Thou fhalt worfhip the Father thy God, and him only fhalt thou ferve;* as entirely excluding himfelf. But his language is, *Thou fhalt worfhip the Lord thy God*, &c. not as particularizing any perfon, but the one effence, in oppofition to that claim of worfhip impudently made by the Devil, Mat. iv. 9. I afk the Doctor's pardon, as he does not admit that there is fuch a being. For he tells us, with almoft unparalleled impiety, that " all that may really " be meant by Jefus being tempted of the devil, may be, " that the improper thoughts mentioned in the courfe of " the narrative, either occurred to himfelf in his private " meditations, or were fuggefted by fome other perfon *." The abfurdity of both thefe fuppofitions is fo obvious, that an illuftration of it would be an infult on the rea. der's underftanding. With refpect to the impiety of the firft, I fhall only obferve, that it fhews, in a ftriking light, what low thoughts Socinians have of him whom, out of compliment, they call their *Saviour*. Not only do they deny him to be the infinitely Holy *God*, but to be perfectly finlefs, as *man*. For it is impoffible that fuch thoughts could occur to one's felf, without any external agency, whe- ther they were indulged or not, without an inward principle of fin. It is not at all furprifing, that the Doctor fhould be fo anxious to get rid of the miraculous conception; as he does not believe that even what was born of Mary was a *holy thing.*

He has a great deal of *probable* reafoning with refpect to Chrift, as the object of prayer. But it is of no avail whatfoever againft the evidence of *facts.* He, indeed, attempts to prove that the firft Chriftians never prayed to their Lord and Saviour. With this view he quotes 1 Pet. iv. 19. *Let them that fuffer according to the will of God, commit the keeping of their fouls unto him in well-doing as unto a faithful Creator* *. But it has been formerly obferved, that even where the name *God* occurs, it is often to be underftood as denoting the whole divine effence; and although Jefus be mentioned in connexion, as *Mediator*, yet not as excluding him from that honour which is his prerogative as *God.* Are we to view him, to whom we commit our fouls, as *a faithful Creator ?* Then, furely, either Socinians call Jefus the author of the new creation in folemn mockery; or he muft be worthy of this truft. For he who makes us new creatures, if there be any truth in the language, muft be as really our Creator as he who gave us being at firft.

Dr P. alfo quotes 1 Pet. v. 10. *The God of all grace who hath called us unto his eternal glory, by Jefus Chrift, after that ye have fuffered a while, make you perfect, ftablifh, ftrengthen, fettle you.* Here, indeed, Chrift is mentioned as *the way.* But becaufe nothing more is faid in this paffage, it will not prove that he has no higher character; it cannot avert the force of other paffages, in which the fame work is afcribed to him, which Dr P. undoubtedly confiders as a proof of Supreme Deity. With this paffage let the Doctor, according to his fyftem, reconcile the following words; *Now, our Lord Jefus Chrift himfelf, and God even our Father,*

* Vol. i. p. 43.

ther,—*comfort your hearts, and ftablifh you in every good
word and work,* 2 Thef. ii. 16, 17.

Our author fays ; " Let us now attend to fome particu-
" lars in the Hiftory of the Apoftles." We cordially ac-
cede to the propofal, being convinced that the more this
hiftory is examined, the more will the falfity of our author's fyftem appear. " When Herod," he fays, " had put
" to death James, the brother of John, and imprifoned Pe-
" ter, we read, Acts xii. 5. that *prayer was made without
" ceafing of the church unto God,* not to Chrift, *for him*."
But the point that the Doctor has yet to prove, is, that this
prayer was exclufively made to the Father. We have at
leaft as good reafon to believe that this prayer was *heard*
and *anfwered by* the Son, as that it was *made to* the Father.
For Peter fays; *Now, I know of a furety, that the Lord
hath fent his Angel, and hath delivered me,* ver. 11. But
our author informs us that " this term, *the Lord,* generally
" fignifies Chrift *." And the moft that can be faid of the
other, is that it *generally* fignifies the Father. But we are
to underftand neither exclufively. For we have as good
evidence that Jefus is the *one Lord,* as our opponents have
that the Father is the *one God.*

We are alfo told that " when Paul and Silas were in pri-
" fon at Philippi, they *fung praifes to God,* not to Chrift,
" Acts xvi. 25." But from the context, it would be moft
natural to think that this term includes Chrift as well as
the Father. For Paul enjoins the jailor to *believe on the
Lord Jefus Chrift,* affuring him that thus he *fhould be faved,*
and in a little we find that this is the fame with *believing in
God,* ver. 31. 34. At any rate, I could not, for my part,
venture to *believe,* or *truft* in a perfon for falvation, from
whom I could not afk it in prayer.

It is added ; " When Paul was warned of what would
" befal him if he went to Jerufalem, Acts xxi. 14. he faid,
                                                    " *The*

* Famil. Illuftr. p. 36.

" *The will of the Lord be done.* This, it must be supposed,
" was meant of God the Father, becaufe Chrift himself
" ufed the fame language, when praying to the Father, he
" faid, *Not my will, but thine be done.*" But the Doctor
has taken only a curfory view of this passage. For it was
not Paul, but the brethren, who fpoke in this manner.
However, becaufe one act of worfhip is fubftantially the
fame with another, exprefsly addreffed to a particular perfon, it will not follow, if there be no other evidence, that
the fame *perfon* is addreffed in both inftances. Nor can it
be juftly concluded that the words, here quoted, could not
refpect Chrift, becaufe he ufed the fame language in addreffing the Father. For Dr P. himfelf cannot deny that the
dying martyr Stephen addreffed the fame prayer to Jefus,
as Jefus at his own death, addreffed to the Father. It is
granted that this language, with refpect to Chrift, *The will
of the Lord be done,* was ufed very differently from that,
Not my will, &c. For in the former inftance his *divine*
will is meant, as being effentially the fame with that of the
Father. But in the latter, he fpoke merely of his *human*
will. According to the Doctor's own acknowledgment,
there muft be *more* probability that the term *Lord* here refpects Chrift, than that it refpects the Father. For he
grants as we have feen, that it *generally* bears the former
fenfe. But the truth is; Dr P. is willing that the term
Lord fhould denote Chrift, when it does not neceffarily refer to any of that *lordfhip* which is peculiar to the divine
nature; that is, when it can be applied to him without its
proper meaning.

It is certainly moft natural to think that the fame perfon
is here meant, as *the Lord,* who, in the verfe immediately
preceding, is called *the Lord* Jefus. An impartial reader
would undoubtedly conclude that the language of the brethren directly referred to that of Paul. He faid, *I am*

　　ready

*ready not to be bound only, but alſo to die at Jeruſalem for
the Name of the Lord Jeſus. And when he would not be
perſuaded, we ceaſed, ſaying, The will of the Lord be done.*
Nor would ſuch a reader ſuppoſe that the brethren aſcribed too much to him, *for whoſe Name* Paul was willing to
ſuffer ſo much. It would naturally occur, that *the Lord*
for whom he was *ready to die*, had ſurely ſomething to ſay
as to the diſpoſal of his lot. But let our author inform us,
if it be not this *Lord Jeſus*, of whom another Apoſtle, as
expreſſing the faith of all believers in his time, declares;
*This is the confidence that we have in him, that if we aſk
any thing* ACCORDING TO HIS WILL, *he heareth us. And
if we know that he hear us, whatſoever we aſk, we know
that we have the petitions that we deſired of him*, 1 John
v. 14, 15.

Dr P. here tranſcribes the whole prayer of the apoſtles,
recorded Acts iv. 24. and carefully inſerts *or ſervant*, where
according to our verſion it is *thy Holy Child Jeſus*. But
what does all this prove, but that which hath never been
denied on the other ſide, that God the Father is properly
addreſſed in prayer? But it cannot prove that he is the
only object.

The Doctor then ſays; " We have now examined ſome
" particulars both of the *inſtructions,* and the *examples* of ſcrip
" ture with regard to the proper object of prayer, in time of
" perſecution," &c *. He here refers to a notion which
ſome have entertained, that " Chriſt is the proper object of
" prayer in time of perſecution." But ſurely he who may
with propriety be addreſſed as the object of worſhip at any
time, may be thus addreſſed at all times.

The Doctor has examined theſe, but he has carefully
paſſed over a great variety of other *inſtructions* and *examples,* which clearly prove that Chriſt is the object of
prayer. We have formerly ſeen that the firſt Chriſtians
were

* Vol. i. p. 43.

were generally known by the defignation of *thofe who called on the Name of Jefus,* and proved that this denotes religious worfhip ; that they prayed to him, when fupplying. the vacancy in the college of the Apoftles, Acts i. 24. that Stephen truly did fo, chap. vii. 59, 60. that Paul was engaged in the fame exercife, chap. xxii. 17. 1 Tim. i. 12. and that he commended or dedicated the elders of the church of Ephefus to the gracious Word of God, as really as to God the Father, Acts xx. 32.

Many other paffages might be mention, which contain the fame proof. We have Paul's own account of his exercife, when buffeted by a meffenger of Satan. *For this thing,* he fays, *I befought the Lord thrice.—And* HE *faid unto me, My grace is fufficient for thee ; my ftrength is made perfect in thy weaknefs.* With the fame breath he adds ; *Moft gladly, therefore, will I rather glory in mine infirmity, that the power of Chrift may reft upon me,* 2 Cor. xii. 8, 9. Surely, the fame *Lord,* whom he befought, anfwered him : and that this was the Lord Chrift, is evident from Paul's calling that *the power* or *ftrength of Chrift,* (for the word is the fame) which *the Lord* had called *his power.* Whatever *the Lord* meant by *his ftrength being made perfect in* Paul's *weaknefs,* Paul himfelf underftood as included in *the ftrength of Chrift refting on him,* or *dwelling in him* as in a tabernacle.

Does not the fame Apoftle view Chrift as the object of prayer, equally with the Father, when he fays ; *Now may God himfelf, and our Father, and our Lord Jefus Chrift, direct our way unto you ?* 1 Thef. iii. 11.

Jefus received this honour from his difciples and others, even during his humiliation. They prayed to him for temporal falvation, which none but God can give, Mat. viii. 25. for mercy, chap. ix. 27. for the increafe of their

faith,

faith, Luke xvii. 5. for the fuppreffion of their unbelief, Mark ix. 24.

The fame glorious Perfon was addreffed by believers, as the objeƈt of prayer, before his incarnation. Jacob fupplicated the God of his fathers as that Angel who had *redeemed* him *from all evil,* and who had power to *blefs,* Gen. xlviii. 15, 16. He was known as *the Name of the God of Jacob,* and under this charaƈter addreffed as the objeƈt of prayer, and as the proteƈtor of his people, Pfal. xx. 1. Now, we have the impartial teftimony of Philo, that the perfonal *Word* was called *the Name* of God.

C H A P. IV.

Of Dr Prieftley's objeƈtion to the Doƈtrine of the Trinity, as implying a Contradiƈtion.

" I ASK then," our author fays, " wherein does the A-
" thanafian doƈtrine of the Trinity differ from a con-
" tradiƈtion? It afferts in effeƈt that nothing is wanting to
" either the Father, the Son, or the Spirit, to conftitute
" each of them truly and properly *God,* each of them being
" equal in eternity, and all divine perfeƈtions ; and yet
" that thefe three are not *three Gods,* but only *one God.*
" They are therefore both *one* and *many* in the fame re-
" fpeƈt, *viz.* in each being *perfeƈt God."* It is granted,
that we are not bound to believe any thing to be a divine
doƈtrine, that is really contradiƈtory to right reafon. But
from the weaknefs, and efpecially from the depravation of
our powers, things may feem contradiƈtions, which are by
no means fo in faƈt. Even reafon may teach us, that it is
unqueftionably our duty to believe a revealed doƈtrine, although it fhould infinitely exceed our comprehenfion.

The

..The objection, produced by Dr P., has been often answered before. The terms of the argument, as it is called, are somewhat altered, but the substance is the same. It is an evident sophism. For the Doctor assumes that each person is considered by Trinitarians as "truly and properly "God," so as to engrofs all divine perfections to himself. In this cafe, each person would have divine perfections of his own, diftinct from thofe of the other persons. But we believe that each perfon is "truly and properly God," as having all divine perfections, though not exclufively. The *equality* afferted, is not that of things perfectly alike, yet fubftantially diftinct; but an equality in the poffeffion of the *fame* things, of the *fame* "eternity, and all divine per- "fections." Therefore, they are not "*one* and *many* in " the fame refpects." For they are *one*, as to abfolute identity of nature and perfections; but *many*, with refpect to the individual and common poffeffion of what is effentially one.

The Doctor is chargeable with an obvious fallacy in the ftructure of his argument. He ufes the term *God* in one fenfe only, as if this were a fair ftate of the invariable practice of Trinitarians. Whereas, according to fcriptural example, they ufe it, in the connexion to which his argument refers, in two different fenfes. In the one, it denotes a *perfon;* in the other, a *nature.* When one perfon is faid to be "truly and properly *God*," the term is ufed *per-* *fonally;* but when the three perfons are faid to be *one God*, *effentially.* He, indeed, blends two diftinct terms, as if they were equally applied to different objects "in the fame " refpect." Thefe are *God*, and *one God.* But one perfon is faid to be "truly and properly *God*," not as excluding the other adorable perfons, but as diftinguifhing the effence of the perfon fpoken of from that of all creatures. The three perfons are faid to be *one God*, not as immediate-

ly

ly oppofed to creatures, but as excluding all diverfity of effence among thefe perfons.

There is another evident fallacy in this argument. Our author throws in a term, in his conclufion, not to be found in the premifes. This is *perfect God*. The introduction of this new term tends greatly to perplex the reader; and feems to give a force to the conclufion, to which it has no claim. Now, this is againft all the rules of reafoning: and it is efpecially unfair, as the expreffion is not commonly ufed by Trinitarians. A believer in the Trinity might fay, that one perfon is *perfectly God;* meaning, that he is completely a divine perfon. But he would not fay, that one is *perfect God*, at leaft in the fenfe affumed in the argument; becaufe, in the idea of God effentially confidered, he includes, not merely all divine perfections, but the different modes of fubfiftence.

It is evident that, in Dr P.'s argument, the *two firft* propofitions are meant to exprefs the principles of Trinitarians. But when thefe propofitions are ftated according to their real principles, it muft appear to every candid reader, that the *conclufion* by no means follows.

" Nothing is wanting to either the Father, the Son, or " the Spirit, to conftitute each of them *a perfon* truly and " properly *God*."

But thefe three perfons, being of the fame effence, are only *one God*.

" Therefore, they are both *one* and *many* in the fame " refpect, *viz.* in each being *perfect God*."

This argument, then, has one character of a fophifm, always given by logicians. The premifes do not contain the conclufion.

" This is certainly," the Doctor fays, " as much a con- " tradiction as to fay that Peter, James, and John, having " each of them every thing that is requifite to conftitute a ‘ complete

" complete man, are yet all together not *three men,* but
" only *one man* *." If the term *man* be ufed, both in the
plural and fingular, in the fame fenfe, it is undoubtedly a
contradiction, to which the other bears no affinity. For
we have fhewn, that the terms, *God,* and *one God,* are ufed
differently, as they are different in fact. *Three perfons* can
never be *one perfon.* But there is a fenfe in which *three
men* may be faid to be *one man;* if the firft expreffion be
ufed *perfonally,* and the fecond with refpect to *nature.* We
often ufe the term *man* to fignify the *human nature* in general; as well as to point out an *individual* poffeffing this nature.
This term is, even in Scripture, ufed to denote both unity
and plurality; although not in the fame refpect. " God
" created *man* in his own image;—*male and female* created
" he *them,*" Gen. i. 27. chap. v. 1, 2. This is the only fenfe
in which there can be any refemblance between the doctrine of a Three-one God, and the example propofed by
Dr P. In this refpect, indeed, all the millions of individuals are but *one,* as having the fame nature. For not
only do they all poffefs thofe effential properties which diftinguifh man from other creatures; but as to body, they
are all originally of the fame fubftance. For God " hath
" made of *one blood* all nations of men," Acts xvii. 26.

We do not, however, affent to what follows; " For the
" ideas annexed to the words *God,* or *man,* cannot make
" any difference in the nature of the two propofitions."
The divine nature is fo infinitely remote from the human,
or any created nature, that God himfelf forbids the comparifon. *To whom then will ye liken me, and make me equal,
and compare me, that we may be like?* Ifa. xlvi. 5. We
dare not ufe fuch fimilitudes, in order to explain a myftery.
For as Dr Young obferves, " A myftery explained, is a
" myftery deftroyed." We advert to them merely as introduced

* Ibid.

troduced by our author, to illuſtrate the falſity, of his pretence, that the doctrine of the Trinity implies a contradiction. As the divine nature is ſo infinitely above the human; although three among men ſhould be in no ſenſe
one, it would by no means prove that this cannot be true,
of God. Therefore, even that ſenſe, in which we have
ſhewn that three perſons may be *one*, with reſpect to man,
falls infinitely ſhort of expreſſing the unity of the divine
nature. For although all the individuals of the human
race have one nature, and are originally of one ſubſtance;
yet the union is not ſo cloſe that the actions of one individual are common to all, which, with reſpect to external
actions, is aſſerted of the divine nature. Beſides, created
perſons are not only *diſtinct* from each other, as to perſonality, ſo that one is not another; but *ſeparate*, ſo that one
exiſts without another. But the divine perſons, although
diſtinct, are not ſeparate; becauſe one is in another. The
Father is in the Son, and the Son in the Father, John
xiv. 10 [*].

On this important ſubject, it is ſtill Dr P.'s unhappineſs,
that he ſeems to think he has diſcovered a *likeneſs* which
he can *compare unto* God [†]. As he *knows the way of the
Spirit*, and has advanced ſo far in diſcovering *the works of
God who maketh all* [‡], he ſeems emboldened to hope that
he may *find out the Almighty* himſelf *unto perfection*. But
how little regard ſoever he may pay to the divine defiance,
as expreſſed in a great many paſſages of Scripture; there is
one authority from which he ought not to differ. " The
" mind of man will never be able to contemplate the
" *being*, perfections, and providence of God, without
" meeting with *inexplicable difficulties*. We may find ſuf-
" ficient reaſon for acquieſcing in the darkneſs which in-
" volves

---

[*] Vid. Hen. Alting. Loc. Com. p. 1. loc. 3. p. 46.
[†] Iſa. xl. 18. [‡] Eccleſ. xi. 5.

" volves thefe great fubjects, but we muſt never expect to
" fee them fet in a perfectly clear light *."

The Doctor further obſerves, in the profecution of his
fubject; " As perfons are apt to confound themfelves with
" the ufe of the words *perfon* and *being*, I ſhall endeavour
" to give a plain account of them †." But the very explanation turns out to be " confufion worfe confounded."—
" The term *being*," he ſays, " may be predicated of every
" thing, and therefore of each of the three perfons in the
" Trinity." The confequence is denied. For the divine
effence is but one thing. *Thefe three are one*, 1 John v. 7.
I, ſaith Chriſt, *and my Father are one*, John x. 30. that is,
one thing; for the word εν is ufed. Therefore, they are
only one *being*. He adds; " For to fay that Chriſt, for
" inſtance, is God, but that there is no *being*, no *fubſtance*,
" to which his attributes may be referred, were manifeſtly
" abfurd." It were fo, indeed. But the *being*, to which
his attributes are referred, is the divine effence, common
to each perfon. Is it lefs abfurd than what is here fuppofed, " to fay that Chriſt is *not* God," and yet to afcribe
divine powers to him; that is, to afcribe *divine attributes*
to him; and yet " to fay—that there is no *being*, no *fub-*
" *ſtance*, to which his attributes may be referred," but the
human nature? The Doctor proceeds:—" and therefore
" when it is faid that each of thefe perfons is by himfelf
" God, the meaning muſt be, that the Father, feparately
" confidered, has a *being*, that the Son, feparately confider-
" ed, has a *being*, and likewife, that the Holy Spirit, fepa-
" rately confidered, has a *being*. Here then are no lefs
" than *three beings*, as well as *three perfons*, and what can
" thefe three beings be but *three Gods?*" All this chain
falls to the ground, becaufe the firſt link is a falfe one. No

Trinitarian

---

* Dr Prieſtley's Inſtitutes of Religion, Pref. p. xiii,
† Ear. Opin. vol. i. p. 49.

Trinitarian fays, that each perfon is *by himfelf*, that is, exclufively, *God*. No Trinitarian *confiders* one perfon as *feparate* from another. They are diftinguifhed as to the modes of perfonal fubfiftence; but they do not exift feparately.

·He further obferves : " By the words *being, fubftance,*
" *fubftratum, &c.* we can mean nothing more than the
" foundation, as it were, of properties, or fomething to
" which, in our idea, we refer all the particular attributes
" of whatever exifts. In fact, they are terms that may be
" predicated of every thing that is the fubject of thought
" or difcourfe, all the difcrimination of things depending
" upon their peculiar properties. So that whenever the
' *properties* differ, we fay that there is a correfponding
" difference in the *things, beings,* or *fubftances,* themfelves.
" Confequently, if the Father, Son, and Spirit, differ in
" any refpect, fo as to have different properties, either in
" relation to themfelves, or to other beings, we muft, ac-
" cording to the analogy of all languages, fay that they
" are three different beings, or fubftances."

To this it is replied, that the fame being may poffefs very different properties. Motion is totally different from thought. The one belongs to body; the other to mind. Yet man, who poffeffes both, is generally allowed to be *one being* only. There are *fome* who will even affert, that foul and body not only conftitute one being, but are effentially the fame principle : and fuch ought certainly to be the laft to refufe a difference of properties in the fame being. Our author *here* ufes the term *being* as equivalent to *thing* or *fubftance*. Now, although different properties are afcribed to the three adorable perfons, it will not follow that they are three different *beings*, that is, three different *fubftances*. For there can be no difference as to fubftance, where there are the fame *effential* properties. But

with

with refpect to the holy Trinity, no difference, or rather, no diftinction is afferted, but as to *perfonal* properties only. To recur to the Doctor's own comparifon, however inadequate ; there are certain *effential* properties that diftinguifh human nature from every other, and that are common to all the individuals poffeffing it, notwithftanding the various *modification* of this one nature, in an inconceivable variety of *perfonal* properties. Now, fuch perfonal properties *only* are afcribed to Father, Son, and Spirit, as neceffarily characterize them in a perfonal refpect.

" Suppofing again," he fays, " that there is an *identity* " of attributes in each of them, fo that, being confidered " one after the other, no difference fhould be perceived in " them, even in idea, (as may be fuppofed to be the cafe " of three men, who fhould perfectly *refemble* one another " in all external and internal properties) and fuppofing, " moreover, that there fhould be a perfect coincidence in " all their thoughts and actions ; though there might be a " perfect *harmony* among them, and this might be called " *unity,* they would ftill *be numerically three.*" The author practically fhews the danger of affimilating things infinitely different. For even, when he employs comparifon, he deftroys it. He firft fuppofes an *identity* of attributes. In a moment, this degenerates into a mere *fimilarity.* The three men who poffefs " an *identity* of attributes—perfectly " *refemble* one another." The fuppofition of *identity* neceffarily fuggefted the idea of abfolute *unity.* But this alfo dies away into mere *harmony,* or agreement. But fuppofing that *identity,* with the idea of which he fets out, the perfons would be, indeed, *numerically three,* as perfons ; but with refpect to effence, *numerically one.* For where there is not a mere refemblance, but an abfolute famenefs of attributes, there is undivided *unity* of nature. This fhews the falfity of his inference ; " Confequently, though " the

" the Father, Son, and Spirit had no real differences, but,
" as has been said, they had the moſt perfect identity of
" nature, the moſt entire unity of will, and conſent of in-
" tellect, and an inceſſant co-operation in the exertion of
" common powers to a common purpoſe, yet would they,
" according to the analogy of language, not be *one God*,
" but *three Gods*; or which is the ſame, they would be
" three beings with equal divine natures, juſt as the three
" men would be three beings, with equal human natures."
In this reaſoning the premiſes deſtroy the concluſion. For
there cannot be three beings, where there is " the moſt
" perfect identity of nature." For that alone is called
perfect identity, which excludes any diſtinction of being.
The Doctor vainly endeavours to ſupport this tottering
ſtructure, by ſuppoſing an abſurdity, *viz.* that the three
men would be *three beings*, with *equal human natures.*"
Theſe three men might indeed be called *three beings*; each
exiſting *ſeparately* from another. But it will not follow,
that three divine perſons muſt be three beings; unleſs it
can be proved, that God has given us *our own* nature as
the ſtandard by which we are to judge of his. But although theſe men might be called three beings, it would
not be ſaid that they had *equal human natures.* Notwithſtanding all the difference between individuals, we ſay that
they have one common nature : and the leſs the difference,
or in other words, the more " perfectly they reſemble one
" another in external and internal properties," the clearer
is the evidence of their poſſeſſing one nature only.

Our author's philoſophy is not much better than his
theology. For he confounds thoſe very terms, which have
been invented for the purpoſe of diſtinction. " The term
" *being*," he ſays, " may be predicated of every thing
" without diſtinction ; but the term *perſon* is limited to in-
" telligent beings. Three men, therefore, are not only
            " three

"ₙthree beings, but, likewife three perfons; the former is
" the *genus*, and the latter the *fpecies*." *Being* cannot be
the *genus*, unlefs it can be faid with propriety, that *thing*,
and *kind of thing*, are terms of the fame import. For as
" the term *being* may be predicated of every thing," *genus*
or *kind* is that term which denotes one clafs of *things* which
differ from others. *Genus* is the firft diftinction under *being*.
When we fpeak of *genus*, we undoubtedly mean the particular *kind* of *being*. Thus, under the univerfal idea conveyed by the term *being*, we fay that *animal* is one *genus*.
Our author is chargeable with a fimilar error, in the definition of *perfon*. This is by no means the *fpecies*. It fignifies an *individual* of a certain fpecies. As *animal* is the
genus, *man* is the *fpecies*, and *perfon* the *individual*. Therefore, the Doctor reafons erroneoufly, when he fays, that
" as *perfon* is a fpecies, comprehended under the genus
" *being*," the Father, Son, and Spirit " muft be three
" beings, as well as three perfons." For the affumption
being falfe, the conclufion cannot be true. As *perfon* is
not a *fpecies*, but only an individual, all that can be inferred, is, that thefe three perfons are three individuals.

There are faid to be two general tefts of the truth or
falfehood of any argument. The firft is, Whether the
premifes contain the conclufion? We have already feen
that Dr P.'s reafoning does not ftand this teft. The fecond
is, Whether in the different members of the argument, the
terms are taken precifely in the fame fenfe? For where-
ever this is not the cafe, the reafoning is fophiftical. Let
us now apply this fecond teft; and we fhall find that Dr
P. pays no refpect to this kind of unity. He firft ufes the
term *being* as the *genus*. " *Being*," he fays, " is the *genus* :"
Then it affumes the ftate of a *fpecies*, according to his
ftrange definition of the latter term. For " the perfon,"
that

that is, the *fpecies*, "is not the lefs a *being* on this account."
One while he makes *perfon* a *fpecies*; then, the *genus*; as
appears from the fame obfervation: " The *perfon* is not
"the lefs a *being* on this account;" that is, the *fpecies* is
not the lefs a *genus.* The end of all this is, that he may
prove the *individual* to be both *genus* and *fpecies.* " As
" perfon is a *fpecies*, comprehended under the genus *being*,
" they muſt be three beings, as well as three perfons;"
that is, adhering to his own definitions, three *genera*, as
well as three *fpecies.* I will prove any thing you pleafe,
if you allow me, not only to ufe terms in whatever fenſe I
choofe to impofe on them, how oppofite foever to that
ordinarily adopted; but to change the fenfe of thefe terms,
as often as I find it neceffary.

But we have another fpecimen of the Doctor's *reafoning*
powers, in the words immediately following what has been
already quoted: " The term. *God* is a fub-divifion under
" the term *perfon*, becaufe we define God to be an intel-
" ligent being, poffeffed of all poffible perfections. Confe-
" quently, if the Father, Son, and Spirit, be each of them
" poffeffed of all poffible perfections, which is not denied,
" they are each of them a *perfon*, each of them a *being*,
" and each of them a *God*; and what is this but making
" *three Gods?*" Our author is fo confident of the foundnefs
of this reafoning, that he adds, in the proper ftyle of gaf-
conade; " Let any Trinitarian avoid this conclufion from
" thefe principles, or affume other principles more juft and
" natural, if he can." But *Te Deum* has been fometimes
fung without a victory. All that is neceffary, in reply,
is, to try how this definition of the term, *God*, will agree
with that nature to which our author wifhes to liken the
divine. " The term *man* is a fub-divifion under the term
" *perfon*, becaufe we define *man* to be an intelligent being
" poffeffed

" poſſeſſed of *certain* perfections. Conſequently, if Peter,
" James, and John, be each of them poſſeſſed of all perfec-
" tions" eſſential to human nature, " which is not denied,
" they are each of them *a perſon*," that is, according to
the former definition, *a ſpecies;* " each of them *a bèing*,"
that is, as alſo formerly defined, *a genus;* " and each of
" them *a man*," that is, a *ſub-diviſion* under the term *per-*
" *ſon;* and what is this but making *three genera*, *three*
" *ſpecies*, and *three ſub diviſions ?*" Although we learn from
the Doctor, that he has taught *Greek*, no man will ſuſpect
that he has ever taught *Logic*.

He ſubjoins; " This definition of the word *perſon*, as
" applied to the doctrine of the Trinity, will perhaps be
" objected to; but if any other definition be given, I will
" venture to aſſert, that it might as well be ſaid that the
" Father, Son, and Spirit are *three Abracadabras*, as
" *three perſons*. They will be equally words without
" meaning." Our author, in his blaſphemous boldneſs,
ſpeaks as if *wiſdom* were to *die with* him. He denies that
words can have any meaning, unleſs uſed in his own ſenſe;
that is, in a ſenſe directly contrary to that in which they
have been uſed, either by learned or unlearned, for thou-
ſands of years. Unleſs you allow *perſon* to be a *ſpecies*, and
the *individual* to be a *ſub diviſion* under *perſon*, according
to the deciſion of this infallible Doctor, your language is
without meaning. For my part, I *object* not to his " defi-
" nition of the word *perſon* as applied to the doctrine of
" the Trinity," but even as applied to the doctrine of human nature.

With reſpect to the explanations which ſome have attempted to give of the mode of the Son's exiſtence, on
which our author animadverts in the remaining part of
this ſection; I do not conſider myſelf as bound to defend
them. All ſuch explanations are beyond our ſphere; and

they have generally darkened counfel by words without knowledge. To attempt to explain a fcriptural doctrine, believed and acknowledged to be a myftery, is nearly as foolifh and prefumptuous as to object to it, becaufe it is a myftery. To fay, that " the divine intellect is fo exerted " on itfelf, that the exiftence of the Son neceffarily flows " from it;" is fpeaking of the things of God without any warrant from God himfelf. If this doctrine of the Trinity be believed, it muft receive our faith, not becaufe we comprehend, but becaufe God has revealed it. On this fubject, for the purpofe of reconciling the minds of others, or of diftinguifhing truth from error, good men have invented various terms, which, I am convinced, have done great injury to the caufe. Even that affertion, that " the Father " communicates the divine effence to the Son," although ufed by almoft every orthodox writer, appears to me unfupported by Scripture, and dangerous in itfelf. To fpeak of a communicated effence, and yet of an underived deity, feems to be a real contradiction. I believe that there is a communion in the divine effence among all the adorable perfons, that it equally belongs to each. But that one perfon owes his divine nature to another, is language to which I can affix no fcriptural idea. There can be no communication of effence on the one hand, without derivation on the other: and how can there be derivation without inferiority? *The Father hath given to the Son to have life in himfelf,* in the fame refpect in which he *hath given him authority to execute judgment alfo,—becaufe he is the Son of man,* John v. 26, 27. The Son, effentially, is as properly the origin of all life as the Father. He is *neceffarily* fo. But the right of holding all divine power in his perfon as God-man, and of exercifing it, in a divine manner, even in the human nature, muft be as really matter of *difpenfation,* as the affumption of that nature. This *authority* is a

voluntary

voluntary gift or *conceſſion.* It is ſometimes, as here, aſcribed to the Father, œconomically viewed as ſuſtaining the
honour of deity in the work of our redemption : at other
times, to God eſſentially conſidered, as in Col. i. 19. where
no particular perſon is mentioned ; *It pleaſed, that in him
all fullneſs ſhould dwell.*

With reſpect to the generation of the Son, our author
inquires, " If, for any incomprehenſible reaſon, this my-
" ſterious *power of generation* be peculiar to the Father,
" why does it not ſtill operate ? Is he not an unchangeable
" being ? the ſame now that he was from the beginning—?
" Why then are not more ſons produced ?" Theſe words
contain their own anſwer. The Father *ſtill operates,* not
in *producing more ſons,* but in the generation of this Son ;
becauſe he is *an unchangeable being.* For we are not to
conceive of this generation, as if it were an act properly
paſt, but as eternally *preſent* in the divine eſſence. Therefore it is thus expreſſed, Pſal. ii. 7. *This day have I begotten
thee.* It is ſpoken of as *paſt,* in condeſcenſion to our weak
apprehenſions, to denote its *perfection.* But as all the *im-
manent* acts of God, as they have been called, that is, thoſe
that are properly *in* God himſelf, which have no relation
to external objects, are eternal ; it is *preſent,* with reſpect
to endleſs duration. For in ſuch acts there is no beginning,
progreſs or end. This *generation,* therefore, is eternally
preſent in the one unalterable *day* of God.

CHAP. V.

*A conſideration of the Argument againſt the Pre-exiſtence of
Chriſt from the Doctrine of Materiality.*

I HAVE formerly examined Dr P.'s objections to the
application of thoſe texts which are brought to prove
that the world was created by Chriſt. He next proceeds

to reafon againft his Pre-exiftence in any fenfe, from the Materiality of man. He refers to his *Difquifitions on Mat- ter and Spirit;* in which he pretends to have " fhewn that " there is no more *reafon* why a man fhould be fuppofed " to have an immaterial principle, than that a dog fhould " have one *." Had the wife man been as great a profi- cient in wifdom as our author, he might have given a far more emphatic reprefentation of the advantage of life, than that which occurs in Eccl ix. 4. He undoubtedly would have faid that " a living *dog* is better than a dead *man.*" Our author is certainly entitled to our acknowledgments, for the exalted ideas he gives us of our nature. And who can refufe that he does honour to his Maker, by giving fo flattering a picture of *the image of God ?*

I fhall not pretend to enter philofophically into this fub- ject. For I am not afhamed to confefs that I *know* not *the way of the Spirit,* any more than I know *how the bones grow in the womb of her that is with child.* The difficulty of imagining any connexion between the *vifible matter* and the *invifible powers* of which a dog, a plant, or a magnet is poffeffed, is the reafon affigned by Dr P. for denying the exiftence of fouls. But as we do not deny thefe *invifible powers,* the effects of which are certain, becaufe we cannot account for their *connexion* with *vifible matter;* we can have no more ground for denying that the *invifible power* may, in fome inftances, be effentially different from the *vifible matter,* yet fo connected with it as to be the fource of operation. Is it inquired, How are we to mark the dif- ference ? It is acknowledged that mere Philofophy leaves us greatly in the dark. But the Doctor's mode of reafon- ing feems to imply a refufal of any aid from Revelation. How much foever I may be at a lofs to account for the operations of irrational creatures, if Revelation informs me,

that

* Vol. i p. 84.

that *the spirit of a beaſt goeth downward*, and that *the beaſts periſh ;* while at the ſame time it aſſures me, that, although *the duſt of man returns to the earth as it was, the ſpirit ſhall return unto God who gave it ;* I certainly ought either entirely to lay aſide Revelation, or to believe that there is an eſſential difference between the frame of man and that of a heaſt ; nay, that, according to the diſtinction made in the language of inſpiration, two principles eſſentially different go to the conſtitution of his frame. I had better deny Revelation at once, than diſbelieve that there is *an innumerable company of angels*, and that *the ſpirits of juſt men made perfect* exiſt in a diſembodied ſtate. I cannot conceive, how God ſhould ſay, *I* AM *the God of Abraham, the God of Iſaac, and the God of Jacob,* if theſe perſons, when this language was uſed, had no more exiſtence than the duſt of the earth ; and far leſs, how Jeſus could make this inference, *God* IS *not the God of the dead, but of the living,* Mat. xxii. 32. For according to Dr P.'s principles, the inference, however little to the purpoſe, ought to have been ; " God *is* not the God of the *living* only, but alſo of " the dead."

The Doctor, however, ſeems fully ſatisfied that his reaſoning " is concluſive againſt the doctrine of *a ſoul,* and " conſequently againſt the whole ſyſtem of pre-exiſtence. " If Peter, James, and John," he ſays, " had no pre-exiſt- " ent ſtate, it muſt be contrary to all analogy to ſuppoſe " Jeſus to have pre-exiſted *." But there is one ſpecies of *analogy,* to which Dr P. finds it not a little difficult to prove that this is *contrary.* I mean *the analogy of faith.* It is to be feared, that this doctrine goes farther than he may be willing to confeſs, even to the denial of *the Father of Spirits.* For if it be inconceivable that a ſpirit ſhould exiſt diſtinctly from matter, he muſt either deny the being of God, or aſſert that God is a material being.

M m 3   The

* Ibid. p. 85, 86.

The latter, indeed, is the natural confequence of the Socinian doctrine. For they afcribe thofe properties to God which belong to matter. They deny that he is a fimple or uncompounded Being. They deny that he is infinite, afcribing extenfion to the divine nature. Some of this perfuafion have gone the length of attributing a bodily fhape to God; as the learned Owen hath proved in his examination of Biddle's Catechifm *. This feems to have been ftill a feature of the Unitarian herefy. For the author of the *Clementine Homilies*, who is claimed by Dr P. as an Unitarian, makes Peter exprefs his own fentiments concerning God in this manner: " He who truly exifts, is he whofe " *form* is borne by the *body* of man; on which account the " heavens, and all the ftars, though more excellent in their " nature, have continued in a ftate of fubferviency to him, " who is inferior according to effence, becaufe of the *form* " of him who is fuperior," *viz.* God †.

On the other hand, Socinians have afcribed the effential properties of God to matter. It feems to be too well-founded a charge, that they hold it to be eternal, in the fame fenfe in which they afcribe eternity to God. They go not fo far as the followers of Ariftotle, who afferted that the world exifted from eternity in a regular ftate. But for once they are *Platonizing Chriftians*. Here they have framed a very curious fyftem. Volkelius affirms that " God is faid to have created the world of nothing, becaufe " he formed it out of Chaos." This is a Socinian Myftery. He made the world *of nothing*, becaufe he made it *of fomething*. He alfo fays that " thefe words, *The earth was* " *without form and void*, defcribe the ftate of things before " the

---

* Page 61—72.

† Ο γαρ οντως ων υτος εςιν, υ την μορφην το ανθρωπυ βαςαζει σωμα, υ εινεκεν ο υρανος και παντες οι αςερες υπεμειναν δυλευειν κατ᾿ υσιαν κρειτλονες οντες, τω κατ᾿ υσιαν χειρονι, δια την τυ κρειτλονος μορφην. Hom. ӡ. fect. ӷ. p. 636.

" the creation *" Dr P. infinuates fomething of the fame nature, when he fays, that " what is called the *Mofaic* " creation was probably—the *re-making*, or *re-conftituting* " of the world, out of a former chaos †.

C H A P. VI.

Of the objection to the Doctrine, that it would be of no Ufe, although it were true.

DR. PRIESTLEY concludes this part of his work with an inquiry into the ufe of the doctrine of the Trinity. According to him, " all that can be faid for it, is that the doc- " trine, however improbable in itfelf, is neceffary to explain " fome particular texts of fcripture ; and that if it had not " been for thofe particular texts, we fhould have found no " *want* of it. For there is neither any fact in nature, nor any " one purpofe of morals (which are the object and end of all " religion) that requires it ‡." He difcovers no occafion for a three-one God ; and there are many who would be plea- fed that there were *no God*. But the wifhes or opinions of either are of no weight in the fcale of truth. If this doc- trine be really "neceffary to explain fome particular texts," and Socinians have never been able to prove the contrary, it ought to be believed, although we fhould not otherwife difcern the ufe of it. There are many of the works of God, the utility of which we cannot perceive. Shall we, therefore, dare to fay that he hath made them in vain? This kind of reafoning has too much the appearance of calling God to *give an account of his matters.* Would it be great prefumption in the clay to fay to the potter, *Why haft thou made me thus?* And is it not unfpeakably greater prefumption to fay, Why *art thou* thus? Why doft thou

exift

---

* Lib. ii. c. 4. ap. Hoornbeck Socin. Confutat. l. iii. c. 1.
† Famil. Illuftr. p. 44.   ‡ Vol. i. p. 87.

exift in this manner, rather than in that? If reafon be fufficiently qualified to be the teft of all that we ought to believe, what is the *ufe* of revelation itfelf?

I cannot prefume to go fo far as fome who have pretended
to *prove* that there could have been no more, and no fewer
divine Perfons than three. This, it would feem, is being
wife above what is written. We know that there are no
more, and no fewer. Therefore, we may fafely conclude
that, according to the incomprehenfible nature of God,
matters could not have been otherwife. Nor can I pretend fully to illuftrate the ufe of this great myftery; and
far lefs, to anfwer all the cavils, or to fatisfy the minds of
thofe who are *become vain in their imaginations.* But as it
would feem that one great defign of the work of redemption was clearly to reveal.the myftery of the Trinity, by
a difcovery of the peculiar operations of the adorable Perfons; he, who " *as a new born babe, defires the unadultera-
ted milk of the word,* will find the doctrine to be of fuch
ufe, that he *may grow thereby,* as to both faith and practice.

Our author fpeaks of *morals,* as if they were the only *object*
of religion. They are, indeed, the *end* of it. But faith is
the *beginning.* For *he that cometh unto God muft believe
that he is,* Heb. xi. 6. Now, we cannot truly believe the
being of God, without believing that *he is,* or *exifts,* according to that revelation which he is pleafed to give of
himfelf in the word. If, therefore, he reveals himfelf as
a three-one God, and we acknowledge one perfon only,
we believe not in God, but in an idol of our own imagination. *Without* this *faith it is impoffible to pleafe him.*
For all outward worfhip is only the clothing of that which
is concealed from the fenfible eye. There is an inward
worfhip of a twofold nature, which, according to the frame
of our fouls, we owe to God. We owe him the homage

of

of the underftanding, and of the will. Unlefs, by faith, we fubject our underftandings to his authority in the revelation which he gives of himfelf, we can never truly honour him with the worfhip of our wills. For the will, when properly regulated, immediately and ftrictly follows the direction of the underftanding. We can neither embrace nor adhere to the true God, unlefs we know him in this character. If we have not juft apprehenfions of him, we radically err as to *morals.* For it is only by faith that we can either know or do what is well-pleafing in his fight. We muft be *transformed, by the renewing of our minds,* THAT *we may prove what is that good, and acceptable, and perfect will of God,* Rom. xii. 2. But the great mean of this transformation is faith, efpecially as *beholding* a *Divine* Saviour in the *glafs* of the word, and depending on the gracious operation of *the Lord the Spirit,* 2 Cor. iii. 18.

It may be faid, that the principles of morality are fo plain, that there can be no difpute, or even doubt about them. But if we entertain wrong apprehenfions concerning the divine perfections, we can have none that are right with refpect to moral duty. The nature of moral evil can never be known to thofe who think that God is *altogether fuch a one as themfelves,* and that he will not require fatisfaction for their fin. Socinians afford a ftriking proof of this. They refufe to believe the teftimony of God concerning his perfections, and the operations flowing from thefe. They materially eject faith from their fyftem of religion. Hence they err as to the end of all *morals.* Now the *end* regulates the nature of every action. They hope to appeafe God, and make an atonement for fin, by their own obedience. This deftroys the action. For the Spirit of God affures us, that *as many as are of the works of the law,* that is, as feek juftification by their own works, *are under the curfe,* Gal. iii. 10. Our repentance and reformation
mation

mation can be no atonement for paſt tranſgreſſion; becauſe we owe the duty of every moment for itſelf. This line of obedience is hopeleſs. For *the Ethiopian may change his ſkin, and the leopard his ſpots, as ſoon as we who have been accuſtomed to do evil, can learn to do well.* In conſe_ quence of refuſing to believe in a Trinity, our author, that he may be conſiſtent with himſelf, finds it neceſſary to deny the miſſion of a divine Perſon, and the whole of that vica- rious work of obedience and ſuffering, by which he *is the end of the law for righteouſneſs to every one that believeth,* and by which alſo he *ſanctifies the people,* enabling them to *walk in newneſs of life.* Or ſhall we rather ſuppoſe that he can ſee no occaſion for a ſecond Perſon to redeem, becauſe he " finds no *want* of " a real redemption ? This we know, *They that be whole need not a Phyſician.*

We have the Doctor's own teſtimony : " Whatever may " be meant by the *redemption of the world,* is not the being " who made it equal to that alſo?" And we never thought of aſcribing it to any other *being.* " If his creatures of- " fend him," he further ſays, " and by repentance and re- " formation become the proper objects of his forgiveneſs, " is it not more natural to ſuppoſe that he has, *within him-* " *ſelf,* a power of forgiving them, and of reſtoring them to " his favour, without the ſtrange expedient of another per- " ſon, fully equal to himſelf, condeſcending to animate a hu- " man body, and dying for them *." It is enough for us to know that God hath expreſsly declared, he *will by no means clear the guilty,* or *hold* ſin *innocent,* Exod. xxxiv. 7. This being the caſe, it is vain to talk about what power he hath *in himſelf.* We know that he hath no power to *deny him- ſelf*: for this would imply imperfection. No creature can make atonement for his own ſin. For there would be much ſin even in his attempts to ſatisfy. And *he that offendeth in one point, is guilty of all.* As the curſe of the

law

* Vol. i. p. 88.

law muft be fuftained, this could be done by none but a divine Perfon.   For *if thou, Lord, fhouldft mark iniquities, O Lord, who fhall ftand?*

The Doctor adds indeed; " We never think of any . " fimilar expedient in order to forgive, with the greateft " propriety and effect, offences committed by our children " againft ourfelves."   But fuppofing this to be true, is there any parallel? Are not all thefe, even the greateft, but a few pence, compared with many talents? We are far from wifhing ftrictly to compare the operations of God with thófe of man.   But he hath condefcended to reprefent his works in language borrowed from creatures, that they might thus be able to form fome apprehenfions of them, ftill remembering that there is an infinite difparity.   In the prefent inftance there is fome refemblance.   A perfon, equal in rank, has often found it neceffary to intercede with an earthly parent for pardon to an undutiful child. How often has this .office been performed by one of the parents towards the other? Even when a parent refolves to forgive, in order to the prefervation of his dignity and authority, does he not fometimes fecretly employ another perfon to intercede for the tranfgreffor? Nay, is it not common among men, that, for the reconciliation of a creditor to a debtor, a third perfon interpofes, and pays the debt, as the only mean of .obtaining deliverance for the latter from the rigour of law? If this be done *voluntarily*, would any one charge the creditor with injuftice? Our author, with confiderable art, confines the comparifon to the conduct of a *parent*.   One in this relation, indeed, is generally apt to err on the fide of indulgence.   But when a very heinous offence is committed by a child againft a parent, the filial tie, inftead of being an excufe, is juftly confidered as a great aggravation.

Perhaps it may be faid, that " even fuppofing the neceffity of infinite fatisfaction, there is no ufe for the doctrine of a plurality of perfons; becaufe, it being granted that the Son, in making atonement, fatisfied his own juftice as God, as well as that of the Father, all this might have been as well done by one perfon. It is indeed true, that the Son fatisfied his own juftice, but not immediately. The atonement was properly directed to God effentially confidered in the perfon of the Father, œconomically acting as *the Judge of all*: whereas the fecond Perfon is to be viewed immediately in this tranfaction, as *emptying himfelf*, and fuftaining *the form of a fervant*. This idea is far more confiftent with the dignity, order and beauty of the divine operations, than if it were fuppofed that one perfon acted as judge and furety, as both inflicting and bearing the punifhment. The Doctor will not refufe, that, according to all juft ideas of human government, the ftate is the fovereign and judge, and that the tranfgreffor is amenable to the whole. Yet for the purpofes of order and dignity, fociety voluntarily vefts its powers in one or more individuals. Thus although the tranfgreffor, in atoning for his crime, may be faid to make fatisfaction to himfelf, in as far as he is a member of the ftate; this fatisfaction is more immediately directed to others, who are the reprefentatives of the whole.

It is alfo more confonant to our ideas of divine propriety, that, on the fuppofition of a gracious purpofe to redeem loft man by an infinite price, the glory of the Godhead fhould be obfcured, as to its difplay, in one perfon only, than that it fhould be thus obfcured in the whole extent of its fubfiftence.

Thofe who affert that there is but one perfon in God, of confequence deny the *miffion* of a divine Perfon. It is faid, that one divine perfon can accomplifh all that is fuppofed to be included in this work? But even among men, when a fovereign treats with rebels, he juftly reckons it more confi-

ftent

ftent with his dignity to employ an ambaffador; while, at the fame time, he generally demonftrates the ferioufnefs of his intentions, and the regard he has for his ungrateful fubjects, by employing one of diftinguifhed rank. And furely the dignity of *God the Judge of all* is more confpicuous in his employing a meffenger, while his love is eminently difplayed in the effential greatnefs of the Perfon fent. The Lord of the vineyard faid, *They will reverence my Son. God hath fpoken unto us—by the Son.* As it is moft confiftent with the glory of God, that he fhould employ a Meffenger, we cannot form an idea of any plan that has fuch a tendency to affect the minds of men with a fenfe of the importance of the gofpel-meffage, as its being delivered by him who is *the fellow* of the Lord of hofts.

While it was the will of God to illuftrate the greatnefs of our falvation by the very manner of its revelation, the infinite diftance of man required that it fhould be revealed in fuch a way as not to overwhelm him with terror. The hiftory of the awful tranfaction at Mount Sinai affords a decifive proof, that God, as preferving his own majefty, could not deal with man without a Mediator. Mofes was indeed admitted to this high office. But it muft be evident to any impartial mind, that it could be only in a typical refpect. For his diftance from God was as great as that of thofe very perfons for whom he acted. Befides, God fuffered him to difcover his unfitnefs for the proper difcharge of this office in different ways. For Mofes himfelf was afraid at the awful difplay of divine glory. *He faid, I exceedingly fear and quake,* Heb. xii. 21. He alfo *fpake unadvifedly with his lips,* and in his anger fmote the rock, inftead of merely fpeaking to it, as God had commanded, Num xx. 10, 11. It being, therefore, the pleafure of God to reveal himfelf *mediately,* and at the fame time with becoming majefty; and no creature being fit to ftand between him

and

and finners, it was only by one partaking of the divine nature that he could make himfelf known. It was only by
this perfon fuftaining the character of a Mediator, that finners could have hope. Whatever Dr P. may *find*, even
the *perfect* and *upright* Job *found the want of* fuch a glorious perfon. Therefore, under a fenfe of fin, of the in-
efficacy of all his own duties to make atonement, and of
the impoffibility of ftanding before his judge, he cries out :
*I am afraid of all my forrows, I know that thou wilt not
hold me innocent.—If I wafh myfelf with fnow-water, and
make my hands never fo clean ; yet fhalt thou plunge me in
the ditch, and mine own clothes fhall abhor me. For he is
not a man as I am, that I fhould anfwer him, and we fhould
come together in judgment. Neither is there any daysman*
betwixt us, that might lay his hand upon us both,* Job ix.
28.—33.

Thofe who acknowledge one perfon only, reject that
wonderful *ladder, fet on the earth, the top of which reaches
to heaven,* Gen. xxviii. 12. We can form no juft idea of
a way into the holieft of all, but through one who effentially is *the Moft Holy.* It is neceffary that this fhould be
a diftinct Perfon from him to whom he is our *way.* Accordingly, God the Son reveals himfelf in this character :
I am the Way,—no man cometh unto the Father but by me.
That our neceffities might alfo be completely fupplied,
while the majefty of the Judge is ftill preferved, we have
another divine Perfon as our guide. Therefore, faith our
Lord ; *When he the Spirit of truth is come, he will guide you
into all truth,* John xvi. 13.

Had God revealed himfelf in fuch majefty as at Mount
Sinai, the revelation would have been loft to finful men.
Had he only manifefted himfelf, as Jefus did on the mount
of

---

* The fame word, μεσιτης, is here ufed by the Seventy, which, in the
New Teftament, denotes the one Mediator.

of transfiguration; the senfes of the hearers would have been overpowered. Had God, confidered according to the Socinian fcheme as one perfon only, revealed himfelf fo as to veil his glory, unbelieving creatures, having no atteftation but his own, would have objected to it, as the Jews did when our Lord bore witnefs of himfelf. But we are fupplied with a ftriking proof that we *do not follow cunningly devifed fables*, becaufe the·divine perfon who appeared in an humble ftate on earth, was folemnly attefted by the voice of another divine perfon *from the excellent glory*, which teftimony was heard and declared by unexceptionable witneffes.

The Doctor can fee nothing that is afcribed to the third Perfon, for which the firft was not fufficient. But it is more congruous to the dignity of God, that one in the character of a Meffenger fhould *ftrive* with guilty and rebellious man, than that this fhould be done by him who fuftains the character of Judge. It was at the fame time neceffary that he, to whom this work was affigned, fhould be able to convince, to illuminate, and to renew the finner.

According to the orthodox fyftem, the perfection of the work of redemption, as to purchafe, has the greateft atteftation poffible; not merely from the infinite veracity of the teftimony, but becaufe it is confirmed by various witneffes, who, perfectly agree in their evidence. Is it faid, that the word of one divine perfon is as·good as that of three? It is, indeed, in itfelf. In the fame manner may it be faid, that the word of God is as good as his oath. But in condefcenfion to human weaknefs, and to filence our unbelief, God hath gracioufly *confirmed his promife by an oath, that we might have a ftrong confolation*, Heb. vi. 17, 18. From the fame gracious motive, he hath given us a threefold teftimony. The great *matter* of our redemption

is

is *eſtabliſhed in the mouth*, not *of two* only, but of *three wit-neſſes*. To the manner of confirming a fact among men the Spirit of inſpiration ſeems to allude, when it is ſaid, *There are three that bear record in heaven.——If we receive the witneſs of men, the witneſs of God is greater*, 1 John v. 7. 9.

Beſides, there could be no vindication of the eſſential dignity of the "Son, as unimpaired by his miſſion and vo-luntary humiliation, equal to that of his having authority to ſend another divine perſon, who had never humbled himſelf in this manner. The Son, continuing to act in an aſſumed character of inferiority, could not ſend the Father, he being ſtill fœderally conſidered as judge. But thoſe who believe in the Holy Trinity can admire the wiſdom of the divine plan, in his ſending the third Perſon. Indeed, the *great ſalvation*, viewed in its neceſſary connexion with the doctrine of the Trinity, appears in a far more clear and glorious manner, than it could otherwiſe have done. Its various parts are far more diſtinctly diſcerned, than if we ſhould ſuppoſe them all to have been accompliſhed by one perſon. The aſcription of the *plan* and *purpoſe* to the Fa-ther arreſts the mind in the contemplation of that infinite wiſdom diſplayed in this work ; of the great obſtacles which were in the way, eſpecially the holineſs and juſtice of God, as well as his faithfulneſs in the threatening ; and of his adorable ſovereignty, in laying hold of our nature, while that of Angels was paſſed by. While the *purchaſe* is aſ-cribed to the ſecond Perſon, we are called to conſider the infinite diſtance that was between him and the accompliſh-ment of his work, the unſpeakable condeſcenſion that was neceſſary, the greatneſs of the evil of ſin, for which nothing could atone but the ſuffering of an infinite perſon, and the tremenduous nature of divine wrath. The aſcription of the *application* of redemption to the Holy Spirit, wonder-

fully

fully tends to affect the mind with a fenfe of that *death in trefpaffes, and in fins*, to which we are fubjected ; as it is not enough that a divine Perfon fhould purchafe redemption, but a perfon of equal dignity muft alfo apply it to our fouls, in the illumination of the darkened underftanding, the conviction of the obdurate confcience, the inclination of the rebellious will, and the fanctification of the carnal affections.

The plan of redemption, as the work of a Trinity of co-equal Perfons, gives us the moft aftonifhing views of divine love. It points out the Father as eternally and infinitely delighting in the fecond Perfon, not only as the Son, but as the Surety of loft man ; as eternally and infinitely expreffing his love to us in the expreffions of his love to our glorious Mediator. This is the account given by perfonal Wifdom : *The Lord poffeffed me in the beginning of his way, before his works of old. I was fet up from ever-lafting;·from the beginning, or ever the earth was.—When he prepared the heavens,—then I was by him, as one brought up with him : and I was daily his delight*, Prov. viii. 22. &c. Both Father and Son are viewed as, in a foederal refpect, holding an eternal and ineffable communion of 'love with the Holy Spirit, who cheerfully engaged, for the completion of the divine purpofe, to be fent by both, to condefcend to ftrive with man, to dwell in him as the Spirit of holinefs, and to reftore that image which fhould be defaced by fin.

Hence alfo we perceive the fecurity of our falvation ; becaufe the New Covenant is made ; not like that of Works, between God and a mutable creature, but between divine Perfons equally unchangeable. We may therefore be affured that nothing *fhall be able to feparate us from the love of God which is in Chriſt Jeſus our Lord,* and that his *Spirit ſhall not depart* from us. Thoſe who deny a Trinity, are ſo far conſiſtent as to refuſe that the ſalvation, which they expect, is *an everlaſting ſalvation.* As they deny that the Meſſiah is JEHOVAH, they diſavow any confidence in that *everlaſting righteouſneſs* which he hath *brought in.* As they diſbelieve that *the counſel of peace* was between JEHOVAH and *the Man whoſe name is the Branch,* they truſt in a covenant, which, according to their own confeſſion, may be, and often is, *broken.*

I may add, that this doctrine diſcovers the *unity* of the divine eſſence in a far more ſtriking light than that of one perſon only. Mere numerical unity does not give us the higheſt idea of perfection. For this unity may exiſt, where there is the greateſt diſorder in the ſubject. But when many perfections, as we ſpeak of them, although apparently oppoſed in their claims and operations, *meet together and embrace each other,* in one eſſence; we have a far more exalted idea of unity. If all theſe perfections exiſt in diſtinct perſons, in a ſtate of infinite harmony, notwithſtanding diſtinct perſonal operations; we have the moſt perfect idea of unity that the mind can conceive. Its perfection is tried by the peculiar operations of theſe perſons, and diſplayed by the abſolute harmony which is the reſult of the whole.

But although we could diſcern no other *uſe* of the doctrine of the Trinity, but that of exerciſing *faith,* it would be ſufficient. This is a power communicated to man, for the expreſs purpoſe of aſſuring him of the truth of things that are beyond his reach, which he has not ſeen, or cannot ſee. For *faith is the demonſtration of things not ſeen,* Heb. xi. 1. We are ſometimes, in an improper ſenſe, ſaid to believe what we have ſeen. We alſo ſpeak of *believing*

certain

certain truths, which are conclusions from facts submitted to our senses, or in consequence of a process of reasoning. But this is not properly called *faith*, but *knowledge*. *Faith* is properly a relative term; and its correlate is *Testimony*. Do we not conclude that many things exist in nature, because we have undeniable evidence; although we cannot understand *how* they exist? And do we not owe as much honour to a divine testimony, as to the testimony of our senses, or the result of our fallible reasonings? When Abraham *believed* a promise *against hope*, did he not act as *irrationally*, as he who believes a doctrine above reason? Was not *every thought brought into captivity*, in the one case, as much as is supposed in the other? However much the conduct of Abraham is extolled in Scripture, he certainly paid as little regard to *reason*, in believing that God had commanded him to sacrifice his son Isaac, as he can do, who believes that God *spared not his* OWN *Son.*

Such a faith has the most certain and extensive influence as to *morality*. The latter, certainly, in a special manner, includes *self-denial*; although this, as far as it implies that we are *not to lean to our own understanding*, cannot be reckoned one of the cardinal virtues of Socinians. When Agur considered that he could *not* tell the name of God, or *his Son's name*, he was convinced that he *had neither learned wisdom, nor had the knowledge of the holy*, Prov. xxx. 3, 4. When God revealed himself to Job, as incomprehensible in his nature and operations, he confessed that he had *uttered things that he understood not, things too wonderful for him, which he knew not;* wherefore he *abhorred himself, and repented in dust and ashes*, Job xlii. 3—6. When Isaiah saw the glory of Christ, as a prelude of his incarnation, he cried out; *Wo is me,—for I am a man of unclean lips!* Isa. vi. 1—5. John xii. 41.

Such

Such a faith naturally fills the mind with greater *reve-rence* of the incomprehenfible majefty of God. Even Seraphs cover their faces with their wings, when they proclaim the thrice holy Lord God Almighty, Ifa. vi. 2, 3. *Wonder* is another exercife of the mind, which properly refpects what we do not fully comprehend. According to the frame of our fouls, it tends greatly to infpire, and to preferve veneration. We generally find that what is thoroughly known, although other circumftances be equal, commands lefs refpect than what is greatly unknown. Admiration, as it regards God, is an act of worfhip, fucceeding faith in an incomprehenfible object. But there is no room for this, in the Socinian fyftem. It leaves nothing in the Saviour, that can entitle him to the name of *Wonderful*. But notwithftanding, he *fhall be admired in all them that believe.*

It muft be allowed that one great mean of attaining perfection is the contemplation of the perfections of God. And furely, that doctrine has the greateft influence on *morals*, which exhibits thefe in the moft ftriking light. That the doctrine of a Three-one God, acting as our Redeemer, has this effect, we have already feen.

No confideration can fo powerfully recommend *unity*, *love, humility*, and difinterefted *benevolence*, as the example of a divine Perfon humbling himfelf for our fakes. Therefore faith the Apoftle'Paul; *Fulfil ye my joy, that ye be like minded, having the fame love, being of one accord, of one mind. Let nothing be done through ftrife or vain glory, but in lowlinefs of mind let each efteem other better than themfelves. Look not every man on his own things, but every man alfo on the things of others. Let this mind be in you, which was alfo in Chrift Jefus : who being in the form of God, thought it not robbery to be equal with God : but made him-*
felf

felf of no reputation, &c. Phil. ii. 2—7. Can any argument more powerfully recommend *forbearance* towards weak brethren. *Even Chrift pleafed not himfelf*, Rom. xv. 3. Throw afide the idea of his divinity, and you lofe the whole force of the argument ; nay, you make it the language of folly. " Jefus had more truft than any other " fervant ever had ; therefore, more obligation to fidelity : " and yet he was not unfaithful to his mafter." What follows from this ? That the more obligation a man is under to another, it is the more furprifing that he fhould prefer the pleafure of his benefactor to his own. " If *even* " Jefus, a mere creature, pleafed not himfelf, but one who " was infinitely *fuperior* to him ; *much more* ought ye to " pleafe your *equals* rather than yourfelves."

Is *love* the *fulfilling of the law ?* Surely, no reprefentation can be given of the love of God, that can have fo conftraining an influence on our hearts, as that of his giving his own Son. Suppofe Jefus to be the moft holy man that ever lived, given to mankind-finners merely to fet them an example ; what a poor idea does this give us of divine goodnefs, compared with that of giving a Son, equal with himfelf, to die for our fins? *Herein is love,—that—he fent his Son to be the propitiation for our fins*, 1 John iv. 10. Can any argument fo powerfully incite to brotherly love, as that of a divine Perfon cheerfully giving himfelf for us, as *an offering and a facrifice ? Hereby perceive we the love of God, becaufe he laid down his life for us : and we ought to lay down our lives for the brethren*, chap. iii. 16. The doctrine of a Trinity in unity, is a moft cogent motive to unity among brethren, and fhews in what the true perfection of a church confifts. How ought it to influence Chriftians to endeavour to have but *one heart*, and *one foul*, when they know that the adorable Perfons, notwithftand-

ing

ing a peculiarity of operation, have eternally manifefted but one will in the work of falvation. That this ought to have the force of an example with us, is evident from the interceffory prayer of our Saviour being recorded for the ufe of the church :—*That they all may be one, as thou, Father, art in me, and I in thee, that they alfo may be one in us,—that they may be one, even as we are one. I in them, and thou in me, that they may be made perfect in one*, John xvii. 21. 23.

Obedience to the holy law could never be recommended by that of a mere man, as much fubjected to its authority as others. But what a ftriking view have we of the dignity of this law, when we confider that Jefus, *although he were a Son*, fo as to be above the law, *yet learned obedience.*

Nothing can have fuch a tendency to illuftrate the guilt and mifery of fallen man, to awaken attention to the great concerns of falvation, and to recommend that holinefs, *without which no man fhall fee the Lord*, as a full perfuafion, not only that the price of our redemption is paid by a divine Perfon, but that it is the fpecial work of another Perfon, equally divine, to *convince us of fin, of righteoufnefs, and of judgment.*

Although Dr P. cannot fee that the Doctrine of the Trinity is of any *ufe*, or that there is " any one purpofe in " *morals* that requires it," an infpired Apoftle confidered the ftedfaft acknowledgment of this myftery, not merely as a *fource* of comfort and union, but as the very *end* of all that comfort and union which the church could attain, of all that love which is the fum and perfection of *morality.*— *I would that ye knew*, he fays, *what great conflict I have for you, and for them at Laodicea, and for as many as have not*

feen

*ſeen my face in the fleſh : that their hearts might be com-
forted, being knit together in love, and unto all riches of the
full aſſurance of underſtanding,* TO THE ACKNOWLEDG-
MENT *of the myſtery of God, and of the Father, and of
Chriſt ; in whom,* or *in which myſtery, are hid all the trea-
ſures of wiſdom and knowledge,* Col. ii. 1, 2, 3.

END OF THE FIRST VOLUME.

Lightning Source UK Ltd.
Milton Keynes UK
UKHW022253191218
334294UK00011B/1251/P